Stevens and Borrie's Elements of Mercantile Law

Edited by T. M. Stevens, M.A., B.C.L.
First edition 1890
Second edition 1897

Edited by Herbert Jacobs, B.A.
Third edition 1900
Fourth edition 1903
Fifth edition 1911
Sixth edition 1920
Seventh edition 1925
Eighth edition 1930
Ninth edition 1934
Tenth edition 1938

Edited by John Montgomerie, B.A.
Eleventh edition, June 1950
(First reprint, September 1953)
Twelfth edition, February 1955
(First reprint, August 1958)
Thirteenth edition, February 1960
(First reprint, October 1963)

Edited by Gordon J. Borrie, LL.M.
Fourteenth edition, May 1965
Fifteenth edition, April 1969
(First reprint, January 1971)
Sixteenth edition, March 1973

Edited by J. K. Macleod, LL.B., PH.D. and
A. H. Hudson, M.A., LL.B., PH.D.
Seventeenth edition, October 1978

Stevens & Borrie's
Elements of Mercantile Law

SEVENTEENTH EDITION BY

J. K. Macleod, LL.B., PH.D.,
of Gray's Inn, Barrister, Professor of Law
at the University of Liverpool

and

A. H. Hudson, M.A., LL.B., PH.D.,
of Lincoln's Inn, Barrister, Professor of Common Law
and Dean of the Faculty of Law
at the University of Liverpool

London · Butterworths · 1978

England
London
Butterworth & Co (Publishers) Ltd
88 Kingsway, WC2B 6AB

Australia
Sydney
Butterworths Pty Ltd
586 Pacific Highway, Chatswood, NSW 2067
Also at Melbourne, Brisbane, Adelaide and Perth

Canada
Toronto
Butterworth & Co (Canada) Ltd
2265 Midland Avenue, Scarborough M1P 4S1

New Zealand
Wellington
Butterworths of New Zealand Ltd
77–85 Customhouse Quay

South Africa
Durban
Butterworth & Co (South Africa) (Pty) Ltd
152–154 Gale Street

USA
Boston
Butterworth (Publishers) Inc
19 Cummings Park, Woburn, Mass 01801

ISBN Casebound 0 406 66086 7
       Limp 0 406 66087 5

Printed in Great Britain by Billing & Sons Limited,
Guildford, London and Worcester

Preface

In preparing this edition no attempt has been made to effect any radical change in the scope and treatment of the law covered by this book. The aim has remained, as in the past, to provide a wide-ranging survey of Mercantile Law in one volume. Indeed the only major topics in Mercantile Law not appearing in this and recent editions have been Company Law and Liquidation, whose bulk is now too great to allow a useful account of them in a work such as this. It is the hope of the editors that this edition will continue to serve the needs of those in commerce for whom, as T. M. Stevens wrote in the preface to the first edition, 'it will frequently happen that a knowledge of Mercantile Law is almost a necessity'.

Changes in the law since the last edition appeared have, however, been so far reaching that even the most restrained approach of necessity involved considerable amendment of and addition to the existing text. That this was inevitable can be appreciated when it is seen that new legislation enacted since the last edition includes the Supply of Goods (Implied Terms) Act 1973, the Fair Trading Act 1973, the Consumer Credit Act 1974, The Trade Union and Labour Relations Act 1974, the Arbitration Act 1974, the Employment Protection Act 1975, the Restrictive Trade Practices Act 1976, the Restrictive Practices Court Act 1976, the Resale Prices Act 1976, the Insolvency Act 1976, the Torts (Interference with Goods) Act 1977, the Patents Act 1977 and the Unfair Contract Terms Act 1977. Responsibility for the administration of much of this legislation so far as it relates to restrictive trade practices and consumer protection is, in fact, in the hands of the former editor of this book, Professor Gordon Borrie, in his capacity as Director-General of Fair Trading.

In order to accommodate this new material without unduly enlarging the book some obsolescent or highly specialised material has either been deleted or given reduced coverage. Apart from the legislation which has already been mentioned, other changes both in statute and in case law have compelled the editors to reconsider the text in many parts of the book and carry still further that process of modernisation on which Professor Borrie embarked in the fourteenth edition and continued in two succeeding editions.

A special problem in the treatment of recent legislation has arisen from the fact that some legislation, though enacted, is not to come into force until an appointed day which may lie some distance in the future. In situations where it seemed both that the appointed day might well come far into the life of this edition and that readers might need full treatment of both the present and the forthcoming law the two bodies of law have been set out in detail. This explains the concurrent treatment of the Consumer Credit Act 1974 and, for instance, the Hire Purchase Act 1965. In other situations where these reasons seemed less pressing only the new law has been dealt with in full.

Mr. and Mrs. Conkerton very kindly read part of the text and made many most helpful comments and suggestions. Our thanks are also due to the publishers for their help in the efficient and speedy production of this edition, and particularly for carrying through the transition to the new numbered-paragraph format.

The law is in general given as it stood on 1 January 1978 though it has proved possible to include a number of later matters. Late in the process of revising for this edition the Court of Appeal decided the case of *H Parsons (Livestock) Ltd v Uttley Ingham & Co Ltd*. It may be that this case will go to the House of Lords and completely overturn the hitherto established views on remoteness of damage, but as this has not yet happened the matter has had to be left over to the next edition.

J. K. MACLEOD
A. H. HUDSON

Faculty of Law
University of Liverpool
1 February 1978

Contents

Contents

Table of Statutes

In the following Tables references are given to Halsbury's Statutes of England (Third Edition) showing the volume and page number at which the annotated Act is printed.

List of Cases

Chapter 1

Introduction

1.01 The law governing commerce in this country traces its origins to the Law Merchant of medieval and early modern times, which was administered in the courts of fairs and markets and the Court of Admiralty but was ultimately received into the common law by great eighteenth-century judges such as Holt CJ and Lord Mansfield.[1] This explains why certain rules of commercial law in matters such as bills of exchange and shipping differ markedly from the corresponding rules for non-mercantile contracts. These anomalous mercantile rules were established when the cosmopolitan Law Merchant prevailed and foreign merchants could not be expected to accept some of the more insular peculiarities of the common law.

---

1 Radcliffe and Cross *The English Legal System* (6th edn) 242–256.

1.02 Unlike the United States and countries of the Continental legal tradition England has no Commercial Code in the sense of general legislative provision for mercantile transactions. English commercial law is a blend of statute, case law and custom,[1] though, as in other fields of law, statute is coming to play a predominant role. Certain specific and important areas of commercial law were codified in the late nineteenth and early twentieth centuries to the extent that complete statutory restatements of the former statute and case law governing the topics in question were enacted by Parliament. These include the Bills of Exchange Act 1882, the Partnership Act 1890, the Sale of Goods Act 1893 and the Marine Insurance Act 1906. When the Law Commission was established to carry out an active policy of law reform one of its declared aims was to further the codification of our law and it embarked upon a project to codify both the English and Scots laws of contract. If this had proved successful it would have had profound consequences for commercial law but the project was suspended in favour of more restricted schemes of reform. Apart from the codifying Acts mentioned above, very large areas of English commercial law are covered by statutory enactments which, if not technically codes, are almost as comprehensive as codes, e.g. bankruptcy. From time to time the process of improving and simplifying the statute book is carried forward by consolidating Acts, which gather together and re-enact statute law governing some specific area of law, e.g. the Companies Act 1948.

1 For the sources of English law and the administration of justice see Walker and Walker *English Legal System* (4th edn). Mozley and Whiteley's *Law Dictionary* (9th edn) will be of help in matters of terminology. James *Introduction to English Law* (9th edn) provides a comprehensive outline both of the modern legal system and the chief divisions of English law.

1.03 Commercial law also spans many areas of judge-made law. Much of commercial law is a specialised application of the law of contract but very considerable contributions have been made by the law of quasi-contract or unjust enrichment, the law of tort, governing liability in damages for certain wrongs arising independently of breach of contract such as negligence and wrongful interference with goods[1] and equity, governing trusts, fiduciary relationships and the special remedies of injunction and specific performance. Entry into the Common Market has provided a further source of commercial law which is likely to be of increasing importance as the years go by.

1 The Torts (Interference with Goods) Act 1977 is to give the comprehensive name of 'wrongful interference with goods' to the torts of conversion, trespass to goods and negligent harm to goods; abolishes detinue and provides a form of judgment where goods are detained; provides that mere denial of title is not to be actionable and that the defence of contributory negligence is not to apply to conversion. It also makes new provision for competing claims to goods. See Halsbury's Statutes, 3rd edn.

1.04 In the past commercial law was almost exclusively civil law in the sense that breach of its rules gave rise to an action for damages, restitution, an injunction or specific performance. In recent years, however, in imposing closer regulatory control over many aspects of commercial activity the State has had increasing recourse to criminal law, especially in the field of consumer protection, e.g. see chapters 14, 15, 18, 19. Although criminal proceedings may result in some measure of compensation for someone aggrieved by conduct penalised by the law, the prime purpose of criminal proceedings is normally to secure the punishment of the accused by imprisonment or fine.

1.05 Prosecution by the State for breach of the criminal law may have any of the following advantages for an aggrieved person:

1. It may be the cheapest and most effective way to cause a cessation of the practice;

2. Conviction at the State's expense may enable the complainant party to obtain an order from the convicting court that he be compensated by the wrongdoer—up to a maximum of £1,000;[1]

3. Where an act is both a crime and a civil wrong, conviction can be used in any subsequent civil action as prima facie proof of the facts necessary for that conviction, thus reducing the cost and increasing the certainty of the outcome of (civil) litigation.[2]

---

1 Powers of the Criminal Court Act 1973, ss. 35, 43 (as amended by the Criminal Law Act 1977, s. 60).
2 Civil Evidence Act 1968, s. 11.

1.06 In addition to proceedings in the ordinary courts, civil or criminal, commercial civil litigation may also take place in arbitral tribunals,[1] usually of the parties' own choosing, where the adjudicator is not normally a member of the judicial staff of the courts, and even if he is a member, is not acting in his ordinary capacity. These tribunals are subject to a measure of supervision by the courts and are attractive to commercial men because hearings may be in private, at times chosen to suit the parties, before a skilled adjudicator with special knowledge of the subject-matter of the dispute, rules of procedure and evidence may be relaxed and the possibilities of expensive appeals may be considerably limited. Arbitration available to a party to a commercial dispute may take one or more of the following forms:

1. Under the Arbitration Act 1950, which is widely used in disputes between business men;

2. Under the power to refer county court proceedings for small sums to arbitration before a county court Judge or Registrar, a scheme which seems to be becoming more popular with private litigants;

3. Private arbitration schemes operated by particular trades or in particular areas, e.g. Consumer Councils of Nationalised Industries.

To the litigant, all these forms of arbitration may offer advantages over the courts in terms of speed, informality, flexibility and cheapness.

---

1 See chap. 34.

Part I

General view of the law of contract

Chapter 2

Contract: types, form and capacity

1. The different types of contract

2.01 In modern law, the word 'contract' generally means an agreement intended by the parties to it to have legal consequences and to be legally enforceable.[1] Thus, there is a contract when one person agrees to sell something to another, when a bank agrees to lend money to a company, and when a builder agrees to repair a damaged chimney. These are common examples of contracts in everyday life, but they are sometimes referred to as *simple contracts* to distinguish them from *specialty contracts* or contracts by deed, and *contracts of record* which are obligations recorded by a court of law in its official records, e.g., judgments and recognisances.

Contracts of record need no further reference and contracts by deed need only a brief further description.[2] The significance of both these types of contract is overshadowed today by the importance of *simple contracts*.

---

1 *Rose and Frank Co v JR Crompton & Bros Ltd* [1923] 2 KB 261, per Bankes LJ, at 282; affd. [1925] AC 445, HL.
2 See para. 2.07, post.

Simple contracts

2.02 A simple contract has been defined above as an *agreement* intended to have legal consequences and to be legally enforceable. Its main essential is mutual agreement and this connotes that (1) *at least two parties* have expressed themselves (2) *with sufficient certainty* (3) *in terms which correspond* upon the subject.

2.03 *Parties.* For an agreement there must be at least two parties, though there may be any number of parties to a multilateral contract,[1] and a number of people may together form one 'party' to a contract.[2] However, a man cannot contract with himself; and, if a person agrees with himself and one or more other persons, the agreement will be construed and enforced as if it had been entered into with the other person or persons alone.[3] The general rule is that the parties may act in person or by way of an agent.[4]

1 E.g. a race or competition: *The Satanita* [1897] AC 59, HL.
2 E.g. a partnership, as to which see generally post, chap. 11; an unincorporated association, as to which see para. 2.22, post; co-contractors generally. Liability of co-contractors may be joint and/or several, depending on the terms of the agreement.
3 Law of Property Act 1925, s. 82.
4 For the law of agency, see post, chap. 10.

2.04   *Certainty*. The details of the bargain must be certain or ascertainable.

In *Scammell (G) and Nephew Ltd v Ouston*,[1]

A agreed to buy a van from B 'on hire-purchase terms': *Held:* no precise meaning could be attributed to these words because there was a wide variety of hire-purchase terms and therefore there was no contract. The parties had never got beyond negotiations.

Similarly, there is no contract if a vital term, such as the price to be paid for goods sold, has not been agreed and remains to be settled by further negotiation.[2]

On the other hand in *Foley v Classique Coaches Ltd*[3]

A agreed to buy petrol from B at a price to be agreed and there was a provision for the submission of any dispute to arbitration. The parties never did agree a price. *Held:* since the price was ascertainable otherwise than by the parties themselves, i.e. by arbitration, the parties had made a concluded contract.

And in an agreement otherwise sufficiently precise a meaningless clause may be ignored. In *Nicolene Ltd v Simmonds*,[4]

A offered to buy some steel bars from B. B agreed to supply them, adding: 'I assume that we are in agreement that the usual conditions of acceptance apply.' B failed to deliver the goods and A sued B for breach of contract. *Held:* since there were apparently no 'usual conditions of acceptance', this meaningless phrase could be ignored. There was a clear concluded contract and B was liable for breach of it.

1 [1941] AC 251, [1941] 1 All ER 14, HL; and see now the Consumer Credit Act 1974, s. 59 (see para. 14.21, note 9, post).
2 *May and Butcher Ltd v R* [1934] 2 KB 17n, HL.
3 [1934] 2 KB 1, CA.
4 [1953] 1 QB 543, [1953] 1 All ER 822, CA.

2.05   *The terms must correspond.*   The parties must be in agreement, a requirement normally expressed by saying that they must be ad idem; and, as will be seen in the next chapter, agreement is normally reached by the process of offer and acceptance.[1] Where all parties say what they mean and mean what they say, then there will literally be a meeting of the minds. But what if this is not the case?

The *general rule* of the Common Law was stated by Blackburn J, in *Smith v Hughes*:[2]

'If, whatever a man's real intention may be, he so conducts himself that a reasonable man would believe that he was assenting to the terms proposed by the other party, and that other party upon that belief enters into the contract with him, the man thus conducting himself would be equally bound as if he had intended to agree to the other party's terms.'

In *Tamplin v James*:[3]

J made a bid at an auction sale for a public-house believing that a certain field was included in the lot. This was a misapprehension on his part. The lot was knocked down to him. There was no ambiguity in the particulars as to what was included in the lot and J was *held* bound to the contract.

Thus, if the outward expressions (objective intentions) of the parties correspond, there will be a contract, even if the mental (subjective) intention of one or both parties is different.[4] This rule is sometimes expressed in terms of the doctrine of estoppel: where a person makes a statement, even though innocently, upon which another relies to his detriment, the speaker cannot subsequently be heard in court to say that the statement was untrue.[5] To use the term of art, he is *estopped* from asserting the untruth of his statement, as where he makes an assertion as to the title of goods[6] or shares[7] sold.

Where the plaintiff seeks an equitable remedy, e.g. specific performance of the contract, and it is argued that mistake[8] precludes the existence of the contract, the court will normally determine the case according to the principles of the common law already examined. If, therefore, at common law, a mistake does not affect the existence of the contract as in *Tamplin v James*[9] the court will be prepared to grant specific performance of it. If, on the other hand, on common law principles, a mistake does prevent a contract from coming into existence specific performance will normally be refused. Thus, in *Webster v Cecil*:[10]

> C had refused to sell land to W at £2,000 but C then wrote offering to sell the land to W at £1,200. C had mistakenly written £1,200 instead of £2,200. W realised C had made his error but immediately purported to accept C's offer to sell at £1,200. *Held:* there was no binding contract of sale at £1,200 as C had made a unilateral mistake in writing down the terms and W knew this. Specific performance was refused.

---

1 See para. 3.02, post.
2 (1871) LR 6 QB 597 at 607.
3 (1880) 15 ChD 215, CA.
4 *Frederick E Rose (London) Ltd v William H Pim, Jnr & Co Ltd* [1953] 2 QB 450, [1953] 2 All ER 739, CA.
5 See per Lord Denman in *Pickard v Sears* (1837) 6 Ad & El 469 at 474. Distinguish equitable estoppel: see para. 3.23, post.
6 *Eastern Distributors Ltd v Goldring* [1957] 2 QB 600, [1957] 2 All ER 525, CA.
7 *Re Bahia and San Francisco Rly Co* (1868) LR 3 QB 584.
8 For further analysis of mistake, see paras. 5.01 et seq.
9 (1879) 15 ChD 215, CA.
10 (1861) 30 Beau. 62.

Form of contract

2.06 A *simple contract* may be

1. Drawn up in writing;
2. Partly written and partly oral;
3. Entirely oral; or
4. Inferred from, and created by the mere conduct of the parties.

The contract may be completely performed at once or it may consist of or include promises to perform or not to perform some act in the future. Thus the purchase of a packet of cigarettes over the counter is a contract which is completed at once, while an order for a suit of clothes to be made involves mutual promises on the part of the tailor to make the suit properly and on the part of the customer to pay for it. The distinction is sometimes expressed by dividing contracts into 'executed' and 'executory' contracts,[1] but even when a contract appears to be completed at once, the effects of it may continue, as when a man buys a bun for a penny and subsequently breaks his teeth on a stone in it.[2]

1 For 'executory' and 'executed' contracts, see para. 3.17, post.
2 *Chapronière v Mason* (1905) 21 TLR 633, CA.

Specialty contracts

2.07 Specialty contracts, also called *deeds*, are contracts under seal. It is necessary that a deed should be written, sealed, and delivered, and the person who executes it must also sign it or place his mark on it.[1] The writing may be by hand or in print, and on paper or parchment. In modern times the seal has become a wafer or a mere piece of wax which has been previously attached to the document.[2] In *Stromdale and Ball Ltd v Burden*,[3] Danckwerts J. said:

'Meticulous persons when executing a deed may still place their finger on the wax seal or wafer on the document but it appears to me that, at the present day, if a party signs a document bearing wax or wafer or other indications of a seal, with the intention of executing the document as a deed, that is sufficient adoption or recognition of the seal to amount to due execution as a deed.'

Delivery of a deed may be
(i) Actual—i.e. handing over the instrument; or
(ii) Constructive—i.e. speaking words importing an intention to deliver,[4] e.g. 'I deliver this as my act and deed'.

Specialty contracts differ from simple (or parol) contracts in the following respects:
(i) No consideration is required.[5]
(ii) Right of action arising out of a contract under seal is normally barred by non-exercise for twelve years; right of action on a simple contract is normally barred in six.[6]

1 Law of Property Act 1925, s. 73. A deed is executed by a company when its seal is affixed in the presence of and attested by its secretary and a director: s. 74.
2 Even the wafer seal would appear to be unnecessary: *First National Securities Ltd v Jones* [1978] 2 WLR 475, CA.
3 [1952] Ch 223, [1952] 1 All ER 59.
4 *Doe d. Garnons v Knight* (1862), 5 B & C 671.
5 See para. 3.18, post.
6 See paras. 8.08 et seq.

2. Contracts requiring a special form

2.08　In general the parties to a contract, even corporations,[1] may make it in any form they choose. Apart from special circumstances, a contract will be equally binding whether it is made under seal, in writing or by word of mouth alone though naturally the terms of a contract will generally be easier to prove if the contract is under seal or otherwise in writing.

Sometimes, however, some special form is necessary; if so, this will be either writing under seal or writing under hand; and sometimes, though a verbal contract may be valid, it may be unenforceable by action unless evidenced by writing.[2]

1　For corporations, see para. 2.22, post.
2　For unenforceability, see para. 2.11, post.

Contracts which must be entered into by deed

2.09　Among these may be mentioned:

1. Gratuitous promises;[1]
2. Leases for upwards of three years.[2]

1　See para. 3.18, post.
2　Law of Property Act 1925, ss. 52 and 54. But a *contract* for a lease is subject to the ordinary rules: see para. 12.05, post.

Contracts which must be in writing

2.10　These include:

1. Bills of exchange and promissory notes; this is required by the Bills of Exchange Act 1882, and was formerly so by the common law;[1]
2. Contracts of marine insurance;[2]
3. Regulated agreements under the Consumer Credit Act 1974.[3]

In addition there are certain transactions, closely connected with or involving contracts, where writing is necessary; for instance, an acknowledgment of a debt so as to start time running again under the Limitation Act must be in writing;[4] transfers of shares in companies are required to be in writing.[5]

1 S. 3 (1), (2). See further chaps. 20, 21, post.
2 See para. 27.06, post.
3 See para. 14.33, post.
4 See para. 8.11, post.
5 Companies Act 1948, s. 75.

Contracts which are unenforceable by action unless evidenced by writing

2.11 By s. 4 of the Statute of Frauds (1677) it was provided that no action could be brought upon any of a number of contracts unless they were evidenced by some *note or memorandum* in writing, signed by the party to be charged, or by his authorised agent. From an early date, however, it was found that the Act was more frequently used as an instrument of frauds than to prevent frauds and the requirements of the Act were repealed in relation to most of the transactions mentioned in it by the Law Reform (Enforcement of Contracts) Act 1954.

There remain only the two following cases where a memorandum is required:

1. A promise to answer for the debt, default, or miscarriage of another person, i.e. a contract of guarantee,[1]
2. A contract for the sale or other disposition of land or any interest in land.[2]

The requirement of a memorandum does not affect the validity of the contract; it merely renders the contract unenforceable by action, unless it is evidenced by writing which fulfils the conditions of the statute, or by part performance.[3] Accordingly, as the contract exists independently of the writing, the writing may be made at any time preceding the commencement of the action.[4] Any document signed by the party to be charged, or his agent,[5] and containing the terms of the contract, is sufficient to satisfy the statute; e.g., a will or an affidavit.[6]

---

1 Statute of Frauds (1677), s. 4. See para. 16.02, post, and generally chap. 16.
2 The rule is now embodied in the Law of Property Act 1925, s. 40: set out para. 12.03, post. The section is not confined to contracts for the *sale* of an interest in land: (*McManus v Cooke* (1887) 35 ChD 681, per Kay J, at 687).
3 The doctrine of part performance is chiefly of significance in the context of sales of interests in land, and will be dealt with in relation thereto: see para. 12.04, post.
4 Contra where the writing is made after commencement of proceedings: *Lucas v Dixon* (1889) 22 QBD 357; *Farr Smith & Co v Messers Ltd* [1928] 1 KB 397.

5 It is not necessary that the principal should have authorised the agent to sign the document as a record of the transaction: *John Griffiths Cycle Corpn Ltd v Humber & Co Ltd* [1899] 2 QB 414, CA. See further para. 12.03, post.
6 *Re Hoyle* [1893] 1 Ch 84, CA.

Note or memorandum

2.12 The note or memorandum must contain details of the contract, including the names of the parties,[1] the subject-matter, the consideration[2] and any other special terms in reasonable detail.[3] It need not be on one piece of paper; it may extend over several, provided that these are so connected and consistent that they can be read together.[4] If the signed paper does not itself contain all the contractual terms, there must be a sufficient reference, express or implied, in that document to some other document or documents, so that when all are read together they comprise a complete note or memorandum, e.g.,

> the term 'our arrangement' was used in a letter, and this was allowed to be connected with an arrangement set out in a previous note, the whole being then taken as the true contract.[5]

This case may usefully be contrasted with *Timmins v Moreland Street Property Co Ltd*[6]

> The buyers of houses sent the seller a cheque for £3,900 payable to the seller's solicitors. The seller gave the buyers a receipt for £3,900 which he (the seller) signed and the receipt contained the terms of the sale. Later the buyers countermanded the cheque and repudiated the contract. *Held:* the document signed by the party to be charged, i.e. the cheque, did not contain all the contractual terms and did not expressly or by implication refer to any other document. In consequence the two documents could not be read together so as to comprise a complete memorandum. Judgment was given for the buyers. (It may well have been different had the cheque been made out in favour of the seller personally as the seller had signed the receipt.)

1 So long as two parties are named who are contractually bound, it does not matter that one is really acting as an agent for someone else. Thus, where an estate agent signed in his own name without qualification a receipt for a deposit which described the property being sold, and contained the names of the estate agent (who was acting for the vendor) and of the purchaser, but not the name of the vendor, it was held to be a sufficient memorandum to bind the vendor: *Davies v Sweet* [1962] 2 QB 300, [1962] 1 All ER 92, CA.

2 The consideration for a guarantee need not be stated: Mercantile Law Amendment Act 1856, s. 3; and see para. 16.02, post.
3 *Pocock v ADAC Ltd* [1952] 1 All ER 294.
4 *Boydell v Drummond* (1809) 11 East, 142.
5 *Cave v Hastings* (1881) 7 QBD 125. It does not matter that the other document contains the words 'subject to contract': *Griffiths v Young* [1970] Ch 675, [1970] 3 All ER 601, CA.
6 [1958] Ch 110; [1957] 3 All ER 265, CA; earlier cases are summarised in the judgments.

2.13 A letter, which would be a sufficient compliance with the statute if it contained the name of the person to whom it is addressed, may be made complete by means of the envelope in which it was sent.[1] And where a signed letter sets out the terms of a contract for the purpose of repudiating it, if the ground of repudiation is not good in law, it will not prevent the letter from being a sufficient memorandum within the statute.[2]

The name of the party charged must be on the paper, but, in addition, the name of the other party, or a sufficient description (with which he may be connected by parol evidence), must be included.[3] Thus, a description of a party as 'the proprietor'[4] or 'personal representative'[5] has been held sufficient; on the other hand, 'vendor' has been considered an insufficient description.[6]

Only the signature of the party sought to be charged is requisite, though in most cases both parties would sign.[7] The signature may be in ink or pencil, printed or stamped;[8] an identifying mark or mere initials will suffice.[9] The signature must be so placed as to show that it was intended to relate and refer to every part of the instrument.[10] If it governs the whole document it need not be at the end—e.g. if a man begins 'I, AB, agree, etc,' and does not sign the paper at the foot, the statute is satisfied.[11] The signature may be that of the party to be charged, or of his duly authorised agent.[12]

---

1 *Pearce v Gardner* [1897] 1 QB 688, CA.
2 *Dewar v Mintoft* [1912] 2 KB 373. Contra where it denies that any contract was ever made: *Thirkell v Cambi* [1919] 2 KB 590, CA. See also the 'subject to contract' cases, para. 12.06, post.
3 *Champion v Plummer* (1805) 1 B & PNR 252; *Williams v Lake* (1860) 2 E & E 349, 29 LJQB 1.
4 *Sale v Lambert* (1874) 18 Eq. 1.
5 Even though it is not stated of whom he is the representative: *Fay v Miller, Wilkins & Co* [1941] KB 360, [1941] 2 All ER 18, CA.
6 *Potter v Duffield* (1874) 18 Eq. 4.
7 *Reuss v Picksley* (1866) LR 1 Ex. 342.
8 *Schneider v Norris* (1814) 2 M & S 286; *Leeman v Stocks* [1951] Ch 941, [1951] 1 All ER 1043.
9 *Baker v Dening* (1838) 8 A & E 94.

10 *Caton v Caton* (1867) LR 2 HL 127, per Lord Westbury.
11 *Evans v Hoare* [1892] 1 QB 593.
12 See further para. 12.03, post.

Variation of contract

2.14 The terms of a valid contract required by the Statute of Frauds to be evidenced in writing cannot be varied orally or by a document which does not comply with the statute.[1] However, a subsequent parol contract may operate to discharge expressly or impliedly the previous written contract, if it discloses an intention not merely to vary the original contract, but to set it aside.[2] A subsequent parol contract which purports not only to discharge the earlier written contract, but also to substitute for it a new one, has the effect of discharging the earlier contract, but if the new one also comes within the provisions of the Statute of Frauds, it will be unenforceable because of the lack of written evidence.

At common law a contract under seal could not be discharged or varied by a parol agreement, but in equity this is now possible.

1 For the ordinary rules on variation of contracts, see para. 3.21, post.
2 *Morris v Baron & Co* [1918] AC 1, HL; *British and Benington's Ltd v NW Cachar Tea Co* [1923] AC 48, HL.

3. Capacity to contract

Presumption of capacity

2.15 Every person is presumed to have capacity to contract, but there are certain persons whose status, age, or condition renders them wholly or partly incapable of binding themselves by a contract—e.g. minors (alternatively referred to as infants). Incapacity must be proved by the party claiming the benefit of it, and until proved the ordinary presumption remains. The incapacity may be such as to make the attempted contract null and void, or it may be such as to render it voidable; in the latter case the contract remains valid until the option to render it invalid is exercised by the person entitled to avoid it.

Minors

2.16 A person under eighteen years of age is a minor and a person is deemed to attain the age of eighteen at the commencement of the eighteenth anniversary of his birth.[1] The policy of the law in relation to minors' contracts is a compromise between the following two principles:

1. To protect minors against their own inexperience; and
2. To do so without causing unnecessary hardship to adults who deal with minors.

Categories of minors' contracts

The present (rather unsatisfactory) law divides minors' contracts into three categories: (a) void contracts; (b) voidable contracts; (c) valid contracts.[2]

---

1 Family Law Reform Act 1969, s. 1 (reducing the age of majority from twenty-one to eighteen).
2 For criticism of the present law see Treitel *Law of Contract* (4th edn) 393–395.

---

a) VOID CONTRACTS

2.17 Some contracts cannot be validly made by a minor. Section 1 of the Infants Relief Act 1874 enacts that:

'All contracts, whether by specialty or by simple contract, henceforth entered into by [minors] for the repayment of money lent or to be lent, or for goods supplied or to be supplied (other than contracts for necessaries), and all accounts stated with infants, shall be absolutely void.'

This section singles out for special treatment the following types of contract:

1. Contracts for *the supply of goods*, which expression probably includes not just sale and exchange, but also simple hire and hire purchase.[1] The section strikes only at credit facilities extended to minors: it is safe to supply goods on cash terms to a minor; and there is no objection to a minor supplying goods on credit to an adult. Moreover, even where goods are supplied on credit to a minor, there is expressly saved by the section the common law liability of a minor for necessaries,[2] which liability also extends to mentally disordered and drunken persons;[2] but in no case can a minor be sued on a bill of exchange or promissory note, even if it is given for necessaries.[3] Probably declaratory of the common

law view of necessaries is the definition found in the Sale of Goods Act 1893 (s. 2) of

'goods suitable to the condition in life of such [minor] or other person,[4] and to his actual requirements at the time of sale and delivery'.[5]

However, because of the difficulty of proving that goods are necessaries,[6] where it is desired to supply goods on credit to a minor it is normal to make an adult surety sign as 'co-principal' or 'indemnifier',[7] though it should be borne in mind that canvassing such business from a minor is now a criminal offence.[8]

2. Contracts for *the repayment of money lent*, including by way of negotiable instrument.[3] This not only renders any loan irrecoverable, but also avoids any mortgage of land or goods executed as security.[9] There are two further statutory protections for minor borrowers. First, the offering of loans to minors is restricted: it is a criminal offence to send to a minor any circular inviting him to borrow money.[8] Second, the legislature has made two attempts to protect fledgling-adults by restricting their power to ratify in early majority loans taken out during minority.[10]

3. *Accounts stated*, i.e. admissions of debt, an anti-avoidance device needed because the admission gave rise to an implied promise to pay. Whilst remaining liable for any entirely distinct tort,[11] a minor cannot be sued for a tort arising out of any contract falling within section 1. Thus, if a minor induces a person to lend him money by fraudulently representing himself to be of full age, he cannot be sued for money lent either on the contract of loan, or in quasi-contract for the return of the capital, or in the tort of deceit.[12] Yet, although the section stipulates that the above types of contract will be 'absolutely void', that expression would appear to be a misnomer in at least two respects. First, it may be that the adult party to such a contract remains bound.[13] Second, property received by the minor under such a void transaction is not necessarily recoverable by the innocent adult.[14]

---

1 *Pearce v Brain* [1929] 2 KB 310 (exchange); cf. *Ballett v Mingay* [1943] KB 281, [1943] 1 All ER 143, CA.

2 Sale of Goods Act 1893, s. 2. For the contractual capacity of mentally disordered and drunken persons, see further para. 2.21, post.

3 *Re Soltykoff* [1891] 1 QB 413, CA. But if a bill is given to a person who has supplied necessaries his right to sue on the *original contract* is not prejudicially affected. Ibid.

4 *Ryder v Wombell* (1868) LR 4 Exch 32.

5 *Johnstone v Marks* (1887) 19 QBD 509, CA.

6 See *Nash v Inman* [1908] 2 KB 1, CA.
7 For sureties, see further para. 16.03, post. However, an adult *guarantor* of a contract void under s. 1 cannot be sued: *Coutts & Co v Browne-Lecky* [1947] KB 104, [1946] 2 All ER 207.
8 Consumer Credit Act 1974, s. 50: see para. 15.15, post.
9 *Nottingham Permanent Benefit, etc, Building Society v Thurstan* [1903] AC 6, HL. But the mortgagee does have a right to be subrogated to the seller: see further paras. 12.10, 17.05, post.
10 Infants Relief Act 1874, s. 2; Betting and Loans (Infants) Act 1892, s. 5.
11 There is obviously difficulty in saying which torts are entirely independent of a contract: see *Fawcett v Smethurst* (1914) 84 LJKB 473; *Ballett v Mingay* [1943] KB 281, [1943] 1 All ER 143, CA.
12 *R Leslie Ltd v Sheill* [1914] 3 KB 607, CA. However, if goods or money obtained by such fraud are still in the infant's possession, he may be required by the court to return them in accordance with the equitable doctrine of restitution.
13 This was the common law; but the general view that it has remained the law notwithstanding the clear words of the Act has been disputed: Treitel *Law of Contract* (4th edn) 381–382.
14 See further below, para. 2.20.

---

b) VOIDABLE CONTRACTS

2.18 Certain classes of contracts are binding on the minor unless he expressly repudiates them during his minority or within a reasonable time[1] after reaching his majority; and the minor's ignorance of his right to repudiate will not relieve him from the consequences of undue delay in exercising that right.[2] What amounts to a reasonable time is in each case to be determined on the particular facts.[3]

This group of contracts consists of those which are incident to interests in permanent property, and includes:

1. *Contracts concerning land.* Whilst precluded by statute from acquiring a legal interest in land,[4] a minor may by contract acquire an equitable interest therein.[5] Thus, a minor who enters into a contract for the sale or purchase of freehold land is bound unless he repudiates.[6] Similarly, in relation to leases, whether made by the minor in the capacity of landlord or tenant, the position is as follows: if he makes a lease and accepts rent after coming of age,[7] or if he continues to occupy under a lease,[8] in either case he will be considered to have adopted the contract; though, had he wished to do so, he could have avoided the lease.[9]

2. *Shares in companies.* If and when a minor who has agreed to subscribe, or has bought, shares in a company, repudiates the bargain, he ceases to be liable for calls and is entitled to have his name removed from the company's register of shareholders.[10] On the other hand, if when he becomes of age he does not repudiate, he will be deemed to have ratified the contract of purchase, and will be liable to be placed on the list of contributories.[11] To

obviate the uncertainties of this situation, quoted companies commonly try to discourage minors from becoming shareholders. 3. *Partnership.* A minor can become a partner, but cannot be responsible for partnership debts during his minority.[12] But he is liable if after reaching majority he fails to repudiate the partnership.[13]

---

1 *Re Blakely Ordnance Co* (1869) LR 4 Ch App 31; and *Ebbett's Case* (1870) LR 5 Ch App 302.
2 *Carnell v Harrison* [1916] 1 Ch 328.
3 *Edwards v Carter* [1893] AC 360, HL, a marriage settlement case.
4 Law of Property Act 1925, s. 1 (6); Settled Land Act 1925, s. 27 (1). For sale of an interest in land between adult parties, see post, chap. 12.
5 *Davies v Beynon-Harris* (1931) 47 TLR 424; Settled Land Act 1925, s. 27 (2).
6 *Whittingham v Murdy* (1889) 60 LT 956.
7 *Baylis v Dineley* (1815) 3 M & S 477 at 481.
8 1 Rolle Abr. 731.
9 Per Gibbs CJ, in *Holmes v Blogg* (1818) 8 Taunt 508.
10 *Steinberg v Scala (Leeds) Ltd* [1923] 2 Ch 452, CA.
11 *Re Blakely Ordnance Co* (1869) LR 4 Ch App 31.
12 *Lovell and Christmas v Beauchamp* [1894] AC 607, HL.
13 *Goode v Harrison* (1821) 5 B & Ald 159 at 160; and see per Lord Herschell, in *Lovell and Christmas v Beauchamp* [1894] AC, at 611.

---

c) VALID CONTRACTS

2.19 There is a well-established rule that beneficial contracts of service are binding on a minor if, taken as a whole, the agreement is not so much to his detriment as to render it unfair that he should be bound by it.[1] This principle, primarily evolved in relation to contracts of employment,[2] has been extended by analogy to contracts of apprenticeship,[3] and any contract under which the minor makes a living by the exercise of some trade or profession, e.g. as an entertainer,[4] author[5] or athlete.[6] But it does not extend to any beneficial contract: if a minor carries on a business, he is not liable on contracts made by him in the course of trade irrespective of whether or not the contract is beneficial to him.[7]

The court, if satisfied that the contract is reasonable and for the benefit of the minor, will enforce its provisions even against him,[8] even if the contract is executory,[9] and will not allow him to repudiate such a contract. If the contract is not reasonable and for the minor's benefit, the court will not enforce it.[10] If a minor's contract of service contains unreasonable stipulations in restraint of trade and these are severable, the void stipulations may be rejected and the operative part of the contract, if otherwise unobjectionable, enforced.[11] An apprentice cannot be sued for damages on his covenant in the deed to serve,[12] but a covenant for the payment of a fair and reasonable premium may be enforced against him[13] and so may a reasonable restrictive covenant not to compete in business after the cessation of the apprenticeship.[14]

1 Smith LJ, in *Flower v London and North Western Rly Co* [1894] 2 QB at 68.
2 *Clements v London and North Western Rly Co* [1894] 2 QB 482, CA. For adult contracts of employment, see further chap. 32, post.
3 *De Francesco v Barnum* (1889) 43 ChD 165, (1890) 45 ChD 430.
4 *Denmark Productions Ltd v Boscobel Productions Ltd* (1967) 111 Sol Jo 715, revsd. on other grounds [1969] 1 QB 699, [1968] 3 All ER 513, CA (Troggs pop group).
5 *Chaplin v Leslie Frewin (Publishers) Ltd* [1966] Ch 71, [1965] 3 All ER 764, CA.
6 *Doyle v White City Stadium Ltd* [1935] 1 KB 110, CA.
7 *Mercantile Union Guarantee Corpn v Ball* [1937] 2 KB 498, [1937] 3 All ER 1, CA.
8 *Clements v London and North Western Rly Co* [1894] 2 QB 482, CA; *Green v Thompson* [1899] 2 QB 1.
9 *Roberts v Gray* [1913] 1 KB 520, CA (contract to tour as professional billiard player).
10 *De Francesco v Barnum* (1889) 43 ChD 165, (1890) 45 ChD 430; *Corn v Matthews* [1893] 1 QB 310, CA.
11 *Bromley v Smith* [1909] 2 KB 235.
12 *Gylbert v Fletcher* (1629) Cro Car 179. The apprentice can sue his master for breach of contract and claim as damages the diminution of his future prospects as well as for loss of earnings. *Dunk v George Waller & Son Ltd* [1970] 2 QB 163, [1970] 2 All ER 630, CA.
13 *Walter v Everard* [1891] 2 QB 369, CA.
14 *Gadd v Thompson* [1911] 1 KB 304.

Recovery of money paid by infants

2.20 Whether a minor can recover money paid under a contract entered into by him which he either avoids, having a right to do so, or which per se is void, probably depends upon whether there has or has not been a total failure of consideration.[1]

1 *Steinberg v Scala (Leeds) Ltd* [1923] 2 Ch 452, CA; *Valentini v Canali* (1890) 24 QBD 166. But see *Chaplin v Leslie Frewin (Publishers) Ltd* [1966] Ch 71, [1965] 3 All ER 764, obiter division of opinion in CA.

Bankruptcy of minors is dealt with in para. 33.02, post.

Mentally disordered and drunken persons

2.21 A contract made with a person who by reason of mental disorder does not know what he is doing is voidable at the mental patient's option, provided that the other contracting party knew or ought to have known at the time of contracting of his disability.[1] A mentally disordered person must pay a reasonable price for necessaries.[2] A contract may in any case be ratified when he recovers from his disorder.

Under the Mental Health Act 1959, the High Court has power to make orders for the management of the property and affairs of those who by reason of mental disorder are incapable of managing their own affairs.

The contracts of elderly people, whose powers are failing, are treated on the same principles. Thus in *Manches v Trimborn:*[3]

> The defendant, an elderly woman, drew a cheque in favour of the plaintiff. She was capable of understanding that she was signing a cheque but, to the plaintiff's knowledge, she was incapable of understanding the transaction to which the cheque related. *Held:* she had a good defence to the action on the cheque.

A person who enters into a contract when to the knowledge of the other party he is in a state of complete drunkenness, so that he does not know what he is doing, may avoid such contract;[4] but it remains good unless he does so.[5] If the contract is for the supply of necessaries at a fair price, in the absence of unfair dealing, it is good.[6]

---

1 *Imperial Loan Co v Stone* [1892] 1 QB 599, CA.
2 Sale of Goods Act 1893, s. 2.
3 (1946) 115 LJKB 305.
4 *Gore v Gibson* (1845) 13 M & W 623.
5 *Matthews v Baxter* (1873) LR 8 Ex 132.
6 Sale of Goods Act 1893, s. 2. See further para. 2.17, ante.

Corporations and companies

2.22 Apart from the special rules about to be considered, a number of people acting together to form one party to a contract are simply regarded by the law as co-contractors in an *unincorporated association,*[1] e.g. a partnership[2] or club; and, in a typical case one of their number will be deputed to contract on behalf of them all.[3] However, there are some circumstances where the law regards the *association* as having become *incorporated*, and as having acquired a legal personality separate from that of its members. In such cases, a contract may be made with the *incorporated association* itself—be it a registered company or other incorporated body—in which case the members of the *association* do not necessarily by that act become parties to the contract,[4] though they may do so.[5]

A *corporation* is an artificial person created by Royal Charter or by Act of Parliament, and endowed with special capacity. It may consist of one person or of many; in the former case it is then known as a corporation sole,[6] and in the latter as a corporation aggregate. The class of corporations aggregate includes various institutions which are holders of charters from the Crown; but, in the commercial world, trading corporations—such as public utilities and nationalised industries—are generally created under special legislation. On the other hand, private enterprise trading organisations normally operate as *registered companies* incorporated under the Companies Act 1948 or earlier Acts superseded by that Act.

Contractual capacity Chartered corporations, i.e. those created by Royal Charter, have the same powers to contract as individuals, whereas statutory corporations, i.e. those created by, or under the terms of, a particular statute, such as companies registered under the Companies Act 1948, have only those powers conferred on them by the statute incorporating them or which are implied by law.[7] Thus, a trading corporation has implied power, in the absence of express restriction, to borrow money for the purpose of its business.[8] In the case of statutory corporations, a contract made in excess of its powers is said to be *ultra vires* and is invalid.[9] The *ultra vires* doctrine does not apply to chartered corporations; and in the case of registered companies the effect of the doctrine has been severely restricted by the European Communities Act 1972, s. 9 (1), which provides that in favour of any person dealing with a company in good faith, any contract made by the directors is deemed to be within the capacity of the company.

Abolition of formal requirements At common law there was a rule that, in general, a corporation must contract under seal. Contracts not made under seal were void.[10] The rule did not apply to companies registered under the Companies Acts, and there were several other exceptions. The rule was finally abolished by the Corporate Bodies' Contracts Act 1960. In any contract made by a corporation after the commencement of this Act, no more formality is required than if the contract were made by an individual.

1 For parties to a contract, see generally para. 2.03, ante.
2 For partnerships, see further chap. 11, post.
3 Cf. *Bradley Egg Farm v Clifford* [1943] 2 All ER 378, CA.
4 *Newborne v Sensolid (Great Britain) Ltd* [1954] 1 QB 45, [1953] 1 All ER 708, CA (pre-incorporation contract; decision now reversed by statute: see para. 10.27, post).
5 It is common to require the operator of a small business trading as a company to contract both on behalf of his company and personally as a means of making him act as surety for the performance of its obligations by his company; for sureties, see further, chap. 16, post.
6 E.g. the vicar of a parish.
7 *Breay v Royal British Nurses' Association* [1897] 2 Ch 272, CA.
8 *General Auction, etc, Co v Smith* [1891] 3 Ch 432.
9 *Ashbury Railway Carriage and Iron Co v Riche* (1875) LR 7 HL 653, HL. See also *Introductions Ltd v National Provincial Bank* [1970] Ch 199, [1969] 1 All ER 887, CA; *Bell Houses Ltd v City Wall Properties Ltd* [1966] 2 QB 656, [1966] 2 All ER 674, CA.
10 *A R Wright & Son Ltd v Romford Corpn* [1957] 1 QB 431, [1956] 3 All ER 785.

Bankrupts

2.23   A person who is made bankrupt is not incapacitated from contracting, but if while undischarged he obtains credit to the extent of £50 or upwards, or trades under a different name from that under which he was adjudged bankrupt, without informing his intended creditor that he is an undischarged bankrupt, or without disclosing the name under which he was adjudged bankrupt, he will be liable to imprisonment.[1]

If a contract is entered into, and one of the parties is adjudged bankrupt, the rights and liabilities under the contract generally pass to his trustee,[2] but the trustee may by disclaimer abandon the contract.[3]

Personal services Contracts requiring the personal services of the bankrupt cannot be enforced by the trustee in bankruptcy against the other party unless the bankrupt is willing to render the services.[4] The rights of the other party are:

1. To prove for loss sustained by non-fulfilment of the contract if the liability of the bankrupt be of a provable nature,[5]

2. In the case of a contract to deliver non-specific goods by instalments, to refuse to deliver instalments after the bankruptcy begins until he is paid for them;[6] and

3. He may apply to the court to have the contract terminated, and the court may rescind it on terms that such party do pay damages to the trustee or prove for damages against the estate, or otherwise.[7]

1 Bankruptcy Act 1914, s. 155. See *R v Doubleday* (1964) 49 Cr App Rep 62.
2 Bankruptcy Act 1914, s. 38; this is subject to the exception that if the contract be one affecting merely the person of the debtor, e.g., to cure, it will not pass to the trustee. See generally post, chap. 33.
3 Ibid, s. 54. See para. 33.32, post.
4 Williams' *Bankruptcy* (18th edn) 316.
5 Bankruptcy Act 1914, s. 30. See para. 33.39, post.
6 Williams' *Bankruptcy* (18th edn) 313.
7 Bankruptcy Act 1914, s. 54 (5). See para. 33.32, post.

Miscellaneous cases

2.24   *An alien enemy* is incapacitated during the continuance of a war from contracting with British subjects, and his power to sue or exercise rights in relation to property in this country is suspended. But an alien enemy may be sued during war, and if sued, he may defend himself.[1]

Foreign sovereigns and states may contract, but the contract cannot be enforced against them unless they consent. However, this sovereign immunity does not extend to separate trading corporations set up by the state, nor to ordinary commercial contracts.[2]

Diplomatic representatives of foreign and Commonwealth countries are to some extent privileged by the Diplomatic Privileges Act 1964 from being sued in the English courts, but the privilege may be waived with the sanction of the Sovereign or the official superior of the representative. Where the privileges and immunities granted by a country to the diplomatic missions of the UK are less than those conferred by the Diplomatic Privileges Act 1964 on the mission of that country, the privileges and immunities granted under the Act may be withdrawn by Order in Council.[3]

A barrister cannot sue for his fees; nor can a Fellow of a College of Physicians, the fellows of which are prohibited by byelaw from recovering at law their expenses, charges or fees.[4]

---

1 *The Hoop* (1799) 1 C Rob 1906; *Porter v Freudenberg* [1915] 1 KB 857, CA; *Robson v Premier Oil & Pipe Line Co Ltd* [1915] 2 Ch 124, CA.
2 *Trendtex Trading Corporation Ltd v Central Bank of Nigeria* [1977] QB 529, [1977] 1 All ER 881, CA; *C Czarnikow Ltd v Centrala Handlu Zagranicznego 'Rolimpex'* [1978] 1 All ER 81, CA, affd Times 6.7.78, HL.
3 Diplomatic Privileges Act 1964, s. 3.
4 Medical Act 1956, s. 27 (2).

Chapter 3

Essentials of a contract

3.01 Before it will be recognised and enforced by the law, every contract must meet all the following requirements: (1) the parties must be in agreement; (2) each party must have given consideration for that agreement (unless under seal); and (3) by that agreement the parties must have intended to create legal relations.

1. Agreement: offer and acceptance

3.02 It has already been seen that a contract requires an agreement between the parties, but that that *consensus ad idem* may be either subjective or objective;[1] another way to put this is to say that each party must actually make, or appear to make, a declaration of willingness to be bound to the other parties on the same terms. As it is sometimes difficult to ascertain whether an agreement has been reached, it is common to reduce the process of reaching agreement into terms of offer and acceptance, though not all agreements can be so analysed.[2] Taking the simple case of negotiations between only two parties,[3] these may be scrutinised for chronological declarations of willingness to be bound to each other in the following way: the first declaration of willingness to be bound on stated terms is an *offer*; and a subsequent declaration by the other party of willingness to be bound on the same terms may be an *acceptance* thereof.[4]

---

1 See para. 2.05, ante.
2 E.g. some multilateral contracts: see *The Satanita* [1897] AC 59, HL.
3 For parties, see further para. 2.03, ante.
4 For the special rules of offer and acceptance applicable to international contracts for the sale of goods, see para. 13.47, post.

A) *Offer*

3.03 An offer may be made to a specific person or group of persons; or it may be made to the general public: it is all a matter of reasonable interpretation of the terms of the offer. In *Carlill v Carbolic Smoke Ball Co*,[1] the facts were these:

> D issued an advertisement in which they offered to pay £100 to any person who should contract influenza after using a certain remedy in a specified manner and for a specified period; P duly used the remedy, and contracted influenza, whereupon the Court of Appeal *held* her entitled to the £100.

Here was a definite offer to anybody who would perform the conditions, and it was accepted by one of the persons to whom it was made.

---

1 [1893] 1 QB 256, CA.

---

a) INVITATION TO TREAT

3.04 It is not always the party who makes the first overture who makes the offer. That party may not himself make a declaration of willingness to be bound, but may instead indicate that he is prepared to receive such declarations from other people. In such cases, the party who makes the first overture is said to be merely issuing an 'invitation to treat'. Whether any particular approach amounts to an offer or only an invitation to treat depends on the speaker's intention, subjective or objective. Of course, there is no such difficulty if the party expressly states his intention, as commonly happens with standard form contracts.[1] Apart from this type of case, it is a matter of ascertaining the intention from all the circumstances of the case. However, in searching for this elusive criterion, there are a number of stereotyped situations where some prima facie rules have been laid down:

a) Auction sales The auctioneer's request for bids is an invitation to treat; each bid is an offer; and, when the auctioneer brings his hammer down on the highest bid, he accepts it.[2]

b) Display of goods for sale Price-marked goods in a shop window are only an invitation to treat, the request for them by the customer amounting to an offer.[3] Similarly, in the case of a self-service shop, the contract is not made when the customer takes the goods off the shelves, but at the check-out.[4]

c) Advertisements Very generally, these fall into two classes. Those advertisements which request an act, such as the supply of information in return for a reward or prize, tend to be offers,[5] whereas those which ask for a reply by would-be acceptors tend

27

to be mere invitations to treat: examples of the latter category are advertisements for tenders,[6] of goods for sale,[7] of scholarship examinations[8] and of price-lists.[9]

d) Sales of shares When a company issues a prospectus, and asks for applications for shares, it does not usually offer to sell them to the public but merely issues an invitation to treat;[10] but it is otherwise where a company sends a shareholder a letter informing him of a 'rights' issue.[11] Transfers of shares are governed by statute.[12]

e) Sales of land.[13]

1 E.g. *Financings Ltd v Stimson* [1962] 3 All ER 386, [1962] 1 WLR 1184, CA (h.p. agreement form). For standard form contracts, see para. 3.13, post.
2 Sale of Goods Act 1893, s. 58 (2), and see further para. 13.48, post. For the position of an auctioneer, see further para. 10.32, post.
3 *Fisher v Bell* [1961] 1 QB 394, [1960] 3 All ER 731 (display of flick-knife: criminal case now reversed by statute).
4 *Pharmaceutical Society of Great Britain v Boots Cash Chemists (Southern) Ltd* [1953] 1 QB 401, [1953] 1 All ER 482, CA.
5 *Williams v Carwardine* (1833) 4 B & Ad 621 (reward poster); *Carlill's Case* (see para. 3.03, ante); *Esso Petroleum Ltd v Customs and Excise Comrs* [1976] 1 All ER 117, [1976] 1 WLR 1, HL ('free gift' with sale); *Thornton v Shoe Lane Parking Ltd* [1971] 2 KB 163, [1971] 1 All ER 686, CA (notice at entrance to car park).
6 *Spencer v Harding* (1870) LR 5 CP 561. Unless tender for a standing order: *Great Northern Rly Co v Witham* (1873) LR 9 CP 16.
7 *Partridge v Crittenden* [1968] 2 All ER 421, [1968] 1 WLR 1204, DC (criminal case).
8 *Rooke v Dawson* [1895] 1 Ch 480.
9 *Grainger & Son v Gough* [1896] AC 325, HL.
10 *Harris' Case* (1872) 7 Ch App 587.
11 *Jackson v Turquand* (1869) LR 4 HL 305.
12 Companies Act 1948, ss. 75–84.
13 See para. 12.05, post.

b) DURATION

3.05 An offer can only be accepted whilst it remains 'alive', and may come to an end in any of the following ways:

a) Revocation by the offeror In English (unlike Continental) law, an offer can generally be withdrawn at any moment *before* acceptance even though expressed to be open for a certain time,[1] unless the offeror has contracted to keep it open (a separate contract of option),[2] bankers' confirmed credits being an apparent exception.[3] However, for revocation to be effective, it must be communicated before acceptance *to* the offeree or his agent,[4] though it need not be communicated *by* the offeror.[5] Revocation generally only takes effect on communication—or receipt where it is sent by post.[4]

b) Rejection An offer is terminated by rejection by the offeree, and for this purpose the proposal of different terms by the offeree (a counter-offer) is prima facie a rejection: thereafter, the original offer cannot normally be accepted.[6] However, this is not the case where the offeree merely tries to get the offeror to modify his offer,[7] or accepts conditionally,[8] or unless the original offeror in rejecting the counter-offer reasserts his offer.

c) Lapse of time An offer expressed to be open for a specified time cannot be accepted thereafter;[9] and, if no time is expressed, an offer impliedly expires at the end of a reasonable time.[10] What is a reasonable time will be indicated by the circumstances: a telegraphed offer may demand a like reply, and an offer to sell perishable goods, or to sell on a fluctuating market, may likewise demand a prompt response.

d) Occurrence of condition Besides lapse of an express time-limit, an offer may determine on the happening of any (expressly or impliedly) stipulated event, e.g. deterioration in condition of goods or life to be insured.[11]

e) Death[12] or liquidation[13] Leaving aside promises of personal service, it seems that prima facie the death of offeror or offeree before acceptance[14] does not preclude the formation of a contract.[15] A corporation cannot die,[16] though its existence (and hence its power to contract) may be liquidated.[13]

---

1 *Routledge v Grant* (1828) 4 Bing 653. See also *Luxor (Eastbourne) Ltd v Cooper* [1941] AC 108, [1941] 1 All ER 33, HL: discussed para. 10.14, post.

2 E.g. *Mountford v Scott* [1975] 1 All ER 198, [1975] 2 WLR 114, CA, and see contracts of hire purchase, discussed para. 14.03 et seq, post.

3 Discussed para. 13.43, post. For an example outside commerce, see *Errington v Errington and Woods* [1952] 1 KB 290, [1952] 1 All ER 149, CA.

4 *Byrne v Van Tienhoven* (1880) 5 CPD 344; *Financings Ltd v Stimson* [1962] 3 All ER 386, [1962] 1 WLR 1184, CA.

5 *Dickinson v Dodds* (1876) 2 ChD 463, CA (reliable indirect information sufficient).

6 *Hyde v Wrench* (1840) 3 Beav 334 (counter-offer by offeree); *Northland Airliners Ltd v Dennis Ferranti Meters Ltd* (1970) 114 Sol Jo 845, CA.

7 *Stevenson v McLean* (1880) 5 QBD 346 (attempt to put words into mouth of offeror).

8 If the offer and acceptance are both subject to the same condition, there is a conditional contract: see para. 7.06, post. But, if the offer is unconditional, a conditional 'acceptance' will be a counter-offer.

9 E.g. 'open for x days', or 'reply by return of post' (for postal rules, see further, para. 3.11, post).

10 *Ramsgate Victoria Hotel Co v Montefiore* (1866) LR 1 Exch 109 (six months too long for share allotment).

11 *Financings Ltd v Stimson* [1962] 3 All ER 386, [1962] 1 WLR 1184, CA (goods); for life insurance, see para. 26.07, post.

12 For the effect of personal incapacity on the power to contract, see para. 2.15, et seq., ante.
13 For the liquidation of companies, see further para. 33.01 (7), post.
14 For the effect of death of a party after acceptance, see para. 8.02, post, and for the effect of bankruptcy after acceptance, see paras. 33.17, 33.32, post.
15 *Bradbury v Morgan* (1862) 1 H & C 249. For continuing guarantees, see para. 16.10 (6), post.
16 See para. 2.22, ante.

B) *Acceptance*

3.06 The second declaration of willingness to be bound—this time by the offeree to the offeror—can only amount to an acceptance if it is on terms which have an identical legal effect to that of the offer (this being a matter of substance, not form),[1] is made whilst the offer is still open[2] and is made by the offeree.[3] Generally speaking, in order to accept the offeree must do both the following:

1 So it does not matter that the offeree merely adds a term which the law would imply anyway, such as the obligation to pay promptly: *Harris' Case* (1872) 7 Ch App 587.
2 For the duration of the offer, see above.
3 For the requirement that only the offeree can accept, see further para. 5.02, post.

a) DISPLAY AN INTENTION TO ACCEPT[1]

3.07 The primary requirement is that the circumstances must show that the negotiations have led to an agreement: the general rule is that the parties must have finished agreeing;[2] but, especially in commercial transactions which have been wholly or partially performed, the courts strive to spell out an agreement,[3] even sometimes to the extent of giving it retrospective effect.[4] However, it does follow from the basic requirement that the would-be acceptor must have knowledge of the offer, so that he cannot accept in ignorance of the offer,[5] nor do cross-offers result in a contract.[6] In the perhaps long series of negotiations between the parties, it may be difficult for the courts, and even for the parties, to say when they have reached agreement;[7] but, once they have reached agreement, the fact that the parties continue negotiations thereafter does not affect the existence of their contract,[8] unless it is possible to spell out of those later negotiations a second contract to rescind or modify the first contract.[9]

1 *Taylor v Allon* [1966] 1 QB 304, [1965] 1 All ER 557, DC (a cautionary insurance tale for drivers).
2 *Scammel v Ouston* [1941] AC 251, [1941] 1 All ER 14, HL (agreement to buy 'on h.p. terms' no contract as those terms not yet settled): see now the Consumer Credit Act 1974, s. 59, para. 14.21. But see *Smith v Morgan* [1971] 2 All ER 1500, [1971] 1 WLR 803.
3 *Hillas & Co v Arcos Ltd* [1932] All ER Rep. 494, HL. But see *Courtney and Fairbairn Ltd v Tolaini Bros (Hotels) Ltd* [1975] 1 All ER 716, [1975] 1 WLR 297, CA; *Bushwall Properties Ltd v Vortex Properties Ltd* [1975] 2 All ER 214, [1975] 1 WLR 1649. And see further para. 13.02, note 20, post.
4 *Trollope and Colls and Holland and Hannen and Cubitts Ltd v Atomic Power Constructions Ltd* [1962] 3 All ER 1035, [1963] 1 WLR 333 (large civil engineering contract substantially executed before agreement reached).
5 *R v Clarke* (1927) 40 CLR 227 (reward case).
6 *Tinn v Hoffmann & Co* (1873) 29 LT 271.
7 E.g. *Brogden v Metropolitan Rly Co* (1877) 2 App Cas 666, HL.
8 *Cranleigh Precision Engineering Ltd v Bryant* [1964] 3 All ER 289, [1965] 1 WLR 1293; *Thoresen Car Ferries Ltd v Weymouth Portland BC* [1977] 2 Lloyd's Rep 614.
9 For rescission and modification of contract by subsequent agreement, see para. 3.21, post.

---

b) COMMUNICATE ACCEPTANCE TO OFFEROR

3.08 The position here in practice differs according to whether the offer also requests a reply or merely performance as follows:

1. Where the offer demands a reply before performance there will be no contract unless and until the offeree communicates his acceptance to the offeror,[1] mere silence by the offeree generally not being deemed consent.[2] Where an offer indicates a particular mode of acceptance, all depends on whether it is prescribed as the *exclusive mode* of acceptance: if so, acceptance is possible in no other way;[3] but if not, any mode of acceptance equally advantageous to the offeror will suffice,[4] e.g. a request to reply 'by return of post' frequently just imposes a time-limit on the offer rather than requiring the acceptance to be conveyed by the Post Office.[5]

2. Where the offer demands *only* performance, any purported communication of acceptance is irrelevant, and performance as requested amounts also to the acceptance even where the offeror is ignorant thereof.[6] This rule may cause difficulty where the requested act is not performable in an instant but over a longish period;[7] and, if it is possible to construe the offer as falling under (3) below it is safer to communicate an acceptance before embarking on performance.

3. Where the offer indicates that it may be accepted either by reply or by performance, then the offeree may choose as between (1) and (2) above, e.g. unsolicited goods.[2]

Where a contract comes into existence on the communication of acceptance, it is normally described as a *bilateral* contract (one involving promises on both sides); and where a contract is concluded by performance, there is said to be a *unilateral* contract (a promise by one side only).[8]

---

1 *Powell v Lee* (1908) 99 LT 284 (leak of school board's resolution to accept did not conclude contract).
2 You cannot force a contract on another simply by saying: 'If I do not hear from you, I will assume you accept': *Felthouse v Bindley* (1862) 11 CBNS 869. But the offeree may take advantage of such an offer and simply accept by performance: see text to footnote 6. This common law defence against inertia selling has now been re-inforced by the Unsolicited Goods and Services Act 1971: see further para. 14.06, post.
3 *Quenerduaine v Cole* (1883) 32 WR 185 (impliedly requiring reply by telegram); *Financings Ltd v Stimson* [1962] 3 All ER 386, [1962] 1 WLR 1184, CA (form stipulated for acceptance by signature).
4 *Manchester Diocesan Council for Education v Commercial and General Investments Ltd* [1969] 3 All ER 1593, [1970] 1 WLR 241.
5 For communications by post, see further para. 3.11, post.
6 *Carlill v Carbolic Smoke Ball Co* [1893] 1 QB 256, CA: see para. 3.03, ante.
7 See para. 3.05, ante.
8 For the effect of this on the rules of consideration, see para. 3.17, post.

3.09 *Conditional assent* An unconditional offer cannot be accepted conditionally, the 'conditional acceptance' in fact being a counter-offer.[1] On the other hand, a conditional offer may be accepted, thus concluding a conditional contract, e.g. a contract of sale only to be performed if a third party approves of the subject-matter,[2] or on the obtaining of a licence;[3] or the parties may enter a binding provisional agreement on the understanding that it is subsequently to be replaced by a formal contract.[4] However, it will be recalled that there is no contract unless and until the parties have finished agreeing,[5] and the condition may indicate that this is not the case,[6] e.g. a sale of an interest in land 'subject to contract'.[7]

---

1 For counter-offers, see para. 3.05, ante.
2 *Marten v Whale* [1917] 2 KB 480, CA (set out para. 7.06, post).
3 Cf. para. 6.02, post.
4 E.g. *Branca v Cobarro* [1947] KB 854, [1947] 2 All ER 101, CA (land—and see note 7 below); *Cory v Patton* (1872) LR 7 QB 304 (insurance slip—and see now the Marine Insurance Act 1906, s. 22: see further para. 27.06, post).
5 See para. 3.07, ante.
6 There are conflicting cases on agreement subject to a satisfactory mortgage: *Lee Parker v Izzet* [1971] 3 All ER 1099, [1971] 1 WLR 1688, and *Lee Parker v Izzet* (No. 2) [1972] 2 All ER 800, [1972] 1 WLR 775. Cf. *The John S Darbyshire* [1977] 2 Lloyd's Rep 457.
7 See further para. 12.06, post.

3.10 *Time of acceptance* Leaving aside postal communications, the general rule is that acceptance dates from the moment of communication,[1] though it has been seen that there are cases where the courts have given it retrospective effect.[2] If the communication is made to the offeror's agent, a distinction must be drawn: if the agent is (or appears to be) authorised to *receive* the acceptance, it takes effect as soon as communicated to him;[1] whereas, if he is only authorised to transmit the acceptance, it must first be communicated to his principal.[3]

---

1 *Entores Ltd v Miles Far East Corpn* [1955] 2 QB 327, [1955] 2 All ER 493, CA. Cf. *The Brimnes* [1975] QB 929, [1974] 3 All ER 88, CA.
2 See para. 3.07, ante.
3 For the powers of an agent, see generally paras. 10.17 et seq., post. Cf. the Post Office.

3.11 *Postal communications* The offer may permit the offeree to respond by post either expressly, or impliedly, e.g. where the offer is by post. In such a case, the special postal rules are prima facie brought into play, but may be ousted by the offer.[1] Where the postal rules apply, then at common law acceptance dates, not from receipt by the offeror, but from posting by the offeree of a properly addressed and stamped letter of acceptance, even if that letter is delayed or lost in the post.[2] Thus, it follows that a revocation of offer is ineffective after the acceptance has been posted; in *Byrne v Van Tienhoven*:[3]

> Defendants posted an offer to sell goods to the plaintiff on October 1st; on the 11th the offer arrived and the plaintiff at once accepted by telegram. On the 8th the defendants had posted a letter withdrawing the offer, and this was received on the 20th. The withdrawal was *held* to be too late.

This illogical exception to the ordinary common law rules of acceptance is based on convenience;[4] it applies to communications by letter or telegram,[5] but not to virtually instantaneous forms of communication such as telephone or teleprinter, where the ordinary rules obtain;[6] and it has been reversed by statute for those international sales of goods which the parties have chosen to have governed by the Uniform Law on Sales.[7]

---

1 *Holwell Securities Ltd v Hughes* [1974] 1 All ER 161, [1974] 1 WLR 155, CA.
2 *Household Fire and Carriage Accident Insurance Co v Grant* (1879) 4 Ex D 216, CA.
3 (1880) 5 CPD 344.
4 Contrast Continental law, where acceptance dates from receipt: but there, a

similar result may be reached by imposing restrictions on the offeror's power to withdraw his offer: see para. 3.05, ante.

5 For letter, see *Grant's Case* (above); for telegram, see *Bruner v Moore* [1904] 1 Ch 305.

6 *Entores Ltd v Miles Far East Corpn* [1955] 2 QB 327, [1955] 2 All ER 493, CA.

7 Uniform Laws on International Sales Act 1967, Sch. 1: see para. 13.47, post.

C) *Constructing a contract*

3.12 It has already been seen that a contract may fail for lack of certainty as to their intention because the parties have not finished agreeing;[1] but this will not be the case just because the contract contains a meaningless phrase,[2] or where the omission can be supplied without any further negotiations between the parties.[3] Moreover, English law obviates the need for business-men to spell out in precise detail all the terms of every contract they make by the following techniques:

1. It categorises the more commonly occurring kinds of contract into e.g. partnership, sale of goods, life insurance, carriage of goods, employment.[4] To each of these established categories,[5] the law attaches a large number of incidents often called 'implied terms',[6] either compulsorily[7] or subject to a contrary intention. It is hence possible for the parties to make quite complicated contracts perhaps by a simple verbal exchange; and, in case of subsequent difficulty, the incidents of such contracts will frequently be easily ascertainable by reference to the law relating to that type of contract.

2. In the absence of any particular statutory provisions[7] or misrepresentation,[8] the parties may incorporate detailed terms (usually written) into an agreement made in simplest form (either oral or written) so as to become part of that agreement in either of the following ways:

a) Incorporation by notice The incorporation is simply a matter of contractual intention: notice to another contracting party (or his agent) will suffice to incorporate terms (irrespective of whether the other party has listened to, or read, them) provided only that the latter realises *before* contracting[9] that the other party intended them to form part of their contract, or ought to have so realised because reasonable steps were taken to bring them to his notice.[10] What are reasonable steps will depend on the circumstances,[11] on whether those terms are unusual or normal,[12] and on whether there is a course of dealings between the parties.[13] But, if such written terms are contradicted by an oral undertaking, the latter may be held to prevail because more attention is commonly paid to what is said than to any notice or document.[14]

b) Incorporation by signed document Where the written terms are embodied in a signed document, the general rule is that there is no obligation to call the attention of the recipient to its terms, and the latter will be bound by the contents of that contractual document regardless of whether he has read them,[15] unless he has reasonably made a fundamental mistake as to what he is signing (the non est factum rule).[16] However, where his signature is only the offer, a recipient can of course revoke that offer at any time before acceptance.[17]

---

1 See para. 3.07, ante.
2 *Nicolene Ltd v Simmonds* [1953] 1 QB 543, [1953] 1 All ER 822, CA (set out para. 2.04, ante).
3 E.g. Sale of Goods Act 1893, s. 9; see para. 13.02, post.
4 The major categories of commercial contract are the subject of later chapters in this book.
5 Where a case does not fall within an established category, it is frequently possible to apply the rules of the nearest such category by analogy; e.g. *Young and Marten Ltd v McManus, Childs Ltd* [1969] 1 AC 454, [1968] 2 All ER 1169, HL.
6 For implied terms and generally, see para. 7.05, post.
7 E.g. the compulsory implied terms found in consumer sales of goods: see further para. 13.19, et seq., post; and similarly see contracts for the carriage of goods, paras. 22.06, 24.06, post.
8 For misrepresentation, see paras. 5.08 et seq., post.
9 *Chapleton v Barry UDC* [1940] 1 KB 532, [1940] 1 All ER 356, CA; *Hollingworth v Southern Ferries* [1977] 2 Lloyd's Rep 70.
10 *Parker v South Eastern Rly Co* (1877) 2 CPD 416, CA (ticket case); *Smith v South Wales Switchgear Ltd* [1978] 1 All ER 18, [1978] 1 WLR 165, HL.
11 E.g. in the ticket cases, it depends on the type of contract for which the ticket is issued: *Chapleton v Barry UDC* [1940] 1 KB 532, [1940] 1 All ER 356, CA (deck-chair—not incorp); *Cockerton v Naviera Anzar SA* [1960] 2 Lloyd's Rep 450 (passenger ship—incorp).
12 *Thornton v Shoe Lane Parking Ltd* [1971] 2 QB 163, [1971] 1 All ER 686, CA (unusual exclusion in car-park ticket).
13 *Spurling v Bradshaw* [1956] 2 All ER 121, [1956] 1 WLR 461, CA; *British Crane Hire Corpn Ltd v Ipswich Plant Hire Ltd* [1975] QB 303, [1974] 1 All ER 1059, CA. Cf. *McCutcheon v David MacBrayne Ltd* [1964] 1 All ER 430, [1964] 1 WLR 125, HL; *Hollier v Rambler Motors (AMC) Ltd* [1972] 2 QB 71, [1972] 1 All ER 399, CA.
14 *Mendelssohn v Normand* [1970] 1 QB 177, [1969] 2 All ER 1215, CA.
15 *L'Estrange v Graucob Ltd* [1934] 2 KB 394.
16 *Saunders v Anglia Building Society* [1971] AC 1004, HL. (Set out para. 5.07, post.)
17 *Financings Ltd v Stimson* [1962] 3 All ER 386, [1962] 1 WLR 1184, CA; and see generally para. 3.05, ante.

D) *Standard Form Contracts*

3.13 The advent of mass production and mass distribution has seen the introduction of standardised contracts. Utilising the legal techniques outlined above for the incorporation of written terms and to some extent bolstered by the (weak) presumption against introducing oral evidence to vary a written contract (the parol evidence rule), many large corporations and trade organisations have evolved sets of uniform terms,[1] a technique copied by Parliament.[2] The objectives of standard forms are as follows:[3]

1. To save time—the business of large organisations would become incredibly complicated if all the terms of every contract had to be negotiated de novo.
2. To allocate risk—this enables contracts the more easily to be costed and sensible provisions to be made for insurance.
3. To exploit economic power, as where a supplier of goods or services has a near monopoly, or there is otherwise a gross inequality of bargaining power.

At this point, the fundamental notion of contract as based on a *consensus*[4] becomes rather strained, and it would appear rather more realistic to regard standard forms as 'a collection of rules made by an organisation and imposed upon all who belong to or deal with it'.[5] Indeed, it begins to resemble a private legislative code; and with increasing frequency there occur situations where the relevant clauses are totally inapposite to the problem which has arisen between the parties.[6] In a judicial survey of this subject, Lord Diplock said:[7]

> 'Standard forms of contracts are of two kinds. The first, of very ancient origin, are those which set out the terms on which mercantile transactions of common occurrence are to be carried out. Examples are bills of lading, charterparties, policies of insurance, contracts of sale in the commodity markets. The standard clauses in these contracts have been settled over the years by negotiations by representatives of the commercial interests involved and have been widely adopted because experience has shown that they facilitate the conduct of trade. Contracts of these kinds affect not only the actual parties to them but also others who may have a commercial interest in the transactions to which they relate, as buyers or sellers, charterers or shipowners, insurers or bankers. If fairness or reasonableness were relevant to their enforceability the fact that they are widely used by parties whose bargaining power is fairly matched would raise a strong presumption that their terms are fair and reasonable.
>
> The same presumption, however, does not apply to the other

kind of standard form contract. This is of comparatively modern origin. It is the result of the concentration of particular kinds of business in relatively few hands. The ticket cases in the 19th century provide what are probably the first examples. The terms of this kind of standard form contract have not been the subject of negotiation between the parties to it, or approved by any organisation representing the interests of the weaker party. They have been dictated by that party whose bargaining power, either exercised alone or in conjunction with others providing similar goods or services, enables him to say: "If you want these goods or services at all, these are the only terms on which they are available. Take it or leave it".'

Perhaps the area of law where standard form contracts have caused most problems is in relation to exclusion clauses.

---

1 E.g. RIBA, Institute of Freight Forwarders; London Grain Trade Assoc.
2 E.g. Sch. 1, Table A of Companies Act 1948.
3 See Treitel *Law of Contract* (4th edn), 136.
4 As to which, see para. 2.05, ante.
5 Cheshire & Fifoot *Law of Contract* (9th edn), 25.
6 The printed terms are pro tanto overridden by any written or oral terms, or by any misrepresentation of those printed terms.
7 *Schroeder Music Publishing Co Ltd v Macaulay* [1974] 3 All ER 616 at 624, HL.

E) *Exclusion clauses*

3.14 Such clauses are to be found in both the types of contract referred to above by Lord Diplock,[1] which may conveniently be termed respectively commercial and consumer transactions. There has long been a clear need for exclusion clauses to be treated differently in the two types of contract. However, whilst Parliament has indeed distinguished between them on an ever-increasing scale, the common law has found it very difficult to develop such selective doctrines. Restrictions on exclusion clauses may be derived from either statute or common law; and they should always be considered in this order, because, if the exclusion be restricted by statute, there may be little point in considering the complexities of the common law.[2]

---

1 *Schroeder Music Publishing Co Ltd v Macaulay* [1974] 3 All ER 616 at 624, HL.
2 Additionally, in many cases, an exclusion clause must *first* be incorporated in

the contract between the parties according to the rules discussed in para. 3.12, ante; otherwise it is likely to be largely ineffective, as it can only operate in tort, e.g. under doctrines of consent or contributory negligence.

3.15 *a) Statute* Whilst a few provisions strike at similar clauses in all, or a wide variety of, types of contract,[1] most are restricted to clauses in particular types of contract.[2] Of the latter, a few positively prescribe the permissible terms of a contract,[3] but the more normal statutory technique is merely to prohibit specified matters, everything else being permissible; and it is in this sphere that the distinction has been drawn between commercial and consumer transactions. Sometimes, the type of contract within the ambit of the Act only falls within one of these categories;[4] whereas in others it plainly comprehends both, in which case the Act may itself draw the distinction between commercial and consumer transactions for the purposes of its treatment,[5] or it may merely enable the Executive to do so.[6] An Act which demonstrates much of the modern thinking on limiting the effect of exclusion clauses is the Unfair Contract Terms Act 1977,[7] which differentiates according to the following situations arising from the operation of a business in the United Kingdom with regard to its domestic transactions:[8]

1. Attempts to retain negligence liability.[9] These are dealt with thus—

   a) In most cases,[10] liability for negligence resulting in death or personal injury can no longer be restricted by contract or notice (s. 2 (1)).

   b) In these cases,[10] liability for other loss or damage resulting from negligence can only be excluded by contract or notice subject to a test of reasonableness (s. 2 (2), (3)).

   c) Negligence liability to consumers can no longer be restricted by what are commonly termed 'Manufacturers' Guarantees' (s. 5).[11]

2. Attempts to protect the weaker contracting party who 'deals as a consumer' (s. 12) or on the other's written standard terms. For most cases,[10] s. 3 provides that the stronger party cannot by contract, except so far as it satisfies the test of reasonableness:

   'a) when himself in breach of contract, exclude or restrict any liability of his in respect of the breach; or

   b) claim to be entitled—

      i) to render a contractual performance substantially different from that which was reasonably expected of him, or

      ii) in respect of the whole or any part of his contractual obligation, to render no performance at all'.

3. In most cases,[10] the reasonableness test is also applied to contractual terms requiring a consumer to idemnify another, whether or not a party to that contract.[12]

4. Contracts for the supply of goods. The rules relating to the exclusion of implied terms in contracts for the sale of goods or hire-purchase are repeated,[13] and are further applied, with adaptation, to analogous contracts for the supply of goods.[14] Finally, the Act deals with the concept of 'reasonableness'. Section 11 (1) lays down the following test of 'reasonableness' for cases (1) (b), (2) and (3):[15]

'the term shall have been a fair and reasonable one to be included having regard to the circumstances which were, or ought reasonably to have been, known to or in the contemplation of the parties when the contract was made';

and s. 11 (5) stipulates that he who asserts must prove that that test is satisfied. Where a term does so comply, s. 9 ousts the common law doctrine of fundamental breach (see below).

---

1 E.g. Misrepresentation Act 1967, s. 3: see para. 5.14, post; Unfair Contract Terms Act 1977; see post.

2 For explanation of the various types of contract, see para. 3.12, ante.

3 E.g. for bills of sale, see para. 17.06, post.

4 E.g. transactions within the Consumer Credit Act 1974: see para. 14.13, post; carriage of persons: see paras. 22.05–22.09, post.

5 E.g. contracts for the supply of goods: see para. 13.27, post.

6 E.g. Fair Trading Act 1973, Part 2: see para. 19.04, post.

7 See the excellent annotations to this Act in Current Law Statutes.

8 The operation of the Act is generally confined to 'business liability' (s. 1 (3)), and does not apply to any of the following: international supply contracts (s. 26); genuinely foreign contracts (s. 27); sea carriage of passengers (s. 28); contractual provisions specifically regulated by statute (s. 29). However, the Act is drafted so as to defeat attempts to achieve indirectly any of the prohibited exclusions (ss. 10, 13).

9 'Negligence' is defined in s. 1 (1).

10 For the most part, ss. 2–4 do not apply to contracts of insurance, transfers of an interest in land or in any patent, trade-mark, copyright, registered design, technical or commercial information or other intellectual property, contracts relating to the formation, dissolution or management of a company or partnership or transfer of shares, or contracts of employment except in favour of an employee except in favour of a person dealing as a consumer. In particular, Sch. 1 contains some further limitation.

11 See further para. 13.28, post.

12 S. 4: see further para. 16.03, post.

13 S. 6: see further para. 13.27, post.

14 S. 7: whether 'the possession or ownership of goods passes', e.g. simple bailment (see para. 14.07, post), contract for work and materials (see para. 13.02, post).

15 This test also applies to s. 3 of the Misrepresentation Act 1967: see para. 5.14, post. But an officially approved clause satisfies the requirement of

reasonableness: s. 29 (2), (3). For the special rules for sale, see para. 13.27, post.

3.16 *b) Common law* There are a number of legal rules which will render an exclusion clause ineffective, even though the clause be incorporated in the transaction:[1]

1. Where the object of the clause is contrary to public policy, as where it purports to exclude liability for fraud.[2]

2. Where the party for whose benefit the clause is expressed to operate gives an over-riding oral undertaking[3] or misrepresents the contents of the clause.[4]

3. Where in a *contractual*—but not a tortious[5]—action there is no privity of contract between the parties, whether the clause purports to confer a benefit or a burden.[6]

Where an exclusion clause cannot be struck down on one of the above grounds, its effect will be a matter of construing the intention of the parties. However, in making this enquiry, the courts will, if the clause is inserted merely for the benefit of one party (the *proferens*), construe the words against him (the *contra proferentem* rule): when faced with such exclusion clauses, the courts have consistently construed them against the *proferens*; and, the more swingeing the clause, the harder the courts have tended to lean against it.[7] This last idea led to the doctrine of fundamental breach, the notion that some breaches of contract may be so serious that no exemption clause, however widely drafted, can protect the guilty party. However, in 1966 the House of Lords indicated that there is no rule of law that a party is unable to rely on an exclusion clause if he has committed a fundamental breach, and that, whilst the courts will examine extremely critically any clause purporting to save a party from liability for such a breach, at the end of the day it is all a matter of construction.[8] For the vast majority of cases, this close judicial scrutiny should suffice to prevent even the most widely drawn exclusion clause from causing too great an injustice; and judicial attempts to retain for the courts a reserve discretion to strike down the most objectionable clauses[9] have probably been rendered unnecessary by statutory developments, particularly the Unfair Contract Terms Act 1977.[10]

---

1 For the rules as to incorporation, see para. 3.12, ante.
2 See the Law Commission Second Report on Exemption Clauses (Law Com 69), paras. 287–289; and see generally para. 5.14, post.
3 *Mendelssohn v Normand* [1970] 1 QB 177, [1969] 2 All ER 1215, CA.
4 *Curtis v Chemical Cleaning and Dyeing Co* [1951] 1 KB 805, [1951] 1 All ER 631, CA. And see generally paras. 5.08 et seq., post.

5 E.g. to an action in the tort of negligence, there may be defences that a notice
   led to consent or voluntary assumption of risk—see *Ashdown v Samuel
   Williams and Sons Ltd* [1957] 1 QB 409, [1957] 1 All ER 35, CA.
6 See generally post, chap. 4.
7 E.g. *Karsales (Harrow) Ltd v Wallis* [1956] 2 All ER 866, [1956] 1 WLR
   936, CA; *Lowe v Lombank Ltd* [1960] 1 All ER 611, [1960] 1 WLR 196,
   CA; *Henry Kendall & Sons Ltd v William Lillico & Sons Ltd* [1969] 2 AC
   31, [1968] 2 All ER 444, HL; *Schuler A.G. v Wickman Machine Tool Sales
   Ltd* [1974] AC 235, [1973] 2 All ER 39, HL.
8 *Suisse Atlantique Societe D'Armement Maritime SA v Rotterdamsche Kolen
   Centrale* [1967] 1 AC 361, [1966] 2 All ER 61, HL.
9 *Harbutt's Plasticine Ltd v Wayne Tank and Pump Co Ltd* [1970] 1 QB 447,
   [1970] 1 All ER 225, CA. See also *Farnworth Finance Ltd v Attryde* [1970]
   2 All ER 774, [1970] 1 WLR 1053, CA and *Kenyon, Son and Craven v
   Baxter Hoare & Co Ltd* [1971] 2 All ER 708, [1971] 1 WLR 519.
10 It is anticipated that there will be few exclusion clauses which will be
   permitted under the 1977 Act, pass the reasonableness test under that Act,
   and yet by reason of s. 9 offer protection against fundamental breaches.

2. Consideration

3.17 When in Tudor times it was settled that the courts would enforce
bargains comprising mutual promises, the judges began to look
round for something which would distinguish those promises
which they would enforce from those which they would not.
Eventually, they arrived at this essentially practical answer: only
where value was given to 'buy' a promise, did the parties
obviously mean business and would that promise be enforced.
That element of value was termed the 'consideration' necessary
to support a promise, and has been defined as[1]

'some right, interest, profit, or benefit accruing to the one
party, or some forbearance, detriment, loss or responsibility
given, suffered or undertaken by the other'.

Reflecting the fact that a contract may be either bilateral or
unilateral,[2] the consideration necessary to support a simple
contract may take either of the following forms:

1. A return promise, which completes a bilateral contract when
given: at that instant, the consideration is said to be *executory* on
both sides, and will only become *executed* some time in the
future.
2. Performance of the requested act, which serves two purposes—it is both the acceptance of the offer and performance of
the requested consideration, so that the offeree's consideration is
said to be *executed* from the outset and to support an *executory*
consideration (the promise) by the offeror.

1 *Currie v Misa* (1875) LR 10 Exch 153 at 162. See further para. 4.01, note 1, post.
2 See para. 3.08, ante.

3.18 Faced with the need to say what minimum was sufficient consideration to support a binding promise, the courts eventually evolved the following rules:

a) Consideration was required for all simple contracts, but not for contracts under seal.[1]

b) Consideration need not be adequate. Whilst demanding *some* consideration, the courts did not pretend to audit the bargain made by the parties: provided a promise was bought by *something* of value, they would not enquire whether *adequate* value had been paid, i.e. whether the parties were getting 'value for money'.

In *Chappell & Co Ltd v Nestlé Co Ltd,*[2]

A promise to supply gramophone records for 1*s* 6*d* plus three chocolate wrappers was held enforceable—the delivery of the wrappers was considered to form part of the consideration.

c) The consideration must be legal.[3]

d) The consideration supplied must be that requested by the offeror as the 'price' for his promise. It must be distinguished (a) from any condition to which the promise is subject,[4] and hence a contract must be distinguished from a conditional gift,[5] and (b) from a motive inducing a promise.[6] The insistence that the consideration be requested logically demands that an offer cannot be accepted in ignorance,[7] and that an executed promise cannot support a subsequent promise—*past* consideration is no consideration.[8] However, both these logical deductions have proved inconvenient: in relation to the former, the courts have sometimes fudged the issue;[9] and, with regard to the latter, exceptions have been created as follows:

i) By statute for negotiable instruments[10] and with regard to the limitation of actions.[11]

ii) At common law by drawing a distinction between *past* and *executed* consideration on the basis that it is good *executed* consideration if given at the request of the person making the subsequent promise,[12] but *past* (and therefore bad) without such a request.[8] Thus, if A promises B £10 for work which has previously been done by B, that promise is binding if A had originally requested the work, but not if he had not.

1 See para. 2.07, ante.
2 [1960] AC 87, [1959] 2 All ER 701, HL.
3 See post, chap. 6.
4 E.g. *Carlill v Carbolic Smoke Ball Co* (set out para. 3.03, ante), using the smoke ball was the consideration, and catching influenza the condition. For conditional contracts, see generally para. 3.09, ante.
5 E.g. 'I will give you £x if you attain 21 yrs of age.'
6 *Bob Guiness Ltd v Salomonsen* [1948] 2 KB 42; but see *Crears v Hunter* (1887) 19 QBD 341, CA. Had the bookmaker promised not to report the punter, there would have been consideration, but the contract would have been void under the Gaming Act 1845: see para. 6.07, post.
7 *R v Clarke* (1927) 40 CLR 227 (reward case—Aust. High Ct.).
8 *Roscorla v Thomas* (1842) 3 QB 234 (seller warranted goods after contract concluded).
9 E.g. *Gibbons v Proctor* (1891) 64 LT 594 (reward case).
10 Bills of Exchange Act 1882, s. 27: see para. 20.17, post.
11 Limitation Act 1939, s. 23 (4): see para. 8.11, post.
12 Possibly this is no exception to the general rule; a promise to pay may be implied from A's request and the £10 may be evidence of what would be the proper sum (*Stewart v Casey* [1892] 1 Ch 104, CA).

3.19 The following are sufficient to support a contract:

1. Payment of money.
2. Compromise of an action.
3. Giving up a claim which has been honestly made, though in fact the claim is one which would not have been successful.[1]
4. Entry into another contract, either with the promisor or a third party.[2]

---

1 Aliter if the claimant knows the claim is bad.
2 For such 'collateral contract' transactions, see para. 4.03, post.

3.20 The following are examples of agreements which do not constitute binding contracts because of the lack of consideration:

1. A promise founded on moral obligation alone;[1]
2. A promise to do what the promisee can legally demand already.

Thus, in *Stilk v Myrick*:[2]

After two seamen had deserted a ship, the remaining seamen agreed to work the ship home in return for a promise of extra wages. *Held:* since the seamen were bound already by their existing contracts to work the ship home, their promise could not constitute consideration for the promise of extra wages and their claim, therefore, failed.

In *Foakes v Beer*:[3]

A debtor agreed to pay a judgment debt by a part payment down, the remainder by instalments, the creditor meanwhile agreeing not to proceed with his legal remedies. The capital sum having been repaid, the creditor claimed interest. The House of Lords *held* that the debtor gave no consideration for an agreement to waive interest, as he could have been made to do what he did independently of his later promise.

On the other hand, if A promises to carry out his existing contractual obligations with B in return for a promise by C, A's performance of those obligations is good consideration for C's promise.[4]

3. A promise to do what the promisor is already bound to do as a matter of public duty. Thus in *Collins v Godefroy*,[5] it was held that a promise to attend court proceedings, given by someone who was bound to attend because a subpoena had been served upon him, could not constitute consideration for a promise of six guineas for his trouble. On the other hand, a party may validly bargain to perform duties over and above his legal duty.[6]

4. Payment of a smaller amount cannot alone be consideration for discharge from an agreement to pay a larger amount.[7]

Similarly, variations in the mode of paying a debt made at the debtor's request for his sole benefit are not consideration which would support a promise.

In *Vanbergen v St. Edmunds Properties Ltd*:[8]

A owed B £208. B at A's request agreed not to serve a bankruptcy notice if A would pay the £208 into a bank in Eastbourne the next day, the bank being chosen solely for the debtor's convenience. A paid the £208 but B not knowing it had been paid served the notice. *Held:* A was not entitled to damages as there was no consideration for B's promise. The choice of the country bank was made entirely for A's convenience.

On the other hand, if it is for the *creditor's* benefit and at his request that a smaller sum is paid at an earlier date than the date when the full sum became due, or at a different place from that where payment is due, there is good consideration for the creditor's promise to take it in full settlement.

---

1 *Eastwood v Kenyon* (1840), 11 A & E 446.
2 (1809), 2 Camp 317. But see *Hartley v Ponsonby* (1857) 7 E & B 872 (so many seamen deserted as to discharge remainder).
3 (1884), 9 App Cas 605. An exception to this rule is compositions with creditors: *Welby v Drake* (1825) 1 C & P 557: see generally para. 33.48, post.
4 *New Zealand Shipping Co Ltd v AM Satterthwaite & Co Ltd* [1975] AC 154, [1974] 1 All ER 1015, PC (see further para. 4.04, post.).
5 (1831), 1 B & Ad 950.

6 *Glasbrook Bros Ltd v Glamorgan County Council* [1925] AC 270, HL (police authority providing police over and above those required to discharge their statutory duty).
7 *Foakes v Beer* (1884) 9 App Cas 605; *D and C Builders Ltd v Rees* [1966] 2 QB 617, [1965] 3 All ER 837, CA. A composition with creditors imports mutual promises by the creditors to reduce their claims: *Good v Cheesman* (1831), 2 B & Ad 328.
8 [1933] 2 KB 223, CA. Similarly, payment of a lesser sum by cheque is no consideration: *D and C Builders Ltd v Rees* [1966] 2 QB 617, [1965] 3 All ER 837, CA.

F) *Variation, waiver and estoppel*

3.21 *a) Variation* Just as a binding contract can be made, so may it be discharged by agreement;[1] and it follows that a contract may be partially discharged or varied by a subsequent contract between the parties.[2] In all cases, however, the new promise to discharge must be supported by consideration: otherwise, it cannot take effect as a binding contract, but only as a waiver or estoppel.

1 For discharge of contracts by agreement, see para. 8.01, post.
2 For the special rules applicable to the variation of contracts required to be evidenced in writing, see para. 2.14, ante.

3.22 *b) Waiver* The common law has long accepted that contractual rights can be expressly or impliedly waived before or after breach by the 'innocent' party without the 'guilty' one giving any consideration for that waiver. The operation of a statutory formulation of this doctrine is illustrated by *Charles Rickards Ltd v Oppenheim*:[1]

> D ordered a Rolls Royce chassis from P, and P agreed to build a body on it by March 20th. After P had failed to complete the work by that date, D continued to press for delivery, but on June 29th gave notice that if the work was not completed within the next four weeks the contract was at an end. After the expiry of that time, D refused to accept delivery of the car.

The Court of Appeal held that time was of the essence of this contract; that this stipulation was impliedly waived by the buyer's request for delivery after March 20th; but that the buyer was entitled to and had made time of the essence again by his notice of June 29th.

1 [1950] 1 KB 616, [1950] 1 All ER 420, CA. This was a decision under the Sale of Goods Act 1893, s. 11 (1) (a): see further para. 13.18, post.

3.23   *c) Estoppel*   At first sight, the promise by a party that he will not insist on his strict contractual rights (which cannot take effect as a variation because of the absence of consideration) looks like an estoppel. Yet, it cannot take effect as a common law estoppel[1] because that doctrine is applicable only to representations of fact, whereas reliance is here being placed on a representation of future intention—that a party will not in the future insist on his strict contractual rights.[2] However, such a promise may be relied upon (by way of defence only) by the other party under the doctrine of *equitable estoppel* developed by the courts since 1947, notwithstanding the lack of consideration. Thus in *Central London Property Trust Ltd v High Trees House Ltd:*[3]

> The plaintiffs by a lease under seal let a block of flats at £2,500 a year. Subsequently when many flats were vacant owing to the war the plaintiffs by letter agreed to accept a reduced rent of £1,250. *Held:* by Denning J, although there was no consideration for the plaintiffs' agreement not to enforce their strict legal right to the full rent, the plaintiffs should not be allowed to go back on that agreement and claim arrears of rent strictly due.

Thus a gratuitous promise by one party to suspend his rights under a contract will prevent him from proceeding to enforce them until he has given reasonable notice of his intention to resume them. This is known as 'equitable estoppel'.[4] The principle does not apply where its application would be inequitable. In *D and C Builders Ltd v Rees.*[5]

> D owed P £482 and when P, in urgent need of money, sought payment, D insisted that his payment by cheque of £300 must be accepted by P 'in completion of the contract'. *Held:* there was no consideration for P's agreement to take less than was due to him, nor was P estopped in the circumstances from claiming the balance of £182.

This last case points to a very real dilemma created for creditors by the doctrine: how is the creditor to know whether the taking of a proffered part-payment (often a wise precaution) will subsequently estop him from recovering the remainder? Moreover, the whole doctrine is in need of clarification: it clearly overlaps with the doctrine of waiver, but their relationship remains uncertain.

1 As to which, see para. 2.05, ante.
2 *Jorden v Money* (1854) 5 HL Cas 185.
3 [1947] KB 130; for the limitations of the doctrine, see *Combe v Combe*, [1951] 2 KB 215, [1951] 1 All ER 767, CA; *Argy Trading Development Co Ltd v Lapid Developments Ltd* [1977] 3 All ER 785, [1977] 1 WLR 444. In *Woodhouse AC Israel Cocoa Ltd SA v Nigerian Produce Marketing Co Ltd* [1972] AC 741 at 758, [1972] 2 All ER 271 at 282; Lord Hailsham LC said the time may soon come when the sequence of cases based on promissory estoppel beginning with the *High Trees House Case* may need to be reviewed and reduced to a coherent body of doctrine by the courts.
4 Denning J's statement of the principle was *obiter*, but it was accepted unenthusiastically by the House of Lords in *Tool Metal Manufacturing Co Ltd v Tungsten Electric Co Ltd* [1955] 2 All ER 675, [1955] 1 WLR 761. The result of these recent cases is to throw doubt on the earlier House of Lords decisions in *Jorden v Money* (1854) 5 HLC 185 and *Foakes v Beer* (1884) 9 App Cas 605; but the doctrine of equitable estoppel has actually been *applied* so seldom as to leave it questionable whether it in fact exists. See further Cheshire & Fifoot *Law of Contract* (9th edn) 84–97.
5 [1966] 2 QB 617, [1965] 3 All ER 837, CA.

3.24   Can one party, A, be discharged from his contractual obligations simply because the other party, B, promises not to enforce them? Mere neglect or delay on the part of B in enforcing his rights probably will not have such an effect,[1] though it is common expressly so to provide in standard form contracts. If A gives consideration for that promise, A will be discharged by reason of the binding contract of variation. However, even in the absence of any consideration given by A, it is clear that B's rights *may* be suspended, and possibly even discharged, by reason of the doctrines of waiver and equitable estoppel. Thus, we are possibly moving towards a situation where a binding contractual promise can only be created with consideration or in a deed, but may be discharged without either of them.[2]

---

1 See *Buckland v Farmar and Moody* (1978) Times 16.2., CA.
2 See *W. J. Alan & Co Ltd v El Nasr Export and Import Co* [1972] 2 QB 189, [1972] 2 All ER 127, CA; *Woodhouse AC Israel Cocoa Ltd SA v Nigerian Produce Marketing Co Ltd* [1972] AC 741 at 758 per Lord Hailsham.

---

3. Intention to create legal relations

3.25   Whilst consideration was originally thought of as the touchstone of those promises which would be enforced,[1] in more recent times this has been found inadequate to deal with all cases. Hence, the courts have developed the doctrine that, not only must there be consideration, but the parties must also intend 'to create legal relations', i.e. intend that their agreement shall be legally enforceable.[2] In the development of this new principle, the courts have drawn a distinction between commercial agreements on the one hand, and domestic or social agreements on the other,[3] though there can be commercial agreements between the members of a family.[4]

---

1 See para. 3.17, ante.
2 *Balfour v Balfour* [1919] 2 KB 571, CA, followed in *Spellman v Spellman* [1961] 2 All ER 498, [1961] 1 WLR 921, CA and *Jones v Padavatton* [1969] 2 All ER 616, [1969] 1 WLR 328, CA (Mother and daughter). See also the Law Reform (Miscellaneous Provisions) Act 1970, s. 1 (contracts to marry).
3 However, it is possible for a domestic or social agreement to create a binding contract where the parties show such an intention: see *Merritt v Merritt* [1970] 2 All ER 760, [1970] 1 WLR 1211, CA, (spouses); *Parker v Clark* [1960] 1 All ER 93, [1960] 1 WLR 286 (house-sharing agreement).
4 E.g. *Snelling v John E Snelling Ltd* [1973] 1 QB 87, [1972] 1 All ER 79.

3.26   Whereas domestic agreements are not usually binding, in the commercial sphere, it is usually assumed that businessmen mean business. Thus, in *Carlill v Carbolic Smoke Ball Co*[1] D's advertisement said that they had deposited £1,000 with their bankers 'to show their sincerity'; and the Court of Appeal therefore held that the advertisement was not a mere advertiser's puff (something of no legal effect), but showed an intention to enter into a binding contract. A case which neatly illustrated the principles is *Rose and Frank v Crompton.*[2]

In 1913, a British manufacturer, D, entered into a franchise agreement with a New York firm, P, whereby D gave P certain rights of selling their product in North America, that agreement containing the following clause—

> 'This arrangement is not entered into ... as a formal or legal agreement, and shall not be subject to legal jurisdiction in the law courts ... , but it is only a definitive expression and record of the purpose and intention of the parties concerned, to which they each honourably pledge themselves'.

After a volume of orders had been executed, D in 1919 without appropriate notice terminated the arrangement whilst some orders were still outstanding. The House of Lords held:

1. The franchise agreement was not legally enforceable because of the express declaration of lack of intention to create legal relations.
2. The outstanding orders once accepted did amount to binding

contracts: they contained nothing to rebut the ordinary presumption that a commercial agreement is intended to be legally enforceable.

Thus, it is well settled that a commercial agreement *can* be made 'binding in honour only', even impliedly; and the football pools, for instance, usually contain an express clause to this effect.[3] However, the onus of proving such an intention lies heavily upon the party to a commercial agreement who asserts it, so that it has been held insufficient to escape legal enforcement to use the ambiguous phrase 'ex gratia'.[4] Labour law appears to be a partial exception: collective agreements are presumed not to be enforceable,[5] whereas individual contracts of employment are binding at law.[4]

---

1 [1893] 1 QB 256, CA (set out para. 3.03, ante). See also *Esso Petroleum Ltd v Comrs of Customs and Excise* [1976] 1 All ER 117, [1976] 1 WLR 1, HL.
2 [1925] AC 445, HL.
3 E.g. *Appleson v H Littlewood Ltd* [1939] 1 All ER 464, CA.
4 *Edwards v Skyways Ltd* [1964] 1 All ER 349, [1964] 1 WLR 349.
5 *Ford Motor Co Ltd v Amalgamated Union Engineering Workers* [1969] 2 QB 303, [1969] 2 All ER 481. This decision was confirmed by the Trade Union and Labour Relations Act 1974, s. 18.

3.27 Finally, a 'binding in honour only' clause must be carefully distinguished from both the following:

1. A clause ousting the jurisdiction of the court and making an agreement enforceable, but *only* by some agency other than the courts: this clause is void on grounds of public policy.[1]
2. An arbitration clause, making the award of an arbitrator a condition precedent to the institution of legal proceedings: such a clause is enforceable.[2]

---

1 *Baker v Jones* [1954] 2 All ER 553, [1954] 1 WLR 1005. See generally para. 6.09, post.
2 *Scott v Avery* (1856) 5 HLC 811. See generally para. 34.04, post.

Chapter 4

The doctrine of privity
and its exceptions

4.01 It follows from the doctrine of consideration discussed in the previous chapter that, if a promise requires consideration before it is enforceable at law, only he who gave consideration for a promise (the promisee) may enforce it in an action for breach of contract against the promisor ('consideration must move from the promisee').[1] Of course, this is not to say that a third party can play no part at all in the performance of a contract: for instance, the actual performance of a contractual promise may be carried out on behalf of the promisor by his servant or other agent;[2] and a third party may be under a tortious duty not to interfere with the performance of that promise,[3] or have a right in tort that the promisor should act carefully.[4] However, returning to the actual enforcement of the contractual promise, the so-called 'privity' rule is logically inescapable, though its inconvenience has led to the development of numerous exceptions.

---

1 Remember that 'the promisee' may consist of more than one person: see para. 2.03, ante. The consideration may move to the promisor, e.g. a bilateral contract (see para. 3.17, ante), but will not necessarily do so, e.g. para. 3.19, case (4).
2 See chap. 10, post.
3 See para. 4.05, post.
4 E.g. *Driver v William Willett (Contractors) Ltd* [1969] 1 All ER 665 (right of employee against his employer's adviser: see generally chap. 32, post); Occupiers' Liability Act 1957, s. 3; Defective premises Act 1972, s. 4; bailment (see para. 14.06, post).

---

1. The doctrine of privity

4.02 The doctrine of privity predicates that a stranger to a contract (i.e. one who is not a party, having given no consideration) can take neither the benefit nor the burden of its terms.

4.03 a) THE BENEFIT

In *Dunlop Pneumatic Tyre Co Ltd v Selfridge & Co Ltd*:[1]

A tyre manufacturer, P, sold tyres to a wholesaler upon condition that on resale he would not only observe P's price list but also extract from his customer a similar undertaking. The wholesaler resold some tyres to retailer, D, extracting such an undertaking; but D resold those tyres below list price.

Whilst the wholesaler could undoubtedly have sued D for breach of contract, P attempted to enforce his resale price maintenance scheme personally against D. However, the House of Lords held that P was not privy to the promise given by D to the wholesaler, and therefore could not enforce it. Resale price maintenance is now regulated by statute,[2] but the general proposition contained in the case is still valid, and its inconvenience has led to the development of the following exceptions:

1. Wide-ranging exceptions were developed at common law to meet the needs of commerce, such as the laws of agency,[3] assignment,[4] negotiable instruments,[5] bankers' confirmed credits,[6] and bailments.[7]

2. Parliament found it necessary to create statutory exceptions in the following fields:

a) Resale price maintenance;[2]

b) Life,[8] fire[9] and motor insurance,[10] the rights of third party beneficiaries against insurers[11] as extended by the Motor Insurance Bureau Scheme,[12] and the insurance of property to its full value by persons with a limited interest in it in the fields of marine insurance[13] and sales of land.[14]

3. With the exception of those categories referred to in (1) above, relatively few exceptions to the privity rule have been allowed at common law:

a) At one stage it looked as though the law of trusts might be developed to provide a general exception by way of the concept of a trust of a promise,[15] but that development was effectively halted by the subsequent insistence on strict proof of a trust.[16]

b) The concept of privity clashed with the needs and concepts of land law, and exceptions were therefore developed so that successors in title might enforce covenants in leases and restrictive covenants generally.[17] An unsuccessful attempt was made to utilise one of the statutory provisions in this field to provide a general exception to the privity rule.[18]

c) The device of the collateral contract, e.g. a promise by A to B made in return for B entering into another (major) contract with either C[19] or B:[20] A is offering to enter a unilateral collateral contract,[21] a promise which B 'buys' by entering the major contract as requested.[22]

Whilst there are thus many exceptions to it, the significance of the privity rule remains this: unless a case can be fitted exactly within one of the established exceptions, the general rule will apply.

---

1 [1915] AC 847, HL.
2 Resale Prices Act 1976: see further para. 28.23, post.
3 See chap. 10, post.
4 See paras. 4.06 et seq., post.
5 See chap. 20, post.
6 See para. 13.43, post.
7 See paras. 14.06 et seq., post.
8 Married Women's Property Act 1882, s. 11: see para. 26.10, post.
9 Fires Prevention (Metropolis) Act 1774, s. 83: see para. 26.14, post.
10 Road Traffic Act 1972, s. 148 (4): see para. 26.06, post.
11 Third Parties (Rights Against Insurers) Act 1930, s. 1; Road Traffic Act 1972, ss. 149, 150: see para. 26.05, post.
12 See para. 26.06, post.
13 Marine Insurance Act 1906, s. 14 (2): see para. 27.03, post.
14 Law of Property Act 1925, s. 47: see para. 26.15, post.
15 See *Lloyd's v Harper* (1880), 16 ChD 290; *Affréteurs Réunis Société Anonyme v Leopald Walford (London) Ltd* [1919] AC 801, HL.
16 See *Vandepitte v Preferred Accident Insurance Corpn of New York* [1933] AC 70, PC; *Re Schebsman* [1944] Ch 83, [1943] 2 All ER 768, CA; *Green v Russell* [1959] 2 QB 226, [1959] 2 All ER 525, CA.
17 See para. 12.08, post.
18 Law of Property Act 1925, s. 56: *Beswick v Beswick* [1968] AC 58, [1967] 2 All ER 1197, HL.
19 *Shanklin Pier Ltd v Detel Products Ltd* [1951] 2 KB 854, [1951] 2 All ER 471; *Andrews v Hopkinson* [1957] 1 QB 229, [1956] 3 All ER 422; *Wells (Merstham) Ltd v Buckland Sand and Silica Ltd* [1965] 2 QB 170, [1964] 1 All ER 41.
20 *City and Westminster Properties (1934) Ltd v Mudo* [1959] Ch 129, [1958] 2 All ER 733; *Esso Petroleum Ltd v Mardon* [1976] 2 QB 801, [1976] 2 All ER 5, CA (set out para. 7.03, post).
21 For unilateral contracts, see para. 3.08, ante. Such collateral contracts must be distinguished from a collateral (minor) promise (= warranty) of the main contract: see paras. 7.08, 13.18, post.
22 See para. 3.19, ante.

4.04   b) THE BURDEN

In *Scruttons Ltd v Midland Silicones Ltd:*[1]

A drum of chemicals was shipped under a contract which limited the carrier's liability to $500. The drum was damaged by the negligence of stevedores engaged by the carrier to unload the cargo, and damage in excess of $500 resulted. The owners of the drum sued the stevedores in the tort of negligence, and the latter sought to plead by way of defence the $500 limitation in the contract of carriage.

The case was a strong one in that there was a clear commercial convenience in allowing the carrier of goods to limit not only his own liability, but also that of all those who he engaged to handle the cargo; and there had indeed been attempts to develop the so-called doctrine of 'vicarious immunity' to provide a specific exception for this case.[2] Notwithstanding this, the House of Lords refused to allow the stevedores the benefit of an exemption clause contained in a contract to which they were not a party, and held them liable for the damages in full. This last case concerns the area where the courts are perhaps under greatest pressure to relax the privity rule, namely, the attempt to confer the benefit of an exclusion clause on a third party. Here, the courts have sought to accommodate the pressure indirectly as follows:

1. Lord Denning in particular has suggested that the objective might be accomplished via the law of agency, by the contracting party making a contract in two capacities: in his own right, so that he could claim the benefit of the exclusion clause, and as agent for the third party so that the latter could do so as well.[3]

2. By allowing a contracting party to apply to court for a stay of proceedings[4] when the other contracting party sues a third party contrary to his contractual promise. Thus, in *Snelling v John G Snelling Ltd*[5]

> X, Y and Z, directors of a company, agreed that if one of them resigned he would forfeit money due to him from the company. X resigned and sued the company for money due to him and the company joined Y and Z as co-defendants. *Held:* although the company was not a party to the agreement between X, Y and Z, X had broken that agreement and with all concerned before the court, further proceedings by X would be stayed and X's claim dismissed.

3. Insistence on the strict letter of the privity rule might be understandable when dealing with contracts for the carriage of passengers,[6] but its manifest inconvenience in relation to the carriage of goods has tempted the Privy Council to achieve vicarious immunity for stevedores indirectly by utilising the device of the collateral contract. In *New Zealand Shipping Co Ltd v AM Satterthwaite & Co Ltd*[7] they held that the exclusion clause could be treated as an offer by the goods' owner to enter into the following collateral contract: if those involved in the performance of the main contract would play their part, e.g. the stevedores unload the goods, the goods' owner would grant them

the benefit of the exclusion clause in the (main) contract of carriage.

---

1 [1962] AC 446, [1962] 1 All ER 1, HL.
2 In *Elder Dempster & Co Ltd v Paterson Zochonis & Co Ltd* [1924] AC 522, HL.
3 See *Morris v CW Martin & Sons Ltd* [1966] 1 QB 716, [1965] 2 All ER 725, CA, obiter; *Scruttons Ltd v Midland Silicones Ltd* [1962] AC 446, [1962] 1 All ER 1, HL, Lord Denning, dissenting.
4 Under s. 41 of the Supreme Court of Judicature (Consolidation) Act 1925.
5 [1973] QB 89, [1972] 1 All ER 79. See also *Gore v Van der Lann* [1967] 2 QB 31, [1967] 1 All ER 360, CA.
6 E.g. *Adler v Dickson* [1955] 1 QB 158, [1954] 3 All ER 397, CA.
7 [1975] AC 154, [1974] 1 All ER 1015, PC. For collateral contracts, see generally para. 4.03, ante; and for the consideration issue, see para. 3.19, ante.

---

2. Interference by third party

4.05   Whilst it is no tort for C simply to dissuade (if there is no conspiracy or use of unlawful means) B from entering into a contract with A,[1] it is a different matter once a contract has been made between A and B: then, interference with that contract by C may subject him to liability in tort. In *Lumley v Gye*:[2]

A singer agreed to sing at a particular theatre for A; and C, without legal justification or excuse, induced her to break the contract. The court held that an action in tort would lie for interfering with an existing contract.

Whilst it seems that the principle does not apply where C is an employee of B who in good faith induces B not to perform his contract with A,[3] it is not confined to contracts of personal service. Thus, in *British Motor Trade Association v Salvadori*:[4]

A sold a car to B, and B promised that if he wished to resell it within a year he would first offer it to A. Without so offering to A, B sold the car within the year to C, who knew of that promise. *Held:* C was liable to A for interfering with the contract between A and B.

However, inducing B to breach his contract with A must be carefully distinguished from the situation where C simply induces B lawfully to terminate his contract with A by giving proper notice:[5] if there is no conspiracy or no use of unlawful means, C commits no tort by so acting.[6] Even within the above constraints, this tort is not committed by C unless his acts constitute the highly technical concept of an 'interference' with the contract between A and B.[7]

Industrial disputes

The primary area where this tort has been litigated is that of industrial disputes. By statute, any act done by a person in contemplation or furtherance of a trade dispute shall not be actionable in tort on the grounds only that it induces another person to break a contract, whether or not that contract be one of employment;[8] and the all-important expression 'trade dispute', which circumscribes the ambit of the provision, is there elaborately defined.[9] It should be noted that the protection is not restricted to contracts of employment,[10] so that it extends, for example, to commercial contracts; nor is it confined to contracts to which a party to a trade dispute is privy, so that 'secondary blacking' is protected.

1 *Midland Cold Storage Ltd v Steer*[1972] Ch 630, [1972] 3 All ER 941.
2 (1853) 2 E & B 216. See also *Hivac Ltd v Park Royal Scientific Instruments Ltd* [1946] Ch 169, [1946] 1 All ER 350, CA: see para. 32.06 post; *Greig v Insole* [1978] 1 WLR 302.
3 *Said v Butt* [1920] 3 KB 497.
4 [1949] Ch 556, [1949] 1 All ER 208.
5 For termination by notice, see para. 8.01, post.
6 *McManus v Bowes* [1938] 1 KB 98, [1937] 3 All ER 227, CA.
7 *DC Thomson & Co Ltd v Deakin* [1952] Ch 646, [1952] 2 All ER 361, CA.
8 Trade Union and Labour Relations Act 1974, s. 13 (1), as amended by the Trade Union and Labour Relations (Amendment) Act 1976.
9 The 1974 Act, s. 29.
10 See chap. 32, post.

3. Assignment of contracts

4.06 CHOSES IN ACTION
The law regards contractual promises as a species of property; but it is a peculiar one in that 'it can only be claimed or enforced by [court] action, and not by taking physical possession'.[1] This is a characteristic which contractual promises share with a large number of other proprietary rights, such as shares in companies, negotiable instruments, policies of insurance, bills of lading, patents, copyrights; and they are collectively known as *choses in action*. If the right is one which, before the Judicature Acts (1873–75) could be claimed only in the Common Law Courts—such as a right to a contract debt, or a right created by statute—it is known as a *legal chose in action*; but, if the right is one which could be claimed only in the Court of Chancery—such as a right to share in a trust fund—it is known as an *equitable chose in action*.

1 *Torkington v Magee* [1902] 2 KB 427, at 430, per Channell J.

4.07 ASSIGNMENT

This is the expression used to describe the transfer of most *choses in action*. Suppose A has agreed to sell a car to B for £500. B has made a promise to pay that price to A; and an assignment would occur where A (the assignor) transfers the benefit of that promise to C (the assignee) in such a way that C can, without the consent of B, enforce payment by B of that £500 to himself (C). Generally speaking, the common law refused to countenance the assignment of *choses in action*, offering only the following possibilities:

1. Novation, whereby A, B and C might all get together and agree that (a) B's debt to A is discharged and replaced by (b) a contract by B to pay C.

2. Acknowledgment, whereby B agrees with A that he will instead pay C, and so notifies C.[1]

3. Power of attorney, whereby A might grant C a (revocable) power of attorney (usually by deed) to sue B for the £500 in A's name.

However, none of the above sufficed to meet the needs of commerce, in that by none of them could C acquire an irrevocable right to the £500 without B's consent; and it was to allow of such a possibility that the equitable doctrine of assignment of *choses in action* was developed. Nowadays, the assignment of many types of *choses in action* is governed by statutory provisions enacted especially for that particular type of *chose*, e.g. shares,[2] negotiable instruments,[3] policies of life[4] or marine[5] insurance, bills of lading,[6] patents,[7] copyrights.[8] However, for those cases where there is no specific statutory provision—and that principally means debts and interests in trust funds—there is available the general provision for statutory assignment discussed below. The foregoing all relates to voluntary assignment. There is also assignment by operation of law,[9] such as the assignment of a bankrupt's contracts to his trustee in bankruptcy,[10] and of a deceased's contracts to his personal representatives.[11] Finally, a distinction must be drawn in the case of voluntary transactions between (a) assignment of rights, (b) assignment of duties and (c) negotiability.

---

1 *Shamia v Joory* [1958] 1 QB 448, [1958] 1 All ER 111.
2 Companies Act 1948, s. 73.
3 See chap. 20, post.
4 See para. 26.07, post.
5 See para. 27.02, post.

6 See para. 23.12, post.
7 See chap. 29, post.
8 See chap. 31, post.
9 There is no assignment by operation of law of contracts relating to purely personal services, rights, and liabilities (*Baxter v Burfield* (1747) 2 Str. 1266).
10 See para. 33.16, post. For voluntary assignment by trustee back to bankrupt, see *Ramsey v Hartley* [1977] 2 All ER 673, [1977] 1 WLR 686, CA.
11 *Otter v Church, Adams, Tatham & Co* [1953] Ch 280, [1953] 1 All ER 168.

Assignment of rights

4.08   *1. Equitable assignments*
Courts of Equity always gave effect to assignments of debts and other *choses in action*. Thus, following the maxim Equity considers as done that which ought to be done, in *Tailby v Official Receiver* it was held that a purported assignment of future book debts:[1]

'operates in equity by way of agreement, binding the conscience of the assignor, and so binding the property from the moment when the contract becomes capable of being performed'.

Nor is any particular form required for an equitable assignment of a *legal chose*: any words (oral or written) which show a clear intention to transfer the subject-matter are sufficient. As Lord Macnaghten said:

'It may be addressed to the debtor. It may be couched in the language of command. It may be a courteous request. It may assume the form of mere permission. The language is immaterial as long as the meaning is plain.'[2]

But the assignment of an *equitable* chose in action requires to be in writing.[3]
The effect of a valid equitable assignment of a chose in action is that the assignee may sue to enforce the right, but he has to join the assignor as co-plaintiff (or, if unwilling to co-operate, as co-defendant) unless the assignment is an absolute assignment of an equitable chose in action. Generally, an assignment is complete in equity as between the assignor and assignee without the assent of, or notice to, the debtor. Thus, in *Holt v Heatherfield Trust Ltd,*[4]

A had a judgment debt against B. A assigned the debt to C. Before notice of the assignment had been given to B, D, a creditor of A, tried to claim the money from B to satisfy his own judgment: *Held:* the debt had been validly assigned in equity to C who therefore had a better title to it than D.

Notice to the debtor is, however, advisable so as to prevent the debtor paying the assignor.[5] If, without having received notice of the assignment, the debtor pays the assignor, the assignee has no right of action against the debtor. It is otherwise if the debtor pays the assignor after having notice of the assignment. Moreover, notice to the debtor is also advisable to obtain priority over any other assignee because if A has made successive assignments of the same *chose*, a subsequent assignee without notice of an earlier assignment will have priority if he is first to give notice to the debtor.[6]

The same effect as an equitable assignment can alternatively be attained by the creation of a trust;[7] and it is common on an equitable assignment so to provide with a view to obtaining priority in the event of A's insolvency.[8]

---

1 (1888) 13 App Cas 523, at 546, per Lord Macnaghten.
2 *William Brandt's v Dunlop Rubber Co* [1905] AC, at 462. But telling the debtor to pay X is only an assignment to X if intended to be an irrevocable transfer of rights to X.
3 Law of Property Act 1925, s. 53 (1).
4 [1942] 2 KB 1, [1942] 1 All ER 404. But see *Warner Bros Records Inc v Rollgreen Ltd* [1976] QB 430, [1975] 2 All ER 105, CA.
5 *Warner Brothers Records Inc v Rollgreen Ltd* [1976] QB 430, [1975] 2 All ER 105, CA.
6 *Dearle v Hall* (1828) 3 Russ. 1.
7 *M'Fadden v Jenkyns* (1842) 1 Ph 153.
8 See *Re David Allester Ltd* [1922] 2 Ch 211.

4.09 *2. Statutory assignments*

The common law rule against assignment was altered by the Judicature Act 1873, s. 25 (6), which was repealed and re-enacted by s. 136 of the Law of Property Act 1925. These Acts provided that a debt or other legal chose in action may be assigned so as to entitle the assignee to sue in his own name without joining the assignor as a party if:

1. The assignment is absolute, and not by way of charge;
2. The assignment is in writing;
3. Notice in writing of the assignment has been given to the debtor.[1]

An absolute assignment of a debt is one where the assignor retains no interest in the property. An assignment by way of charge is not an absolute assignment, but an assignment by way of mortgage with a proviso for redemption is within s. 136. Thus, in *Durham Brothers v Robertson,* [2]

> A, a builder, had a claim for a contract debt against B, and when borrowing money from C he assigned the debt to C as security for the loan 'until the money lent be repaid'. This was *held* to be an asssignment by way of charge of B's debt.

It would not be appropriate in such a case for C to sue B without joining A as a party since the court would need to examine the state of accounts between A and C in order to determine whom B should pay.

If, on the other hand, A had assigned the debt to C as security for the loan unconditionally but with a proviso for reassignment upon repayment of the loan, there would have been an absolute assignment. Until the debtor B had notice of the reassignment, both B and any court would be entitled to assume that B should pay the debt to C.

Clearly, the assignment of a debt is only *absolute* within the terms of the section if it is an assignment of the assignor's entire interest. Even the assignment of a definite part of a debt is not an absolute assignment. [3]

Of course, if an assignment is not absolute and, therefore, cannot be valid as a legal assignment under s. 136 of the Law of Property Act, it may be valid as an equitable assignment. [4] Similarly, there will only be an equitable assignment where A purports to assign the *future* hire rent under a hire purchase agreement—this not being an existing chose because the hirer has not bound himself to continue the hiring [5]—or where A purports to make his assignment simply by way of deposit with the intention of creating a charge over the hire purchase agreement to secure a loan from C. [6]

---

1 The notice must actually reach the debtor; *Holt v Heatherfield Trust Ltd* [1942] 2 KB 1, [1942] 1 All ER 404.
2 [1898] 1 QB 765.
3 *Williams v Atlantic Assurance Co* [1933] 1 KB 81, [1932] All ER Rep. 32, CA, approving *Re Steel Wing Co* [1921] 1 Ch 349.
4 E.g. *Durham Bros v Robertson* (set out above).
5 See *Tailby v Official Receiver* (1888) 13 App Cas 523, HL. For h.p. agreements, see para. 14.03, post.
6 See *Independent Automatic Sales Ltd v Knowles and Foster* [1962] 3 All ER 27, [1962] 1 WLR 974.

4.10 *3. Points common to both equitable and legal assignments*
a) *'Subject to equities'* Every assignment (whether legal or equitable) is 'subject to equities'. This means that when sued by

the assignee, the debtor can raise against him all defences (including rights of set-off) that he could have raised against the assignor at the time he received notice of the assignment. A claim for damages against the assignor arising out of the contract under which the assigned debt arises, is an equity which may be set up by way of defence in an action by the assignee for the debt.[1] But if the assignor induced the defendant to enter into the contract by fraud and the latter is not in a position or does not claim to rescind it, the defendant cannot set off the damages for fraud to which he is entitled against the assignor as an answer in whole or in part to the claim of the assignee.[2]

b) Consideration Where the provisions of s. 136 have been complied with a voluntary assignment will confer the legal right to sue.[3] However, as an equitable assignment normally takes effect as a contract to assign, if there is any doubt at the outset as to the existence of consideration given by C for an equitable assignment, it is a wise precaution to effect the assignment by deed.[4]

c) No assignment of some rights Some rights, such as the right to sue for damages in tort and rights under personal contracts like contracts of employment, cannot be assigned at all.[5]

Cozens-Hardy, LJ, in *Tolhurst v Associated Portland Cement Manufacturers Ltd*, said:

'The section relates to procedure only. It does not enlarge the class of choses in action, the assignability of which was previously recognised either at law or in equity.'[6]

---

1 *Newfoundland (Govt) v Newfoundland Rly Co* (1888) 13 App Cas 199, PC. Cf. *Business Computers Ltd v Anglo-African Leasing Ltd* [1977] 2 All ER 741, [1977] 1 WLR 578.
2 *Stoddart v Union Trust* [1912] 1 KB 181.
3 *Re Westerton* [1919] 2 Ch 104.
4 For what amounts to consideration, see paras. 3.17 et seq., ante. Cf. *Olsson v Dyson* (1969) 120 CLR 365, Aust. HC.
5 *Nokes v Doncaster Amalgamated Collieries Ltd* [1940] AC 1014, [1940] 3 All ER 549, HL.
6 [1902] 2 KB at 676 (affd [1903] AC 414, HL).

Assignment of duties

4.11 A person cannot assign his obligation to perform any contract so as to shift from himself the liability for non-performance, although he may where the contract so allows[1] perform by the act of his agent,[2] e.g. a buyer of goods need not personally hand over the price to the seller.[3] The distinction is this: whilst vicarious performance may be permissible as a way of discharging a promise, the original promisor remains contractually liable for that performance.

The person to whom performance is due may consent to a *novation* creating a new contract under which the original contractor gets his release and the liability of another is substituted. Thus, when there is a change in the membership of a partnership, the creditors of the partnership may agree to release the obligations of the retiring partners for existing debts in return for the partnership as newly constituted taking on the liability.[4]

---

1 The contract may expressly or impliedly prohibit vicarious performance, e.g. a commission to paint a picture.
2 For agency, see chap. 10.
3 For a buyer's duty to pay the price, see para. 13.36, post.
4 See para. 11.11, post.

Negotiability

4.12   A distinction must be drawn between assignability and negotiability. Negotiability implies *both*:

1. That the contract (*e.g.* the liability embodied in a cheque) may be passed from hand to hand without notice of the transfer to the party under liability; *and*
2. That the bona fide transferee for value of a negotiable instrument holds it free from any defects in title which might have affected the prior holders, and not subject to equities.

The law on this subject is dealt with in the chapter on 'Negotiable Instruments' (chapter 20).

Chapter 5

Mistake, misrepresentation and undue influence

1. Mistake

5.01   Much of the confusion which surrounds the subject of mistake in the law of contract stems from the fact that we describe as 'mistakes' phenomena which may have a fundamentally different effect: the crucial question is this—did the mistake prevent the parties from reaching any agreement? Additionally, there is a special rule for documents mistakenly signed.

A) *Mistake preventing agreement being reached*

Mistake as to identity, subject-matter or terms may prevent any agreement being reached between the parties:[1]

---

1 For the process of reaching agreement between the parties by way of offer and acceptance, see paras. 3.03 et seq., ante.

5.02   *1) Mistake as to identity*
It is a fundamental of the law of contract that an offer can only be accepted by the person(s) to whom it is made: an offer made by A to B cannot be accepted by C.[1] This rule has in particular been invoked where a rogue has induced another to sell the rogue his goods, and the rogue has then resold the goods to a bona fide purchaser. As we shall see later, the issue of which of the two innocent parties is to lose may depend on whether there was a contract made between the seller and the rogue.[2] This is an enquiry fraught with difficulty because the seller intends in his own mind to do two things which are (unbeknown to him) contradictory—that being the essence of the successful fraud; and the issue for the courts is which represents the seller's *predominant* intention. Thus, in *Cundy v Lindsay*:[3]

A rogue Blenkarn ordered goods from L by the following fraud: there was a well-known firm of Blenkiron & Co carrying on business at 123 Wood Street; the rogue hired rooms at 37 Wood Street, and signed his written order sent from No 37 in such a way that it could be read as Blenkiron; and L fulfilled the order without checking the address. Thus, L intended to do two things which were in fact contradictory: (1) to deal with the addressee at 37 Wood Street; and (2) to deal with the genuine firm of Blenkiron.

The House of Lords held that L's predominant intention, as a matter of construction of the correspondence, was to deal with the genuine firm; and, as the offer was made to them, it could not be accepted by the rogue. In this sort of situation, the transaction between L and the rogue is described as being a 'void contract', meaning there never was any contract at all. Of course, before this sort of fraud can lead to a void contract, the fraud must involve the use of two separate identities: it is otherwise if the rogue merely used an alias, not the name of a real person. In *King's Norton Metal Co Ltd v Edridge, Merrett & Co Ltd*:[4]

The plaintiffs agreed to sell goods on credit to one Wallis who had ordered goods in the name of 'Hallam and Co.' This was merely an alias used by Wallis. The goods were despatched to Wallis and he sold them to the defendant. *Held:* the contract between the plaintiffs and Wallis was valid. The plaintiffs could not establish they intended to contract with someone other than Wallis, and their mistake was one as to the creditworthiness rather than as to the identity of the other party.

In both these cases, the parties dealt with one another by correspondence and it was simply a matter of eliciting the intention of the seller by interpreting the correspondence. However, where parties deal with one another face to face, the process of interpretation is aided by a presumption that the seller intends to deal with the person in front of him (the rogue). Thus in *Lewis v Averay*:[5]

L advertised his car for sale in a newspaper. A man came to see L about the car, saying he was 'Richard Green' and purporting to be a well-known actor of that name. L agreed to sell his car to this man in return for a cheque for £450. The man was allowed to drive away the car and he promptly sold it to A. The cheque was dishonoured. *Held:* where the transaction is between parties face to face there is a presumption in law that there is a contract even though a fraudulent impersonation has been made. L therefore had no right to recover the car from A.

---

1 For the process of reaching agreement between the parties by way of offer and acceptance, see paras. 3.03 et seq., ante.
2 See paras. 13.11 et seq., post.
3 (1878) 3 App Cas 459.
4 (1897) 14 TLR 98.
5 [1972] 1 QB 198, [1971] 3 All ER 907, CA, following *Phillips v Brooks* [1919] 2 KB 243, cf. *Ingram v Little* [1961] 1 QB 31, [1960] 3 All ER 332, CA.

5.03 *2) Mistake as to subject-matter*
There is no contract where one party intends the contract to deal with one thing, and the other with something different.[1] Thus, in *Scriven Bros & Co v Hindley*:[2]

> A bid for a lot at an auction sale which consisted of tow but A thought he was bidding for hemp. The lot was knocked down to him. Both tow and hemp were being sold at the auction, but the bales were not properly described in the auctioneer's catalogue and the samples were confusingly marked. *Held:* contract void.

Similarly, where the agreement contains a patent ambiguity as to the subject-matter, it may be found that the parties never reached any real agreement,[3] a rule possibly extending to latent ambiguities. In *Raffles v Wichelhaus*:[4]

> A agreed to buy cotton from B to arrive 'ex *Peerless* from Bombay'. There were two ships of that name coming from Bombay—A had one in mind, B the other. The terms of the contract could apply to either and it was *held* that the contract was void.

However, in deciding whether the parties have reached agreement over the subject-matter, what generally matters is not what they intend in their minds, but their apparent intention.[5] Moreover, the same is true even if both parties make the same mistake, so that in *Rose v Pim*:[6]

> A agrees to buy 'horsebeans' from B. Both A and B wrongly believe that 'horsebeans' are the same thing as 'feveroles' which a customer has ordered from A. There is a binding contract between A and B.

---

1 For the special rule for documents mistakenly signed, see para. 5.07, post.
2 [1913] 3 KB 564.
3 *Falck v Williams* [1900] AC 176, PC. Cf. *Ireland v Livingstone* (1872) LR 5 HL 395 (see para. 10.18, post).

4 (1864) 2 H & C 906.
5 *Tamplin v James* (1880) 15 ChD 215; set out para. 2.05, ante.
6 *Frederick E Rose (London) Ltd v William H Pim Jnr & Co Ltd* [1953] 2 QB
   450, [1953] 2 All ER 739.

5.04 *3) Mistake as to terms*
Where, applying the objective test, one party is offering to
contract on one set of terms and the other thinks that he is
contracting on different terms, there is a mistake as to the terms,
and hence no agreement. What has really happened, although
neither party realised it, is that the offeree made a counter-offer
instead of accepting.[1] However, this situation must be carefully
distinguished from that where there is simply a mistake as to the
quality of what is being offered.[2] In *Smith v Hughes:*[3]

P, a farmer, asked D, a trainer of racehorses, if he would like
to buy a quantity of oats, showing him a sample. After
delivery of the bulk corresponding with that sample, D
complained that the oats were new, and therefore useless for
feeding to racehorses. P, who knew the oats were new—he had
no old oats—sued for the price. There was a conflict of
evidence as to whether, during the negotiations, the parties
had spoken of a sale of 'oats' or 'old oats'.

The court drew the following distinctions:
1. If both P and D used the word 'old', there would be a contract
for the sale of old oats, and P would be in breach in delivering
new oats;
2. If P offered to sell 'those oats' (new) and D offered to buy
'old oats', then the parties never reached agreement, there being
a mistake of offer and acceptance;
3. If neither party used the word 'old', there was a contract for
the sale of 'those oats' (new), D being mistaken in his own mind
in thinking them old—a mistake as to quality.[2]

1 For counter-offers, see para. 3.05, ante.
2 For mistakes as to quality, see below.
3 (1871) LR 6 QB 597 (the issue was not decided, and the case sent back for
   retrial).

B) *Mistake not preventing agreement being reached*

5.05 Even where a mistake does not prevent the parties from reaching
agreement, it may nevertheless affect the contract, though the

extent to which it does so may differ as between common law and equity.

a) MISTAKE AT COMMON LAW
Leaving aside mistakenly signed documents,[1] the following types of mistake must be considered:

1) Impossibility

The most obvious example is factual impossibility, where the parties contract in respect of some object, both mistakenly thinking that it exists. There are two possible explanations of their intentions:

1. the contract is void from the outset, neither party being bound;[2] or
2. one party in effect guaranteed the existence of the object, being liable for its non-existence.[3]

Similarly, a contract may be void for legal impossibility if it provides for the doing of something which cannot, as a matter of law, be done, e.g. where one mistakenly agrees to buy one's own property;[4] but this should be distinguished from the situation where there is a contract for the sale of goods then owned by a third party, of which the likeliest explanation is that the seller is guaranteeing that he can obtain the goods. Again, a contract may be void because, although physically and legally possible, it is commercially impossible, as where there is a contract to view an already-cancelled procession.[5]

2) Mistake as to quality

The leading case is *Bell v Lever Bros Ltd*:[6]

> B and S were employed by Lever Bros on five-year service contracts and Lever Bros wished to dispense with their services before the expiry of this period. Lever Bros made compensation agreements with B and S under which they received £50,000 for loss of office. Lever Bros later discovered that B and S had committed certain breaches of duty which, had Lever Bros known of these breaches earlier, would have entitled them to dismiss B and S without compensation. The House of Lords accepted that these breaches were not in the minds of B and S at the time of the compensation agreements. The House *held* that despite the mistake of both parties, i.e. the assumption that the services of B and S could only be dispensed with by compensation agreements, these agreements were valid contracts. The parties were mistaken only as to the quality of the service contracts (which were the subject-matter

of the compensation agreements), i.e. their mistake was only as to whether the service contracts were voidable.

Whilst their Lordships did admit of the possibility of such mistakes so fundamental as to render a contract void at common law, any such doctrine would plainly be very restricted indeed—the mistake has to be more fundamental than that in B's case, between a £30,000 contract and a worthless (because voidable) one. There is a sound policy reason behind this strict view: were it not so, a party could always escape from a bad bargain on a plea that he had 'made a mistake' as to the value of what he was getting.

---

1 See para. 5.07, post.
2 *Couturier v Hastie* (1856) 5 HL Cas 673. This was the orthodox view of what the case decided, and was embodied in s. 6 of the Sale of Goods Act 1893: see para. 13.04, post.
3 *McRae v Commonwealth Disposals Commission* (1950) 84 CLR 377 (Aust. HC).
4 *Cooper v Phibbs* (1867) LR 2 HL 149 (a case in equity, see para. 5.06, post).
5 *Griffith v Brymer* (1903) 19 TLR 434. Cf. frustration: see para. 8.02, post.
6 [1932] AC 161, HL.

---

b) MISTAKE IN EQUITY

5.06   Whilst at common law the effect of mistake—if it operates at all—is to render the contract void *ab initio* (from the outset), equity is much more flexible, offering the following remedies in appropriate cases:

1) Specific performance
In an action for specific performance,[1] equity will generally follow the common law. Thus, if the contract is valid at law notwithstanding the mistake, specific performance will normally be awarded;[2] whereas, if it is void, this remedy will normally be refused.[3] However, as equitable remedies are discretionary, a court may refuse specific performance because of the mistake notwithstanding that the contract is valid at common law, e.g. where it is the carelessness of the party seeking specific performance that led the other to make the mistake;[4] or it may award the remedy on terms as a middle course, e.g. with a cash allowance to cover the mistake.[5]

2) Rescission
Where on common law principles a contract is void, the court may, in order to do justice, impose equitable terms on the parties in setting the contract aside, as in *Cooper v Phibbs*:[6]

> A took a lease of a fishery from B, both parties mistakenly believing B owned it. Actually the fishery belonged to A, but B had incurred expense in improvements. *Held:* the lease would be set aside on terms that A would reimburse B's expenses.

However, equity may go further than the common law and set aside a contract, i.e. rescind it, for a mistake which the common law would not regard as sufficient to render that contract void *ab initio.* In *Solle v Butcher:*[7]

> The parties agreed to the lease of a flat in the common belief that owing to alterations it was no longer subject to the Rent Acts restricting the amount of rent chargeable and that a rent of £250 was permissible. However, they were mistaken as to this belief, for the flat was still subject to the Rent Acts and the legal rent was £140. *Held:* the lease was not void at common law—the mistake was only as to the quality of the flat—but it would be set aside on equitable principles on terms that were just to both parties.

Before this jurisdiction can be exercised, there must be a mistake as to a state of affairs existing at the time the contract was made,[8] and it is not even clear that it extends beyond the Rent Acts.[9]

3) Rectification

Where parties have reached an agreement (which need not be a concluded binding contract) and this is then embodied in a document but this document fails to record the agreement accurately, though they both mistakenly think it does, either party may ask the court to rectify the written document in order to bring it into line with their prior agreement.[10] However, although a contract will normally be rectified only if *both* parties have made a mistake as to its contents,[11] a party may be granted the remedy of rectification on proof that he believed a certain term was included and the other party concluded the contract with the omission of that term in the knowledge that the other party believed the term was included.[12]

---

1 For the remedy of specific performance, see para. 7.32, post.
2 *Tamplin v James* (1880) 15 ChD 215, CA—set out para. 2.05, ante.
3 *Webster v Cecil* (1861) 30 Beav 62—set out para. 2.05, ante.
4 *Denny v Hancock* (1870) 6 Ch App 1.
5 But not where the mistake is 'substantial': *Flight v Booth* (1834) 1 Bing NC 370.
6 (1867) LR 2 HL 149 (decision probably confined to mistakes as to private rights, *not* the general law).
7 [1950] 1 KB 671, [1949] 2 All ER 875, CA.

8 *Amalgamated Investments and Property Co Ltd v John Walker & Sons Ltd* [1976] 3 All ER 509, CA: for discussion of the doctrine of frustration, see para. 8.02 et seq., post.
9 *Solle v Butcher* was followed in *Grist v Bailey* [1967] Ch 532, [1966] 2 All ER 875. Lord Denning MR, also purported to follow *Solle v Butcher* in *Magee v Pennine Insurance Co Ltd* [1969] 2 QB 507, [1969] 2 All ER 891, CA, but it is not clear whether the other majority judge, Fenton Atkinson LJ, supported Lord Denning's reasoning.
10 *Joscelyne v Nissen* [1970] 2 QB 86, [1970] 1 All ER 1213, CA.
11 *Riverlate Properties Ltd v Paul* [1975] Ch 133, [1974] 2 All ER 656, CA.
12 *A Roberts & Co Ltd v Leicestershire County Council* [1961] Ch 555, [1961] 2 All ER 545.

C) Mistake in signing a written document

5.07 If anyone signs a written document which is radically different in effect from the document he thinks he is signing and this mistake has been induced by a misrepresentation, he may plead *non est factum* (it is not my deed) and he is not bound by it.[1]

In *Foster v Mackinnon*:[2]

M, 'a gentleman far advanced in years and of poor sight', was induced by C to sign a piece of paper described by C as 'a guarantee'. In fact, the document was a bill of exchange and M's signature appeared to be that of an endorser and, therefore, to make him liable to a later holder for value. *Held:* M was not bound by his signature as he had signed the paper under a mistake as to its nature.

However, it is difficult for an adult literate person to succeed in the defence of *non est factum* and the defence is not available if the signer is negligent. The signer must at least take reasonable care to find out the general effect of the document before signing. The House of Lords has recently clarified the law in *Saunders v Anglia Building Society*:[3]

An elderly lady had mislaid her spectacles and did not read the document she was asked to sign by her nephew which she mistakenly thought was a deed of gift of her house to him so that he could raise money on it. In fact the document was an assignment of the house to her nephew's business associate, and the latter mortgaged it to the defendants but defaulted in his repayments. The elderly lady sought a declaration that she was not bound by her signature. *Held:* The effect of the document was not so fundamentally different from the document she thought she was signing as to enable her to plead *non est factum* and her action failed.

1 *Mercantile Credit Co Ltd v Hamblin* [1965] 2 QB 242, [1964] 3 All ER 592.
2 (1869) LR 4 CP 704.
3 [1971] AC 1004, [1970] 3 All ER 961. The distinction formerly drawn between the character and the contents of the document was regarded by the House of Lords as unsatisfactory.

2. Misrepresentation

5.08   If one party to a contract has been induced to enter that contract by a misrepresentation made by the other party to the contract (or his agent), the representee (the first party) may have some remedy *under that contract*; but this cannot be the case where the misrepresentation was made by a stranger to the contract thereby induced.[1]

1 *Gross v Lewis Hillman Ltd* [1970] Ch 445, [1969] 3 All ER 1476, CA. A stranger to a contract is one who has not given consideration for, and is not privy to, a contract: see para. 4.02, ante. Such a stranger might, however, be liable to the representee in the torts of deceit or negligent misstatement.

The meaning of misrepresentation

5.09   A misrepresentation is an untrue statement of fact made by one party to a contract, A, to the other thereto, B, which is a factor inducing B to enter into the contract between them. The state of mind in which A makes the misrepresentation will be considered later.[1] But at the outset, there must be distinguished a misrepresentation (which contains the ingredients analysed below) from a 'mere puff'. The latter is mere 'sales talk', which everybody should recognise as such, and upon which no reliance should be placed. In each case, it is a question of fact whether there was only such indiscriminate praise,[2] or an assertion seriously meant.[3]

a) Untrue statement   It is possible for the representation to be made by conduct so that if A induces B to give him credit by dressing up as a military officer, the contract is voidable for misrepresentation. Normally, however, the representation is a statement made orally, or in writing. The general rule is that silence cannot amount to a misrepresentation, but the assertion of a half-truth may be a misrepresentation. Lord Cairns in *Peek v Gurney*[4] said:

'There must, in my opinion, be some active misstatement of

fact, or, at all events, such a partial and fragmentary statement of fact, as that the withholding of that which is not stated makes that which is stated absolutely false'.

Thus, in *Dimmock v Hallett*[5] the vendor of farms induced the sale by the statement that they were let to tenants: this was true so far as it went, but the statement amounted to a misrepresentation because the tenants had given notice to quit. Further, where a representation is made during negotiations which, though true at the time it is made, becomes untrue before the contract is made, it amounts to a misrepresentation—if, therefore the person who made the statement fails to disclose the change, the contract is voidable.[6] In some contracts there is a positive obligation on a party to disclose all material facts within his knowledge. These contracts, known as contracts *uberrimae fidei*, of which insurance contracts are the most important, are referred to below.[7]

b) Of fact This excludes untrue statements of law so that if A induced B to buy goods from him by falsely stating that the law no longer permitted goods to be taken on hire-purchase, the contract is not voidable.[8] A statement of intention may amount to a promise,[9] though it is usually not a statement of fact; but, if it can be proved that the stated intention was not in fact held, there is a misrepresentation of fact. As Bowen LJ said in *Edgington v Fitzmaurice*:[10]

'The state of a man's mind is as much a fact as the state of his digestion'.

Similarly, a mere statement of opinion is not a statement of fact; but, where the facts are not equally known to both parties and an opinion stated by the party who knows the facts best is not in fact held, or there are no reasonable grounds for such opinion, the opinion amounts to a misrepresentation of fact.[11] Thus where the vendor of a hotel described it as let to 'Mr. Flack, a most desirable tenant' and as Bowen LJ put it, Mr. Flack paid his rents only 'in driblets under pressure', the vendor's statement of opinion was held to amount to a misrepresentation of fact.[12]

c) Inducement The statement by A must have been intended by A to be acted upon and it must actually have been relied on by B as at any rate one of the factors that induced B to make a contract with A. If B is not deceived by, or does not rely on, the representation, the contract will not be set aside.[13] So too if A tells B that the horse which A is proposing to sell to B has two eyes and B knows the horse does not have two eyes, there is no operative misrepresentation. But if B was not aware of the falsity of A's statement, it is no ground for refusing B a remedy that B had every opportunity of discovering the truth. In *Redgrave v Hurd*:[14]

> A solicitor, A, made false statements of fact about the finances of his firm and an intending partner, B, relied on these statements when entering into partnership. *Held:* B was entitled to have the partnership contract rescinded on the ground of misrepresentation although A had given B the opportunity of examining certain papers from which B could have discovered the true position.

---

1 See paras. 5.10, 5.12, post.
2 E.g. *Dimmock v Hallett* (1866) 2 Ch App 21; *Bisset v Wilkinson* [1927] AC 177, PC.
3 E.g. *Carlill v Carbolic Smoke Ball Co* [1893] 1 QB 256, CA (set out para. 3.03, ante).
4 (1873) LR 6 HL 377, 403.
5 (1866) 2 Ch App 21.
6 *With v O'Flanagan* [1936] Ch 575, [1936] 1 All ER 727. Cf. *Wales v Wadham* [1977] 2 All ER 125, [1977] 1 WLR 199.
7 Para. 5.15, post.
8 Contra private rights: see para. 5.06, ante.
9 For contractual promises, see para. 7.02, post.
10 (1885) 29 ChD 459, 483.
11 *Brown v Raphael* [1958] Ch 636, [1958] 2 All ER 79.
12 *Smith v Land and House Property Corporation* (1884) 28 ChD 7.
13 *Smith v Chadwick* (1884) 9 App Cas 187.
14 (1881) 20 ChD 1.

Types of misrepresentation

5.10   The crucial thing in determining the remedies which may be available for misrepresentation is A's state of mind when he made that misrepresentation.

a) FRAUDULENT MISREPRESENTATION AND REMEDIES THEREFOR

A fraudulent misrepresentation is a statement of fact made by A knowing it is false, or without belief in its truth, or recklessly, without caring whether it is true or false. In *Derry v Peek*:[1]

> A company issued a prospectus, stating that the company had a right to use steam power for its tramway cars; in fact, the consent of the Board of Trade was required before steam could be used, and when, afterward, consent was applied for, it was refused. The directors believed the truth of their statements, and pleaded that they had reasonable ground for

believing them to be true. *Held:* not a fraudulent misrepresentation.

In this case in the House of Lords it was definitely settled that, in order to maintain an action for deceit, a false statement must be either—

1. Untrue to the knowledge of the person making it; or
2. Untrue in fact and not believed to be true by the person making it; or
3. Untrue in fact and made recklessly—e.g. without any knowledge on the subject, and without caring whether it is true or false.

But an untrue statement honestly made without any reasonable grounds for belief in its truth is not sufficient; in other words, in an action for deceit the plaintiff must prove actual dishonesty, not mere negligence or blundering.

If the representation is made innocently by an agent but his principal knew of facts which rendered it untrue, that will only amount to fraud if the principal authorised it or deliberately concealed the facts from the agent in the hope that the latter would make the representation in question. In *Armstrong v Strain:*[2]

> An estate agent made a representation to the plaintiff about a house, which was untrue. The owner knew the facts but did not know of the agent's statements or authorise them. *Held:* there was no fraud for there is no way of combining an innocent principal and an innocent agent so as to produce dishonesty.

If the representation in fact is fraudulent within the definition above given, honesty of motive in making it will not be an answer to an action of deceit.[3]

---

1 (1889) 14 App Cas 337, HL.
2 [1952] 1 KB 232, [1952] 1 All ER 139, CA.
3 *Polhill v Walter* (1835) 3 B & Ad 114; *Foster v Charles* (1830) 7 Bing. 105.

Remedies

5.11 A defrauded person has several remedies open to him. He may:

1. Rescind the contract, e.g. by communication with the fraudulent party or by conduct which manifests unequivocally his intention no longer to be bound by the contract or by obtaining a court order of rescission.[1] At one time it was thought that communication with the fraudulent party was essential unless a court order was obtained; but in *Car and Universal*

Finance Co Ltd v Caldwell,[2] the Court of Appeal held that where a car owner was induced by fraud to sell it to a rogue who disappeared, the owner had rescinded the sale when he asked the police to try to recover the car.

2. Resist any action to enforce the contract.

3. Sue for damages in the tort of deceit in which case he must prove that he has suffered actual damage.[3] This right is normally open to the defrauded person irrespective of whether he is rescinding the contract or affirming it.[4] The measure of damages comprehends all loss flowing directly from the fraud.[5]

Fraud as to credit It remains to note that s. 6 of the Statute of Frauds Amendment Act 1828 was passed to prevent evasion of the requirement of s. 4 of the Statute of Frauds[6] (that guarantees must be evidenced in writing) by alleging that an oral representation was made fraudulently and suing for damages in an action for deceit. The Amendment Act applies to *fraudulent* misrepresentations only and not to cases where the claim is based upon any contractual or other breach of duty;[7] it prevents an action being brought on a fraudulent misrepresentation as to a person's character made to enable him to get credit, etc. unless the misrepresentation is in writing and signed by the party to be charged.

---

1 Unlike rescission for innocent misrepresentation (as to which see below), the remedy is not here limited by the need to make restitution; but it is subject to the other limitations there discussed (except lapse of time).

2 [1965] 1 QB 525, [1964] 1 All ER 290, CA.

3 *Derry v Peek* (1889) 14 App Cas 337 (set out para. 5.10, ante).

4 Anyone induced to subscribe for shares in a company may only claim damages if he also rescinds the contract: *Holdsworth v City of Glasgow Bank* (1880) 5 App Cas 317.

5 *Doyle v Olby (Ironmongers) Ltd* [1969] 2 QB 158, [1969] 2 All ER 119, CA (fraudulent inducement to buy a business—damages included reasonable expenses of running it).

6 See para. 2.11, ante.

7 *Banbury v Bank of Montreal* [1918] AC 626; *WB Anderson & Sons Ltd v Rhodes (Liverpool) Ltd* [1967] 2 All ER 850.

---

b) INNOCENT MISREPRESENTATION AND REMEDIES THEREFOR

5.12 Any misrepresentation which is made with an honest belief in its truth is an innocent misrepresentation. Neither the common law nor equity gave a remedy in damages for innocent misrepresentation *simpliciter,* but, in equity rescission of contract was permitted, and at common law damages could be sought for the tort of negligent misstatement.[1] However, the availability of damages to the representee has been increased in the following two respects by the Misrepresentation Act 1967: (1) where rescission is claimed, the court is given power to award damages instead (see below); and (2) the representee may claim damages as of right in respect of a negligent misrepresentation. Thus, s. 2 (1) provides that

'Where a person has entered into a contract after a misrepresentation has been made to him by another party thereto and as a result thereof he has suffered loss, then, if the person making the representation would be liable to damages in respect thereof had the misrepresentation been made fraudulently, that person shall be so liable notwithstanding that the misrepresentation was not made fraudulently, unless he proves that he had reasonable ground to believe and did believe up to the time the contract was made that the facts represented were true.'

It will be observed that in respect of this statutory tort the burden of proof is reversed: whereas at common law, the representee must prove that the representation was made negligently,[1] under s. 2 (1) it is for the representor to disprove negligence.

---

1 *Hedley Byrne & Co v Heller & Partners* [1964] AC 465, [1963] 2 All ER 575, HL; *Esso Petroleum Co Ltd v Mardon* [1975] QB 819, [1975] 1 All ER 203, CA (set out para. 7.03, post); *Howard Marine and Dredging Co Ltd v A Ogden & Sons (Excavations) Ltd* [1978] 2 WLR 515, CA.

Remedies

5.13 1. *Rescind the contract*, e.g. by B communicating with the party who made the misrepresentation, A, or by conduct which manifests unequivocally B's intention not to be bound by the contract, or by B obtaining a court order of rescission. In some cases, e.g. where the seller of a second-hand car innocently misrepresent the mileage done in the car since its engine was last overhauled, rescission of the contract may be an unduly drastic remedy, and the court now has the power to award damages instead under s. 2 (2) of the Misrepresentation Act 1967. For the future, it may therefore do this,

'if of opinion that it would be equitable to do so, having regard to the nature of the misrepresentation and the loss that would be caused by it if the contract were upheld, as well as to the loss that rescission would cause to the other party.'

In any case, there are a number of circumstances in which the right to rescind a contract for misrepresentation is lost:

a) *By affirmation* The person to whom the misrepresentation has been made (B) loses his right to rescind the contract if he has affirmed it expressly or by conduct after he has knowledge of the untruth of the representation.[1] Unreasonable delay by B after he has knowledge of the untruth is evidence of affirmation.[2]

b) Third party rights The right to rescind is lost if a third party has acquired rights in the subject-matter of the contract for value before B has manifested his intention to rescind the contract.[3]

c) Restitution impossible Where the parties cannot be restored to their original position, rescission is not permissible for innocent misrepresentation (though it is otherwise where there is fraud). Thus, in *Lagunas Nitrate Co v Lagunas Syndicate*,[4] rescission was refused where a change in the parties' position had resulted from the plaintiffs *working* certain nitrate deposits purchased from the defendants after misrepresentation by the defendants.

d) Lapse of time This is no bar to rescission in the case of fraudulent misrepresentation, but where the misrepresentation is innocent, the lapse of such time as would enable a reasonable person to discover the truth does mean that the right to rescind is lost. In *Leaf v International Galleries*:[5]

> The seller of a picture misrepresented it as being one painted by Constable. The purchaser claimed rescission to recover the purchase price five years after the sale. *Held:* although there was no evidence of affirmation as the purchaser had only just discovered the falsity, it was too late for him to rescind.

Until the Misrepresentation Act 1967, the mere execution or performance of a contract had been held in some cases[6] to bar the right to rescind for innocent misrepresentation; but these cases have been reversed by s. 1 of this Act.[7]

2. *Resist any action to enforce the contract.*

3. *Claim damages.*[8] It is convenient to think in terms of *three* types of misrepresentation with regard to the award of damages:

a) Fraudulent misrepresentation (see para. 5.10, ante).

b) Negligent misrepresentation, where damages may be claimed as of right either at common law (see ante, para. 5.12, ante) or under s. 2 (1) of the Misrepresentation Act 1967.[9]

c) Non-negligent innocent misrepresentation, where damages lie in the discretion of the court under s. 2 (2).[10]

---

1 *Long v Lloyd* [1958] 2 All ER 402, [1958] 1 WLR 753, CA.
2 Cf. *Allen v Robles* [1969] 3 All ER 154, [1969] 1 WLR 1193, CA.
3 See *Car and Universal Finance Co Ltd v Caldwell* [1965] 1 QB 525, [1964] 1 All ER 290, CA, and *Lewis v Averay* [1972] 1 QB 198, [1971] 3 All ER 907, CA (set out para. 5.02, ante), and see para. 13.14, post.

4 [1899] 2 Ch 392. Contra in case of natural deterioration.
5 [1950] 2 KB 86, [1950] 1 All ER 693.
6 *Seddon v NE Salt Co* [1905] 1 Ch 326; *Angel v Jay* [1911] 1 KB 666.
7 The Act also provides in s. 1 that the right to rescind is not lost because the representation has become a term of the contract: see also para. 7.01, post.
8 Normally rescission and damages cannot both be claimed at the same time: *Horsler v Zorro* [1975] Ch 302, [1975] 1 All ER 584.
9 See para. 5.12, ante, and *Watts v Spence* [1976] Ch 165, [1975] 2 All ER 528; *Andre and Cie SA v ETS Michel Blanc and Fils* [1977] 2 Lloyd's Rep. 166; *Howard Marine and Dredging Co Ltd v A Ogden & Sons (Excavations) Ltd* [1978] 2 WLR 515, CA. Presumably, there may also be a claim for rescission in a proper case.
10 Where the court refuses to grant damages in the exercise of this discretion, the only possible monetary claim is for an indemnity. Such claim, however, does not cover all the natural consequences of the misrepresentation but only the expense of carrying out the actual obligations of the contract: *Whittington v Seale-Hayne* (1900), 82 LT 49. A claim for indemnity may only be made if the plaintiff is entitled to rescind, and is an equitable remedy.

Avoidance of exemption clauses

5.14 No contractual clause exempting a party from liability for fraudulent misrepresentation is effective. In the case of attempts to exclude liability for innocent misrepresentation,[1] it is provided by s. 3 of the Misrepresentation Act:[2]

'If a contract contains a term which would exclude or restrict:
(a) any liability to which a party to a contract may be subject by reason of any misrepresentation made by him before the contract was made, or
(b) any remedy available to another party to the contract by reason of such a misrepresentation;
that term shall be of no effect except in so far as it satisfies the requirement of reasonableness as stated in section 11 (1) of the Unfair Contract Terms Act 1977; and it is for those claiming that the term satisfies that requirement to show that it does.'

1 The Act leaves standing the ordinary common law rules as to what amounts to a misrepresentation: see para. 5.09, ante. It is thus possible to prevent there being any misrepresentation: *Overbrook Estates Ltd v Glencombe Properties Ltd* [1974] 3 All ER 511, [1974] 1 WLR 1335.
2 As substituted by s. 8 of the Unfair Contract Terms Act 1977. For the test of reasonableness in that Act, see para. 3.15, ante. And see *Howard Marine and Dredging Co Ltd v A Ogden & Sons (Excavations) Ltd* [1978] 2 WLR 515, CA.

Contracts uberrimæ fidei

5.15 There is a certain group of contracts which are voidable by a party misled who enters into them unless each party had disclosed to the other every material fact within his own knowledge, or that of his agent, at the time when the contract is made.[1] These are styled contracts *uberrimæ fidei*. They include:

1. All contracts of insurance,[2] and are not limited to contracts of marine, fire and life[3] insurance;
2. Where there is a fiduciary or confidential relationship between the parties,[4] e.g. principal and agent,[5] partners,[6] fiduciary relationship.[4]
3. *Directors' liability in respect of statements in a prospectus.*

Section 43 of the Companies Act 1948 applies to statements made in a prospectus inviting persons to subscribe for shares in or debentures of a company, and entitles persons so subscribing on the faith of untrue or misleading statements to proceed for damages against any of the following (subject to certain specific defences):

1. Directors at the time of issuing the prospectus;
2. Persons who have authorised their names to be placed on a prospectus as being directors or as having agreed (at once or after an interval) to become directors;
3. Promoters—i.e. persons being parties to the preparation of the prospectus, and not being engaged in such preparation merely in a professional capacity;
4. Any person who authorised the issue of the prospectus.

---

1 *Mackender v Feldia AG* [1967] 2 QB 590, [1966] 3 All ER 847, CA.
2 *Seaton v Heath* [1899] 1 QB 782, CA, reversed on the facts sub nom. *Seaton v Burnand* [1900] AC 135, HL. See generally, chaps. 26, 27, post.
3 *London Assurance v Mansel* (1879) 11 ChD 363.
4 *Boardman v Phipps* [1967] 2 AC 46, [1966] 3 All ER 721, HL. And see also undue influence, para. 5.16, post.
5 *Regal (Hastings) Ltd v Gulliver* [1967] 2 AC 134, [1942] 1 All ER 378, HL. See further para. 10.11, post.
6 See para. 11.14, post.

---

3. Duress and undue influence

5.16 If one party, A, has been induced to enter into the agreement by some unfair pressure brought to bear upon him by the other party, B, A may be able to escape from the agreement on this ground.

Duress The common law took a very narrow view as to what constituted duress, restricting it to actual or threatened violence to the person, or imprisonment. Where B acts in such a manner to induce A by duress to contract with him, this should logically negative A's consent to the agreement,[1] hence making the alleged contract void *ab initio*.[2] However, the cases have thus far treated duress as having the same effect as the concurrent equitable jurisdiction to relieve against undue influence, the facts of the cases being such that it made no difference.

Undue influence Where A has exercised improperly some power he possesses over the mind of B so as to induce B to contract with him, equity has long intervened to rescind the agreement, which is described as being 'voidable' at the instance of A.[3] Out of this jurisdiction arose the special rules about unconscionable bargains which applied particularly to moneylenders. This last area was put in statutory form in 1900 and has since been re-enacted as 'extortionate credit bargains' in the Consumer Credit Act 1974.[4] The equitable jurisdiction to intervene arose wherever a contract was induced by undue influence, this being presumed in the case of certain designated confidential relationships between A and B, e.g. solicitor-client, trustee-beneficiary. In the absence of such a relationship, the onus of proving undue influence is upon the person who claims it was exercised, e.g. by such as threatening to have A's son charged with forgery[5] or playing on A's fears concerning the state of his father's health.[6] In *Lloyds Bank Ltd v Bundy*:[7]

A was an elderly farmer whose sole asset was his farmhouse, and who had been guaranteeing to the Bank the overdraft on his son's failing business account. The assistant manager of the Bank went to see A at his home, taking with him completed forms for a further guarantee of sums desperately needed by A's son and which the Bank required to be secured by a charge for £11,000 on the farm. The manager told A that the Bank would only continue to support his son if A signed them. After the business failed, the Bank took steps to enforce the guarantee and charge.

The Court of Appeal set aside both guarantee and charge on the grounds that A looked to the bank for financial advice; and that, as it was in the Bank's interest that A signed, the assistant manager could not discharge the duty of giving independent advice. Going further than was strictly necessary, Lord Denning MR may have given a pointer to future developments in this area of the law when he put a new, and potentially much wider, gloss on the decided cases, explaining that they all contain a common single thread:[8]

'They rest on inequality of bargaining power. By virtue of it, the English law gives relief to one who, without independent advice, enters into a contract on terms which are very unfair or transfers property for a consideration which is grossly inadequate, when his bargaining power is grievously impaired by reason of his own needs or desires, or by his own ignorance or infirmity, coupled with undue influences or pressures brought to bear on him by or for the benefit of the other'.

---

1 *Scott v Sebright* (1887) 12 PD at 24.
2 *Lanham* 29 MLR 615.
3 Rescission is subject to the usual limitations: see para. 5.13, ante.
4 See para. 15.18, post.
5 *Williams v Bayley* (1866) LR 1 HL 200.
6 *Mutual Finance Ltd v John Wetton & Sons Ltd* [1937] 2 KB 389, [1937] 2 All ER 657.
7 [1975] QB 326, [1974] 3 All ER 757, CA.
8 Ibid, at pp. 339, 765.

Chapter 6

Contracts which the law treats as invalid

6.01 Notwithstanding that the parties may have thought they were in agreement,[1] there may be no contractual promise enforceable in the courts by them for any of the following reasons (inter alia):

1. No agreement was ever reached by reason of mistake, the supposed contract being *void ab initio*, i.e. the alleged contract never existed.[2]

2. The agreement reached does not amount to a contract because of the absence of consideration, or lack of intent to create legal relations.[3]

3. The agreement reached does amount to a contract, but one which is *voidable ab initio* by reason of misrepresentation or undue influence, i.e. there was initially a binding contract, but one liable to be set aside *(rescinded)*[4] and, if it is set aside, the effect will be as if it never existed.[5]

4. The agreement reached does amount to a contract, but it is *unenforceable*, e.g. under the rules introduced by the Statute of Frauds (1677), the courts will recognise the existence of the contract, but will do nothing to enforce it at common law.[6]

5. There was a binding contract initially, but it has been discharged for one of the reasons considered in chapter 8, in which case the contract is said to have been *avoided*[7] (rescinded).[4]

Leaving aside the above permutations, there are some situations where the agreement reached will not be unreservedly enforced (if at all) because the law finds it objectionable, and therefore treats it as invalid. Such situations must be subdivided because the effects of the invalidity are not the same in all cases. However, in respect of all of them there is a presumption in favour of validity: it is doubtful whether any contract will be invalid unless it falls within one of the classes mentioned below; and, if there is any serious doubt, the courts incline towards supporting rather than upsetting a contract.

1 See paras. 3.02–3.16, ante.
2 See paras. 5.02–5.04, ante.
3 See paras. 3.17–3.27, ante.
4 Alternative expression for this situation: *Buckland v Farmar and Moody* (1978) 122 Sol Jo 211, CA.
5 See paras. 5.09–5.16, ante.
6 See paras. 2.11–2.14, ante. Cf. the making of regulated agreements by unlicensed traders under the Consumer Credit Act 1974, where the Act expressly sets out the degree of unenforceability (para. 15.08).
7 See para. 8.01, post.

---

1. Contracts illegal by statute or common law

Contracts illegal by statute

6.02 Contracts forbidden by statute are invalid, whether they are forbidden expressly or impliedly.

a) Express prohibition   For instance, it is a criminal offence to enter into an instalment credit contract in relation to goods, e.g. of hire-purchase, credit sale or hiring, without there being paid the minimum deposit or for a 'repayment' period exceeding the maximum laid down: any contract contravening these provisions, which are commonly known as the 'Term Controls',[1] is invalid.[2]

b) Implied prohibition   Where a contract is not expressly prohibited by statute, it is a matter of construction of the statute whether it is aimed at the contract so as to make it impliedly forbidden.[3] Nor is a contract illegal merely because a statute is contravened. In *Archbolds (Freightage) Ltd v S Spanglett Ltd*:[4]

> X engaged Y to carry whisky for X from Leeds to London. Unknown to X, Y used a van which had no A licence and Y was thus in contravention of the Road Traffic Act. The whisky was stolen owing to negligence on the part of Y's driver. *Held:* the contract was not illegal and Y was liable to X for the loss. Holroyd Pearce LJ said: 'To hold the contract illegal would injure the innocent, benefit the guilty and put a premium on deceit.'

c) Licences   If a statute imposes a penalty for entering into a certain kind of contract, and the purpose of the penalty is merely to obtain revenue (as distinct from protecting the public), the contract is not illegal.[5] If a contract is illegal in the absence of a licence, it cannot be enforced;[6] but, if one of the parties made himself responsible for the obtaining of a licence (either expressly or impliedly), the innocent party may be able to sue him on a 'collateral warranty' to that effect.[7]

1 Contained in Statutory Orders made under the Emergency Laws (Reenactments and Repeals) Act 1964, s. 1; see further para. 14.07, post.
2 *Bowmakers Ltd v Barnet Instruments Ltd* [1945] KB 65, [1944] 2 All ER 579, CA.
3 *St John Shipping Corpn v Joseph Rank Ltd* [1957] 1 QB 267, [1956] 3 All ER 683 (see para. 23.22, post).
4 [1961] 1 QB 374, [1961] 1 All ER 417, CA. See also *Shaw v Groom* [1970] 2 QB 504, [1970] 1 All ER 702, CA.
5 *Smith v Mawhood* (1845) 14 M & W 452.
6 Or the contract may have been made conditional on the obtaining of a licence: see para. 3.09, ante, and para. 13.46, post.
7 *Strongman (1945) Ltd v Sincock* [1955] 2 QB 525, [1955] 3 All ER 90, CA.

6.03   THE EFFECT OF ILLEGALITY
This may depend on whether the illegality affects the very formation of the contract, or merely its performance.
a) *Illegal as formed*   Where the very creation of the contract is prohibited, it is *illegal ab initio*, and neither party can acquire any rights under it at common law. Thus, in *Re Mahmoud and Ispahani:* [1]

There was a contract for the sale of linseed oil at a time when a statutory order provided that no person should buy or sell it without a licence. The seller held a licence; and the buyer untruthfully alleged to the seller that he too had one. *Held:* the contract was illegal, the honest belief of the seller being irrelevant, so that the seller's action for non-acceptance failed.

Of course, the Statute imposing the prohibition can always expressly provide as to the effect of its contravention. [2]
b) *Illegal as performed*   Into this category fall contracts which are lawful in their formation, but which are performed by one of the parties in a manner prohibited by statute. Here, the courts will not allow the party responsible for the illegality any rights or remedies under the contract. In *Anderson Ltd v Daniel:* [3]

Statute required that the seller of artificial fertiliser give his buyer an invoice stating the percentage of certain chemicals contained. A seller who failed to do so was not allowed to sue for the price.

Similar treatment has been meted out by the courts to one who was privy to, or condoned, the illegality. [4] However, if the other party is innocent, he will be allowed to enforce the contract. [5]

1 [1921] 2 KB 716.
2 E.g. collective enforcement of resale price maintenance agreements: see para. 28.21, post.
3 [1924] 1 KB 138, CA.

4 *Ashmore, Benson, Pease & Co Ltd v Dawson Ltd* [1973] 2 All ER 856, [1973] 1 WLR 828, CA.
5 See *Re Trepca Mines Ltd* (No 2) [1963] Ch 199 at 220–221, [1962] 3 All ER 351 at 356, CA; and see further para. 6.05, post.

Contracts illegal at common law

6.04 Certain types of contract are forbidden at common law on grounds of public policy, and are accordingly illegal. Leaving aside the vexed question of whether the courts can create new heads of public policy,[1] the following categories of case are well-established:

a) A contract to commit a crime or tort The doctrine has been applied to contracts whose object was to obtain goods by false pretences,[2] or to defraud prospective shareholders,[3] or to deceive a third party, as by giving a false reference for public or private employment in return for a commission.[4] Of a somewhat similar nature are those where a claim is made under an insurance policy, but the facts giving rise to the insured event amount to a crime. It is settled that a claim will not lie under a life insurance policy where the insured committed suicide;[5] or under an accident policy where the insured committed manslaughter and was subsequently held liable to the deceased's widow in damages.[6] However, motor insurance is exceptional: a motorist has been held entitled to his indemnity where his driving was so negligent as to amount to manslaughter;[7] and a third party deliberately injured may exercise the statutory right to compensation from the driver's insurers.[8]

b) A contract that is sexually immoral Quite apart from a contract to do something sexually immoral, this rule also catches contracts innocent in themselves where an immoral purpose is intended. Thus, in *Pearce v Brooks:*[9]

> Where a brougham was hired out to a prostitute, and the evidence showed that the payment to be made was not to depend upon amounts earned, yet that the owner knew of the immoral object for which the carriage was hired, the court declared the contract illegal and *held* that the owner could not recover the hire charges.

c) A contract prejudicial to public safety This head covers two distinct categories. First, trading with an enemy in time of war is illegal: this includes anyone voluntarily residing, or carrying on business, in enemy territory in time of war;[10] and, whilst such a contract made during wartime is *void ab initio,* one previously made is simply avoided as from outbreak of war.[11] Second, this head covers contracts which have for their object the commission of an offence in a foreign and friendly country. Thus, in *Regazzoni v KC Sethia (1944) Ltd:* [12]

> A agreed to buy jute bags from B. They were to be shipped from India to a European port; and it was intended that they should be resold to a South African customer. Export to South Africa was prohibited by the Indian government. *Held:* the contract was illegal and could not be enforced in the English Courts.

d) Contracts prejudicial to the administration of justice Contracts illegal under this head include an agreement not to appear at the public examination nor to oppose the discharge of a bankrupt,[13] to give false evidence in court,[14] or to compromise a prosecution for a 'public offence',[15] such as false pretences,[16] forgery[17] or rape.[18] Two items which require particular mention are agreements 'improperly to stir up litigation' by aiding one party (maintenance)[19] and agreements to finance litigation in return for a share of anything recovered (champerty);[20] although, since 1967 neither will amount to either a criminal offence or a tort, this is without prejudice to any rule of law whereunder these activities are to be treated as contrary to public policy.[21] Not all financial aid to litigation is regarded as being improper, and therefore 'maintenance', e.g. test cases,[22] class actions;[23] and there is presently debate as to whether some form of contingent fee for lawyers ('champerty') should be legalised.

e) A contract liable to corrupt public life Amongst other activities objectionable under this head are contracts for the sale of public offices,[24] to procure a title to be conferred on another (even in consideration of a gift to charity),[25] or to use one's position and influence to obtain a benefit from the Government.[26]

f) A contract to defraud the Revenue Whilst a person may lawfully arrange his affairs to pay as little tax as possible (tax avoidance), he may not conceal or misrepresent the facts in order to do so (tax evasion). Thus, in *Miller v Karlinski:* [27]

> the terms of a contract of employment were that the employee should receive a salary of £10 weekly and repayment of his expenses, but that he should be entitled to include in his expenses account the amount of income tax due in respect of his weekly salary. *Held:* in an action to recover arrears of salary, the contract of employment was illegal.

This rule applies to both national taxes and local rates,[28] and to exchange control regulations.[29]

1 See Cheshire & Fifoot *Law of Contract* (9th edn) 331–332; Treitel *Law of Contract* (4th edn) 316–319.
2 *Berg v Sadler and Moore* [1937] 2 KB 158, [1937] 1 All ER 637.
3 *Begbie v Phosphate Sewage Co Ltd* (1876) 1 QBD 679, CA. See also *Scott v Brown, Doering, McNab & Co* [1892] 2 QB 724 (agreement to rig stock market).
4 *Waldo v Martin* (1825) 4 B & C 319. See also *Brown, Jenkinson & Co Ltd v Percy Dalton (London) Ltd* [1957] 2 QB 621, [1957] 2 All ER 844, CA.
5 *Beresford v Royal Insurance Co Ltd* [1938] AC 586, [1938] 2 All ER 602, HL. See Suicide Act 1961.
6 *Gray v Barr* [1971] 2 QB 554, [1971] 2 All ER 949, CA.
7 *Gray v Barr* [1971] 2 QB 554, [1971] 2 All ER 949, CA.
8 *Hardy v Motor Insurers Bureau* [1964] 2 QB 745 at 761, CA, per Lord Denning MR. For the statutory right to compensation, see para. 26.06, post.
9 (1866) LR 1 Exch 213.
10 *Sovracht (V/O) v Van Udens Scheepvart en Agentuur Maatschappij (NV Gebr.)* [1943] AC 203, [1943] 1 All ER 76, HL. For the purposes of the Trading with the Enemy Act 1939, involuntary residence is sufficient: *Vamvakas v Custodian of Enemy Property* [1952] 2 QB 183, [1952] 1 All ER 629.
11 *Kuenigl v Donnersmarck* [1955] 1 QB 515, [1955] 1 All ER 46.
12 [1958] AC 301, [1957] 3 All ER 286, HL.
13 *Kearley v Thomson* (1890) 24 QBD 742, CA.
14 *R v Andrews* [1973] 1 QB 422, [1973] 1 All ER 857, CA.
15 Contra where the offence is of a 'private' nature—where the injured party has a choice of criminal or civil proceedings: *Fisher & Co v Apollinaris* (1875) 10 Ch App 297.
16 *Jones v Merionethshire Permanent Building Society* [1892] 1 Ch 173. See Theft Act 1968, ss. 15 and 16.
17 *Brook v Hook* (1871) LR 6 Exch 89.
18 *R v Panayiotou* [1973] 3 All ER 112, [1973] 1 WLR 1032, CA.
19 *Re Trepca Mines Ltd (No 2)* [1963] Ch 199 at 219, CA, per Lord Denning MR.
20 See *Re Thomas* [1894] 1 QB 747, CA.
21 Criminal Law Act 1967, ss. 13 and 14.
22 See *Martell v Consett Iron Co Ltd* [1955] Ch 363, [1955] 1 All ER 481, CA.
23 See *Wallersteiner v Moir (No 2)* [1975] QB 373, [1975] 1 All ER 849, CA.
24 *Garforth v Fearon* (1787) 1 Hy. Bl. 328.
25 *Parkinson v College of Ambulance Ltd and Harrison* [1925] 2 KB 1. See now the Honours (Prevention of Abuses) Act 1925.
26 *Montefiore v Menday Motor Components Co Ltd* [1918] 2 KB 241.
27 (1945) 62 TLR 85. See also *Napier v National Business Agency Ltd* [1951] 2 All ER 264.
28 *Alexander v Rayson* [1936] 1 KB 169, *Edler v Auerbach* [1950] 1 KB 359, [1949] 2 All ER 692.
29 As to which, see para. 13.45, post.

6.05 THE EFFECT OF ILLEGALITY

Besides the usual distinction as to whether the contract is illegal as formed, or merely as performed, there is also relevant here an intention to break the law—and in this context all parties are assumed to know the law.[1]

a) Illegal as formed   The contract is illegal *ab initio*,[2] though it is not totally devoid of effect:

1. The general rule is that neither party can sue on the illegal contract,[3] or under any collateral contract,[4] though it may be that a party who has entered the contract under an innocent mistake as to the facts which make it illegal can sue in tort.[5]

2. The general rule is that title passes under an illegal contract notwithstanding the illegality, so that money[6] or goods[7] transferred cannot be recovered; but property may be recovered, either by one who belongs to a class that the statute was designed to protect,[8] or if the action can be pursued without reference to the illegal contract.[9]

b) Illegal as performed   The guilty party cannot rely upon the contract,[10] or the illegal part there;[11] but the rights of the innocent party remain unaffected by the illegality. Thus, in *Marles v Philip Trant & Sons Ltd (No 2):*[12]

> X agreed to sell to D spring wheat, but delivered winter wheat. D innocently resold the wheat as spring wheat to P; but D performed the resale contract illegally in that he did not supply an invoice with the goods. *Held:* P succeeded against D, and D against X for breach of the respective contracts of sale.

---

1 *JM Allan (Merchandising) Ltd v Cloke* [1963] 2 QB 340, [1963] 2 All ER 258, CA.
2 *Re Mahmoud and Ispahani* [1921] 2 KB 716, CA: set out above, para. 6.03.
3 *Snell v Unity Finance Ltd* [1964] 2 QB 203, [1963] 3 All ER 50, CA; *Yin v Sam* [1962] AC 304, PC.
4 *Spector v Agenda* [1973] Ch 30, [1971] 3 All ER 417.
5 *Belvoir Finance Ltd v Stapleton* [1971] 1 QB 210, [1970] 3 All ER 664, CA.
6 *Taylor v Chester* (1869) LR 4 QB 309; *Berg v Sadler and Moore* [1937] 2 KB 158, [1937] 1 All ER 637, CA.
7 *Kingsley v Stirling Industrial Securities Ltd* [1967] 2 QB 747, [1966] 2 All ER 414, CA.
8 *Kiriri Cotton Co Ltd v Dewani* [1960] AC 192, [1960] 1 All ER 177, PC.
9 *Amar Singh v Kulubya* [1964] AC 142, [1963] 3 All ER 499, PC. *Bowmakers Ltd v Barnet Instruments Ltd* [1945] KB 65, [1944] 2 All ER 579, CA.
10 *Anderson Ltd v Daniel* [1924] 1 KB 138, CA: set out above, para. 6.03.
11 *Geismar v Sun Alliance and London Insurance Ltd* [1977] 3 All ER 570.
12 [1954] 1 QB 29, [1953] 1 All ER 651, CA.

2. Contracts rendered void by statute

6.06 There are cases where a statute provides that contracts contravening its terms shall be, not illegal, but void. Two such classes of cases will be dealt with later: restrictive trading agreements,[1] and contraventions of the Registration of Business Names Act 1916;[2] but some consideration must be given here to gaming and wagering contracts.

Gaming and wagering contracts

By the Gaming Act 1845, s. 18:

> 'all contracts or agreements, whether by parole or in writing, by way of gaming or wagering, shall be null and void; and no suit shall be brought or maintained in any court of law or equity for recovering any sum of money or valuable thing alleged to be won upon any wager, or which shall have been deposited in the hands of any person to abide the event on which any wager shall have been made.'

Securities deposited with a stockbroker to *secure* payment of 'differences' in favour of the broker are not deposited to 'abide the event', and may be recovered from the stockbroker;[3] but not money so deposited if it has been appropriated to losses, because that is equivalent to a voluntary payment with knowledge of the facts.[4] Money deposited with a stakeholder to abide the event of a wager may be recovered if its return is demanded before it has been paid over to the winner.[5]

It has been held that:[6]

> 'The essence of gaming and wagering is that one party is to win and the other to lose upon a future event which at the time of the contract is of an uncertain nature—that is to say, if the event turns out one way A will lose, but if it turns out the other way he will win.'

This definition cannot be treated as exhaustive and must be read as subject to the qualification that neither of the parties has any other interest in the contract than the sum or stake he will win or lose.[7] An insurance contract is not a wager because the insured must have an insurable interest in the subject-matter of the insurance.[8] There cannot be more than two parties or two sides to a wager and each side must stand to win or lose. The Horserace Totalisator Board cannot lose on bets placed with it so such bets are not void and the Board is entitled to sue for lost bets.[9] A multipartite agreement to contribute to a sweepstake is not a wager, but may be illegal as a lottery.

---

1 See chap. 28, post.
2 See para. 11.06, post.
3 *Universal Stock Exchange v Strachan* [1896] AC 166, HL.
4 *Strachan v Universal Stock Exchange* [1895] 2 QB 697.
5 *Hampden v Walsh* (1876) 1 QBD 189.
6 *Thacker v Hardy* (1879) 4 QBD, at 695, per Cotton LJ.
7 See *Weddle, Beck & Co v Hackett* [1929] 1 KB 321, at 329–334.
8 See para. 26.01, post.
9 *Tote Investors Ltd v Smoker* [1968] 1 QB 509, [1967] 3 All ER 242; *Ellesmere v Wallace* [1929] 2 Ch 1, per Russell LJ. In this case the earlier judicial definitions of gaming and wagering were exhaustively discussed.

6.07   The Gaming Act makes void not only the original bet but also any subsequent promise to pay the bet even if supported by a fresh consideration.[1]

Gaming and wagering contracts are *void* but not *illegal*;[2] so that a partnership formed for the purpose of carrying on a bookmaker's business is not *per se* illegal.[3] No offence is committed in making a wager, but the courts will not enforce the contract. Thus it will be entirely at the option of the promisor whether or not he pays the debt: he may do so if he likes; if he does, the money cannot be recovered.

It would follow from this, that if an agent is employed to make the bet, the principal cannot set up the statute as a defence to an action by the agent for money paid in respect of a loss; the agent could sue on the implied contract to indemnify him in regard to moneys properly expended for his principal, as there is no violation of the law in paying bets at the request of the principal;[4] and until the Gaming Act 1892 such was the law; but by that Act it is provided that:

'any promise, express or implied, to pay any person any sum of money paid by him under or in respect of any contract or agreement rendered null and void by the [Gaming Act 1845], or to pay any sum of money by way of commission, fee, reward, or otherwise in respect of any such contract, or of any services in relation thereto or in connection therewith, shall be null and void, and no action shall be brought or maintained to recover any such sum of money.'

Whilst this statute does not enable an agent who has *received* money for bets made by him on behalf of another to retain it,[5] it does save from liability an employee (or other agent) who should have *taken* wagers in cash.[6]

1 *Hill v Hill (William) (Park Lane) Ltd* [1949] AC 530.
2 See *Saxby v Fulton* [1909] 2 KB, at 227, per Buckley LJ.
3 *Jeffrey v Bamford* [1921] 2 KB 351.
4 *Read v Anderson* (1884) 13 QBD 779.
5 *De Mattos v Benjamin* (1894) 63 LJQB 248.
6 *AR Dennis & Co Ltd v Campbell* [1978] 1 All ER 1215, CA.

6.08   Negotiable securities such as cheques given in payment of bets on games and horse races, or for the repayment of money knowingly lent for gaming, are deemed to have been given on an *illegal* consideration; as between immediate parties they are unenforceable, but holders in due course may sue upon them.[1] By the Gaming Act 1968, s. 16 (4), a cheque accepted in exchange for cash or tokens to be used by a player in gaming on licensed or registered premises is valid and enforceable even between the parties. Money lent without security in England expressly for the purpose of paying betting debts is irrecoverable, but not if it is merely lent to enable the borrower to pay the debts with no obligation upon him to do so.[2] Probably, money lent without security in England for the purpose of gaming in this country is recoverable if the gaming is legal under the Gaming Act 1968 provided there is no obligation on the borrower to use the loan for wagering.[3] However the Gaming Act 1968, s. 16 (1) provides that where gaming takes place on licensed premises the licensee shall not make any loan to enable someone to take part in gaming or in respect of losses incurred by anyone in gaming.

Although money lent in a foreign country for the purpose of gambling abroad, where the game in question is not illegal, e.g. to play roulette at Monte Carlo, may be recovered by action in England,[4] if a negotiable instrument payable in England be given for the amount advanced, the security will be bad.[5]

---

1 See the Gaming Act 1710, as amended by the Gaming Act 1835. Negotiable instruments given in payment of other kinds of bets are not enforceable as between the immediate parties but any subsequent holder for value may sue upon them.
2 *Re O'Shea, ex parte Lancaster* [1911] 2 KB 981; *Macdonald v Green* [1951] 1 KB 594, [1950] 2 All ER 1240; *CHT Ltd v Ward* [1965] 2 QB 63, [1963] 3 All ER 835 (lender paying winner direct unable to recover loan).
3 *CHT Ltd v Ward* [1965] 2 QB 63, [1963] 2 All ER 835. Contra if the loan is secured by a cheque—then it seems neither the loan nor the cheque may be sued on: *Carlton Hall Club Ltd v Laurence* [1929] 2 KB 153.
4 *Saxby v Fulton* [1909] 2 KB 208, CA; *Société Anonyme des Grands Etablissements de Touquet Paris-Plage v Baumgart* (1927) 96 LJKB 789.
5 *Moulis v Owen* [1907] 1 KB 746, CA.

3. Contracts void at common law

6.09 Certain types of contract are treated as invalid at common law on grounds of public policy.

a) Contracts to oust the jurisdiction of the court A contract which purports to destroy the right of any party thereto to submit questions of law to the courts is *pro tanto void*. Thus, in *Baker v Jones*:[1]

> The rules of the British Amateur Weightlifters' Association provided that the council of the Association should be the sole interpreter of its rules. *Held:* the contract between the member and the Association on the basis of those rules could not exclude the jurisdiction of the courts, the objectionable clause would be ignored, and the court therefore had jurisdiction to determine whether the interpretation of its rules adopted by the Association was correct in law.

Similarly, an agreement may be invalid in so far as it attempts to exclude mandatory rules of law: so an agreement on accounting procedure as between two companies may be invalid if one of them goes into liquidation;[2] and a promise by an employee to release his employer from the statutory duty to provide safe working conditions is invalid.[3]

However, this is not to say that no ouster of the courts can be valid. Whilst the parties cannot agree that their agreement shall only be enforceable privately, they can agree that it shall not be enforceable at all: it may be couched as a mere 'gentleman's agreement', with no intention to create legal relations.[4] Alternatively, many commercial agreements provide that any dispute shall be referred first to a domestic tribunal, a provision whose effect was explained by Lord Denning as follows:[5]

> 'Parties cannot by contract oust the ordinary courts from their jurisdiction. They can, of course, agree to leave questions of law, as well as questions of fact, to the decision of the domestic tribunal. They can, indeed, make the domestic tribunal the final arbiter on questions of fact, but they cannot make it the final arbiter on questions of law. They cannot prevent its decisions being examined by the courts. If parties should seek, by agreement, to take the law out of the hands of the courts and put it into the hands of a private tribunal, without any recourse at all to the courts in the case of error of law, then the agreement is to that extent contrary to public policy and void'.

Accordingly, it is competent for the parties to provide that any disagreement shall first be referred to arbitration;[6] or to stipulate that their dispute shall be justifiable by a foreign tribunal, under what is called a 'choice of laws clause'.[7]

b) *Contracts prejudicial to the status of marriage* Under this head are rendered void contracts in restraint of marriage,[8] marriage brokerage contracts,[9] as well as contracts tending to prejudice existing marriages.[10]

c) *Contracts in restraint of trade.*

---

1 [1954] 2 All ER 553, [1954] 1 WLR 1005. See further para. 34.04, post.
2 *British Eagle International Airlines Ltd v Compagnie Nationale Air France* [1975] 2 All ER 390, [1975] 1 WLR 758, HL.
3 *Baddeley v Earl Granville* (1887) 19 QBD 423.
4 See paras. 3.25–3.27, ante.
5 *Lee v Showman's Guild of Great Britain* [1952] 2 QB 329 at 342, [1952] 1 All ER 1175 at 1181, CA.
6 See para. 34.04, post.
7 See para. 9.01, post.
8 *Re Michelhan's Will Trusts* [1964] Ch 550, [1963] 2 All ER 188.
9 *Hermann v Charlesworth* [1905] 2 KB 123, CA.
10 E.g. some separation agreements.

Contracts in restraint of trade

6.10 A contract in restraint of trade is one which unreasonably restricts a person from freely exercising his trade, skill or profession; and for a long time the courts have tended to invalidate such provisions as being against public policy.

a) THE CONTRACTS DESCRIBED

In *Esso Petroleum Co Ltd v Harper's Garage (Stourport) Ltd:*[1]

Esso had solus agreements with the Garage whereby the Garage agreed to buy all the petrol for their filling stations from Esso. With regard to one filling station, the agreement was to last four and a half years, and with regard to the other filling station for twenty-one years. On the latter Esso had a mortgage to secure £7,000 lent to the Garage which could not be redeemed till the twenty-one years was up. *Held:* the agreements were in restraint of trade and had to be justified by the test of reasonableness. The crucial consideration was the length of period each agreement was to last and in the circumstances the agreement in regard to the first filling station was valid but that relating to the second was invalid and the Garage was entitled to redeem the mortgage on it and buy petrol for it elsewhere.

The House of Lords pointed out that the following two independent questions were involved in determining whether the agreement was unreasonably in restraint of trade:

1. Is the contract so restrictive of the promisor's liberty to trade that it must be treated as prima facie invalid? It is well established that the following categories—considered further below—are so invalid: namely, restraints on employees, vendors of businesses, within trade associations and in respect of franchise agreements. On the other hand, certain classes of restrictive agreement have been consistently treated as valid by the courts, e.g. sole agencies, tied (public) house agreements and restrictive covenants in conveyances. The difficulty that remains is to find some criterion upon which to determine the answer to this question in respect of arrangements that do not fall within one of these established categories, e.g. the *Esso Case*.

2. Is it reasonable? Even where a contract would be invalid under (1) above, it is nevertheless valid if the restrictive clause can be justified as being reasonable in the interests of both the parties and the public. The starting point will be the nature and extent of the restraint intended by the parties—a matter going beyond the mere words of the contract.[2] Once this is established, the reasonableness of the provision is a matter of law for the court; but the promisee may adduce evidence of any special circumstances which he alleges to justify the restraint,[3] though only facts existing at the date of contracting are relevant.[4] The promisee must show that he is seeking to protect some legitimate interest of his,[5] the restraint must be no wider than is reasonably necessary to protect that interest,[6] and that restraint must be balanced against the quantum of consideration accruing to the promisor.[7] Moreover, the degree of justification required will not necessarily remain constant as between the different categories of promisor's interest, e.g. a purchaser of a business is likely to be able to exact a wider restraint to protect his goodwill than will an employer to protect his trade secrets.[8]

---

1 [1968] AC 269, [1967] 1 All ER 699, HL.
2 E.g. see *Home Counties Dairies Ltd v Skilton* [1970] 1 All ER 1227, [1970] 1 WLR 526, CA; *Marion White Ltd v Francis* [1972] 3 All ER 857, [1972] 1 WLR 1423, CA.
3 *Sir WC Leng & Co Ltd v Andrews* [1909] 1 Ch 763 at 770–771, per Fletcher Moulton LJ. As to admissibility of general economic evidence, see *Texaco Ltd v Mulberry Filling Station Ltd* [1972] 1 All ER 513, [1972] 1 WLR 814.
4 *Gledow Autoparts Ltd v Delaney* [1965] 3 All ER 288 at 295, CA, per Diplock LJ.
5 The doctrine extends beyond the confines of contract to e.g. the Jockey Club, Football League, or a trade or professional Association.
6 *Herbert Morris Ltd v Saxelby* [1916] 1 AC 688 at 710, HL, per Lord Parker. See also *Greig v Insole* [1978] 1 WLR 302.

7 *Esso Petroleum Ltd v Harper's Garage (Stourport) Ltd* [1968] AC 269 at 300, 318, 323, HL.
8 See *Mason v Provident Clothing and Supply Co Ltd* [1913] AC 724, HL.

6.11 *a) Restraints on employees* In only two situations have the courts accepted that the employer has a legitimate interest requiring protection as against his employee.[1] First, he is entitled to protect his trade secrets, whether they be secret processes,[2] or special problem-solving techniques;[3] but it is not yet clear to what extent commercial 'know-how' will be protected.[4] Second, an employer is allowed to protect himself against his trade customers being enticed away by an ex-employee, but only where the employee during the course of his employment acquired not merely knowledge of these customers,[5] but also influence over them.[6] In deciding whether a restraint is reasonable, the courts pay particular attention to the following two factors:
i) The area of the restraint. Everything depends on the sphere of operation of the employer's business, so that a restraint has been allowed extending throughout the United Kingdom.[7] But generally speaking only a much smaller area of restraint has been proved justifiable; for instance, an invalid restraint was imposed on the manager of a Cambridge butcher's shop not to carry on a similar business within a five mile radius of the shop,[8] or upon an Islington canvasser not to trade within twenty-five miles of London.[9]
ii) The duration of restraint. Whilst there have been instances where a lifetime's restraint has been supported,[10] usually only a much shorter duration is appropriate.[11]

Nor will the courts allow indirect evasion of their rules as to the limits of permissible restraints on employees. The employer cannot secure for himself a greater degree of protection than would be allowable here either by placing the restriction in his pension plan,[12] or by making an agreement with a rival business not to employ those who had previously been employed by the other.[13]

b) Restraints on vendors of businesses As a vendor of a business would prima facie be well placed to set up a competing business, he may be unable to obtain a price that adequately reflects the value of the custom that he has built up (the goodwill)[14] unless he can by the terms of the sale bind himself not to do so. Accordingly, the courts look more favourably on such restraints than is the case in respect of employees: but they insist that there must be a genuine sale of a business;[15] and that the restrictive covenant only protects the business sold.[16] Even assuming such a genuine interest worthy of protection, the restraint must still be reasonable; and here the courts again pay special attention to the factors of time and area.[17]

c) *Restraints within trade associations* Businessmen have frequently in the past formed associations with the object of restricting output or maintaining the selling price of certain commodities. The common law was fairly well disposed towards such restraints,[18] so long as the arrangements were kept within reasonable bounds.[19] But nowadays this field has been largely pre-empted by statute.[20]

d) *Restraints in franchise agreements* The common law has no objection to sole agency agreements, provided they are reasonable.[21] In relation to the supply of goods, the principles applicable are well illustrated by the *solus* agreements of the petrol trade;[22] and in relation to exclusive services by *A Schroeder Music Publishing Co Ltd v Macaulay:*[23]

> P, a young and unknown song-writer, entered a standard form contract with D, a music publisher, whereunder P for 10 years assigned the world copyright of any composition produced to D; but D did not undertake to exploit all or any such composition; and D alone might terminate the agreement by one month's notice. The House of Lords held that the total commitment of P and lack of obligation on D made the agreement an unreasonable restraint of trade.

The operation of the restraint of trade doctrine in this field too has been largely pre-empted by statute.[20]

---

1 See *Eastham v Newcastle United Football Club* [1964] Ch 413, [1963] 3 All ER 139.

2 *Forster & Sons Ltd v Suggett* (1918) 35 TLR 87.

3 *Commercial Plastics Ltd v Vincent* [1965] 1 QB 623, [1964] 3 All ER 546, CA.

4 See *Blanco White* 15 Conv. 89, 26 Conv. 366. The other protective device offered by the law is public registration as a patent or copyright: see chaps. 29, 31, post.

5 So restrictions have been disallowed on a grocer's assistant, or an employee who might never meet the customers.

6 Restrictions have been held valid on a solicitor's clerk, a tailor's cutter-fitter, a milk roundsman, a brewery manager, an estate agent's clerk.

7 *E Underwood & Son Ltd v Barker* [1899] 1 Ch 300. See also *Lamson Pneumatic Tube Co v Phillips* (1904) 91 LT 363 (Eastern Hemisphere).

8 *Empire Meat Co Ltd v Patrick* [1939] 2 All ER 85, CA.

9 *Mason v Provident Clothing and Supply Co Ltd* [1913] AC 724, HL.

10 *Fitch v Dewes* [1921] 2 AC 158, HL (within 7 miles of Tamworth, where he served as solicitor's managing clerk).

11 *Stenhouse Australia Ltd v Phillips* [1974] AC 391, [1974] 1 All ER 117, PC; *M and S Drapers (A Firm) v Reynolds* [1956] 3 All ER 814, [1957] 1 WLR 9, CA.

12 *Bull v Pitney-Bowes* [1966] 3 All ER 384, [1967] 1 WLR 273.
13 *Kores Manufacturing Co Ltd v Kolok Manufacturing Co Ltd* [1959] Ch 108, [1958] 2 All ER 65, CA.
14 For an exposition of goodwill in relation to partnerships, see para. 11.21, post.
15 *Vancouver Malt and Sake Brewing Co Ltd v Vancouver Breweries Ltd* [1934] AC 181, PC.
16 *British Concrete Co Ltd v Schelff* [1921] 2 Ch 563.
17 See *Goldsoll v Goldman* [1915] 1 Ch 292, CA (set out para. 6.11, post.); *Nordenfelt v Maxim Nordenfelt Guns and Ammunition Co* [1894] AC 535, HL.
18 E.g. *English Hop Growers v Dering* [1928] 2 KB 174, CA; *Birtley and District Co-operative Society Ltd v Windy Nook and District Industrial Co-operative Society Ltd (No 2)* [1960] 2 QB 1, [1959] 1 All ER 623.
19 *McEllistrim v Ballymacelligott Co-Op Agricultural and Dairy Society* [1919] AC 548, HL; *Pharmaceutical Society of Great Britain v Dickson* [1970] AC 403, [1968] 2 All ER 686, HL.
20 See chap. 28, post.
21 See *Martin-Baker Aircraft Co Ltd v Canadian Flight Equipment Ltd* [1955] 2 QB 556, [1955] 2 All ER 722 (set out below, para 10.07).
22 *Esso Petroleum Co Ltd v Harper's Garage (Stourport) Ltd* [1968] AC 269, [1967] 1 All ER 699, HL (set out para. 6.10, ante); *Shell UK Ltd v Lostock Garage Ltd* [1977] 1 All ER 481, [1976] 1 WLR 1187, CA. Cf. *Cleveland Petroleum Co Ltd v Dartstone Ltd* [1968] 1 All ER 201, [1969] 1 WLR 116, CA.
23 [1974] 3 All ER 616, [1974] 1 WLR 1308, HL. See also *Clifford Davis Management Ltd v WEA Records Ltd* [1975] 1 All ER 237, [1975] 1 WLR 61, CA; *Budget Rent a Car International Inc v Mamos Slough* (1977) 121 Sol Jo 374, CA.

b) THE LEGAL CONSEQUENCES

6.12 Where a contract is found to be unreasonably in restraint of trade, it is prima facie invalid; but that does not mean that such contracts are totally void. The invalidity goes no further than is necessary to satisfy the requirements of public policy. Of course, if the objectionable clause forms the whole of the consideration, where it is struck down in toto there will be no contract left; but it is otherwise where there remains a valid consideration because the contract originally contained more than one consideration to support the promise which it is sought to enforce.[1] Furthermore, even where the whole of the consideration is contained in one clause only, the courts have power to sever the objectionable parts of the clause, leaving the rest standing unaffected. Thus, in *Goldsoll v Goldman:*[2]

When X sold an imitation jewellery business to Y, X agreed that he would not for two years deal in real or imitation jewellery in any part of the UK, France, USA, etc. *Held:* the covenant as drafted was void, but it could be severed by removing from it the reference to 'real' jewellery and the reference to countries other than the UK. The remaining part of the covenant was enforceable.

However, a court will not order severance if this would affect the meaning of the rest of the contract, nor if it involves altering or adding words. Moreover, the courts are reluctant to sever unreasonably wide covenants contained in contracts of employment.[3]

A contract in restraint of trade is part of the goodwill of a business, and for this reason is treated as assignable in the absence of any special provision to the contrary; it accordingly passes with the goodwill so as to enable the purchaser to enforce the contract in his own name.[4] If a contract of employment is repudiated on the part of the employer by the wrongful dismissal of the employee, the latter is no longer bound by a clause restrictive of his right to trade.[5]

---

1 *Goodinson v Goodinson* [1954] 2 QB 118; [1954] 2 All ER 255, CA.
2 [1915] 1 Ch 292.
3 *Attwood v Lamont* [1920] 3 KB 571. This is because of the lack of bargaining equality between the parties. But see *T Lucas & Co Ltd v Mitchell* [1972] 3 All ER 689, CA.
4 *Jacoby v Whitmore* (1883) 49 LT 335.
5 *General Billposting Co v Atkinson* [1909] AC 118, HL. The compulsory winding-up of a company is equivalent to a wrongful dismissal (*Measures Bros Ltd v Measures* [1910] 2 Ch 248).

Chapter 7

Performance and breach

1. Terms of the contract

7.01 In the course of the negotiations which precede a contract, it is common for the parties to make certain statements of fact (representations). If the representor made a promise to that effect which became part of a contract between the parties, then the representation is said to be a *contractual term*: performance of that term is required in accordance with the rules discussed later in this chapter; and it will be seen that the normal remedy for a breach of a contractual term is an action for damages. However, if the representation did not become a contractual term, it is said to be a *mere representation*; and the remedies available to the representee where the representation was untrue were considered in chapter 5.

As will be seen later in this chapter, the common law required strict performance of a contractual term: if the promisor failed to perform, he was prima facie liable to pay damages irrespective of whether the breach was due to any fault on his part. However, where the statement did not attain contractual status, but remained a mere misrepresentation, the common law would only allow damages as follows: if the representee could prove that the representation was made fraudulently (always a difficult matter), he might recover damages in the tort of deceit;[1] or, if the representee could prove negligence, then since 1963 he has been allowed an action for the tort of negligent misstatement.[2] As was seen in chapter 5, the Misrepresentation Act 1967 made the following major changes as regards this remedy:

1. It in effect reversed the burden of proof in the case of negligent misrepresentation, making the representor liable unless he could disprove negligence (s. 2 (1)).

2. Even where the representor disproved negligence, the representee might at the discretion of the court be allowed damages in lieu of his common law right to rescind (s. 2 (2)).

3. It extended the common law right to rescind.[3]

Accordingly, whereas before 1967 a substantial number of misrepresentees would be remediless unless they could prove that a representation amounted to a contractual term, this is less true under the Act. To this extent, it is today less important to prove that a misrepresentation has become a contractual term. Nevertheless the dichotomy between contractual terms and mere representations remains significant because the remedies for breach of contract and misrepresentation remain different in some respects.

---

1 *Derry v Peek* (1889) 14 App Cas 337, HL.
2 *Hedley Byrne & Co Ltd v Heller & Partners Ltd* [1964] AC 465, [1963] 2 All ER 575, HL.
3 See para. 5.13, ante.

Contractual term or mere representation?

7.02 The distinction is a difficult one to determine, and is said to depend on the intention of the parties, as inferred from all the facts. It appears from the decided cases that a statement is more likely to be interpreted by the courts as a contractual term if it is made by someone with particular knowledge of the facts and was made close to the time when the contract was completed. In *Oscar Chess Ltd v Williams*:[1]

> W, a private individual, offered to sell a car to the plaintiff car dealers. He described the car as a 1948 model, which was the year given in the car's registration book, and the sale was completed. Eight months after the sale, it wass discovered that the car was a 1939 model and that the registration book had been fraudulently altered by a previous owner. *Held:* since W did not have any personal knowledge of the car's age, nor any expert knowledge of cars in general, it was not reasonable to interpret his statement as a contractual promise but only as a misrepresentation. Owing to the delay since the sale, rescission for misrepresentation would not be granted, and there being no fraud, damages were not available either.

Contrast *Bannerman v White*:[2]

> When B offered hops for sale, W asked if any sulphur had been used in their cultivation, adding that he would not even ask the price if sulphur had been used. B assured W that no sulphur had been used and the sale was completed. It was

later learned that sulphur had been used in the treatment of some of the hops and W refused to accept them. *Held:* B's statement was clearly intended by both parties to be a term of the contract, in fact a condition, and W was entitled to repudiate the contract. Even if W had delayed before seeking a remedy, he would still have been entitled to damages for breach of a contractual term.

---

1 [1957] 1 All ER 325, [1957] 1 WLR 370, CA.
2 (1861) 10 CB (NS) 844. See also *Dick Bentley Productions Ltd v Harold Smith (Motors) Ltd* [1965] 2 All ER 65, [1965] 1 WLR 623, CA; *J Evans & Son (Portsmouth) Ltd v Andrea Merzario Ltd* [1976] 2 All ER 930, [1976] 1 WLR 1078, CA.

7.03   These two cases illustrate the simple issue of whether or not a representation by A becomes a contractual term of the ('major') contract with B induced thereby. But there is another possibility: notwithstanding that the representation does not become a term of that major contract between A and B, it might amount to a collateral contract between them.[1] The potential of the collateral contract device in this direction was illustrated by the case of *Esso Petroleum Ltd v Mardon*:[2]

Esso developed a new retail petrol site, and then negotiated a three year lease of the site to M. During the negotiations, L, an employee of Esso who had 40 years' experience of the trade, estimated to M that the throughput of the petrol station would be in the order of 200,000 gallons by the third year of operation. Throughput never exceeded 86,502 gallons.

The Court of Appeal held Esso liable on *both* the following grounds:
1. L's estimate was a negligent misstatement;[3] and
2. M signed the lease as consideration for a collateral contract of warranty by Esso as to the throughput.

---

1 For collateral contracts, see para. 4.03, ante.
2 [1976] QB 801, [1976] 2 All ER 5, CA. Cf. *Howard Marine & Dredging Co Ltd v A Ogden & Sons (Excavations) Ltd* [1978] 2 WLR 515, CA.
3 See para. 5.12, ante.

Express and implied terms

7.04   When searching for the contents of a contract, there will be many provisions in respect of which a careful enquiry to distinguish between misrepresentations and terms will be unnecessary. Except in so far as they imply a statement of present fact, promises as to the future cannot amount to misrepresentations which might give rise to the remedies considered in chapter 5; the sole issue is likely to be whether such promises were incorporated in the contract.[1] Similarly, where a party seeks to rely upon express terms which he alleges to have been incorporated into the contract, if these have not been read by the other party, there will be no question of their inducing entry into the contract, and the sole issue will be incorporation.[1] The relevance of these various rules can be illustrated by reference to a transaction involving a standard form of contract:[2] whether the terms printed on that standard form are part of the contract is a matter of incorporation;[1] whereas, whether a statement which induced the consumer to enter that standard-form contract is also an express term of that contract, or of a collateral contract or a mere representation depends on the matters discussed above.

---

1 See para. 3.12, ante.
2 As to which, see para. 3.13, ante.

7.05   Besides these express terms, the contract may also contain some 'implied' terms, an expression used to describe all the following separate (but overlapping) categories of terms that might be imported into the transaction:
1. Terms implied in fact, i.e. those terms which must necessarily be implied from the express terms used by the parties. For instance, a common matter of dispute is whether there is an implied term that a company which has entered into a contract to sell its products over a fixed period will continue to carry on business throughout that period.[1]
2. Terms implied by custom. Unless there is an express provision to the contrary,[2] where all the parties are in business in a particular trade the courts assume that the parties to a commercial contract intend to incorporate therein any relevant trade custom.[3] Indeed, a fairly constant process is observable: first, a particular custom is shown to exist, and the parties to have relied upon it; second, all contracts within that particular trade are thereafter presumed to have incorporated it in the absence of a

contrary intention;[4] and third, when it is well settled the matter is put into statutory form as in (3) below.[5]

3. Terms implied by statute.[6]

4. Terms implied by the courts, especially on one of the following grounds:

a) By analogy. For instance, in contracts for the sale of goods, there is a statutory implied term as to the fitness of those goods for the purpose supplied[7] and the courts have implied a similar term into analogous transactions, so that in *Samuels v Davis*[8] it was held that where a dentist undertakes to make a denture for reward there is an implied term that it will be reasonably fit for the purpose.

Scott LJ said in delivering judgment:

'In my view it is a matter of legal indifference whether the contract was one for the sale of goods or one of service to do work and supply materials. In either case, the contract must necessarily, by reason of the relationship between the parties and the purpose for which the contract was entered into, import a term that, given reasonable co-operation by the patient, the dentist would ... produce a denture which could be used by the patient for the purpose of eating and talking in the ordinary way'.

b) In respect of the various classes of contracts which do not have statutorily implied terms under (2) above, the courts have tended to develop their own battery of implied terms (excludable by contrary intention), often justifying the development on the basis of what is reasonable in the circumstances.[9] A fruitful source of controversy over such developments are contracts of employment.[10]

c) To give 'business efficacy' to the contract. The leading case is *The Moorcock*:[11]

In return for landing charges, wharfinger D agreed to allow shipowner P to discharge his vessel from D's jetty. The jetty extended into the Thames; and both parties realised that the vessel must ground at low water. When the tide ebbed, the vessel settled on a ridge of hard ground beneath the mud and suffered damage.

Notwithstanding that D had no control over the river bed, the Court of Appeal held that he had impliedly promised that the river bottom was, so far as reasonable care could make it, safe for the vessel to berth—otherwise, Bowen LJ explained, P would simply be buying 'an opportunity of danger'. In *Reigate v Union Manufacturing Co (Ramsbottom)*[12] Scrutton LJ said:

'an implied term is not to be added because the court thinks it would have been reasonable to have it inserted in the contract. A term can only be implied if it is necessary in the business sense to give efficacy to the contract; that is, if it is such a term that it can confidently be said that if at the time the contract was being negotiated someone had said to the parties, "What will happen in such a case," they would both have replied, "Of course, so and so will happen; we did not trouble to say that; it is too clear".'

Whilst the *Moorcock* doctrine is still used by the courts,[13] it is only used to justify the implication of terms to the minimum extent necessary to give 'business efficacy' to the transaction—a concept far narrower than that which would be reasonable.[14] Furthermore, it is fatal to such an argument that one party does not know the facts from which it is sought to deduce the term, so that an attempt by a trade union to imply the 'Bridlington Agreement' into its contract with a union-member failed when it was proved that the member had never heard of that agreement.[15]

---

1 *Hamlyn & Co v Wood & Co* [1891] 2 QB 488, CA. Contrast *General Publicity Services Ltd v Best's Brewery Co Ltd* (1951) 2 TLR 875, CA.
2 *Les Affréteurs Réunis Société Anonyme v Leopold Walford (London) Ltd* [1919] AC 801, HL.
3 E.g. *Produce Brokers Co Ltd v Olympia Oil and Cake Co Ltd* [1916] 1 AC 314, HL; *Cunliffe-Owen v Teather and Greenwood* [1967] 3 All ER 561, [1967] 1 WLR 1421. Sale of Goods Act 1893, new s. 14 (4) (see para. 13.22, post). Where only one party is in a particular trade and the other is ignorant of the custom, the effect may be to prevent the formation of any agreement at all because the parties are never ad idem.
4 E.g. see para. 10.15, post.
5 E.g. Marine Insurance Act 1906, ss. 33–41 (see paras. 27.32, et seq., post).
6 See para. 3.12, ante.
7 See para. 13.22, post.
8 [1943] 1 KB 526, [1943] 2 All ER 3. See also *Charnock v Liverpool Corpn* [1968] 3 All ER 473, [1968] 1 WLR 1498, CA (term in contract of repairs implied that repairs would be effected with reasonable expedition) followed in *Brown and Davis Ltd v Galbraith* [1972] 3 All ER 31, [1972] 1 WLR 997, CA; *Young and Marten Ltd v McManus, Childs Ltd* [1969] 1 AC 454, [1968] 2 All ER 1169, HL.
9 Per Lord Denning MR in *Greaves & Co (Contractors) Ltd v Baynham Meikle & Partners* [1975] 3 All ER 99, at 103, CA. But it does not follow that, conversely, a term will be implied simply because it would be reasonable for the contract to contain it: *Liverpool City Council v Irwin* [1977] AC 239, [1976] 2 All ER 39, HL.
10 See paras. 32.06–32.09, post.
11 (1889) 14 PD 64, CA.
12 [1918] 1 KB 592 at 605. And see dicta of Mackinnon LJ in *Shirlaw v Southern Foundries (1926) Ltd and Federated Foundries Ltd* [1939] 2 KB 206, 227, [1939] 2 All ER 113, 124.

13 E.g. *Gardner v Coutts & Co* [1967] 3 All ER 1064, [1968] 1 WLR 173;
   Greig v Insole [1978] 1 WLR 302.
14 *Shell UK Ltd v Lostock Garage Ltd* [1977] 1 All ER 481, [1976] 1 WLR
   1187, CA. And see further note 9 above.
15 *Spring v National Amalgamated Stevedores and Dockers Society* [1956] 2
   All ER 221, [1956] 1 WLR 585. See also *Gallacher v Post Office* [1970] 3
   All ER 712.

---

2. Performance

A) Conditions

7.06 Unfortunately, the word *condition* is used in several different
senses in our law, without any consistent attempt either to
distinguish between the different ideas comprehended within the
expression or to attain uniformity of terminology.

Conditions precedent

The contractual promises made by a party may be expressed to
be subject to a *condition precedent,* which *condition* may be
precedent[1] to either (1) contract, or (2) performance.[2]
a) *Conditions precedent to contract*   In *Pym v Campbell:*[3]

> D agreed in writing to buy from P a share of an invention.
> When P sued for breach, D was allowed, by way of an
> exception to the parol evidence rule, to give oral evidence that
> he had signed the agreement subject to the approval of Dr
> Abernethie, an expert. When he saw it, Dr Abernethie did not
> approve the invention.

Thus, the approval of Dr Abernethie was a condition precedent
to the actual agreement: unless and until he approved, there was
no agreement. The result is thus similar to the situation where
the parties have not finished agreeing.[4]
b) *Condition precedent to performance*   In *Martin v Whale:*[5]

> P agreed to buy a plot of land from X, subject to P's solicitor
> approving of 'title and restrictions'. At the same time, the
> parties entered into a linked agreement for the sale of P's car
> to X. X took possession of the car and disposed of it to D; and
> the solicitor subsequently disapproved X's title to the land. It
> was held that X had 'agreed to buy' the car, and could
> therefore pass a good title to D.

So, even before P's solicitor pronounced on the title to the land, there was a contract for the sale of the car, but the performance of that contract was suspended pending the solicitor's action.

Whether a condition is precedent to contract, or merely to performance is a matter of intention; and, in view of the difficulties that may be caused, it is therefore prudent for the parties to spell out their intention in this regard.

1 Alternatively, a contract may be subject to a *condition subsequent*, if the obligations of the contract are to cease on the happening of a certain event: *Head v Tattersall* (1871) LR 7 Exch 7. This may be the explanation of contracts terminable on notice (see para. 8.01, post), e.g. contracts of hire-purchase terminable by the owner by notice on the happening of certain events (see generally paras. 14.03 et seq., post); contracts of employment (see generally chap. 32, post).
2 The conditional contracts discussed here must be carefully distinguished from conditional acceptance of an unconditional offer: see para. 3.09, ante.
3 (1856) 6 E & B 370. As to the parol evidence rule, see para. 3.13, ante.
4 As to which, see para. 3.07, ante.
5 [1917] 2 KB 480, CA (see further para. 13.16, post). See also *Carlill v Carbolic Smoke Ball Co* [1893] 1 QB 256, CA (catching the disease: see para. 3.03, ante).

Conditions and warranties

7.07 As will be seen later, the breach of any contractual promise will give the innocent party the right to an action for damages.[1] However, where the breach is of a more serious nature, the innocent party may additionally be entitled to '*avoid*' the contract; that is, to be discharged from the obligation of *future* performance,[2] though the contract probably remains in existence for the assessment of damages.[3] Where the innocent party is entitled to *avoid* the contract, the two remedies of *avoidance* and damages are not alternative, but complementary—whether the contract is discharged as to future performance merely affects the amount of damages recoverable, e.g.:

Suppose a contract worth £100 to the innocent party in the circumstance where avoidance would give him £90 worth. The innocent party can either:
1. avoid and claim £10 damages (£90 + £10 = £100); or
2. affirm the contract but claim £100 damages.

1 See para. 7.27, post.
2 Distinguish contracts that are *rescinded*, which are void *ab initio*: see para. 6.01, ante.
3 See para. 7.22, post.

7.08 When deciding whether to allow the innocent party to *avoid* for breach, a court is, in the absence of authority, faced with two approaches.

a) Classify the term broken More popular in the nineteenth century, this approach required the court to classify the term broken according to whether or not it goes[1]

> 'so directly to the substance of the contract or (is) so essential to its very nature that (its) non-performance may fairly be considered by the other party as a substantial failure to perform the contract at all'.

If breach of the term would amount to a 'substantial failure to perform', then that term is called a *condition*, and the breach gives the innocent party the right to *avoid*; whereas, if it does not amount to a 'substantial failure to perform', the term is called a *warranty*, and breach only gives the innocent party the right to damages.[2] Of course, the courts will not always have to apply the above test to ascertain whether a particular term is a *condition* or a *warranty*: in the case of many terms, there will be precedents which decide which it is; and, where an implied term is imported by statute, Parliament will frequently specify the status of the term.[3] Where the law leaves them free to do so, the parties may expressly assign the status of *condition* or *warranty* to a particular term,[4] this being commonly done in the case of standard-form contracts;[5] but such clauses are likely to be read *contra proferentem*[6] so that, for instance, it will not necessarily be conclusive expressly to designate a term a *condition*.[7]

b) Classify the breach A new approach developed in the 1960's with the case of *Hong Kong Fir Shipping Co Ltd v Kawasaki Kisen Kaisha Ltd*:[8]

> P chartered their ship to D for twenty-four months. When delivered, her engine-room staff were too few and too incompetent to cope with her antiquated machinery, so that P were in breach of their implied undertaking to provide a seaworthy vessel. When the ship broke down for the second time on her first voyage, and D discovered repairs would take fifteen weeks, they repudiated the charter. *Held:* a wrongful repudiation.

Diplock LJ said:

> 'No doubt there are many simple contractual undertakings, sometimes express but more often because of their very simplicity ... to be implied, of which it can be predicated that every breach of such an undertaking must give rise to an event which will deprive the party not in default of substantially the whole benefit which it was intended he should obtain from the

contract. And such a stipulation ... is a condition. So too there may be other simple contractual undertakings of which it can be predicated that *no* breach can give rise to (such) an event ... ; and such a stipulation ... is a warranty.

'There are, however, many contractual undertakings of a more complex character which cannot be characterised as being "conditions" or "warranties". ... Of such undertakings, all that can be predicated is that some breaches will and others will not give rise to (such) an event ... ; and the legal consequences of a breach ... , unless provided for expressly in the contract, depend upon the nature of the event to which the breach gives rise and do not follow automatically from a prior classification of the undertaking as a "condition" or a "warranty".'

In other words, the court should not classify the term—from which it would have followed that even the most insignificant breach of condition would give a right to *avoid*, whereas even the most serious breach of warranty would only give a right to damages—but should instead await the breach, and then measure that breach against the value of performance of the whole contract. For convenience, these may be called 'innominate terms'.

---

1 *Wallis, Son and Wells v Pratt and Haynes* [1910] 2 KB 1003, at 1012, CA, per Fletcher Moulton LJ; affd. by HL [1911] AC 394.
2 An instance of the inconsistency or historic survival of terminology is that this nomenclature is not adhered to e.g. in the case of marine insurance contracts: see para. 27.32, post.
3 E.g. the Sale of Goods Act 1893 as amended: see paras. 13.19 et seq., post.
4 E.g. *Dawsons Ltd v Bonnin* [1922] 2 AC 413, HL(S) (set out para. 26.04, post).
5 As to which, see para. 3.13, ante.
6 See para. 3.16, ante.
7 *L Schuler AG v Wickman Machine Tool Sales Ltd* [1974] AC 235, [1973] 2 All ER 39, HL.
8 [1962] 2 QB 26, [1962] 1 All ER 474, CA. For the undertaking as to seaworthiness, see further para. 23.04 (a), post. See also *Tradax Internacional v Goldschmidt SA* [1977] 2 Lloyd's Rep. 604.

7.09   In many cases, there will be an authority which stipulates whether a particular term is a *condition*, a *warranty*, or an *innominate term*; and that will settle the matter. But what where there is no such guidance? Plainly, the two approaches are mutually inconsistent: the first directs the court to classify the term when the contract is made; whereas the second requires that the judge hold his hand and measure the breach. Moreover, the first has the advantage of predictability; whereas the second has the advantage of flexibility. Nor is it simply the case that the nineteenth century preference for predictability has been replaced by a modern enthusiasm for flexibility. Thus, in *The Mihalis Angelos*:[1]

> Owners of a ship promised the charterers that it would be expected ready to load 'about July 1st' at the port of Haiphong. On July 17th it was clear that it would be some time before the ship would reach Haiphong and the charterers cancelled the charterparty. *Held:* the clause that the ship would be ready to load was a condition of the contract and its breach entitled the charterers to repudiate the contract.

In this case, the Court of Appeal emphasised the advantages of predictability and certainty in commercial transactions; whereas the advantages of a flexible approach were extolled by the Court of Appeal in *The Hansa Ford*.[2]

---

1 [1971] 1 QB 164, [1970] 3 All ER 125, CA.
2 [1976] QB 44, [1975] 3 All ER 739, CA (see para. 13.18, post).

B) The obligations of performance

Introductory

i) The time of performance

7.10   The general rule is that performance should be complete, and according to the terms of the agreement. Where no time for performance is fixed, there is an implied undertaking that the performance shall be completed within a reasonable time, having regard to the circumstances of the particular case.[1] Where a time for performance is fixed, the other party is entitled to treat the contract as discharged if performance is not completed within the time fixed only if time is of the *essence of the contract*, i.e. a condition of the contract.[2] However, in mercantile contracts, the time of performance of other terms, e.g. as to delivery date, is generally of the essence of the contract. Thus, failure by the seller of goods to meet a delivery date entitles the buyer to repudiate the contract.

---

1 *Charnock v Liverpool Corpn* [1968] 3 All ER 473, CA.
2 For sale of goods, this rule is embodied in s. 10 of the Sale of Goods Act 1893: see para. 13.30, post.

ii) Waiver of performance

7.11 It has already been seen that a party may waive, or be equitably estopped from insisting on, strict performance.[1] Such waivers are particularly common in relation to the contractual time for performance. Take a typical case, a contract for the sale of goods whereunder time of delivery was of the essence, but the seller has failed to meet that date. Even if:

> the buyer waives the seller's breach (as by continuing to press for delivery) the buyer may again make time of the essence of the contract by giving reasonable notice that he will not take delivery after a certain date. The buyer will then be entitled to refuse to take delivery unless delivery is made by that date.[2]

1 See paras. 3.22–3.24, ante.
2 *Charles Rickards Ltd v Oppenheim* [1950] 1 KB 616, [1950] 1 All ER 420, CA (set out para. 3.22).

iii) Variation of performance

7.12 It has already been seen that the parties may together vary a contractual promise by subsequent contract, provided that there is consideration for the variation; and, as a promise may be varied, so may it be completely discharged by subsequent agreement.[1] A common example is a contract to discharge an obligation to pay money, where the basic rule is that payment of a lesser sum is no satisfaction of a greater.[2]

From the viewpoint of a party minded to take a relaxed view of a failure by the other party to perform according to the strict letter of the agreement, there is always the danger that the 'accidental' presence of consideration may turn what was intended as a mere waiver into a binding contract of variation; and it is for this reason common to find a provision in a standard-form contract to the effect that no such relaxation or indulgence is intended to be a variation.[3] Moreover, in the case of tender of a sum less than his debt by the debtor, the creditor is faced with this further difficulty: whilst it will be seen below that the creditor is not bound to accept a lesser sum, he may wish to do so on the maxim that 'a bird in the hand, etc'; and, whilst in so doing he may with care avoid creating any accord and satisfaction, he may subsequently find that he is equitably estopped from recovering the remainder.[4]

1 See para. 8.01, post.
2 See para. 3.20, ante.

3 For standard-form contracts, see para. 3.13, ante.
4 See para. 3.24, ante.

---

iv) Set-off

7.13 To an action for non-performance there are various defences, but these, as a rule, arise out of circumstances which are sufficient to discharge the contract and will therefore be examined in chapter 8—e.g. impossibility. But *set-off* is not of such a nature: it is a right on the part of a defendant to avail himself of a debt due to him from the plaintiff in extinction or reduction of the claim in the action, and so to avoid the consequence of non-performance. A claim for any monetary sum (whether liquidated or not) may be made by way of set-off but the claim and the set-off must exist between the same parties in the same capacity. Claims that cannot be raised by way of set-off, e.g. a claim for a sum in excess of the plaintiff's claim, may generally be made the subject of a counter-claim. Such questions belong rather to the law of procedure than of contract.

Payment

7.14 This may be defined as the performance of a contract by delivery of money or of some negotiable instrument.

A debtor is bound to seek his creditor,[1] and is not entitled to wait until demand has been made.[2] This obligation may, of course, be varied by special agreement, and then, in addition to the demand, the debtor is entitled to an allowance of a reasonable time to enable him to fetch the money.[3]

---

1 *Fessard v Mugnier* (1865) 34 LJCP 126. For the special position between banker and customer, see para. 10.31, post.
2 For the effect of payment to an agent, see para. 7.17, post.
3 *Massey v Sladen* (1869) LR 4 Ex. 13.

---

a) TENDER

7.15 When money is tendered, the whole amount should be offered, without imposing conditions;[1] but a tender may be made *under protest*, so as to reserve any right of the debtor to dispute the amount[2] and save him from some costs. A debtor who is always ready to pay and actually offers to do so in effect performs his contract, so that tender is a defence to an action to recover a debt if the money is brought into court.[3]

1 *Dixon v Clarke* (1847) 5 CB 365; *Evans v Judkins* (1815) 4 Camp. 156.
2 *Scott v Uxbridge Rly Co* (1866) LR 1 CP 596; *Greenwood v Sutcliffe* [1892] 1 Ch 1, CA.
3 The costs of the action thereafter incurred will be borne by the creditor: *Griffiths v School Board of Ystradyfodwg* (1890) 24 QBD 307.

---

b) MODES OF PAYMENT

7.16 *a) Payment in cash* The primary obligation is to make payment by legal tender, the law allowing that debts of any amount may be paid by Bank of England notes[1] or (less commonly) gold coins. Small sums may be paid in accordance with the terms of the Coinage Act 1971.[2] Further, the exact amount must be produced, as a creditor cannot be compelled to give change.[3] But in all the above examples the creditor may waive his strict rights, and on slight evidence uncontradicted by other facts the court would probably infer that he had done so with regard to his right to either or both of legal tender,[4] or that actually tendered.[5]

If payment is made in accordance with the direction of the creditor, the debtor will not be liable if the money is lost.[6] Thus, if (but only if) a debtor is expressly or impliedly requested or authorised by his creditor to make a payment through the post (as by a posted demand for payment), then although the money may be lost in course of transit and never reach the creditor, it will amount to payment.[7] But apart from special directions, a request to remit money through the post only authorises the debtor to do so in the manner in which a prudent person would make the remittance in the ordinary course of business, and the sending of a large sum in Treasury notes, which were stolen before they reached the creditor, has been held not to discharge the debt.[8]

Again, where the debtor gives an order on a third person to pay to the creditor, the payment is complete if the creditor, without consulting the debtor, arranges special terms with the third party, and in consequence loses the money.[9] The following are examples of payments which are good, though not made in the usual way:

1. Money paid by consent of the creditor for his benefit by the debtor;[10]
2. Payment in goods according to agreement.[11]

b) Payment by cheque or other negotiable instrument[12] Apart from agreement, the creditor cannot be compelled to take, nor the debtor to make himself liable on a negotiable instrument in payment. Prima facie, payment by negotiable instrument is presumed to be conditional and suspends the creditor's rights:[13] if the instrument is not taken up, the original liability revives;[14]

while, if the bill is met, the payment relates back to the time when it was given.[15] However, if a buyer offers cash, but the vendor prefers a bill, the payment is absolute, and all right of action upon the original consideration goes and the vendor must sue on the bill.[16] A third possibility is that a bill of exchange is merely given by way of collateral security,[17] in which case none of the creditor's remedies are suspended.[18]

Payment by cheque (properly drawn and suitably crossed) has these advantages: not only is the cashed cheque its own receipt,[19] but where a lost cheque is not known to have come into the hands of a holder in due course (this can be prevented by crossing it 'not negotiable'[20]) the creditor can require a duplicate cheque on giving the usual indemnity.[21]

---

1 Currency and Bank Notes Act 1954, s. 1 (2).
2 By s. 2, the following coinage shall be legal tender up to the amounts indicated: cupro-nickel or silver in denominations of more than 10p (£10); or the same in denominations of not more than 10p (£5); bronze (20p).
3 *Robinson v Cook* (1816) 6 Taunt. 336.
4 *Polglass v Oliver* (1831) 2 Cr & J 15.
5 *Douglas v Patrick* (1789) 3 Term Rep 683.
6 *Eyles v Ellis* (1827) 4 Bing. 112.
7 *Thairlwall v Great Northern Rly Co* [1910] 2 KB 509; *Norman v Ricketts* (1886) 3 TLR 182, CA. See also *Pennington v Crossley & Son* (1897) 77 LT 43, CA; *International Sponge Importers Ltd v Watt (Andrew) & Sons* [1911] AC 279, HL(S).
8 *Mitchell-Henry v Norwich Life Insurance Co* [1918] 2 KB 76, CA.
9 *Smith v Ferrand* (1827) 7 B & C 19, 24.
10 *Waller v Andrews* (1837) 3 M & W 312, 318.
11 *Cannan v Wood* (1836) 2 M & W 465, 467; but see the Truck Acts 1831–1896 (para. 32.13, post) which, subject to exceptions, forbid the payment of wages in kind to 'workmen'.
12 For negotiable instruments, see generally chap. 20.
13 *Bolt and Nut Ltd v Rowlands, Nicholls & Co Ltd* [1964] 2 QB 10, [1964] 1 All ER 137, CA.
14 If the debtor after giving a bill commits an act of bankruptcy the original debt revives, though the bill has not yet matured (*Re Raatz* [1897] 2 QB 80).
15 *Marreco v Richardson* [1908] 2 KB, at 593, per Farwell LJ. But see *Re Hone* [1951] Ch 85, [1950] 2 All ER 716.
16 *Cowas-Jee v Thompson* (1845) 5 Moo. PCC 165.
17 Such surety devices are considered further in para. 16.03, post.
18 *Modern Light Cars Ltd v Seals* [1934] 1 KB 32.
19 Cheques Act 1957, s. 3. But see Chalmers *Bills of Exchange* (13th edn) 308.
20 See further para. 21.04, post.
21 See para. 20.18, post.

---

c) THE RULES OF PAYMENT

7.17 *a) Who may pay* It is the duty of the debtor to pay, but a third party may do so for him.[1] In this latter case, the debtor should either give his authorisation or ratification,[2] though either may be implied from the facts. Until such affirmation by the debtor, the money may be repaid to the payer, and then the original debtor's liability does not cease.[3]

b) *To whom payment may be made* The payment should be made to the creditor, and if there are several joint creditors then to any one of them. If one of several joint creditors collusively with the debtor forgives the debt, the release may be set aside by the court.

Payments may be made to the creditor's agent. However, the general rule is that until the agent hands over the money this does not amount to payment to his principal, so that if this is not done for some reason, e.g. agent's fraud or insolvency, the debtor must pay again.[4] Exceptionally, payment to the agent will discharge the debtor, but only if made:

1. in and according to the usual course of business:[5] and
2. before the principal gives notice that he requires payment to be made to himself.[6]

Further, when an agent has a lien on the proceeds of goods sold by him in his own name, e.g. as a factor or auctioneer, payment to the principal is no defence to an action by the agent for the price unless the contract of sale permitted payment direct to the principal.[7]

An express authority to an agent to sell goods does not necessarily authorise him to receive payment.[8]

c) *Appropriation of payments* If a debtor owes more than one debt to a creditor, and makes a payment insufficient to satisfy the whole indebtedness, the money is appropriated as follows:

1. First, to whichever debt the debtor desires, provided he exercises his option at the time of payment,[9] making this clear to the creditor;[10]
2. Second, if the debtor, with knowledge of his right of election,[11] chooses not to exercise it, the creditor may do so at any time, though his appropriation is revocable until communicated,[12] and this right of appropriation lasts up until the very last moment.[13] Provided there is a genuine debt, the creditor may appropriate the payment to it, though the right of action is unenforceable, e.g. because the agreement was not evidenced in writing as required by the Statute of Frauds, or the right of action is gone, for instance a debt barred by the Limitation Act.[14] The creditor must, however, have some legal or equitable claim, though it may not be enforceable by action; he cannot appropriate a payment to a demand arising out of a contract forbidden by law,[15] nor does his right to appropriate remain after a judgment which does not give effect to it.[16]
3. If there is a current account between the parties, the law

recognises the following presumption, known as the *rule in Clayton's Case*:[17] monies are deemed to be paid out in the order in which they are paid in.[18] However, this presumption may be rebutted by proof of a contrary intention or agreement between the parties.[19]

---

1 An acknowledgment by the third party to the creditor may enable the creditor to enforce this arrangement: see para. 4.07, ante.
2 *Simpson v Eggington* (1855) 10 Exch 845 at 847.
3 *Walter v James* (1871) LR 6 Exch 124 (see para. 10.04, post).
4 *Heald v Kenworthy* (1855) 10 Exch 739; *Irvine & Co v Watson & Sons* (1880) 5 QBD 414, CA. See further para. 10.26, post.
5 *Saunderson v Bell* (1834) 2 C & M 304; *Catterall v Hindle* (1867) LR 2 CP 368, Ex Ch.
6 *Gardiner v Davis* (1825) 2 C & P 49.
7 *Williams v Millington* (1788) 1 H. Bl. 81; *Robinson v Rutter* (1855) 4 E & B 954.
8 *Butwick v Grant* [1924] 2 KB 483.
9 *Croft v Lumley* (1858) 5 E & B 648.
10 *Leeson v Leeson* [1936] 2 KB 156.
11 *Waller v Lacy* (1840) 1 M & G 54.
12 *Simson v Ingham* (1823) 2 B & C 65 (mere undisclosed entry in creditor's accounts). But for transactions within the Consumer Credit Act 1974, see para. 14.35(b), post.
13 *The Mecca* [1897]: AC 286; *Seymour v Pickett* [1905] 1 KB 715 (when in the witness box).
14 *Mills v Fowkes* (1839) 5 Bing. NC 455.
15 *Lamprell v Guardians of Billericay Union* (1849) 3 Exch 283 at 307; *A Smith & Son (Bognor Regis) v Walker* [1952] 2 QB 319, [1952] 1 All ER 1008, CA.
16 *Smith v Betty* [1903] 2 KB 317.
17 *Devaynes v Noble (Clayton's Case)* (1816) 1 Mer. 572.
18 *Deeley v Lloyds Bank Ltd* [1912] AC 756, HL.
19 *The Mecca* [1897] AC 286, HL; *Devaynes v Noble, (Clayton's Case)* (1816) 1 Mer. 585 at 608; *Henniker v Wigg* (1869) LR 4 QB 792; *Re Hallet's Estate* (1880) 13 ChD 696.

7.18 *d) Current Accounts* In the case of a current account between banker and customer the rule in *Clayton's Case* may operate to the disadvantage of the banker unless care is taken to prevent it from so doing. Thus,

> where a mortgage is given to a bank to secure a running account and the customer subsequently creates a second mortgage on the property in favour of a third person, the banker cannot, after notice of such second mortgage, make *further* advances to the prejudice of the second mortgagee.[1]

If the banker continues the account, all further advances will be unsecured: all payments in will be appropriated to the previous advances secured by the mortgage, so that in the end the banker may find that the security has been wholly or in part satisfied, while the debt in substance remains unpaid; for there is no ground of presuming any intention on the part of the bank to apply payments in to the unsecured items in order of date in priority to the secured items.[2]

The same result may happen in the case of a continuing guarantee which has been determined by notice. However, if the banker does not wish to enforce immediate payment of the secured balance, he can avoid the operation of the rule in *Clayton's Case* by the simple device of breaking the account and opening a new and distinct account for fresh transactions.[3]

---

1 *Hopkinson v Rolt* (1861) 9 HL Cas. 514. But by s. 94, Law of Property Act 1925, notice of the second mortgage would not prevent the bank claiming priority if it was under a contractual obligation to allow the overdraft.
2 *Deeley v Lloyds Bank* [1912] AC 756, HL.
3 Remarks of Lord Selborne, *Re Sherry* (1884) 25 ChD at 702.

7.19   *e) Trust moneys* As against a beneficiary under a trust, a trustee who has mixed trust money with his own moneys in his banking account may not set up the rule in *Clayton's Case*, and it will be presumed that in drawing from the bank he drew on his own and not on the trust money.[1] However, if the trustee exhausts his own money and draws out part of the trust moneys, the beneficiary is only entitled to that part of the credit balance which represents the lowest sum to which the trust moneys have at any time reduced. This is the position despite the fact that the trustee has afterwards paid further money into the account, unless he has expressly appropriated such further moneys to the replacement of the amount improperly withdrawn.[2] Where the contest is between two claimants to a mixed fund consisting of moneys belonging to both, the rule in *Clayton's Case* applies if the money has been paid into an active banking account. Otherwise the claimants share *pari passu*.[3] The position is the same where an innocent party has received trust money without consideration and mixed it with his own.[4]

f) Payment by instalments See chapter 14, post.

---

1 *Re Hallett's Estate* (1880) 13 ChD 696.
2 *James Roscoe (Bolton) Ltd v Winder* [1915] 1 Ch 62.
3 *Re Stenning* [1895] 2 Ch 433; *Diplock, Re Diplock v Wintle* [1948] Ch 465, [1948] 2 All ER 318, CA; *affd. sub nom. Ministry of Health v Simpson* [1951] AC 251, [1950] 2 All ER 1137, HL.
4 *Re Diplock,* ante.

Interest

7.20 Interest is not generally allowed at common law in the absence of agreement, but in certain cases a creditor is entitled to simple interest. Compound interest is never allowed, unless by express or implied contract.[1]

However, simple interest is chargeable as of right (1) where there is an express or implied agreement to pay it; (2) where the usage of trade allows it; (3) on money obtained by fraud and retained by fraud;[2] (4) on a judgment debt[3] or arbitration award[4] (5) when by Act of Parliament it is provided that interest shall be payable.

In any proceedings tried in any court of record[5] for the recovery of any debt or damages, the court may, if it thinks fit, order that there shall be included in the sum for which judgment is given interest at such rate as it thinks fit on the whole or any part of the debt or damages for the whole or any part of the period between the date when the cause of action arose and the date of the judgment. The above powers were conferred on the court by s. 3 of the Law Reform (Miscellaneous Provisions) Act 1934, but the statute does not authorise the giving of compound interest, or apply to any debt upon which interest is payable as of right.

---

1 *Fergusson v Fyfe* (1841) C & F 121.
2 *Johnson v R* [1904] AC 817.
3 Judgments Act 1838, s. 17 amended by the Administration of Justice Act 1970, s. 44 and the Judgment Debts (Rate of Interest) Order 1971 (S.I. 1971 No. 491).
4 Arbitration Act 1950, s. 20: see further para. 34.17, post.
5 An arbitrator has the same power (*Chandris v Isbrandtsen-Moller Co Inc* [1951] 1 KB 240, [1950] 2 All ER 618, CA).

---

3. Breach of contract

7.21 Upon any breach of contract, there is always a right of action for damages, for, even where no actual damage can be proved, nominal damages will be awarded.[1] However, in addition,[2] the innocent party, A, may have the right to avoid the contract if the guilty party, X, is in total breach, either by reason of a repudiation or a seriously defective performance; but these rules are modified in the case of lump sum and severable contracts.

1 For damages, see further para. 7.27 et seq., post.
2 See para. 7.07, ante.

---

a) TOTAL BREACH

7.22 Leaving aside lump sum contracts, a total breach may come about in either of the following ways:

a) *Seriously defective performance* As has been seen, A will have a prima facie right to avoid the contract where there is a breach of condition, or a breach of innominate term, by X which deprives A of substantially the whole benefit of the contract.[1]

b) *Repudiation* A will have a prima facie right to avoid where there is an unequivocal refusal by X to perform his contract: this repudiation may be express;[2] or it may be implied, as where X completely fails to perform his side of the bargain, or incapacitates himself from so doing.[3] Whilst X may repudiate at the time when performance is due, he may also repudiate before that time—this is called an '*anticipatory breach*' (see below).

Where there is such a total breach by X, this does not automatically bring the contract to an end,[4] except possibly where further performance is impossible by reason of the breach:[5] it is thought that the general rule is that A merely has the option to treat the contract as discharged, the contract remaining binding on both parties unless and until A elects to avoid it.[6] Thus, when A discovers the breach by X, he has a right of election as follows:[7]

a) *To treat the contract as discharged* The effect of this is that A may thereafter refuse to perform his part of the contract,[8] and successfully resist any action brought upon the contract by X,[9] whilst at the same time maintaining an action for damages against X—usually for compensation for the lost value of performance.[10]

b) *Not to treat the contract as discharged* Apart from the possible exception noted above,[5] A may elect not to 'accept' the 'offer' by X to bring the contract to an end, in which case the contract continues binding on both parties—unless, perhaps, there is a 'continuing breach' of a hiring agreement,[11] or an *anticipatory breach* of any type of contract (see below). The logical outcome of A so electing not to treat the contract as discharged was demonstrated in *White and Carter (Councils) Ltd v McGregor*:[12]

A agreed to display advertisements for X's garage for three years. Later the same day, X repudiated the agreement but A declined to accept the repudiation, proceeded with the advertisement display, and sued for the contract price. *Held:* A was not obliged to accept the repudiation or sue for damages but was entitled instead to carry out his side of the contract as he had, and claim the full contract price.

1 See para. 7.08, ante.
2 E.g. *Overstone Ltd v Shipway* [1962] 1 All ER 52, [1962] 1 WLR 117, CA.
3 E.g. by reselling, or by self-induced frustration.
4 *Heyman v Darwins Ltd* [1942] AC 356, [1942] 1 All ER 337, HL.
5 *Harbutt's Plasticine Ltd v Wayne Tank and Pump Co Ltd* [1970] 1 QB 447, [1970] 1 All ER 225, CA: for impossibility of performance, see further para. 8.02 et seq., post. For the question of whether a wrongly dismissed employee is compelled to treat his contract of employment as discharged, see Cheshire & Fifoot *Law of Contract* (9th edn) 575–576.
6 Per Diplock LJ in *R V Ward Ltd v Bignall* [1967] 1 QB 534 at 548, CA.
7 For the manner in which this election may be exercised, see *Car and Universal Finance Co Ltd v Caldwell* [1965] 1 QB 525, [1964] 1 All ER 290, CA: see para. 5.11, above.
8 In this sense, performance by X was a condition precedent to A's obligation to perform: see generally para. 7.06, ante.
9 See *General Billposting Co Ltd v Atkinson* [1909] AC 118, HL (see para. 6.11, ante).
10 The fact that A purports to treat himself as discharged by reason of some act by X insufficient in law to give A such a right does not matter provided a sound alternative ground in fact exists; but, where X's act did not amount to a total breach, then A's purported avoidance on such insufficient grounds will itself be a repudiation.
11 See *Yeoman Credit Ltd v Apps* [1962] 2 QB 508, [1961] 2 All ER 281, CA.
12 [1962] AC 413, [1961] 3 All ER 1178, HL(S).

b) ANTICIPATORY BREACH

7.23 Where X repudiates the contract at a time before performance by him is due, A's normal right of election to avoid or affirm is modified in that he does not need to await the time for performance but may exercise his right of election immediately.

a) To treat the contract as discharged Immediately X repudiates, A may treat the contract as discharged and sue for damages, notwithstanding that the time for performance has not yet arrived. Thus, in *Hochster v De la Tour:*[1]

On April 12, A was engaged to act as a courier to X, the employment to begin in June. In May, X wrote to inform A that his services would not be required. On May 22, A commenced an action for damages which succeeded.

In such an action, A is entitled to damages in lieu of performance, including damages in respect of those terms which would have been performed by X after the anticipatory breach was accepted as discharging the contract.[2]

b) Not to treat the contract as discharged If A does not accept the repudiation by X, but instead keeps the contract open, X may again change his mind and perform his side of the contract

when the time for performance arrives; but, if X remains
adamantly set against performance, A may be able to obtain an
order of specific performance.[3] However, the fact that the
contract remains open may operate to the advantage of either
side as regards A's claim for damages: as damages are measured
at the time appointed for performance,[4] A is, in a sense,
gambling on the market; and a frustrating event[5] intervening in
the period between the anticipatory breach and the time for
performance will discharge both parties without any liability to
damages.[6]

---

1 (1853) 2 E & B 678.
2 *Moschi v Lep Air Services Ltd* [1973] AC 331, [1972] 2 All ER 393, HL.
3 *Hasham v Zenab* [1960] AC 316, PC.
4 *Roper v Johnson* (1873) LR 8 CP 167. As to damages, see paras. 7.27 et seq.,
   post.
5 See para. 8.02, post.
6 *Avery v Bowden* (1855) 5 E & B 714.

---

c) LUMP SUM CONTRACTS

7.24 If X agrees with A to do an entire work for a specified sum, and
the entire work is not carried out by X, the general rule is that
this amounts to a total breach of contract and therefore prima
facie X can recover nothing for any part of the work he has done.
In circumstances where X has conferred a benefit on A, the
effect may be unjustly to enrich A: X cannot sue under the
contract, because he has not fully performed the condition
precedent upon which his right to sue depends;[1] nor may he
claim on a *quantum meruit* basis (i.e. for what the benefit is
worth) where such a claim would be inconsistent with his
contract.[2]

However, in recognition of the hardship thus created, the
common law will, by way of exception to this rule of 'entire
contracts', allow X a right of action notwithstanding his own
failure to make complete performance in all the following cases:
(1) where it has been so agreed, as where A is only entitled to
damages in respect of X's breach; (2) where A has wrongfully
prevented X from completing performance;[3] (3) where the
contract is divisible—being in reality a series of little contracts
(see below); (4) (possibly) where there has been *substantial
performance*;[4] or (5) (possibly) where the contract has been
frustrated.[5]

---

1 For conditions precedent, see para. 7.06, ante.

2 *Sumpter v Hedges* [1898] 1 QB 673, CA. See also *Forman & Co v The Ship 'Liddesdale'* [1900] AC 190, PC; *Vigers v Cook* [1910] 2 KB 475, CA.
3 *Planché v Colburn* (1831) 8 Bing 14.
4 *H Dakin & Co Ltd v Lee* [1916] 1 KB 566; *Hoenig v Isaacs* [1952] 2 All ER 176 CA, cf. *Bolton v Mahadeva* [1972] 2 All ER 1322, [1972] 1 WLR 1009, CA. It has been held by the Divisional Court and Scrutton LJ, that this principle does not apply against a surety who has only guaranteed payment of the contract price on the work being 'duly executed': *Eshelby v Federated European Bank Ltd* [1932] 1 KB 254 at 433, CA.
5 See para. 8.06, post.

---

d) PARTIAL BREACH

7.25 Where X is only in partial breach of contract, he can always sue A for any damages suffered, or *quantum meruit* for any work done.[1] However, unless it is a *lump sum contract*, A is not entitled to avoid the contract and refuse performance of his promises—that would be a wrongful repudiation on his part.

---

1 *Planché v Colburn* (1831) 8 Bing 14.

7.26   Particularly where the contract provides for performance by instalments, it may be difficult to know whether a serious breach or repudiation by X in respect of one instalment will amount to a *total breach* of the whole contract. The rule is that it is a matter of construction whether X's breach is a *total breach*, in which case A can avoid the whole contract, or whether it is a *partial breach* in which case A is entitled to a remedy in damages for the particular breach, but is not entitled to treat the contract as discharged.[1] Lord Blackburn in *Mersey Steel and Iron Co v Naylor*, said:

'The rule of law ... is that, where there is a contract in which there are two parties, each side having to do something ... If you see that the failure to perform one part of it goes to the root of the contract, goes to the foundation of the whole, it is a good defence to say, "I am not going to perform my part of it." ... But Mr. Cohen contended that whenever there was a breach of a material part of the contract, it necessarily went to the root of the matter. I cannot agree with that at all'.[2]

Frequently it happens that the contract is divisible into various stipulations, e.g.:

to deliver cargo at certain stated intervals, on March 1st, April 1st, and so on, in which case the question whether the breach of one of them constitutes repudiation of the contract depends mainly on the ratio of the instalment to the whole contract and the probability of repetition of the breach.[3]

If, however, the parties expressly agree that breach of a single term shall entitle the other party to treat the contract as abandoned, the general rule is inapplicable.[4] And if a party shows by his acts, or otherwise, an intention not any longer to be bound by his contract, this gives the other a right to refuse further performance, though, so far, one term only has been broken. In the case of *Freeth v Burr:*[5]

> The plaintiff agreed to buy from the defendants some iron, to be delivered in two instalments, net cash within a fortnight of delivery; after delivery, and when the first payment was due, plaintiff refused to pay, mistakenly believing he had a right of set-off for late delivery. It was *held*, that the buyer's acts did not exhibit an intention 'to abandon and altogether to refuse performance of the contract', so as to justify the defendant's refusal to continue performance as the buyer had acted bona fide under a mistake of law; the defendant's remedy was in damages for breach of contract.[6]

The House of Lords approved the principle in *Mersey Steel and Iron Co v Naylor.*[7]

---

1 See notes to *Pordage v Cole* (1669) 1 Wm. Saund. 548 (ed. 1871). For sales of goods, see now the Sale of Goods Act, s. 31 (2): see para. 13.36, post.
2 (1884) 9 App Cas 434, 443. See also *Warinco AG v Samor SPA* [1977] 2 Lloyd's Rep. 582.
3 In some cases each instalment is treated as a separate contract: see *Jackson v Rotax Motor and Cycle Co* [1910] 2 KB 937, CA, and contrast *Thorpe v Fasey* [1949] Ch 649, [1949] 2 All ER 393.
4 *Cutter v Powell* (1795) 6 Term Rep 320.
5 (1874) LR 9 CP 208.
6 *Freeth v Burr* (1874) LR 9 CP 208, 213; see also *Withers v Reynolds* (1819) 2 B & Ad 882; *Simpson v Crippin* (1873) LR 8 QB 14; and cf. *Honck v Muller* (1881) 7 QBD 92, CA.
7 (1884) 9 App Cas 434. See also *Thorpe v Fasey* [1949] Ch 649, [1949] 2 All ER 393; *Peter Dumanil & Co Ltd v James Ruddin Ltd* [1953] 2 All ER 294, [1953] 1 WLR 815, CA.

---

4. Remedies

A) *Damages*

7.27   Whenever a contractual term is broken, the injured party is entitled to claim damages in respect of *loss* caused by the breach:[1] it follows that there can be no double recovery, even though the wrong-doing may give rise to more than one cause of action.[2] However, damages cannot be claimed in respect of every loss which may result from the breach. The loss must not be too remote:

'The damages should be such as may fairly and reasonably be considered either arising naturally, i.e. according to the usual course of things, from such breach of contract itself, or such as may reasonably be supposed to have been in the contemplation of both parties at the time they made the contract, as the probable result of the breach of it'.[3]

In *Victoria Laundry (Windsor) Ltd v Newman Industries Ltd*:[4]

B agreed to sell to A, a laundry company, a boiler to be delivered on a certain date, but delivered it five months late. B was aware of the nature of A's business. A claimed (1) for loss of profits that would have been earned through the extension of the business, and (2) for loss of his highly lucrative dyeing contracts. *Held:* A was entitled to damages for loss under head (1); but since B had no knowledge of the particular dyeing contracts made by A, A was entitled under head (2) only to a normal rate of profit from dyeing contracts and not to the exceptional profit A would actually have made.

In *The Heron II*:[5]

A chartered a ship from B to carry 3,000 tons of sugar from Constanza to Basrah with the intention of selling the sugar at Basrah. B made deviations in breach of the contract so that the sugar arrived in Basrah nine days later than expected and the price obtainable for the sugar was some £4,000 less than it would have been had the sugar arrived on time. B did not know of A's intention to sell the sugar in Basrah but the House of Lords *held* that B must have realised it was *not unlikely* that the sugar would be sold on arrival at the then market price and that prices were apt to fluctuate daily. A was entitled to his loss of profit as damages for B's breach of contract.

Moreover, if the *kind* of damage caused by a breach of contract is not too remote, it is immaterial that its *results* are far more serious than could have been reasonably contemplated.[6]

---

1 For the power to award damages in lieu of specific performance, see para. 7.32, note 1, post.
2 *Cullinane v British "Rema" Manufacturing Co Ltd* [1954] 1 QB 292, [1953] 2 All ER 1257, CA (see also para. 13.33, note 10, post).
3 *Hadley v Baxendale* (1854) 9 Exch 341.
4 [1949] 2 KB 528, [1949] 1 All ER 997, CA.
5 [1969] 1 AC 350, [1967] 3 All ER 686. The House of Lords said that the rule in tort—that all damage reasonably foreseeable was recoverable (*The Wagon*

Mound No. 1 [1961] AC 388, [1961] 1 All ER 404, PC)—was not the same as the rule in contract enunciated in *Hadley v Baxendale* (1854) 9 Exch 341. But see *H Parsons (Livestock) Ltd v Uttley Ingham & Co Ltd* [1978] 1 All ER 525, [1977] 3 WLR 990, CA (see also para. 13.33, post), and the contrary view of Lord Denning MR.

6 *Vacwell Engineering Co Ltd v BDH Chemicals Ltd* [1971] 1 QB 111, [1970] 3 All ER 553; *Wroth v Tyler* [1974] Ch 30, [1973] 1 All ER 897.

---

i) Assessment of damages

7.28 Assuming that the loss is not too remote from the breach of contract, the amount of damages recoverable is prima facie[1] the amount necessary to put the injured party in the same position (so far as money can do it) as if the contract had been performed[2] or—exceptionally—returning him to the position he was in before the contract was made;[3] and, in an appropriate case, damages may include a sum for mental distress.[4] Nevertheless, such damages are solely in respect of what the guilty party was contractually bound to do; so a wrongfully dismissed employee can recover nothing in respect of discretionary bonuses.[5]

Although when a breach of contract has occurred the injured party is entitled to damages sufficient to compensate him for his loss, he is himself under a duty to take any reasonable steps which would mitigate his loss and to bring into account any sums which thereby are, or should be saved.[6] Thus, in *Brace v Calder*:[7]

B agreed to work for a partnership C & Co for a certain period. Before the period expired, two of the four partners retired. The remaining partners continued the business and were willing to continue to employ B, but B refused. *Held:* The dissolution of the partnership caused by the retirements was a wrongful dismissal of B, but B was entitled to nominal damages only since he had failed to mitigate his loss by accepting the offer of continued employment.

In commercial contracts it is generally reasonable to accept an offer from the party in default;[8] but that does not require the innocent party to go so far as to give up property obtained,[9] nor to forgo his right of election on anticipatory breach.[10]

An estimate of damages may be based on probabilities, but a court will not award damages of a problematical character upon the assumption that numerous events of a contingent nature would have happened.[11] However, although damages which are incapable of assessment cannot be recovered, the fact that they are difficult to assess with certainty of precision, does not deprive the plaintiff of the right to recover them. The Court must do its best to estimate the loss, and a contingency may be taken into account. In *Chaplin v Hicks*:[12]

> The defendant advertised that he would employ, as actresses at remunerative salaries, twelve ladies to be selected by him out of fifty whom the readers of various newspapers, in which the candidates' photographs were published, had adjudged to be the most beautiful. The plaintiff won her section and became one of the fifty eligible for selection by the defendant; but the defendant made an unreasonable appointment which the plaintiff could not keep, and proceeded to select twelve out of the forty-nine who were able to keep the appointment. The jury assessed the plaintiff's damages at £100 for the loss of her chance of obtaining a prize and the Court of Appeal refused to disturb the verdict.

---

1 Subject to any liquidated damages clause. Such clauses are restricted by the rule against penalties, as to which see paras. 7.30, 14.05, post.
2 *Wertheim v Chicoutimi Pulp Co* [1911] AC 301, PC. The damages should be awarded in the currency which best expresses the injured party's loss: *Services Europe Atlantique Sud v Stockholms Rederiaktierolag Svea* [1978] 2 WLR 887, CA.
3 Including even pre-contract expenditure: *Anglia Television Ltd v Reed* [1972] 1 QB 60, [1971] 3 All ER 690, CA.
4 *Jarvis v Swan's Tours* [1973] 1 QB 233, [1973] 1 All ER 71, CA; *Jackson v Horizon Holidays Ltd* [1975] 3 All ER 92, [1975] 1 WLR 1468, CA; *Heywood v Wellers* [1976] QB 446, [1976] 1 All ER 300, CA; *Cox v Phillips* [1976] 3 All ER 161, [1976] 1 WLR 638.
5 *Lavarack v Woods of Colchester Ltd* [1967] QB 278, [1966] 3 All ER 683, CA.
6 *British Westinghouse and Electric Manufacturing Co v Underground Rail Co Ltd* [1912] AC 673, HL; *Nadreph Ltd v Willmett & Co* [1978] 1 All ER 746.
7 [1895] 2 QB 253, CA (see also paras. 11.15, note 7, 32.12, note 6, post).
8 *Payzu Ltd v Saunders* [1919] 2 KB 581 at 589, CA, per Scrutton LJ.
9 *Strutt v Whitnell* [1975] 2 All ER 510, [1975] 1 WLR 870, CA.
10 *White and Carter (Council) Ltd v McGregor* [1962] AC 413, [1961] 3 All ER 1178, HL(S) (set out para. 7.22, ante). But see *Hounslow London Borough Council v Twickenham Garden Developments Ltd* [1971] Ch 233, [1970] 3 All ER 326.
11 *Sapwell v Bass* [1910] 2 KB 486.
12 [1911] 2 KB 786.

---

ii) Effect on damages of tax liability

7.29 Since damages are compensatory, whenever a claim for damages includes a claim for loss of income, the income tax that would have been payable on such income must be taken into account.[1] In *Parson v BNM Laboratories Ltd*:[2]

P claimed damages for wrongful dismissal from his employment, the loss of salary and commission amounting to £1,200. *Held:* That sum must be reduced by £320 being the amount of income tax which would have been payable on the lost salary and commission.

---

1 *British Transport Commission v Gourley* [1956] AC 185, [1955] 3 All ER 796, HL.
2 [1964] 1 QB 95, [1963] 2 All ER 658, CA. See Law Reform Committee, Seventh Report *(Effect of tax liability on damages),* Cmnd 501. Where the damages for loss of earnings exceeds £5,000, the court will have to take account of the fact that the excess is taxable under the Income and Corporation Taxes Act 1970, ss. 187, 188 (3).

---

iii) Liquidated damages

7.30 If the parties to a contract agree that, in the event of a breach, the party in default shall pay a specified sum to the other party, that sum is recoverable on breach if it is a genuine pre-estimate of the probable loss which will be caused by the breach. The sum is then termed 'liquidated damages', and even if the actual loss incurred is greater, only that sum may be claimed.[1] If, however, the sum specified as payable on breach is not a genuine pre-estimate of loss but is meant instead to deter a party from breaking the contract, the sum is known as a 'penalty' and is not recoverable. In this latter case, the plaintiff will instead recover damages assessed in accordance with the general principles already discussed.

In determining whether the sum fixed is in the nature of damages, or of a penalty, the court looks not to the name by which the parties have called it, but to its actual nature, e.g.

if the parties fix a very large sum, and call it damages for non-payment of a small sum, the court will regard it as a penalty;[2]

and the same view will be taken by the court if the sum fixed is extravagant, exorbitant or unconscionable in regard to any possible amount of damages or any kind of damage which may be conceived to have been within the contemplation of the parties when they made the contract.

Further, a sum payable on one event only will in general be regarded as liquidated damages;[3] but if payable on the breach of one or more stipulations of different degrees of importance, the presumption is that the parties intended the sum to be penal.[4] But even in the latter case, if the damage is the same in kind for every possible breach, is incapable of being precisely estimated, is a fair pre-estimate of the probable damage and not uncon-

scionable, the sum named will not be treated as a penalty. In
Dunlop Pneumatic Tyre Co Ltd v New Garage, etc Co Ltd:[5]

> Purchasers of tyres agreed not to tamper with the marks on
> them, not to sell them below listed prices, not to exhibit
> without consent, and to pay £5 as 'liquidated damages' for
> every breach. *Held:* The £5 sum was recoverable as liquidated
> damages and was not a penalty.

It is for consideration whether the rule against penalties can
be used to strike down clauses providing for the payment of
penal sums upon the happening of events other than breaches of
contract.[6]

---

1 See *Cellulose Acetate Silk Co v Widnes Foundry (1925) Ltd* [1933] AC 20.
2 See *Kemble v Farren* (1829) 6 Bing 141. See also *Alder v Moore* [1961] 2 QB
  57, [1961] 1 All ER 1.
3 *Clydebank, etc Co v Don José Castaneda* [1905] AC 6.
4 *Lord Elphinstone v Monkland, etc Co* (1886) 11 App Cas 332; *Law v
  Redditch Local Board* [1892] 1 QB 127; *Strickland v Williams* [1899] 1 QB
  382; *Willson v Love* [1896] 1 QB 628; *Pye v British Automobile Syndicate*
  [1906] 1 KB 425.
5 [1915] AC 79, HL; followed in *Robophone Facilities Ltd v Blank* [1966] 3 All
  ER 128, [1966] 1 WLR 1428, CA.
6 *Bridge v Campbell Discount Co Ltd* [1962] AC 600, [1962] 1 All ER 385, HL.
  See further the Law Commission Working Paper *Penalty Clauses and
  Forfeiture of Monies Paid* (WP No. 61).

---

iv) Foreign currency

7.31 Since an English judgment must normally make an award
expressed in sterling, it is necessary to decide the date for
conversion into English currency of damages for breach of
contract which had in the first instance to be assessed in foreign
currency. The proper date for conversion into English money of a
loss proved in foreign currency is the date when it was incurred,
and not the date when the judgment is pronounced. An
alteration in the rate of exchange subsequent to a breach of
contract is not an element in the assessment of damages;[1] but the
hardship of this rule is mitigated by the power of the courts to
award judgment in a foreign currency in an appropriate case.[2]

---

1 *SS Celia v SS Volturno* [1921] 2 AC 544; *Di Ferdinando v Simon, Smits &
  Co* [1920] 3 KB 409.
2 *Miliangos v George Frank (Textiles) Ltd* [1976] AC 443, [1975] 3 All ER
  801, HL; *Price v Strange* [1977] 3 All ER 371, [1977] 3 WLR 943, CA.

B) *Specific performance*

7.32 This is a discretionary remedy granted formerly by courts of
equity but now by all courts, where the innocent party elects to
affirm the contract after breach, but damages of themselves will
not be a sufficient compensation.[1] It is used mostly with regard
to contracts concerning land, but in certain cases the courts will
compel performance of other contracts. Thus, a contract for the
sale of a thing of rare beauty, or of one with regard to which
there is an exceptional value—e.g. heirlooms—may be ordered
to be specifically performed.[2] But specific performance of an
agreement will not be granted:

1. If the contract is for personal services, e.g. a contract of
employment.[3]

2. If the constant supervision of the court would be necessary to
secure obedience to the order. Thus, where the lessor of a flat
broke a contractual term to provide a resident porter with certain
defined duties, the court declined to order specific performance.[4]

3. If it would be unenforceable against the person asking for
specific performance, e.g. where the plaintiff seeking specific
performance of an agreement to sell land is a minor.[5]

---

1 *Capital and Suburban Properties Ltd v Swycher* [1976] 1 Ch 319, [1976] 1 All
ER 881, CA. For the rights of the innocent party where the party in default
fails to perform an order of S.P. see also *Biggin v Minton* [1977] 2 All ER
647, [1977] 1 WLR 701. For the award of damages in lieu of specific
performance, see the Chancery Amendment Act 1858; *Horsler v Zorro* [1975]
Ch 302, [1975] 1 All ER 584, discussed 91 LQR 337; and *Wroth v Tyler*
[1974] Ch 30, [1973] 1 All ER 897.

2 *Dowling v Betjemann* (1862) 2 John & H 544. See also Sale of Goods Act
1893, s. 52, para. 13.32, post; *Beswick v Beswick* [1968] AC 58, [1967] 2 All
ER 1197, HL.

3 It has been suggested that this principle is weakening: Cheshire & Fifoot *Law
of Contract* (9th edn) 615–616. However, by the Trade Union and Labour
Relations Act 1974, s. 16, no court may compel an employee to work either by
way of an order of specific performance or injunction. On a complaint of
'unfair dismissal' an industrial tribunal may order a complainant employee to
be re-engaged but if this order is disobeyed the tribunal is empowered only to
award compensation: Employment Protection Act 1975, s. 72.

4 *Ryan v Mutual Tontine Westminster Chambers Association* [1893] 1 Ch 116.

5 *Flight v Bolland* (1828) 4 Russ. 298.

C) *Injunction*

7.33 This too is a discretionary remedy which a court may award
where damages would not be an adequate remedy.[1] An

injunction is a court order restraining a party to a contract from acting in breach of it. Thus, if an employee is bound by a valid covenant in restraint of trade, his employer may obtain an injunction to prevent him from acting in breach of it.[2] Disobedience to the order is punishable as a contempt of court.

It has been noted that a court will not grant an order of specific performance of a contract for personal services and it follows from this that no court will award an injunction to restrain a servant from breaking his promise to serve as this would indirectly amount to compelling him to perform a personal contract. Even where A has entered into a negative stipulation, i.e. an express promise not to enter into other employment, no injunction will be ordered if the effect of granting it would be to compel A to serve. In *Page One Records Ltd v Britton:*[3]

A group of pop musicians, The Troggs, agreed to let X manage their careers and not to let anyone else act as their manager. After a year, The Troggs repudiated their contract with X and X sought an injunction to restrain The Troggs from engaging someone else as their manager. *Held:* an injunction would in effect compel The Troggs to continue to employ X and this would amount to enforcing performance of a contract for personal services. The injunction sought was, therefore, refused.

---

1 *Sky Petroleum v VIP Petroleum* [1974] 1 All ER 954, [1974] 1 WLR 576. It will only be granted where just and equitable to do so: see *Shell UK Ltd v Lostock Garage Ltd* [1977] 1 All ER 481, [1976] 1 WLR 1187, CA.

2 See further para. 6.10, ante.

3 [1967] 3 All ER 822, [1968] 1 WLR 157. Cf. *Lumley v Wagner* (1852) 1 DM & G 604 and *Warner Bros Pictures Incorporated v Nelson* [1937] 1 KB 209, [1936] 3 All ER 160 (injunction preventing film star from working for X would not compel her to work for Y with whom she was already in contract because she could instead pursue another albeit less remunerative occupation). And see *Hill v CA Parsons & Co Ltd* [1972] Ch 305, [1971] 3 All ER 1345, CA: para. 32.12, post.

Chapter 8

Termination of contract and limitation of actions

1. Termination of contract

A) *By performance*

8.01 See paras. 7.06 et seq., ante.

B) *By agreement*

The obligations under any contract may be discharged and the contract terminated by mutual agreement, which mutual agreement to discharge may be found in either the original agreement or a subsequent agreement.

i) *By the original agreement*
The original agreement may provide for its discharge on the happening of some event other than performance, e.g. notice.[1] Thus, a sale or return transaction envisages that the transferee may not complete the purchase, but may instead discharge his obligations by returning the goods;[2] or a seller of goods may exercise an express power of resale;[3] or a contract for the supply of goods on instalment terms may provide for its automatic termination in the event of the transferee's insolvency;[4] and, of course, in a contract of hire-purchase the hirer has by definition the right to terminate the transaction at will.[5]

ii) *By subsequent agreement*
On ordinary principles, any duty created by one simple contract may be discharged by another simple contract.[6] If neither party has yet performed his obligations under the original contract, the mutual release of promises will provide the necessary consideration.[7] If, however, A has performed his side of the contract, any promise by A to release B from his obligations will usually[8] only amount to a binding contract if supported by some fresh

consideration (or under seal), in which event it is usually termed an '*accord and satisfaction*'.[9]

An agreement to discharge a contract which is supported by consideration does not generally have to be in any particular form, so that an oral agreement is effective to discharge a written contract. There are special rules where the original contract is one required by law to be evidenced in writing and the later agreement is intended not merely to terminate it (in which case the agreement of discharge may be oral) but is intended to vary it or substitute a fresh agreement.[10]

---

1 There are two ways in which a promise may be discharged by notice: (1) where there was actually just a series of offers, those not already accepted being revocable e.g. continuing guarantees (see para. 16.10 (6), post); (2) where a contractual promise is subject to a condition subsequent that it be terminable by notice (see para. 7.06, note 1, ante).
2 For sale or return transactions, see para. 13.08, post.
3 See Sale of Goods Act 1893, s. 48 (4): see para. 13.38, post.
4 See generally paras. 14.02 et seq., post.
5 See para. 14.03, post.
6 E.g. a novation: see para. 4.07, ante. For variation not amounting to a discharge, see para. 3.21, ante.
7 E.g. *Pearl Mill Ltd v Ivy Tannery Co Ltd* [1919] 1 KB 78, DC.
8 Except for cases falling within s. 62 of the Bills of Exchange Act 1882: see para. 20.30, post.
9 The *accord* is the agreement to discharge the existing obligation, and the *satisfaction* is the consideration necessary to support it. E.g. *bunge SA v kruse* [1977] 1 Lloyd's Rep. 492, CA.
10 See para. 2.14, ante.

C) *By breach*

8.02 See paras. 7.21 et seq., ante.

D) *Frustration*

If, between the time when a contract is made and when it is completed, an event occurs which destroys the basis of the contract, but which is not the fault of either party, the contract is said to be frustrated and, therefore, terminated. The parties are excused from further performance and neither is liable to the other in damages or otherwise.[1] Thus, in *Poussard v Spiers and Pond*:[2]

An actress, engaged to play a leading role in an operetta, was prevented through illness from taking up her role until a week after the season began. *Held:* the contract had terminated and no action lay against her for breach of contract.

In *Taylor v Caldwell:* [3]
An agreement to let a music-hall for four days was held to be terminated when the music-hall was burnt down before the first day for which it had been let.

If a contract is made on the basis that a certain event will take place, the contract will be discharged by frustration should that event not occur. In *Krell v Henry:* [4]

A hired out the use of a room to B so that B could watch the coronation procession of Edward VII. When the procession was cancelled, it was held that the contract between A and B terminated.

However, the doctrine has no application unless the happening of the event is assumed by both parties to be the *sole basis* of the contract. So,

a person, who hired a steamship for the purpose of seeing an intended royal naval review of Edward VII *and* for a day's cruise round the fleet, was held not entitled to refuse payment on ground that the review had been cancelled. [5]

Clearly, if further performance of a contract is rendered illegal, for example, because an Act of Parliament has been passed having this effect, the contract is frustrated. Similarly a contract with someone abroad is frustrated if war is declared and performance of the contract would involve trading with the enemy. Even temporary prohibition of a contract by lawful Government action may cause frustration of it. [6] Thus in *Metropolitan Water Board v Dick, Kerr & Co:* [7]

The Ministry of Munitions in the exercise of statutory powers conferred by the Defence of the Realm Act required contractors to cease work under a contract for the construction of a reservoir and to place their plant at the disposal of the Ministry of Munitions. By its terms the contract enabled the engineer to grant an extension of time for completion where the contractors had been unduly delayed or impeded; but the House of Lords *held:*
1. That this provision did not apply here; and
2. That the contract had ceased to be operative because the character and duration of the interruption would make it when resumed a completely different contract based on changed conditions.

If only a part of the contract becomes impossible of performance, that may not be regarded as going to the length of preventing substantial performance of the contract as a whole.[8]

Impossibility arising from a lawful act of Her Majesty's Government will excuse performance, e.g.

if the Government has requisitioned specific goods in the hands of the seller before the property in them has passed to the buyer, the seller will be excused from carrying out his contract.[9]

---

1. The doctrine of frustration does not apply to an event for which the parties have expressly and completely provided in their contract, as is commonly done in standard form contracts. Cf. *The Eugenia* [1964] 2 QB 226, [1964] 1 All ER 161, CA; *Tradax Export SA v Andre and Cie SA* [1976] 1 Lloyd's Rep. 416, CA; *V Berg & Son v Vanden Avenne-Izegem PVBA* [1977] 1 Lloyd's Rep. 499, CA.
2. (1876) 1 QBD 410. See also *Condor v The Barron Knights Ltd* [1966] 1 WLR 87; *Marshall v Harland and Wolff Ltd* [1972] 2 All ER 715, [1972] 1 WLR 899; *Hare v Murphy Bros* [1974] 3 All ER 940, CA. Contrast *Mount v Oldham Corpn* [1973] QB 309, [1973] 1 All ER 26, CA.
3. (1863) 3 B & S 826.
4. [1903] 2 KB 740, CA.
5. *Herne Bay Steam Boat Co v Hutton* [1903] 2 KB 683, CA.
6. For export/import licences, see para. 13.46, post.
7. [1918] 1 AC 119, HL.
8. *Eyre v Johnson* [1946] KB 481, [1946] 1 All ER 719. For sale of goods, see further para. 13.04, post.
9. *Re Shipton Anderson & Co and Harrison Bros & Co's Arbitration* [1915] 3 KB 676.

8.03 *Change not fundamental* Mere delay, difficulty or loss of profit will not of themselves discharge the parties from their contract. An uncontemplated turn of events making the contract more difficult to perform is not sufficient. In *Davis Contractors Ltd v Fareham UDC:*[1]

Contractors agreed to build 78 houses for the UDC within eight months. Owing to a severe labour shortage, completion of the work took twenty-two months and the cost of the work exceeded the contract price agreed. The contractors argued that the contract had been frustrated and therefore they were not confined to the contract price, but were entitled to a larger sum based on the extra costs incurred. *Held:* The contract had not been frustrated.

In *Tsakiroglou & Co Ltd v Noblee and Thorl GmbH:*[2]

A contract made in October 1956, provided for the sale and delivery of groundnuts from the Sudan to Germany, shipment to be made November/December 1956. The Suez Canal was closed from November 1956 to April 1957, and shipment via the Cape of Good Hope would have involved the sellers in additional expense. The sellers failed to deliver. *Held:* The sellers were liable for breach of contract. The contract had not been frustrated by the closing of the Suez Canal because the change of circumstances was not sufficiently fundamental.

---

1 [1956] AC 696, [1956] 2 All ER 145, HL. See also *Amalgamated Investment and Property Co Ltd v John Walker & Sons Ltd* [1976] 3 All ER 509, CA; *Exportelisa SA v Giuseppe & Figli Soc Coll* [1977] 2 Lloyd's Rep. 494.
2 [1962] AC 93, [1961] 2 All ER 179, HL. See also *The Eugenia* [1964] 2 QB 226, [1964] 1 All ER 161, CA; *Intertradex SA v Lesieur-Tourteaux SARL* [1977] 2 Lloyd's Rep. 146.

8.04   *Self-induced frustration*   It follows from the definition of frustration, given above, that if one party to a contract deliberately brings about the event which destroys the basis of the contract, the doctrine of frustration has no application: it is probable that the contract is automatically discharged, as with frustration (see below); but the party bringing about that event is then liable in damages.[1] Thus, in *Maritime National Fish Ltd v Ocean Trawlers Ltd:*[2]

The appellants chartered from the respondents a trawler which could only fish with an otter trawl, both parties knowing that an otter trawl could only be used with a Canadian Government licence. Subsequently, the Canadian Ministry of Fisheries allowed the appellants three licences for trawlers which could be used with otter trawls and the appellants applied these licences to three other trawlers that they owned. *Held:* The charter contract was not frustrated because it was the appellants' own action that prevented them using the chartered trawler with otter trawls. They were still liable for the contract charges.

---

1 See para. 7.22, ante.
2 [1935] AC 524, PC. See also *Hare v Murphy Bros* [1974] 3 All ER 940, CA. It is uncertain whether the negligent as distinct from deliberate action of a party which destroys the basis of the contract also prevents the operation of the doctrine of frustration. Whether such a licensing refusal is a frustrating event or self-induced may cause difficulty where one of the contracting parties is a government agency: see *C Czarnikow v Centrala Handlu Zagranicznego Rolimpex* [1977] 3 WLR 677, [1978] 1 All ER 81, CA; affd [1978] 3 WLR 274, HL.

8.05 *Contracts to transfer an interest in land* There is considerable uncertainty as to whether the doctrine of frustration has any application to leases. A number of cases do establish that if, during the continuance of a lease, the premises are burnt down by fire or requisitioned by the Government in wartime, the obligations under the lease, for example, the tenant's obligation to pay rent, continue.[1] The reason is that the basis of the contract is the *estate* in land and whatever happens, that continues to exist. However, two Law Lords *obiter* in *Cricklewood Property and Investment Trust Ltd v Leighton's Investment Trust Ltd*[2] expressed the view that if after a building lease, for say 99 years, was executed, the land is permanently zoned as open space, the lease would be discharged by frustration.

Similar difficulty exists in deciding whether frustration applies to contracts to *sell* interests in land;[3] whilst it has been held that a compulsory purchase notice did not frustrate a contract of sale,[4] the issue of whether it *could* do so should turn on the same principle as is involved with leases.

1 *Redmond v Dainton*, [1920] 2 KB 256.
2 [1945] AC 221, [1945] 1 All ER 252, HL.
3 For contracts for the sale of land, see chap. 12, post.
4 *Hillingdon Estates Co v Stonefield Estates Ltd* [1952] Ch 627, [1952] 1 All ER 853.

8.06 *Effect of frustration* The effect of frustration at common law was that the contract automatically came to an end and that any obligation that arose before the frustrating event remained enforceable.[1] However, in 1942 the House of Lords ruled that money paid for a consideration that had *wholly* failed was recoverable.[1] But this did not prevent injustices where one party had incurred expense in carrying out part of the contract. Now, the Law Reform (Frustrated Contracts) Act 1943, provides that upon frustration, except in so far as it is expressly provided for by the contract the following results ensue:

1. All sums paid or payable in pursuance of the contract before its discharge are recoverable or cease to be payable;
2. The court may make an allowance in respect of expenses incurred by the other party if it deems it just to do so, but only up to the amounts paid or payable before the frustrating event occurred;
3. Where one party has benefited by acts of partial performance done by the other party, the court may order him to pay such a sum as is reasonable in all the circumstances.

The Act has no application to contracts for the carriage of goods by sea, to voyage charter parties, to contracts of insurance, or to contracts for the sale of goods which perish before the risk passes to the buyer.[2]

1 *Fibrosa Spolka Akcyjna v Fairbairn Lawson Combe Barbour Ltd* [1943] AC 32, [1942] 2 All ER 122, HL.
2 See chaps. 13, 23, 26–27, post.

E) *Miscellaneous*

8.07   A contract may be terminated—

1. By merger. Where a judgment is obtained for breach of contract, the original cause of action is merged in the judgment and no further action is possible for breach of the contract, even if fresh damage results;[1]
2. By bankruptcy (unless the contract is one which the trustee in bankruptcy can and does adopt), so far as the contract gives rise to a debt provable in bankruptcy;[2]
3. If the contract is in writing, by an unauthorised alteration in a material part made by a party seeking to enforce the contract.[3]

1 *Conquer v Boot* [1928] 2 KB 336.
2 See Bankruptcy Act 1914, s. 54: see para. 33.32, post.
3 *Pattinson v Luckley* (1875) LR 10 Exch 330. As to alterations of negotiable instruments, see the Bills of Exchange Act 1882, s. 64: see para. 20.33, post.

2. Limitation of actions

8.08   The Limitation Act 1939 provides that as a general rule actions founded on simple contract or tort shall not be brought after the expiration of six years from the date on which the cause of action accrued, while an action on a contract under seal must be brought within twelve years of the accrual of the cause of action. A judgment debt is similarly barred after twelve years and interest on the judgment debt cannot be recovered more than six years after it accrued due.

If the damages claimed include damages for personal injuries, the time limit is in any event reduced to three years;[1] and to cover the position where the injuries resulting from a tort or breach of contract only become manifest after a considerable time-lag, the Limitation Acts allow an action to be brought despite the expiry of even that time-limit in certain circumstances. It is provided that the three years run from whichever is the later of the date of accrual of the cause of action, or of the plaintiff's (or his personal representative's) knowledge of his injury; and 'knowledge' is defined as 'first knowledge of the following facts':[2]

'(a) that the injury in question was significant, and
(b) that the injury was attributable in whole or in part to the act or omission which is alleged to constitute negligence, nuisance or breach of duty, and
(c) the identity of the defendant, and
(d) if it is alleged that the act or omission was that of a person other than the defendant, the identity of that person and the additional facts supporting the bringing of an action against the defendant

and knowledge that any act or omission did or did not, as a matter of law, involve negligence, nuisance or breach of duty is irrelevant.'

Moreover, notwithstanding that the plaintiff falls outside the time-limit as above extended, in a personal injury case the court is given power to override the limitation period and allow the action to proceed having regard to the relative prejudice which its decision would cause the parties.[3]

---

1 Limitation Act 1939, s. 2 A (as amended by the Limitation Act 1975).
2 Limitation Act 1939, s. 2 A (6) (as amended).
3 Ibid., s. 2 D.

8.09 *Parties under disability* The running of time may be suspended if the parties are under certain disabilities. If a plaintiff, when the cause of action arises, is a minor, or is of unsound mind;[1] the period of limitation does not begin to run against him until he ceases to be under such disability or he dies, whichever event first occurs.[2] But where the time has once begun to run, no subsequent disability i.e. becoming of unsound mind, will suspend the operation of the statute.[3] If there are several joint creditors, the disability of some will not prevent time running against the others.

---

1 For these disabilities, see further paras. 2.15–2.21, ante.
2 Limitation Act 1939, ss. 22 (as amended), 31 (2). In claims for personal injury, there is no extension of time at all for a minor if he was 'in the custody of a parent' at the time the cause of action accrued. The word 'custody'

denotes a state of fact and it is irrelevant that such custody is inadequately exercised: *Todd v Davison* [1972] AC 392, [1971] 1 All ER 994, HL.
3 *Homfray v Scroope* (1849) 13 QB 509, 512. And see the Limitation Act 1939, s. 22, proviso (a).

8.10 *Concealed fraud or mistake* If the action is based on fraud, or the right of action has been concealed by fraud, or is for relief from the consequences of a mistake, the period of limitation does not begin to run until the plaintiff has discovered the fraud or the mistake or could with reasonable diligence have discovered it.[1] 'Fraud' in relation to concealment has a somewhat wider meaning than the fraud which would give rise to a separate cause of action. It means conduct on the part of the defendant which hides from the plaintiff his cause of action so that it would be inequitable for the defendant to rely on the lapse of time as a bar to the claim. Thus in *Archer v Moss:*[2]

> The defendant developer agreed to build a house for the plaintiff on a concrete raft foundation. Eight years later the plaintiff discovered that the foundation was not as specified in the contract and that the house was unsafe. *Held:* the plaintiff was entitled to sue because his right of action had been concealed by the defendant's fraud in covering up the bad work so that it might not be discovered for a long time.

Where mistake is relied on, it must be an essential ingredient in the action.[3]

1 Limitation Act 1939, s. 26.
2 [1971] 1 QB 406, [1971] 1 All ER 747, CA. See also *Beaman v ARTS Ltd* [1949] 1 KB 550, [1949] 1 All ER 465, and *King v Victor Parsons & Co* [1973] 1 All ER 206, [1973] 1 WLR 29, CA.
3 *Phillips-Higgins v Harper* [1954] 1 QB 411, [1954] 2 All ER 51, CA.

8.11 *Revival of the remedy*
Although the right of action is already barred by lapse of time, it may be revived by acknowledgement of the debt, or by (what is much the same) part payment provided it is clearly referable to the contract. The effect of such revival is that, 'the right shall be deemed to have accrued on and not before the date of the acknowledgement or the last payment'.[1] However, neither an acknowledgement nor a part payment is effective to revive a cause of action unless it concerns a 'debt or other liquidated pecuniary sum', so the debt must be quantified in figures or it must be liquidated in the sense that it is capable of assessment

by calculation or by extrinsic evidence without further agreement of the parties. In *Good v Parry*:[2]

A landlord who had received no rent from a tenant of certain premises since 1951, claimed in 1962 for arrears of rent as from 1951. A letter had been sent to the landlord in 1957, signed by the tenant's agent, saying: 'the question of outstanding rent can be settled as a separate agreement as soon as you present your account'. *Held:* the letter was merely an admission that there might be some justified claim, but it was not an acknowledgement of a liquidated debt. The landlord's claim for arrears of rent was statute-barred except for arrears due from the last six years.

An acknowledgement must be in writing signed by the debtor or his agent and must be made to the creditor or his agent.[3] A payment made before the period of limitation has expired binds all persons liable for the debt, but a payment made after the expiration of the period binds only the person making the payment and his assigns.[4] An acknowledgement or payment by one of several personal representatives binds the estate.[5]

a) *Acknowledgements* The acknowledgement must be made by the debtor or his agent before the action is brought to the creditor or his agent,[3] but it may be sufficient if it is contained in a balance sheet which a company sends to a creditor who is also a shareholder.[6] A bare admission of liability is sufficient even if coupled with a refusal or a conditional offer to pay—it need not amount to an implied promise to pay.[7]

b) *Part payment* A payment to revive a debt must be clearly referable to the contract. If a debtor owes his creditor several distinct debts, and, in making a payment to the creditor, does not appropriate it to any particular debt, the appropriation by the creditor towards a statute-barred debt does not revive his right of action for the balance of that debt. But, a payment of part of the amount owing on a current account and made 'generally on account' starts time running afresh on the whole amount outstanding because the balance is a single debt.[8]

The Act of 1939 does not affect actions for which a period of limitation is prescribed by any other enactment.[9] The Crown, public authorities, and the corporations created under nationalization Acts are now in the same position as other persons or bodies.[10]

---

1 Limitation Act 1939, s. 23 (4).
2 [1963] 2 QB 418, [1963] 2 All ER 59.
3 Limitation Act 1939, s. 24. It can only bind a joint debtor if the acknowledgor acted as his agent: ibid., s. 25 (5), (8).

4 Ibid., s. 25 (6), (8).
5 Ibid., s. 25 (7).
6 *Ledingham v Bermejo Estancia Co Ltd* [1947] 1 All ER 749; *Jones v Bellegrove Properties Ltd* [1949] 2 KB 700, [1949] 2 All ER 198, CA. But it depends on the circumstances: *Consolidated Agencies Ltd v Bertram Ltd* [1965] AC 470, [1964] 3 All ER 282, PC; *Re Gee & Co (Woolwich) Ltd* [1975] Ch 52, [1974] 1 All ER 1149. A director cannot make an acknowledgement to himself so as to bind the company: *Re Coliseum (Barrow) Ltd* [1930] 2 Ch 44, [1930] All ER Rep. 221. Nor will the auditors' certificate be an acknowledgement to him: *Re Transplanters (Holding Co) Ltd* [1958] 2 All ER 711, [1958] 1 WLR 822.
7 But see *Re Flynn (No. 2)* [1969] 2 Ch 403, [1969] 2 All ER 557.
8 *Re Footman Bower & Co Ltd* [1961] Ch 443, [1961] 2 All ER 161. The balance is regarded as a single and undirected debt although, under the rule in *Devaynes v Noble, Clayton's Case* (para. 7.17, ante) a payment of part of the amount due on a current account has to be appropriated to the earliest outstanding debt which is not statute-barred.
9 Limitation Act 1939, s. 32.
10 Law Reform (Limitation of Actions, etc.) Act 1954, ss. 1, 5.

Chapter 9

Foreign law

1. Proper law of the contract

Conflict of laws

9.01 A dispute sometimes arises as to what is to be the law by which a contract or some part of it is to be governed. The uncertainty may be brought about by a variety of causes: for instance, the contract may be entered into in one country with a view to its being wholly or partly performed in another, and the laws of the two countries may materially differ as to the validity or effect of one or more stipulations in the contract.

It is impossible either to exhaust the circumstances which may give rise to the dispute or to lay down hard and fast rules for the determination of any particular case, but all the authorities agree that the point to be ascertained is:

> What was or must be presumed to have been the intention of the parties with respect to the system of law which is to govern the contract?

Choice of laws clause The most satisfactory evidence of the intention of the parties is, of course, that appearing on the face of the contract, and it is only where this leaves the question in doubt that there is any occasion to resort to other considerations. If the parties to a contract expressly agree that it is to be governed by Ruritanian law, then provided that the intention so expressed is bona fide and legal, Ruritanian law is 'the proper law of the contract', irrespective of whether the contract or the parties to it have any connection with Ruritania.[1]

Further, if instead of a contract expressly providing that it should be governed by the law of Ruritania, it states that the courts of Ruritania are to have jurisdiction in any dispute arising out of the contract or that any disputes are to be settled by arbitration in Ruritania, Ruritanian law may still be 'the proper law of the contract'. In *Hamlyn Co v Talisker Distillery*:[2]

A contract was entered into in England between parties residing in England and Scotland respectively, but was mainly to be performed in Scotland, the House of Lords largely based their judgment upon the following clause in the contract:

'Should any dispute arise out of this contract the same to be settled by two members of the London Corn Exchange or their umpire in the usual way'.

This was considered to be a clear indication that the parties contemplated that the contract should be interpreted according to the rules of English law. English law was the proper law of the contract.

However, the House of Lords has recently made it clear that any presumption arising from an arbitration clause may be rebutted, e.g. by evidence that the contract is more closely connected with some country other than the one where arbitration is to take place.[3]

---

1 *Vita Food Products Incorporated v Unus Shipping Co* [1939] AC 277, [1939] 1 All ER 513.
2 [1894] AC 202. Followed in *NV Kwik Hoo Tong Handel Maatschappij v James Finlay and Co Ltd* [1927] AC 604, and *Tzortzis v Monark Line A/B* [1968] 1 All ER 949, [1968] 1 WLR 406, CA.
3 *Compagnie d'Armement Maritime SA v Compagnie Tunisienne de Navigation SA* [1971] AC 572, [1970] 3 All ER 71, HL.

9.02 *Other factors*[1] Where the doubt is not removed by the language of the contract, the broad rule is that the court will apply the system of law with which the contract, on an objective assessment, has its closest and most real connection.[2] This may be the legal system prevailing in the place where the contract is made.[3] It may give way to the law of the place where the contract is to be performed (*lex loci solutionis*) if *both* parties have to perform their obligations in a country other than that where the contract is made.[4] This may not be so, however, where each party has to perform his obligations in different countries. In the case of *Jacobs v Credit Lyonnais:*[5]

A contract was made in England by a French company carrying on business in England to sell a quantity of esparto to another company carrying on business in England. The esparto was to be shipped from Algeria but payment was to be made in England. Owing to an insurrection in Algeria and the consequent military operations, the collection and transport of this particular merchandise was prevented, at a time when the contract had not been wholly completed, thereby excusing further performance according to the French law of 'force majeure'.

It was, however, decided that the proper law of the contract was English, and by English law the obligation to deliver being absolute the subsequent impossibility afforded no defence to an action for damages. Conveyances of immovables, i.e. interests in land, are governed by the lex situs, the system of the country where they are located, but the proper law of a contract to convey immovables may be chosen in the ordinary way, provided it does not conflict with the lex situs.[6]

In regard to formalities compliance with the lex loci contractus (the place of contracting) as distinct from the proper law, may suffice for contracts generally, this being an alternative to compliance with the formal requirements of the proper law.[7]

The foregoing rules for ascertaining the proper law of the contract, i.e. the law by which the parties intended it to be governed, may apply to cases where a Sovereign State is a party to the contract, although due weight must be given to that circumstance. Accordingly where a loan was issued by the British Government in the United States, the rights and obligations under the contract were held to be governed by American law, because the proper inference from the terms of the loan and the relevant surrounding circumstances was that the parties intended that should be so.[8]

---

1 It is not now correct to term these presumptions. See Cheshire *Private International Law* (9th edn) 216 citing *Coast Lines v Hudig and Veder Chartering NV* [1972] 2 QB 34, [1972] 1 All ER 451.

2 *Bonython v Commonwealth of Australia* [1951] AC 201, PC; *James Miller & Partners Ltd v Whitworth Street Estates Ltd* [1970] AC 583, [1970] 1 All ER 796, HL; *Offshore International v Banco Central SA* [1976] 3 All ER 749, [1977] 1 WLR 399.

3 *Peninsular and Oriental Steam Navigation Co v Shand* (1865) 3 Moo. PCCNS 272.

4 *Benaim & Co v Debano* [1924] AC 514, [1924] All ER Rep. 103.

5 (1884) 12 QBD 589.

6 See *Cheshire* op. cit. pp. 511–512.

7 See *Cheshire* op. cit. pp. 225–226.

8 *R v International Trustee* [1937] AC 500, [1937] 2 All ER 164.

9.03   Where the proper law of a contract is the law of a part of the United Kingdom only because it has been chosen by the parties but apart from that would be the law of some other country, then those sections of the Unfair Contract Terms Act 1977 which govern the avoidance of liability for negligence, contractual liability, unreasonable indemnity clauses and liability arising from the sale and supply of goods do not operate as part of the proper law. Where, however, a contract term selects the law of some other country and it appears to the court that the choice was made to evade the Act or that one of the parties who was habitually resident in the United Kingdom dealt as a consumer and the essential steps necessary for the making of the contract were taken there then the Act applies.[1]

The Act does not apply to 'international supply contracts'. These are contracts for the sale of or transfer of possession or ownership in goods where the places of business of the parties, or if they have none their habitual residences, are in the territories of different states. The Channel Islands and the Isle of Man are different states from the United Kingdom for this purpose. Moreover, either the goods must at the time of the conclusion of the contract be in course of carriage or about to be carried from the territory of one state to another or the acts constituting offer and acceptance must have been done in the territories of different states or the contract must provide for the goods to be delivered to the territory of a state other than that within whose territory those acts were done.[2]

---

1 Unfair Contract Terms Act 1977, s. 27. See generally para. 3.15, ante.
2 Ibid., s. 26.

---

2. Illegality

9.04 If a contract is illegal by the proper law, the English courts will refuse to enforce it.[1] Furthermore, it seems that the English courts will refuse to enforce a contract which is illegal by the law of the country where performance is to take place, even though it is valid by the proper law. This is certainly so if the proper law of the contract is English. Thus in *Ralli Brothers v Compania Naviera Sota y Aznar*:[2]

> An English firm chartered a Spanish ship to çarry jute from India to Spain, freight payable in part in pesetas in Barcelona. After the contract was made, Spanish law prohibited payment of freight at more than a certain fixed sum which was below the freight charges provided for in this contract. *Held:* The English courts could not allow a claim for any excess over the freight permitted by Spanish law, although the proper law of the contract was English.

Probably, if a contract is legal by the proper law of the contract, it will be upheld though its terms are illegal by the lex loci contractus.[3]

However, whatever the proper law of a contract, an English court will not enforce it if it contravenes certain fundamental principles of justice and morality as accepted by the common law. Thus, a contract which prejudices the relations of the United Kingdom with other countries[4] or a champertous agreement[5] will not be upheld by the English courts although the proper law may regard the contract as valid. Moreover, an English court will not enforce a contract if it is contrary to an English Act of Parliament if the Act's provisions were intended to have extra-territorial effect.[6] Statutes concerning wagering contracts and the Sale of Goods Act have no effect on contracts where the proper law is not English.[7]

---

1 *Kahler v Midland Bank Ltd* [1950] AC 24, [1949] 2 All ER 621.
2 [1920] 2 KB 287. See also *Regazzoni v KC Sethia (1944) Ltd* [1958] AC 301, [1957] 3 All ER 286.
3 *Re Missouri SS Co* (1889) 42 ChD 321.
4 *Regazzoni v KC Sethia (1944) Ltd* [1958] AC 301, [1957] 3 All ER 286. See *Cheshire* op. cit., pp. 148–159.
5 *Grell v Levy* (1864) 16 CB (NS) 73.
6 *Boissevain v Weil* [1950] AC 327, [1950] 1 All ER 728.
7 *Saxby v Fulton* [1909] 2 KB 208.

---

3. The lex fori

9.05 Whatever law governs the interpretation of the contract, anything which relates to the remedy to be enforced must be determined by the lex fori, the law of the place where proceedings on the contract are brought. The practice of those courts must be followed, their rules as to the admissibility of evidence will apply, and so will any provision which bars the remedy, such as the Limitation Act 1939.[1] If the remedy is barred by lapse of time according to the law of the country in which enforcement is sought, it does not matter that it is not so barred by the proper law.[1] Where parties accepted Scottish arbitration, Scottish law was the lex fori and therefore governed the arbitration so that, for example, the arbiter then had no jurisdiction to state a case for the High Court.[2]

Conversely, an action on a foreign contract may be maintained here, even though the time has expired for enforcing the contract in the foreign country, provided that the period laid down by the English statute has not been exceeded.[3] It would be otherwise if the foreign statute destroyed the debt as well as the remedy.[3] If an action is brought in England on a contract which by English law has to be evidenced in writing (e.g. a contract relating to land), there must be a sufficient note or memorandum of the contract whatever is the proper law of the contract.[4]

Foreign law will not be judicially noticed in the English courts.[5] It must be proved, as a fact, by the evidence of a competent witness;[6] until the contrary be proved, the general law of a foreign State is presumed to be the same as the English law.[7] But questions of foreign law must be decided by the judge and not by a jury.[8]

---

1 *Don v Lippmann* (1838) 5 Cl & F 1.
2 *James Miller & Partners Ltd v Whitworth Street Estates Ltd* [1970] AC 583, [1970] 1 All ER 796, HL. See now Administration of Justice (Scotland) Act 1972, s. 3.
3 *Harris v Quine* (1869) LR 4 QB 653.
4 *Leroux v Brown* (1852) 12 CB 801.
5 As to Common Market Law see European Communities Act 1972, s. 3.
6 Civil Evidence Act 1972, s. 4.
7 *Dynamit Aktiengesellschaft v Rio Tinto Co* [1918] AC 260 at 292 et seq.
8 Judicature Act 1925, s. 102; County Courts Act 1959, s. 97.

---

4. Foreign judgments

Registration and enforcement

9.06 Judgments given in the superior courts of foreign or Commonwealth countries, which accord substantial reciprocity of treatment to judgments given in the superior courts of the United Kingdom, can be registered as of right and enforced under the provisions of Part I of the Foreign Judgments (Reciprocal Enforcement) Act 1933 in cases where the Act has been extended by Order in Council to the country in which the judgment was obtained.[1] The judgment must be final and conclusive as between the parties and must be for a sum of money, not being a sum payable for taxes or in respect of a fine or other penalty. If the requirements of the Act are satisfied, the High Court must, on the application of the judgment creditor[2] made within six years of the date of the judgment, order it to be registered.

On registration the judgment will for the purposes of execution (or, e.g., as the basis of a bankruptcy petition) be of the same force and effect as if it had been originally given in the registering court and entered on the date of registration; and the sum for which the judgment is registered will carry interest.

The registration of a foreign judgment will be set aside on the application of any party against whom it may be enforced on the following grounds:

1. The judgment is not one to which the Act applies; or
2. The court pronouncing judgment had no jurisdiction over the defendant; or
3. The judgment debtor, being the defendant before the foreign court, did not receive notice of the proceedings in sufficient time to enable him to appear and he did not appear; or
4. The judgment was obtained by a fraud on the court;[3] or
5. The enforcement of the judgment would be contrary to public policy;[4] or
6. The rights under the judgment are not vested in the person who applied for registration.

Registration *may* be set aside if the English court is satisfied that the matter had already been the subject of a final judgment of a competent court. Registration of a foreign judgment is only conclusive as to the question litigated in the foreign court. Hence if that question was procedural this does not prevent the substantive merits of the case being litigated in an English court.[5]

A foreign judgment which can be registered cannot be enforced by action.[6]

---

1 Earlier Acts, the Judgments Extension Act 1868, and the Administration of Justice Act 1920, contain limited provisions for the registration of judgments of the Courts of Scotland, Northern Ireland, and the Commonwealth. The 1933 Act will eventually supersede the 1920 Act, which applies to the Commonwealth, since the 1933 Act is being extended to further countries.
2 Or any person in whom the rights under the judgment have become vested (s. 11).
3 See, e.g., *Syal v Heyward* [1948] 2 KB 443, [1948] 2 All ER 576.
4 Foreign Judgments (Reciprocal Enforcement) Act 1933, s. 4. A mere technical defect in the judgment such as failure to set out as required by the lex fori the steps taken to bring the action to the notice of the defendant will not render the foreign judgment a nullity nor is the award of a compensatory sum which is not a fine or other penalty contrary to public policy: *SA Consortium General Textiles v Sun and Sand Agencies* [1978] 2 WLR 1.
5 Ibid., s. 8, and *Black-Clawson v Papierwerke Waldhof-Aschaffenburg Aktiengesellschaft* [1975] AC 591, [1975] 1 All ER 810, HL.
6 Ibid., s. 6. Special provision has been made by the European Communities (Enforcement of Community Judgments) Order 1972 for the registration and enforcement of the judgments of tribunals of the EEC. This does not apply to courts of the member states.

Enforcement by action

9.07 Except in cases where the enforcement of foreign judgments by action is prohibited by the Foreign Judgments (Reciprocal Enforcement) Act 1933 because it is registrable under that Act, any *final* judgment of a foreign, Commonwealth or colonial court, which has *jurisdiction* over the subject-matter and the parties will be acted on here as conclusive of any matter of law or fact thereby decided provided the judgment was for a definite sum. It may also be enforced by action here unless the foreign proceedings are in conflict with English views of natural justice,[1] or the judgment was obtained by fraud.[2]

In actions *in personam* the courts of this country will treat the defendant as subject to the jurisdiction of a foreign court in the following cases:

1. Where he was present in the foreign country when the action began;

2. Where he has voluntarily submitted to the jurisdiction of the foreign court by appearing as plaintiff, or by entering an appearance, or by agreeing expressly or perhaps impliedly to submit to its jurisdiction.[3]

But possession of property abroad is not sufficient to give the foreign court jurisdiction in a personal action.[4] In actions *in rem*, jurisdiction normally belongs to the courts of the country where the *res* is situated but no foreign judgment relating to immovables (land) abroad will be enforced in England.[5]

The fraud of the plaintiff in obtaining the judgment may be pleaded as a defence to an action brought on the foreign judgment, even though the defendant relied on this in the foreign proceedings and the merits of the foreign judgment are therefore being reopened.[6]

An English court will also grant an injunction restraining a person who is subject to its jurisdiction from enforcing a judgment of a foreign court which he has obtained by breach of contract or fraud. In doing so the English court does not set aside the judgment or purport to interfere with the foreign court; such injunction is directed only against the *person* over whom the English court has jurisdiction.[7]

It was once a general rule that English courts would only give judgment in sterling.[8] This was first abandoned for plaintiffs living in a Common Market country[9] and then for cases where the proper law, the money of account measuring the obligation, and the money of payment all were of the same country.[10] The Administration of Justice Act 1977 repealed a number of statutory provisions which contemplated judgment being in sterling.[11]

Sovereign immunity It is doubtful how far the general rule that a foreign sovereign is immune from suit in English courts, except when there is submission to the jurisdiction, is subject to exception in commercial transactions.[12]

---

1 *Pemberton v Hughes* [1899] 1 Ch 781. A mere irregularity in procedure will not affect the validity of the foreign judgment.
2 *Vadala v Lawes* (1890) 25 QBD 310.
3 *Emanuel v Symon* [1908] 1 KB 302 at 309, per Buckley LJ. See Cheshire *Private International Law* (9th edn), 636–637.
4 *Emanuel v Symon* [1908] 1 KB 302. See *Cheshire* pp. 641–642.
5 See *Cheshire* p. 645.
6 *Godard v Gray* (1871) LR 6 QB 139; and see *Syal v Heyward* [1948] 2 KB 443, [1948] 2 All ER 576.
7 *Ellerman Lines v Read* [1928] 2 KB 144.
8 *Re United Railways of Havana and Regla Warehouses Ltd* [1961] AC 1007, [1960] 2 All ER 332.
9 *Schorsch Meier GmbH v Hennin* [1975] QB 416, [1975] 1 All ER 152, CA.
10 *Miliangos v George Frank (Textiles) Ltd* [1976] AC 443, [1975] 3 All ER 801, HL.
11 S. 4.
12 *Trendtex Trading Corpn v Central Bank of Nigeria* [1977] QB 529, [1977] 1 All ER 881.

Part II

Agency and partnership

Chapter 10

Agency

1. Introductory

10.01 An agent is 'he who is employed to do anything in the place of another',[1] and the person who employs him is called the principal. Most frequently, an agent, A, is employed for the purpose of bringing about a contract between his principal, P, and another person, usually referred to as the third party, T. In the language of commerce a person who buys goods and resells them is frequently described as an agent, e.g. a motor dealer may be described as sole agent for a particular make of car, but that does not necessarily mean that he is acting in *law* as agent for the manufacturer. In practice, such a dealer buys the cars from the manufacturer and sells on his own account to a purchaser so that he is selling not as an agent at all but as his own principal. An agent may or may not be a servant of the principal, and this distinction may have important results in considering how far the agent is entitled to be given work to enable him to earn his commission and how far is he entitled to notice.[2] In commerce, an agent who is not an employee may well belong to one of several well-known categories: these categories, together with the chief variations in their legal characteristics, will be discussed later.[3]

Capacity Those who do not have legal capacity to make contracts[4] cannot get rid of their disabilities by the employment of agents, but if, for example, a minor can lawfully do an act on his own behalf, so as to bind himself e.g. in a contract for necessaries, he can instead appoint an agent to do it for him.[5] Moreover, incapacity to contract for himself will not prevent a person from being appointed agent to contract for another. Thus, a minor can make a contract on behalf of an adult principal for the purchase of non-necessary goods though he could not validly make such a contract for himself.

1 Comyns' Digest, Attorney A.
2 See *Bauman v Hulton Press* [1952] 2 All ER 1121, para. 32.07, post.
3 Paras. 10.29, et seq., post.
4 See paras. 2.15, et seq., ante.
5 *G(A) v G(T)* [1970] 3 All ER 546 at 549 per Lord Denning MR.

2. The principal/agent relationship

1. Appointment of agents

a) BY CONTRACT OF AGENCY

10.02 A contract of agency created before A purports to act on behalf of P is by far the most common way in which the relationship of principal and agent comes into existence. Such a contract between P and A may be created expressly or by implication.

a) Express contract of agency Some such contracts are elaborate affairs, often being drawn on a standard form,[1] e.g. partnership agreements,[2] franchise agreements. However, as a rule, no formal mode of appointment is required; in fact, the vast majority of agencies are created verbally, often without any detailed arrangement at all, and unless these were recognised by law, mercantile business could hardly proceed. The agent does not have to be appointed in writing merely because his task is to bring about a contract which itself has to be evidenced in writing such as a contract for the sale of land.[3] But if the agent is to have authority to contract under seal (e.g. to execute a conveyance), the authority must also be under seal, and it is then called a power of attorney, though the want of a deed will be of no avail as a defence to a principal who is present and allows the agent to enter into the contract for him.[4]

b) Implied contract of agency There are many situations in commerce where, notwithstanding that the parties have not gone to the trouble of entering into an express contract of agency, one may be implied.[5] Thus, Lord Pearson in *Garnac Grain Co v HM Faure and Fairclough Ltd*[6] said:

'They will be held to have consented if they have agreed to what amounts in law to such a relationship, even if they do not recognise it themselves and even if they profess to disclaim it. ... Primarily one looks to what they said and did at the date of the alleged creation of the agency. Earlier words and conduct may afford evidence of a course of dealing in existence at that time and may be taken into account more generally as historical background'.

The issue turns upon the presumed intention of P and A, a

criterion which may cause some uncertainty and difficulty—as witness the relationship between the dealer and the financier in a financed instalment credit transaction.[7]

---

1 For standard-form contracts generally, see para. 3.13, ante.
2 For partnership, see chap. 11.
3 *Heard v Pilley* (1869) 4 Ch App 548. For sales of land see chap. 12.
4 *Ball v Dunsterville* (1791) 4 Term Rep. 313.
5 E.g. *Hely-Hutchinson v Brayhead* [1968] 1 QB 549, [1967] 3 All ER 98, CA; *Townsend Carriers v Pfizer* (1977) 33 P & CR 361.
6 [1968] AC 1130 at 1137; [1967] 2 All ER 353 at 358, HL.
7 See *Branwhite v Worcester Finance Ltd* [1969] AC 552, [1968] 3 All ER 104, HL. For the intervention of statute see paras. 10.33, 14.47–14.49, post.

---

b) BY ESTOPPEL

10.03 Whilst there may be no contract of agency between P and A, P may have represented to T that such a contract of agency existed. Such a representation will not affect the relationship between P and A being here considered, but it will estop P from denying as against T that A was his agent,[1] thus enabling A to bind P to a contract with T.[2]

---

1 For estoppel, see para. 2.05, ante.
2 See para. 10.19, post.

---

c) BY RATIFICATION

10.04 Although there may be no contract of agency in existence at the time when the 'agent' purports to contract on behalf of his 'principal' with T, when the lack of authority is discovered, P may 'ratify' A's act either expressly or by implication. Perhaps the commonest situation of ratification is where an already-appointed agent 'accidentally' exceeds his authority, and P subsequently impliedly ratifies when, with knowledge of this excess, he performs part of the agreement negotiated with T.

However, ratification is only possible if aertain conditions are satisfied:

1. The agent in making the contract must purport to act as an agent and name or clearly identify his principal—a contract made by someone in his own name with an undeclared intention to make it on behalf of another, for whom he then had no authority to act, cannot be ratified.[1]
2. The principal must be in existence and competent to make the contract when the contract is made. Thus—

A principal who was an enemy alien when the contract was made cannot ratify it after he ceases to be an enemy alien.[2]

Similarly, a company cannot adopt or ratify a contract entered into on its behalf before the company was incorporated;[3] but it may make a new contract to the same effect, unless such contract would be ultra vires.[4]

3. Generally, a principal can only ratify if, at the time of ratification, he could lawfully do the act himself. Thus, in *Grover and Grover Ltd v Mathews*:[5]

A contract of fire insurance had been taken out by A on P's behalf (without authority) and P purported to ratify this contract *after* a fire had taken place. *Held:* the purported ratification was ineffective.

Apart from this point ratification must be either within any time fixed for ratification or, if none, within a reasonable time.

4. Void contracts cannot be ratified. Therefore a company cannot ratify a contract purported to have been made on its behalf if that contract was then ultra vires the company.[4] But an issue of shares intra vires the company, though voidable because made by the directors for improper motives, is ratifiable by the company.[6]

5. Where ratifying, the principal must either have full knowledge of the facts or be shown to have adopted the agent's acts, whatever they were.[7]

Effect of ratification If a contract is properly ratified, the ratification dates back to the time when the act was done. In consequence, it has been held that where T's offer is unconditionally accepted without authority by A, P may ratify even after T has purported to revoke his offer.[8] There is authority for saying that this is not so, if A's acceptance is made expressly or impliedly subject to ratification[9] or if A and T by mutual consent cancel the transaction before P ratifies;[10] or if a third party has acquired vested proprietary rights prior to ratification;[11] or to enable P to sue for breach occurring before ratification.[12]

It may be added that where an agent makes a contract in the name of his principal, but with the intention of fraudulently taking the benefit of the contract for himself, the principal may nevertheless ratify and enforce the contract as against the other parties to it.[13]

---

1 *Keighley, Maxsted & Co v Durant* [1901] AC 240, HL.
2 *Boston Deep Sea Fishing and Ice Co Ltd v Farnham* [1957] 3 All ER 204, [1957] 1 WLR 1051.
3 *Kelner v Baxter* (1866) LR 2 CP 174. The European Communities Act 1972,

s. 9 (2), makes the promoter liable on the contract, but does not make the company liable.

4 *Ashbury Railway Carriage and Iron Co v Riche* (1875) LR 7 HL 653: see further para. 2.22, ante.

5 [1910] 2 KB 401. But see the Marine Insurance Act 1906, s. 86: para. 27.09, post.

6 *Bamford v Bamford* [1970] Ch 212, [1969] 1 All ER 969, CA.

7 *Marsh v Joseph* [1897] 1 Ch 213.

8 *Bolton Partners v Lambert* (1889) 41 ChD 295, CA.

9 *Watson v Davies* [1931] 1 Ch 455; *Warehousing and Forwarding Co of East Africa Ltd v Jafferali and Sons Ltd* [1964] AC 1, [1963] 3 All ER 571, PC.

10 *Walter v James* (1871) LR 6 Exch 124 (see para. 7.17, ante).

11 *Bird v Brown* (1850) 4 Exch 124.

12 *Kidderminster Corpn v Hardwick* (1873) LR 9 Exch 13. But are these last three propositions reconcilable with the later decision in *Bolton Partners v Lambert* (1889) 41 ChD 295?

13 *Re Tiedemann and Ledermann Frères* [1899] 2 QB 66.

---

d) OF NECESSITY

10.05 In an emergency, A may have power to bind P without prior authority, and even though P refuses to ratify A's actions. In *Great Northern Rly Co v Swaffield*:[1]

> The railway company incurred the expense of stabling a horse after it had been carried to its destination and there was no one to receive it. Although the company had no express or implied authority to incur such expense, it was entitled to claim an indemnity from the owner of the horse as an agent of necessity.

No one may claim to be an agent of necessity unless it is impossible or impracticable to communicate with the principal in order to obtain his instructions.[2] In any case, any action taken must be reasonably necessary in the circumstances and taken in good faith in the interests[3] of the principal.[4] With modern communications, it may be thought that there are likely to be relatively few circumstances where the doctrine of agency of necessity may be operative.

---

1 (1874) LR 9 Exch 132.

2 *Springer v Great Western Rly Co* [1921] 1 KB 257.

3 *Prager v Blatspiel, Stamp and Heacock Ltd* [1924] 1 KB 566, [1924] All ER Rep. 524.

4 *Sachs v Miklos* [1948] KB 23, [1948] 1 All ER 67, CA.

---

e) BY COHABITATION

10.06 At common law, a husband might be liable for debts contracted by his wife under one or more of three cases:[1]

1. She may have been expressly or impliedly authorised by him to contract on his behalf (see ante).
2. He may have held her out to a particular tradesman as having authority to pledge his credit (see ante, agency by estoppel).
3. If she was deserted by her husband without means she used to be entitled, as a so-called 'agent of necessity', to pledge his credit for necessaries.

This third category was rendered unnecessary by social security legislation and maintenance rights for deserted wives; and accordingly it was abolished in 1970.[2]

---

1 Report on Financial Provisions in Matrimonial Proceedings (Law Com. 25) para. 108.
2 Matrimonial Proceedings and Property Act 1970, s. 41 (1).

---

2. Termination of agency

10.07   This may occur either by the act of the parties themselves or by operation of law.

a) BY ACT OF THE PARTIES

Apart from termination by mutual agreement,[1] an agency may as a general rule, be terminated by the unilateral action of either party. Thus, irrespective of any express words in the agency contract, P can revoke A's authority so that any further acts of A, purporting to be done on P's behalf, will render A liable to third parties for pretending to have an authority that has been withdrawn from him, i.e. for *breach of warranty of authority*;[2] and A cannot thereafter do acts to earn commission under the contract of agency now terminated.[3] But it must be noted that the principal may well be liable to T on contracts entered into on his behalf after the termination of the agency, unless he has caused notice of such termination to reach third parties, who may act on the faith of the previous authority, until such a time has elapsed or such circumstances have happened, as would lead a reasonable man to infer that the agent's authority had been countermanded. This liability will be based on the principle of estoppel.

So, in the case of a partnership (which is in many respects a kind of agency), the partner who leaves the firm but remains ostensibly a member, is liable for debts incurred after his retirement.[4]

However, although either party to an agency contract may unilaterally bring it to an end, such action may well be a breach of the agency contract for which damages are payable. Thus, if the agent is engaged for a fixed period, revocation of his authority before the end of that period is a breach.[5]

If the agent is a salaried servant of the principal he will have an implied right to reasonable notice in the absence of agreement to the contrary.[6] Even where the agent is not a servant of the principal, a term *may* be implied that he is entitled to notice and therefore unilateral revocation of his authority is a breach of contract. In *Martin-Baker Aircraft Co Ltd v Canadian Flight Equipment Ltd*:[7]

> The plaintiff appointed M sole selling agent of their products. The agreement imposed various duties on M but contained no provision for determination except in the case of misconduct. *Held:* the agreement was neither terminable summarily nor permanent but could be terminated by reasonable notice which in the particular case meant twelve months' notice. The contract was analogous to a master-servant contract because M was a sole selling agent, had to expend much time and money, and was subject to restrictions as to sale of other persons' goods.

A limit to this power of revocation at any time is found where an '*interest* has been coupled with an authority'; e.g. when the principal has entered into an agreement to give something to a person, and has appointed the latter an agent to collect and secure it for himself. In such case the authority cannot be revoked. So, although the authority of an agent to sell goods is generally revocable[8] it will become irrevocable if the agent has made advances to his principal in consideration of the latter giving him authority to sell at the market price and retain his advances out of the proceeds.[9]

Further, by virtue of the Powers of Attorney Act 1971, s. 5, the donee of a power of attorney who acts in pursuance of the power at a time when it has been revoked shall not, by reason of the revocation, incur any liability (either to the donor or to any other person) if at that time he did not know that the power had been revoked. Where a power of attorney has been revoked and a person without knowledge of the revocation deals with the donee of the power, the transaction between them shall, in favour of that person, be as valid as if the power had then been in existence.

---

1 For discharge by subsequent agreement, see para. 8.01, ante.
2 See further para. 10.23, post.
3 For the issue of whether the agent prior to termination has done a commission-earning act, see para. 10.14, post.

4 Partnership Act 1890, s. 36. See para. 11.12, post.
5 *Turner v Goldsmith* [1891] 1 QB 544, CA.
6 *Bauman v Hulton Press* [1952] 2 All ER 1121, and see further chap. 32.
7 [1955] 2 QB 556, [1955] 2 All ER 722.
8 *Smart v Sanders* (1848) 5 CB 895.
9 *Raleigh v Atkinson* (1840) 6 M & W 670. See also Powers of Attorney Act 1971, s. 4.

10.08   b) BY OPERATION OF LAW

Subject to exceptions depending upon the special terms of the appointment and the types of irrevocable agency just referred to (agency coupled with an interest and the provisions of the Powers of Attorney Act 1971):

1. Death: The principal's death generally puts an end to the authority of the agent. A case illustrating this is *Smout v Ilbery*[1] in which:

> It was decided that a butcher was unable to recover from the husband's estate the price of meat supplied to a woman, at a time when her husband, supposed to be alive, was in reality dead; her authority to buy was gone.

2. Bankruptcy: The agent's authority is generally revoked by the bankruptcy of his principal; not necessarily by that of himself.

3. Insanity: The insanity of the agent will determine his authority, and the insanity of the principal seems equivalent to a revocation, but if third parties have dealt with the agent on the faith of an authority previously given, and without notice of a determination or revocation, the principal will be precluded from denying the continuance of the authority. Thus, in *Drew v Nunn*:[2]

> P gave his wife authority to buy, then became insane. When he had recovered, P repudiated her contracts, but was held liable in an action for the price because his subsequent insanity did not relieve him from the consequences of the representation he had previously made by giving his wife a general authority to buy, upon the faith of which the plaintiff acted.

4. Supervening illegality or frustration: Thus, a contract of agency involving personal services is terminated if the principal or agent is compelled to join the armed forces because he is no longer available to perform his duties.[3] Similarly, a contract of agency is terminated by destruction of the subject-matter, so that the employment of an estate agent to let a house is determined if the house is burnt down.

5. Expiration of the time agreed upon for its continuance;

6. Complete performance; e.g. when an agent to procure a buyer has procured one who is accepted.

1 (1842), 10 M & W 1. In so far as this case decided that the agent would not be liable in such circumstances for damages for breach of warranty of authority, it must be treated as overruled. See para. 10.23, post.
2 (1879) 4 QB 661. But see *Yonge v Toynbee* [1910] 1 KB 215, CA.
3 *Marshall v Glanvill* [1917] 2 KB 87; *Morgan v Manser* [1948] 1 KB 184, [1947] 2 All ER 666.

3. Rights and duties of agent as against principal

DUTIES OF AN AGENT TO HIS PRINCIPAL

10.09 a) *To obey his principal's instructions* Unless he is acting gratuitously the agent is liable in damages for failure to do what he has agreed to do.[1] Provided what the agent has agreed to do is not illegal,[2] then whether the agent is acting gratuitously or not, if he proceeds to carry out the agency, he must do so as agreed and comply with his principal's lawful instructions or be liable in damages.

1 *Turpin v Bilton* (1843) 5 Man. & G. 455.
2 *Cohen v Kittell* (1889) 22 QBD 680.

10.10 b) *To exercise due care and skill* The exact amount of skill and care required varies with the circumstances, but generally a man who undertakes to act for another must not show less diligence than he would have shown if exercising his own affairs. If, in addition, he is engaged upon an understanding that he must show special skill, he is liable to indemnify his principal if he does not show this skill, even though he has done his best.[1] In this respect a difference is to be observed between a gratuitous and a paid agent. Whilst the gratuitous agent is not bound to proceed to carry out the agency work at all, he is liable if he is negligent in carrying out a matter actually commenced. Even then, however, the responsibility may not be so great as that of a paid agent, for it seems that whereas the latter is liable for ordinary negligence, the voluntary agent is liable in damages only if he is guilty of 'gross negligence',[2] unless, indeed, his profession is such as to imply skill, in which case, if he enters upon the work at all, he must do so with that skill:[3] perhaps a modern way of putting this would be to say that the standard of care required varies as between the circumstances outlined.

1 See further chap. 32.
2 *Beauchamp v Powley* (1831) 1 Mood. & R. 38; *Doorman v Jenkins* (1835) 2

Ad. & EL. 256; and see per Crompton J in *Beal v South Devon Rly Co* (1864) 3 H & C 337 at 341, 342.
3 Lord Loughborough in *Shiells v Blackburne* (1789) 1 Hy. Bl. 158.

10.11 c) *To act in good faith* Whatever the agent does must be done in good faith for the benefit of his principal. An agent must never place himself in such a position as to cause his duty and his interest to conflict.[1] It is for this reason that he must not act for the advancement of his personal interests nor turn himself into a principal without his principal's assent. Therefore, if a broker is employed to buy as an agent, he may not sell his own goods to his principal unless the latter assents.[2] For the same reason an agent cannot accept commission from both parties to a contract without the fullest disclosure to and the consent of each principal.[3]

Secret profits It follows also that an agent must not make any secret profit out of the agency. He stands in a fiduciary position and anyone who acquires profits by reason of such position and by reason of the opportunity of knowledge resulting from it must account for it to the person to whom he stands in fiduciary relationship.[4] It is not necessary that the principal should have suffered any loss or even that the agent should have been acting directly in his principal's business. In *Reading v A-G*:[5]

> A soldier wearing uniform rode on civilian lorries carrying illicit spirits. His presence ensured that the lorries were not inspected by the police. He received £20,000 for this service. *Held:* the Crown could claim this sum as the soldier had used his authority as a means of obtaining a profit for himself.

A sub-agent who is aware that he is being employed by an agent of the principal stands in a fiduciary relationship to the principal, and will be accountable to him for any secret commission received, even though no privity of contract has been established between the sub-agent and the principal.[6]

An agent who takes a secret commission is a debtor to his principal for the amount thus received; but the principal cannot claim that the agent is trustee for him of the actual money, and so cannot follow the money into and claim the investment in which the agent has placed it; the principal's remedy is to bring an action and get judgment for an amount equivalent to that received by the agent.[7] An agent who receives a secret profit must not only account for it to his principal, but also normally forfeits his right to commission in respect of the transaction in connection with which the corrupt bargain was made.[8] However, if the agent has acted bona fide, then although he will have to give up to his principal any secret profit, he may be permitted to retain his remuneration.[9]

Bribes are a particular kind of secret profit. A bribe is a payment to the agent by a third party who knows the agent is acting as such and the payment is kept secret from the principal. An agent who receives a bribe may be dismissed without notice[10] and may be required to pay the bribe over to his principal or pay damages.[11] The fact that the principal could recover from his agent a bribe received, will not of itself prevent him from proceeding for damages against the third party who paid the bribe and the agent for conspiracy to defraud[11]—they are jointly and severally liable.[12] And further, where a contract has been entered into with an agent who has been induced to accept a bribe, the principal may refuse to be bound by the contract, irrespective of any effect the bribe may have had on the agent's mind.[13] The agent or third party, or both, may also be prosecuted under the Prevention of Corruption Acts, but proof of corrupt motive is necessary for conviction.[14]

Misuse of confidential information It is part of the agent's duty of good faith not to misuse confidential information. An agent may not employ, save in his principal's interest, materials and information which the agent has obtained or been supplied with only for his principal and in the course of his agency;[15] he owes a duty to keep secret information given to him and documents entrusted to him for the purpose of his agency. But an agreement not to disclose offences which ought to be divulged to a third party in the interests of justice is contrary to public policy, and disclosure will not expose the original recipient of the information to an action for damages.[16]

---

1 E.g. *Henry Smith & Son v Muskett* (1977) 121 Sol Jo 618.
2 *Lucifero v Castel* (1887) 3 TLR 371; *Armstrong v Jackson* [1917] 2 KB 822; *Kimber v Barber* (1873) LR 8 Ch App 56.
3 *Fullwood v Hurley* [1927] 1 KB 498; *Anglo-African Merchants Ltd v Bayley* [1970] 1 QB 311, [1969] 2 All ER 421; *North and South Trust Co v Berkeley* [1971] 1 All ER 980, [1971] 1 WLR 471 (practice criticised of Lloyd's insurance brokers, agents of insured, acting also for underwriters).
4 *Regal (Hastings) Ltd v Gulliver* [1967] 2 AC 134, [1942] 1 All ER 378, HL; *Phipps v Boardman* [1967] 2 AC 46, [1966] 3 All ER 721, HL; *English v Dedham Vale Properties Ltd* [1978] 1 All ER 382.
5 [1951] AC 507, [1951] 1 All ER 617, HL.
6 *Powell v Evan Jones & Co* [1905] 1 KB 11. See also para. 10.12, post.
7 *Lister v Stubbs* (1890) 45 ChD 1.
8 *Andrews v Ramsay & Co* [1903] 2 KB 635.
9 *Hippisley v Knee Brothers* [1905] 1 KB 1.
10 *Boston Deep Sea, etc Co v Ansell* (1888) 39 ChD 339.
11 But the claims to recover the bribe and damages for loss are in the

alternative: *Maheson S/o Thambiah v Malaysia Government Officer's Co-operative* [1978] 2 WLR 444, PC.

12 *Mayor of Salford v Lever* [1891] 1 QB 168, CA; *Grant v Gold, etc, Syndicate, Ltd* [1900] 1 QB 233.

13 *Shipway v Broadwood* [1899] 1 QB 369.

14 The Acts of 1906 and 1916, as amended.

15 *Lamb v Evans* [1893] 1 Ch 218, CA; *Robb v Green* [1895] 2 QB 315. See also para. 32.06, post.

16 *Howard v Odham's Press* [1938] 1 KB 1, [1937] 2 All ER 509.

10.12 *d) To act personally* A further duty of the agent is prima facie to do the work himself, and not to commit it to others for performance, for the old maxim applies—*Delegatus non potest delegare.*[1] But this needs some modification, for though it applies where personal trust is put in the agent, or where personal skill is required, yet in many cases it does not, especially under these circumstances:

1. Where custom sanctions delegation;
2. Where delegation is necessary to proper performance;
3. Where there is an agreement, express or implied, to allow it.

The leading case on this part of the subject is *De Bussche v Alt*:[2]

> There, a plaintiff (resident in England) consigned a ship to G & Co in China, for sale on certain terms, and G & Co, with the knowledge of the plaintiff, employed the defendant in Japan to sell it.

A point arose in the action whether or not the delegation was good, and Thesiger LJ, in giving the judgment of the court, said:

> 'The maxim (*delegatus non potest delegare*) when analysed, merely imports that an agent cannot, without authority from his principal, devolve upon another obligations to the principal which he has himself undertaken to personally fulfil; and that, inasmuch as confidence in the particular person employed is at the root of the contract of agency, such an authority cannot be implied as an ordinary incident in the contract. But the exigencies of business do from time to time render necessary the carrying out of the instructions of a principal by a person other than the agent originally instructed for the purpose ... And we are of opinion that an authority to the effect referred to may and should be implied, where from the conduct of the parties to the original contract of agency, the usage of trade, or the nature of the particular business which is the subject of the agency, it may reasonably be presumed that the parties to the contract of agency originally intended that such authority should exist, or where in the course of the employment

unforeseen emergencies arise which impose upon the agent the necessity of employing a substitute'.

In this case, the agent was authorised to create privity of contract between his principal and the sub-agent in Japan, but the general rule is that the sub-agent is the agent's agent and no privity is created between the principal and the sub-agent.[3] In consequence, therefore, the sub-agent cannot normally claim remuneration or indemnity from the principal and the principal cannot normally claim in contract against the sub-agent if the latter has displayed a lack of due care.[4]

---

1 E.g. *John McCann & Co v Pow* [1975] 1 All ER 129, [1974] 1 WLR 1643, CA.
2 (1878) 8 ChD 286.
3 *Calico Printers' Association Ltd v Barclays Bank* (1931) 145 LT 51 (Wright J). For the doctrine of privity, see para. 4.02, ante.
4 However, since the House of Lords decision in *Hedley Byrne & Co Ltd v Heller and Partners Ltd* [1964] AC 465, [1963] 2 All ER 575, the lack of privity would seem not to prevent an action in the tort of negligence against the sub-agent, at any rate where the agent gives the sub-agent possession of the principal's goods and there is lack of care as to their safety: *Gilchrist Watt and Sanderson Pty Ltd v York Products Pty Ltd* [1970] 3 All ER 825, [1970] 1 WLR 1262, PC.

10.13 *e) To account to the principal* The agent must not intermix his affairs with those of the principal, e.g. he should not pay money received as agent into his own private account[1] and he must always account to his principal for money received on the latter's behalf.[2]

---

1 *Gray v Haig* (1854) 20 Beav, 219.
2 *De Mattos v Benjamin* (1894) 63 LJQB 248.

RIGHTS OF AN AGENT AS AGAINST HIS PRINCIPAL

10.14 An agent has a right to the remuneration agreed upon, or if none has been fixed, then in cases where a contract to pay for his services is to be implied from the circumstances, the agent is entitled to be paid what is usual and customary in the business in which he has been employed, or, in the absence of custom or usage, to a reasonable remuneration.

Where the terms on which commission is to be paid are clearly stated in the contract there is no room for an implied term. So in *Luxor (Eastbourne) Ltd v Cooper:*[1]

An agent was employed on terms that he should be paid a

commission on completion of a sale. He produced a person ready able and willing to buy but the owners refused to sell. *Held:* the agent was not entitled to commission.

In that case there was no room for an implied term that the agent should be paid on the basis of a *quantum meruit* or that the owner would accept a reasonable offer. If the agency contract is intended to attract commission on no more being done than the provision of an offer, then that result must be stated in quite clear and precise terms.[2]

Thus, if an estate agent is engaged on the basis that commission will be paid to him by the vendor 'on introducing a purchaser', that means someone who does purchase and not one who merely makes a definite offer to purchase.[3] Once there is a binding contract of sale, however, the vendor cannot wrongfully withdraw from it except at the risk of having to pay his agent commission, because it is his own fault that the sale has not been completed.[4] If it is not the vendor but the purchaser who withdraws, the case is entirely different and no commission is payable.[5]

In *Midgley Estate Ltd v Hand*,[6] commission was payable to the agents as soon as someone introduced by them 'shall have signed a legally binding contract effected within a period of three months from this date'. The person introduced signed a legally binding contract within that period but was unable to raise the money to complete the purchase. The Court of Appeal ruled that, on the terms of the agents' contract, they had earned their commission; the terms were clear and unambiguous.

Where an agent is to be paid commission 'on securing an offer to purchase', normally at not less than a specified price, commission is payable as soon as such an offer is made.[7] The effect of an agent being appointed 'sole agent' is that commission is payable even if the ultimate purchaser is introduced by another agent but not if the vendor himself sells. If the agent is given 'the sole right to sell', it seems that he may claim commission even if the owner himself sells.

Generally speaking, when a contract of agency is terminated, no further commission is payable to the agent in respect of business done thereafter even though the principal obtains the benefit of making contracts with persons introduced by the agent before such termination.[8] It is, however, a matter of construction: if commission is payable on all business done with persons introduced by the agent 'as long as we do business', the obligation is a continuing one;[9] and such a continuing obligation may even be implied.[10] However, the court may decline to order an account to be taken every year till 'the crack of doom'.

Instead it may award compensation to be assessed on the basis that after termination of the agency the agent is entitled to go on receiving commission on repeat orders with a reduction to take account of expenses saved.[11]

On termination of an agency, the agent may, depending on the construction of the contract, be required to repay any commission paid to him on account if it has not actually been earned by him before the agency terminated.[12]

---

1 [1941] AC 108, [1941] 1 All ER 33, HL.
2 See *Dennis Reed Ltd v Goody* [1950] 2 KB 277, [1950] 1 All ER 919, CA; *Christie Owen and Davies Ltd v Stockton* [1953] 2 All ER 1149, [1953] 1 WLR 1353.
3 *Jones v Lowe* [1945] KB 73, [1945] 1 All ER 194.
4 *EP Nelson & Co v Rolfe* [1950] 1 KB 139, [1949] 2 All ER 584, CA.
5 *Dennis Reed Ltd v Goody* [1950] 2 KB 277, [1950] 1 All ER 919, CA.
6 [1952] 2 QB 432, [1952] 1 All ER 1394, CA. See also *Ackroyd & Sons v Hasan* [1960] 2 QB 144, [1960] 2 All ER 254, CA; and *Wilkinson Ltd v Brown* [1966] 1 All ER 509, [1966] 1 WLR 194, CA; *Christie Owen and Davies Ltd v Rapacioli* [1974] QB 781, [1974] 2 All ER 311, CA; *Hoddell v Smith* (1975) 240 Estates Gazette 295, CA.
7 Provided it is a firm and unconditional offer: *Bennett, Walden & Co v Wood* [1950] 2 All ER 134, CA; and see *Drewery and Drewery v Ware-Lane* [1960] 3 All ER 529, [1960] 1 WLR 1204, CA.
8 *Nayler v Yearsley* (1860), 2 F & F 41.
9 *Wilson v Harper* [1908] 2 Ch 370; see also *Sellers v London Counties Newspapers* [1951] 1 KB 784, [1951] 1 All ER 544, CA.
10 *British Bank for Foreign Trade v Novinex Ltd* [1949] 1 KB 623, [1949] 1 All ER 155, CA.
11 *Roberts v Elwells Engineers Ltd* [1972] 2 QB 586, [1972] 2 All ER 890, CA.
12 *Bronester Ltd v Priddle* [1961] 3 All ER 471, [1961] 1 WLR 1294.

10.15 An agent is entitled to be indemnified for losses and liabilities incurred by him in the course of the agency. Thus, in one case,

> where the agent was made liable in damages for seizing goods improperly, and it was shown that he did it bona fide, and at the command of his principal, he was adjudged to be entitled to indemnity.[1]

So if a principal directs his agent to engage in any enterprise in which by any particular custom or usage of the market, liabilities are incurred, the agent will be entitled to be indemnified against these unless the custom is inconsistent with the contract.[2] To this last proposition limits have to be placed:

1. If the loss is caused by default of the agent himself, his right disappears;[3]
2. The custom must be one that is well known; so notorious in

the market that those dealing there may easily ascertain it, and may well be supposed to have knowledge of it;[4]

3. The custom must be legal and reasonable, or else express knowledge of the custom should be shown to exist.[5]

It has even been held that when a person at the request of another incurs some liability, which, though not legally enforceable, is paid in consequence of some moral pressure (e.g. danger of expulsion from a society), the principal may be legally liable to indemnify his agent.[6]

---

1 *Toplis v Crane* (1838) 5 Bing. NC 636; see also *Henderson & Co v Williams* [1895] 1 QB 521, CA.
2 *Whitehead v Izod* (1867) LR 2 CP 228, per Willes J. See *Bernard Thorpe & Partners v Flannery* (1977) 244 Estates Gazette 129, CA.
3 *Duncan v Hill* (1873) LR 8 Ex. 242; *Ellis v Pond* [1898] 1 QB 426.
4 *Grissell v Bristowe* (1868) LR 3 CP 112, revsd. on other grounds LR 4 CP 36.
5 *Neilson v James* (1882) 9 QBD 546; *Perry v Barnett* (1885) 14 QBD 467; on appeal 15 QBD 388; *Seymour v Bridge* (1885) 14 QBD 460.
6 *Read v Anderson* (1884) 13 QBD 779 (revsd. on facts by Gaming Act 1892).

10.16 An agent has a right to a lien, the particular kind varying with the class of agent. See para. 17.11, post. Finally, in some cases an agent has a right to stop goods *in transitu*[1] as when, being agent of the consignee, he has made himself liable for the price by having pledged his own credit.[2] This right may not be exercised if the general balance between the principal and agent is in favour of the former.

---

1 Para. 13.38, post.
2 *Hawkes v Dunn* (1830) 1 C & J 519.

---

3. Authority of an agent

10.17 In considering the authority of an agent two questions arise: firstly, the extent of the actual authority of the agent; and, secondly, the degree to which the principal may become bound to third parties by acts of the agent which are outside that authority. If the agent acts within his actual authority to effect a contract with a third party, then the third party and the principal are bound by it; if the agent exceeds his actual authority, he is guilty of a breach of duty and may be liable both to dismissal and to indemnify his principal.

Actual authority

10.18 The actual authority of an agent to bind his principal to a contract with a third party will be derived from the terms of the contract of agency between P and A.[1] It has already been seen that that contract of agency may be express or implied.[2] Likewise, the powers of A under that contract may be express or implied: the extent of A's express powers is simply a matter of construction of the words used; but the boundaries of his implied powers may cause some difficulty.[3] Thus, a man put in charge of a shop will have implied authority to order goods for the purposes of the trade carried on, to receive payment from customers, and to give receipts; but an agent to sell does not necessarily have implied authority to receive payment,[4] and even an agent who is appointed to receive a debt may be authorised, not to accept a cheque, but to take cash only.[5] Again, it is now settled that an estate agent has no implied authority from the vendor to receive a deposit from a prospective purchaser.[6]

Where the terms of A's authority are clearly stated in the contract of agency, there is no room for implied terms.[7] However, if the authority is ambiguous and A bona fide adopts one interpretation and acts upon it, P cannot repudiate the transaction on the ground that he meant the authority to be taken in the other sense.[8] Moreover, even though A exceeds his actual authority—whether by acting when he has no authority, or in excess of his actual authority—P may subsequently ratify A's acts on the conditions set out above.[9]

---

1 If an agent was acting within his actual authority, it is no defence to P that A was using that authority to his own ends: *Hambro v Burnand* [1904] 2 KB 10.
2 See para. 10.02, ante.
3 For implied terms in general, see para. 7.05, ante.
4 *Butwick v Grant* [1924] 2 KB 483. For the effect of payment by T to A in these circumstances, see para. 10.25, post.
5 E.g. *Williams v Evans* (1866) LR 1 QB 352.
6 *Sorrell v Finch* [1977] AC 728, [1976] 2 All ER 371, HL.
7 *Catlin v Bell* (1815) 4 Camp. 183; *Jonmenjoy Coondoo v Watson* (1884) 9 App Cas 561.
8 *Ireland v Livingstone* (1872) LR 5 HL 395. But compare *Falck v Williams* [1900] AC 176, PC (see para. 5.03, ante).
9 See para. 10.04, ante.

Estoppel

10.19 Over and above the actual authority with which A is endowed by reason of the contract of agency just considered, A may have extra authority to bind P to T arising by reason of the doctrine of estoppel. Where P has represented to T that A has authority to bind P, then, notwithstanding that A has no actual authority, P may be estopped as against T from denying that A's act was authorised. Thus, in *Pickering v Busk:*[1]

> A broker was employed by a merchant to buy hemp; the broker did so, and, at the merchant's request, the hemp was left at the broker's wharf; the broker sold the goods, and the purchaser was *held* to have obtained a good title to the goods on the ground that the broker was the apparent agent, and that the merchant was estopped by his conduct from denying the agency.

Before such an estoppel can arise, *all* the following requirements must be satisfied:

1) P must make *a representation* to T. This representation may be express or implied. For instance, it may be implied from the circumstances of A's appointment to a particular position: where the appointment would normally give the agent an implied authority, then, notwithstanding that the contract of agency negatives such an implication, in publicly acknowledging the appointment P may be impliedly representing that A has the authority. Thus, in *Panorama Developments (Guildford) Ltd v Fidelis Furnishing Fabrics Ltd:*[2]

> A was the duly appointed Company Secretary of P Ltd. In that capacity, he purported to order self-drive cars on various dates. As the cars were in fact for his own use, P Ltd refused to pay for them. *Held:* P Ltd liable on basis that, by appointing A Company Secretary, P Ltd were holding A out as being authorised to sign contracts connected with the administrative side of the business.

On ordinary principles the representation must be of existing fact: it is insufficient that it be as to P's future intention,[3] or of law;[4] and in this context it must be a representation that A is authorised to act as agent on behalf of P in the relevant transaction.[5]

2) The representation must be made *by P*, or by another agent authorised to do so.[6] An agent cannot bind his principal simply because he, the agent, insists to T that he has P's authority. No matter that P has 'enabled' A to make the representation, e.g. in

the sense that P has put A in the situation where A has the necessary credibility; in *Farquharson Bros & Co v King & Co:*[7]

A, a confidential clerk in the employ of P, perpetrated a series of frauds over four years as follows: he instructed a warehousekeeper to transfer some of P's goods to the order of Brown; and, under the name of Brown sold and delivered the goods to T. *Held:* as T had never heard of P, there could be no question of estoppel, and P could deny A's authority to sell.

3) P must make the representation *to* T. It is insufficient that P makes the representation, but T does not obtain knowledge of it. Thus, in *MacFisheries Ltd v Harrison:*[8]

H, the licensee of a public house, sold his lease to S, but left his name over the door. M supplied goods to S for sale in the public house. After S's bankruptcy, M sought to make H liable for the price on the grounds that S purchased as H's agent. *Held:* the action failed as, whilst H's name over the door might amount to a representation, M admitted that he did not notice it.

Nor is it sufficient that T merely has constructive knowledge of P's representation, as where that representation is contained in the articles of a company—which T had not actually read, but of which he is deemed to have constructive notice.[9]

4) T must *rely on* the representation. No estoppel will be raised if T knew the representation to be untrue;[10] and this may be so even where the representation is contained in a document incorporated in a contract between P and T which T has not necessarily read.[11]

---

1 (1812) 15 East 38. See also *Eastern Distributors Ltd v Goldring* [1957] 2 QB 600, [1957] 2 All ER 525, CA (set out in para. 13.12, post).

2 [1971] 2 QB 711, [1971] 3 All ER 16, CA.

3 *Jorden v Money* (1854) 5 HL Cas 185.

4 So for P to show T the agency contract and innocently misrepresent its effect in law will not raise an estoppel against P.

5 For P to represent that A is the owner of P's goods brings another rule into play: see Sale of Goods Act 1893, s. 21 (1), para. 13.12, post.

6 E.g. *Henderson & Co v Williams* [1895] 1 QB 521, CA.

7 [1902] AC 325, HL.

8 (1924) 93 LJKB 811.

9 *Freeman and Lockyer v Buckhurst Park Properties (Mangal) Ltd* [1964] 2 QB 480, [1964] 1 All ER 630, CA.

10 *Overbrooke Estates Ltd v Glencombe Properties Ltd* [1974] 3 All ER 511, [1974] 1 WLR 1335, CA.

11 This is the purpose behind the commonly found clause in standard-form contracts that A has no authority to vary the terms contained therein. But see *Lowe v Lombank Ltd* [1960] 1 All ER 611, [1960] 1 WLR 196, CA.

Mercantile agency

10.20 Since the nineteenth century, it has been clearly settled at
common law that for an owner of goods simply to give possession
of them to another will not without more estop the owner from
setting up his title where that other purports to dispose of the
goods to a bona fide purchaser.[1] Whilst such a rule protects
ownership, it is inconvenient to commercial men whose
overriding interest is that the bona fide purchaser shall get a
good title. Accordingly, they secured a limited exception to the
common law rule, whereby entrusting one's goods to a factor
raises a sort of statutory estoppel in the event of that factor
disposing of them to a bona fide purchaser. As a statutory
exception, it is strictly construed, and will not operate unless all
its requirements are satisfied.

This statutory exception is now to be found in the Factors Act
1889, which purports to apply to both 'goods' and 'documents of
title to goods', which expression is defined by s. 1 (4) of the Act
to include:[2]

> 'any bill of lading, dock warrant, warehouse-keeper's certi-
> ficate, and warrant or order for the delivery of goods, and any
> other document used in the ordinary course of business as
> proof of the possession or control of goods, or authorising or
> purporting to authorise, either by endorsement or by delivery,
> the possessor of the document to transfer or receive goods
> thereby represented'.

The exception purports to deal with the situation where such
goods or documents of title are entrusted to what it terms a
'mercantile agent', which the Act defines as an agent

> 'having in the customary course of his business as such agent
> authority either to sell goods, or to consign goods for the
> purpose of sale, or to buy goods, or to raise money on the
> security of goods'.[3]

The expression comprehends factors, brokers, dealers and
auctioneers.[4] A mere servant or shop assistant is not a mercantile
agent, but the fact that a person is acting for one principal only
and has no general occupation as an agent does not exclude him
from filling that character.[5]

The key provision of the 1889 Act in relation to mercantile
agents is as follows:

> 'Where a mercantile agent is, with the consent of the owner,[6]
> in possession[7] of goods or of the documents of title to goods,
> any sale, pledge,[8] or other disposition of the goods, made by
> him[9] when acting in the ordinary course of business of a

mercantile agent, shall, subject to the provisions of this Act, be as valid as if he were expressly authorised by the owner of the goods to make the same; provided that the person[10] taking under the disposition acts in good faith,[11] and has not at the time of the disposition notice that the person making the disposition has not authority to make the same'.[12]

These provisions only apply if the mercantile agent is in possession of goods or of the documents of title to goods in his capacity *as* a mercantile agent, i.e. for some purpose connected with a possible sale, such as display. They do not apply if the mercantile agent is given possession for some other purpose, such as repair or safe custody;[13] nor where the person in possession is not a mercantile agent. Thus, where documents of title to goods are pledged[14] to a bank, who re-delivers those documents to the pledgor under a *trust receipt*,[15] the effect of an unauthorised disposition of the documents to a third party acting in good faith is as follows: where the pledgor is a mercantile agent, he is a joint owner in possession with the consent of the other joint owner (the bank), and can pass a good title to a third party under s. 2 (1);[16] but the third party will not obtain a good title where either the pledgor is not a mercantile agent[17] or he is not authorised by the trust receipt to dispose of the goods on behalf of the bank.[18]

If the owner withdraws his consent, a disposition to any person acting in good faith will nevertheless remain good, provided such person has not at the time of the sale or disposition received notice of such withdrawal.[19] The agent who, by reason of being or having been in possession of goods with the owner's consent, obtains possession of the documents of title to them, is deemed to hold these documents with the owner's consent.[20]

Section 3 enacts that:

'A pledge of documents of title to goods shall be deemed to be a pledge of the goods;'

but when a mercantile agent pledges goods as security for a debt or liability due from the pledgor to the pledgee before the time of the pledge, the pledgee can acquire no further right to the goods than could have been enforced by the pledgor at the time of the pledge.[21]

---

1 *Johnson v Credit Lyonnais Co* (1877) 3 CPD 32, CA.
2 The Registration Document (log-book) of a motor vehicle is not a document of title: *Joblin v Watkins and Roseveare (Motors) Ltd* [1949] 1 All ER 47; *Sargent (Garages) Ltd v Motor Auctions (West Bromwich) Ltd* [1977] RTR 121 at 121, CA. It is now clear that, in relation to a motor vehicle, 'goods'

refs simply to the vehicle itself (regardless of the log-book): *Stadium Finance Ltd v Robbins* [1962] 2 QB 664, [1962] 2 All ER 633, CA.

3 See Factors Act 1889, s. 1 (1).

4 In fact, it covers most of the particular types of agent listed in the fifth section (see paras. 10.29 et seq., post).

5 *Lowther v Harris* [1927] 1 KB 393.

6 Such consent is presumed, unless there is evidence to the contrary (Factors Act 1889, s. 2 (4)). The fact that the consent has been obtained by fraud does not exclude the section. See *Pearson v Rose and Young* [1951] 1 KB 275, [1950] 2 All ER 1027; *Du Jardin Ltd v Beadman Brothers* [1952] 2 QB 712, [1952] 2 All ER 160.

7 I.e., when the goods or documents are in his actual custody, or in the custody of some other person subject to his control, or for him, or on his behalf (ibid., s. 1 (2)).

8 Including lien or giving security on goods or documents (Factors Act 1889, s. 1 (5)).

9 Or his clerk or other person authorised in the ordinary course (s. 6).

10 In the case of joint purchasers, the transaction will not be upheld unless they have all acted in good faith (*Oppenheimer v Fraser* [1907] 2 KB 50).

11 *Heap v Motorists' Advisory Agency Ltd* [1923] 1 KB 577.

12 Factors Act 1889, s. 2 (1).

13 *Pearson v Rose and Young Ltd* [1951] 1 KB at 288, [1950] 2 All ER at 1032, per Denning LJ, cf. the interpretation of the Sale of Goods Act 1893, s. 25 (1): see para. 13.15, post.

14 For pledges, see generally, para. 17.02, post.

15 An agreement whereby the pledgor promises to hold the documents on trust for the bank, the effect being that the pledgor and the bank are joint owners of the goods and the pledgor holds any proceeds on trust for the bank. See para. 17.02, post.

16 *Lloyds Bank Ltd v Bank of America, National Trust and Savings Association* [1938] 2 KB 147, [1938] 2 All ER 63, CA.

17 *Mercantile Bank of India Ltd v Central Bank of India Ltd* [1938] AC 287, [1938] 1 All ER 52, PC.

18 See *Babcock v Lawson* (1880) 5 QBD 284, CA.

19 Factors Act 1889, s. 2 (2).

20 Ibid., s. 2 (3).

21 Factors Act 1889, s. 4: i.e. antecedent debts are excluded.

10.21 The effect of section 2 (1) is illustrated by *Oppenheimer v Attenborough & Son*:[1]

The plaintiff was induced to entrust a parcel of diamonds to a diamond broker (a mercantile agent) upon the representation that the broker could sell them to X at an agreed minimum price. Instead, the broker pledged the diamonds to the defendant, who took in good faith and for value. Evidence was given that diamond brokers employed to sell diamonds had no authority to pledge them, and that it was unheard of in the trade to employ a broker to pledge diamonds.

The Court of Appeal found in favour of the pledgee, holding that it was irrelevant that the pledgee thought the pledgor was acting as a principal, and that such pledging was unheard of in the diamond trade. Their Lordships appeared to draw this distinction: when considering the mercantile agent's *acquisition* of the goods, it must be considered whether the owner actually intended to satisfy the requirements of s. 2 (1) as to acquisition—a subjective test; whereas, in deciding whether the *disposition* was 'in the ordinary course of business', the test is objective—does the transaction look all right to the transferee? However, the courts have shown some reluctance to apply this distinction in cases where a rogue mercantile agent has obtained possession of a motor vehicle (without the log-book) with the consent of the owner, and then sold it to a bona fide purchaser: in two cases, the Court of Appeal suggested that such a disposition could not be in the ordinary course of business;[2] but more recently it has been re-affirmed that the proper test is whether the transaction looks all right to a transferee.[3]

---

1 [1908] 1 KB 221, CA.
2 *Pearson v Rose and Young Ltd* [1951] 1 KB 275, [1950] 2 All ER 1027, CA; *Stadium Finance Ltd v Robbins Ltd* [1962] 2 QB 664, [1962] 2 All ER 633, CA.
3 *Astley Industrial Trust Ltd v Miller* [1968] 2 All ER 36.

Usual authority

10.22   Usual authority is that authority which A derives from the nature of his office; and its extent is normally derived from the class of agents to which A belongs. Unfortunately, the term 'usual authority' is used in a number of different senses as follows:

1. Implied actual authority—A has been appointed to such a post, so therefore he has impliedly been granted such an authority as usually goes with such a post (see ante).
2. Authority by estoppel—notwithstanding that A's actual authority has been limited, by appointing A to such a post P has represented to the outside world (including T) that A has such authority as usually goes with the post (see ante).
3. Usual authority—notwithstanding that A has no actual or estoppel authority, the fact of his appointment gives him a usual authority such as normally goes with the post.

This last category—if it exists—establishes a further head of authority by which A may bind P to T. A must actually be the duly appointed agent of P, but acting in excess of the actual authority granted to him by P; and T must be unaware that A is acting as an agent at all. In the leading case of *Watteau v Fenwick*:[1]

> A was manager of P's beerhouse and P forbad him to purchase cigars for the business from third parties. A did order cigars from T on credit, such being within the authority usually given to such an agent. T was unaware A was an agent and unaware of the secret limitation on his authority. *Held:* T could claim the price of the cigars from P.

---

1 [1893] 1 QB 346. But see *Daun v Simmins* (1879) 41 LT 783, CA; *Kinaham v Parry* [1911] 1 KB 459, CA. Cf. Partnership Act 1890, s. 5, para. 11.09, post.

BREACH OF WARRANTY OF AUTHORITY

10.23 An agent who represents himself to have an authority from a principal which he really does not possess, or exceeds that which he does possess, is liable to an action at the suit of third parties for breach of warranty of authority, provided the want of authority was not known to such parties.[1] Nor is it different if the agent bona fide supposed himself to have authority;[2] even though his original authority has ceased by reason of facts of which he has no knowledge or means of knowledge, e.g. by the death or insanity of his principal, or in the case of a company by its dissolution.[3] However, it must be borne in mind that A does not warrant that P will perform, but merely that he has authority to bind P.[4]

This doctrine is not limited to cases where the professing agent purports to *contract* on behalf of an alleged principal: any person who suffers damage by acting on the untrue assertion of authority may sue for breach of the implied warranty. Thus, in *Starkey v Bank of England*:[5]

> A broker, acting innocently under a forged power of attorney for the transfer of Consols, required the Bank of England in performance of their statutory duty to transfer the Consols in their books. Upon discovery of the forgery, the true owner of the Consols compelled the bank to make good the loss, and the bank was held entitled to indemnity from the broker.

It will be observed that the bank made no contract of any kind, but simply performed a duty upon the faith of the alleged agency.

But in cases where a breach of warranty of authority, or an undertaking to indemnify, is sought to be implied the facts must not be such as to negative that implication.[6]

1 *Collen v Wright* (1856) 7 E & B 301, on appeal (1857) 8 E & B 647; *Firbank's Executive v Humphreys* (1887) 18 QBD 54; *Halbot v Lens* [1901] 1 Ch 344; *Salvesen v Rederi Aktiebolaget Nordstjernan* [1905] AC 302; *Yonge v Toynbee* [1910] 1 KB 215, CA.
2 *Polhill v Walter* (1832) 3 B & Ad 114. As to the measure of damages, see *Meek v Wendt* (1888) 21 QBD 126; and *Re National Coffee Palace Co* (1883) 24 ChD 367, CA.
3 *Yonge v Toynbee* [1910] 1 KB 215, CA.
4 But see the case of a *del credere* agent: see para. 10.30, post.
5 [1903] AC 114. Apart from agency, a person who presents a forged transfer for registration impliedly undertakes to indemnify the company or corporation against any loss resulting therefrom (*Sheffield Corporation v Barclay* [1905] AC 392). In *Bank of England v Cutler* [1908] 2 KB 208, CA, a broker who identified as the registered holder of certain stock a person who was fraudulently personating such holder, was held liable to indemnify the bank for the consequent loss on the ground that his conduct amounted to a request to the bank to permit the entry and registration of the forged transfer.
6 *Gowers v Lloyds and National Provincial Foreign Bank Ltd* [1938] 1 All ER 766, CA.

4. Who can sue and be sued

10.24 Whether P, or A, or both, are liable on a given contract with T is a matter depending upon the intention of the parties and authority of the agent.

Generally, A is not liable on the contract with T,[1] but P is liable. However, to this rule many exceptions are found, most of them depending upon the rule that if by his conduct one person causes another to believe that a principal is being dealt with, he cannot put that other in a worse position by any subsequent disclosure of his character as agent; e.g.:

> A owes B money, and B buys goods to the amount, supposing A to be vendor; A cannot afterwards, by showing himself to be an agent only, prevent B from setting off the debt against the price.

1 But only for breach of warranty of authority (see para. 10.23, ante), under a collateral contract or for negligent misstatement or deceit.

RELATIONS WITH THIRD PERSONS WHERE EXISTENCE OF PRINCIPAL DISCLOSED
10.25 Here, in the absence of evidence to the contrary, the principal, and he alone, has liabilities and rights regardless of whether his identity is disclosed. However, under certain circumstances, A may be liable on the contract with T, e.g.:

1. If he agrees to be so;[1]
2. Where the principal does not exist, or is not in a condition to be bound by the contract[2] (see para. 10.27, post);
3. If the contract is by deed, and the agent executes it in his own name though he describes himself as signing 'for and on behalf of' another.
4. When the custom of trade makes him liable.

If the contract has been reduced into writing it is a question of construction whether the agent contracted personally, or for a principal; and, where a person signs a contract in his own name, without qualification, he is prima facie to be deemed to be contracting personally. But where the signature is accompanied by representative words, e.g. 'on account of' or 'as agent', then whether the principal is named or not, the qualified signature must be taken as intended to negative personal liability, although other words and clauses in the body of the document may indicate the contrary.[3]

If upon the terms of a written contract the agent appears as principal, he is bound, though as a fact it was known at the time that he was bargaining as agent only, unless he can show that the contract was so drawn up by mistake; and this follows from the general rule, that oral evidence cannot be admitted to vary a written contract.[4]

It was thought at one time that where a home agent contracted on behalf of a foreign principal there was a presumption that the agent alone could sue and be sued unless the contrary intention plainly appears from the contract itself or the surrounding circumstances;[5] but the Court of Appeal has now held that no such presumption exists.[6] The nationality of the principal is merely one factor in determining whether T has shown he is willing to treat P as a party to the contract and if so whether A is a party too.

An agent may sue on a contract even if his principal is disclosed, if he has an interest (e.g. lien) in the proceeds; for this reason an auctioneer may sue for the price of goods.[7]

Settlement with the agent If the principal owes money to the third party under the contract, then generally speaking he remains liable although he has paid his agent.[8] In *Irvine & Co v Watson and Sons*:[9]

> P employed A to buy oil; A bought some from T, saying it was for principals, but not naming them; the terms were cash on delivery; it was not an invariable custom to pay on delivery; the oil was delivered and P, supposing the cash had been paid (which was not the fact), settled with A; when A became insolvent, T sued P for the price. *Held:* P must pay, though if

T had led P to believe that the agent and they had settled matters, P would have been protected.

---

1 See, e.g. *International Rly Co v Niagara Parks Commission* [1941] AC 328, [1941] 2 All ER 456. It is a question of fact whether an agent of an *unnamed* principal is personally liable: *N and J Vlassopulos Ltd v Ney Shipping Ltd* [1977] 1 Lloyds Rep. 478, CA.
2 Even if his signature is accompanied by representative words: see Powell *Law of Agency* (2nd edn) 249.
3 *Gadd v Houghton* (1876) 1 Ex D 357; *Ariadne SS Co v James McKelvie & Co* [1922] 1 KB 18, CA; affd. sub nom *Universal Steam Navigation Co v J McKelvie & Co* [1923] AC 492, HL. There are special rules for negotiable instruments, see para. 20.07, post.
4 *Basma v Weekes* [1950] AC 441 at 454, [1950] 2 All ER 146 at 152, PC; and see *Wake v Harrop* (1861) 6 H & N 768, affd. (1862) 1 H & C 202 as to mistake.
5 Lord Tenterden in *Thomson v Davenport* (1829) 9 B & C 78 at 87.
6 *Teheran-Europe Co Ltd v ST Belton (Tractors) Ltd* [1968] 2 QB 545, [1968] 2 All ER 886, CA.
7 *Williams v Millington* (1788) 1 Hy Bl 81; *Chelmsford Auctions Ltd v Poole* [1973] 1 QB 542, [1973] 1 All ER 810, CA; and see para. 10.32, post.
8 *Macfarlane v Giannacopulo* (1858) 3 H & N 860. For the rules of payment, see generally para. 7.14 et seq., ante.
9 (1880) 5 QBD 414, CA.

RELATIONS WITH THIRD PERSONS WHERE EXISTENCE OF PRINCIPAL UNDISCLOSED

10.26   In this case the general rule is that either A or P may sue T on the contract;[1] and T may sue either A, or P—when he discloses his existence.[2]

If the principal sues upon the contract, he must do so subject to any right of set-off that the third party may have acquired against the agent before he knew him to be acting for a principal.[3] In *Rabone v Williams*:[4]

Factors sold to W, and when the undisclosed principal sued, W claimed to set-off a debt due by the factors to him, and the claim was allowed.

This set-off cannot be allowed if the third party was aware that the agent was really such, although he was not aware of the identity of the principal;[5] thus in the case of a sale he should show that the contract was made by a person to whom the principal had entrusted possession of the goods, that that person sold them as his own goods in his own name, and that he (the buyer) believed the agent to be the principal, and that the set-off claimed accrued before he was undeceived.[6] As the doctrine of constructive notice does not extend to ordinary commercial transactions, a person dealing with an agent in the honest belief that he is the principal is not affected by mere notice of facts which might on inquiry lead to the discovery of the existence of a principal.[7]

However, if in the contract the agent expressly or impliedly contracts that he is the only principal, there is no right of action in the actual principal; the agent alone can sue or be sued. In *Humble v Hunter*:[8]

> An agent entered into a charter-party and described himself as 'owner' of the ship; it was held that evidence was not admissible to show that another was principal, nor could that other sue on the contract. For if the principal allows the agent to represent himself as principal, the agent alone can sue on the contract made.

Subject to this, the third party (as stated above) may bring his action against either the agent or the undisclosed principal, and oral evidence will be admitted to show that a written contract purporting to be made by a certain person is in reality made by him as agent. The liability of principal and agent is alternative and not joint, and though the creditor may be entitled to elect against which of them he will enforce his remedies, any unequivocal acts showing an intention to hold one of them liable will discharge the other.[9] Thus, if the creditor obtains judgment on the contract against the principal, he cannot afterwards get judgment against the agent, nor, if he gets it against the agent, can he afterwards succeed against the principal.[10] Possibly the remedy against the undisclosed principal may be lost if the principal has settled with the agent before the third party was aware that there was a principal: in *Armstrong v Stokes*:[11]

> P engaged A to buy goods and A bought from T without disclosing he was acting as an agent. P paid A the price of the goods but A did not pass this on to P. *Held:* P was not liable to T as P had paid the price to A at a time when T did not know of P and was giving credit to A alone.

---

1 See, e.g. *Nash v Dix* (1898) 78 LT 445; *Dyster v Randell & Sons* [1926] Ch 932.
2 See, e.g. *Heald v Kenworthy* (1855) 10 Exch 739 (P had already paid A before agency discovered, but held bound to pay T again).
3 *George v Clagett* (1797) 7 Term Rep, 359, and for a later example, see *Montagu v Forwood* [1893] 2 QB 350.
4 (1785) 7 TR 360, n.
5 (1887) 12 App Cas 271.
6 *Semenza v Brinsley* (1865) 18 CBNS 467; *Borries v Imperial Ottoman Bank* (1874) LR 9 CP 38.
7 *Greer v Downs Supply Co* [1927] 2 KB 28.
8 (1848) 12 QB 310. See also *Said v Butt* [1920] 3 KB 497. Cf. *Formby Bros v*

Formby (1910) 102 LT 116, CA; *Fred. Drughorn Ltd v Rederiaktiebolaget Transatlantic* [1919] AC 203; *Epps. v Rothnie* [1945] KB 562, [1946] 1 All ER 146.

9 *Scarf v Jardine* (1882) 7 App Cas 345. The institution of proceedings against either the principal or the agent does not necessarily amount to a binding election so as to bar proceedings against the other: *Clarkson Booker Ltd v Andjel* [1964] 2 QB 775, [1964] 3 All ER 260, CA.

10 *Kendall v Hamilton* (1879) 4 App Cas, per Cairns LC, at 514. Quaere whether he can get the judgment set aside and then sue the other?

11 (1872) LR 7 QB 598. This decision was criticised by the Court of Appeal in *Irvine & Co v Watson & Sons* (1880) 5 QBD 414, discussed in para. 10.25, ante; and it appears to be contrary to *Heald v Kenworthy* (1855) 10 Exch 739 (see note 2, ante).

RIGHTS AND DUTIES WHEN THE PRINCIPAL IS NON-EXISTENT

10.27 Although an agent expressly contracting as such cannot generally sue in his own name, he may be able to do so where he purports to act for an unnamed principal but there is none, the supposed agent being the real principal.[1] Similarly, where a person purports to make a contract for a non-existent company, it may at common law be possible to infer that he intended to assume personal liability;[2] but pre-incorporation contracts are now dealt with by s. 9 (2) of the European Communities Act 1972, which provides:

'Where a contract purports to be made by a company, or by a person or agent for a company, at a time when the company has not been formed then subject to any agreement to the contrary the contract shall have effect as a contract entered into by the person purporting to act for the company or as agent for it, and he shall be personally liable on the contract accordingly'.

1 *Schmaltz v Avery* (1851) 16 QBD 655. The agent could not have enforced the contract himself if he had purported to contract for a named principal whose identity was material. For corporations, see generally para. 2.22, ante.

2 *Kelner v Baxter* (1866) LR 2 CP 174. But see *Holman v Pullin* (1884) Cab & El 254 (no such inference drawn).

EQUITABLE LIABILITY OF PRINCIPAL FOR MONEY BORROWED WITHOUT AUTHORITY

10.28 In some cases where an agent borrows money on behalf of another without any authority or in excess of his authority, although the mere fact of the borrowing may impose no liability on the principal, yet the lender acting in good faith has an equitable right to recover against the principal any part of the money borrowed which has in fact been applied in paying legal debts and obligations of the principal.[1] The lender is subrogated to the position of P's creditor. And even where the agent is known to have no authority to borrow, yet to the extent to which the money borrowed is applied to payment of legal debts of the principal, the lender may assert this equitable right.[2]

This equity may also protect an agent who pays his principal's debts without authority. Thus, where a bank contrary to instructions honoured the cheques of a company on the signature of one director only, the cheques having been drawn in favour of and the proceeds received by ordinary trade creditors of the company, so that its liabilities were not thereby increased, the bank on being sued by the company for the amount of the cheques was held entitled to take credit for such payments.[3]

---

1 *Blackburn, etc, Building Society v Cunliffe, Brookes & Co* (1883) 22 ChD 61; affd. sub nom *Cunliffe Brooks & Co v Blackburn, etc, Building Society* (1884) 9 App Cas 857; *Bannatyne v MacIver* [1906] 1 KB 103.
2 *Reversion Fund and Insurance Co v Maison Cosway* [1913] 1 KB 364.
3 *Liggett (Liverpool) Ltd v Barclays Bank Ltd* [1928] 1 KB 48.

---

5. Particular types of agents

10.29 Many of the types of agent referred to in this section fall within the statutory expression 'mercantile agent', and therefore have their powers to dispose of goods increased by the Factors Act 1889 (see para. 10.20, ante).

a) FACTORS AND BROKERS

The distinction between factors and brokers was important in nineteenth century commerce, though both categories were employed to sell goods and might bring into play the rules relating to unnamed and undisclosed principals.[1] However, their powers differed in a number of respects. A factor was entrusted with the possession of goods for the purposes of sale,[2] and thus came within the Factors Act 1889;[3] he had a general lien over the goods and proceeds in respect of the balance of his charges;[4] and he was entitled to sell in his own name.[5] On the other hand, a broker was not granted possession or control over goods, being merely a negotiator empowered to effect contracts of sale or purchase for others;[6] and he therefore fell outside the Factors Act,[3] and normally had no general lien[7] and no power to sell in his own name.[8]

Factors flourished in the nineteenth century, but have since tended to fall away. They should not be confused with the modern, computer-based, debt-collecting business termed 'factoring'.[9]

The special position of insurance brokers, who must now be registered as such,[10] is beyond the scope of this work.[11]

---

1 See paras. 10.25–10.26, ante.
2 See the judgment in *Stevens v Biller* (1884) 25 ChD 31.
3 See *Cole v North Western Bank Ltd* [1928] 1 KB 48.
4 *Drinkwater v Goodwin* (1775) 1 Cowp 251; and see para. 17.11, post.
5 Subject to the ordinary rules for undisclosed principals.
6 *Stevens v Biller* (ante), at p. 37.
7 Except for insurance brokers, who have a lien on the policy for their general balance: *Mann v Forrester* (1814) 4 Camp. 60.
8 See *Baring v Corrie* (1818) 2 B & Ald. 137 at 143, 148.
9 See Biscoe *Law and Practice of Credit Factoring*.
10 Insurance Brokers (Registration) Act 1977.
11 See *Chitty on Contracts*, 24th edn, Vol. 2, paras. 3936–3937.

---

b) DEL CREDERE AGENTS

10.30 A *del credere* agent is an agent for sale who undertakes to pay if the buyer becomes insolvent; but such an agent does not guarantee the due performance of the contract in the sense that the seller may sue him in respect of any breach by the buyer other than his failure to pay. Such disputes must be fought out between the principals, the agent only guaranteeing that the buyer will prove solvent and not default in payment.[1]

The *del credere* agent will be liable though the arrangement has not been reduced to, or evidenced by, writing, as his guarantee promise is only part of the larger contract of agency and the courts have held that the provisions of the Statute of Frauds are excluded in such a case.[2]

---

1 *Thomas Gabriel & Sons v Churchill and Sim* [1914] 3 KB 1272.
2 *Sutton & Co v Grey* [1894] 1 QB 285, CA, and para. 16.05, post.

---

c) BANKERS

10.31 The banker is the agent of the customer to pay sums of money as ordered, but the ordinary relationship between banker and customer is that of debtor and creditor; the banker being creditor when the customer's account is overdrawn, the customer being the creditor when the balance is in his favour.[1] However the ordinary rule that a debtor must seek his creditor[2] does not apply; and the obligation to pay does not arise until the customer or banker, as the case may be, has made a demand for payment upon the other. Accordingly, the period of limitation will only commence to run from the date of such demand.[3]

The customer is entitled to draw cheques on the banker to the extent of the money standing to his credit;[4] the banker has a general lien on all securities of the customer deposited with him as banker to secure any sum in which the customer may be indebted to the banker unless there be an express contract, or circumstances that show an implied contract inconsistent with lien.[5] With regard to bills of exchange: a banker has authority to pay bills accepted by the customer and made payable at his bank,[6] but he is not bound to do so;[7] but, if he pays out on a bill or cheque not drawn by the customer i.e. a forgery, he is not generally entitled to debit his customer's account.[8]

A banker is under a qualified duty to keep secret the state of his customer's account, his customer's transactions and information relating to the customer acquired through keeping the account, and disclosure (except with the consent of the customer) is only justifiable:

1. Where made under compulsion of law;[9]
2. Where made in pursuance of a duty to the public;
3. Where necessary to protect the interests of the banker.[10]

The banker's duty of secrecy continues after the closing of the customer's account.

If a bank, with its customer's express or implied assent, answers enquiries regarding the customer's credit, it owes a duty of care to the enquirer and will be liable for loss suffered as a result of careless misstatements unless it has excluded liability, for example, by giving the advice 'without responsibility'.[11]

---

1 *Foley v Hill* (1848) 2 H of L Cas. 28.
2 See para. 7.14, ante.
3 *Joachimson v Swiss Bank Corporation* [1921] 3 KB 110.
4 *Pott v Clegg* (1847) 16 M & W 321. When the cheque has been paid it becomes the property of the drawer, but the banker may keep it so long as it is wanted as a voucher. For cheques, see chap. 21.
5 *Brandao v Barnett* (1846) 12 Cl & F 787.
6 *Kymer v Laurie* (1849) 18 LJQB 218. For bills, see chap. 20.
7 Lord Macnaghten in *Bank of England v Vagliano* [1891] AC, at 157, HL. The position of a banker who pays a forged instrument or a genuine instrument with a forged indorsement is dealt with, para. 21.05, post.
8 For an exceptional case where he may do so, see para. 10.28 n. 3, ante.
9 Bankers' Books' Evidence Act 1879 and Paget *Law of Banking* (8th edn), 167–172.
10 *Tournier v National Provincial and Union Bank of England* [1924] 1 KB 461. By statutory authority, the Inland Revenue is empowered in certain circumstances to require a banker to give information about a customer's account.
11 *Hedley Byrne & Co Ltd v Heller & Partners Ltd* [1964] AC 465, [1963] 2

All ER 575, HL. But see now the Unfair Contract Terms Act 1977: para. 3.15, ante.

---

d) AUCTIONEERS

10.32 An auctioneer is a person employed to sell property by auction.[1] The following points should be noticed:

1. It seems that, where an auctioneer advertises goods to be sold by auction, he is not liable for breach of contract to prospective purchasers where the lots are withdrawn before the auction.[2]

2. He is an agent for the seller (with authority to do all such acts as come within an auctioneer's province),[3] and when the goods have been knocked down, for the buyer also, and his signature is then sufficient to satisfy the requirements of s. 40 of the Law of Property Act 1925.[4]

3. At common law he gave no warranties as to the property on behalf of the seller unless expressly so authorised,[5] but that position has now been overtaken by statute with regard to undertakings by the seller.[6]

4. The auctioneer may himself sue for or receive the price of goods sold by auction even where the principal is disclosed:[7] he undertakes to give possession in return for the price.[8]

5. He must not delegate his authority.[9]

6. He should sell only for cash,[10] and at the best price; but he is entitled to sue on any cheque taken for the deposit and drawn in favour of himself.[11]

7. He is responsible to his principal for loss sustained through his delivering the goods without receiving the price,[12] and he is answerable for the proper storage of goods whilst they are with him.

8. He has possession of the goods, and a lien on them.[12]

9. He has implied authority to sell goods without reserve,[13] but if a sale is notified as being subject to reserve and the auctioneer knocks down goods to a 'buyer' at less than the reserve price the buyer has no right to the goods and cannot sue the auctioneer for breach of warranty of authority.[14]

10. An auctioneer who sells on behalf of A goods which really belong to B, and who delivers the goods to the purchaser, is liable in damages for conversion at the suit of B, though he acted without knowledge of B's rights.[15] If the true owner recovers the goods from the person to whom the auctioneer has sold them, the auctioneer may be liable to that purchaser.[16]

---

1 As to contracts for the sale of goods made by auction: see para. 13.48, post.
2 *Harris v Nickerson* (1873) LR 8 QB 286. But he might be liable in the torts of deceit or negligent misstatement.

3 E.g. he may be bound to sell the goods under descriptions supplied by his principal: *Brown v Drapper & Co* (1975) 233 Estates Gazette 929, CA.
4 See paras. 12.03, 12.05, post.
5 Where there is a sale of unascertained goods, and the auctioneer acts on behalf of an unnamed principal, the auctioneer may give certain undertakings as to his principal's title: see per Salter J in *Benton v Campbell, Parker & Co* [1925] 2 KB 410.
6 See the Supply of Goods (Implied Terms) Act 1973 and the Unfair Contract Terms Act 1977, discussed below, paras. 13.19 et seq.
7 *Chelmsford Auctions Ltd v Poole* [1973] 1 QB 542, [1973] 1 All ER 810, CA. As to land, he may only receive the deposit: *Sykes v Giles* (1839) 5 M & W 645.
8 Per Salter J in *Benton v Campbell, Parker & Co* [1925] 2 KB 410; for the ordinary rule as to delivery and payment, see para. 13.30, post.
9 See para. 10.12, ante.
10 Unless it is customary to accept a cheque, and he acts without negligence in taking one: *Farrer v Lacy Hartland & Co* (1885) 31 ChD 42.
11 *Pollway Ltd v Abdullah* [1974] 2 All ER 381, [1974] 1 WLR 493, CA (see further para. 20.17, post).
12 *Williams v Millington* (1788) 1 Hy Bl 81 at 84. See para. 10.25, ante.
13 In which case, the auctioneer will be liable for breach of contract if he knocks the goods down to the seller: *Warlow v Harrison* (1859) 1 E & E 309—probably for breach of warranty of authority, as to which see para. 10.23, ante. For a dispute as to the highest bidder, see *Tully v Irish Land Commission* (1961) 97 ILTR 174.
14 *McManus v Fortescue* [1907] 2 KB 1, cf. *Fay v Miller, Wilkins & Co* [1941] KB 360, [1941] 2 All ER 18, CA.
15 *Consolidated Co v Curtis & Son* [1892] 1 QB 495 at 500: *RH Willis & Son v British Car Auctions Ltd* [1978] 2 All ER 392, [1978] 1 WLR 438, 62, CA.
16 For breach of warranty of authority: see para. 10.23, ante, and for conversion, see para. 1.03, ante.

---

e) Others

10.33 *i) freight forwarders*
Freight forwarders, who are sometimes called forwarding agents, are intermediaries who arrange the through transport of goods, typically in international sale transactions and on standard-form contracts.[1]

ii) dealers in credit transactions
A dealer who negotiates a regulated agreement within the ambit of the Consumer Credit Act 1974 may by the terms of that Act be deemed the agent of the creditor under that regulated agreement for certain purposes.[2]

---

1 See Hill *Freight Forwarders.* For international sales, see paras. 13.39, et seq., post; and for standard-form contracts, see para. 3.13, ante.
2 See paras. 14.47–14.49, post. For the difficulties at common law, see para. 10.02, ante.

Chapter 11

Partnership[1]

1. Introductory

11.01 As a broad generalisation, a person wishing to engage in business is offered the following choices of medium by the law: he may operate as a sole trader, relying on agents[2] and other employees[3] to do for him that which he cannot do himself; or he may enter into a partnership with one or more equals, their relationship being codified in the Partnership Act 1890, and that partnership may in turn utilise agents[2] and other employees;[3] or he may obtain for his business separate legal personality by registering it under the Companies Acts 1948 and 76, that separate legal person operating through agents[2] and other employees.[3] Nowadays, registered companies tend to be a more popular business medium than a partnership, probably largely because of the advantages thereby obtained in respect of the raising of share and loan capital, limitation of liability and taxation. Hence the device of the partnership most commonly appears within those professions and trades which are prevented by their trade organisation from operating through the medium of a registered company and thus from obtaining limited liability at the expense of their clients.

The Partnership Act 1890 is a statute which has codified the main principles of the law of partnership; and, though it does not contain the whole of that law,[4] the main principles of it are authoritatively stated by the statute.[5] One of the advantages of the partnership medium not available to the same extent in respect of registered companies is the ability to keep the business affairs of the partnership secret—particularly the accounts; and it is common for partnerships to avail themselves further of this advantage by including in their partnership agreement a provision for arbitration in the event of a dispute.[6] The relative success of the Partnership Act as a piece of drafting, combined with the relative infrequency with which arbitrated partnership disputes have been referred to the courts since 1890, has resulted in a paucity of litigation such as might lead to an underestimate of the present degree to which partnerships are utilised, and to obscure the present areas of tension within the field of partnership.

---

1 In this chapter, the references to sections are to those of the Partnership Act 1890.
2 For the law of agency, see ante, chap. 10.
3 For the contract of employment, see post, chap. 32.
4 See ibid, s. 46.
5 As amended by the Limited Partnerships Act 1907: dealt with para. 11.22, post.
6 For arbitration agreements generally, see post, chap. 34.

---

2. Definition of a partnership

11.02   Section 1 of the Partnership Act 1890 defines partnership as follows:

'Partnership is the relation which subsists between persons carrying on a business in common with a view of profit.'

The section goes on to exclude expressly incorporated companies (those having separate legal personality from their members), whether incorporated in the normal way (under the Companies Acts 1948 and 1976) or under any other Act of Parliament, e.g. the public utilities, or (more exceptionally) by letters patent or Royal Charter.

Distinctions from a company Partnerships must be distinguished from trading companies, which are almost invariably incorporated under the Companies Acts and are governed by a completely different code of law. The main practical difference between a registered company and a partnership is that the formation and existence of a partnership depends upon mutual trust and the personal relationship of the members to each other, whereas the formation and existence of a registered company does not depend to any extent on this; further, whilst in a partnership every member is entitled and likely to take part in the management of the business, in a company the management is left to specified officers.[1] In law, the essential difference is that a company is regarded as being a separate entity from its members,[2] while a partnership is not, although, as a matter of procedure, many things can be done in the name of the firm. 'The firm' is simply a short name substituted for the names of the members composing the partnership and every partner is liable *personally* to the full extent of his fortune for any debt of the firm. When an action is brought against partners in the firm's name, it is still in effect an action against each of the individual partners.[3]

Limit on numbers By the Companies Act 1948, a banking partnership may not consist of more than ten persons but the Companies Act 1967 allows a banking partnership of not more than twenty persons each of whom is for the time being authorised by the Department of Trade to be a member of such partnership.[4]

With regard to other partnerships, the general rule is that the partnership may not consist of more than twenty persons but this restriction does not apply to partnerships of solicitors, or accountants or members of a recognised stock exchange. The Department of Trade has powers by regulations to exempt other types of partnerships from the general rule.[5]

---

1 In partnerships, the investors are normally active participants in the running of the firm, and it is unusual to have a sleeping partner; whereas in the case of registered companies it is by no means normal for shareholders as such to participate in the management, especially in the larger companies.
2 *Salomon v Salomon & Co* [1897] AC 22, HL.
3 See per James LJ, in *Re Shand, Ex parte Corbett* (1880) 14 ChD 122.
4 Companies Act 1948, s. 429 as amended by Companies Act 1967, s. 119.
5 Companies Act 1948, s. 434 as amended by Companies Act 1967, s. 120. Various regulations have been made exempting from the general rule partnerships of specified descriptions such as estate agents and actuaries.

11.03 *How to identify a partnership* In many cases, it will be clear from the formal partnership agreement (as to which see para. 11.07, post) that there is a 'partnership' within the meaning of section 1. However, in addition to defining 'partnership' in a general way, and then expressly excluding bodies which would otherwise answer the terms of the definition, the Act seeks to help in the difficult borderline cases by laying down certain further rules for determining the existence of a partnership. These rules, set out in section 2, define the principles applicable to the consideration of typical cases, and serve very materially to elucidate and explain the meaning of 'partnership'. They are as follows:

'(1) Joint tenancy, tenancy in common, joint property, common property, or part ownership does not of itself create a partnership as to anything so held or owned, whether the tenants or owners do or do not share any profits.

(2) The sharing of gross returns does not of itself create a partnership, whether the persons sharing such returns have or

have not a joint or common right or interest in any property from which or from the use of which the returns are derived.

(3) The receipt by a person of a share of the profits of a business is prima facie evidence that he is a partner in the business, but the receipt of such a share, or of a payment contingent on or varying with the profits of a business, does not of itself make him a partner in the business, and in particular—

(a) The receipt by a person of a debt or other liquidated amounts by instalments or otherwise out of the accruing profits of a business does not of itself make him a partner in the business or liable as such:

(b) A contract for the remuneration of a servant or agent of a person engaged in a business by a share of the profits of the business does not of itself make [him] a partner in the business or liable as such:

(c) A person being the widow or child of a deceased partner, and receiving by way of annuity a portion of the profits made in the business in which the deceased person was a partner, is not by reason only of such receipt a partner in the business, or liable as such:

(d) The advance of money by way of loan to a person engaged or about to engage in any business on a contract with that person that the lender shall receive a rate of interest varying with the profits, or shall receive a share of the profits arising from carrying on the business, does not of itself make the lender a partner with the person or persons carrying on the business or liable as such. Provided that the contract is in writing, and signed by or on behalf of all the parties thereto:[1]

(e) A person receiving by way of annuity or otherwise a portion of the profits of a business in consideration of the sale by him of the goodwill of the business is not by reason only of such receipt a partner in the business or liable as such.'

---

1 The absence of a written and signed contract will not automatically make the lender a partner, but the fact that the lender is to share in the profits is then prima facie evidence of partnership—the whole agreement will be looked at to ascertain the real intention of the parties.

11.04 Whether a given person is or is not a partner depends upon the facts of the case and the intention of the parties. At one time it was considered that receipt of part of the profits was of itself conclusive proof of partnership, but this is not so.[1] In *Cox v Hickman*:[2]

> A trader owed money to many creditors, who entered into an arrangement with him, whereby he agreed to carry on the business under their superintendence, and grądually to pay off their debts out of a share of the profits. The case was carried up to the House of Lords, where it was *held*—somewhat against what then seemed the current of authority—that such an arrangement did not constitute a partnership *per se*, and it would only be a partnership if the debtor carried on the business for and on behalf of the creditors, so as to constitute the relation of agent and principal between them. On the facts, there was no partnership.

The Act now states the law as declared in *Cox v Hickman*. If the 'lender' is to have a voice in the management, or he is to be repaid only out of the business, or he is to take an interest in the capital, the agreement probably will be considered a partnership.

It is clear that partnership is not the same as co-ownership; the former may include the latter, but the converse will not apply. They may be thus distinguished:

1. Co-ownership is not necessarily the result of agreement, partnership is; e.g. A gives land to B and C in common; B and C are not partners, but may become so by agreement among themselves. So the co-owners of a ship are not necessarily partners, and it needs an agreement, express or implied, to make them so;
2. Co-ownership does not, of necessity, involve the idea of working for profit, partnership does;
3. A co-owner has a right of free disposition over his property without the consent of his co-owner; a partner who desires to replace himself by another cannot, in the absence of agreement, do so without the consent of his co-partner.

Sharing profits is strong, though not conclusive, evidence of partnership;[3] and it may be that an agreement to share losses is even more cogent, but again not conclusive.[4] At the same time the court will look at the whole of the evidence, and draw the fair inference of fact; only when nothing more is known than that profits or losses are shared, does it *necessarily* follow that there must be a partnership.[3] Persons who work together with a view to forming a company are not normally partners within the meaning of section 1 of the Partnership Act 1890. In *Keith Spicer Ltd v Mansell*:[5]

> M and B agreed to form a limited company and, in the three weeks prior to its formation decided to do certain acts so that

the company could start business at once on its formation. B ordered goods from KS Ltd intending them to be used by the company and M and B opened a bank account in the name of the proposed company; B became insolvent and KS Ltd sued M for the price of the goods on the basis that M and B were partners when they were ordered. *Held:* M and B were not partners and M was therefore not liable for the price of the goods.

It may be difficult to determine whether discussions with a view to partnership or other evidence tending to point towards a partnership necessarily establish that a partnership in fact exists.[6]

---

1 *Mollwo, March & Co v Court of Wards* (1872) LR 4 PC 419.
2 (1860) 8 HL Cas. 268.
3 *Badeley v Consolidated Bank* (1888) 38 ChD 238; and see *Davis v Davis* [1894] 1 Ch 393, 399, 401; *Hollom v Whichelow* (1895) 64 LJQB 170; *King v Whichelow*, ibid, 801; *Canny Gabriel Castle Jackson Advertising v Volume Sales (Finance)* (1974) 131 CLR 321 (High Ct of Australia).
4 See *Ross v Parkyns* (1875) LR 20 Eq 331; *Walker v Hirsch* (1884) 27 ChD 460.
5 [1970] 1 All ER 462; [1970] 1 WLR 333, CA. Cf. *Kelner v Baxter* (1866) LR 2 CP 174: see para. 10.27, ante.
6 *Floydd v Cheney* [1970] 1 Ch 603, [1970] 1 All ER 446.

11.05 *Postponement of lender's rights in case of insolvency* The Act further provides that if any person to whom money has been advanced on a contract[1] to pay a rate of interest varying with the profits, or any buyer of a goodwill who has engaged to pay the vendor a portion of the profits in consideration of the sale, shall be adjudged a bankrupt, or enter into an arrangement to pay his creditors less than 100 pence in the pound, or die in insolvent circumstances, the claims of any such lender or vendor of goodwill shall be postponed to the rights of the ordinary creditors.[2]

---

1 Whether such contract is in writing or not (*Re Fort* [1897] 2 QB 495).
2 Partnership Act 1890, s. 3. For goodwill, see para. 11.21, post.

---

3. The firm name

11.06 In the case of a firm having a place of business in the United Kingdom, if the firm name does not consist of the true surnames of all partners who are individuals and the corporate names of all partners who are corporations without any addition except the true christian names or initials of the individual partners,[1] the firm must be registered under the Registration of Business Names Act 1916. The particulars requiring registration include the business name and the general nature and principal place of the business, and in respect of every individual partner must disclose: his christian name and surname; his present nationality; his usual residence; and any other business occupation that he follows; and in respect of every corporation which is a partner the corporate name and registered office must be stated. Particulars of changes in the constitution of the firm must also be registered.

If there is default in registration the firm cannot sue on any contract entered into while it was in default, unless the court grants relief against the disability, but if the firm is sued on such a contract it will not be precluded from asserting rights under the contract by way of counter-claim or set-off.[2] The court may, e.g. if satisfied that the default was accidental or that on other grounds it is just and equitable to grant relief, grant relief generally; or it may do so as respects any particular contract in the course of proceedings to enforce it, and if such relief is granted it will operate retrospectively so as to validate the contract *ab initio* and all subsequent proceedings in respect of it.[3] The title to property of which the defaulter has obtained complete possession is not affected.[4]

All registered firms must publish particulars of the names and nationality of the partners in their trade catalogues, trade circulars, show cards and business letters.[5]

---

1 The Act also applies where a partner has changed his name (except in the case of a woman who marries) but subject to exceptions in s. 116 (4) of the Companies Act 1947 where, e.g., twenty years have elapsed since the change of name.
2 Registration of Business Names Act 1916, s. 8.
3 *Re Shaer* [1927] 1 Ch 355.
4 *Daniel v Rogers* [1918] 2 KB 228.
5 Registration of Business Names Act 1916, s. 18, as amended by the Companies Act 1947, s. 123, Sch. IX, Part II.

---

4. Formation of the contract

11.07   The contract is formed by consent alone, and no particular formality is required. The agreement may therefore be oral or implied from conduct, but in that case the court will not imply into the agreement more terms than are strictly necessary.[1]

However, the general practice is to have a written agreement containing the terms on which the partners are to carry on their business, and this document is styled the *Articles of Partnership,* if under seal, or a *Partnership Agreement,* if not under seal. In practice, most trades and professions likely to operate by way of partnerships have their own model form of contract.[2] The rights and duties of the parties to a partnership agreement are considered later (para. 11.14 et seq., post), as is the property of the firm (para. 11.18, post).

1 *Miles v Clark* [1953] 1 All ER 779, [1953] 1 WLR 537.
2 E.g. *Phoenix v Pope* [1974] 1 All ER 512, [1974] 1 WLR 719. For standard-form contracts generally, see para. 3.13, ante.

5. Who may be partners

The broad rule that anyone who is *sui iuris* may be a partner is subject to a number of qualifications.

11.08 1. Alien *enemies* or persons adhering to the enemy may not be partners of an Englishman, and a partnership between such persons and an Englishman is dissolved when war breaks out;[1] but, where for the purpose of winding up the affairs of a dissolved partnership an action is brought to recover a debt due to the firm, an alien enemy partner may be joined as a co-plaintiff.[2]
2. Insanity of a partner will not ipso facto dissolve an already existing partnership, but it will be a ground on which the court may decree dissolution.[3]

A minor may be a partner, and, unless he repudiates the contract during his minority or within a reasonable time of becoming 18 (as he may), he remains a member of the firm, though he does not thereby render himself personally liable to creditors for partnership debts contracted during his minority.[4] However, an infant partner cannot prevent partnership debts being discharged out of the partnership assets, including any capital which he may have supplied.

New partners may be admitted, provided the legal number is not exceeded,[5] but, of course, the consent of all the existing partners must first have been obtained, either in the original articles or agreement or by subsequent agreement.[6]

1 *Stevenson & Sons v Aktiengesellschaft für Cartonnagen-Industrie* [1917] 1 KB 842, CA. This case went to the House of Lords, where it was not disputed

that the partnership had been dissolved by the outbreak of war. As to the rights of the enemy partner, see para. 11.17, post.

2 *Rodriguez v Speyer Bros* [1919] AC 59.
3 Partnership Act 1890, s. 35.
4 *Lovell v Beauchamp* [1894] AC, at 611, per Herschell LC.
5 Para. 11.02, ante.
6 Partnership Act 1890, s. 24 (7).

---

6. Rights and duties of the partners in relation to third parties

11.09 *Liability on contracts* Every partner is an agent of the firm and his other partners for the purpose of the business of the partnership; and, in general, every partner who does any act for carrying on in the usual way business of the kind carried on by the firm binds the firm and his partners.[1]

But partners are not liable (*a*) on a contract entered into by a partner outside the scope of the business of the firm, unless the partner was, in fact, specially authorised to make the contract,[2] or (*b*) on a contract entered into by a partner without authority if the third party either knows the partner has no authority or does not know or believe him to be a partner.[3]

The liability on a partnership debt is joint, not several.[4] But the estate of a deceased partner is severally liable in due course of administration for the debts and obligations of the firm while he was a partner, subject to the prior payment of his separate debts.[5] This must not be misunderstood. As a general rule every partner is liable for every penny of the firm's debts, and the creditor has the option to sue any or all of them. If he obtains judgment against the firm, he may issue execution against the property of the members, and is not confined to satisfaction out of the joint property. The liability is joint, but all are liable. He may sue each partner separately, but if he obtains *judgment* against any of them he cannot enforce the judgment against any but those against whom it was pronounced, nor can he afterwards get judgment against the others; for the liability, being a joint—i.e. a single liability, has become merged in the judgment. Nor are his rights different, where he does not get any payment under the judgment. Thus in *Kendall v Hamilton*:[6]

A and B (partners) borrowed money from C; eventually C sued them on the loan, and obtained a judgment which was not satisfied. Afterwards C discovered that D was a partner with A and B at the date of the loan, but it was *held* that C had lost his remedy against D, as the joint liability had merged in a judgment which was not pronounced against D.

Had D been dead, and his estate been in course of administration, D's estate would have been severally liable, i.e. liable on a separate contract to the same effect as the joint one, and this would not have been merged by a judgment against the other contractors.

The above doctrine of merger has no application where there are distinct causes of action; so that if a partner gives his own cheque for the price of goods sold to the firm, the creditor may, if the cheque is dishonoured, recover judgment upon it, without prejudicing his rights to sue the firm or any member of it for the price of the goods, if his judgment on the cheque remains unsatisfied.[7]

1 Partnership Act 1890, s. 5.
2 Partnership Act 1890, s. 7.
3 Ibid, ss. 5, 8. Cf. the rule in ordinary agency law that if an agent acts within his usual authority for an undisclosed principal the principal is bound even though the agent has acted contrary to secret restrictions on his authority: *Watteau v Fenwick* [1893] 1 QB 346; para. 10.22, ante.
4 Ibid, s. 9; and see *Kendall v Hamilton* (1897) 4 App Cas 504; *Badeley v Consolidated Bank* (1887) 34 ChD 536; reversed on another point, 38 ChD 238, CA.
5 Ibid, s. 9. In *Bagel v Miller* [1903] 2 KB 212 M's estate was held not liable for the price of goods ordered by the firm at a time when M was a partner but the goods were not delivered until after M's death, since the obligation to pay only accrued on delivery.
6 (1879) 4 App Cas 504.
7 *Wegg Prosser v Evans* [1895] 1 QB 108.

11.10 *Implied authority of a partner*   It is settled that all partners are bound by the acts or admissions of one, if done within the scope of the business. Story says:

'a partner, indeed, virtually embraces the character both of a principal and of an agent'.[1]

And in *Baird's Case,*[2] James LJ, said:

'as between the partners and the outside world (whatever may be their private relations between themselves), each partner is the unlimited agent of every other in every matter connected with the partnership business, or which he represents as partnership business, and not being in its nature beyond the scope of the partnership.'

But a partner is an agent only so far as he is acting upon, and within the scope of, the firm's ordinary affairs; that the act is useful to the firm is not sufficient, neither is it necessary; the act done must be a furtherance of the ordinary business of the firm.[3]

Even then (as has already been pointed out), the firm will not always be bound, for if a partner attempts to make a firm liable, though within his apparent authority, the firm will not be bound, if in fact he has no authority, and if this was known to the other contracting party, or by the exercise of reasonable diligence could have been known; e.g.:

A partner gives a partnership security in discharge of a private debt; the recipient must show that he took it without knowledge, and without such negligence as would amount to knowledge.

In *Kendal v Wood*, Cockburn CJ, said, that in a case such as this, the recipient would deal with the partner at his peril.[4]

The apparent authority of a partner may be explained as follows:[5]

1. Every partner may bind his firm by any of the following acts:
   a) He may sell any goods or personal chattels of the firm;
   [Legal estate in land must be conveyed by all the partners, or by one authorised by *deed*.]
   b) He may purchase on account of the firm any goods of a kind necessary for or usually employed in the business carried on by it;[6]
   c) He may receive payment of debts due to the firm,[7] and give receipts and releases for them;
   d) He may engage employees for the partnership business.
2. If the partnership is in trade, that is, if the business is one which depends on the buying and selling of goods,[8] every partner may *also* bind the firm by any of the following acts:
   a) He may make, accept and issue bills and other negotiable instruments in the name of the firm;[9]
   [A member of a *non-trading* partnership may bind the firm by negotiable instruments, but only in those cases where it is shown to be within the usual course to issue negotiable instruments, the burden of showing this being on the person attempting to make the firm liable.]
   b) He may borrow money on the credit of the firm;
   c) He may, for the purpose, pledge any goods or personal chattels belonging to the firm.
3. A partner has no implied authority to bind the firm by a deed,[10] or to give a guarantee in the name of the firm,[11] or to bind the firm by a submission to arbitration.[12]

The authority continues even after a dissolution, so far as is necessary properly to wind up the business and complete pending transactions, save that a bankrupt partner cannot bind the firm by his acts.[13] And where one of two partners dies, the surviving partner may carry on the business for the purpose of finally winding it up, and may mortgage the real or personal property of the late firm for the purpose of securing a partnership debt.[14]

---

1 *Partnership* § 1.
2 (1870) 5 Ch App, at 733.
3 *Mercantile Credit Co Ltd v Garrod* [1962] 3 All ER 1103.
4 (1871) LR 6 Ex. 243, CA.
5 Drake, *Law of Partnership* (2nd edn) 36–40.
6 A partner has no implied authority to make his co-partners partners with other persons in another business. But where a partner in a firm of produce merchants agreed with X to buy and re-sell potatoes on joint account, Megarry J, *held* the partner had implied authority to bind his co-partners to such joint venture or partnership with X—such partnership was not 'another business': *Mann v D'Arcy* [1968] 2 All ER 172, [1968] 1 WLR 893.
7 In the absence of express or implied authority, a private debt due to one partner is not discharged by payment to the firm of which he is a member: *Powell v Brodhurst* [1901] 2 Ch 160.
8 *Higgins v Beauchamp* [1914] 3 KB 1192 at 1195, per Lush J, in which case it was *held* that the business of cinema proprietors was not a trading business and in consequence a partner had no implied authority to borrow on behalf of the firm.
9 See para. 20.07, post. When a partner's individual name coincides with the firm's name and he does not carry on a separate business, his acceptance of a bill of exchange is prima facie the acceptance of the firm: see *Yorkshire Banking Co v Beatson* (1880) 5 CPD 109.
10 *Steiglitz v Eggington* (1815) Holt NP 141.
11 *Brettel v Williams* (1849) 4 Exch 623.
12 *Stead v Salt* (1825) 3 Bing 101.
13 Partnership Act 1890, s. 38.
14 *Re Bourne* [1906] 2 Ch 427.

11.11   *Outgoing partners*   When a partner retires, the other partners may agree to hold him free of all liabilities already incurred: if assented to by the creditors, this will give him a complete release; but if the creditors are not parties to this agreement, then, so far as they are concerned, he is still a debtor,[1] though he may have rights of indemnity against his former partners. Agreement by the creditors to release a retired (or deceased) partner may be implied from a course of dealing with the firm as newly constituted.[2] Such an agreement, express or implied amounts to a *novation*.[3]

If a member of a firm agrees with his partners on retirement that he shall in future be regarded merely as a surety for the firm's existing debts, the creditors who know this must treat the retiring partner as a surety, and may release him if they give time to the other parties.[4]

A change in the constitution of a firm will prima facie terminate a continuing guarantee given to the firm or to a third party in respect of the transactions of the firm so far as relates to future transactions.[5]

Incoming partners A new partner is not liable for debts incurred before he entered the firm[6] save by special agreement. Thus:

> If on June 1st A & Co owe B £500 and on June 2nd C joins A & Co, agreeing to give a premium and to be liable for existing debts B cannot sue C unless he, B, is a party to the contract, and gives consideration; e.g. agrees, if C makes himself responsible, to give time to the firm or to release an old partner.[7]

---

1 Partnership Act 1890, s. 17 (2), (3).
2 *Rouse v Bradford Banking Co* [1894] 2 Ch at 54; and see *Re Head* [1893] 3 Ch 426, with which cf. *Bilborough v Holmes* (1877) 5 ChD 255.
3 See para. 4.07, ante.
4 *Rouse v Bradford Banking Co* [1894] AC 586. This is the ordinary rule in respect of sureties: see para. 16.10 (2), post.
5 Partnership Act 1890, s. 18.
6 Ibid, s. 17 (1).
7 See *Rolfe v Flower* (1866) LR 1 PC 27 (a case where such an arrangement was implied).

11.12 *Persons liable as partners by holding out* Generally speaking, the partners alone are liable, but there are classes of persons who, although not partners, are treated by law as such; they are, in fact, estopped by their conduct from denying themselves to be members of the debtor firm.[1]

Those who, not being partners, are so treated, have been styled *quasi*-partners, and they become such by virtue of the rule in section 14 (1):

> 'Everyone who by words spoken or written or by conduct represents himself, or who knowingly suffers himself to be represented, as a partner in a particular firm, is liable as a partner to anyone who has on the faith of any such representation given credit to the firm, whether the representation has or has not been made or communicated to the person so giving credit by or with the knowledge of the apparent partner making the representation or suffering it to be made.'

The contract is made on his credit, and he is therefore as answerable as a partner if loss is incurred thereby. An example of this is to be found in the case of *Martyn v Gray*:[2]

> Where A introduced B to C as the moneyed partner; B was not a partner, but he stood by, and did not deny the statement, and he was *held* answerable for a loss incurred.

However, representations of this kind cannot be used against a man unless his conduct causes others to alter their position on the faith of them.

Upon the principle of '*holding out*', where two persons, who though not in fact partners have traded as such, become bankrupt, the assets of the business will be administered as joint estate.[3] The executors of a deceased partner are not bound by the mere use of the old partnership named by the survivors.[4]

A retiring member is not as such liable for debts contracted subsequently to his retirement, but he may be so if he continues an apparent member of the firm as regards persons who are not aware that he had ceased to be a partner. In order to escape liability for future transactions of the firm, he should give actual notice to persons who were in the habit of dealing with it, but a notice in the *London Gazette* will be sufficient as regards persons who had no dealings with the firm before the date of the dissolution or change,[5] and it is advisable in the case of local firms to give further notice through the local papers. Moreover, a partner who retires is not liable for debts contracted after his retirement to persons who did not know he was a partner. This is so even where the partner has taken an active part in managing the firm's business but the third party who deals with the firm after his retirement only learns of his membership of the firm after he has retired.[6] In *Tower Cabinet Co Ltd v Ingram*:[7]

> X and Y carried on a partnership business and both their names were on the firm's notepaper. The partnership was dissolved but no notice was put in the London Gazette. After the dissolution X continued to trade in the firm name and ordered goods from T using the old notepaper without Y's authority. T sought to make Y liable on the contract. *Held:* there was no holding out under s. 14 as Y had not *knowingly* suffered himself to be represented as a partner and, as T did not know Y to be a partner before Y's retirement, s. 36 (3) relieved him from liability as an apparent partner.

---

1 For the doctrine of estoppel, see generally para. 2.05, ante.
2 (1863) 14 CB NS 824.
3 *Re Pulsford, ex parte Hayman* (1878) 8 ChD 11.
4 Partnership Act 1890, s. 14 (2). See also *Bagel v Miller* [1903] 2 KB 212, para. 11.09, ante.
5 Partnership Act 1890, s. 36 (1), (2).
6 Ibid, s. 36 (3).
7 [1949] 2 KB 397, [1949] 1 All ER 1033.

11.13 *Liability for torts* This rests on a somewhat different footing, for only those who are actual members of the firm are held liable for the consequences; and the principle of 'holding out' has no application. Even true partners are not answerable for all wrongs of their co-partners, but only if the wrongful act was committed whilst the partner was acting with his co-partner's authority, or in the ordinary course of the firm's business: in these cases the firm is liable to the same extent as the partner who has committed the wrong. In *Hamlyn v Houston & Co*:[1]

> It was within the ordinary course of a business firm of grain merchants to obtain information by legitimate means as to contracts made by competing firms. One partner in the business bribed the clerk of a competitor to disclose such information thereby inducing the clerk to break his contract of employment. *Held:* the firm was liable in damages to the competitor.

The firm is also liable if the tort is misapplication of property, and either the money was received by the misapplying partner within the scope of his apparent authority, or was received by the firm, and misapplied by one or more of the partners whilst in its custody.[2]

The liability rests upon the fundamental principle, that within a certain limit, dependent upon the nature of partnership business, each member of the firm is agent for the rest.[3] The liability for wrongs is 'joint and several'. A judgment against one partner is therefore not a bar to a subsequent action against the others.[4]

The cases decided on this point are numerous and sometimes difficult to distinguish. The following are fair specimens, and will, for present purposes, sufficiently illustrate the rules:

> Two solicitors are partners, and a client hands money to one of them to be invested on a specific security; this partner misappropriates the money, and the other is entirely ignorant of the transaction; nevertheless he is liable, for it is within the ordinary scope of a solicitor's business to receive money to invest on specific securities.[5] Had the money been given to invest at discretion the case would have been different, such investments not being part of a solicitor's work.[6]

If a partner, being a trustee, improperly employs trust-property in the business of the firm, the other partners are not liable to replace the trust-property: provided that:

1. Any partner will be liable who has notice of the breach of trust; and
2. Trust-money may be followed and recovered from the firm if still in its possession or under its control.[7]

1 [1903] 1 KB 81. See also *Mercantile Credit, Co Ltd v Garrod* [1962] 3 All ER 1103.
2 Partnership Act 1890, ss. 10, 11.
3 Ibid, s. 12.
4 Law Reform (Married Women and Tortfeasors) Act 1935, s. 6.
5 *Blair v Bromley* (1847) 2 Ph 354. See also *Lloyd v Grace Smith & Co* [1912] AC 716, HL (where fraud committed by employee of partnership).
6 *Harman v Johnson* (1853) 22 LJQB 297. See also *Cleather v Twisden* (1885) 28 ChD 340; *Rhodes v Moules* [1895] 1 Ch 236 and *Meekins v Henson* [1964] 1 QB 472, [1962] 1 All ER 899.
7 Partnership Act 1890, s. 13.

7. Rights and duties of the partners as between themselves

11.14 It has been said already that it is usual for the partnership agreement to be comprised in written Articles of Partnership or a Partnership Agreement.[1] The rights and duties of the partners will then be regulated by the written terms; but a number of rights and duties are implied by s. 24 and these are operative subject to any express agreement to the contrary. It is a basic obligation that each partner will observe the utmost fairness and good faith towards his fellow partners.

The mutual rights and duties of the partners, whether contained in an agreement or implied by the Act, may be varied at any time by the consent of the partners and such consent (which must be unanimous) may be inferred from a course of dealing.[2]

When the express partnership expires by effluxion of time, and the partners continue together, there is an implied arrangement that the partnership shall continue on the old terms so far as applicable, and the same rule applies when surviving partners continue the business after the death of a member of the old firm.[3] Nevertheless, if the partnership is for a fixed term, and is carried over, the new partnership will be at will only, and its continuance on the old terms will be presumed only so far as these are consistent with the incidents of a partnership at will.[4]

1 See para. 11.07, ante.
2 Partnership Act 1890, s. 19.
3 *Neilson v Mossend Iron Co* (1886) 11 App Cas 298, decided on the particular words of the articles.
4 Partnership Act 1890, s. 27. See *Stekel v Ellice* [1973] 1 All ER 465, [1973] 1 WLR 191.

11.15   Amongst the rights of a partner implied by law (so far as they are unmodified by agreement), are:

1. The right to take part in the management of the business.[1] No remuneration can ordinarily be claimed,[2] but compensation for extra trouble caused by the wilful inattention of a co-partner to business may be allowed to the partner or partners upon whom the additional burden is thrown.[3]

2. To have the business carried on according to agreement. Its nature cannot be changed without the unanimous consent of all the partners; in ordinary matters connected with the business, a majority will bind the others.[4]

3. To prevent the admission of a new partner. No person can be introduced as a partner without the consent of all those who, for the time being, are members of the firm.[5] A partner may assign his share of profits, or may mortgage it;[6] this will only enable the other partners to demand a dissolution if the agreement so provides.

Where a fixed term has been agreed on, a partner may retire only with the consent of all the partners, but where it is a partnership 'at will', any partner may retire by giving notice to the other partners.[7]

A majority of the partners cannot expel any partner unless a power to do so has been conferred by *express* agreement.[8]

4. To be indemnified by the firm against personal liabilities incurred and payments made by him in the ordinary and proper conduct of the business; or in or about anything necessarily done for the preservation of the business or property of the firm; e.g. a partnership is formed to work a mine, and the business cannot be continued until a new shaft is sunk; a partner who pays the cost required is entitled to indemnity.[9]

5. To have interest at the rate of five per cent per annum on any actual payment or advance to the firm made by him beyond the capital he has agreed to subscribe, from the date of such payment or advance.[10] Apart from agreement, express or implied, no partner is entitled to receive interest on his capital; and if there is a mere agreement to pay interest and nothing more, such interest will only be payable out of profits, i.e. it will not be treated as an outgoing or loss of the business.[11]

6. To have the books kept at the principal place of business of the firm, and to be allowed to examine and copy them whenever he may desire.[12] The right of a partner to examine the books is not personal to himself, and he may employ an agent to whom no reasonable objection can be taken to examine the books on his behalf; but the agent must undertake not to make use of the information so acquired except for the purpose of advising his principal.[13]

7. In the absence of any special agreement, the partners are entitled to share equally in the capital and profits of the business, and must contribute to the losses equally.[14]

8. To be dealt with by his colleagues with the utmost good faith in all partnership matters. A number of rules exemplify this principle. Thus:

a) Partners are bound to render true accounts and full information of all things affecting the partnership to any partner or his legal representatives.[15]

b) Every partner must account to the firm for any benefit he may derive which is obtained by him (without the assent of the others) from any transaction concerning the partnership or from any use by him of the partnership property, name or business connection.[16] Thus,

A, B, C and D are partners in business as sugar refiners, A being also in trade for himself as a sugar merchant, the other partners being cognisant, and not objecting; A, without the knowledge of the firm, sells sugar at a profit to it. *Held:* he must account for and share this profit with the partnership.[17]

c) A partner who carries on a *competing* business without the consent of the others, must account for and pay over to the firm all profits made by him therein.[18]

d) If in the sale by one partner to another of a share in the partnership business, the purchaser knows, and is aware that he knows, more about the partnership accounts than the vendor, he must put the vendor in possession of all material facts and not conceal what he alone knows; and unless such information is furnished the sale may be set aside.[19]

---

1 Partnership Act 1890, s. 24 (5).
2 Ibid, s. 24 (6).
3 *Airey v Borham* (1861) 29 Beav 620.
4 Ibid, s. 24 (8).
5 Ibid, s. 24 (7).
6 For the rights of the assignee or mortgagee, see s. 31 of the Partnership Act 1890.
7 Ibid, s. 26. See *Brace v Calder* [1895] 2 QB 253 (para. 7.28, ante).
8 Ibid, s. 25; and see *Re A Solicitor's Arbitration* [1962] 1 All ER 772, [1962] 1 WLR 353.
9 Ibid, s. 24 (2), and *Re German Mining Co, Ex parte Chippendale* (1853) 4 De GM & G 36.
10 Ibid, s. 24 (3).
11 Ibid, s. 24 (4).
12 Ibid, s. 24 (9).
13 *Bevan v Webb* [1901] 2 Ch 59.
14 Ibid, s. 24 (1). See *Hodson v Cashmore* (1972) 226 Estates Gazette 1203.
15 Ibid, s. 28.
16 Ibid, s. 29.

17 *Bentley v Craven* (1853) 18 Beav 75; and see *Featherstonehaugh v Fenwick* (1810) 17 Ves 298; *Thompson's Trustee in Bankruptcy v Heaton* [1974] 1 All ER 1239, [1974] 1 WLR 605.
18 Partnership Act 1890, s. 30.
19 *Law v Law* [1905] 1 Ch 140.

11.16   *After dissolution*[1]   When the partnership is dissolved, new rights accrue to its members:
1. A public notification of the dissolution may be demanded by any partner, and, as the practice of the *Gazette* Office is to require the signature of all the partners, any partner may take action to compel a recalcitrant member to sign.[2]
2. Each partner has an equitable lien on the property owned by the firm at the date of dissolution, entitling him to have it applied in payment of the firm's debts, and then in payment of what may be due to the partners.[3] If a partner has been induced to enter the partnership by fraud or misrepresentation, and has, on that ground, rescinded the partnership contract, he will be entitled to repayment of the amount given by him for his share, after the partnership liabilities have been satisfied; and to secure payment of that amount he has a lien on the surplus assets.[4]
3. In settling the accounts between the partners after a dissolution, *subject to any agreement*, the assets of the firm (including sums contributed by partners to make up deficiencies of capital) must be distributed in the following order:

a) In paying the debts and liabilities of the firm to persons who are not partners;[5]
b) In paying partners rateably what is due from the firm to them for advances as distinguished from capital;
c) In paying each partner rateably what is due from the firm to him in respect of capital;[6]
d) In distributing the ultimate residue among the partners in the proportion in which profits are divisible.[7]

Losses (including deficiencies of capital) must be paid first out of profits; next out of capital; if this is exhausted, then individually by the partners, in the same proportions as the profits would have been divided had any existed.[7]

Where partners have contributed unequal capitals and have agreed to share profits and losses equally, if the assets are insufficient to repay each partner the whole of his capital and one of the partners is unable to contribute his share of the loss, the solvent partners are not bound to contribute for him. This, in *Garner v Murray*:[8]

G, M and W became partners on the terms that they should contribute the capital in unequal shares and divide the profits equally. On a dissolution, after satisfying all liabilities to creditors and the advances of the partners, the assets were insufficient to make good the capital. A larger sum was due to G than to M. Nothing could be recovered from W. *Held:* that the true principle of division was for each partner to be treated as liable to contribute an equal third share of the deficiency, and then to apply the assets in paying to each partner rateably what was due to him in respect of capital.

4. Any partner may, on dissolution, require that the property, including the goodwill,[9] shall be sold, and he may restrain any other partner from doing anything tending directly to decrease the value, e.g. using the firm's name, when an attempt is being made to sell the goodwill. And the goodwill may be sold when a partner dies, for the right to it does not vest in the survivors.[10]

5. When one partner on entering into a partnership for a fixed term pays a premium, and before the expiration of the term the firm is dissolved otherwise than by the death of a partner, the court may order a return of all or a certain amount of this premium, but not when the dissolution is wholly or chiefly due to the misconduct of the partner who paid the premium, nor when the firm has been dissolved by an agreement containing no provision for a return of any part of the premium.[11] The entire question is in each case in the discretion of the court and such order will be made as, under the circumstances, will work justice. In *Atwood v Maude*:[12]

> One partner took another into business with him for a fixed term, asking a premium as compensation for the latter's inexperience. After two years the original partner demanded a dissolution on the ground of the latter's incompetence, whereupon the new partner sued the original partner for a dissolution and a return of the premium, and the court awarded dissolution and a return to the former of such part of the premium as bore the same proportion to the total amount as the unexpired period of the term bore to the total term agreed upon.

From this judgment it appears that the court will ordinarily order the return of the premium, having regard to the terms of the contract, the position of the parties, and their conduct, and that the amount will be calculated on a proportion similar to that taken in the case mentioned.

6. When a member of a firm ceases to be a partner, he is entitled to a settlement in due course and the amount due is deemed to be a debt accruing due at the date of the dissolution or retirement, unless otherwise agreed.[13]

1 For dissolution, see para. 11.19, post.
2 Partnership Act 1890, s. 37.
3 Ibid, s. 39. The right of a partner to have the goodwill sold when the firm has been dissolved is referred to para. 11.16 (4).
4 Partnership Act 1890, s. 41. He is also entitled to stand in the place of creditors for any payment made by him in respect of partnership liabilities, and is entitled to be indemnified by the person guilty of the fraud against all the debts and liabilities of the firm (ibid).
5 Or liability to a partner which does not arise out of the partnership: *Brenner v Rose* [1973] 2 All ER 535, [1973] 1 WLR 443 (landlord).
6 On the issue of capitalising profits, see *Smith v Gale* [1974] 1 All ER 401, [1974] 1 WLR 9.
7 Ibid, s. 44.
8 [1904] 1 Ch 57.
9 See para. 11.21, post.
10 *Smith v Everett* (1859) 27 Beav 446.
11 Partnership Act 1890, s. 40.
12 (1868) LR 3 Ch 369.
13 Partnership Act 1890, s. 43.

11.17 If the continuing or surviving partners trade with the capital or assets of the firm without any final settlement of accounts, the outgoing partner or his estate is, in the absence of agreement to the contrary,[1] entitled to such share of the profits made since the dissolution as the court may find to be attributable to the use of the outgoing partner's share of the assets, or, at the option of the outgoing partner or his representatives, to interest at the rate of five per cent per annum on the amount of such share.[2] If profits are claimed they are not to be measured by the amount to which a partner would have been entitled before his retirement or death, but by his proportionate interest in the assets (including goodwill) used in carrying on the business, and subject to a proper allowance to the continuing partner or partners for personal superintendence and management.[3]

Where a partnership between a British subject and an alien enemy has been dissolved by the outbreak of war, and the business in England is continued by the English partner with the aid of the alien partner's share of the capital, the latter is not deprived of the rights conferred by s. 42, but nothing can be paid to him until after the conclusion of peace.[4]

---

1 It is advisable to provide for such an event in the articles of partnership, and to fix in them the basis upon which an outgoing partner's share or his rights in the goodwill are to be valued.
2 Partnership Act 1890, s. 42.
3 *Manley v Sartori* [1927] 1 Ch 157. See also *Pathirana v Pathirana* [1967] 1 AC 233, PC.
4 *Stevenson & Sons Ltd v Act Für Cartonnagen-Industrie* [1918] AC 239, HL.

8. Property of the firm

11.18   The assets which are to make up the property of the firm should be defined as fully as possible in the articles of partnership or partnership agreement.[1] Unless otherwise agreed, all property and rights and interests in property originally brought into the partnership stock or acquired, whether by purchase or otherwise, on account of the firm, or for the purposes and in the course of the partnership business, is partnership property.[2] It must be held and applied by the partners exclusively for the purpose of the partnership and in accordance with the partnership agreement;[3] and property bought with the money of the firm is deemed, unless a contrary intention appears, to be partnership property.[4]

During the continuance of the firm, the members are joint owners of the property, i.e. each owns the whole, and the property is not divided up into portions which belong separately to the members.[5] In ordinary cases of joint ownership, when one joint owner dies, his co-owners succeed to his share: but in the joint ownership arising out of partnership this is not so, and the representative of the deceased succeeds to his interest.

If land is conveyed to partners for partnership purposes, the partners hold the legal estate as joint tenants on trust for sale. As between the partners, and as between the beneficiaries on intestacy of a deceased partner, it is treated as personalty not realty.[6]

Assignment of share[7]   A partner who assigns his share of the property to another person, either absolutely or by way of mortgage, gives, according to the terms of the assignment, the assignee the right to receive, in whole or in part, the share of profits and (on dissolution) of the property which would have come to that partner; but the assignee cannot during the continuance of the partnership, inspect the firm's books or interfere in the business.[8]

The assignee cannot complain of a bona fide agreement subsequent to the assignment to pay salaries to the partners even though this may diminish the profits;[9] he must also accept the account of profits agreed to by the partners, but on a dissolution he is entitled to have an account taken for the purpose of ascertaining the value of the share assigned, irrespective of any agreement between the partners themselves as to the value of such share.[10]

---

1 Whether property is partnership property depends on the intention of the parties: see *Miles v Clark* [1953] 1 All ER 779, [1953] 1 WLR 537 (court

only willing to imply into the contract minimum necessary to give it business efficacy; see para. 7.05, ante).

2 Particular difficulty has been experienced in deciding whether land held by the partners as co-owners is partnership property: see Partnership Act 1890, s. 20 (3); *Waterer v Waterer* (1873) LR 15 Eq 402; *Davis v Davis* [1894] 1 Ch 393; and see further Drake *Law of Partnership* (2nd edn) 79–84.

3 Partnership Act 1890, s. 20 (1).

4 Ibid, s. 21.

5 For conversion of partnership property (cheques), see *Souhrada v Bank of New South Wales* [1976] 2 Lloyd's Rep. 444 (NSW).

6 Partnership Act 1890, s. 22: *Re Fuller's Contract* [1933] Ch 652.

7 For assignment of choses in action generally, see paras. 4.06 et seq., ante.

8 Ibid, s. 31.

9 *Re Garwood's Trusts* [1903] 1 Ch 236.

10 *Watts v Driscoll* [1901] 1 Ch 294.

---

9. Dissolution

11.19 The rights and duties consequent upon dissolution have already been considered;[1] it now remains to show how, when, and on what grounds it is brought about. It may be caused in any of the following ways:

1. At the will of any *one* partner where no fixed term has been agreed upon.[2] If the partnership was constituted by deed, the partner desiring to terminate the partnership must give notice in writing; in other cases verbal notice will suffice.[3] But a partnership where no fixed term has been agreed upon, or a partnership entered into for an undefined time, may not be a partnership at will, if the partners have made an agreement to the contrary, e.g. that the partnership should be terminated 'by mutual arrangement only'.[4]

2. By effluxion of the time agreed upon as the term, or if entered into for a single adventure or undertaking, by the termination of that adventure or undertaking.[5]

3. Transfer of a partner's interest—

   a) By bankruptcy or death, unless otherwise agreed (as it frequently is);[6]

   b) At the option of the other partners, if any partner suffers his share to be charged by the court for his separate debt on the application of any of his creditors;[7] but the other partners have power to redeem any share of the partnership charged, or buy any share of the partnership ordered to be sold, on behalf of the creditor.[8]

4. Occurrence of an event making the partnership illegal:[9] e.g. war breaking out between the countries in which the different members of the partnership are trading.

5. Fraud, making the original contract voidable.[10]

6. In addition, the court may decree a dissolution of partnership in any of the following cases:

a) Where it appears necessary or expedient to the court with regard to a partner who is under a mental disability;[11]

b) Permanent incapacity of a partner to perform his part of the contract;[12]

c) Misconduct of a partner calculated to prejudice the business, wilful or persistent breach of the agreement, or such other conduct as makes it not reasonably practicable for the other members to continue in partnership with him;[13]

d) When the business can only be carried on at a loss;[14]

e) Whenever the court thinks it just and equitable to decree dissolution.[15]

In the cases of permanent incapacity, misconduct and persistent breach of agreement, a partnership cannot be dissolved on the application of the partner who is in fault, but a partnership may be dissolved on the application of a partner who is under a mental disability, as well as at the instance of the other members.

---

1 See para. 11.16, ante.
2 Partnership Act 1890, ss. 26 (1), 32 (c).
3 Ibid, s. 26 (2).
4 *Moss v Elphick* [1910] 1 KB 846, CA.
5 Partnership Act 1890, s. 32 (a), (b).
6 Ibid, s. 33 (1).
7 Ibid, s. 33 (2).
8 Ibid, s. 23.
9 Ibid, s. 34.
10 *Redgrave v Hurd* (1881) 20 ChD 1, CA: set out para. 5.09, ante.
11 Mental Health Act 1959, s. 103 (1) (f).
12 Partnership Act 1890, s. 35 (b).
13 Ibid, s. 35 (c), (d). For a case where there was a retirement rather than a dissolution, see *Sobell v Boston* [1975] 2 All ER 282, [1975] 1 WLR 1587.
14 Ibid, s. 35 (e).
15 Ibid, s. 35 (f).

Administration of partnership estates

11.20 The following rules apply to the administration of the estates of bankrupt and insolvent partners. The partnership property is termed the *joint estate,* and the separate properties of the individual partners the *separate estates.*

The general rule is:

That joint estate is applied in payment of the debts of the partnership, and separate estate in payment of the individual debts of the partner to whom it belongs; if in either case any surplus remains, the surplus of a separate estate will be transferred to the joint estate, if that is deficient; the joint estate surplus being dealt with as part of the respective separate estates in proportion to the right and interest of each partner in the joint estate.[1]

Thus:

A and B are partners; A owes his separate creditors £100, and his separate estate is £75. B owes £150, and has £175; the firm's debts are £500, and assets £450. The separate creditors of A take the £75, those of B take £150 of the £175, the joint creditors taking the remaining £25 of B's separate estate as well as the whole of the joint estate (£450).

Again:

If A and B are partners, and A is insolvent, B being solvent, the joint creditors will recover the full amount from B, B being then allowed to prove against A's estate to the amount which he has paid beyond his proportion.

Similar principles hold in the administration of the estate of a deceased partner in the Chancery Division.

Exceptions:

1. If there is no joint estate and no solvent partner, the joint creditors may prove against the separate estates on an equal footing with the separate creditors.[2]

2. If anyone is defrauded by the partners or one of them so that the firm is liable for the fraud, he may prove his debt at his election *either* against the joint estate *or* against the separate estates of the fraudulent partners.[3]

3. When a partner has fraudulently, and without the consent of the others, converted partnership property to his own use, the joint estate may prove against that partner's separate estate in competition with the separate creditors, even though it is not shown that the separate estate has benefited by the conversion.[4]

As regards the fraudulent conversion, it was said by Jessel MR, in *Lacey v Hill,* that:

'it is not necessary for the joint estate to prove more than ... that this overdrawing was for private purposes, and without the knowledge, consent, privity, or subsequent approbation of the other partners. If that is shown, it is prima facie a fraudulent appropriation within the rule'.[5]

And such consent or knowledge must have been real, not constructive, for it is the better opinion that the doctrine of constructive notice is not applicable here.[6]

4. If a joint creditor petitions against a partner in respect of his joint debt and that partner is adjudged bankrupt, he is allowed as petitioning creditor to prove his joint debt in competition with the separate creditors.[7]

5. Where a partner has carried on a distinct and separate trade and has incurred a debt to the firm or become a creditor of the firm, one estate can prove against the other.

Proof by solvent partner against estate of bankrupt co-partner Partners may not compete in an administration with the firm's creditors, either against the joint or against any of the separate estates. But if a solvent partner has paid off the joint creditors or if there is no possibility of a surplus in the separate estate of the co-partner so that the firm's creditors could never obtain anything from him, the solvent partner may prove for a contribution *pari passu* with the separate creditors of his co-partner.[8]

Secured creditor A creditor of the firm who holds a security for the debt on the separate property of a partner may prove against the joint estate and retain his security against the separate estate, provided he does not receive in the whole more than the full amount of his debt. And a separate creditor of a partner holding a security on the joint property is in a corresponding position. The reason of the above rule is that the surrender of the security would not augment the estate against which proof was being made.[9]

---

1 See Bankruptcy Act 1914, s. 33 (6).
2 *Re Budgett, Cooper v Adams* [1894] 2 Ch 557.
3 *Re Collie, ex parte Adamson* (1878) 8 ChD 807; possibly against the estate of an innocent partner (*Re Stratton, ex parte Salting* (1884) 25 ChD 148).
4 See *Read v Bailey* (1878) 3 App Cas 94.
5 (1876) 4 ChD 543.
6 See *Lacey v Hill* (1876) 4 ChD 537, CA, and Drake *Law of Partnership* (2nd edn) 175 et seq.
7 Bankruptcy Act 1914, s. 114.
8 *Re Head, ex parte Head* [1894] 1 QB 638.
9 *Re Turner* (1882) 19 ChD 105.

---

10. Goodwill

11.21 The nature of goodwill is intimately connected with the law of partnership, and questions concerning it arise so frequently in partnership matters, that it may be very properly discussed here.

The term is one which is seldom misunderstood, but it is not easy to give a definition of it. Lord Macnaghten in *Trego v Hunt*,[1] says:

'What "goodwill" means must depend on the nature and character of the business to which it is attached. Generally speaking, it means much more than what Lord Eldon took it to mean in the particular case actually before him of *Cruttwell v Lye*[2] where he says: "The goodwill which has been the subject of sale is nothing more than the probability that the old customers will resort to the old place." Often it happens that the goodwill is the very sap and life of the business, without which the business would yield little or no fruit. It is the whole advantage, whatever it may be, of the reputation and connection of the firm, which may have been built up by years of honest work or gained by lavish expenditure of money.'

In some forms of business, the goodwill is personal,[3] e.g. made by the skill of the person owning it; whilst in others, the goodwill attaches itself rather to the property than to the owner's person, e.g. the goodwill of a well-situated public-house.[4] Some businesses depend so entirely upon personal skill and influence, that goodwill in the ordinary sense can hardly exist.[5] A personal goodwill is capable of transfer, and so is the other kind, and this latter attaches itself to the property, and may go with it, e.g. to a mortgagee.[6]

Where a person assigns the goodwill of a business to another, without expressly binding himself not to compete with the assignee, whether he does so as sole owner of the goodwill or as a partner transferring his interest therein to his co-partner, the legal position may be summed up as follows:

1. The person who acquires the goodwill alone may represent himself as continuing or succeeding to the business of the vendor.
2. But the assignor may nevertheless carry on a similar business in competition with the purchaser, though not under a name which would amount to a representation that he was carrying on the old business.
3. The assignor may publicly advertise his business, but he may not personally or by circular solicit the customers of the former firm; although he may deal with customers of the old firm, he must not *solicit* those who do not come to him of their own accord.[7]

The rule against the soliciting of old customers does not apply to an involuntary alienation, e.g. to the sale of a person's business by his trustee in bankruptcy,[8] or by the trustee under a deed of assignment for the benefit of creditors;[9] but it applies to the executor of a deceased partner who sells the goodwill to the surviving partner in pursuance of an obligation imposed by the partnership deed.[10]

The way in which the goodwill should be dealt with on the dissolution of a firm has already been mentioned,[11] as has the validity of restrictions on competition agreed in a sale of goodwill.[12]

---

1 [1896] AC, at 23, 24. See also per Warrington J, in *Hill v Fearis* [1905] 1 Ch, at 471.
2 (1810) 17 Ves 346.
3 *Cooper v Metropolitan Board of Works* (1884) 25 ChD 472.
4 *Re Kitchen, Ex parte Punnett* (1881) 16 ChD 226, CA.
5 E.g. *Austen v Boys* (1858) 27 LJ Ch 714. However, in *Arundell v Bell* (1883) 31 WR 477 Baggallay LJ, thought that something might exist analogous to a goodwill; and it is doubtful if the earlier case is still good law.
6 *Cooper v Metropolitan Board of Works*, ante; cf. *Re Bennett* [1899] 1 Ch 316.
7 *Trego v Hunt* [1896] AC 7; *Curl Bros Ltd v Webster* [1904] 1 Ch 685.
8 *Walker v Mottram* (1882) 19 ChD 355.
9 *Green & Sons Ltd v Morris* [1914] 1 Ch 562.
10 *Boorne v Wicker* [1927] 1 Ch 667.
11 Para. 11.16 (4), ante.
12 See para. 6.10, ante.

---

11. Limited partnerships

11.22 From 1 January 1908 it became lawful to form limited partnerships under the Limited Partnerships Act 1907; but they have always been rare because of the greater advantages of private limited companies which were introduced by the Companies Act of the same year.

A limited partnership is not a legal entity distinct from the individuals who compose the firm.[1] It must consist of one or more:

i) *General* partners, liable for all the debts and obligations of the firm, and

ii) *Limited* partners, who shall at the time of entering into partnership contribute a sum as capital, or property valued at a stated amount.

The following points should be noted:

1. A limited partner is not liable for debts beyond the amount so contributed, but he must not during the continuance of the partnership, either directly or indirectly, draw out or receive back any part of his contribution, and if he does so he will be liable for the debts of the firm up to the amount so drawn out or received back.

2. A body corporate may be a limited partner.[2]

3. Unless a limited partnership is so registered with the Registrar of Joint Stock Companies, every limited partner will be liable as a general partner.[3]

4. A limited partner must not take any part in the management of the business, and he cannot bind the firm, but he may inspect the books, look into the state and prospects of the business, and advise with the partners thereon. If a limited partner does take part in the management of the business he will be liable as a general partner for debts incurred while he so takes part in the management.[4]

5. Unless the agreement specifies otherwise, a limited partner may only assign his share with the consent of the general partners.[5]

6. A partner may be introduced without the consent of the limited partner.[6]

7. *Dissolution*

a) The general partners may not dissolve the partnership by reason of a limited partner suffering his share to be charged for his separate debt.[7]

b) A limited partner may not dissolve the partnership by notice.[8]

c) The death or bankruptcy of a limited partner does not dissolve the partnership, and the insanity of a limited partner is only a ground for dissolution if his share cannot be otherwise ascertained and realised.[9]

---

1 *Re Barnard* [1932] 1 Ch 269; and see para. 11.02, ante, as to the meaning of the word 'firm'.
2 Limited Partnerships Act 1907, s. 4.
3 Ibid, s. 5.
4 Ibid, s. 6 (1).
5 Ibid, s. 6 (5) (b).
6 Ibid, s. 6 (5) (d).
7 Ibid, s. 6 (5) (c).
8 Ibid, s. 6 (5) (e).
9 Ibid, s. 6 (2).

Part III

Sale and credit

Chapter 12

Sale of land

1. Introduction

12.01 The single most important difference between land and other property is this: in the case of property other than land (goods or choses in action[1]), what is dealt with is the property itself; whereas, in the case of land it is interests in the land, rather than the land itself, which are bought and sold. The law recognises a great number of interests in any one piece of land, perhaps because land is permanent in a way different from all other property and normally of considerable value.

Broadly speaking, interests in property may be of two kinds.

a) Concurrent interests More than one person may at the same time hold an interest in any sort of property. They may have the same interest, in which case they are *co-owners* of that interest. Alternatively, the various rights in property may be distributed between different people, as where one has 'ownership' whilst another has possession: in relation to goods, this last arrangement is termed a *bailment*;[2] and in respect of land it is called a *lease* (see below).

b) Successive interests This is the situation where persons are each in succession entitled to the enjoyment of property. Successive interests in land are where, e.g. A holds land for life (*a life estate*), but on his death it is to pass to B (*a reversion or remainder*). Except behind a trust, successive interests cannot exist in property.

The law relating to land is very complicated precisely because so many interests—concurrent or successive—may exist and have to be regulated. However, it is here only necessary to refer to the two interests in land which are of most significance to commerce.

a) Freehold This is the greatest interest in land which is capable of subsisting in law, i.e. the nearest thing permitted to complete ownership, and is technically termed an estate in *fee simple absolute in possession.*

b) Leasehold This interest arises where the freeholder (*landlord*) grants the possession of land to another (*the tenant*) for a period of certain duration e.g. 99 years or for a period capable of being rendered certain, e.g. periodic tenancy, or where a leaseholder in turn sublets part of the period of his lease;[3] and this is technically an estate called a *term of years absolute*.

Every transfer of property for value involves two aspects: first, the contract to transfer the property; and second, the actual transfer (*conveyance*) of the property. In the case of property other than land, the two stages are normally telescoped into one, the contract acting as its own conveyance, e.g. sales of goods.[4] However, it is otherwise in respect of sales of interests in land, and accordingly the two elements of contract and conveyance will be dealt with separately.

Thus far, discussion has concerned the transfer of property for the purposes of occupation, but there are also transfers made by way of security. The essence of such transactions (*a mortgage*) is that the owner of the property transfers proprietary rights therein to another by way of security for the repayment of a loan to that other (*the mortgagee*), the borrower (*mortgagor*) normally retaining possession of the property throughout. There are different sets of statutory rules governing mortgages according to whether or not the subject-matter of the mortgage is land. Mortgages of goods will be dealt with later,[5] and reference has already been made to assignments by way of mortgage or charge of choses in action;[6] but mortgages (or charges) of land will form the last section of this chapter. Finally, it should be remembered that, whilst a mortgage of an interest in land as a device for raising money is analytically distinct from a sale of an interest in land, in practice most sales of an interest in land are financed by mortgages of that interest taken out (granted) at the time of purchase; and in this context it makes no difference whether the sale price is advanced by the vendor or by an independent third party.

---

1 For choses in action, see para. 4.06, ante.
2 For bailments, see para. 14.06, post.
3 For the special rule that most leases must be under seal, see para. 2.09, ante.
4 See para. 13.06, post.
5 See paras. 17.05 et seq., post.
6 See paras. 4.08 et seq., ante.

2. The contract

A) *Types of contract*

12.02 There are three main types of contract that may be used for the sale of an interest in land.

a) An open contract In an open contract, only the essential terms are expressly agreed between the parties, the remaining terms being left to the general law: the essential terms are (1) the parties, (2) the property, (3) the consideration, and (4) in the case of a lease, its commencement and duration.[1] However, it is possible for the parties to specify as much detail as they like, so that a contract can be partly formal and partly open.

b) A contract by correspondence In the case of contracts by correspondence, s. 46 of the Law of Property Act 1925 provides that the Lord Chancellor's Statutory Form of Conditions shall govern the contract, subject to any contrary intention expressed in the correspondence.[2] This provision amounts to a statutory recognition of the inconveniences of the open contract.

c) A formal contract Within the limits allowed by law, it is always open to the parties to make a contract in such terms as they think fit. In practice, it is normal to use one of the standard forms of conditions, e.g. the Law Society's Conditions of Sale, or the National Conditions of Sale, the standard form being amended to suit the circumstances. The utilisation of such standard forms is by far the most common mode of contracting for sales of interests in land.

---

1 Per Lord Denning MR in *Harvey v Pratt* [1965] 2 All ER 786 at 788, [1965] 1 WLR 1025 at 1027, CA. And see *Bigg v Boyd Gibbins Ltd* [1971] 2 All ER 183, [1971] 1 WLR 913, CA.
2 See *AM Prichard* (1974) 90 LQR 55.

B) *Form of contract*

12.03 According to s. 40 (1) of the Law of Property Act 1925:

'No action may be brought upon any contract for the sale or other disposition of land or any interest in land, unless the agreement ... or some memorandum or note thereof, is in writing, and signed by the party to be charged or by some other person thereunto by him lawfully authorised'.

The nature of this statutory requirement that the contract should be *evidenced* by a written note or memorandum has already been considered.[1] It remains to be considered when a party can be bound by the signature of his agent for the purposes of s. 40. Whether a person is the duly authorised agent of another for this purpose is to be determined by the general law of agency.[2] It is not necessary that the principal should have authorised the agent to sign the document as a record of the transaction:[3]

> The signature of counsel to a pleading may constitute a sufficient memorandum of a contract by his client, although the pleading was signed without the slightest intention of bringing about that result.[4]

A person may be agent for both parties, but if he is himself one of the parties, he cannot be agent to sign for the other. An auctioneer is agent to sign for the vendor, and for the buyer also just after the lot has been knocked down to the buyer; his signature will then bind both parties unless indeed he is himself the vendor.[5] This authority to sign cannot be revoked after the fall of the hammer;[6] nor does it continue for an indefinite period after the sale.

A signature made a week after the auction was held to be too late;[7] but the auctioneer need not sign in the auction room if his signature can be fairly said to be part of the transaction of sale.[8]

Absence of such a note or memorandum as will satisfy s. 40 (1) does not preclude the existence of a contract,[9] but it merely results in that contract being unenforceable by action.[10] Thus, if the purchaser repudiates such a contract the vendor is entitled to retain any deposit paid by the purchaser. Moreover, the entire rule is expressly made subject to the doctrine of part-performance (s. 40 (2)).

---

1 See paras. 2.11 et seq., ante.
2 See ante, chap. 10.
3 *John Griffiths Cycle Corpn v Humber & Co Ltd* [1899] 2 QB 414, CA.
4 *Grindell v Bass* [1920] 2 Ch 487; *Farr Smith & Co v Messers Ltd* [1928] 1 KB 397.
5 *Farebrother v Simmons* (1822) 5 B & Ald 333.
6 *Van Praagh v Everidge* [1902] 2 Ch 266; *revsd* on another point [1903] 1 Ch 434.
7 *Bell v Balls* [1897] 1 Ch 663.
8 *Chaney v Maclow* [1929] 1 Ch 461.
9 *Law v Jones* [1974] Ch 112, [1973] 2 All ER 437, CA, overruled on another point by the case in the next note.
10 *Tiverton Estates Ltd v Wearwell Ltd* [1975] Ch 146, [1974] 1 All ER 209, CA.

PART PERFORMANCE

12.04 Notwithstanding that no action is available at common law for damages because there is no writing sufficient to comply with s. 40 of the Law of Property Act 1925, it is possible to obtain a court order of specific performance of an agreement relating to land, provided that there has been part performance of the agreement by the plaintiff with the defendant's consent. Thus, in *Rawlinson v Ames*:[1]

> The plaintiff agreed orally to let his flat to the defendant for twenty-one years and to make certain alterations whose execution the defendant supervised. Later, the defendant refused to take the flat. *Held:* the plaintiff was entitled to an order of specific performance because, although there was no written evidence of the contract, the plaintiff had partly performed the contract with the defendant's consent by doing acts which were explicable only on the basis of some such contract as the plaintiff alleged had been made.

Equivocal acts, like the mere payment of money, which are explicable on other grounds than the existence of a contract such as that alleged by the plaintiff, are not treated as acts of part performance.[2] However, it is not necessary for the plaintiff to show that his acts establish the exact terms of the contract he alleged. Thus, in *Kingswood Estate Co Ltd v Anderson*:[3]

> The elderly tenant of a house, living with her invalid son, enjoyed security of tenure under the Rent Acts. She agreed to give up possession to the landlords in return for an oral tenancy of a flat in which they could live for the rest of their lives. After they moved to the flat, the landlords served a four weeks' notice to quit. *Held:* although the contract relating to the flat was oral, the tenant's acts in leaving the controlled premises and entering into possession of the flat were sufficient acts of performance to defeat the landlords' claim for possession.

1 [1925] Ch 96.
2 *Steadman v Steadman* [1976] AC 536, [1974] 2 All ER 977, HL.
3 [1963] 2 QB 169, [1962] 3 All ER 593, CA; followed in *Wakeham v Mackenzie* [1968] 2 All ER 783.

C) *Formation of contract*

12.05 Generally speaking, the formation of a contract for the sale of an interest in land is subject to the ordinary rules for the formation of contracts already considered.[1] If it is of vital importance to the parties that a binding contract be entered into at an early date, it is quite feasible for them to enter into an open contract, or a contract by correspondence.[2] Similarly, where land is sold by auction, it is normal to get the buyer to whom the property has been knocked down immediately thereafter to sign a formal contract.[3] Indeed, there is nothing to prevent the parties immediately entering into a binding informal agreement on the basis that it will subsequently be replaced by a more formal agreement.[4]

---

1 See paras. 3.02, ante, et seq. For infants, see para. 2.18 (1), ante.
2 See para. 12.02, ante.
3 For formal contracts, see para. 12.02, ante; and for the position of auctioneers, see para. 10.32, ante.
4 E.g. *Branco v Cobarro* [1947] KB 854, [1947] 2 All ER 101, CA.

12.06 On the other hand, in many cases the prospective purchaser will want to assure himself on a number of points, e.g. survey, mortgage finance, title and legal restrictions, before he enters into a binding contract to purchase. He may therefore wish to make any agreement expressly subject to conditions; and it will then be a matter of interpretation whether those conditions are precedent to contract, i.e. no contract until they materialise, or merely to performance.[1] However, it will commonly be that the prudent prospective purchaser does not even wish to enumerate the conditions to be satisfied before he enters into a binding contract, but instead wishes to give himself time to take legal advice on all aspects of the transaction, and to reconsider the transaction generally; and his use of the phrase 'subject to contract' has been hallowed by usage as being effective to achieve such a result. Indeed, it is the normal practice for a prospective purchaser of an interest in land expressly to make an (oral or written) offer to purchase 'subject to contract'—a number of similar phrases have been held to have the same legal effect; and, because the practice is so common, it has been held that the parties may impliedly make their agreement subject to contract,[2] though there are risks for the purchaser in leaving the matter to implication.[3]

Where the parties do make their agreement 'subject to contract', there is a strong presumption that, even though that agreement be in a signed writing, it does not conclude a binding contract at that stage.[4] The usual expectation of the parties is that a definitive binding contract should thereafter come into existence in the following way: (1) the solicitors to the parties agree between themselves the terms of a draft contract; (2) the vendor's solicitor prepares, in duplicate, the engrossments (formal copies) of the draft contract; (3) each solicitor obtains his client's signature to one of the engrossments; (4) finally the two solicitors exchange the signed engrossments.[5] Where this procedure is followed, the two solicitors may effect stage (4) by meeting and formally exchanging contracts, whereupon the first document delivered is the offer and the second the acceptance; but more commonly there is an exchange by post, in which case the first document posted is the offer, and the second the acceptance, so that the earliest moment at which a binding contract would normally come into existence would be when the second document was put in the post—either party being at liberty to withdraw from the transaction until then.[6] Exceptionally an agreement initially made 'subject to contract' may become binding at an earlier stage than that just outlined, e.g. where both parties employ the same solicitor[7] or waive the condition.[8]

1 See note 6 to para. 3.09, ante. For the special opportunity given to a debtor to withdraw from a prospective regulated land mortgage, see the Consumer Credit Act 1974, s. 58. This right is in lieu of a right of cancellation: see para. 14.34, post. Conceptually distinct is the limited statutory right to terminate the agreement granted to the debtor (buyer) in respect of a regulated conditional sale of land by the Consumer Credit Act 1974, s. 99: see para. 14.35, post.
2 *Tevanan v Norman Brett (Builders) Ltd* (1972) 223 Estates Gazette 1945.
3 The court might reject the implication and find a binding contract: *Law v Jones* [1974] Ch 112, [1973] 2 All ER 437, CA. For implied terms in contracts, see generally para. 7.05, ante.
4 *Eccles v Bryant* [1948] Ch 93, [1947] 2 All ER 865, CA. Contrast *Storer v Manchester City Council* [1974] 3 All ER 824, [1974] 1 WLR 1403, CA.
5 Per Lord Greene MR in *Eccles v Bryant* (ante), at 97, 866.
6 *Eccles v Bryant* (ante). For offer and acceptance, see generally paras. 3.02, et seq., ante.
7 *Smith v Mansi* [1962] 3 All ER 857, [1963] 1 WLR 26, CA; *Earl v Mawson* (1974) 232 Estates Gazette 1315, CA.
8 *Griffiths v Young* [1970] Ch 675, [1970] 3 All ER 601, CA; as explained in *Tiverton Estates Ltd v Wearwell* [1975] Ch 146, [1974] 1 All ER 209, CA.

3. The conveyance

12.07 This stage is the formal performance of the contract previously made for the sale of an interest in land, and is virtually always entrusted to a solicitor.[1] 'The work of the conveyancer is twofold. First, he investigates titles by examining documents and making inquiries and searches. Secondly, he drafts conveyances and other legal documents'.[2] The contract will have given the purchaser an equitable title,[3] and it is therefore advisable for him to insure the property for its full value from that moment.[4] The formal conveyance is needed to transfer the legal title in the interest sold to the purchase, and hence make him secure in his purchase: otherwise, unless he had registered and estate contract he runs the risk of being defeated by a subsequent bona fide purchaser of a legal estate in that same property without notice of his purchase.[5]

The actual steps taken after contract to effect conveyance will depend on whether the title to the interest conveyed is registered or unregistered. Where the title to the land remains unregistered, conveyancing will be in the traditional manner: the vendor proves his title by producing the chain of transfers stretching back in time from himself at least fifteen years to a good root of title;[6] and the final link will then be added to that chain by a conveyance from the vendor to the purchaser in return for the price. However, since 1925 increasing areas of the country have been covered by the new system of land registration under the Land Registration Acts 1925 to 1971. In the case of registered land, the owner will have 'traded-in' his documents of title in return for a title in the Land Registry; and, when he sells that interest, his title can be proved by a mere inspection of the Register and the conveyance will be by way of a simple Standard Form document. Because of its greater simplicity, a transfer of registered land will normally be cheaper than in respect of unregistered land.

Whilst the above account relates to the theory of conveyancing, it is increasingly becoming the modern practice for the crucial investigations on behalf of the purchaser to be made before he enters into the contract to purchase, the conveyancing stage tending to become more of a formality. From the viewpoint of the purchaser, this increases the importance of ensuring that the initial agreement is made 'subject to contract'.[7]

---

1 They have been granted a statutory monopoly of remunerated conveyancing: Solicitors Act 1974, s. 22.
2 Megarry *Manual of the Law of Real Property* (5th edn) 303.
3 *Walsh v Lonsdale* (1882) 21 ChD 9.
4 If the vendor has kept the property insured, the purchaser may be entitled to the benefit thereof: Law of Property Act 1925, s. 47; see para. 26.15, post. For the cautionary tale of a tenant who relied on his landlord to insure, see *Argy Trading Development Co Ltd v Lapid Developments Ltd* [1977] 3 All ER 785, [1977] 1 WLR 444.
5 *Bailey v Barnes* [1894] 1 Ch 25.
6 Law of Property Act 1969, s. 23.
7 See para. 12.06, ante.

12.08   A conveyance will normally contain covenants restricting the use to which the grantee can put the land. It has already been pointed out that these restrictive covenants are enforceable by and against the successors in title of the original grantor and grantee, thus constituting an important exception to the ordinary rules of privity of contract.[1] A full examination of this part of land law is not, however, properly within the scope of this work.[2]

---

1 Para. 4.03, ante.
2 Cheshire *Modern Law of Real Property* (12th edn), 592.

---

4. Mortgages

12.09   The object of a mortgage[1] is that, if the lender (*mortgagee*) remains unpaid, he is protected even against the insolvency of the borrower (*mortgagor*) because he has a claim on the property secured for satisfaction of his debt which takes precedence over the claims of other creditors. The classic mortgage involved a conveyance of the legal or equitable interest in property to the lender with a provision for redemption, i.e. reconveyance to the borrower on repayment of the loan. However, a device regarded for most practical purposes as a species of mortgage is a charge, whereby the borrower (*chargor*) conveys nothing and merely grants the lender (*chargee*) certain rights over property as security for a loan.[2] In either case, the borrower on making the mortgage or charge retains an equity of redemption: this is an equitable interest in the property amounting to his rights of ownership subject only to the loan, and thus worth the market value of the property, less the loan. The borrower may deal with this equity of redemption just like any other interest in land, e.g. he can sell or mortgage it; but, if he wants to sell the property, he may prefer to repay (*redeem*) the loan and sell free of the mortgage or charge. It is a general rule that the lender cannot prevent the borrower from redeeming the mortgage or charge[3] on payment of the capital sum plus a reasonable rate of interest,[4] and free from all conditions in the mortgage;[5] but this rule against clogging the equity of redemption does not apply where the borrower is a limited company.[6]

---

1 For an explanation, see para. 12.01, ante.
2 See *London County and Westminster Bank Ltd v Tompkins* [1918] 1 KB 515.
3 *Salt v Marquess of Northampton* [1892] AC 1.

4 *Cityland and Property (Holdings) Ltd v Dabrah* [1968] Ch 166, [1967] 2 All ER 639.

5 For the limitation of restrictions during the currency of the mortgage as being in restraint of trade, see para. 6.10, ante.

6 *Companies Act* 1948, s. 89; *Knightsbridge Estates Trust Ltd v Byrne* [1940] AC 613, [1940] 2 All ER 401, HL.

12.10   By the Law of Property Act 1925, only two methods of creating *legal* mortgages of freehold or leasehold land are now possible:[1]

1. By a lease or sublease, subject to a provision for cesser on redemption; or

2. By a charge by deed expressed to be by way of legal mortgage.[2]

In practice, (2) is the more popular method of mortgaging property today, being shorter and simpler. However, where the borrower has only an equitable interest in property to utilise as security, he may create an equitable mortgage or charge by outright conveyance of the property secured. Moreover, the more informal rules of equity—which looks to the intention of the parties rather than to the mere form—may be utilised to create informal mortgages or charges: not only may this save an intended formal transaction which does not strictly comply with the rules, but it may be used to create an informal mortgage or charge simply by a deposit of the title deeds for the purpose of giving security.[3]

Unless the parties have otherwise agreed, a mortgagee or chargee has five (cumulative) remedies for enforcing his security as follows, these remedies now being regulated by the Law of Property Act 1925:[4] to sue for the repayment of capital after due date; to foreclose, thereby destroying the borrower's equity of redemption and acquiring the latter's interest;[5] to sell[6] the property mortgaged or charged free from the equity of redemption, repay himself, and hand over any surplus to the borrower (or next subsequent incumbrancer);[7] to take possession[8]—a step normally only taken as a prelude to the exercise of the power of sale; or to appoint a receiver to recover any income of the property, e.g. rent.[6] Furthermore, during the continuance of the mortgage or charge, the lender has the following rights, inter alia: to all fixtures attached to the land; to take out fire insurance at the borrower's expense;[9] to *consolidate* or *tack* two or more mortgages or charges which he holds or makes in respect of the same borrower.[10]

1 Ss. 85 (1), 86 (1). For mortgage brokers within the Consumer Credit Act 1974, see para. 14.27, post.
2 On transfer of charges, see Consumer Credit Act 1974, s. 177.
3 *Bozon v Williams* (1829) 3 Y & J 150 at 161.
4 Where the agreement is a regulated one within the Consumer Credit Act 1974 (see para. 14.13, post) and the mortgagee is not a Building Society or other exempt person, he may have to serve a preliminary notice before exercising any of these rights by reason of the Consumer Credit Act 1974, ss. 76, 87, 98 (see para. 14.37, post); or he may be required to obtain a court order under the Consumer Credit Act 1974 (s. 126) in circumstances where one is not required by the Law of Property Act 1925 (see para. 14.22, post). For the position where the mortgagor is a minor, see para. 2.17, ante.
5 Remedy not available to an equitable chargee: *Re Lloyd, Lloyd v Lloyd* [1903] 1 Ch 385, CA. See also s. 99 of the Consumer Credit Act 1974 (see para. 14.36, post).
6 The power only exists where the mortgage or charge was made by deed.
7 Whilst this right does not arise automatically on an equitable mortgage or charge, it is possible to achieve it by conveyancing devices.
8 See also Consumer Credit Act 1974, s. 92 (2): see para. 14.40, post.
9 Law of Property Act 1925, ss. 101 (1), 108.
10 The highly technical subjects of *consolidation* and *tacking* are beyond the scope of this work, but it should be noted that they make it dangerous to purchase mortgaged/charged property without careful enquiry.

12.11   Where a borrower is insolvent, it becomes vitally important to determine the order of priority of the various creditors, for that may decide which creditors will suffer the loss of the deficiency. The rules of bankruptcy regulating the competing claims of creditors in general will be dealt with in chapter 33, including the rights of secured creditors.[1] It remains to point out here what the mortgagee or chargee of land must do to secure for himself the status of a secured creditor.[2] Apart from mortgagees who are protected by taking possession of the title deeds to the mortgaged property, a mortgage relating to a legal estate requires registration as a land charge:[3] priority ranks according to registration;[4] and an unregistered mortgage is 'void as against a purchaser of the land charged therewith',[5] even if he has actual notice of it.[6] Furthermore, if the borrower is a limited company, any charge (including one created by a deposit of title deeds)[7] must *also* be registered in the Companies Register:[8] otherwise, the loan is immediately repayable and the charge void as against any liquidator and all creditors of the company.[9]

1 See para. 33.43, post.
2 For the parallel requirements for a mortgage of goods, see paras. 17.06, 17.10, post.
3 Mortgages of equitable interests in any property (land, goods or choses in action) date from the order in which notice is served on the owner of the

property: *Dearle v Hall* (1828) 3 Russ 1. For choses in action, see para. 4.08, ante; and for goods, see paras. 17.06, 17.10, post.

4 Law of Property Act 1925, s. 97.

5 Land Charges Act 1972, s. 4 (5).

6 Law of Property Act 1925, s. 199.

7 *Re Wallis and Simmonds (Builders) Ltd* [1974] 1 All ER 561, [1974] 1 WLR 391.

8 Land Charges Act 1972, s. 3 (7); Law of Property Act 1969, s. 26.

9 Companies Act 1948, s. 95; and see *Re Molton Finance Ltd* [1968] Ch 325, [1967] 3 All ER 843, CA. See further para. 17.10, post.

Chapter 13

Sale of Goods

13.01 The law relating to the sale of goods was codified by the Sale of Goods Act 1893, an enactment largely declaratory of the common law[1] and expressly saving the common law except in so far as is inconsistent with the express provisions of the Act (s. 61 (2)). The 1893 Act (SGA) has been subsequently amended by the Supply of Goods (Implied Terms) Act 1973 (SOGIT) and the Unfair Contract Terms Act 1977 (UCTA).

---

1 This will strengthen the argument for the application of the SGA rules by analogy to similar transactions; and see now UCTA, s. 7.

---

1. The contract of sale

a) A CONTRACT OF SALE OF GOODS

13.02 This is a:

'contract whereby the seller transfers, or agrees to transfer, the property in goods to the buyer for a money consideration, called the price'.[1]

a) A contract The SGA makes no attempt to interfere with the ordinary rules concerning the formation of contract;[2] but there are separate statutory provisions for unsolicited goods[3] and for adoption in international sales.[4]

b) A contract of sale The object of the contract must be to 'transfer the property in goods', this being defined by s. 62 (1) as the 'general property[5] in goods, and not merely a special property', e.g. a pledge.[6] However, the agreement to transfer the general property may be absolute, or it may be conditional in the sense that its performance is dependent on a condition precedent.[7] The insistence of the SGA on a promise to transfer the general property in goods from the promisor to the promisee distinguishes a sale from the following transactions: a bailment;[8] a pledge;[6] a mortgage,[9] or an agency.[10]

c) Goods These are defined as including 'all chattels personal other than things in action and money. ... The term includes emblements, industrial growing crops, and things attached to or forming part of the land which are agreed to be severed before sale or under the contract of sale.'[11] It follows from the definition that sales of ships are included.[12] A sale of minerals is not included unless they are already detached from the land.[13] 'Emblements' and 'industrial growing crops' are crops that are not naturally growing but are grown by the industry of men. 'Things attached to or forming part of the land' include things that are growing naturally on the land such as timber.[14]

The goods which form the subject of a contract of sale may be either *existing goods* owned or possessed by the seller, or goods to be manufactured or acquired by the seller after the making of the contract of sale. The latter are referred to in the Act as *future goods.*[15]

This requirement of *goods* enables the contract of sale to be technically distinguished from a sale of skill and labour e.g. the sale by an artist of the portrait which he paints under that contract.[16] Whilst the SGA implied terms do not strictly apply to such a situation, they have been applied at common law by analogy.[17]

d) Price Section 1 (1) requires that the transfer of goods be for 'a money consideration, called the price'. If the price consists of goods, the transaction is one of barter, not sale. However, the mere fact that part of the price is made up of goods, e.g. a part-exchange, does not make the transaction one of barter: the test seems to be the intention of the parties—if they intend a sale, it does not matter that it is agreed that some goods be accepted *in lieu of* part of that price.[18]

In the usual case, the amount of the price will be specified in the contract; but it may be left to be fixed in a manner thereby agreed, or may be determined by the course of dealings between the parties.[19] Under all other circumstances a reasonable price is presumed to have been intended.[20] A reasonable price is not necessarily the market price; what is reasonable depends on the circumstances of each particular case.[21] If the price is to be fixed by the valuation of a third party, and that third party cannot, or does not value, the agreement is avoided; except that:

1. So far as goods have already been delivered to and appropriated by the buyer, he must pay a fair price for them; and
2. If the third party is prevented from making the valuation by the act of a party to the contract of sale, that party may be sued for damages.

1 SGA, s. 1 (1).
2 1 See paras. 3.02, et seq., ante. For minors' contracts for necessaries, see paras. 2.16, et seq., ante.
3 Unsolicited Goods and Services Act 1971; see para. 14.06, post.
4 Uniform Law on International Sales Act 1967: see para. 13.47, post.
5 The 'general property' roughly approximates to the ownership of goods, but is more accurately regarded as a bundle of rights: see para. 13.06, post.
6 'Special property' is a more limited interest than general property. For instance, in a pledge, the pledgor retains the general property in the goods pledged, whilst the pledgee acquires a special property in them. For pledges, see paras. 17.02, et seq., post.
7 SGA, s. 1 (2). E.g. *Marten v Whale* [1917] 2 KB 480, CA (para. 7.06, ante).
8 See para, 14.06, post.
9 For mortgages of goods, see paras. 17.05, et seq., post.
10 Under a contract of agency, the agent may contract to sell or buy *for* his principal, and that contract does not transfer the property in any goods: for agency, see chap. 10.
11 SGA, s. 62 (1). For things in action, see paras. 4.06, et seq., ante.
12 *Behnke v Bede Shipping Co Ltd* [1927] 1 KB 649.
13 *Morgan v Russell & Sons* [1909] 1 KB 357.
14 These may also amount to an interest in land and have to comply with the rules relating to tranfers of interests in land: as to which, see chap. 12.
15 SGA 1893, s. 5 (1). There may be a contract for the sale of goods the acquisition of which by the seller depends upon a contingency which may or may not happen (ibid, s. 5 (2)).
16 *Robinson v Graves* [1935] 1 KB 579, CA.
17 *Young and Marten Ltd v McManus, Childs, Ltd* [1969] 1 AC 454, [1968] 2 All ER 1169, HL; *Gloucestershire County Council v Richardson* [1969] 1 AC 480, [1968] 2 All ER 1181, HL.
18 *GJ Dawson (Clapham) Ltd v Dutfield* [1936] 2 All ER 232.
19 S. 8 (1). For the offence by a seller of giving a misleading indication of the price, see the Trade Descriptions Act 1968, s. 11 (see para. 18.09, post); and for the law on price control and maintenance, see chap. 28, post.
20 S. 8 (2). But the fact that there is no expressly agreed price may be evidence that the parties have not yet finished agreeing: *May and Butcher Ltd v R* (1929) [1934] 2 KB 17, HL; and see para. 3.07, ante.
21 S. 9.

---

b) SALE AND AGREEMENT TO SELL

13.03   The definition in s. 1 (1) draws a distinction between a *sale* and an *agreement for sale*. Where the transfer of property takes place at once, the contract is called a sale, and where the transfer of property is to take place at a future time or subject to some condition that has to be fulfilled, such as payment of the price, the contract is an agreement to sell.[1] An agreement to sell becomes a sale when the time elapses or the conditions are fulfilled subject to which the property in the goods is to be transferred.[2]

---

1 S. 1 (3).

2 S. 1 (4). As to the effect of the passing of property, see paras. 13.06, et seq., post.

---

c) MISTAKE AND FRUSTRATION

13.04 The Act draws a sharp distinction according to whether a contract of sale is impossible of performance at the time it is made, and then deals with just one instance of such impossibility; namely, where the contract is, or becomes, impossible of performance by reason of the perishing of the goods which are its subject-matter.

a) Mistake If at the time of the contract for the sale of specific goods, i.e. goods identified and agreed on at the time of the contract, the goods have perished without the knowledge of the seller, the contract is void.[1] 'Perishing' includes physical destruction and theft, even of part of the goods only if they were sold as an indivisible whole.[2]

b) Frustration If there is an agreement to sell specific goods and later, without any fault on the part of the seller or buyer, they perish before the risk of loss passes to the buyer, the agreement is avoided, i.e. frustrated;[3] and as will be seen, the risk of loss generally passes to the buyer at the same time as ownership.[4] In all other cases, however, the matter is governed by the common law on the question of when such a contract will be frustrated;[5] and as to the effect of frustration the position is as follows: the parties may be excused from performing any part of the contract which has become impossible of performance,[6] whilst remaining liable to perform the rest,[7] the court having the advantage of a statutory discretionary power of apportionment.[8]

---

1 SGA, s. 6. For another view of the situation, see para. 5.05, ante.
2 *Barrow, Lane and Ballard, Ltd v Phillip Phillips & Co Ltd* [1929] 1 KB 574.
3 S. 7.
4 Para. 13.06, post.
5 Compare *Howell v Coupland* (1876) 1 QBD 258, CA; *Blackburn Bobbin Ltd v TW Allen & Sons Ltd* [1918] 1 KB 540; affd. [1918] 2 KB 467, CA; *Intertradex SA v Lesieur-Tourteaux SARL* [1977] 2 Lloyd's Rep 146. See generally para. 8.02, ante.
6 *Howell v Coupland*, ante.
7 *HR and S Sainsbury Ltd v Street* [1972] 3 All ER 1127, [1972] 1 WLR 834.
8 See para. 8.06, ante.

2. Form of contract

13.05 A contract for the sale of goods may be in any form; whatever the price, it may be made by word of mouth or in writing, partly in writing and partly by word of mouth, or merely implied from the conduct of the parties.[1] Exceptionally, some formalities may be required; for instance, where the buyer does not take possession of the goods immediately, but is given a receipt;[2] or where there is a sale of a ship, or a share therein;[3] or where there is a consumer instalment credit contract.[4]

---

1 SGA, s. 3. S. 4, dealing with the formalities of sales generally was repealed by the Law Reform (Enforcement of Contracts) Act 1954: see para. 2.11, ante.
2 See the Bills of Sale Act 1878 (para. 17.06, post).
3 Merchant Shipping Act 1894, s. 24: see para. 25.03, post.
4 See the Consumer Credit Act 1974 (paras. 14.12, et seq., post).

---

3. Transfer of property from seller to buyer

13.06 Whilst the object of a contract of sale is to transfer the general property in goods from seller to buyer,[1] English law has rejected the idea that that property should automatically pass, either at the time of contract or delivery: instead, it was settled that the matter should be left to the agreement between the parties.[2] Thus, whilst the conveyance need not take place at the time when the contract is made, it remains true that in the case of goods[3] the contract of sale suffices to effect the conveyance.[4]

The concept of the property in goods must be distinguished from the title to goods: an enquiry as the whereabouts of property is the proper one in a dispute between seller and buyer, whereas the issue of best title is crucial where the owner's goods have come into the hands of a bona fide purchaser.[5] Perhaps the best way of looking at the concept of property is as a bundle of rights.[6] Amongst these rights, the most important are as follows:

1) The basic rule is that only the person with the property in goods can pass the best title, so that, if a case cannot be fitted within one of the exceptions, the basic rule applies.[5]

2) Prima facie, the risk in goods lies on the owner: res perit domino.[7] Section 20 provides:

> 'Unless otherwise agreed,[8] the goods remain at the seller's risk until the property therein is transferred to the buyer, but when the property therein is transferred to the buyer, the goods are at the buyer's risk whether delivery has been made or not.[9]

Provided that where delivery has been delayed through the

fault of either seller or buyer the goods are at the risk of the party in fault as regards any loss which might not have occurred but for such fault.[10]

Provided also that nothing in this section shall affect the duties or liabilities of either seller or buyer as a bailee ... of the goods of the other party.'[11]

3) Generally, the seller can only sue for the price when the property has passed, and is otherwise left to claim damages.[12]

4) On the insolvency of a party, the general rule is that any goods in which he has the property will fall into his bankruptcy.[13] Thus, where an insolvent seller has retained the property in goods, his buyer who has pre-paid the price will be reduced to claiming in the bankruptcy for a dividend;[14] but a buyer who has not paid the price is relatively safe, in that he can simply offer to buy the goods from the trustee in bankruptcy for cash.[15]

---

1 See para. 13.02, ante.
2 See ss. 1 (4) and 17.
3 Contra sales of land: see para. 12.01, ante.
4 Contra transfers of choses in action (see para. 4.09, ante) and mortgages or pledges of goods (see paras. 17.06, 17.02, post).
5 See para. 13.11, post.
6 See Atiyah *Sale of Goods* (5th edn) 141–145.
7 For the special rules for international sales, see paras. 13.39, et seq., post.
8 Specific provision as to the passing of risk is commonly found in standard form contracts: as to which, see generally, para. 3.13, ante.
9 E.g. *Rugg v Minett* (1809) 11 East 210 (sale of goods lying in a warehouse; goods destroyed by fire before delivery). For the special rules for delivery at a distant place, see para. 13.39, post.
10 E.g. *Demby Hamilton & Co v Barden* [1949] 1 All ER 435. Where the contract envisages a delay in delivery, the court may infer an intention that the risk pass immediately notwithstanding that the property remains in the seller: *Sterns Ltd v Vickers Ltd* [1923] 1 KB 78, CA.
11 Where one party to the sale is bailee of the goods for the other, the former owes the latter the ordinary duty of care of a bailee for value: see para. 14.06, post. Where there is a third party bailee, he may be sued on the terms of a bill of lading by the buyer notwithstanding the latter's lack of privity under the Bills of Lading Act 1855: see para. 23.12, post.
12 See para. 13.36, post.
13 See paras. 33.16, et seq., post.
14 See generally para. 33.47, post.
15 As the trustee's duty is to realise the assets, he will generally agree, in which case the buyer need only prove in the bankrupt seller's estate for any consequential loss flowing from the seller's breach of contract. Contra, where the contract price was substantially below the market value of the goods, in which case the trustee may disclaim the contract entirely as onerous property (as to which, see para. 33.32, post).

THE RULES FOR THE PASSING OF PROPERTY

13.07 For the purposes of determining when the property in goods is to pass under a contract of sale, the SGA makes a distinction between *specific* goods and *unascertained* goods. Specific goods are defined as goods identified and agreed upon at the time the contract of sale is made.[1] Unascertained goods are not expressly defined in the Act but it may be inferred that they are goods which become ascertained at any time *after* the contract is made.[2]

---

1 S. 62 (1). See *Kursell v Timber Operators Ltd* [1927] 1 KB 298, CA.
2 The test is: Can the buyer at the time of contracting point to any particular item and say 'That is, or is to be, mine by virtue of this contract'.

SALE OF SPECIFIC GOODS

13.08 The cardinal question when the goods are specified or ascertained is, what is the intention of the parties? If an answer to this can be obtained, the time when the property passes is fixed by that answer, for the intention of the parties governs the matter;[1] and where that intention does not otherwise appear, the following rules for ascertaining it are laid down in s. 18 of the SGA:

Rule 1—'Where there is an unconditional contract for the sale of specific goods in a deliverable state,[2] the property in the goods passes to the buyer when the contract is made, and it is immaterial whether the time of payment or time of delivery, or both, be postponed'.[3]

A buyer is not necessarily entitled to possession of the goods because the property in them has passed, the general rule being that the seller is entitled to retain possession until the buyer has paid the price,[4] and, anyway, postponement of the time of payment or delivery or both may be evidence of a contrary intention.[5]

Rule 2—'Where there is a contract for the sale of specific goods and the seller is bound to do something to the goods, for the purpose of putting them in a deliverable state, the property does not pass until such thing be done, and the buyer has notice thereof'.[6]

For instance, if the seller is to repair or alter the goods, the property passes only when the repairs or alterations are done and the buyer has notice of that fact, because the sale is of *repaired* or *altered* goods.[7]

Rule 3—'Where there is a contract for the sale of specific goods in a deliverable state, but the seller is bound to weigh, measure, test, or do some other act or thing with reference to the goods for the purpose of ascertaining the price, the property does not pass until such act or thing be done, and the buyer has notice thereof'.[8]

This rule does not apply if the 'weighing, measuring, or testing' is to be done by the buyer,[9] and it has in fact rarely been applied.

Rule 4—'When goods are delivered to the buyer on approval or "on sale or return" or other similar terms[10] the property therein passes to the buyer:

1. When he signifies his approval or acceptance to the seller or does any other act adopting the transaction.

2. If he does not signify his approval or acceptance to the seller but retains the goods without giving notice of rejection, then, if a time has been fixed for the return of the goods, on the expiration of such time, and, if no time has been fixed, on the expiration of a reasonable time. What is a reasonable time is a question of fact'.

If the buyer pledges the goods, he does an 'act adopting the transaction',[11] but the property will not pass if there is an express term in the contract that the property will not pass until the goods are paid for, because all the rules are subject to contrary intention shown in the contract.[12]

In *Poole v Smith's Car Sales (Balham) Ltd:*[13]

A car was left by the plaintiff with the defendant dealers on 'sale or return' terms in August 1960. After several requests, the car was returned in November 1960 in a damaged state owing to unauthorised use by the defendants' servants. *Held:* as the car had not been returned within a reasonable time, the property in the car had passed to defendants under s. 18, r. 4. The defendants were therefore liable for the price agreed.

---

1 SGA, s. 17 (1). See for example, *Re Anchor Line (Henderson Bros) Ltd* [1937] 1 Ch 1, CA.
2 I.e. in a state in which the buyer is bound to accept (ibid, s. 62 (4)).
3 E.g. *Dennant v Skinner* [1948] 2 KB 164, [1948] 2 All ER 29.
4 SGA, s. 28: see para. 13.30, post.
5 E.g. *Lacis v Cashmarts* [1969] 2 QB 400, DC.
6 E.g. *Underwood Ltd v Burgh Castle Brick and Cement Syndicate* [1922] 1 KB 123 and 343, CA.
7 E.g. *Phillip Head & Sons Ltd v Showfronts Ltd* (1969) 113 Sol Jo 978 (sale and laying of carpet).
8 E.g. *Hanson v Meyer* (1805) 6 East 614.
9 *Nanka Bruce v Commonwealth Trust Ltd* [1926] AC 77, PC.
10 Distinguish h.p. agreement, as to which see para. 14.03, post.
11 *Kirkham v Attenborough* [1897] 1 QB 201.
12 *Weiner v Gill* [1906] 2 KB 574, CA; *Genn v Winkel* (1912) 107 LT 434, CA.
13 [1962] 2 All ER 482, [1962] 1 WLR 744, CA.

SALE OF UNASCERTAINED GOODS

13.09 The contract is here merely an executory agreement, and until the goods are ascertained, i.e. identified after the contract as being in accordance with the agreement, the property does not pass:[1] nor does the buyer appear to obtain thereby any equitable rights in the goods.[2] Such cases will include a contract to sell part of a greater quantity, e.g. sale of so many tons of hay out of a certain year's produce and a sale of goods of a certain kind, e.g., a new Ford Capri 1978. Rule 5 of s. 18 shows that generally the property in unascertained goods will not pass until goods of the description agreed are *appropriated* to the contract.

Rule 5—'1) Where there is a contract for the sale of unascertained or future goods by description, and goods of that description and in a deliverable state are unconditionally appropriated to the contract, either by the seller with the assent of the buyer, or by the buyer with the assent of the seller, the property in the goods thereupon passes to the buyer.[3] Such assent may be express or implied, and may be given either before or after the appropriation is made.

2) Where, in pursuance of the contract, the seller delivers the goods to the buyer or to a carrier or other bailee or custodian (whether named by the buyer or not) for the purpose of transmission to the buyer, and does not reserve the right of disposal, he is deemed to have unconditionally appropriated the goods to the contract'.[4]

If the seller sends notice of appropriation to the buyer and the latter does not reply promptly, it must be inferred that he assents to the appropriation and the property in the goods will be deemed to pass on the expiration of a reasonable time after receipt of the notice.[5]

It follows from Rule 5 that if the thing sold is in course of manufacture the prima facie rule is that the property in it does not pass to the buyer before completion.[6] But the parties may expressly or impliedly agree by the contract itself or during the course of the construction of the chattel that the property in the partly finished article shall pass to the purchaser, and such an agreement is generally presumed where payments are to be made in respect of particular stages of manufacture coupled with the fact that the buyer has agreed to accept the corpus so far as completed, e.g. by inspecting and approving it. This kind of question has arisen most frequently in connection with ship-building contracts. Materials provided by the manufacturer ready to be incorporated into the fabric of the subject-matter of the sale cannot be regarded as 'sold' unless they have been fixed or in a reasonable sense made part of the corpus, or unless there is evidence of a separate agreement that the property in the unfinished materials should pass.[7]

---

1 SGA 1893, s. 16.
2 *Re Wait* [1927] 1 Ch at 636, per Atkin LJ: see further paras. 13.33, 17.14, post.
3 Compare *Aldridge v Johnson* (1857) 26 LJQB 296; *Re Wait* [1927] 1 Ch 606, CA.
4 See e.g. *Wardar's (Import and Export) Co Ltd v W. Norwood & Sons Ltd* [1968] 2 QB 663, [1968] 2 All ER 602, CA; *Edwards v Doin* [1976] 3 All ER, 705, DC.
5 *Pignataro v Gilroy* [1919] 1 KB 459, DC.
6 *Carlos Federspiel & Co SA v Charles Twigg & Co Ltd* [1957] 1 Lloyd's Rep 240.
7 *Re Blyth Shipbuilding and Dry Docks Co Ltd* [1926] Ch 494; *McDougall v Aeromarine of Emsworth Ltd* [1958] 3 All ER 431, [1958] 1 WLR 1126.

RIGHT OF DISPOSAL RESERVED

13.10 If when selling specific goods or when appropriating goods to a contract for the sale of unascertained goods, the seller reserves the right of disposal to the goods, i.e. retains a *jus disponendi*, until some condition is satisfied (generally that the price be paid) the property will not pass until that condition is fulfilled.[1] The Act also deals specifically with two common instances of this principle in relation to international sales, providing two ways in which the seller who ships goods may utilise the bill of lading.[2] First, where goods are shipped, and by the bill of lading the goods are deliverable to the order of the seller, the seller is prima facie deemed to reserve the right of disposal.[3] Second, if a purchaser receives the bill of lading together with a bill of exchange for acceptance, this is evidence of intention on the part of the vendor not to part with the goods till acceptance of the bill;[4] but upon acceptance of the bill or payment of the price, the property will vest in the buyer, the seller's conditional appropriation of the goods having thereby become unconditional.[5]

---

1 SGA, s. 19 (1).
2 For international sales, see further paras. 13.39, et seq., post; and for bills of lading, see paras. 23.08 et seq., post.
3 SGA, s. 19 (2); and see *Wait v Baker* (1848) 2 Exch 1; *Turner v Trustees of the Liverpool Docks* (1851) 6 Exch 543.
4 *The Parchim* [1918] AC 157, PC. For bills of exchange, see chap. 20, post.
5 SGA, s. 19 (3).

4. Transfer of title

13.11 The transactions dealt with here involve the situation where goods belonging to A are transferred by B to C. Both A and C may be entirely blameless; and, where B has disappeared or is insolvent, the problem is to determine whether A or C is entitled to the goods, and hence which is reduced to pursuing a (worthless) right against B.

As a general rule, only the owner (A) is capable of passing a good title in goods to a buyer: *nemo dat quod non habet*; so that in the normal case better title will remain in A.[1] There are however a number of exceptions to this rule, whereunder a bona fide purchaser (C) may acquire a good title.

In *Bishopsgate Motor Finance Corpn Ltd v Transport Brakes Ltd*,[2] Denning LJ said:

> 'In the development of our law, two principles have striven for mastery. The first is the protection of property. No one can give a better title than he himself possesses. The second is the protection of commercial transactions. The person who takes in good faith and for value without notice should get a good title. The first principle has held sway for a long time, but it has been modified by common law itself and by statute so as to meet the needs of our times.'

---

1 SGA 1893, s. 21 (1). E.g. *Mercantile Bank of India Ltd v Central Bank of India Ltd* [1938] AC 287, [1938] 1 All ER 52, PC.
2 [1949] 1 KB 322 at 336–337, [1949] 1 All ER 37 at 46, CA.

GENERAL EXCEPTIONS

13.12 *a) Agency* If the seller of good sells them under the authority[1] of or with the consent of the owner,[2] the buyer obtains a good title.[3] Moreover, a buyer obtains a good title if the owner of goods is precluded by his conduct from denying the seller's authority to sell. In *Eastern Distributors Ltd v Goldring*:[4]

> M, the owner of a Bedford van, wished to purchase a car, but could not raise the deposit. Accordingly, the car dealer suggested they pretend to the finance company (C) that M wished to hire both the van and the car. C accepted the proposal in respect of the van; but M subsequently sold the van to A. *Held:* whilst ownership would normally have passed from M to A, C had obtained a good title by estoppel because M and A were precluded from denying the dealer's authority to sell to C.

But merely permitting someone else to have possession of goods does not estop the owner from denying that person's authority to sell.

In *Central Newbury Car Auctions, Ltd v Unity Finance, Ltd*:[5]

> Dealer A purchased a car, in the log-book of which the previous registered owner, Ashley, had not signed his name. A did not register himself as owner because he intended to resell the car. Subsequently, a rogue, B, tricked the dealer into parting with possession of the car and log-book, and then offered the car to C, giving the name of Ashley. By this time, B had signed the log-book in the name of Ashley. C compared the signature in the log-book with that which B provided in his presence, and then completed the purchase. *Held:* B had no title and therefore gave none to C; and A was not estopped from denying B's title simply because he transferred possession of the car and log-book to B.

b) Sale by mercantile agent This exception is dealt with in para. 10.20, ante.

c) Sale under special common law or statutory powers of sale Thus a sale by a pledgee of an unredeemed pledge,[6] by a repairer of uncollected goods,[7] or by an unpaid seller,[8] or of a guest's goods by an innkeeper whose bill is unpaid[9] give the purchaser a good title as against the pledgor, owner, buyer or guest respectively.[10] A court has wide powers under the Rules of the Supreme Court to order a sale of goods.

---

1 For the rules of agency, see para. 10.17, et seq., ante.
2 Compare *Mordaunt v British Oil and Cake Mills Ltd* [1910] 2 KB 502; *DF Mount Ltd v Jay and Jay (Provisions) Co Ltd* [1960] 1 QB 159, [1959] 3 All ER 307.
3 SGA 1893, s. 21 (1).
4 [1957] 1 QB 600, [1957] 2 All ER 525, CA. For agency by estoppel, see para. 10.19, ante; for an instance where no estoppel was found, see para. 14.03, n. 5, post.
5 [1957] 1 QB 371, [1956] 3 All ER 905, CA. See also *J Sargent (Garages) Ltd v Motor Auctions (West Bromwich) Ltd* [1977] RTR 121, CA.
6 See paras. 17.03–17.04, post.
7 Torts (Interference with Goods) Act 1977, s. 12; see further para. 17.12, post.
8 SGA, s. 48: see para. 13.38 (iii), post.
9 Innkeepers Act 1878: see para. 17.11, post.
10 But, apart from the reputed ownership doctrine, a trustee in bankruptcy cannot pass a better title than the bankrupt had: see paras. 33.16, et seq., post.

SPECIAL EXCEPTIONS

13.13 *Sale in market overt* When goods are sold in 'market overt' to a bona fide purchaser (C), without notice of the seller's (B's) defect or want of title, and according to the usage of the market, the sale is binding on the true owner (A), though he neither sold them nor authorised their sale.[1] Goods are sold in 'market overt' if they are sold in a recognised market established by grant or prescription or under statutory powers. The sale need not be effected by a trader if sales by private treaty habitually take place in the market.[2] But by custom sales by a trader in a shop in the City of London made in the ordinary course of his business on any day except Sunday are treated as being made in market overt.[3]

1 SGA 1893, s. 22 (1). NB: SGA ss. 22 (2) and 24 have been repealed.
2 *Bishopsgate Motor Finance Corpn Ltd v Transport Brakes Ltd* [1949] 1 KB 322, [1949] 1 All ER 37, CA. Cf. *Reid v Metropolitan Police Comr* [1973] 1 QB 551, [1973] 2 All ER 97, CA.
3 *Hargreave v Spink* [1892] 1 QB 25.

13.14 *Sale under a voidable title* Where the seller (B) of goods has a voidable title, e.g. because he has obtained the goods by fraud, but his title has not been avoided at the time of the sale,[1] the buyer (C) acquires a good title to the goods, provided he buys them in good faith and without notice of the seller's defect of title.[2]

1 See *Car and Universal Finance Co Ltd v Caldwell* [1965] 1 QB 525, [1964] 1 All ER 290, CA (see para. 5.11, ante).
2 SGA 1893, s. 23. See *Lewis v Averay* [1972] 1 QB 198, [1971] 3 All ER 907, CA (set out in para. 5.02, ante).

13.15 *Sales be sellers in possession* The policy behind this exception is that, where the seller (B) has sold the same goods to a number of people in succession, the first buyer to get actual possession (C) shall have the best title. Accordingly, the SGA provides that where a person (B) having sold goods 'continues or is in possession' of the goods or the documents of title[1] thereto, delivery or transfer of the goods or documents of title by such vendor or his mercantile agent,[2] under any sale, pledge, or other disposition thereof, has the same effect as if such vendor or other person were expressly authorised by the owner (A) of the goods to make the same, provided that the person to whom the sale or disposition has been made (C) acts bona fide and without notice of the previous sale.[3] The Court of Appeal held in *Worcester Works Finance Ltd v Cooden Engineering Co Ltd*[4] that 'continues ... in possession' means continuity of physical possession and it is irrelevant whether B remains in possession as a bailee or a trespasser or whether A has consented or not to the seller remaining in possession.

---

1 'Document of title' has the same meaning as in the Factors Act 1889 (SGA 1893, s. 61). As to what the expression includes, see para. 10.20, ante. The registration book of a motor car is not a document of title.
2 For the meaning of this, see para. 10.20, ante.
3 SGA 1893, s. 25 (1). A similar provision is to be found in the Factors Act 1889, s. 8.
4 [1972] 1 QB 182, [1971] 3 All ER 708, CA, following *Pacific Motor Auctions Proprietary Ltd v Motor Credits (Hire Finance) Ltd* [1965] AC 887, [1965] 2 All ER 105, PC.

13.16 *Sales by buyers in possession* The policy behind this exception is similar to the previous one; namely, that a 'buyer' who has been allowed to take possession of goods before the property in them passed to him should be able to pass a good title. Hence, the SGA provides that where a person having bought or agreed to buy goods (B) obtains *with the consent of the seller*, (A) possession of the goods or the documents of title to the goods, the delivery or transfer by that person, or by a mercantile agent acting for him, of the goods or documents of title, under any sale, pledge, or other disposition thereof, to any person (C) receiving the same in good faith and without notice of any lien or other right of the original seller in respect of the goods, has the same effect as if the person making the delivery or transfer (B) were a mercantile agent in possession of the goods or documents of title with the consent of the owner (A).[1]

1) 'Agreed to buy'. It was early settled that this phrase comprehended the typical conditional sale, whereby the price was payable by instalments and the property did not pass until payment was completed;[2] but the supposed injustice of this rule in consumer transactions prompted Parliament to reverse it—*but only for such cases*.[3] However, the inconvenience of the former rule[2] led the instalment credit trade to devise the hire purchase (h.p.) contract, and it was quickly established that under a h.p. agreement the hirer had not 'agreed to buy',[4] a ruling again partially countered by Parliament—this time only in respect of motor vehicles (see para. 13.17, post).

2) The seller's (A's) consent to the buyer's (B's) possession. The issue here is whether 'consent' is to be given the same meaning as in the case of the mercantile agency exception.[5]

3) The effect of the exception. Its operation is illustrated by *Cahn v Pockett's Bristol Channel Steam Packet Co Ltd*:[6]

> The seller of goods (A) forwarded to the buyer a bill of lading indorsed in blank, together with a draft for the price for acceptance. The buyer (B) did not accept the draft, but transferred the bill of lading to the plaintiffs (C), who took it in good faith and for value. A stopped the goods *in transitu*. The Court of Appeal *held* that C had acquired a good title to the goods, as, although it was not intended that any property should pass to B until acceptance of the draft, B had nevertheless obtained possession of the documents of title with the consent of A.

Where operative, this exception is expressed to 'have the same effect as if the person making the transfer were a mercantile agent in possession ... with the consent of the owner', an obvious reference back to s. 2 (1) of the Factors Act 1889.[7] When it first considered this provision, the Court of Appeal took the view that it merely incorporated the result of s. 2 (1); namely, that the disposition by B should be as valid as if he were expressly authorised by A to make it.[8] However, more recently they have taken the view that the reference also requires that the disposition by B should be made by him when acting in the ordinary course of business of a mercantile agent;[9] and, as most buyers do not dispose of goods in such a manner, very few sales will fall within this exception so that the development of h.p. agreements was unnecessary.[10]

---

1 S. 25 (2). A similar provision is to be found in the Factors Act 1889, s. 9.

2 *Lee v Butler* [1893] 1 QB 318, CA. See also *Marten v Whale* [1917] 2 KB 480, CA (set out para. 7.06, ante).

3 By s. 54 of the Hire-Purchase Act 1965. See now the amendment made to s. 25 (2) of the SGA by Sch. 4 of the Consumer Credit Act 1974. Conditional sales which are regulated agreements within the CCA are considered para. 14.02, post.

4 *Helby v Matthews* [1895] AC 471, HL. For h.p. agreements, see para. 14.03, post.

5 Compare *Inglis v Robertson* [1898] AC 616, HL(S); and *Du Jardin v Beadman Bros Ltd* [1952] 2 QB 712, at 716, per Sellers J.

6 [1899] 1 QB 643, CA (the court also applied the similar provisions found in the Factors Act 1889, s. 10 and the proviso to s. 47 of the SGA: see para. 13.38, post).

7 See paras. 10.20–10.21, ante.

8 *Lee v Butler* [1893] 2 QB 318, CA.

9 *Newtons of Wembley Ltd v Williams* [1965] 1 QB 560, [1964] 3 All ER 532, CA (by the freak chance that the buyer disposed of the goods in the Warren Street car market, that requirement was here satisfied).

10 Twelfth Report of the Law Reform Committee (Cmnd. 2958, 1966), para. 24.

13.17 *Protection of purchasers of vehicles* If a motor vehicle has been let under a hire-purchase agreement or has been agreed to be sold under a conditional sale agreement and, before the property has passed to the debtor, he (B) disposes of the vehicle to a 'private purchaser' (C) who takes the vehicle in good faith and without notice of the hire-purchase agreement or conditional sale agreement, the disposition has effect as if the title of the owner, seller or creditor (A) had been vested in the debtor (B) immediately before the disposition.[1] Further, where the disposition is to 'a trade or finance purchaser', i.e. C is a dealer in motor vehicles or a finance company, then if the person who is the first private purchaser of the vehicle after that disposition is a purchaser in good faith and without notice of the hire-purchase or conditional sale agreement, the disposition to the first purchaser has effect as if the title of A had been vested in B immediately before he disposed of it to the original purchaser (C).[2] A private purchaser of a vehicle which is still subject to a hire-purchase agreement is protected if he honestly believes that, although the vehicle was once subject to such an agreement, the instalments have been paid off.[3]

Sale after delivery of writ of execution Where a writ of execution has been delivered to the sheriff to be executed, the sheriff (A) has a legal right to seize them to sell and thus satisfy the judgment debt. But while the writ remains unexecuted, the debtor (B) is able to pass a good title to the goods to anyone (C) who purchases them in good faith for valuable consideration without notice of the writ.[4]

---

1 Hire-Purchase Act 1964, s. 27, as reproduced in Sch. 4 of the Consumer Credit Act 1974. A 'conditional sale agreement' means an agreement in which the total purchase price is payable by instalments, and the property is to remain in the seller until such conditions as to payment of instalments or otherwise, as may be specified in the agreement, are fulfilled: Hire-Purchase Act 1964, s. 29 (1). A 'private purchaser' means someone buying the vehicle or taking it on hire-purchase who does not carry on the business of purchasing vehicles for resale or of providing finance by purchasing vehicles in order to dispose of them under hire-purchase or conditional sale agreements: ibid, s. 29 (2); and see *Stevenson v Beverley Bentinck Ltd* [1976] 2 All ER 606, [1976] 1 WLR 483, CA.
2 In this case, the private purchaser may be materially aided by the presumptions of good faith, etc, found in s. 28.
3 *Barker v Bell* [1971] 2 All ER 867, [1971] 1 WLR 983, CA.
4 SGA 1893, s. 26, amended by the Administration of Justice Act 1965, s. 22. Once the writ is executed, e.g. by the sheriff seizing the debtor's goods, the debtor cannot pass title to the goods even though he is left temporarily in possession of them: *Lloyds and Scottish Finance Ltd v Modern Cars and Caravans (Kingston) Ltd* [1966] 1 QB 764, [1964] 2 All ER 732.

5. Conditions and warranties

DEFINITIONS

13.18 There is more in a contract for the sale of goods than simply payment of the price and delivery of the goods. For instance:

> A may buy a second-hand motor car and then find that the seller had no title to it; or that it is a 1970 model when it was said to be a 1975 model; or that it is so defective that it is only fit for the scrap-heap.

A's rights in these events may be covered expressly in the contract;[1] but more probably nothing will have been said about them, so that it will be a matter of implication.[2] Furthermore, if the innocent party (A) is not content with damages for breach of contract, but wishes to escape from (*avoid*) the contract, it will be necessary to determine the status of the contractual term broken: Is it a condition, a warranty, or an innominate term?[3]

The only contribution provided by the SGA on this issue is to define a 'warranty' simply in terms of its effects as:[4]

> 'An agreement with reference to goods which are the subject of a contract of sale, but collateral to the main purpose of such contract, the breach of which gives rise to a claim for damages, but not to a right to reject the goods and treat the contract as repudiated.'

Whilst 'condition' is nowhere expressly defined in the Act, it is inferentially defined by s. 11 as a term, breach of which will give rise to a right to reject and rescind, again a definition solely in terms of effect. When it is asked how to distinguish between a 'condition' and a 'warranty', s. 11 unhelpfully says that that is a matter of intention, adding:[5]

> 'A stipulation may be a condition, though called a warranty in the contract'.

Although the SGA obviates the problem to some extent by expressly assigning the status of condition or warranty to the statutory implied terms considered below, in all other cases reference must be made back to the common law, [3] the only contribution of the Act being the provision that:[6]

> 'Where a contract of sale is subject to any condition to be fulfilled by the seller, the buyer may waive the condition, or may elect to treat the breach of condition as a breach of warranty, and not as a ground for treating the contract as repudiated'.

---

1 For express terms, see para. 7.04, *ante*.

2 See para. 7.05, ante.
3 *Cehave NV v Bremer Handelgesellschaft mbH* [1976] QB 44, [1975] 3 All ER 739, CA; and see paras. 7.07–7.09, ante.
4 S. 62 (1).
5 S. 11 (1) (b).
6 S. 11 (1) (a).

IMPLIED CONDITIONS AND WARRANTIES

13.19 The common law started from the strict position that the buyer must make express stipulations or take his chance: *caveat emptor*. However, the common law gradually modified this stand, and the terms which it was prepared to imply in favour of the buyer were codified in the SGA. They have subsequently been re-codified in a manner much more advantageous to the buyer by the SOGIT.[1]

1 As amended by the Consumer Credit Act 1974, Sch. 4. The SOGIT has been drafted so as to insert new implied terms into the SGA. These implied terms are not negatived by any promises unless inconsistent therewith: new s. 55 (2) of the SGA, as renumbered by SOGIT, s. 4.

i) Implied terms as to title

13.20 Into every contract of sale, the new s. 12 prima facie imports three implied terms:

a) An implied condition as to title The Act lays down that there is:[1]

> 'an implied condition on the part of the seller that in the case of a sale he has a right to sell the goods, and in the case of an agreement to sell, he will have a right to sell the goods at the time when the property is to pass'.

This obviously covers the situation where the seller does not own the goods he is purporting to sell (regardless of his innocence or otherwise);[2] but it has been decided that an owner of goods has 'no right to sell' them where they bear marks or labels which infringe a registered trade mark.[3] A breach of this condition entitles the buyer to recover the price as upon a total failure of consideration, and irrespective of whether he has enjoyed possession of the goods for a period. In *Rowland v Divall*:[4]

> P bought a car from D, and two months later sold it to X. After a further two months, it was discovered that the car had been sold to D by a thief. P refunded his price to X and sued D, claiming to rescind the contract with D and recover his price from D. *Held:* there had been a total failure of

consideration, as P had received no part of that for which he bargained, so that P was entitled to recover the price he paid.

b) An implied warranty as to encumbrances The Act lays down that there is:[5]

'an implied warranty that the goods are free, and will remain free until the time when the property is to pass, from any charge or encumbrance not disclosed or known to the buyer before the contract is made'.

c) An implied warranty as to quiet enjoyment The Act lays down that there is an implied warranty that:[6]

'the buyer will enjoy quiet possession of the goods except so far as it may be disturbed by the owner or other persons entitled to the benefit of any charge or encumbrance so disclosed or known'.

If it had been required that all contracts of sale contain these three implied terms, it would have been virtually impossible to deal in goods to which there was no clear title. Accordingly, the Act allows the seller to limit his implied undertakings as to title as follows:

1) He may contract to 'transfer only such title as he or a third person may have'.[7] Where the seller goes further, and does not even promise to transfer to the buyer such title as he has, it is questionable whether the contract amounts to a sale of goods within the SGA.[8]

2) In cases falling within (1) above, the Act lays down that there shall[9] be two implied warranties as follows:[10]

a) 'that all charges or encumbrances known to the seller and not known to the buyer have been disclosed to the buyer before the contract is made'; and
b) 'that the buyer's quiet possession will not be disturbed by the seller, or by any third person whose title the seller is contracting to transfer, or by their privies'.

---

1 S. 12 (1) (a) of the SGA, as amended by s. 1 of SOGIT.

2 *Rowland v Divall* [1923] 2 KB 500, CA.

3 *Niblett v Confectioners' Materials Co* [1921] 3 KB 387, CA.

4 [1923] 2 KB 500, CA. For the implications of this decision, see *Butterworth v Kingsway Motors Ltd* [1954] 2 All ER 694, [1954] 1 WLR 1286.

5 S. 12 (1) (b) of the SGA, as amended by s. 1 of SOGIT. See *Lloyds and Scottish Finance Ltd v Modern Cars and Caravans Ltd* [1966] 1 QB 764, [1964] 2 All ER 732.

6 S. 12 (1) (b) of the SGA, as amended by s. 1 of SOGIT. See *Mason v Burningham* [1949] 2 KB 545, [1949] 2 All ER 134, CA; *Microbeads AG v Vinhurst Road Markings* [1975] 1 All ER 529, [1975] 1 WLR 218, CA.

7 New s. 12 (2), as supplied by s. 1 of SOGIT.

8 Because the Act defines a sale as an agreement to transfer the property in goods: see para. 13.02, ante.

9 These two implied warranties may not be excluded: see para. 13.27, post.

10 New s. 12 (2), as supplied by s. 1 of SOGIT.

---

ii) Implied conditions as to description

13.21   According to the new s. 13 (1) of the SGA:[1]

'Where there is a contract for the sale of goods by description, there is an implied condition that the goods shall correspond with the description; and if the sale be by sample, as well as by description, it is not sufficient that the bulk of the goods corresponds with the sample if the goods do not also correspond with the description'.

Leaving aside sales by sample,[2] it will be observed that the undertaking is limited to 'sales by description'. This expression is apt to cover all those cases 'where the purchaser has not seen the goods, and buys them relying on the description alone, whether the goods be specific or unascertained',[3] but it also comprehends goods which the buyer sees before contracting. In *Beale v Taylor*:[4]

The seller of a car advertised it as a 'Herald Convertible, white, 1961 ...' The buyer saw the car before agreeing to buy it and later discovered that while the rear half of the car was part of a 1961 Herald Convertible, the front half was part of an earlier model. *Held:* buyer entitled to damages for breach of the condition implied by s. 13 of the Sale of Goods Act.

Furthermore, there may be a sale by description even though the seller gives no express description, for the goods may describe themselves, whether by label or appearance; and this notion has been explicitly extended to self-service sales.[5]

Where there is a sale by description, the following points should be noted: first, whilst any descriptive statements *may* form part of the contract description, it does not follow that they *necessarily* will do so, this depending on the intention of the parties;[6] second, if the description has a special meaning by trade usage, then the goods may have to comply with that usage rather than the ordinary meaning;[7] third, the undertaking is implied whether or not the seller sells in the course of a business;[8] and fourth, there are limitations on the seller's ability to exclude the undertakings.[9] Furthermore, the extent of the seller's duty in respect of this undertaking is dependent on the degree of precision of description: if the description is vague, the duty may be minimal; and the more precise the description, the more onerous the duty.[10]

Nor does the undertaking comprehend all contractual statements as might form part of the description of the goods, but only those going to the identity of the goods, i.e. where the goods would have a different identity without that description. This limitation is particularly relevant with regard to descriptive statements as to quality: unless goods in breach of such a promise are of a different identity, the complaint must be couched in terms of the implied undertakings as to quality and fitness referred to below.[11]

---

1 As renumbered by s. 2 of SOGIT. For the criminal offence of applying a false trade description to goods, see paras. 18.02, et seq., post.
2 As to which, see para. 13.25, post.
3 *Varley v Whipp* [1900] 1 QB 513.
4 [1967] 3 All ER 253, [1967] 1 WLR 1193, CA.
5 New s. 13 (2) of the SGA, as supplied by s. 2 of SOGIT.
6 I.e. whether they are mere representations or contractual terms: as to which issue see para. 7.02, ante.
7 E.g. a promise to supply Eau de Cologne is not satisfied by tendering sewage-water from the Rhine. If the trade usage is only known to one of the parties, there may be no agreement: see generally paras. 3.02, et seq., ante.
8 Contra the undertakings as to quality and fitness: see para. 13.22, post.
9 See para. 13.27, post.
10 E.g. *Arcos Ltd v Ronaasen & Son Ltd* [1933] AC 470, HL (held not *de minimis*: as to which, see para. 13.22 (5), post).
11 *Ashington Piggeries Ltd v Christopher Hill Ltd* [1972] AC 441, [1971] 1 All ER 847, HL (set out para. 13.23, post). Cf. *Reardon Smith Line v Yngvar Hansen-Tangen* [1976] 3 All ER 570, [1976] 1 WLR 989, HL.

---

iii) *Implied conditions as to quality and fitness*

13.22 These two undertakings have the following points in common:
1) Except in the case of sales by sample,[1] or undertakings annexed by usage[2] or by any other enactment:[3]

'there is no implied condition or warranty as to the quality or fitness for any particular purpose of goods supplied under a contract of sale'.

2) The statutory undertakings apply not just to the contract goods, but also to other goods 'supplied under the contract of sale'. Thus, in *Wilson v Rickett, Cockerell & Co Ltd*:[4]

A ton of coalite was sold to the plaintiff. The consignment included a piece of coal in which explosive was embedded. *Held*: the consignment considered as a whole was 'unmerchantable' having defects unfitting it for its only proper use—burning.

3) The statutory undertakings only apply to goods supplied by a seller 'in the course of a business'. Whilst private sales are thus

clearly excluded,[5] except where a private seller sells through the services of an auctioneer,[6] the provision unfortunately appears to contain an ambiguity in relation to business sales: Is it restricted to sales of stock-in-trade, or does it extend to all 'across-the-counter' sales, including sales of plant and machinery?[7]

4) If it is contemplated by the parties that something be done to the goods before they are used, e.g. kits, they must comply with the undertakings after, but not necessarily before, that has been done.[8]

5) There are some departures from the strict terms of the contract which are said to be *de minimis*; i.e., so small that businessmen and therefore lawyers will ignore them.[9]

6) The goods supplied must comply with the undertakings not just at the time of sale, but also thereafter as follows: in the case of goods bought for resale, for long enough for the buyer to dispose of them in the ordinary course of business;[10] and in the case of goods bought for consumption, for a reasonable amount of usage.[11]

7) In the case of domestic sales, but not international sales,[12] there are limitations on the seller's power to exclude these undertakings.[13]

---

1 See para. 13.25, post.
2 New s. 14 (4), as renumbered by s. 3 of SOGIT. See generally para. 7.05, ante.
3 E.g. Trading Stamps Act 1964: see para. 13.26, post.
4 [1954] 1 QB 598, [1954] 1 All ER 868, CA (the coal sold was all right; but the complaint was that a free detonator was also supplied).
5 It is an offence under Part 2 of the Fair Trading Act 1973 to disguise a business sale so that the buyer thinks it is a private sale: S.I. 1977, No. 1918; and see generally para. 19.08, post.
6 New s. 14 (5), as supplied by s. 3 of SOGIT: see further para. 13.48, post.
7 E.g. suppose the seller is a green-grocer; rhubarb is part of his stock-in-trade, but his delivery van is plant and machinery.
8 *Heil v Hedges* [1951] 1 TLR 512 (sale of partly-cooked pork chops).
9 But the departure will have to be very small: see *Jackson v Rotax Cycles Ltd* [1910] 2 KB 937, CA; *Arcos Ltd v Ronaasen & Son Ltd* [1933] AC 470, HL.
10 *Mash and Murrell Ltd v Joseph Emmanuel Ltd* [1961] 1 All ER 485, [1961] 1 WLR 862, revsd. on facts [1962] 1 All ER 77, [1962] 1 WLR 16, CA.
11 *Crowther v Shannon Motor Co* [1975] 1 All ER 139, [1975] 1 WLR 30, CA. (The relevant time for testing compliance is as at sale, but failure within a reasonable period thereafter will be evidence of lack of compliance.)
12 See para. 13.39, post.
13 See para. 13.27, post.

13.23   a) *Implied condition as to fitness*   According to new s. 14 (3) as amended:[1]

'Where the seller sells goods in the course of a business and the buyer, expressly[2] or by implication, makes known[3]—

(a) to the seller, or

(b) where the purchase price or part of it is payable by instalments and the goods were previously sold by a credit-broker to the seller, to that credit-broker,[4]

any particular[5] purpose for which the goods are being bought, there is an implied condition that the goods supplied under the contract are reasonably fit for that purpose, whether or not that is a purpose for which such goods are commonly supplied, except where the circumstances show that the buyer does not rely, or that it is unreasonable for him to rely, on the skill or judgment of the seller or credit-broker'.

This seller's duty of fitness is a strict one: it matters not that he could not have discovered the defect by the exercise of reasonable care;[6] nor that he promised two contradictory things;[7] nor even that the buyer himself was unaware of the possibility of harm.[8] However, the duty is only that the goods be 'reasonably fit', and this must be tested in relation to the purpose for which the goods are supplied and with regard to the degree of precision with which the buyer's purpose is specified. In *Ashington Piggeries Ltd v Christopher Hill Ltd*:[9]

P was a manufacturer of animal feedstuffs. D, a mink farmer, asked P to make up a new mink food compound in accordance with a formula to be supplied by D, and to be called 'King Size'. P made it clear that he knew nothing about mink, but did suggest that herring meal should be substituted for one of the other ingredients. After a year's satisfactory deliveries, P began to obtain herring meal from a new source, N. Unknown to any of the parties, the meal contained DMNA, a substance produced in the meal by chemical reaction and highly toxic to mink. D's mink died.

The House of Lords found that there was no breach of the undertaking as to description,[10] but held each seller liable to his buyer as follows: (a) P was liable to D for breach of *both* the undertakings as to fitness and merchantability; and (b) N was liable to P for breach of the undertaking as to fitness, but *not* merchantability.[11] With regard to fitness, each seller was liable to his buyer because, not only was DMNA highly toxic to mink, but it was also in some degree toxic to all other domestic animals and poultry: the answer might have been otherwise had DMNA been toxic only to mink,[12] though even in such circumstances it is arguable that the seller's duty is merely to warn of possible hazards,[13] or perhaps that there is no liability at all because the buyer has not relied on the seller's skill and judgment (see below). The undertaking as to fitness is subject to the following qualifications:

1) Knowledge of particular purpose. With regard to the implication of knowledge, the effect of the cases would appear to be as follows: if the goods have only one ordinary user, the seller is impliedly promising that the goods are fit for that use;[14] if they have more than one ordinary user, there is no promise that they are fit for any particular one of those uses unless the buyer specified that use;[15] and, whilst the undertaking is expressly made applicable to extraordinary user, the buyer must specify that extraordinary user to obtain the benefit of the undertaking.[16]

2) Reliance. Once the buyer has shown that his purpose has been made known to the seller, the undertaking will be imported unless the seller can show *either* non-reliance,[17] *or* unreasonable reliance.[18] Moreover, there may be a partial reliance: a contract to manufacture an article in accordance with the buyer's specifications may be silent on some matters, and in respect of these the buyer is impliedly relying on the seller.[19]

---

1 New s. 14 (3) of the SGA, as substituted by s. 3 of SOGIT and again amended by Sch. 4 of the Consumer Credit Act 1974. For the criminal offence of applying a false trade description to goods, see paras. 18.02, et seq., post.
2 The *Ashington Piggeries Case* (see note 9), as between P and D.
3 The buyer does not *have* to give the information, it being sufficient that the seller was aware of it: The *Ashington Piggeries Case* (see note 9), as between N and P.
4 The amended version also contains a definition of 'credit-broker': see further para. 14.27, post.
5 'Particular' does not mean just 'special', as opposed to 'general' purpose: The *Ashington Piggeries Case* (see note 9), as between N and P.
6 The *Ashington Piggeries Case* (see note 9)—the possibility of DMNA being produced in this way was then virtually unknown.
7 *Baldry v Marshall* [1925] 1 KB 260, CA (sale of Bugatti car promised suitable for touring: such cars are not suitable for this purpose).
8 The *Ashington Piggeries Case* (see note 9), as between P and D.
9 [1972] AC 441, [1971] 1 All ER 847, HL.
10 The goods had the contract identity, viz. 'King Size' and 'herring meal' respectively: see para. 13.21, ante.
11 See para. 13.24, post.
12 E.g. *Griffiths v Peter Conway Ltd* [1939] 1 All ER 685, CA.
13 E.g. *Vacwell Engineering Co Ltd v BDH Chemicals Ltd* [1971] 1 QB 88, [1969] 3 All ER 1681.
14 E.g. *Wilson v Rickett Cockerell & Co Ltd* [1954] 1 KB 598, [1954] 1 All ER 868, CA (set out in para. 13.22, ante).
15 E.g. *Baldry v Marshall* [1925] 1 KB 260, CA; *Henry Kendall & Sons Ltd v William Lillico & Sons Ltd* [1969] 2 AC 31, [1968] 2 All ER 444, HL.
16 E.g. *BS Brown & Son Ltd v Craiks Ltd* [1970] 1 All ER 823, [1970] 1 WLR 752, HL.

17 But this is a matter of fact, not form: *Lowe v Lombank Ltd* [1960] 1 All ER 611, [1960] 1 WLR 196, CA.

18 E.g. considering the relative known expertise of the parties.

19 E.g. *Cammell Laird & Co Ltd v Manganese Bronze and Brass Co Ltd* [1934] AC 402, HL.

13.24 *b) Implied condition as to merchantable quality* According to the new s. 14 (2):[1]

'Where the seller sells goods in the course of a business, there is an implied condition that the goods supplied under the contract are of merchantable quality,[2] except that there is no such condition—

(*a*) as regards defects specifically drawn to the buyer's attention before the contract is made; or

(*b*) if the buyer examines the goods before the contract is made, as regards defects which the examination ought to reveal'.

The concept of 'merchantable' was explained in 1815 as meaning that the goods must do more than comply with their description,[3] and must:[4]

'be saleable in the market under the denomination mentioned in the contract'.

Thereafter, the common law largely concentrated on developing a definition in terms of saleability, eventually deciding that goods are merchantable if they are:[5]

'in such an actual state that a buyer fully acquainted with the facts and therefore knowing what hidden defects exist and not being limited to their apparent condition would buy them without abatement of the price obtainable for such goods if in reasonable sound order and condition and without special terms'.

Whilst this approach made sense where the buyer bought the goods for resale, it proved inadequate in respect of goods bought for consumption. Accordingly, a statutory definition in terms of usability was introduced in 1973:[6]

'Goods of any kind are of merchantable quality ... if they are as fit for the purpose or purposes for which goods of that kind are commonly bought as it is reasonable to expect having regard to any description applied to them, the price (if relevant) and all the other relevant circumstances. ...'

The effect of this statutory test appears to be as follows: if the goods have only one ordinary use, they are unmerchantable if unfit for that use;[7] but if the goods have more than one ordinary use, they are not unmerchantable merely because they are unfit for the buyer's particular purpose as long as they are fit for one of their ordinary uses;[8] and, if the buyer requires the goods for some unusual purpose, they may be merchantable (because fit for some ordinary use) and yet unfit for the purpose required,[9] or they may be fit for the unusual purpose whilst unmerchantable (because unfit for ordinary use).[10] Moreover, the statutory test is sophisticated in that it allows the court to take into account the contract description,[11] the price (if relevant),[12] and 'all the other relevant circumstances'.[13] Nor is the statutory test expressed to be exclusive: whilst it will, no doubt, be the appropriate one where goods are bought for consumption, it would seem to allow the common law saleability test to be applied where goods are bought for resale.[14] Finally, the statutory undertaking as to merchantability is subject to the following qualifications:

1) Specified defects. Even where the seller is entirely prohibited from excluding his liability,[15] it remains open to him to escape liability for breach of this undertaking in respect of defects specified in the contract.

2) Examination. Where the buyer has made a pre-contractual examination of the goods, there is no undertaking in respect of defects which *that examination* ought to have revealed.

---

1 New s. 14 (2) of the SGA, as substituted by s. 3 of SOGIT.

2 There are conflicting decisions on the meaning of the word 'quality': see *Niblett v Confectioners' Materials Co* [1921] 3 KB 387, CA; *Sumner, Permain & Co v Webb & Co* [1922] 1 KB 55, by the same CA.

3 As to which, see para. 13.21, ante.

4 Per Lord Ellenborough in *Gardiner v Gray* (1815) 4 Camp. 144 at 145.

5 Per Dixon J in *Australian Knitting Mills v Grant* (1933) 50 CLR 387, 418, approved by Lords Guest, Pearce and Wilberforce in *Henry Kendall & Sons v William Lillico & Sons Ltd* [1969] 2 AC 31, [1968] 2 All ER 444, HL.

6 New s. 62 (1) (A) of the SGA, introduced by s. 7 of SOGIT. Cf. *Henry Kendall & Sons v William Lillico & Sons Ltd* [1969] 2 AC 31; [1968] 2 All ER 444, HL.

7 E.g. *Wren v Holt* [1903] 1 KB 610, CA (beer); *Grant v Australian Knitting Mills Ltd* [1936] AC 85, PC (woollen underpants); *Wilson v Rickett Cockerell Ltd* [1954] 1 KB 598, [1954] 1 All ER 868, CA (coalite); *Godley v Perry* [1960] 1 All ER 36, [1960] 1 WLR 9 (catapult); *Lee v York Coach and Marine* [1977] RTR 35, CA (car).

8 E.g. *Sumner, Permain & Co v Webb & Co* [1922] 1 KB 55, CA (Indian Tonic Water saleable anywhere other than Argentina). Compare the *Ashington Piggeries Case* (see para. 13.23, ante, as between P and D, on basis that DMNA toxic in some degree to all animals; but not as between N and P, where it was not argued on appeal that DMNA *not* toxic to some other animals.

9 E.g. *B.S. Brown & Son Ltd v Craiks Ltd* [1970] 1 All ER 823, [1970] 1 WLR 752, HL (industrial cloth unfit for dresses).

10 E.g. where purpose-built.

11 E.g. *McDonald v Empire Garage (Blackburn) Ltd* [1975] CLY 3050.

12 Contra if the market has simply turned: *Cehave NV v Bremer Handel-gesellschaft mbH* [1976] QB 44, [1975] 3 All ER 739, CA.
13 See *Henry Kendall & Sons v William Lillico & Sons Ltd* [1969] 2 AC 31, [1968] 2 All ER 444, HL; and the *First Report on Exemption Clauses* (Law Com 12) paras. 41–44.
14 Cf. the *Cehave Case (above); the McDonald Case* (above).
15 See para. 13.27, post.

---

iv) *Implied conditions in sales by sample*

13.25 Section 15 (2) imports the following undertakings in sales by sample:

1) *That the bulk shall correspond with the sample in quality;* the correspondence must be complete.[1] It is not sufficient that with a small amount of labour and expense the bulk could be made to correspond with the sample.[2]
2) *That the buyer shall have a reasonable opportunity of comparing the bulk with the sample before acceptance;*[3] and
3) *That the goods shall be free from any defect rendering them unmerchantable, which would not be apparent on reasonable examination of the sample.*[4]

Sale by sample does not of necessity take place whenever a sample is shown; sale by sample takes place when there is a term in the contract, express or implied, to that effect;[5] the whole of the circumstances must be looked to.

Lord Macnaghten, in *Drummond v Van Ingen*, laid it down that:

'The office of the sample is to present to the eye the real meaning and intention of the parties with regard to the subject-matter of the contract which, owing to the imperfection of language, it may be difficult or impossible to express in words. The sample speaks for itself. But it cannot be treated as saying more than such a sample would tell a merchant of the class to which the buyer belongs, using due care and diligence, and appealing to it in the ordinary way and with the knowledge possessed by merchants of that class at the time. No doubt the sample might be made to say a great deal more. Pulled to pieces and examined by unusual tests which curiosity or suspicion might suggest, it would doubtless reveal every secret of its construction. But that is not the way in which business is done in this country'.[6]

---

1 But see *Hookway v A Isaacs & Son* [1954] 1 Lloyd's Rep 491; *Steels and Busks Ltd v Bleeker Bik & Co Ltd* [1956] 1 Lloyd's Rep 228.
2 *(E & S) Ruben Ltd v Faire Bros & Co Ltd* [1949] 1 KB 254, [1949] 1 All ER 215.

3 Place of delivery is, prima facie, the place of inspection (*Perkins v Bell* [1893] 1 QB 193).

4 For a reasonable inspection, see *Godley v Perry* [1960] 1 All ER 36, [1960] 1 WLR 9. For the concept of merchantability, see para. 13.24, ante.

5 SGA 1893, s. 15 (1). For contracts conditional on buyer's approval of sample, see *Wood Components of London v James Webster & Bro Ltd* [1959] 2 Lloyd's Rep 200; *John Bowron & Son Ltd v Rodema Canned Foods Ltd* [1967] 1 Lloyd's Rep 183.

6 (1887) 12 App Cas 284 at 297. See also *Heilbutt v Hickson* (1872) LR 7 CP 438.

---

v) Implied undertakings in trading stamp transactions

13.26 It should be noted that when anyone redeems trading stamps for goods, certain *warranties* are implied by the Trading Stamps Act 1964, s. 4:[1]

a) the promotor of the trading stamp scheme has a right to give the goods in exchange,

b) the person obtaining the goods shall have and enjoy quiet possession of them,

c) the goods shall be free from any charge or encumbrance in favour of any third party, not declared or known to the person obtaining the goods,

d) the goods shall be of merchantable quality except that if the person obtaining the goods has examined the goods before or at the time of redemption, there shall be no implied warranty as regards defects which the examination ought to have revealed.

This provision is subject to the terms on which redemption is made, so far as these terms expressly exclude or modify these implied warranties.

---

1 As amended by Sch. 4 of the Consumer Credit Act 1974.

EXCLUSION CLAUSES

13.27 Assuming that an exclusion clause has been incorporated into the contract of sale according to the ordinary common law rules,[1] it has already been seen that there are a number of general common law and statutory restrictions on its effectiveness.[2] However, in relation to sales some special statutory restrictions were introduced in 1973, and are now to be found in the Unfair Contract Terms Act 1977 (UCTA), to which the old principle of freedom of contract is expressly made subject.[3] However, this compulsory element does rct apply to international supply contracts;[4] but a choice of laws clause[5] cannot be used to dress up what is really a domestic transaction as an international contract 'wholly or mainly' for the purpose of avoiding the restrictions below.[6]

Where there is a domestic transaction, then attempts to exclude liability for breach of the implied undertakings in the SGA are restricted as follows: there is a total prohibition against contracting out of the implied undertakings as to title to any greater extent than that allowed by s. 12;[7] whereas rather different treatment is accorded to attempts to contract out of the implied undertakings as to description (s. 13), merchantability and fitness (s. 14), and in respect of sales by sample (s. 15).[8] In respect of the latter category, the Act first draws a distinction according to whether or not the buyer is in the particular transaction 'a person dealing as a consumer', which expression is defined to exclude all 'sales by auction or competitive tender',[9] but to include all other cases—except where the seller proves to the contrary (s. 12 (3))—which satisfy the test laid down by s. 12 (1) as follows:

'A party to a contract "deals as consumer" in relation to another party if—

(a) he neither makes the contract in the course of a business[10] nor holds himself out as doing so;[11] and

(b) the other party does make the contract in the course of a business;[10] and

(c) ... the goods passing under or in pursuance of the contract are of a type[12] ordinarily[13] supplied for private use or consumption'.[14]

Where the buyer 'deals as a consumer', the undertakings cannot be excluded or restricted by reference to any contract term;[15] but in all other cases the limitation is simply that the exclusion is only valid in so far as it satisfies the test of reasonableness. Unlike the other provisions of the Act introducing such a test,[16] there are here laid down 'guidelines' for the application of the reasonableness test.[17]

---

1 UCTA, s. 11 (2), and see para. 3.12, ante.
2 See paras. 3.14–3.16, ante.
3 New s. 55 (1) of the SGA, as amended by s. 4 of SOGIT.
4 S. 26 of UCTA. See further generally, paras. 13.39, et seq., post.
5 See para. 9.01, ante.
6 S. 27 of UCTA. See further para. 9.03, ante.
7 See para. 13.20, ante.
8 See paras. 13.21–13.25, ante.
9 S. 12 (2). For sales by auction generally, see para. 13.48, post.
10 For a discussion of 'in the course of business', see para. 13.22 (3), ante.
11 E.g. where the buyer represents that he is a trader to get a trade discount.
12 This distinguishes between, e.g. different models or qualities made by same manufacturer for trade and domestic use respectively.

13 There is no guidance as to what standard to adopt.
14 There may be difficulty with goods frequently used in either category, e.g. small vans.
15 S. 6 (2). It is an offence for a retailer to erect a sign suggesting that he may do so, e.g. 'no cash refunds': S.I. 1976, No. 1813, made under Part 2 of the Fair Trading Act 1973; as to which, see para. 19.08, post.
16 See para. 3.15, ante.
17 S. 11 (2) and Sch. 2; and see *Rasbora Ltd v JCL Marine Ltd* [1977] 1 Lloyd's Rep 645.

MANUFACTURER'S PRODUCT LIABILITY

13.28 Where a retailer sells goods obtained from a manufacturer, which owing to some latent defect cause injury to the ultimate buyer or consumer, the latter can recover damages from the retailer in contract[1] and in certain circumstances from the manufacturer in tort.[2]

The manufacturer's liability is based on actionable negligence,[3] the existence or non-existence of which is immaterial to the contractual liability of the retailer.

A manufacturer of products which he sells in such a form as to show that he intends them to reach the ultimate consumer in the form in which they left him with no reasonable possibility of intermediate examination, and with the knowledge that the absence of reasonable care in the preparation or putting up of the products will result in an injury to the consumer's life or property, owes a duty to the consumer to take that reasonable care.[4]

Attempts by manufacturers to exclude even this negligence-based liability have been avoided by s. 5 of the UCTA; and the issue presently under debate is whether they should be made strictly liable to consumers.[5]

1 For breach of the implied undertakings, see paras. 13.20, et seq., ante. If the goods are dangerous, the sale may amount to a criminal offence under, e.g. the Consumer Protection Acts 1961–71.
2 E.g. *Grant v Australian Knitting Mills Ltd* [1936] AC 85, PC. The action will normally have to be in tort because there is no privity of contract between manufacturer and consumer, except under some collateral contract, e.g. under a 'Manufacturer's Guarantee': for privity and collateral contracts, see paras. 4.02, et seq., ante.
3 Whilst a seller remains strictly liable in contract: see *Daniels and Daniels v White & Sons Ltd* [1938] 4 All ER 258. As for negligence liability the last case should be compared with *Hill v James Crowe (Cases) Ltd* [1978] 1 All ER 812.
4 *M'Alister (or Donoghue) v Stevenson* [1932] AC 562, HL; and see further *Street on Torts* (6th edn) 173–179.
5 See *Liability for defective products* (Law Comm. No. 82, Cmnd 6831).

6. Rights of the buyer

13.29 The rights of each party corresponds to the duties of the other; it suffices, therefore, to deal with the rights of each. The buyer's rights fall under two heads:

1. He is entitled to delivery, and
2. He is entitled to have any conditions and warranties observed.

DELIVERY

13.30 Delivery is defined in s. 62 of the Act as the

'voluntary transfer of possession from one person to another'.

The vendor must deliver the goods in accordance with the terms of the contract of sale.[1] The expenses of and incidental to putting the goods into a deliverable state must be borne by the seller unless otherwise agreed.[2]

Delivery does not necessarily involve placing the buyer in actual possession; it may be *constructive,* as by handing to the buyer the key of the warehouse in which bulky goods are stored. Again, the seller may agree to retain physical possession of the goods, but on terms which change his possession from that of owner to that of bailee. The transfer of a document of title, e.g. a bill of lading, is a symbolic delivery of the goods.[3] If the goods are in the possession of a third person, there is no delivery by the seller to the buyer, unless and until such third person acknowledges to the buyer that he holds the goods on his behalf ('attornment'); but this rule is not to affect the operation of the issue or transfer of any document of title to goods.[4]

The vendor must, in the absence of special agreement, deliver the goods upon payment or tender of the price; for subject to agreement to the contrary, *delivery of the goods and payment of the price are concurrent conditions.*[5] If credit is allowed he must deliver at once;[6] but in the latter case, if the buyer becomes insolvent before he gets actual possession, the vendor may retain the goods,[7] and as to future deliveries, Mellish LJ said:

'The seller, notwithstanding he may have agreed to allow credit for the goods, is not bound to deliver any more goods under the contract, until the price of the goods not yet delivered is tendered to him'.[8]

Though the vendor is bound to deliver, he cannot, in the absence of agreement to do so, be compelled to carry or send the goods to the buyer. *The place of delivery is, apart from any express or implied agreement,*[9] *the seller's place of business, if he has one; if not, his residence;* though if the goods sold are specific goods which to the knowledge of the parties when the contract is made are in some other place, then delivery should be made at the place where the goods are located at the time of sale.[10]

Where the seller is bound to send the goods to the buyer, and no time is fixed by contract, he must deliver within a reasonable time.[11] Demand or tender of delivery must be made at a reasonable hour; what is a reasonable hour is a question of fact.[12] *Delivery to a carrier. If the seller is authorised or required to send goods to the buyer delivery to a carrier is prima facie delivery to the buyer,*[13] but if the seller agrees to deliver at a fixed place, the carrier who takes the goods there is agent for the seller, and there is no delivery till their arrival.[14] The seller must, unless otherwise authorised by the buyer, make a reasonable contract with the carrier having regard to the nature of the goods and the circumstances of the case—should the seller fail to do this and the goods are lost or damaged, the buyer may decline to accept and pay for them, or hold the seller responsible in damages.[15]

Where the seller is required to deliver goods at the buyer's premises, he discharges his obligations if he delivers them there without negligence to a person apparently having authority to receive them.[16]

A stipulation as to time *of payment* is not of the essence of the contract, i.e. is not a condition unless a different intention appears from the terms of the contract.[17] Other stipulations as to time in mercantile contracts are usually construed as conditions.[18] In particular, a stipulation as to time of *delivery* is generally construed as a condition, so that if the seller fails to deliver on time, the buyer may treat the contract as repudiated.[19]

---

1 SGA 1893, s. 27.
2 Ibid, s. 29 (5).
3 See *Dublin City Distillery Co v Doherty* [1914] AC 823, where the authorities on constructive delivery are reviewed by Lord Atkinson.
4 SGA 1893, s. 29 (3).
5 Ibid, s. 28. For instalment deliveries, see para. 13.32, post.
6 For payment by instalments, see para. 14.02, post.
7 *Bloxam v Sanders* (1825) 4 B & C, at 948; and see 'Lien' and 'Stoppage *in Transitu*,' para. 13.38 (ii), post.
8 *Re Edwards, ex parte Chalmers* (1873) 8 Ch App 289.
9 For delivery at a distant place, see para. 13.39, post.
10 SGA 1893, s. 29 (1).
11 Ibid, s. 29 (2).
12 Ibid, s. 29 (4).
13 Ibid, s. 32 (1).
14 *Dunlop v Lambert* (1838) 6 Cl & F 600 at 621. Similarly in c.i.f. contracts (see para. 13.41, post) delivery of the goods is deemed to take place not when the goods are given to the carrier but when the documents relating to them are handed to the buyer.

15 SGA 1893, s. 32 (2); *Thomas Young & Son Ltd v Hobson & Partners* (1949) 65 TLR 365.
16 *Galbraith and Grant Ltd v Block* [1922] 2 KB 155.
17 SGA 1893, s. 10. But as to delivery and payment being concurrent conditions, see ante.
18 *Bowes v Shand* (1877) 2 App Cas 455 at 463.
19 See *Jacobson Van Den Berg & Co (UK) Ltd v BIBA Ltd* (1977) 121 Sol Jo 333, CA.

13.31 *Delivery of wrong quantity* When delivery is made it must be of the exact quantity. *If too little is delivered* the buyer may return the whole or keep the goods and pay for them at the contract rate.[1]

If too much is delivered the buyer may retain the goods included in the contract and reject the rest, or reject the whole. Alternatively, he may accept the whole delivery. In this case there is virtually a new contract, and he must pay for the whole of the goods at the contract rate.[2]

If the contract goods are sent with other goods of a different description the buyer can keep the contract goods or reject the whole. He cannot keep the other goods except by agreement.[3]

Frequently the contract, in naming the quantities, includes some such expression as 'say about', 'more or less', etc., and the effect of this is to allow in favour of the seller a reasonable variation between the contract quantity and the amount delivered.[4] And the usage of the trade or the course of dealing between the parties may import such terms into the contract.[5] Each case stands by itself, and words of quantity may be merely words of estimate and not of contract.[6]

In the absence of agreement to the contrary a buyer cannot be compelled to take delivery by instalments.[7]

1 SGA 1893, s. 30 (1).
2 Ibid, s. 30 (2).
3 Ibid, s. 30 (3); *Re Moore & Co and Landauer & Co* [1921] 2 KB 519, CA.
4 *McConnel v Murphy* (1874) LR 5 PC 203; *Miller v Borner* [1900] 1 QB 691. Contrast *Morris v Levison* (1876) 1 CPD 155.
5 SGA 1893, s. 30 (4); *Margaronis Navigation Agency Ltd v Henry W Peabody & Co of London Ltd* [1965] 2 QB 430, [1964] 3 All ER 333.
6 *Re Harrison and Micks Lambert* [1917] 1 KB 755. See also *Tebbitts Bros v Smith* (1917) 33 TLR 508, CA.
7 SGA 1893, s. 31 (1). For instalment deliveries, see para. 13.32, post.

RIGHTS UPON BREACH OF THE CONTRACT[1]

13.32 *Remedy for non-delivery* Where the seller wrongfully neglects or refuses to deliver the goods to the buyer, the buyer's remedy is an action for damages, and the damages will be the estimated loss directly and naturally resulting, in the ordinary course of events, from the seller's breach of contract.[2] Where there is an available market for the goods in question, it is assumed that the buyer will go out and buy a replacement; so the buyer is prima facie entitled to recover the difference between the contract price and the market price at the time when they ought to have been delivered, or, if no time was fixed, at the time of the refusal to deliver.[3] Any sub-contracts made by the buyer are generally ignored: in *Williams Brothers v Agius*:[4]

> The seller failed to deliver coal, the contract price of which was 16s 3d per ton. The buyer had made a contract to resell the coal at 19s a ton. At the date of the seller's refusal to deliver the market price for such coal was 23s 6d per ton. *Held:* buyer entitled to 7s 3d per ton as damages the sum necessary to enable him to buy coal on the market and comply with his resale obligations.

Where there is no available market for the goods, the buyer's damage will, as stated, depend on the loss directly and naturally resulting from the breach but if special circumstances are known to the seller, e.g., the non-delivery will mean loss to the buyer of a sub-contract, such special damages may also be claimed.[5]

If the seller fails to deliver in accordance with the contract goods which he knew were required to carry out a sub-contract, and the buyer becomes thereby unable to carry out the same, the latter is entitled to recover from the seller not only loss of profit on the resale but also the costs, etc., of reasonably defending an action against him by the sub-purchaser.[6]

Instalment deliveries. If the agreement was to deliver by stated instalments, to be separately paid for, and the seller makes defective deliveries in respect of one or more instalments, it is in each case a question depending on the terms of the contract, whether the buyer is entitled to repudiate the contract, or has merely a right to damages.[7] The main tests to be considered are (i) the quantitative ratio which the breach bears to the contract as a whole, and (ii) the degree of probability that such a breach will be repeated. But a single breach may be so serious as to involve repudiation of the contract.[8]

Specific performance Where chattels are unique or of peculiar importance, the court, on the buyer's application, may order specific performance of a contract to deliver them; the judgment to this effect may be unconditional, or upon such terms and conditions as to damages, payment of the price and otherwise, as to the court may seem just.[9] Accordingly, the court may order specific performance of a contract for the sale of a ship which is of peculiar or practically unique value to the purchaser.[10] In any case, however, the goods must be 'specific', i.e. identified and agreed upon at the time the contract is made[11] or 'ascertained', i.e. identified in accordance with the agreement after the contract has been made.[12]

---

1 See the remarks on 'BREACH OF CONTRACT,' paras. 7.21, et seq., ante, which are, in the main, applicable to the present subject.

2 SGA 1893, s. 51 (1), (2). See *H Parsons (Livestock) Ltd v Uttley Ingham & Co Ltd* [1978] 1 All ER 525, [1977] 3 WLR 990, CA (see generally para. 7.27, ante).

3 Ibid, s. 51 (3) and see *Tai Hing Cotton Mill Ltd v Kamsing Knitting Factory* [1978] 1 All ER 515, [1978] 2 WLR 62, PC. Where the seller has committed an anticipatory breach of a contract to deliver goods within a reasonable time, the relevant market price is that prevailing at the time when delivery ought to have been made, subject to a duty to mitigate on the part of the buyer (if he accepted the seller's repudiation) by buying at once if the market is rising assuming there is a reasonable opportunity to do so: *Garnac Grain Co v HMF Faure and Fairclough and Bunge Corpn* [1967] 2 All ER 353, HL.

4 [1914] AC 510, HL.

5 SGA 1893, s. 54; *Patrick v Russo-Grain Export Co* [1927] 2 KB 535; *Victoria Laundry (Windsor) Ltd v Newman Industries Ltd* [1949] 2 KB 529, [1949] 1 All ER 997, CA (set out in para. 7.27, ante).

6 *Agius v Great Western Colliery Co* [1899] 1 QB 413; *Hammond v Bussey* (1888), 20 QBD 79.

7 SGA 1893, s. 31 (2). And see para. 7.26, ante.

8 *Maple Flock Co Ltd v Universal Furniture, etc, Ltd* [1934] 1 KB 148, CA.

9 SGA 1893, s. 52. Cf. injunctions: see para. 7.33, ante.

10 *Behnke v Bede Shipping Co* [1927] 1 KB 649. Contrast *Cohen v Roche* [1927] 1 KB 169, where Hepplewhite chairs were held not to have sufficient value as antiques to justify an order for specific delivery; and see *Societe des Industries Metallurgiques SA v Bronx Engineering Co Ltd* [1975] 1 Lloyd's Rep 465, CA.

11 SGA 1893, s. 62 (1).

12 *Re Wait* [1927] 1 Ch 606, per Atkin LJ.

13.33 *Breach of condition* Unless the buyer waives the condition and claims damages only, the breach of it entitles him to repudiate the contract.[1] If the buyer waives a condition to deliver goods within a stipulated time, he cannot afterwards abruptly cancel the contract without first giving notice to the seller fixing a reasonable time for delivery.[2] Unless there be a term of the contract, express or implied, to the contrary, if the contract is not severable[3] and the buyer has accepted[4] the goods or part of them, the buyer is bound to treat the breach of condition as a breach of warranty.[5] However, where a buyer rejects goods for breach of condition after he has paid the price, he is not entitled to retain possession of the goods until the money paid has been returned.[6]

Breach of warranty The buyer may not on account of this repudiate the contract, but he may:

1. Set up the breach of warranty in diminution or extinction of the price, and
2. He may bring an action against the seller, and claim damages for the breach.[7]

The measure of damages for breach of warranty is the estimated loss directly and naturally resulting in the ordinary course of events from the breach of warranty.[8] In *Bostock & Co v Nicholson & Sons*:[9]

> The plaintiffs claimed damages against the defendants for breach of warranty in not supplying sulphuric acid commercially free from arsenic. The acid, which contained arsenic in large quantities, was used by the plaintiffs in the manufacture of brewing sugar, which the plaintiffs sold to brewers. The defendants did not know the purpose for which the acid was bought. In consequence of the poisonous nature of the sugar, the plaintiffs became liable to pay damages to the brewers and the goodwill of their business was entirely destroyed. The plaintiffs recovered as damages, under sub-s. (2) of s. 53,
>
> (i) the price paid for the impure acid;
> (ii) the value of the goods spoilt by being mixed with it.

The other heads of damage were held not to fall within the measure laid down by the sub-section.

In the case of breach of warranty of quality, prima facie the measure of damages is the difference between the value of the goods at the time of delivery to the buyer, and the value they would have had if they had answered the warranty.[10] Larger damages will be claimable if, e.g. the defects cause personal injury or damage to property.

If the seller commits a breach by late delivery then prima facie the buyer is entitled to the difference between the market price at the time the goods ought to have been delivered and the (lower) market price of the goods when they are actually delivered plus any damage, e.g. for loss of use naturally arising or reasonably contemplated by the parties.[11] Where, however, the buyer has made a resale contract at a price higher than the market price at the time of actual delivery the damages may be reduced to the difference between the market price at the time the goods ought to have been delivered and the resale price.[12]

---

1 SGA 1893, s. 11 (1) (a) (set out in para. 13.18, ante).
2 *Hartley v Hymans* [1920] 3 KB 475; *(Charles) Rickards Ltd v Oppenheim*

[1950] 1 KB 616, [1950] 1 All ER 420, CA; and see generally, para. 3.22, ante.

3 *J Rosenthal & Sons Ltd v Esmail* [1965] 2 All ER 860, [1965] 1 WLR 1117, HL; and see further *Chitty on Contract* (24th edn) Vol. 2, para. 4578. For instalment contracts see para. 13.32, ante.

4 As to what is 'acceptance', see para. 13.35, post.

5 SGA 1893, s. 11 (1) (c), as amended by the Misrepresentation Act 1967, s.4 (1).

6 *JL Lyons & Co v May and Baker* [1923] 1 KB 685.

7 SGA 1893, s. 53 (1).

8 Ibid, s. 53 (2). *H Parsons (Livestock) Ltd v Uttley Ingham & Co Ltd* [1978] 1 All ER 525, [1977] 3 WLR 990, CA. And see further para. 7.27, ante.

9 [1904] 1 KB 725. Especially where there is a chain of claims, the costs may be a very significant item: e.g. *Kasler and Cohen v Slovouski* [1928] 1 KB 78.

10 SGA 1893, s. 53 (3). But see *Cullinane v British 'REMA' Manufacturing Co Ltd* [1954] 1 QB 292, [1953] 2 All ER 1257, CA, analysed [1970] JBL 19.

11 Where no available market, see *Kwei Tek Chao v British Traders and Shippers (No. 2) Ltd* [1954] 2 QB 459, [1954] 3 All ER 165.

12 *Wertheim v Chicoutimi Pulp Co Ltd* [1911] AC 301, PC.

---

7. Rights of the seller

13.34 The seller is entitled to be paid; and unless otherwise agreed, delivery of the goods and payment of the price are concurrent conditions.[1] The seller is also entitled to have the goods accepted subject to the right of the buyer to examine the goods, if he has not previously done so, to see if they comply with the contract.[2]

---

1 SGA 1893, s. 28. See para. 13.30, ante.

2 As to which see paras. 13.18, et seq., ante.

ACCEPTANCE

13.35 By the SGA, s. 34, where goods are delivered to a buyer which he has not previously examined he is not deemed to have accepted them until he has had a reasonable opportunity of examining them. There is acceptance by the buyer either:[1]

1. When he intimates to the seller that he accepts them,[2] or

2. Except where s. 34 provides otherwise, when after delivery of the goods to him, he does any act in relation to them which is inconsistent with the ownership of the seller,[3] or

3. Except where s. 34 provides otherwise, when after the lapse of a reasonable time, he retains the goods without intimating to the seller that he has rejected them.[4]

Once a buyer has 'accepted' the goods, he is bound to treat any breach of condition as a breach of warranty. If the buyer, having had an opportunity of examining the goods, despatches all or part of them to a sub-buyer that is an act which is inconsistent with the ownership of the seller. If the buyer, however, has not had an opportunity to examine them, despatch of all or part of them to a sub-buyer is not *acceptance* of the goods because this part of s. 35 is made subject to s. 34.

Under ordinary circumstances a seller cannot compel the buyer to return rejected goods; he is entitled only to notice of the rejection.[5] If the contract is broken by the buyer, the seller acquires other rights—viz., the right to bring an action against the buyer, and, in some cases, rights against the goods.

---

1 SGA 1893, s. 35, as amended by the Misrepresentation Act 1967, s. 4 (2).
2 In the case of a c.i.f. contract, the buyer has two rights of acceptance—in respect of (1) the documents and (2) the goods: see para. 13.41 n. 5, post.
3 E.g. where he cannot place the goods at the seller's disposal, as where a sub-buyer refuses to return them.
4 E.g. *Leaf v International Galleries* [1950] 2 QB 86, [1950] 1 All ER 693, CA; *Long v Lloyd* [1958] 2 All ER 402, [1958] 1 WLR 753, CA; *Lee v York Coach and Marine* [1977] RTR 35, CA.
5 SGA, s. 36.

---

a) ACTIONS AGAINST THE BUYER

13.36 *a) For breach of contract* Where the property in the goods has passed to the buyer[1] the seller may,

1. If the buyer makes default in payment,[2] bring an action for the price;[3] or
2. If the buyer neglects or refuses to accept, he may bring an action for damages for not accepting the goods.[4]

Where the property in the goods has not passed to the buyer, the action which generally lies is one for not accepting;[4] but, where the price is payable on a day certain, irrespective of delivery, and the buyer wrongfully neglects or refuses to pay the price, the seller may maintain an action for the price, although the property in the goods has not passed, and the goods have not been appropriated to the contract.[5]

The damages for non-acceptance will be such as directly and naturally result in the ordinary course of events from the breach.[6]

Where there is an available market for the goods in question, the measure of damage is prima facie to be ascertained by the difference between the contract price and the market or current price at the time or times when the goods ought to have been accepted.[7]

Where there is no available market, e.g. where goods are

made to a special specification of the buyer, the measure of damages will be the loss of profit expected by the seller.[8]

Similarly, if supply of the kind of goods being sold exceeds demand, there is no 'available market' and, should a buyer break his contract, the seller is entitled to his loss of profit on the sale.[9] It is otherwise if demand exceeds supply because the seller makes just as many deals as he would have done if the buyer did not break his contract—nominal damages only are then awarded.[10]

When the seller is ready to deliver the goods, and requests the buyer to take delivery, and the buyer does not within a reasonable time after such request take the goods, he is liable to the seller for any loss occasioned by his neglect or refusal to take delivery, and also for a reasonable charge for the care and custody of the goods.[11] However, if the contract is to deliver by stated instalments, refusal to accept or to pay for one or more instalments may entitle the seller to treat the contract as at an end, and sue as for a total breach, or it may give a right to sue only for damages arising from the particular default; the right of the seller in this respect depends upon the terms of the contract in each case.[12]

---

1 Ante, paras. 13.06–13.10, ante.
2 For the situation where the contract provides for postponement of payment, see para. 14.02, post.
3 SGA 1893, s. 49 (1). For price, see para. 13.02, ante.
4 Ibid, s. 50 (1).
5 Ibid, s. 49 (2).
6 Ibid, s. 50 (2).
7 Ibid, s. 50 (3).
8 *Re Vic Mill Ltd* [1913] 1 Ch 465, CA; *Lazenby Garages Ltd v Wright* [1976] 2 All ER 770, [1976] 1 WLR 459, CA. Cf. *Interoffice Telephones Ltd v Robert Freeman Co Ltd* [1958] 1 QB 190, [1957] 3 All ER 479, CA.
9 *WL Thompson Ltd v Robinson (Gunmakers) Ltd* [1955] Ch 177, [1955] 1 All ER 154.
10 *Charter v Sullivan* [1957] 2 QB 117, [1957] 1 All ER 809, CA.
11 SGA 1893, s. 37.
12 Ibid, s. 31 (2); *Payzu Ltd v Saunders* [1919] 2 KB 581, CA. For instalment contracts generally, see para. 7.26, ante, and chap. 14, post.

13.37 *b) In tort* It is tortious for the buyer wrongfully to dispossess the seller of the goods, detain or dispose of them.[1] Such actions will be wrongful where the seller was in possession or had an immediate right to possess,[2] and the buyer—whether innocently or not[3]—dealt with the goods in a manner inconsistent with the seller's right to them.[4] A satisfied judgment will act rather like a forced sale;[5] but, whereas in a contract action the buyer may be required to pay the price,[6] in this tort action he will be liable for damages calculated by reference to the value of the goods: it is true that the prima facie measure of damages is likewise market *value* or replacement cost;[7] but this sum may be reduced where the buyer has an interest in the goods[8] or increases their value.[9]

---

1 In so far as it amounts to a 'wrongful interference with goods' within the meaning of the Torts (Interference with Goods) Act 1977; as to which, see para. 1.03, ante.

2 For the moment when the seller is bound to deliver, see para. 13.30 ante. For competing rights to the goods, see now s. 8 of the 1977 Act.

3 *Hollins v Fowler* (1875) LR 7 HL 757; *Moorgate Mercantile Co Ltd v Finch and Read* [1962] 1 QB 701, [1962] 2 All ER 467, CA.

4 E.g. unjustifiable seizure; destruction or alteration; disposition *and* delivery. For the position of co-owners, see now s. 10 of the 1977 Act; and for contributory negligence, pledge and denial of title, see now s. 11 of the 1977 Act.

5 *USA v Dollfus Mieg* [1952] AC 582, [1952] 1 All ER 572, HL; and s. 5 of the 1977 Act.

6 See para. 13.36, ante.

7 Depending on whether there is an available market: *Leibosch Dredger v Edison SS (Owners)* [1933] AC 449. HL; *J and E Hall Ltd v Barclay* [1937] 3 All ER 620, CA.

8 *Belsize Motor Supply Co v Cox* [1914] 1 KB 224.

9 *Greenwood v Bennett* [1973] QB 195, [1972] 3 All ER 586, CA; and ss. 6 and 9 of the 1977 Act.

---

b) REMEDIES AGAINST THE GOODS

13.38 The rights of the 'unpaid seller' against the goods granted by Part IV of the SGA are as follows: (1) lien; (2) stoppage in transitu; (3) resale. In this part of the Act, 'seller' includes any person in the position of a seller;[1] and an '*unpaid*' seller means one to whom the whole price has not been paid or tendered, or who has been conditionally paid by means of a negotiable instrument which has been subsequently dishonoured.[2]

i) Lien

This is the seller's right to hold goods of which he has possession, but not ownership, when the price has not been paid.[3] If the property in the goods has not passed to the buyer, the unpaid seller has a right of withholding delivery, similar to and co-extensive with lien.[4]

The unpaid seller may retain possession of the goods until he is paid or tendered the price in the following cases,[5] viz:

1. Where the goods have been sold without any stipulation as to credit;

2. Where the goods have been sold on credit, but the term of credit has expired;

3. Where the buyer becomes insolvent—i.e. when he has ceased to pay his debts in the ordinary course of business, or cannot pay his debts as they become due.[6]

And if the goods have been part delivered, the unpaid seller may exercise his right of lien on the remainder, unless such part delivery has been made under such circumstances as to show an agreement to waive the lien.[7] It has been decided that if the seller breaks his contract to deliver whilst the buyer is solvent, nevertheless he will be entitled to retain the goods if the buyer subsequently becomes insolvent.[8]

Lien is lost if:

1. The seller delivers the goods to a carrier or other bailee for the purpose of transmission to the buyer without reserving the right of disposal;[9] or

2. If the buyer or his agent lawfully obtains possession of the goods;[9] or

3. If the seller waives his lien;[9] or

4. If the documents of title to the goods come into the hands of a bona fide purchaser.[10]

ii) Stoppage in transitu

This differs from *lien* chiefly in two points:

1. It can be exercised[11] only when the buyer is insolvent;[12] and

2. Only when the goods have left the possession of the seller.[13]

It is the right[14] conferred on the unpaid seller who has parted with goods to stop them, on insolvency of the buyer, before they have reached the buyer's actual or constructive possession, and to resume possession of the goods and retain them until payment or tender of the price.[15] However, the right is lost if the documents of title to the goods come into the hands of a bona fide purchaser.[16] The general result of the stoppage is to restore the right of possession to the vendor; to place him, in fact, in a position similar to that which he had lost by parting with possession of the goods. The sale is not thereby rescinded.[17] However, whilst an important right in the armoury of the unpaid seller in the eighteenth and nineteenth centuries, stoppage in transit has been less used in recent times. In the field of international sales,[18] it may have been rendered more or less obsolete by the system of payment by bankers' confirmed credits and government export guarantees;[19] and, as regards domestic transactions, it has never applied to the Post Office—who offer their own alternative, the 'cash on delivery' service[20]—and in other cases the tendency is rather to utilise instalment credit contracts.[21]

iii) Resale

As the contract of sale is not usually rescinded by the exercise of the right of lien or of stoppage *in transitu*, it follows that, as a rule, re-sale is not allowable. But, if, notwithstanding this, the unpaid seller re-sells, although this is generally a breach of contract, the new buyer acquires a good title as against the original and defaulting buyer.[22] In certain cases the unpaid vendor is entitled to re-sell, viz:

1. Where the right was expressly reserved in the contract of sale;[23] or
2. Where the goods are perishable;[24] or
3. Where the unpaid seller gives notice to the buyer of his intention to re-sell, and the buyer does not, within a reasonable time, pay or tender the price.[24]

In these cases the seller may re-sell and claim damages from the buyer for any loss occasioned by the buyer's breach of contract. The exercise by the unpaid seller of a right of resale under these provisions rescinds the original contract so that any profit made by the unpaid seller on resale is his to keep.[25]

---

1 Including an agent of the seller to whom the bill of lading has been indorsed, or a consignor or agent who has himself paid or is responsible for the price: s. 38 (2). For bills of lading, see generally paras. 23.08 et seq., post.
2 S. 38 (1). For dishonour of negotiable instruments, see para. 20.20, post.
3 S. 39 (1). For liens, see generally, paras. 17.11 et seq., post.
4 S. 39 (2).
5 S. 41.
6 S. 62 (3). For bankruptcy generally, see chap. 33, post.
7 S. 42; and for waiver of contractual rights generally, see para. 3.22, ante. However, if in a severable contract, one instalment is delivered and not paid for, the seller has no lien over another instalment which is paid for.
8 See *Valpy v Oakeley* (1851) 16 QB 941.
9 S. 43.
10 The proviso to s. 47: see further para. 13.16, ante.
11 For the manner of exercise, see s. 46 (1).
12 For 'insolvent buyer', see ante.
13 I.e. from the moment his lien is 'lost'. For the duration of the transit, see s. 45.
14 For the duties of the carrier, see s. 46 (2).
15 S. 44, i.e. his lien is resurrected.
16 The proviso to s. 47: see further para. 13.16, ante.
17 S. 48 (1).
18 As to which, see generally paras. 13.39, et seq., post.
19 See Schmitthoff *Export Trade* (6th edn) chap. 22.
20 See part 8, Inland Post Regulations 1963.
21 As to which, see chap. 14, post.

22 S. 48 (2).
23 S. 48 (4).
24 S. 48 (3).
25 *RV Ward Ltd v Bignall* [1967] 1 QB 534, [1967] 2 All ER 449, CA.

---

8. International sales

a) CONTRACTUAL TERMS

13.39 International contracts for the sale of goods are frequently made on standard terms,[1] which will commonly make provision as to which system of law is to govern the transaction,[2] and for arbitration in the event of disputes.[3] Assuming that English Law applies, the contract of sale will in general be governed by the rules previously considered in this Chapter for ordinary sales; and in this section comment will only be made where the law differs therefrom.

i) Risk

Whilst the general rule is *res perit domino,*[4] where goods are delivered at a distant place, deterioration necessarily incident to the course of transit will fall on the buyer, though the seller agrees to deliver at his own risk,[5] but loss caused by failure on the part of the seller to see that perishable goods are fit to go on the journey must be made good by the seller.[6]

When goods are sent by sea, the seller must give such notice to the buyer as may enable him to effect any usual insurance of them during their sea transit, otherwise the goods shall be deemed to be at the risk of the seller.[7] This applies to a sale under an f.o.b. contract, although delivery is complete when the goods are put on board.[8]

ii) Exclusion clauses

Whilst there are substantial restrictions on the ability of a seller to exclude his liability in a domestic sale,[9] there is no such limitation on freedom of contract in respect of 'international sales',[10] meaning for this purpose contracts satisfying *both* the following criteria:

a) Parties Sales must be:[11]

'made by parties whose places of business (or, if they have none, habitual residences) are in the territories of different States (the Channel Islands and the Isle of Man being treated for this purpose as different States from the United Kingdom)'.

b) Goods/contract The transaction must *also* satisfy *one* of the following requirements:[12]

'(a) the goods in question are, at the time of the conclusion of the contract, in the course of carriage, or will be carried, from the territory of one State to the territory of another; or
(b) the acts constituting the offer and acceptance have been done in the territories of different States; or
(c) the contract provides for the goods to be delivered to the territory of a State other than that within whose territory those acts were done'.

---

1 For standard form contracts, see para. 3.13, ante.
2 For choice of law clauses, see para. 9.01, ante.
3 For arbitration clauses, see post, chap. 34.
4 See para. 13.06, ante.
5 SGA 1893, s. 33.
6 *Beer v Walker* (1877) 46 LJKB 677; *Mash and Murrell Ltd v Joseph I Emanuel Ltd* [1961] 1 All ER 485, [1961] 1 WLR 862 (revd. on the facts [1962] 1 All ER 77 *n*, [1962] 1 WLR 16 *n*); *Cordova Land Co Ltd v Victor Bros* [1966] 1 WLR 793.
7 SGA 1893, s. 32 (3).
8 *Wimble Sons & Co v Rosenberg & Sons* [1913] 3 KB 743.
9 See para. 13.27, ante.
10 UCTA, s. 26 (1) and (2).
11 UCTA, s. 26 (3).
12 UCTA, s. 26 (4).

---

b) TYPES OF CONTRACT

13.40 Where contracts of sale involve the shipment of goods from one country to another, certain obligations of the contract are generally indicated by the initials or words 'f.o.b.'; 'c.i.f.'; or 'ex ship'. Such descriptions of the contract carry with them legal effects founded on the custom of merchants adopted into the law by the decisions of the courts.

FOB contracts These initials mean '*free on board*'. Thus, a clause in the contract might run, 'Sold to A B 200 bags of rice f.o.b. Antwerp'. Under such a contract the seller must put the goods on board at Antwerp at his own expense for the account of the buyer; and when on board, whether the goods are specific or unascertained, they are at the risk of the buyer, who is considered to be the shipper.[1] The buyer must name a ship or authorise the seller to select one, and it is the seller's duty to give the buyer sufficient notice to enable him to protect himself by insurance against loss during the sea transit.[2] Property in the goods will normally pass to the buyer as soon as they are put on board but not if loaded together with other goods of the same description.

---

1 *Cowasjee v Thompson* (1845) 5 Moo. PCC 165; *Brown v Hare* (1858), 3 H & N 484, on appeal, (1859) 4 H & N 822; *Inglis v Stock* (1885) 10 App Cas 263.
2 S. 32 (3); see para. 13.39, post.

13.41 *CIF contracts* The initials c.i.f. stand for the words, *cost, insurance, freight*. Thus, if a merchant agrees to sell goods 'at £2 per ton c.i.f. Manchester Docks', that sum will include the price of the goods, the premium for insuring them and the freight payable for carrying them to their named destination, Manchester.

The obligations undertaken by the seller under a c.i.f. contract, in the absence of provision to the contrary, were summarised by Lord Atkinson[1] as follows:

The seller must:

1. Make out an invoice of the goods sold;
2. Ship at the port of shipment goods of the description contained in the contract;[2]
3. Procure a contract of affreightment under which the goods will be delivered at the destination contemplated by the contract;[3]
4. Arrange for an insurance upon the terms current in the trade which will be available for the benefit of the buyer,[4]
5. With all reasonable despatch send forward and tender to the buyer these shipping documents, namely, the invoice, bill of lading and policy of insurance, delivery of which to the buyer is symbolical of delivery of the goods purchased, entitling the seller to payment of their price.

Property in the goods normally passes when the documents are handed over to the buyers and payment is made, though the buyer is entitled to reject the documents if they do not conform with the contract.[5]

A c.i.f. contract usually provides for payment of 'cash against documents' and the fact that the goods have not arrived at the time when the documents are tendered does not excuse the buyer from making immediate payment; but this does not prejudice the buyer's right to reject the goods and recover the money paid by him if on arrival the goods are found not to be in conformity with the contract.[6]

So, a vendor under an ordinary c.i.f. contract who has shipped appropriate goods can effectively tender proper documents to the buyer and require payment, although the seller knows at the time that the goods have been lost at sea. This is because the risk passes to the buyer as soon as the goods are put on board.[7]

The seller's obligation to insure must be strictly complied with. If he does not effect an insurance the buyer is not bound to accept and pay for the goods, although they arrive safely at their destination.[8]

If under a c.i.f. contract the bill of lading has been falsely dated so as to make it appear that the goods were shipped in accordance with the contract, and the buyer is thereby induced to accept the documents, he can, on subsequently discovering the fact, recover the difference between the market price and the contract price of the goods as damages for breach of the seller's implied obligation to deliver a correct bill of lading.[9]

In practice the buyer frequently agrees to accept documents other than those required under a strict c.i.f. contract, e.g. a certificate of insurance instead of a policy or a delivery order instead of a bill of lading. Such deviations must be expressly provided for in the contract and it must be made clear whether or not the seller is to be entitled to sue for the price on tender of the substituted documents.[10]

---

1 *Johnson v Taylor Bros & Co* [1920] AC, at 155, 156.
2 See *V Berg & Son v Vanden Avenne-Izegem PVBA* [1977] 1 Lloyd's Rep 499, CA.
3 For contracts for the carriage of goods, see post, chaps. 22–24.
4 For contracts of insurance, see post, chaps. 26, 27.
5 *Kwei Tek Chao v British Traders Ltd (No. 2)* [1954] 2 QB 459, [1954] 3 All ER 165. Thus, the buyer under a c.i.f. contract has two rights to reject: (1) to reject the documents; (2) to reject the goods. For the buyer's right to reject generally, see para. 13.35, ante.
6 *E Clemens Horst Co v Biddell Bros* [1912] AC 18.
7 *C Groom Ltd v Barber* [1915] 1 KB 316.
8 *Orient Co Ltd v Brekke and Howlid* [1913] 1 KB 531.
9 *Finlay & Co v NV Kwik, etc Maatschappij* [1929] 1 KB 400; *Kwei Tek Chao v British Traders and Shippers Ltd (No. 2)* [1954] 2 QB 459, [1954] 3 All ER 165.
10 See *Comptoir D'Achat et de Vente du Boerenbond Belge SA v Luis de Ridder Limitado, The Julia* [1949] AC 293, [1949] 1 All ER 269.

13.42 *Sales 'ex ship'* Lord Sumner in delivering the judgment of the Privy Council described the characteristics of these contracts in the following words:

> In the case of a sale 'ex ship' the seller has to cause delivery to be made to the buyer from a ship which has arrived at the port of delivery and has reached a place therein, which is usual for delivery of goods of the kind in question. The seller has

therefore to pay the freight, or otherwise to release the shipowner's lien and to furnish the buyer with an effectual direction to the ship to deliver. Till this is done the buyer is not bound to pay for the goods. Till this is done he may have an insurable interest in profits, but none that can correctly be described as an interest 'upon goods,' nor any interest which the seller, as seller, is bound to insure for him. If the seller insures, he does so for his own purposes and of his own motion. The mere documents do not take the place of the goods under such a contract.[1]

---

1 *Yangtsze Insurance Association v Lukmanjee* [1918] AC, at 589. See also *Commercial Fibres (Ireland) v Zabaida and Zabaida* [1975] 1 Lloyd's Rep 27 ('ex-warehouse' contract).

---

c) MEANS OF PAYMENT

13.43 *Bankers commercial credits (Letters of credit)* In contracts where it is the buyer's duty to pay cash against documents, it is commonly made a condition that the buyer shall open a credit in the seller's favour. This means that the buyer must instruct his own bank (the 'issuing bank') to open a credit in the seller's favour at a bank (the 'correspondent bank') in the seller's country. The issuing bank then instructs the correspondent bank to pay the seller (or accept a bill of exchange drawn by the seller) when he hands over the shipping documents. If the buyer's obligation is to provide a 'confirmed credit', then the seller is entitled to obtain the correspondent bank's undertaking of liability under the credit (in addition to the liability assumed by the issuing bank) before shipment. In every case the buyer must provide the credit a reasonable time before the first day of shipment,[1] and if shipment is to take place between two dates the credit must remain open for the whole of that period[2] even if the choice of the exact date is left to the buyer.[3] The banker for his part will be entitled to indemnity from the buyer but only if he complies exactly with his instructions, or if deviation from them is subsequently ratified expressly or by conduct.[4] The banker may refuse to pay the seller if the documents tendered do not on the face of them clearly correspond to what he has been instructed to accept.[5] But if 'clean' bills of lading are presented, the bank is not concerned to see that conditions on the back of them have been complied with.[6]

The object of a confirmed credit is to provide an assurance in advance that the seller will be paid and to enable him to discount bills at the best rate. The credit is sometimes made transferable and the seller may be relying on it to obtain the goods themselves. If that fact is known to the buyer and he fails to provide the credit, the measure of damages will be the loss of the profit which would have been made.[7] A confirmed letter of credit constitutes a contract between the correspondent bank and the seller and the buyer cannot cancel it even if he claims that the seller is in breach of the contract of sale.[8]

---

1 *Sinason-Teicher Inter-American Grain Corpn v Oilcakes and Oilseeds Trading Co Ltd* [1954] 3 All ER 468, [1954] 1 WLR 1394, CA.
2 *Pavia & Co SPA v Thurmann-Nielsen* [1952] 2 QB 84, [1952] 1 All ER 492, CA.
3 *Ian Stach Ltd v Baker Bosley Ltd* [1958] 2 QB 130, [1958] 1 All ER 542.
4 *Bank Melli Iran v Barclays Bank (Dominion, Colonial and Overseas)* [1951] 2 TLR 1057.
5 *Rayner & Co Ltd v Hambro's Bank Ltd* [1943] 1 KB 37, [1942] 2 All ER 694.
6 *British Imex Industries Ltd v Midland Bank Ltd* [1958] 1 QB 542, [1958] 1 All ER 264; *Edward Owen Engineering Ltd v Barclays Bank International Ltd* [1978] 1 All ER 976, CA.
7 *Trans Trust SPRL v Danubian Trading Co Ltd* [1952] 2 QB 297, [1952] 1 All ER 970, CA.
8 *Hamzeh Malas & Sons v British Imex Industries Ltd* [1958] 2 QB 127, [1958] 1 All ER 262, CA.

13.44   *Export guarantees*   The main object of the ECGD[1] guarantee is to 'insure' the seller against his buyer's failure to pay the price for specified reasons,[2] which include the buyer's insolvency (commercial risk) or orders of his government (political risk).[3] It serves a purpose similar to a commercial credit with these differences:

a) Whilst a commercial credit is furnished by the buyer at his expense, an export guarantee involves a premium paid by the seller; and
b) Whilst a commercial credit enables the seller to obtain the price irrespective of any defect in the goods, this is not generally the case with an export guarantee.

Export guarantees may be classed into three groups:

1. Supplier's credit policies amount in law to insurance policies taken out by the sellers rather than guarantees,[4] so that, if ECGD pays out, it is subrogated to the sellers' rights.[5] Whilst sales of consumer and engineering goods are usually dealt with under a general comprehensive policy taken out by the seller for a period, supplies of capital goods or for major projects are usually covered by specific policies; but, in either case only a proportion of the risk is covered.[6]
2. Suppliers' credit finance, designed to assist suppliers to obtain banking finance for their exports at reduced rates of interest.

This can be achieved by the supplier making an assignment by way of charge of his policy under (1) to the bank.[7] However, as the banker will then take subject to the equities,[8] he may prefer a direct 'guarantee' issued to him by the ECGD,[9] and with this arrangement the ECGD will require the seller to sign a recourse agreement in respect of risks not covered by (1).[10]

3. Buyer's credit financing, by way of a 'guarantee' extended to a banker who makes finance available to an overseas buyer and involves four contracts: (a) of sale; (b) between overseas buyer and UK banker for finance;[11] (c) between banker and the ECGD;[9] (d) a 'premium agreement' between the ECGD and the seller. Under this scheme, the seller obtains no cover in his own right as against the default or insolvency of the buyer; but on the other hand, the ECGD's right of recourse as against the seller is restricted to the latter's default under the contract of sale by the 'premium agreement'.

---

1 The Export Credits Guarantee Department of the Department of Trade and Industry: see s. 7 of the Export Guarantees Act 1968.
2 See the Export Guarantees Act 1968; the Export Guarantees and Payments Act 1970; and the Overseas Investment and Export Guarantees Act 1972; the Export Guarantees Act 1975; the Export Guarantees and Overseas Investment Act 1978. See also the 1934 Berne Union and the relevant EEC Directives.
3 Special insurance is available under the 1972 Act in respect of risks of war, expropriation, restrictions on remittance, etc.
4 Thus, it is a contract *uberrimae fidei:* as to which, see para. 5.15, ante.
5 See *Re Miller, Gibb & Co Ltd* [1957] 2 All ER 266, [1957] 1 WLR 703; *L Lucas Ltd v Export Credits Guarantee Department* [1974] 2 All ER 889, [1974] 1 WLR 909, HL: see further paras. 26.03, 27.30, post.
6 Usually up to a max. of 90%: see e.g. *Hill and Lichtenstein Ltd v Export Guarantee General Manager* [1972] NZLR 802 (SC).
7 See *Paul and Frank Ltd v Discount Bank (Overseas) Ltd* [1967] Ch 348, [1966] 2 All ER 922.
8 As to which, see para. 4.10, ante.
9 It is unclear whether the contract is technically one of indemnity or insurance.
10 E.g. the buyer does not pay by reason of the seller's breach.
11 Normally by the buyer granting the banker promissory notes to the value of the (instalments of the) price. For promissory notes, see paras. 21.10, et seq., post.

13.45 *Exchange control* The object of exchange control legislation is to protect the economy, and it seeks to do so by two methods: first, by control over the acquisition by local residents of gold and foreign currency; and second, by restricting the credit terms a local exporter may offer and requiring him to make early remittance of the price.[1] The approach of the legislation is to prohibit certain acts without Treasury permission, that discretionary dispensing power being delegated to the Bank of England.[2] Such prohibitions include the following: against the payment, e.g. by an importer, in any currency to a resident of an external territory,[3] whether payment is made within the UK[4] or elsewhere;[5] against compensation deals;[6] against the export of goods to any destination in any external territory;[7] against breach of the duty of a UK resident, e.g. exporter, to collect debts due by residents of external territories—though this does not prevent the discounting of negotiable instruments and trading debts to UK bankers, confirming houses or factors;[8] against the *issue* of negotiable instruments, e.g. by an importer, to enable the payee to obtain foreign currency,[9] or their endorsement.[8]

---

1 See the Exchange Control Act 1947, and regulations made thereunder.
2 Generally, contracts falling within the ambit of the 1947 Act are not illegal, but contain an implied term that they are conditional on Treasury consent: s. 33; and see *Contract and Trading Co (Southern) Ltd v Barbey* [1960] AC 224, [1959] 3 All ER 846, HL. *Aliter*, if it is clear that the parties propose to, or do, perform without obtaining Treasury consent: *Shaw v Shaw* [1965] 1 All ER 638, [1965] 1 WLR 537, CA. For the effect of such illegality on any contract, see para. 6.05, ante, and for offences, see Sch. 5 of 1947 Act.
3 This is anywhere outside the Scheduled Territories (basically the British Isles).
4 S. 5, which also covers, e.g. payment by a UK Bank of a cheque drawn by a resident of an external territory in favour of a UK resident.
5 S. 6, which includes the use by a UK resident of foreign currency earned overseas to make payments for ordinary purchases outside the UK.
6 S. 7. See *Shaw v Shaw* (above).
7 S. 23. In practice, the Treasury has granted a general dispensation in respect of most classes of exports; but all other cases require Special Permission.
8 S. 24 Prohibitions include assignment of debts to a resident of an external territory.
9 S. 4, which covers bills of exchange, promissory notes, banker's drafts, traveller's cheques, banker's confirmed credits.

---

d) SPECIAL RULES
i) Export/Import Licences

13.46 Where the export or import of goods requires a licence, the parties may have expressed an intention as to who is to apply for that licence, and what is to happen if one is not forthcoming.

Subject to any such clear intention, the position with regard to the duty to obtain a licence is as follows:

1. In ex-works or ex-store contracts, it is the buyer's duty to obtain a licence.

2. In ex-ship contracts, it is the seller's duty to obtain any

necessary export licence, but the buyer's to obtain any import licence.

3. In f.o.b. and c.i.f. contracts, it is generally the seller's duty to obtain an export licence;[1] but, where a UK buyer buys for export, the duty may be on him.[2] Similarly, it will normally be the buyer's duty to obtain an import licence.[3]

Once it is decided on whom lies the duty to obtain the necessary licence, the effect of failure to obtain that licence depends on whether or not that duty is absolute. Where the duty is absolute, the party under that duty will on failure to obtain a licence prima facie[4] be liable for non-performance of the contract of sale, i.e. to make or take delivery.[5] However, that party may excuse such non-performance if he can show (a) that the duty was merely to use his best endeavours to obtain a licence and (b) that he has done so:[6] the contract is then frustrated.[7]

---

1 See *A V Pound & Co Ltd v MW Hardy & Co Inc* [1956] AC 588, [1956] 1 All ER 639, HL; *Peter Cassidy Seed Co Ltd v Osuustukkuk-Auppa IL* [1957] 1 All ER 484, [1957] 1 WLR 273.
2 *HO Brandt & Co v HN Morris & Co Ltd* [1917] 2 KB 784, CA.
3 *Mitchell Cotts & Co (Middle East) Ltd v Hairco Ltd* [1943] 2 All ER 552, per Scott LJ at 554–555, CA.
4 *C Czarnikow Ltd v Centrala Handlu Zagranicznego 'Rolimpex'* [1978] 1 All ER 81, CA.
5 The *Peter Cassidy Case* (above).
6 *Re Anglo-Russian Merchant Traders and John Batt & Co (London)* [1917] 2 KB 679, CA. But see *Ross T Smyth & Co (Liverpool) Ltd v WN Lindsay (Leith) Ltd* [1953] 2 All ER 1064, [1953] 1 WLR 1280; *Brauer & Co (Great Britain) Ltd v James Clark (Brush Materials) Ltd* [1952] 2 All ER 497, CA; *Agroexport State Enterprise for Foreign Trade v Compagnie Europeene de Cereales* [1974] 1 Lloyd's Rep 499.
7 See generally paras. 8.02, et seq., ante.

---

ii) Uniform Laws

13.47 The Uniform Laws on International Sales Act 1967 was designed to give effect to two Conventions signed at The Hague in 1964, whose objective was to achieve some uniformity in the laws which in different states apply to contracts for the international sale of goods. The two Conventions are incorporated in the Act as Schedules, and deal respectively with sales law (Schedule 1) and the formation of contracts for such sales (Schedule 2). Thus, these two Uniform Laws are part of English Law[1] and available whenever the transaction is governed by English Law;[2] but they are applicable *only* where the parties have expressly so chosen.[3] Whilst the Uniform Laws are primarily intended to apply to international sales of goods,[4] the parties can also choose to make their domestic sales under these rules—though this can only be done to the extent that it does not affect the application of mandatory provisions of English Law.[5]

a) The Uniform Law on the International Sale of Goods (ULIS) This contains provisions governing the obligations of the seller[6] as regards making delivery,[7] conformity of the goods with the contract,[8] handing over documents,[9] undertakings as to title,[10] contracts of carriage and insurance;[11] the obligations of the buyer[6] as regards payment of the price,[12] taking delivery;[13] and also provisions common to the obligations of seller and buyer with regard to usage,[14] delivery and payment,[15] frustration,[16] damages,[17] preservation of the goods,[18] and the passing of risk.[19]

b) The Uniform Law on the Formation of Contracts for the International Sale of Goods (ULFC) This contains provisions with regard to an offer and acceptance[20] leading to an international contract for the sale of goods as follows: usage,[21] absence of form,[22] the definition of an offer as opposed to an invitation to treat,[23] duration of offer,[24] definition of acceptance[25] and its distinction from counter-offer,[26] communication of acceptance,[27] and death of a party.[28]

---

1 Uniform Law on International Sales Act 1967, ss. 1 (2), 2 (2).
2 See ante, chap 9.
3 Ibid, s. 1 (3).
4 For the definition, see Sch. 1, Arts. 1, 5–7; Sch. 2, Art. 1. This definition is almost identical in substance to that of the UCTA: as to which, see para. 13.39, ante.
5 Sch. 1, Art. 4. For example, see exclusion clauses: see para. 13.27, ante.
6 See ULIS, Arts. 18, 56. For remedies, see ibid, Arts. 10, 55, 70, 75–81. The innominate term approach is adopted: see para. 7.08, ante.
7 ULIS, Arts. 19–32, 90.
8 Ibid, Arts. 33–49.
9 Ibid, Arts. 50–51.
10 Ibid, Arts. 52–53. Despite terminology, they do not deal with the passing of property: see Art. 8.
11 Ibid, Art. 54.
12 Ibid, Arts. 57–64, 69.
13 Ibid, Arts. 65–68.
14 Ibid, Art 9. This will enable the parties to use the common types of contract f.o.b. etc: as to which, see para. 13.40, ante.
15 Ibid, Arts. 71–73.
16 Ibid, Art. 74.
17 Ibid, Arts. 82–89.
18 Ibid, Arts. 91–95.
19 Ibid, Arts. 96–101.
20 For the common law rules of offer and acceptance, see paras. 3.03, et seq., ante.
21 ULFC, Art. 2.1; but it may not be provided that silence is to amount to acceptance: Art. 2.2.
22 Ibid, Art. 3. See also ULIS, Art. 15. For the common law rules, see paras. 2.06, et seq., ante.
23 ULFC, Art. 4.

24 Ibid, Arts. 5, 8.2–3, 9.
25 Ibid, Art. 6.
26 Ibid, Art. 7.
27 Ibid, Arts. 8.1, 10, 12.
28 Ibid, Art. 11.

---

9. Sales by auction

13.48 When goods are sold by auction each lot is prima facie deemed to be the subject of a separate contract of sale. Anyone who makes a bid is in law making an offer to buy and there is acceptance if the auctioneer knocks down the goods to the last bidder. Thus, the sale is complete when the hammer falls, or as otherwise customary, and after that time the bid may not be retracted. The seller or his agent may bid, but only if an express notification to that effect is given; a contravention of this rule makes the sale fraudulent. The seller may notify that he has placed a reserve price on the goods.[1] Sales effected through an auctioneer are business sales for the purpose of importing the implied undertakings as to description, fitness and quality,[2] and for the purpose of allowing the exclusion of these undertakings so far as is reasonable.[3]

i) The protection of sellers

By the Auctions (Bidding Agreements) Act 1927 sellers are to some extent protected from loss resulting from agreements designed to stifle competition and bring about a sale of goods at a lower price than might otherwise have been obtained. By this Act a dealer[4] who gives or offers any gift or consideration to another person as a reward for abstaining or having abstained from bidding at an auction, or any person who accepts or attempts to obtain such reward, is guilty of a punishable offence; but this does not prevent a dealer previously to the auction from entering into an agreement in writing with other persons to purchase goods bona fide on a joint account, if before the purchase the dealer deposits a copy of the agreement with the auctioneer.[5]

If goods have been sold at an auction to a person who is a party to a prohibited bidding agreement (assuming one of the parties to that agreement is a dealer), the seller may avoid the contract and, if the goods are not returned to him, he may recover compensation from *any* party to the prohibited agreement.[6]

ii) The protection of buyers

The misdescription of auctioned goods may amount to an offence,[7] as may the actual holding of a mock or 'Dutch' auction.[8]

---

1 SGA 1893, s. 58. As to auctioneers, see para. 10.32, ante; and as to offer and acceptance, see para. 3.04, ante.
2 New s. 14 (5) of the SGA: see para. 13.22 (3), ante.
3 UCTA, s. 12 (2): see para. 13.27, ante.
4 I.e., a person who in the normal course of his business attends sales by auction for the purpose of purchasing goods with a view to reselling them: Auctions (Bidding Agreements) Act 1927, s. 1 (2).
5 Auctions (Bidding Agreements) Act 1927, s. 1 (1).
6 Auctions (Bidding Agreements) Act 1969, s. 3.
7 Applying a false trade description to goods: see paras. 18.02 et seq., post.
8 See the Mock Auctions Act 1961, and *Allen v Simmons* [1978] 1 WLR 879, DC.

Chapter 14

Domestic instalment transactions

14.01 This chapter is concerned with the situation where a person (the consumer) wishes to acquire from a supplier the possession and use of goods without himself finding the full price or value from his own resources at or before the moment of delivery. It is possible that the consumer may envisage paying that full price or value by way of a lump sum some time after delivery to himself, but more likely that he will envisage the periodic payment by himself of much smaller sums. The first section is concerned with the types of contract that may be utilised as between supplier and consumer to achieve this objective; the second section is an account of the manner in which the transaction may be financed by a third party (the financier); and there follows an analysis of the legal effect of these arrangements.

1. Types of instalment contract

A) *Instalment sales*

14.02 The supplier and consumer may enter into a contract for the sale of goods which is subject to all the rules considered in chapter 13, except in so far as they are varied below. However, such contracts differ from an ordinary sale in these fundamental characteristics: first, they provide for payment of the price by (normally approximately equal) instalments—perhaps after an initial deposit;[1] second, they will oust the ordinary presumption that delivery and payment are concurrent terms,[2] providing for early delivery and subsequent payment of instalments of the price;[3] and third, the transactions are normally conducted by way of standard form contracts.[4] Moreover, since 1938, the legislature has recognised that such contracts have much in common with hire-purchase (h.p.) agreements, and have accordingly sought to extend the h.p. controls to some such sales.[5]

In practice, there is a clear dichotomy according to whether or not in an instalment sale there is a reservation of the property in the goods:[6] transactions without such a reservation are conveniently termed 'credit sales', and those with such a reservation 'conditional sales'.[7]

a) CREDIT SALES

Where the property in goods passes on or before delivery, the buyer clearly has a good title that he could pass to another[8] or that might fall into his insolvency.[9] For the purpose of the statutory control of instalment contracts, there was introduced a category now termed a 'credit-sale agreement' and defined as:[10]

'an agreement for the sale of goods, under which the purchase price or part of it is payable by instalments, but which is not a conditional sale agreement'.

As will be seen later, the statutory control does not extend to all agreements falling within this definition.[11]

b) CONDITIONAL SALES

Where the contract (usually expressly) reserves the property in the goods (usually until payment of the full price), the buyer has no property to transfer to another (whether by way of sale, pledge or insolvency).[12] However, he may be able to pass a good title to a bona fide purchaser for value by way of one of the exceptions to the nemo dat rule: the conditional buyer may be a person 'who has agreed to buy' goods; and it was, of course, to meet this threat that the h.p. form of agreement was invented.[13] Nevertheless, it was thought that conditional sales had so much in common with h.p. agreements in this regard that this rule was partially reversed,[14] and a new limited exception to the nemo dat rule was created for dispositions of motor vehicles to bona fide 'private purchasers' made by one who was a conditional buyer or hirer under a h.p. agreement of that vehicle.[15]

Another approach available to the unpaid seller is to accept that he may lose title to the goods to a bona fide purchaser from the conditional buyer, and instead try to trace the proceeds of that sub-sale. In *Aluminium Industrie Vaassen BV v Romalpa Aluminium Ltd*:[16]

A manufacturer, D, bought from P some aluminium foil under a conditional sale which provided that ownership of items made by D out of the foil would also remain in P as 'surety' for the price. Upon D's insolvency, P sought to trace the proceeds of sales of items made out of the foil. *Held:* in the light of the fiduciary relationship created by the terms of the conditional sale, P was entitled to trace the proceeds into D's bank account.

The tracing of proceeds into a bank account has already been examined;[17] and the effect of this decision is to by-pass the statutory system of registration of charges on a company's property[18] with the following practical result: in the event of the company's insolvency, its bankers debts, which will normally have taken a first charge over its bank accounts to secure loans to the company, may be postponed to the company's ordinary trade creditors.

For the purpose of the statutory control of instalment contracts, there was introduced a category now termed a 'conditional sale agreement' and defined as:[10]

'an agreement for the sale of goods or land under which the purchase price or part of it is payable by instalments, and the property in the goods or land is to remain in the seller (notwithstanding that the buyer is to be in possession of the goods or land) until such conditions as to payment of instalments or otherwise as may be specified in the agreement are fulfilled'.

These statutory controls in respect of agreements for the sale of land have already been dealt with;[19] and in respect of conditional sales of both goods and land it will be seen later that the statutory controls do not extend to all agreements falling within this definition.[11]

---

1 For the controls on minimum deposit and maximum repayment period, see para. 14.07, post. Deposits are frequently paid by way of a 'trade-in', but that does not prevent the transaction being a sale: see para. 13.02 (d), ante.

2 S. 28 of the SGA: see para. 13.30, ante.

3 Distinguish instalment deliveries and matching payments, where s. 28 of the SGA is observed: as to these, see further para. 13.32, ante.

4 See para. 3.13, ante.

5 See paras. 14.43–14.44, post.

6 For the incidents of property, see para. 13.06, ante.

7 Outside the ambit of the legislation above referred to, these expressions are not terms of art.

8 See para. 13.11, ante.

9 See para. 33.16, post.

10 See now s. 189 (1) of the Consumer Credit Act 1974: these agreements may be constituted by two or more documents—ibid, s. 189 (4). Cf. the definition in s. 1 (1) of the Hire Purchase Act 1965.

11 See paras. 14.13–14.14, 14.43–14.44, post.

12 See para. 13.11, ante, and para. 33.17, post.

13 See para. 13.16, ante, and para. 14.03, post.

14 See para. 14.44, post.

15 See para. 13.17, ante.

16 [1976] 2 All ER 552, [1976] 1 WLR 676, CA.

17 See para. 7.19, ante.
18 As to which, see para. 17.09, post.
19 See para. 12.10, ante.

B) *Hire-purchase agreements*

14.03   A hire-purchase (h.p.) agreement is an agreement, usually in standard-form,[1] by an owner of goods to hire them out to a 'hirer'[2] and give to the hirer an option to purchase them conditional on his completing the necessary payments for the goods and complying with the terms of the agreement.[3] Normally, the h.p. price (which equals rentals plus option charge) is roughly equivalent in total to the cash price of the goods plus interest, and is paid as follows: the hirer will make an initial payment or deposit (say about 30 per cent of h.p. price) and is thereupon given immediate possession of the goods; the remainder of the h.p. price is paid by way of rent (say monthly) for the hiring of the goods over a period (say two years); and, when all the instalments have been paid the hirer is permitted to exercise the option to purchase (thereby 'converting' the transaction from one of hire to one of sale) for a further nominal sum.

In many cases, the owner under the h.p. agreement will be purchasing from a third party the goods which are to be let under the h.p. agreement as part of that transaction;[4] and he will therefore be concerned to ensure that he obtains a good title to the goods. As a person purchasing goods in these circumstances cannot with safety rely upon obtaining title under any of the exceptions to the nemo dat rule, he will normally first consult the organisation next referred to.

Hire Purchase Information Ltd   This is a non-profit-making company formed in 1938 by the main finance houses for the purpose of maintaining a voluntary register of motor vehicles subject to h.p. agreements, and subsequently extended to cover a wide range of goods the subject of instalment credit contracts. The House of Lords has recently decided that a mistaken reply by this Organisation that a particular vehicle was not subject to any instalment credit contract raised no title by estoppel in favour of the enquirer as against an owner forgetting to register such a contract.[5] Accordingly, attempts to turn the Organisation into a de facto compulsory private enterprise title registration system would now appear to have been defeated; and hopes for the provision of an effective registration system must now wait on a reform of the chattel mortgage laws.[6]

Assuming his title, the major concern of the owner under a

h.p. agreement will be to preserve that title until the option to purchase is exercised, the danger being that the hirer will before that date transfer the goods to another. Obviously, the hirer has during this period no property in the goods; and it has long been settled that he is not one who has 'agreed to buy', so that he cannot transfer a good title to a bona fide purchaser or pledgee.[7] Moreover, the effect of the reservation of property is also to save the goods from the hirer's other creditors: first, it will normally prevent the transaction from amounting to a chattel mortgage;[8] second, it will usually save the goods from the hirer's bankruptcy;[9] and third, an adequate form of words preserves the goods from the hirer's landlord's distress.[10]

For the purpose of the statutory control of instalment contracts, a definition was provided, the present one being as follows:[11]

'"hire-purchase agreement" means an agreement, other than a conditional sale agreement, under which—

(a) goods are bailed or (in Scotland) hired in return for periodical payments by the person to whom they are bailed or hired, and

(b) the property in the goods will pass to that person if the terms of the agreement are complied with and one or more of the following occurs—

(i) the exercise of an option to purchase by that person,

(ii) the doing of any other specified act by any party to the agreement,

(iii) the happening of any other specified event'.

As will be seen later, the statutory control does not extend to all agreements falling within this definition.[12]

---

1 Despite a large measure of uniformity of terms, it would appear that the terms of a h.p. agreement are insufficiently settled to save an 'agreement to buy on h.p. terms' from failing on grounds of uncertainty: *Scammell v Ouston* [1941] AC 251, [1941] 1 All ER 14, HL; and see generally para. 3.07, ante.

2 Under the Consumer Credit Act 1974, he is described as the 'debtor': see para. 14.14, post.

3 A hybrid between the contracts of sale (see para. 13.02, ante) and bailment (see para. 14.06, post), h.p. would appear to be a form of contract *sui generis*: per Goddard J in *Karflex Ltd v Poole* [1933] 2 KB 251 at 264, 265.

4 See lender credit, methods (2) and (3): see para. 14.10, post.

5 *Moorgate Mercantile Co Ltd v Twitchings* [1977] AC 890, [1976] 2 All ER 641, HL; and see generally para. 13.12, ante.

6 See paras. 17.05 et seq., post.

7 *Helby v Matthews* [1895] AC 471. However, he may pass a good title under such other exceptions to the rule of *nemo dat quod non habet* as sale in market overt, or a disposition of a motor vehicle to a private purchaser under

the provision of ss. 27–29, Hire-Purchase Act 1964. See paras.13.13, 13.17, ante.
8 *McEntire v Crossley Bros Ltd* [1895] AC 457, HL. For chattel mortgages, see further paras. 17.05 et seq., post.
9 Aside from the occasional goods falling within the reputed ownership doctrine: see further para. 33.22, post.
10 See *Smart Bros Ltd v Holt* [1929] 2 KB 303, DC.
11 See now s. 189 (1) of the Consumer Credit Act 1974: these agreements may be constituted by two or more documents—ibid, s. 189 (4). Cf. the definition in s. 1 (1) of the Hire Purchase Act 1965.
12 See paras. 14.13–14.14, post.

---

a) OBLIGATIONS OF THE OWNER

14.04 Subject to the terms of the agreement, the owner is under a common law duty to deliver the goods to the hirer. Indeed, the hiring does not commence until goods of the contract description are delivered to the hirer,[1] there being an implied term that the goods will remain in substantially the same state from the time the offer is made until delivery;[2] and breach of these duties entitles the hirer to repudiate the agreement.[3] However, unless the goods are of a special or unique kind, the hirer's only other remedy for breach is damages, not specific performance.[4]

Upon this common law form, the Supply of Goods (Implied Terms) Act 1973 (SOGIT) imposes the following implied terms, which are almost identical with those applicable in the case of sales of goods:[5] there are implied undertakings as to title,[6] description,[7] fitness and merchantable quality,[8] and in contracts by sample.[9] Moreover, in respect of exclusion clauses, the Unfair Contract Terms Act 1977 (UCTA) imposes identical restrictions to those applicable in respect of a contract for the sale of goods.[10]

---

1 *Karsales Ltd v Wallis* [1956] 2 All ER 866, [1956] 1 WLR 936, CA.
2 *Karsales Ltd v Wallis* (above); *Financings Ltd v Stimson* [1962] 3 All ER 386, [1962] 1 WLR 1184, CA.
3 In the case of a motor vehicle, failure to supply the log book means that the hire-purchase contract does not come into operation: *Bentworth Finance Ltd v Lubert* [1968] 1 QB 680, [1967] 2 All ER 810, CA.
4 See generally para. 7.32, ante.
5 See paras. 13.19–13.25, ante.
6 SOGIT, s. 8.
7 Ibid, s. 9.
8 Ibid, s. 10.
9 Ibid, s. 11.
10 See para. 13.27, ante.

b) OBLIGATIONS OF THE HIRER

14.05 Subject to the terms of the agreement, the hirer is under the following obligations:

1) *To take delivery of the goods.* If a hirer declines to take the goods he is liable in damages, but the owner has no right to wait and sue for the instalments as they would have become due had the hirer taken delivery.[1]

2) *To take care of the goods.* The hirer is liable in damages if the agreement is determined and the goods are in a damaged state unless he can prove that he has taken reasonable care of them. In assessing damages in respect of such article:

> 'there ought to be evidence as to what its general condition and value were at the inception of the contract and, similarly, evidence as to what its general condition and value were at the termination of the contract'.[2]

The hirer is not liable for fair wear and tear.

3) *Liability for loss or damage irrespective of negligence.* An action in tort lies against a hirer if he deals with the goods in a manner inconsistent with the owner's title, such as disposing of them or wrongfully withholding possession from the owner after the agreement has been terminated.[3] If the hirer deals with the goods in a way clearly not authorised by the owner, he is strictly liable for any damage to the goods occurring thereafter.

4) *To pay instalment charges.* The essence of hire-purchase is that the hirer is not bound to *buy* the goods and must be given some option to terminate the agreement and return the goods. If he exercises that option, he must pay all instalments due at that time, together with any further sum which the agreement lawfully requires under a 'minimum payment' clause should be paid on that event.[4]

5) *Damages for default.* Should the hirer default in making his payments as required in the agreement, he is liable for all arrears, and the owner is invariably entitled under the agreement to terminate the agreement and to resume possession of the goods. The hirer is also liable in damages for loss consequent on his breach. The measure of damages depends on whether, by words or conduct, the hirer has repudiated the agreement or not. If he has repudiated the agreement, e.g., by writing a letter to the effect that he cannot go on with the agreement, and this repudiation has been accepted by the owner,[5] the measure of damages is the difference between the hire-purchase price (less any 'option money') and the sum of the sale price reasonably obtained and any payments paid by or due from the hirer to date.[6] A discount is made to take account of the fact that the owner obtains accelerated receipt of his capital outlay.[7] If,

however, the hirer has not repudiated the agreement but is merely in arrears with one or more instalments, or the owner has not accepted the hirer's repudiation but exercises a contractual right to terminate the agreement, the owner may only claim against the hirer the amount of instalments in arrears, damages for any failure on the part of the hirer to take reasonable care of the goods, and the cost of repossessing them.[8]

Where the agreement itself provides by a 'minimum payment' clause that, on default by the hirer, if the owner exercises his contractual right to end the agreement, the hirer must pay not only the arrears due but some further fixed sum, the court will only allow such sum to be claimed if it represents a genuine pre-estimate of the loss likely to follow from the hirer's default. Otherwise the sum will be irrecoverable as a 'penalty' and the owner will be confined to a claim for damages assessed by the court on the principles already discussed.[9]

5) *To make certain payments in the event of bankruptcy, levy of execution, etc.* The agreement may provide that if any distress or execution is levied against the hirer or a receiving order is made against him, the owner may terminate the agreement and retake possession of the goods. Such a term is enforceable and the court has no power to grant equitable relief to the hirer in such a case.[10] Should the agreement also provide that, on such event, the hirer must make certain further payments after the owner repossesses the goods, such sum may be recoverable.[11]

---

1 *National Cash Register Co Ltd v Stanley* [1921] 3 KB 292, DC.
2 Per Davies LJ in *Brady v St Margaret's Trust* [1963] 2 QB 494, [1963] 2 All ER 275, CA.
3 This is a conversion, or 'wrongful interference with goods': see generally para. 13.37, ante.
4 *Associated Distributors Ltd v Hall* [1938] 2 KB 83, [1938] 1 All ER 511, CA. Lords Denning and Devlin *obiter* said that case was wrongly decided: *Bridge v Campbell Discount Co Ltd* [1962] AC 600, [1962] 1 All ER 385, HL. In *United Dominions Trust (Commercial) Ltd v Ennis* [1968] 1 QB 54, [1967] 2 All ER 345 at 348, CA, Lord Denning said that a hirer is not to be taken to exercise this option to terminate unless he does so consciously, knowing of the consequences, and avowedly in exercise of the option.
5 The hirer's repudiation of the agreement is not 'accepted' by the owner if the owner seeks to enforce a minimum payment clause in the agreement: *United Dominions Trust (Commercial) Ltd v Ennis* [1968] 1 QB 54, [1967] 2 All ER 345, CA.
6 *Yeoman Credit Ltd v Waragowski* [1961] 3 All ER 145, [1961] 1 WLR 1124, CA.
7 *Overstone Ltd v Shipway* [1962] 1 All ER 52, [1962] 1 WLR 117.
8 *Financings Ltd v Baldock* [1963] 2 QB 104, [1963] 1 All ER 443, CA; *Brady v St Margaret's Trust* [1963] 2 QB 494, [1963] 2 All ER 275, CA.
9 *Bridge v Campbell Discount Co Ltd* [1962] AC 600, [1962] 1 All ER 385,

HL; *Anglo-Auto Finance Co Ltd v James* [1963] 3 All ER 566, [1963] 1 WLR 1042, CA.
10 *Kelly v Lombard Banking Co Ltd* [1958] 3 All ER 713, [1959] 1 WLR 41, CA.
11 *Re Apex Supply Co Ltd* [1942] Ch 108, [1941] 3 All ER 473; doubted by Somervell LJ, in *Cooden Engineering Co Ltd v Stanford* [1953] 1 QB 86, at 98, [1952] 2 All ER 915, at 921.

---

c) *Simple hiring*

14.06 Simple hiring is a species of bailment.

a) BAILMENT GENERALLY

Bailment is the delivery of the possession of goods on a condition, express or implied, that they shall be returned to the bailor or dealt with according to his directions as soon as the purpose for which they were bailed is ended. There are many common everyday transactions of bailment—the deposit of goods for safe custody or storage, the leaving of goods for the purposes of cleaning or repair, the hiring out of goods, the pledge of goods as a security for money lent,[1] and the carriage of goods.[2] In practice the relationship between bailor and bailee is usually based on contract but this is not necessarily so.[3] Thus, there is a bailment where the carrier or repairer of goods is acting gratuitously and if the bailee of goods, B, delivers possession of them to a sub-bailee, C, with the owner's consent, there is a bailment relationship between the owner and C and C owes the owner the same duties as B does.[4] In *Gilchrist Watt and Sanderson Property Ltd v York Products Property Ltd*:[5]

> Shipowners carried two cases of clocks belonging to the plaintiffs from Hamburg to Sydney. The two cases were unloaded by the defendants but one of the cases was missing when the plaintiffs were ready to take delivery. *Held:* the defendants owed a duty of care to the plaintiffs although there was no contract between them—the defendants' obligation was the same as that of a bailee whether or not it could with strict accuracy be described as being the obligation of a bailee.

The principal liabilities of a bailee are:
1. To allow the bailor to repossess the goods bailed when proper demand for them is made by the bailor. Failure on the part of the bailee to do this renders him liable to the bailor in tort;[6] and the bailee is also liable for any loss or damage to the goods occurring while he is wrongfully detaining the goods irrespective of negligence.[7] Where the goods bailed are entrusted by the

bailee to his servant who steals them the bailee is liable for their loss to the bailor.[5]

2. To take reasonable care of the goods bailed.[8] It was at one time felt that the degree of care required depended on the type of bailment and, in particular, on whether it was a gratuitous bailment or a bailment for reward. However, in the case of *Houghland v RR Low (Luxury Coaches) Ltd*,[9] the Court of Appeal held that the standard of care required of a bailee is the same whether the bailment is gratuitous or for reward. Ormerod, LJ said:

> 'The question that we have to consider in a case of this kind, if it is necessary to consider negligence, is whether in the circumstances of this particular case a sufficient standard of care has been observed by the defendants or their servants.'

Moreover, the onus of proof is on the bailee. Thus, if the goods bailed are lost or returned to the bailor in a damaged state, the bailee is liable in damages unless he can prove that all reasonable care was taken by himself, by his servants and by any independent contractor to whom he has entrusted the goods.[10] Furthermore, the bailee is liable for any loss or damage, irrespective of negligence, if the loss or damage occurs after the bailee has dealt with the goods in a manner fundamentally inconsistent with the bailment.[11] On the other hand, a bailment must be distinguished from a mere licence. If a barber's shop or café provides hooks on which a customer may leave his coat but no employee of the proprietors of the shop or café takes possession of the coat from the customer, there is no bailment and hence, no duty of care on the part of the proprietors. In *Ashby v Tolhurst*:[12]

> The plaintiff left his car at the defendant's car park after paying the one shilling charge. On the plaintiff's return, he was informed by the attendant that someone had come for the car on his behalf. The plaintiff claimed for the loss of his car. *Held:* the relationship between the owners of the car park and the car owner was that of licensor and licensee, not of bailee and bailor, so that no duty of care arose.

During the currency of a bailment at will, i.e. where there is no fixed term, both the bailor and bailee have the right to sue in tort any third party who wrongfully interferes with their title to the goods.[13]

However, where the bailment is for a fixed term, then during the continuance of the bailment the bailor has no such right:[14] indeed, the bailee has a right of action even as against the bailor,[15] and as against a third party may recover the full value of the goods notwithstanding his limited interest.[16]

Unsolicited goods

Where someone receives unsolicited goods and he has no reasonable cause to believe they were sent to him with a view to their being acquired for the purposes of a trade or business, he has certain rights under the Unsolicited Goods and Services Act 1971 to treat the goods as an unconditional gift to him.[17] The conditions are that he does not agree to acquire or return them and either that (a) during the six months' period from delivery the sender did not take possession and the recipient did not unreasonably refuse repossession or that (b) not less than thirty days before the end of the six months' period the recipient gave notice to the sender and during the thirty days the sender did not take possession and the recipient did not unreasonably refuse repossession.

---

1 For pledges, see paras. 17.02–17.04, post.
2 For the carriage of goods, see chaps. 22–24.
3 Bailments may therefore operate outside the constraints of the doctrine of privity: see para. 4.03 (1), ante.
4 *Morris v CW Martin & Sons Ltd* [1966] 1 QB 716, [1965] 2 All ER 725, CA.
5 [1970] 3 All ER 825, [1970] 1 WLR 1262, PC.
6 For conversion or 'wrongful interference with goods': see generally para. 13.37, ante.
7 *Shaw & Co v Symmons & Sons Ltd* [1917] 1 KB 799.
8 *Coggs v Bernard* (1703) 2 Ld Raym 909.
9 [1962] 1 QB 694, [1962] 2 All ER 159, CA.
10 *British Road Services Ltd v Arthur V Crutchley & Co Ltd* [1968] 1 All ER 811, CA. The ordinary negligence liability of a bailee may be excluded by contractual terms, but such terms may be ineffective if there has been a fundamental breach of contract because the bailee may be unable to discharge the burden of proof; see *Woolmer v Delmer Price Ltd* [1955] 1 QB 291, [1955] 1 All ER 377; *Levison v Patent Steam Carpet Cleaning Co Ltd* [1977] 3 All ER 498 [1977] 3 WLR 90, CA. See also para. 3.15, ante.
11 *Edwards v Newland & Co* [1950] 2 KB 534, [1950] 1 All ER 1072, where the bailee stored goods in a warehouse other than the one in which he contracted to store them, and was held liable for consequent loss irrespective of negligence.
12 [1937] 2 KB 242, [1937] 2 All ER 837, followed in *Tinsley v Dudley* [1951] 2 KB 18, [1951] 1 All ER 252, CA.
13 For a right of action in conversion, see *Manders v Williams* (1849) 4 Exch 339 (bailor); *The Winkfield* [1902] P. 42, CA (bailee); and for the new 'wrongful interference with goods', see the Torts (Interference with Goods) Act 1977, s. 1 (see generally para. 13.37, ante). Mere denial of title is no longer conversion: ibid s. 11 (3).
14 The bailor cannot sue in conversion for the full value of the goods (*Gordon v Harper* (1796) 7 Term Rep. 9), but may sue for damage so his reversionary

interest (*Mears v London and South Western Rly Co* (1862) 11 CBNS 850); and see now s. 1 of the 1977 Act (ante).
15 *Roberts v Wyatt* (1810) 2 Taunt 268.
16 *The Winkfield* (ante); and see now s. 7 of the 1977 Act (ante).
17 For his common law rights, see para. 3.08, ante.

---

b) SIMPLE HIRING AGREEMENTS

14.07 The expression 'simple hiring' is commonly used to distinguish a hiring from a h.p. agreement: the latter does, but the former does not, include an option to purchase.[1] However, in neither case is the transferee a person who has 'agreed to buy' and hence able to pass a good title to a bona fide purchaser,[2] though there is another exception to the nemo dat rule applicable in respect of motor vehicles let on h.p.—but not under a simple hiring.[3] In modern times there has also been a tendency to use simple hiring agreements made for virtually the entire useful life of the goods hired to serve as an alternative to the instalment sale[4] or h.p. agreement;[5] and this has led Parliament to invent a category termed a 'consumer hire agreement'.[6] Furthermore, in respect of both long and short-term hirings, there has developed the practice of describing the agreement by different appellations according to context, of which the following are examples:

1) 'Charter' is the expression that has long been used in relation to the hiring of ships, and over the years there has been developed a separate body of law relating to charterparties.[7]
2) 'Leases' of goods:[8] 'finance leases' are closely akin to sales, being long-term contracts for a total rental close to the price at which the goods would be sold;[9] whereas 'operating leases' have more in common with orthodox hiring arrangements.[10]
3) 'Contract-hire' is the terminology employed for the hiring of motor vehicles for a length of time less than in (2) but greater than in (4).
4) 'Rental agreement' is the expression used in relation to the short term hiring of motor vehicles and the indefinite hiring of televisions.

Leaving aside charterparties,[7] the common law rules are the same for all forms of simple hiring, though in practice these rules are frequently ousted or varied by elaborate standard form contracts.[11]

a) *Obligations of the owner* Whilst there are no statutorily implied terms,[12] the common law will imply terms as follows: of quiet possession;[13] of reasonable fitness for the purpose required.[14] But, like sale and h.p.,[15] there is a statutory limitation on the ability of the owner to exclude these undertakings.[16]

b) *Obligations of the hirer* Besides the ordinary obligations of a bailee mentioned above,[17] the hirer is under an obligation to accept delivery of the goods.[18]

Terms controls As part of the economic regulator, the Government is empowered[19] to regulate the minimum deposit and maximum repayment period of all three types of instalment contract (sale, h.p. and hiring); and entry into a contract whose terms breach these controls will render that contract illegal.[20]

---

1 The distinction is vital: see *Galbraith v Mitchenell Estates Ltd* [1965] 2 QB 473, [1964] 2 All ER 653; and for statutory intervention, see paras. 14.29, et seq., post. For the option to purchase in h.p. agreements see para. 14.03, ante.
2 See para. 14.03, ante.
3 See para. 13.17, ante.
4 As to which, see para. 14.02, ante.
5 As to which, see para. 14.03, ante.
6 CCA, s. 15: see para. 14.14 (b), post.
7 See paras. 23.02, et seq., post.
8 Cf. leases of land: see chap. 12, ante.
9 E.g. of plant and machinery to be used as part of the fixed assets of a business.
10 Shorter-term leases, usually of specialist equipment together with ancillary services.
11 As to which, see generally para. 3.13, ante.
12 For statutory implied terms, for sales, see paras. 13.19–13.25, ante; and for h.p., see para. 14.04, ante.
13 *Lee v Atkinson and Brooks* (1609) Yelv. 172.
14 The duty is not strict, unlike the analogous statutory undertaking: *Hyman v Nye* (1881) 6 QBD 685; *White v John Warrick & Co Ltd* [1953] 2 All ER 1021, [1953] 1 WLR 1285, CA.
15 See paras. 13.27, 14.04, ante.
16 Unfair Contract Terms Act 1977, s. 7: see para. 3.15, ante.
17 See para. 14.06, ante.
18 Where there is no available market for hiring them elsewhere, the measure of damages is the full rate of hire for the agreed period, minus a sum for accelerated payment: *Robophone Facilities Ltd v Blank* [1966] 3 All ER 128, [1966] 1 WLR 1428, CA.
19 Under the Emergency Laws (Re-enactments and Repeals) Act 1964, s. 1.
20 *Bowmakers Ltd v Barnet Instruments Ltd* [1945] KB 65, [1944] 2 All ER 579, CA; and see generally paras. 6.03–6.05, ante.

---

2. Methods of financing instalment transactions

14.08 Bearing in mind that this chapter is concerned with the supply of goods on instalment terms in a domestic, as opposed to an international,[1] transaction, that transaction will be seen to have two facets: first, there is the sale aspect, though it has been seen that not all instalment contracts are technically sales; and second, the transferee is in effect, though not always in law, being loaned the price of the goods. Accordingly, the transactions may be divided according to whether or not the 'sale' and 'loan' aspects are both being supplied by the same person.

---

1 As to which, see paras. 13.39, et seq., ante.

---

a) VENDOR CREDIT

14.09 Where one person supplies both the goods and the 'loan', the transaction may be set up in either of the following ways:

1) The supplier and consumer enter into one of the three forms of instalment contract examined above; or

2) The supplier and consumer enter into a contract of sale combined with one of the following accounting systems (the consumer usually being supplied with a 'credit card' to denote the arrangement in force):

a) An open account, e.g. monthly, whereby the consumer pays the entire price for all goods purchased during the preceding month on a designated day in each month.

b) A revolving or budget account, whereby the consumer agrees to make regular payments of an agreed amount (e.g. £10) and is then allowed to purchase goods from the supplier up to the value of a designated multiple (say 8 times) of that sum (£80), it being agreed that the credit shall never exceed that sum, but that new purchases on credit may be made in so far as the credit falls below that amount.

b) LENDER CREDIT

14.10 Where one person supplies the goods (the supplier) and another supplies the 'loan' (the financier) to the consumer, the transaction may be set up in any of the following ways:

1) The financier lends the 'price' of the goods to the consumer, and the consumer ther purchases the goods for cash from the supplier. The Clearing Banks have long used this method (via overdraft or personal loan); but other financiers used to eschew it because their loan contracts were governed by the Money-lenders Acts.

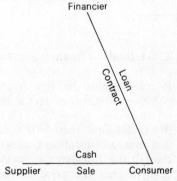

2) The supplier makes a cash sale of the goods to the financier, who then enters into an instalment contract with the consumer. This form of financing was popular in respect of motor vehicle transactions financed by other than the Clearing Banks because the financier thereby avoided the Moneylenders Acts.

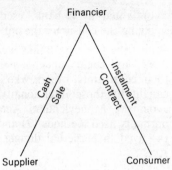

3) The supplier enters into an instalment contract with the consumer, and subsequently assigns the benefit of the contract to a financier in return for the outstanding price (less a discount), it being common to make the assignment, e.g. monthly in respect of blocks of agreements (block discounting). This method was commonly used by non-clearing bank financiers in respect of items of a comparatively small unit value, e.g. electrical goods, and, if properly conducted, also avoided the Moneylenders Acts.

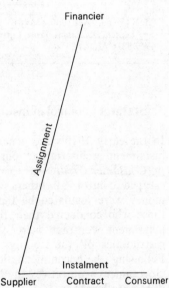

4) Check or voucher trading, whereby the financier supplies to the consumer a check/voucher (say for a face value of £20) in return for regular payments (say £1 p.w.), the consumer exchanges the check/voucher for goods to its face value with a supplier, and the latter recovers the face value of the check/voucher (less a discount) from the financier. This form of trading does escape the Terms Controls, but it was never clear whether it fell within the Moneylenders Acts.

5) Credit cards are used by consumers to authenticate their signatures when obtaining goods or services on credit, and include the following classes:

    a) Issued by a supplier—see vendor credit (2).
    b) Issued by a bank, and used to guarantee cheques—no element of credit being involved.

c) Issued by a bank, used to guarantee cheques, but also giving the consumer the option to pay by instalments.

Whilst the Clearing Banks were exempt from the Moneylenders Acts,[1] and could hence develop methods (1) and (5) free from their constraints, others who made a business of lending were caught by those intentionally onerous Acts.[2] Thus, it was to avoid the Moneylenders Acts 1900–27 that other financiers normally used methods (2) and (3); and the operators of method (4) lived in perpetual danger of being found to infringe those Acts.

---

1 Moneylenders Act 1900, s. 6 (d).
2 See *United Dominions Trust Ltd v Kirkwood* [1966] 2 QB 431, [1966] 1 All ER 968, CA.

---

3. Statutory control of instalment transactions

14.11 In the early 1970's the general picture of statutory control of instalment credit transactions charted by the *Crowther Report on Consumer Credit*[1] was this: whilst the Clearing Banks totally escaped control, all others who made a business of lending money were regulated by the Moneylenders Acts; whereas all those who conducted their financing via one of the forms of instalment contract were subject in some degree to the restrictions of the totally dissimilar Hire-Purchase Acts.[2] Following the recommendations of the *Crowther Report*, the Government's objectives in the projected reforming legislation were as follows:[3]

1. To establish trade discipline over the whole field by licensing, whereas previously such a control had only existed under the Moneylenders Acts for those within their ambit; and
2. To extend to all forms of instalment transaction similar legislative controls irrespective of the technical classifications such as instalment contracts or moneylending; and
3. To provide 'truth in lending'.

These objectives were embodied in the Consumer Credit Act 1974 (CCA), which is intended to be brought into force by degrees;[4] but in this transitional period both the old and new law must be considered.

---

1 Cmnd. 4596 (1971).
2 Hire-Purchase Act 1965; Advertisements (Hire-Purchase) Act 1967.

3 See the White Paper 'Reform of the Law on Consumer Credit' 1973 (Cmnd. 5427).
4 S. 192. For the transitional provisions, see ibid, Sch. 3. For the implementation to date, see Guest and Lloyd *Encyclopedia of Consumer Credit*; Goode *Consumer Credit Legislation.*

The Consumer Credit Act 1974

14.12 In one sense, the CCA is radical,[1] in that it makes a fresh start in attempting to cover almost the whole field of consumer instalment transactions with some entirely new terminology, which it lists and explains by way of helpful examples in Schedule 2.[2] Yet in another sense, the CCA is building on the previous statutory protections: many of the ideas of the Moneylenders Acts and the Hire Purchase Acts have been adapted to cover a wide range of transactions whilst being expressed in the new terminology. However, it should be noted that the CCA does *not* make chattel mortgages easier,[3] *nor* abolish the concept of h.p.,[4] *nor* deal with implied terms,[5] *nor* affect third party rights,[6] *nor* interfere with the fair trading rules,[7] *nor* alter the terms controls on instalment credit contracts.[8] Furthermore, neither is all the rest of consumer credit law to be found in the Act, despite its 193 sections and five schedules: the policy of the Act is to confine itself to general principles, leaving the details to be filled out by statutory instruments—themselves likely to be as voluminous as the Act.[9]

1 For a commentary on the Act by the draftsman, see Bennion *Consumer Credit Control.*
2 But see s. 188: in the event of conflict, the Act prevails over the examples. For repeals, see Scheds. 4 and 5.
3 For chattel mortgages, see paras. 17.05, et seq., post.
4 As to which, see paras. 14.03–14.05, ante.
5 Except to extend the obligations to third parties in some circumstances: see further para. 14.49, post. For the implied terms, see paras. 13.19–13.25, 14.04, ante.
6 For the nemo dat rule and exceptions thereto, see paras. 13.11–13.17, ante; and the rules on insolvency, see chap. 33, post.
7 As to which, see chap. 19, post.
8 As to which, see para. 14.07, ante.
9 For the general powers in relation to statutory instruments, see ss. 179–182. For the instruments for the time being in force, see Guest and Lloyd *Encyclopedia of Consumer Credit;* Goode, *Consumer Credit Legislation.*

THE AMBIT OF THE ACT

14.13 Leaving aside the subjects of pledges[1] and sureties,[2] the ambit of the CCA is generally confined to 'regulated agreements',[3] which expression means:[4]

'a consumer credit agreement, or consumer hire agreement, other than an exempt agreement'.

'Exempt agreements' are defined by s. 16, and include:

a) Agreements made by Building Societies, local authorities, etc., secured on land;[5]

b) Agreements in which the number of payments, or charge for credit, as the case may be, does not exceed that specified by Order;

c) Certain hiring agreements relating to e.g. gas meters;

d) Certain agreements which have 'a connection with a country outside the United Kingdom'.

Thus, the nub of the Act is built around the concepts of *regulated,* i.e. non-exempt, *consumer credit* and *consumer hire* agreements, though for both categories there are the following partial exemptions:

1) 'Small agreements', which are basically those where the maximum credit or rental does not exceed £30, and where the transaction involves no real security, i.e. there is no h.p., conditional sale or mortgage agreement.[6] Generally, small agreements are relieved from, e.g., most of the requirements as to formalities,[7] and the automatic duty to supply periodic statements of account.[8]

2) 'Non-commercial agreements', which are those 'not made by the creditor or owner in the course of a business carried on by him'.[9] Besides the same exemptions as for 'small agreements', 'non-commercial agreements' are also outside, e.g. the licensing provisions[10] and connected-lender liability.[11]

3) Bank overdrafts may be exempted from most of the requirements as to formalities.[12]

---

1 As to which, see para. 17.04, post.

2 As to which, see chap. 16, post.

3 The agreement must be made on or after 1.4.77: SI. 1977 No. 325.

4 S. 189 (1), including where the agreement is to be gathered from more than one document (s. 189 (4)). For commencement, see Sch. 3, para. 1. The provisions of the Act likewise apply where there is more than one party on either or both sides (ss. 185, 186); and the Act provides specifically for transactions which fall within more than one of its categories—'multiple agreements' (s. 18).

5 For mortgages of land, see generally para. 12.09, ante.

6 S. 17. There are special provisions for running-account credit (s. 17 (2):

which concept is explained in para. 14.14, post) and anti-avoidance (s. 17 (3), (4)).

7 S. 74 (2).
8 S. 78 (7).
9 S. 189 (1). 'A person is not to be treated as carrying on a particular type of business merely because occasionally he enters into transactions belonging to a business of that type': s. 189 (2).
10 Because he is not carrying on a business as required by s. 21 (1): see further para. 15.05, post.
11 Under s. 75: as to which, see para. 14.49, post.
12 S. 74 (1) (b), (3).

14.14 Returning to the two major categories of regulated agreement, these are as follows:

a) Consumer credit agreement This is defined as a non-exempt agreement between an individual ('the debtor') and any other person ('the creditor') by which the creditor provides the debtor with credit not exceeding £5,000.[1] Thus, it requires the following:

1. An agreement for the provision of 'credit' by a creditor (not that the prospective debtor be bound to take the credit). Section 9 lays down that 'credit' includes a 'cash loan, and any other form of financial accommodation', and expressly provides that the hire rent in h.p. is 'credit'.

2. To an 'individual', which expression includes 'a partnership or other unincorporated body of persons not consisting entirely of bodies corporate'.[2] Like the Hire-Purchase Acts, the CCA does not apply to goods acquired by a limited company.

3. By a 'creditor', which expression is defined as meaning:[3]

'the person providing credit under a consumer credit agreement or the person to whom his rights and duties under the agreement have passed by assignment or operation of law'.

Again, this extension to assignees follows the Hire-Purchase Acts.

4. Of credit not exceeding £5,000. Once again following the Hire-Purchase Acts, the ambit of the Act is fixed by reference to a financial limit, there being power to inflation-proof that figure by statutory order;[4] but the CCA differs from that earlier Act in this regard: the limit denotes the amount of credit extended, not the amount the debtor has to repay, so that deposit, interest and credit charges do not form part of the credit.[5] Moreover, the CCA has the extra refinement of expressly comprehending both the following:

a) 'Fixed-sum credit', which includes loans of a fixed amount and the hire-rent in h.p.[6]

b) 'Running-account credit', whose complicated definition[7] includes overdrafts, credit-card facilities and other revolving credit arrangements.[8] As the amount of the credit to be utilised will be unknown at the outset of the arrangements, there is a complicated provision to determine which running-account credits are to be regulated.[9]

b) Consumer hire agreement This is defined as a non-exempt agreement made by a person ('the owner') with an individual ('the hirer') for the bailment of goods to the hirer, and which agreement contains all the following characteristics:[10]

1. It is not a h.p. agreement—h.p. being a form of consumer credit.

2. It must be capable of subsisting for more than three months —this excludes short-term hirings, but covers indeterminate ones, e.g. from week to week.

3. It must not require the hirer to make payments which in total and without breach of the agreement exceed £5,000 (inflation-proofed[4]): it does not matter that the hirer elects to pay more; the test is whether the agreement requires him to do so.

---

1 S. 8; and see examples 5, 6, 7, 15, 19 and 21 of Sch. 2.
2 S. 189 (1). It includes joint debtors: s. 185.
3 S. 189 (1). It makes provision for joint creditors: s. 186.
4 S. 182: see further, para. 14.30, post.
5 S. 9.
6 Ss. 10 (1) (b); 9 (3).
7 S. 10 (1) (a). Illustrated by examples 15, 16, 18 and 23 in Sch. 2.
8 See paras. 14.09–14.10, ante.
9 S. 10 (2), (3).
10 S. 15. Owner includes assignee therefrom: s. 189 (1). See examples 20 and 24 in Sch. 2.

THE NEW CONCEPTS OF THE CCA

14.15 In essence, the concepts of the CCA are modelled on the *Crowther Report*,[1] and the explanation of many of the new classifications will be found there. The concept of 'consumer hiring' could not be taken much further; and the provisions in relation thereto will be dealt with later.[2] However, the wide-ranging concept of 'consumer credit' was sub-divided according to the following functional and overlapping distinctions:

a) 'Restricted-use'/'unrestricted-use' credit The test laid down by section 11 is whether or not the debtor is in fact free to use the credit as he wishes (regardless of whether that use would be a breach of contract): Does the debtor get his hands on the money, or otherwise acquire freedom of use?[3] The Crowther Report recommended that the borrower of unrestricted-use

(UU) credit might need particular protection in that he was likely to be borrowing in straightened circumstances to meet existing commitments;[4] and the CCA therefore distinguished between these and restricted-use (RU) agreements, though making little use of the distinction except in relation to categories (c) and (d) below.[5]

b) *'Debtor-creditor'/'debtor-creditor-supplier' agreement* (see below).

c) *'Credit-token' agreements* Such agreements are defined as:[6]

'a regulated agreement for the provision of credit in connection with the use of a credit-token'.

A credit-token is:[7]

'a card, check, voucher, coupon, stamp, form, booklet or other document or thing given to an individual by a person carrying on a consumer credit business,'

which enables the individual to obtain cash, goods or services either (a) from the card-issuer himself, or (b) from a third party, the card-issuer paying the third party in return for payment to him by the individual, e.g. bank cards, check or voucher trading. Besides all the usual restrictions on regulated consumer credit agreements, credit-token agreements are also subject to the following special restrictions: a prohibition on giving unsolicited credit-tokens;[8] special cancellation and copies provisions;[9] the earliest point at which the debtor may become liable for the use (or misuse) of a credit-token;[10] special limitations on the debtor's liability for misuse of a credit-token, usually to a maximum of £30;[11] and special documentation.[12]

d) *'Linked' transactions* There may be a host of satellite agreements surrounding the entry into a regulated consumer credit or consumer hire agreement, e.g. maintenance or insurance. Expressly excluding from this category agreements for the provision of security,[13] s. 19 elaborately defines what amount to 'linked transactions'.[14] The intention is that, where other provisions of the CCA interfere with the enforcement of the regulated agreement, they may likewise affect these satellite transactions.[15]

---

1 Cmnd. 4596 (1971). See esp. para. 5.2.10.
2 See para. 14.45, post.
3 See examples 8, 10, 12, 13, 14, 16, 17 and 18 of Sch. 2.
4 Cmnd. 4596 (1971), para. 6.2.21.
5 Ss. 19 (1) (c); 45; 58 (2); 69; 71; 72; 74 (2).
6 S. 14 (2).
7 Ss. 14 (1); 189 (1); and see examples 3, 14 and 16 of Sch. 2.

8 S. 51 (1), thereby granting a statutory monopoly of decreasing value to the existing operators.
9 Ss. 63 (4); 64 (2); 70 (5); 85: for the general provisions, see paras. 14.33–14.34, post.
10 Ss. 66; 171 (4).
11 Ss. 84; 171 (4).
12 S. 179: for the general provisions, see para. 14.33, post.
13 As to the provisions relating to sureties, see paras. 16.12, et seq., post.
14 See example 11 of Sch. 2.
15 E.g. ss. 57 (1); 69 (1); 70 (1); 96; 171 (2).

'DEBTOR-CREDITOR'/'DEBTOR-CREDITOR-SUPPLIER' AGREEMENTS

14.16 This is the major dichotomy of regulated consumer credit agreements, and is in essence a distinction as to whether in an instalment transaction the credit is provided by:

a) the supplier of the goods or somebody connected with him; or

b) an entirely independent third party.

It will be observed that the distinction is not between vendor and lender credit: some forms of lender credit fall within (a) and some within (b). The vital issue is whether or not the lender is connected with the supplier, i.e., whether the goods plus finance are being supplied as one business package, or as two separate ones: if they are part of a single package, then they will generally stand or fall together under the CCA; whereas, if they are two truly independent operations, a transgression of the CCA by one will generally not affect the other.

The vital, but difficult, matter of the connection between the financier (creditor) and supplier is dealt with by s. 187, which points out that such a connection can arise in either of the following ways:

a) There may be a 'pre-existing arrangement' between creditor and supplier, e.g. for the creditor to finance transactions for the latter; *or*

b) The transaction between consumer and supplier may be entered into 'in contemplation of future arrangements between a creditor or supplier', e.g. in the hope that a financier will finance the transaction.

Section 187 provides that there will be a 'pre-existing arrangement' between a creditor and a supplier 'if the consumer credit agreement is entered into in accordance with, or in furtherance of, arrangements previously made' between the creditor and supplier, or an 'associate' of either of them,[1] the expression 'associate' being extremely widely defined.[2]

1 Where the creditor is an associate of the supplier, there is a presumption that there is a pre-existing relationship between them: s. 187 (5).
2 Ss. 184; 189 (1).

14.17 Based on the dichotomy of whether or not there is such a pre-existing or contemplated arrangement between a creditor and supplier, the CCA then seeks to define the two categories in a very complicated manner.

a) 'Debtor-creditor' agreement Where there is no such relationship between creditor and supplier, s. 13 christens the arrangement between consumer and creditor a 'debtor-creditor' (DC) agreement; but it does so by requiring a DC agreement to fall within one of the following three categories:

a) An RU credit agreement to finance a transaction between the debtor and the supplier, but not made by the creditor under a pre-existing or contemplated arrangement between himself and the supplier.

E.g. a bank bridging or personal loan, the money being paid by the bank direct to a third party named by the debtor.

b) An RU credit agreement to refinance any existing indebtedness of the debtor's, whether to the creditor or another person.

E.g. a moneylender pays off a bank overdraft on behalf of the debtor.

c) A UU credit agreement which is *not* made by the creditor under a pre-existing or contemplated arrangement between himself and the supplier in the knowledge that the credit is to be used to finance a transaction between the debtor and the supplier.

E.g. a pledge, a bank overdraft, or any other loan where the creditor does not know where the money is going.[1]

---

1 See also examples 8, 16, 17, 18, 21 of Sch. 2.

14.18 *b) 'Debtor-creditor-supplier' agreement* Where the supply of goods and credit is a joint venture, s. 12 christens the arrangement between the debtor and creditor/supplier a 'debtor-creditor-supplier' (DCS) agreement; but it does so by requiring a DCS agreement to fall within one of the following three categories:

a) An RU credit agreement to finance a transaction between

the debtor and the creditor, whether forming a part of that agreement or not.

E.g. any of the forms of vendor credit referred to above.[1]

b) An RU credit agreement to finance a transaction between the debtor and supplier and made by the creditor under a pre-existing or contemplated arrangement between himself and the supplier.

E.g. all forms of lender credit by methods (2), (3) and (4), and also lender credit by method (1) where the lender pays the supplier direct, or by method (5 (c)) where a credit card is used to purchase goods.[2]

c) A UU credit agreement which *is* made by the creditor under a pre-existing or contemplated arrangement between himself and the supplier in the knowledge that the credit is to be used to finance a transaction between the debtor and the supplier.

This is really an anti-avoidance device aimed at the situation where there is in reality a joint venture for the supply of credit and goods, but the debtor is technically free to use the credit as he wishes.[3]

Inter alia, the DC/DCS dichotomy is important for the following reasons: it is an offence to canvass DC agreements off trade premises;[4] the disclosure requirements will vary according to whether it is a DC or DCS agreement;[5] cancellation of a DCS agreement extends to the agreement for the supply of goods[6] and there are special provisions for the return of those goods and the deposit;[7] and if the debtor in a DCS agreement has a claim against the supplier in respect of misrepresentation or breach of contract, he has a like claim against the creditor.[8]

---

1 See para. 14.09, ante.
2 For the forms of lender credit, see para. 14.10, ante. See also example 16 of Sch. 2.
3 See also example 8 of Sch. 2.
4 S. 49 (1): see further para. 15.15, post.
5 See further paras. 14.32–14.33, 15.15–15.16, post.
6 Ss. 19 (1) (b); 69 (1); and see further para. 14.34, post.
7 Ss. 70 (3); 71 (1).
8 Ss. 56; 75; and see further paras. 14.48–14.49, post.

THE MAJOR AREAS OF CCA CONTROL

14.19 Leaving aside pawnbroking[1] and contracts of surety[2] and consumer credit intermediaries,[3] the major areas of control are as follows:

a) Machinery for enforcement This embraces the following elements:

a) Criminal sanctions for breach. Breach of many of the provisions of the CCA (or regulations made thereunder) is a criminal offence of strict liability,[4] though that in itself does not lead to any further sanctions.[5] Furthermore, like the other two major consumer protection statutes of recent years,[6] the CCA not only imposes strict criminal liability, but also, where that liability is imposed on a body corporate, the brains behind that company commit a like offence;[7] and the CCA further incorporates, almost common-form,[6] defences to that strict liability.[8]

b) Centralised control. One of the major recommendations of the *Crowther Report* was for the appointment of a Credit Commissioner, working under the aegis of a single Government Department;[9] and this proposal was accepted in a modified form by grafting these functions onto the Office of Fair Trading (OFT), first set up under the Fair Trading Act 1973,[10] now under the aegis of the Department of Prices and Consumer Protection.[11] The CCA places upon the Director General of Fair Trading (DG) the following functions:[12]

1. The administration of the licensing system;[13]
2. The supervision of the working and enforcement of the Act at local authority level (see below);
3. To act as a central enforcement agency where the issue is one of a national rather than a local complexion;
4. To keep under review, and from time to time advise the Government on, the workings of the Act, and also on social and commercial developments in the consumer credit field;[14]
5. To make annual and other reports.[15]

c) Local authority enforcement. Another of the defects found by the *Crowther Report* was a lack of enforcement on the ground.[16] To remedy this, Parliament applied the solution already successfully adopted for the Trade Descriptions Act 1968, placing the task upon the local weights and measures authorities.[17] As a result, the spasmodic and uneven enforcement of the old law should be replaced by a reasonably uniform and regular enforcement of the new. The CCA provides an (almost common-form[18]) administrative system as follows:

1. Powers of entry and inspection, backed if necessary by warrant, are granted to local authority inspectors,[19] together with a power to seize goods;[20]
2. A power to make test purchases;[21]
3. Obstruction of an inspector is an offence;[22]
4. Notification to the DG of convictions.[23]

1 See para. 17.04, post.
2 See paras. 16.12, et seq., post.
3 As to which, see paras. 14.25, et seq., post.
4 For sentences, see s. 167 and Sch. 1.
5 S. 170. Thus, there is no possibility of an action for breach of statutory duty, nor for pleading that the agreement is illegal (see generally chap 6, ante).
6 See the Trade Descriptions Act 1968, ss. 23–25; and the Fair Trading Act 1973, ss. 24, 25, 132: see paras. 18.16–18.19, 19.07, post.
7 S. 169.
8 S. 168.
9 Cmnd. 4596 (1971), chap. 7.1.
10 See para. 19.01, post.
11 The 4 divisions of the OFT are Consumer Affairs, Consumer Credit, Monopolies and Mergers, Restrictive Trade Practices (for last two, see chap. 28).
12 Ss. 1, 4, 5, 6, 7. Subject to the control of the Secretary of State (s. 2) and the supervision of the Council on Tribunals (s. 3).
13 See paras. 15.05, et seq., post.
14 If the information gathered by the DG discloses any unfair 'consumer trade practice', he may initiate the procedure under Part 2 of the Fair Trading Act 1973 for the making of a statutory order prohibiting that practice: see further paras. 19.04, et seq., post.
15 S. 5. But see s. 174.
16 Cmnd. 4596 (1971), chap. 7.4.
17 S. 161. But see s. 174. The common nomenclature is now 'Trading Standards Depts.'
18 See paras. 18.20, 19.07, post.
19 S. 162.
20 S. 162. Compensation is available in the event of acquittal: s. 163.
21 S. 164.
22 S. 165.
23 S. 166. If the DG finds that a trader is persistently breaking the law, he may seek a court order against him under Part 3 of the Fair Trading Act 1973 (see paras. 19.09, et seq., post) or call in question whether he is a 'fit person' to hold a licence (see para. 15.09, post).

14.20   *b) Truth-in-lending* Following the recommendations of the *Crowther Report*,[1] the CCA attempts to force disclosure of the true cost of credit. As a first step, it has enabled the Secretary of State to make regulations governing the components to be taken into account in calculating the 'total charge for credit'.[2] This concept is important for the following reasons:

1. When expressed as a percentage, to fix the low cost credit category of exempt agreement;[3]
2. To establish the amount of credit, and hence whether an agreement is regulated;[4]
3. To decide whether or not a credit bargain is extortionate;[5]
4. To publicise the total charge for credit expressed both as a sum of money and as a percentage by way of the advertisement and documentation regulations.[6]

1 Cmnd. 4596 (1971), paras. 6.5.15–21.
2 S. 20; and see S.I. 1977 No. 327. HMSO have produced *Consumer Credit Tables.*
3 See para. 14.13, ante.
4 See para. 14.14, ante.
5 See para. 15.18 (2), post.
6 Ss. 44, 52, 53, 55, 60: see paras. 14.32–14.33, post.

14.21 *c) Transactional control prior to default* The CCA envisages the following types of transactional control exercised even prior to default by the debtor or hirer:

1. The legal regulation of interest rates: low interest rates may render a transaction exempt;[1] and high interest rates may lead to plea to a court of an 'extortionate credit bargain',[2] or to the DG that the creditor is not a 'fit person' to hold a licence.[3]
2. Entry into a credit or hire agreement,[4] default rendering an agreement 'improperly executed', and hence 'enforceable against the debtor or hirer on an order of the court only' (s. 65).
3. Documentation[5] and copies.[6]
4. Formation of a regulated agreement. The common law rules for the formation of agreement[7] are varied with regard to assent,[8] revocability,[9] agency to receive notice of withdrawal[10] and revocation by post.[11]
5. Cancellation[12] and contracting out of the Act.[13]
6. Implied terms. Whilst there is no alteration in the statutorily implied terms in sale and h.p.,[14] liability for breach of those undertakings and for misrepresentations by the supplier is extended to the creditor.[15]
7. Right to terminate.[16]
8. Accelerated settlement. The debtor is granted a right of early settlement, together with a statutory rebate.[17]

1 See para. 14.13, ante.
2 See para. 15.18 (b), post.
3 See para. 15.09 (a), post.
4 See para. 14.33, post.
5 S. 60: see para. 14.33, post.
6 Ss. 62, 63: see para. 14.33, post.
7 See paras. 3.02, et seq., ante.
8 S. 61: see para. 14.33, post.
9 A promise not to revoke his offer by a debtor or hirer is void: s. 59. For the special right of withdrawal from a land mortgage, see s. 58: see para. 12.06, ante.
10 S. 57 (3): see para. 14.47, post.
11 Ss. 57 (4), (1); 69 (7).
12 Ss. 67–73: see para. 14.34, post.
13 S. 173.
14 As to which, see paras. 13.19–13.25, ante.

15 Ss. 56, 75: see paras. 14.47–14.49, post.
16 Ss. 99–102: see para. 14.36, post.
17 Ss. 94–97.

14.22 *d) Transactional 'default' control* In favour of the defaulting debtor or hirer, the CCA imposes the following restrictions on the freedom of action of his creditor or owner:

1. Obligatory preliminary notices. It is a principle of the Act that the debtor or hirer shall always receive a seven-day notice before the creditor or owner takes any of the following actions: (a) demands earlier payment of any sum; (b) recovers possession of any goods or land; (c) treats any rights conferred on the debtor or hirer by the agreement as terminated, restricted or deferred; (d) terminates the agreement; (e) enforces any security.[1]

2. Death provisions.[2]

3. Court orders.[3] The Act envisages the following types of court order:

a) Enforcement Orders where the creditor or owner has himself infringed the Act in any of a number of listed ways;[4] or, notwithstanding that the creditor or owner is not in breach, where he wishes to exercise certain rights on the death of the debtor or hirer,[2] or seeks to repossess protected goods,[5] or seeks to enforce a regulated land mortgage.[6]

b) Time Orders (see below).

1 Ss. 76, 87, 98; see para. 14.37, post.
2 S. 86: see para. 14.38, post.
3 To come into force on a date to be appointed: Sch. 3, paras. 41, 43. For jurisdiction, see s. 141; for the power to make declarations, see s. 142; for onus of proof, see ss. 171, 172; for service of documents, see s. 176.
4 S. 127 (1): by entering an improperly executed agreement or security agreement; where there is a failure to serve a required copy notice on a surety; where a negotiable instrument is wrongly taken as security. The court has a wide discretion as to enforcement: see s. 127 (2)–(5).
5 Ss. 90–92: see para. 14.39, post.
6 S. 126: see para. 12.10, ante.

TIME ORDERS

14.23 This is the major weapon granted to the courts by the CCA for the control of regulated agreements, and is available in any of the following cases: on an application for an enforcement order; after service of an obligatory preliminary notice; in an action brought by a creditor or owner to enforce a regulated agreement or any security, or recover possession of any goods or land to which a regulated agreement relates.[1] The Act continues:[1]

'A time order shall provide for one or both of the following, as the court considers just—

(a) the payment by the debtor or hirer or any surety of any sum owed under a regulated agreement or a security by such instalments, payable at such times, as the court, having regard to the means of the debtor or hirer and any surety, considers reasonable;

(b) the remedying by the debtor or hirer of any breach of a regulated agreement (other than non-payment of money) within such period as the court may specify'.

The Act then makes elaborate supplementary provisions with regard to Time Orders as follows:

a) Where an offer to pay by instalments is made by the debtor or hirer and accepted by the creditor or owner, the court may give effect thereto without hearing evidence of means.[2]

b) Whilst a Time Order is in force, the creditor or owner cannot take any further action (save as allowed by the court); and, if the debtor or hirer complies with the Order, the breach to which it relates shall be treated as not having occurred.[3]

c) On application of any person affected by a Time Order, the court may vary or revoke the Order.[4]

d) The court may impose conditions in the Order,[5] or may:[6]

'include such provisions as it considers just for amending any agreement or security in consequence of a term of the order'.

---

1 S. 129.
2 S. 130 (1).
3 S. 130 (5).
4 S. 130 (6).
5 S. 135.
6 S. 136.

14.24 Furthermore, special powers are granted to the court in relation to instalment credit contracts as follows:

a) Conditional sale and h.p. agreements

a) An order may deal with future instalments of price or hire-rent.[1]

b) After the making of a Time Order, the debtor or hirer in possession shall be treated as a bailee of the goods under the terms of the agreement, notwithstanding that the agreement has been terminated.[2]

c) The court is empowered to make an order protecting the property pending proceedings.[3]

d) Instead of making a Time Order, the court may, if it considers it just, either[4]

1. Order the return of the goods to the creditor ('Return Order'); or

2. Split the goods as between creditor and debtor ('Transfer Order').

b) Hiring agreements Where under a consumer hiring agreement the court makes an order for the return of the goods to the owner, or where the owner has repossessed the goods and the hirer has applied to the court, the court may, if it appears just to do so, having regard to the extent of the enjoyment of the goods by the hirer, order that:[5]

'(a) the whole or part of any sum paid by the hirer to the owner in respect of the goods shall be repaid, and

(b) the obligation to pay the whole or part of any sum owed by the hirer to the owner in respect of the goods shall cease'.

---

1 S. 130 (2).
2 S. 130 (4). Nevertheless, he is deemed to be in adverse possession of the goods so that the creditor can mount an action to recover possession: s. 134: see further para. 14.40, post.
3 S. 131.
4 S. 133.
5 S. 132: see further para. 14.45, post.

CONSUMER CREDIT INTERMEDIARIES

14.25 The CCA seeks to control not just the parties to regulated agreements, but also the various intermediaries and parties to ancillary transactions which surround regulated agreements. These are collectively termed 'ancillary credit businesses',[1] and fall into the following categories:

---

1 Ss. 145 (1); 189 (1). Lawyers acting in contentious business are excluded: ss. 146 (1)–(4).

14.26 *a) Credit reference agency*, which is defined as:[1]

'a person carrying on a business comprising the furnishing of persons with information relevant to the financial standing of individuals, being information collected by the agency for that purpose'.

With the widespread use of computers to effect a nationwide

pre-contract reference service to prospective creditors, it was felt necessary to protect consumers against inaccurate prejudicial information; and two steps were taken in this regard. First, all credit reference agencies have been made subject to most of the licensing provisions.[2] Second, the prospective debtor has been given the power of access to his record, and rectification thereof.[3]

---

1 S. 145 (8). This category does not appear to include banks, who simply collect information in the course of their business.
2 S. 147–150: see further paras. 15.05, et seq., post.
3 Ss. 157–160. Now in force.

14.27   *b) Credit brokerage,* which is defined as:[1]

'the effecting[2] of introductions[3]—

(a) of individuals desiring to obtain credit—

(i) to persons carrying on businesses to which this sub-paragraph applies,[4] or

(ii) in the case of an individual desiring to obtain credit to finance the acquisition or provision of a dwelling occupied or to be occupied by himself or his relative,[5] to any person carrying on a business in the course of which he provides credit secured on land, or

(b) of individuals desiring to obtain goods on hire to persons carrying on businesses to which this paragraph applies,[6] or

(c) of individuals desiring to obtain credit, or to obtain goods on hire, to other credit-brokers'.

The Act does not regulate the introduction of companies to credit or hiring facilities because they are not 'individuals',[7] but it does embrace the following types of brokerage:

a) Regulated consumer credit or consumer hire agreements,[8] and will thus include a supplier of goods financing his business by way of lender credit transactions with consumers;[9]

b) Most types of exempt consumer credit agreement;[10]

c) Mortgage brokers in respect of the acquisition of land;[11]

d) Other credit brokers.[12]

As credit-brokers did not themselves purport to lend money, they never fell within the ambit of the Moneylenders Acts;[13] and the Hire-Purchase Acts only applied to them in so far as they indulged in vendor credit or one form of lender credit.[14] However, under the CCA they will now be subject to the following restrictions: they are subject to most of the licensing provisions;[15] a curb is placed on excessive brokerage fees;[16] there is a complete prohibition on canvassing off trade premises either

DC agreements[17] or ancillary credit services;[18] they are subject to similar restrictions on seeking business as prospective creditors;[19] and credit-brokerage agreements are subject to the same controls as regulated agreements in respect of disclosure, documentation, copies, etc.[20]

---

1 Ss. 145 (2); 189 (1).
2 Occasional transactions are to be ignored: s. 189 (2).
3 Except where an agent is appointed on a commission-basis (i.e. *not* an employee) to canvass DCS agreements or hiring agreements: s. 146 (5) e.g. mail order company agents.
4 To consumer credit agreements as set out in s. 145 (3).
5 For 'relative', see ss. 184; 189 (1).
6 To consumer hire agreements as set out in s. 145 (4).
7 See s. 189 (1).
8 Ss. 145 (2) (a) (i), (3) (a). See para. 14.14, ante.
9 See para. 14.10, ante.
10 Ss. 145 (2) (a) (i), (3) (b). See para. 14.13, ante. To meet attempts to avoid the Act by declaring a foreign law applicable to the agreement there is an anti-avoidance device: s. 145 (3) (c).
11 S. 145 (2) (a) (ii). See para. 12.09, ante.
12 S. 145 (2) (c). An anti-avoidance device.
13 See para. 15.02, post.
14 See paras. 14.09, 14.10 (3), ante.
15 Ss. 147–150; not yet in force. But see generally paras. 15.05, et seq., post.
16 If no agreement results from the introduction, any brokerage fee over £1 is recoverable on certain conditions: s. 155.
17 S. 49: see para. 15.15, post.
18 Ss. 153, 154.
19 Ss. 151, 152, which refer back to the following sections: ss. 44–47, 52–54; and see para. 15.15, post.
20 S. 156, which refers to disclosure (s. 55), form and content (ss. 60, 179), signing (s. 61), copies (ss. 62, 63, 180), improperly executed agreements (s. 65) and enforcement orders (s. 127).

14.28   *c) Debt-adjusting, debt-counselling, debt-collecting* The Act defines these three separate, but overlapping, categories of ancillary credit business as follows:

1. Debt-adjusting is:[1]
   'in relation to debts due under consumer credit agreements or consumer hire agreements—
   > (a) negotiating with the creditor or owner, on behalf of the debtor or hirer, terms for the discharge of a debt, or
   > (b) taking over, in return for payments by the debtor or hirer, his obligation to discharge a debt, or
   > (c) any similar activity concerned with the liquidation of a debt'.

2. Debt-collecting is:[2]

'the taking of steps to procure payment of debts due under consumer credit agreements or consumer hire agreements'.

3. Debt counselling is:[3]

'the giving of advice to debtors or hirers about the liquidation of debts due under consumer credit agreements or consumer hire agreements'.

However, in all three cases, there are exempted from these categories persons who engage in the above activities but playing only one of the following roles;[4] (a) creditor or owner otherwise than by assignment;[5] (b) assignee of the general business (other than a debt-collecting business) of the creditor or owner; (c) supplier;[6] (d) credit-broker who has acquired the business of the supplier; (e) one who would be a credit-broker if he were not an independent canvasser.[7] Apart from the limitation on brokerage fees, these three categories are subject to all the same restrictions as credit-brokers.[8]

---

1 Ss. 145 (5); 189 (1). E.g. banker, accountant, solicitor.
2 Ss. 145 (7); 189 (1). E.g. factoring: and see note 5 post.
3 Ss. 145 (6); 189 (1). E.g. Citizens Advice Bureaux.
4 S. 146 (6).
5 So, the provision does not save financiers engaged in lender credit method (3) (see para. 14.10, ante): they are not creditors under regulated agreements because they grant credit to suppliers; but they are debt-collectors.
6 E.g. supplier financing his business as in previous note.
7 I.e. falling within s. 146 (5): see para. 14.27, note 3, ante.
8 See para. 14.27, ante. The licensing provisions are already in force for all three of these categories.

---

4. Transactional control of instalment contracts/debtor-creditor-supplier agreements

14.29   Presently, the transactional control of instalment credit contracts is to be found in the Hire-Purchase Acts; but, during the life-time of this edition, these should be superseded by the provisions of the Consumer Credit Act 1974 (CCA), which is intended to be brought into force by degrees.[1] Accordingly, for the present both the old and new law must be borne in mind. However, this is not likely to cause too much difficulty: in this area, the CCA provisions tend to be modelled on the old Hire-Purchase Acts provisions (apart from the nomenclature); and the major difference is that the CCA provisions are applicable to a wider range of transactions.[2]

1 See para. 14.11, ante. For the transitional provisions, see generally ibid Sch. 3. For the provisions and Regulations for the time being in force, see para 14.11, note 4, ante.
2 For the ambit of the CCA, see paras. 14.13–14.14, ante.

Hire-purchase agreements

14.30 The definition of h.p. in the CCA is somewhat more sophisticated than that found in the previous legislation.[1] Leaving aside advertisements (see below), the ambit of the previous legislation—the Hire-Purchase Act 1965 (HPA)—compared with the CCA as follows:[2] both are restricted to agreements under which the hirer is not a registered company,[3] and within an upper financial limit—now £5,000 in both cases.[4]

---

1 The CCA definition is set out para. 14.03, ante, and amounts to the provision of RU credit for a DCS agreement (see paras. 14.15, 14.18, ante). There was a different, but basically similar, definition under the previous Acts: see the HPA, s. 1; the Advertisements (Hire-Purchase) Act 1967, s. 7 (1).
2 It must be borne in mind that the HPA was largely restricted to instalment credit *contracts*, whereas the CCA extends to instalment credit *transactions*: for transactions, see paras. 14.09–14.10, ante.
3 HPA, s. 4; CCA, ss. 8 (1), 15 (1).
4 HPA, s. 2 (as amended); CCA, ss. 8 (2), 15 (1). Note that the former includes the deposit, whereas the latter does not.

---

a) SEEKING BUSINESS

14.31 The Advertisements (Hire-Purchase) Act 1967 requires certain information to be included in any advertisement[1] of goods available for disposal on h.p., or credit sale, if the advertisement contains an indication that a deposit is payable, or that no deposit is payable, or of the amount of one or more of the instalments. The information required consists of:

a) the total number of instalments payable;
b) the length of the period in respect of which each instalment is payable; and
c) if any instalments are payable before delivery of the goods, the number of instalments so payable.

The Act applies irrespective of whether the hire-purchase price or total purchase price exceeds £5,000 and 'credit sale' is so defined as to *include* conditional sales.[2]

Where the amount of the deposit or of any instalment is given in the advertisement or a sum is stated as the hire-purchase price or total purchase price, the advertisement must also state the cash price of the goods, the amount of each instalment, either a statement that there is no deposit or a statement of the amount of the deposit expressed as a sum of money or as a fraction or percentage of a stated sum, and the hire-purchase price or total purchase price of the goods.

If the advertisement contains a fraction represented as the rate of interest to be borne by the hirer or buyer, the advertisement must contain not only the details already referred to but also the instalments must be expressed as instalments of equal amounts, the fraction must be expressed as a specified amount per cent per annum and the amount so specified must be not less than the amount calculated in accordance with a prescribed formula.[3]

---

1 'Advertisement' is defined ibid, s. 7 (3). Cf. the wider definition in the CCA, s. 189 (1).

2 For conditional and credit sales, see further paras. 14.43–14.44, post.

3 The formula is set out in the Advertisements (Hire-Purchase) Act 1967, Sch. 1, Part III.

14.32 *The CCA.* Part IV of the CCA is to apply, subject to the dispensing power of the Secretary of State:[1]

'to any advertisement,[2] published for the purposes of a business carried on by the advertiser,[3] indicating that he is willing—
    (a) to provide credit,[4] or
    (b) to enter into an agreement for the bailment or (in Scotland) the hiring of goods by him';[5]

provided that the advertiser carries on a business[6] relating to the provision of one of the following:[7] (i) consumer credit or consumer hire agreements;[8] (ii) credit secured on land to individuals.[9] In respect of advertisements which fall within this definition, the Secretary of State is empowered to make Regulations as to their form and content,[10] including the true cost;[11] and there is also a prohibition on advertisements which convey information (including the advertiser's intention) which in a material respect is false or misleading.[12] Furthermore, where the advertisement indicates a willingness to provide RU credit relating to goods,[13] the advertiser must also be prepared to supply the goods for cash.[14] Breach of any of the foregoing rules amounts to an offence.[15] For further restrictions on seeking business, see para. 15.15, post.

---

1 CCA s. 43 (5).

2 For the definition of 'advertisement', see CCA, s. 189 (1). The rules relating to such advertisements are to be brought into force on a day to be appointed: ibid. Sch. 3, para. 8.

3 For the definition of 'advertiser', see CCA, s. 189 (1).

4 This does not include advertisements which refer only to unsecured credit agreements in excess of £5,000, or credit agreements for any amount secured on land or available only to bodies corporate: CCA, s. 43 (3).

5 This does not include advertisements which indicate that they are not prepared to enter consumer hire agreements: CCA s. 43 (4).

6 This does not include one who only occasionally enters into such agreements: CCA, s. 189 (2).

7 CCA s. 43 (2). To meet attempts to avoid the Act by declaring a foreign law applicable, there is an anti-avoidance device: ibid s. 43 (2) (c).

8 As to which see para. 14.14, ante.

9 Note the absence of any financial limit. For agreements secured on land, see further para. 12.09–12.10, ante.

10 CCA, s. 44; and see also ibid, ss. 52–54. No such Regulations have yet been made: breach will be an offence (s. 167 (2)): and see further para. 14.19, ante.

11 See further CCA, s. 20: see para. 14.20, ante.

12 CCA, s. 46.

13 For RU credit, see para. 14.15, ante.

14 CCA, s. 45.

15 CCA, s. 47. See further para. 14.19, ante.

---

b) ENTRY INTO THE AGREEMENT[1]

14.33 *a) Statement of cash price* By s. 6 of the HPA, before any h.p. agreement is entered into, the owner must state in writing to the prospective hirer, a price at which the goods may be purchased by him for cash, i.e., the cash price. If the hirer has inspected the goods or like goods and tickets or labels were attached to or displayed with the goods clearly stating the cash price, or if the hirer has selected the goods by reference to a catalogue, price list, or advertisement, which has clearly stated the cash price, then s. 6 is deemed to have been complied with.

Similar requirements may be embodied in Regulations made under the CCA,[2] any regulated agreement made in breach being improperly executed.[3]

b) Documentation Under the HPA, an owner may not enforce a h.p. agreement unless the agreement is signed by the hirer himself and by or on behalf of all other parties to the agreement.[4] The agreement must contain a statement of the hire-purchase price,[5] the cash price of the goods to which the agreement relates, the amount of each of the instalments, the date upon which each instalment is payable, and must contain a list of the goods to which the agreement relates sufficient to identify them.[6] The agreement must also contain a notice in the terms prescribed in the Schedule 1 to the Act, explaining the hirer's statutory right to terminate the agreement and the statutory restrictions on the owner's right of repossession.[6] The Department of Trade has made regulations prescribing the type size, the colour of the paper and lettering used and that a 'box' in red print be used for the hirer's signature.[7] Similar requirements may be embodied in Regulations made under the CCA,[8] contravention rendering the regulated agreement improperly executed.[9]

c) Copies Under the HPA, where a hirer under a h.p. agreement signs the agreement at 'appropriate trade premises', i.e. premises at which the owner normally carries on business or goods of a similar description are normally offered or exposed for sale in the course of a business carried on at these premises, then if the agreement is signed by or on behalf of all other parties immediately after or immediately before the hirer signs, it is sufficient if a copy is there and then delivered to the hirer. Otherwise, the hirer must be given a copy of the document he is asked to sign in the form in which it was when presented or sent to him (the 'first statutory copy') *and* a copy of the agreement (the 'second statutory copy') must be delivered or sent to him within seven days of the making of the agreement.[10] Where the hirer signs elsewhere than at 'appropriate trade premises', e.g. at his home, he must always be given or sent both a copy of the document in the form he signs it (the 'first statutory copy') *and* be sent by post a copy of the agreement (the 'second statutory copy') within seven days of the making of the agreement. Both copies must contain statements of the hirer's right of cancellation, considered below.[11] Similar requirements are to be found in the CCA,[12] contravention rendering the regulated agreement improperly executed.[13]

Effect of non-compliance Where the provisions of ss. 5 to 9 of the HPA are not complied with, the owner is not entitled to enforce the hire-purchase agreement or any contract of guarantee relating thereto, nor does he have any right to recover the goods from the hirer, nor may any security given by the hirer or guarantor be enforceable against the hirer or guarantor by any holder thereof.[14] However, provided that there is an agreement signed by the hirer and by or on behalf of all other parties to the agreement, if the court is satisfied that a failure to comply with any of the other requirements as to the formation of the agreement has not prejudiced the hirer, the court may dispense with that requirement for the purposes of the action.[15] Where a regulated agreement under the CCA is improperly executed, the consequences are specified by s. 65 as follows:

'(1) An improperly-executed regulated agreement is enforceable against the debtor or hirer on an order of the court only.[16]

(2) A retaking of goods or land to which a regulated agreement relates is an enforcement of the agreement'.[17]

---

1 All the provisions of the CCA dealt with in this section are subject to s. 74 of the Act.
2 Under CCA, s. 55. No Regulations have yet been made.
3 CCA, s. 55 (2): see further below.
4 HPA, s. 5.
5 For 'total purchase price', see HPA, s. 58, and *Mutual Finance Co Ltd v Davidson* [1963] 1 All ER 133, [1963] 1 WLR 134, CA.
6 HPA, s. 7 (1).
7 HPA, s. 7 (2); and S.I. 1965, No. 1646.
8 CCA, ss. 60, 61 (including any security provided by him: s. 105 (9)). No Regulations have yet been made. For the special rules on formation of contract, see para. 14.21, ante.
9 CCA, s. 61 (1): see further below.
10 HPA, s. 8. For 'appropriate trade premises', see para. 14.34, post.
11 HPA, s. 9.
12 CCA, ss. 62, 63; 180.
13 CCA, ss. 62 (3), 63 (5): see further below.
14 The hirer cannot be sued in conversion merely for refusing to give up possession when the owner is in breach of these provisions (HPA, s. 52). If he parts with possession to a third party both he and the third party may be liable in conversion (*Eastern Distributors Ltd v Goldring* [1957] 2 QB 600, [1957] 2 All ER 525, CA). See now the Torts (Interference with Goods) Act 1977.
15 HPA, s. 10. There is no dispensing power in respect of the requirements in s. 9 that the second statutory copy of an agreement signed otherwise than at appropriate trade premises be sent by post to the hirer (unless it is merely that the seven-day period has not been complied with) and that the statutory copies contain statements of the hirer's right of cancellation.
16 For enforcement orders, see CCA, s. 127: see para. 14.22, ante.
17 The court is here empowered to make a time order (CCA, s. 129): see para. 14.23, ante.

---

c) CANCELLATION

14.34 *a) Under the HPA* Where the customer signs a hire-purchase agreement (or a document which would constitute such an agreement if executed by or on behalf of the owner of the goods) at a place other than 'appropriate trade premises', he may serve a notice of cancellation of the agreement on the owner or his agent at any time before the end of four days beginning with the day on which he receives the 'second statutory copy' of the agreement.[1] 'Appropriate trade premises' means premises at which the owner normally carries on a business, or goods of a similar description are normally offered or exposed for sale in the course of a business carried on at those premises. Any contractual provision restricting this right is void. The effect of a notice of cancellation being served is to rescind the agreement, or to constitute a revocation of any offer to enter into such agreement if the agreement has not yet been effected. Notice of cancellation shall be deemed to be served at the time when it is posted, if it is sent by post and addressed to a person specified in the first or second statutory copy of the agreement, or addressed to the owner or the owner's agent. Notice may alternatively be served on the owner or the owner's agent by other means than by post.

Consequences of cancellation. When the hirer exercises his right of cancellation he is under no obligation to deliver any goods in his possession to which the agreement relates except at his own premises and in pursuance of a written and signed request.[2] In the meantime, he is under an obligation to take reasonable care of them.[3] Any payment made by the hirer in pursuance of the agreement is recoverable by him and he has a lien over the goods in his possession until such sum is recovered.[4]

b) Under the CCA The draftsman of the CCA adopted this idea with enthusiasm, applying it across the much wider field of regulated agreements unless secured on land, and re-christening them 'cancellable agreements'.[5] The excessively complicated provisions run to several pages of statutory text.[6] Whilst agreements secured on land are never cancellable,[5] the debtor is instead given a special right of withdrawal.[7]

---

1 HPA, s. 11.
2 HPA, s. 13.
3 The obligation ceases if twenty-one days have elapsed since service of the notice of cancellation unless the hirer has within that time received a written and signed request for delivery and has unreasonably refused or failed to comply with it.
4 HPA, s. 14. There are provisions in s. 15 concerning the effect of the notice of cancellation where goods have been given in part-exchange.
5 CCA, ss. 67, 189 (1). For the duty to give notice of cancellation rights, see ibid, s. 64.
6 CCA, ss. 67–73. To come into force on a day to be appointed: ibid, Sch. 3, para. 13.
7 CCA, s. 58: see para. 12.06, ante.

---

d) DURING THE CURRENCY OF THE AGREEMENT

14.35   *a) Requirements as to information* At any time before the final payment has been made under a hire-purchase agreement, the hirer is entitled, by making a request in writing and on the payment of twelve and one half pence, to have the owner supply him with a copy of the agreement together with a statement containing certain particulars relating to the amounts paid, due, and to become payable under the agreement.[1] Failure by the owner to comply with this provision, without reasonable cause, and so long as the default continues, means that the agreement cannot be enforced against the hirer, nor can any contract of guarantee be enforced, nor can the owner enforce any right to recover the goods.[2] No security given by the hirer or by any guarantor is enforceable.[2] Conversely, if the agreement requires the hirer to keep the goods comprised in the agreement under his possession or control, the hirer must, on receipt of a request in writing from the owner, inform him where the goods are.[3] Under the CCA, similar provisions are to be found (except in non-commercial agreements[4]) as follows: in favour of the debtor or hirer, there are rather more sophisticated obligations to provide information,[5] breach being an offence[6] and also rendering the agreement unenforceable whilst the default continues;[7] whilst in favour of the creditor or owner, failure to provide the requisite information is simply an offence.[8]

b) *Appropriation of payments* Where a hirer has two or more hire-purchase agreements with the same owner and owes money at a given date on two or more of them, he may specify, when making a payment insufficient to satisfy his total debt, which debt he is paying.[9] If he does not so specify the payment must be appropriated by the owner in the proportion which the sums due at the time under each agreement bear to one another.[10] Similar provisions are to be found in the CCA.[11]

c) *Variation of agreement* Whilst there was no single provision dealing with the variation of agreements within the ambit of the HPA,[12] there is such a provision for regulated agreements within the CCA.[13] Furthermore the debtor is given the right to make a rebated early settlement.[14]

---

1 HPA, s. 21 (1), (3)–(5).
2 HPA, s. 21 (2).
3 HPA s. 24.
4 See para. 14.13, ante.
5 CCA, ss. 77–79. To come into force on a day to be appointed: ibid, Sch. 3, para. 17.
6 See further para. 14.19, ante.
7 CCA, ss. 77 (4), 78 (6), 79 (3).
8 CCA, s. 80; and see further para. 14.19, ante.
9 For the common law, see para. 7.17, ante.
10 HPA, s. 51.
11 CCA, s. 81. To come into force on a day to be appointed: Sch. 3, paras. 18 and 1.
12 For the common law, see para. 3.21, ante. For variation by court order on an application to recover protected goods, see para. 14.40, post.
13 CCA, s. 82: already in force.
14 CCA, ss. 94–97.

e) THE CONSUMER'S RIGHT TO TERMINATE

14.36   *a) Under the HPA*   At any time before the final payment under the agreement falls due, the hirer may determine the agreement by giving notice in writing to any person entitled or authorised to receive the sum payable under the agreement (frequently, the dealer).[1] The hirer's liability if he gives such notice, without prejudice to any liability already accrued, is to pay the amount if any by which one-half of the hire-purchase price exceeds the total of the sums paid and the sums due in respect of the hire-purchase price immediately before termination, or such lesser sum as may be specified in the agreement.[2] However, if the court is satisfied that a sum less than the amount by which one-half of the hire-purchase price exceeds the total of the sums paid and the sums due in respect of the hire-purchase price immediately before termination would be equal to the loss sustained by the owner in consequence of the termination, the court may make an order for the payment of that sum.[3] If the hirer has failed to take reasonable care of the goods, he is liable to pay damages for the failure.[4] Any provision in the agreement excluding or modifying the hirer's statutory right to terminate the agreement is void.[5]

b) Under the CCA   Similar provisions as to termination by the debtor are to be found in the CCA,[6] with an extension to conditional sales in respect of land.[7]

1 HPA, s. 27.
2 HPA, s. 28 (1).
3 HPA, s. 28 (2).
4 HPA, s. 28 (3).
5 HPA, s. 29 (2) (b).
6 CCA, ss. 99, 100, 102, 103. To come into force on day(s) to be appointed: ibid, Sch. 3, paras. 29, 30, 32.
7 See the definition of conditional sale (para. 14.02, ante); and see further para. 12.10, ante.

f) PRELIMINARY NOTICES BY OWNER

14.37   Without counterpart in the HPA, the CCA will require the creditor to serve preliminary notices before taking certain courses of action.[1] A hire-purchase agreement will normally provide expressly for, e.g. termination of the agreement in the following circumstances:

1) On default by the hirer. If the creditor wishes to take *any* of these courses of action[1] *by reason of any breach* by the debtor or hirer of a regulated agreement, the CCA will normally[2] require the service on the debtor or hirer of a preliminary seven-day notice[3] in due form:[4] if before the date specified for that purpose

in the default notice the debtor or hirer makes good the default, the breach shall be treated as not having occurred.[5]

2) In the absence of default, on the happening of specified events:

a) In so far as the death of the debtor or hirer is the specified event, the matter is subject to s. 86 of the CCA.[6]

b) On the happening of certain other specified events.[7] The CCA here divides the cases according to what action the creditor wishes to take:[8] where he wishes to terminate the agreement, he will normally[9] be required to serve a preliminary seven-day termination notice in due form;[10] but for certain lesser actions,[11] another form of notice will normally[12] be required in due form.[13]

In all cases, a creditor wishing to proceed following due service of a preliminary seven-day notice is *also* subject to the restrictions considered below.

---

1 These courses of action are listed para. 14.22, ante.
2 There are exceptions for overdrafts (CCA, s. 87 (2)), the crystallisation of floating charges (ibid, s. 87 (3): see further para. 17.09, post) and such cases as may be specified by Regulation (ibid, s. 87 (4)).
3 CCA, s. 87 (1). To come into force on a day to be appointed: Sch. 3, paras, 23, 35.
4 CCA, s. 88.
5 CCA, s. 89.
6 See para. 14.38, post.
7 What these are depends on the wording of the agreement: for examples, see para. 14.05, ante.
8 But in no case does the debtor have the right to retrieve the situation such as he has upon breach.
9 There are exceptions for overdrafts (CCA, s. 98 (2), (4)) and such cases as may be specified by Regulation (ibid, s. 98 (5)).
10 CCA, s. 98 (1), (3), (6). To come into force on a day to be appointed: Sch. 3, paras. 28 and 35.
11 These are: (a) demanding earlier payment, (b) recovering possession, or (c) treating any right conferred on the debtor as terminated, restricted or deferred.
12 There are exceptions for overdrafts (CCA, s. 76 (2), (4)) and such cases as may be specified by Regulation (ibid, s. 76 (5)).
13 CCA, s. 76 (1), (3), (6). To come into force on a day to be appointed: Sch. 3, para. 17.

---

g) DEATH OF CONSUMER

14.38 *a) Under the HPA* If a hire-purchase agreement provides that on the death of the hirer the agreement shall terminate or be terminable, or the owner shall have the right to recover possession, or any sum shall be payable or any right of the hirer shall cease to be exercisable or shall be restricted or postponed, it shall to that extent be void.[1] Detailed statutory provisions restrict the recovery of possession of goods after the hirer's death if one-third of the hire-purchase price has been paid or tendered before or after his death.[2]

b) Under the CCA, which makes a fresh start on this problem. Leaving aside bank current accounts and the situation where life assurance is built into a regulated transaction,[3] the CCA makes provision for the death of the debtor or hirer by drawing a distinction according to whether or not at the time of the death the regulated agreement was 'fully secured':[4] if so, the creditor or owner is not entitled *by reason of the death* to take any of the specified actions to realise his assets;[5] whereas, if the agreement is 'only partly secured or unsecured', he can take such actions, but only on a court order.[6]

---

1 HPA, s. 30.
2 HPA, Sch. 3.
3 CCA, s. 86 (3), (4), (5).
4 CCA, ss. 86, 128. To come into force on day(s) to be appointed: ibid, Sch. 3, paras. 22, 43.
5 CCA, s. 86 (1), (6). The specified prohibited actions are those which would normally require a default notice: as to which, see para. 14.37, post.
6 CCA, s. 86 (2). The court may make such order (ibid, s. 128), 'only if, the creditor or owner proves that he has been unable to satisfy himself that the present and future obligations of the debtor or hirer under the agreement are likely to be discharged'.

---

h) CONSUMER'S DEFAULT

14.39 *a) Under the HPA* The Act first avoids any contractual provision whereby the owner or any person acting on his behalf may enter premises for the purpose of taking possession of goods let under a hire-purchase agreement or that relieves the owner from any liability for such entry.[1] Also void is any provision whereby anyone acting on the owner's behalf in connection with the formation or conclusion of a hire-purchase agreement is deemed to be the agent of the hirer or whereby an owner is relieved from liability for the acts or defaults of anyone acting on his behalf in connection with the formation or conclusion of a hire-purchase agreement.[2]

However, where the agreement provides that it shall terminate or be terminable, or that the owner shall have the right to recover possession if the hirer defaults in the payment of one or more instalments, such 'specified consequences' will not follow on such default, unless a notice of default is served on the hirer (by post or otherwise), giving him at least seven days in which to make the payments due.[3] The 'specified consequences' will only follow if the notice is not complied with.

'Protected Goods.' Part III of the Hire-Purchase Act 1965 contains provisions restricting the owner's right to recover possession of goods when one-third of the hire-purchase price has been paid. By s. 33 the phrase 'protected goods' is used to describe goods where for the time being the following conditions are fulfilled:

1. That the goods have been let under a hire-purchase agreement;
2. That one-third of the hire-purchase price has been paid (whether in pursuance of a judgment or otherwise) or tendered by or on behalf of the hirer or a guarantor; and
3. That the hirer has not terminated the hire-purchase agreement or the bailment by virtue of any right vested in him.

The owner may not enforce any right to recover possession of 'protected goods' from the hirer otherwise than by court action.

Should the owner contravene this provision, the agreement determines, and the hirer and any guarantor are entitled to recover from the owner any sums paid under the agreement or contract of guarantee or under any security given in respect thereof.[4]

The action has to be commenced in the county court of the district where the hirer resides or carries on business or resided or carried on business at the date on which he last made a payment.[5] On the hearing of the action the court may:

1. Make an order for the specific delivery of all the goods to the owner; or
2. Make an order for the specific delivery of all the goods to the owner but postpone the operation of the order on condition that the hirer or any guarantor pays the unpaid balance of the hire-purchase price at such times and in such amounts as the court thinks just; or
3. Make an order for the specific delivery of a part of the goods to the owner and for the transfer to the hirer of the owner's title to the remainder of the goods.[6]

If the second type of order is made, i.e. a 'postponed order', the court may revoke the postponement or vary the conditions of the postponement at any time.[7]

If at any time the court has made an order for specific delivery of goods to the owner (including a 'postponed order') which has not been complied with and the owner has not recovered possession of all such goods, the owner may apply to the same court to revoke the order and instead to make an order for the payment of a sum equal to the balance of the outstanding payments subject to a discount for accelerated receipt.[8] Even if the owner has recovered possession, he may apply to the court for an order requiring the hirer to pay any instalments accrued due before the action for repossession was brought and for any sum payable under a valid minimum payment clause.[9]

---

1 HPA, s. 29 (2) (a).
2 HPA, s. 29 (2), (d) and (e).
3 HPA, s. 25. The Court of Appeal held in *Eshun v Moorgate Mercantile Co Ltd* that a notice was invalid if it failed to refer to the provision of the agreement under which the notice was given, did not specify the consequences of non-payment of arrears due, and failed to give the date of service of the notice: [1971] 2 All ER 402, [1971] 1 WLR 722, CA.
4 HPA, s. 34 (2). In *Mercantile Credit Co v Cross* [1965] 2 QB 205, [1964] 1 All ER 603, the Court of Appeal held that the owner does not contravene s. 34 if he serves the hirer with a termination notice telling the hirer to surrender possession of the goods and the hirer acquiesces by doing as he is asked. Nor is s. 34 contravened if the owner retakes possession after the hirer has abandoned the goods: *Bentinck v Cromwell Engineering Co* [1971] 1 QB 324, [1971] 1 All ER 33, CA.
5 HPA, s. 49 (1).
6 HPA, s. 35 (4).
7 HPA, s. 39.
8 HPA, s. 42.
9 HPA, s. 44. Such a clause is void if it subjects the hirer to a liability greater than that specified in s. 28. See para. 14.36, ante.

14.40   *b) Under the CCA*   The restrictions upon any contractual right of the creditor or owner to repossess goods let or sold under a regulated agreement are as follows:

1) An obligatory preliminary seven-day default notice, whereunder the debtor or hirer may remedy the default.[1]

2) Limitation on the recovery of goods or land[2] except with the permission of the debtor or hirer given at the time.[3] Section 92 (1) provides[4]—

> 'Except under an order of the court, the creditor or owner shall not be entitled to enter any premises to take possession of goods subject to a regulated hire-purchase agreement, regulated conditional sale agreement or regulated consumer hire agreement'.

Any contravention is actionable as a breach of statutory duty.[5]

3) In respect of 'protected goods',[6] the creditor is not entitled at any time before the debtor terminates the agreement[7] to recover possession of the goods from the *debtor* except on an order of the court.[8] Recovery of goods in contravention of this provision shall terminate the regulated h.p. or conditional sale agreement and:[9]

'the debtor shall be released from all liability under the agreement, and shall be entitled to recover from the creditor all sums paid by the debtor under the agreement'.

Where the creditor seeks repossession by court action, the court is empowered to make a Time Order,[10] or may instead make a Return Order or a Transfer Order[11]—with or without conditions.[12]

4) Against charging default interest.[13]

---

1 See para. 14. 37, ante.
2 For restrictions in respect of land, see s. 92 (2): and see further para. 12.10, ante.
3 Whilst an entry and repossession *clause* is void (CCA, s. 173 (1)), consent may be given at the time by the debtor or hirer (ibid, s. 173 (3)).
4 To come into force on a day to be appointed: CCA, Sch. 3, para. 25; and see para. 35.
5 CCA, s. 92 (3).
6 For the new definition of 'protected goods', see CCA s. 90. Note the special provisions for variation of agreements (ibid, s. 90 (4)) and death of the debtor (ibid, s. 90 (6)).
7 For termination of the agreement by the debtor, see para. 14.36 ante.
8 CCA, s. 90 (1), (5). To come into force on a day to be appointed: Sch. 3, para. 24. The debtor has adverse possession: ibid, s. 134.
9 CCA, s. 91 (b).
10 CCA, s. 129 (1) (c). For Time Orders, see para. 14.23, ante.
11 CCA, s. 133; see para. 14.24, ante.
12 Taking into account the power to impose conditions (CCA, s. 135), it is possible to make the equivalent of a postponed order under the HPA. Cf. The HPA Orders: para. 14.39, ante.
13 CCA, s. 93: see further para. 15.17, post.

---

i) GUARANTEES AND INDEMNITIES

14.41 *a) Under the HPA* A contract of guarantee relating to a hire-purchase agreement and any security given by such guarantor is not enforceable unless, within seven days of the making of the contract of guarantee or of the hire-purchase agreement, whichever is the later, there is delivered or sent to the guarantor a copy of the hire-purchase agreement and a copy of a note or memorandum of the contract of guarantee.[1] If a court is satisfied that failure to comply with this requirement has not prejudiced the guarantor and that it would be just and equitable to do so, the court may dispense with the requirement. A guarantor is given similar rights to require information to be provided as has the hirer.[2] For the purposes of these provisions and of other provisions in the Hire-Purchase Act, any contract made at the request (express or implied) of the hirer to *indemnify* the owner against any loss that he may incur under the hire-purchase agreement, is to be treated in the same way as a contract of guarantee.[3]

b) *Under the CCA* An entirely new system is created by the CCA.[4]

---

1 HPA, s. 22.
2 See para. 14.35, ante.
3 HPA, s. 58 (1).
4 CCA, ss. 105–113; and see paras. 16.14, et seq., post.

---

j) NEGOTIABLE INSTRUMENTS

14.42 Without counter-part in the HPA, the CCA forbids[1] the use of negotiable instruments,[2] *other than bank notes and cheques,*[3] to discharge any sum payable,[4] or as security therefor,[5]

    a) by the debtor or hirer under a regulated agreement, or
    b) by any person as surety in relation to the agreement;[6]

and it further forbids the negotiation of cheques for such purposes except to bankers.[7] The penalties for contravention are as follows: the regulated agreement or security therefor under which any sum is payable is enforceable only on a court order;[8] a person who takes any cheque or other negotiable instrument in contravention of this prohibition cannot be a holder in due course;[9] and, if the debtor or hirer becomes liable on such an instrument to a holder in due course, e.g. a banker, the creditor or owner shall indemnify the protected person in respect of that liability.[10] The object of these important provisions is to prevent circumvention of the consumer's statutory protections in lender credit by the use of the rule that the holder in due course takes free of the equities.[11]

---

1 There are savings for the following categories: non-commercial agreements (CCA, s. 123 (5)); international contracts (ibid, s. 123 (6)), as to which see paras. 13.39, et seq., ante.
2 For negotiable instruments, see generally post, chaps. 20, 21. Ss. 123–125 are to come into force on a date to be appointed: ibid, Sch. 3, para. 40.
3 For cheques and bank notes, see chap. 21, post.
4 CCA, s. 123 (1), (3).
5 See CCA, s. 123 (4).
6 CCA, ss. 105–113; and paras. 16.14, et seq., post.
7 CCA, s. 123 (2). For 'bankers', see para. 21.01, post.
8 CCA, s. 124.
9 CCA, s. 125 (1) and (2). For 'holders in due course', see para. 20.16, post.
10 CCA, s. 125 (3). But 'Nothing in this Act affects the rights of the holder in due course of any negotiable instrument': ibid, s. 125 (4).
11 For lender credit, see para. 14.10, ante.

Other instalment credit contracts

a) CREDIT SALE AGREEMENTS

14.43 Whilst the statutory definition of 'credit sale' under the HPA required that the price be payable by five or more instalments,[1] there is no such requirement under the CCA;[2] but in both cases the ambit of the statutory category is restricted by an upper financial limit and to non-corporate buyers.[3]

Under both the HPA and CCA, 'credit sales' (as respectively defined) are subject to restrictions as follows: in respect of seeking business,[4] entry into the agreement,[5] cancellation,[6] during the currency of the agreement,[7] guarantees and indemnities;[8] but, to save imposing burdens on the creditor out of all proportion to the amounts involved, the provisions as to entry and cancellation do not apply to small agreements,[9] Additionally, under the CCA, credit sales are subject to the requirements as to preliminary notices,[10] death of the buyer[11] and negotiable instruments.[12]

---

1 HPA, s. 1 (1).
2 See para. 14.02, ante.
3 See para. 14.14, ante. They amount to the provision of RU credit for a DCS agreement: see paras. 14.15, 14.18, ante.
4 The Advertisements (Hire-Purchase) Act 1967; the CCA, ss. 43–47. See paras. 14.31–14.32, ante.
5 HPA, ss. 5–9; CCA, ss. 55, 60–63. See para. 14.33, ante.
6 HPA, ss. 11–15; CCA, ss. 67–73. See para. 14.34, ante.
7 HPA, ss. 21, 24, 51; CCA, ss. 77, 81, 82, 94–97. See para. 14.35, ante.
8 HPA, ss. 22, 58 (1); CCA, ss. 105–113. See para. 14.41, ante, and paras. 16.14, et seq., post.
9 HPA, s. 2 (3) and (4); CCA, s. 74 (2). For 'small agreements' under the CCA, see para. 14.13, ante.
10 CCA, ss. 76, 89, 98. See para. 14.37, ante.
11 CCA, s. 86 (2): see para. 14.38, ante.
12 CCA, ss. 123–125: see para. 14.42, ante.

---

b) CONDITIONAL SALE AGREEMENTS

14.44 Whilst neither the HPA nor CCA statutory definitions of 'conditional sales' require the price to be payable by any particular number of instalments,[1] the CCA definition extends to sales of land.[2] In the case of both Acts, the ambit of the statutory category is restricted by an upper financial limit and to non-corporate buyers.[3]

Where a conditional sale agreement falls within the ambit of the Acts, it is subject to all the same statutory restrictions as a credit sale agreement. Additionally, the Acts have largely assimilated conditional sales with h.p. agreements where such agreements fall within their ambit. First, the Acts have provided that a buyer under a conditional sale is not one who has 'agreed to buy' for the purposes of the exception to the nemo dat rule.[4] Second, they have subjected such conditional sales to restrictions in respect of the death of the buyer[5] and on the buyer's default,[6] and granted the conditional buyer a statutory right of termination.[7]

---

1 See para. 14.02, ante.
2 For sales of land, see chap. 12, ante.
3 See para. 14.14, ante. They amount to the provision of RU credit for a DCS agreement.
4 HPA, s. 54; and the Factors Acts 1889, s. 9 and Sale of Goods Act 1893, s. 25 (2) (the last two as amended by Sch. 4 of the CCA). As to this rule, see para. 13.16, ante.
5 HPA, s. 30, and Sch. 3; CCA, ss. 86, 128. See para. 14.38, ante.
6 HPA, ss. 25, 29, 33, 34, 45; CCA, ss. 87–89, 90–93, 129–136. See para. 14.39, ante.
7 HPA, ss. 27, 28; CCA, ss. 99, 100, 102–103; see para. 14.36, ante. But not in respect of land: CCA, s. 99 (3).

---

c) CONSUMER HIRE AGREEMENTS

14.45 Whilst the HPA was inapplicable to simple hiring agreements, it has been explained above that the practice has developed of utilising such contracts to serve the same purpose as h.p. agreements;[1] and therefore, the CCA sought to control those agreements which it termed 'consumer hire agreements'.[2] Accordingly, the CCA has made applicable all the same restrictions as in the case of credit sales,[3] including all the judicial controls.[4] However, despite the incidence of ownership of goods let on hire, it was not possible to utilise the further rules in respect of conditional sales. Instead, the CCA introduced separate provisions as follows:

1. A right of termination is granted to the hirer.[5]
2. There is a financial relief for the hirer where the owner recovers possession of the goods to which the agreement relates.[6]

---

1 See para. 14.07, ante.
2 CCA, s. 15: see para. 14.14, ante.
3 As to which, see para. 14.43, ante. By way of exception, the provision as to supplying information to the hirer is to be found in the separate s. 79.
4 CCA, Part IX: see para. 14.22, ante.
5 CCA, s. 101. To come into force on a day to be appointed: Sch. 3, para. 31.
6 CCA, s. 132; set out in para. 14.24, ante: to come into force on a day to be appointed (Sch. 3, para. 43). Note that the rules against extortionate credit bargains (as to which, see para. 15.18, post) are not applicable to consumer hire agreements.

Lender credit transactions

14.46   Under some types of lender credit, the supplier of the goods is not in law a party to the contract whereunder the goods are supplied to the consumer;[1] and this state of affairs may operate harshly on the consumer where he was induced to enter the transaction by a misrepresentation by the supplier, though the common law had attempted to mitigate the difficulty by granting the consumer a right of action against the supplier either in the tort of negligence or under a collateral contract of warranty.[2] This, and further difficulties[3] arising from the fact that there were three parties involved in the transaction,[1] has led to the development of a number of statutory provisions.

1 For lender credit, see para. 14.10, ante. For transactions effected by unlicensed brokers, see para. 15.08, post.
2 *Andrews v Hopkinson* [1957] 1 QB 229, [1956] 3 All ER 422. Foll.; *Yeoman Credit Ltd v Odgers* [1962] 1 All ER 789, [1962] 1 WLR 215, CA.
3 The common law solved the problem of allowing the consumer to recover the deposit from the financier: *Branwhite v Worcester Works Finance Ltd* [1969] 1 AC 552, [1968] 3 All ER 104, HL.

a) DEEMED AGENCY

14.47   *a) Under the HPA* Any representations (whether constituting a condition or warranty or not) with respect to the goods to which a hire-purchase agreement relates, made to the hirer by the dealer who conducted the antecedent negotiations, are deemed to have been made by him as agent of the owner.[1] Such dealer is also deemed to be the owner's agent for the receiving of any notice of cancellation or notice of revocation of a customer's offer to enter into a hire-purchase agreement, or any notice given by a hirer, claiming to rescind the agreement, for example for misrepresentation.[2] Any contractual provision excluding or restricting these statutory provisions is void.[3]
b) Under the CCA there are similar provisions.[4]

1 HPA, s. 16.
2 HPA, ss. 12 (3) and 31.
3 HPA, s. 29 (3).
4 CCA, ss. 56 (2), (3); 57 (3); 69 (6); 102 (1); 173 (1); 175.

b) NEGOTIATIONS BY THE SUPPLIER

14.48   The deemed agency provisions were not sufficient to enable the consumer to plead the supplier's misrepresentations as against the financier in all forms of lender credit,[1] nor to permit him to exercise in all such circumstances his various statutory rights, e.g. of withdrawal, cancellation. The position would now appear to be adequately covered by s. 56 of the CCA, which is already in force.

The key to s. 56 is the wide definition of 'antecedent negotiations' as:[2]

'any negotiations with the debtor or hirer—
(a) conducted by the creditor or owner in relation to the making of any regulated agreement,[3] or
(b) conducted by a credit-broker in relation to the goods sold or proposed to be sold by the credit-broker to the creditor before forming the subject-matter of a debtor-creditor-supplier agreement within section 12 (a),[4] or
(c) conducted by the supplier in relation to a transaction financed or proposed to be financed by a debtor-creditor-supplier agreement within section 12 (b) or (c),[5]
and "negotiator" means the person by whom negotiations are so conducted with the debtor or hirer'.[6]

Moreover, such negotiations:[7]

'shall be taken to begin when the negotiator and the debtor or hirer first enter into communication (including communication by advertisement), and to include any representations made by the negotiator to the debtor or hirer and any other dealings between them'.

Building on this wide definition, s. 56 (2) provides that negotiations with the debtor which fall within s. 56 (1) shall be deemed to be conducted by the negotiator in the capacity of agent of the creditor as well as in his actual capacity.[8] Any attempt to avoid this provision is void.[9]

---

1 See para. 14.10, ante.
2 S. 56 (1); and see Sch. 2, examples 1, 2, 3, 4.
3 For regulated agreements, see paras. 14.13–14.14, ante. By s. 189 (1), a prospective creditor or owner are included. At common law, it will include servants and agents of these categories.
4 I.e. lender credit method (2): see para. 14.10, ante. For DCS agreements, see para. 14.18, ante.
5 I.e. the other forms of lender credit: see previous note.
6 At common law 'negotiator' will include his agents and servants.
7 S. 56 (4). Includes both contractual statements and misrepresentations, whether made by advertisement or otherwise: see s. 189 (1), 'representation'.
8 See also s. 75 of the CCA, para. 14.49, post.
9 S. 56 (3).

c) SHODDY GOODS

14.49 By reason of the deemed agency provisions and s. 56, the financier in a lender credit transaction would in some circumstances be liable for breaches of express or implied terms in the contract for the supply of the goods. However, one of the most contentious recommendations of the *Crowther Report* was that this should be the case in all lender credit transactions where the financier was 'connected with' the supplier;[1] and this view was adopted by s. 75 of the CCA, which is already in force. Section 75 (1) provides that:

'If the debtor under a debtor-creditor-supplier agreement falling within section 12 (b) or (c) has, in relation to a transaction financed by the agreement, any claim against the supplier in respect of misrepresentation or breach of contract, he shall have a like claim against the creditor who, with the supplier, shall accordingly be jointly and severally liable to the debtor'.

Where the financier is an original party to the contract for the supply of goods to the consumer,[2] s. 75 thus reinforces s. 56 in relation to the financier's liability (see ante); but for other lender credit situations s. 75 imposes a new liability to a 'like claim'.[3] Because it is recognised that the real fault in such cases will lie with the supplier, the Act allows the financier to have recourse to the supplier.[4] Moreover, by way of exception, s. 75 does not apply to a claim:[5]

'(a) under a non-commercial agreement,[6] or
(b) so far as the claim relates to any single item to which the supplier has attached a cash price not exceeding £30 or more than £10,000'.[7]

---

1 Cmnd. 4596 (1971), para. 6.6.24.
2 I.e. lender credit method (2): see para. 14.10, ante. For DCS agreements, see para. 14.18, ante.
3 The financier may utilise any defences available to the supplier. But the consumer is not limited to claiming damages: e.g. he may rescind, or sue in quasi-contract.
4 S. 75 (2), (5).
5 S. 75 (3). But if the creditor is himself a party to the supply contract, he will be liable on ordinary principles, e.g. for breach of implied terms.
6 See para. 14.13, ante.
7 The limits, which refers to the *cash* price will save many small transactions, e.g. credit or check card, and large industrial transactions, e.g. aircraft.

Chapter 15

Moneylending/debtor-creditor agreements

15.01 The subject-matter of this chapter is the legal regulation of the business of lending money, a matter which used to be governed by the Moneylenders Acts 1900–27, and is now to be governed by the Consumer Credit Act 1974 (CCA), the latter not yet being fully in force.[1]

---

1 See para. 14.11, ante.

---

1. Ambit of the legislation

The Moneylenders Acts

15.02 The expression 'moneylender' includes every person whose business is that of moneylending, or who advertises or announces himself or holds himself out in any way as carrying out that business.[1] However, the expression 'moneylender' does not include:

1. A pawnbroker;[2] or
2. A friendly society; or
3. Any person bona fide carrying on the business of banking or insurance[3]. A certificate given by the Department of Trade that a person can properly be treated as being a person bona fide carrying on the business of banking is conclusive evidence that he is so carrying on that business;[4] or
4. Any person bona fide carrying on any business not having for its primary object the lending of money, in the course of which and for the purposes whereof he lends money;[5] or
5. Any body corporate for the time being exempted from the Moneylenders Acts by order of the Department of Trade.

1 Moneylenders Act 1900, s. 6.
2 For exceptions, see para. 17.04, note 1, post.
3 For insurance, see post, chaps. 26, 27. For banking businesses see *United Dominions Trust Ltd v Kirkwood* [1966] 2 QB 431, [1966] 1 All ER 968, CA; and for bankers, see para. 21.01, post.
4 Moneylenders Act 1900, s. 6, as amended by the Companies Act 1967, s. 123. The Department of Trade's certificate may be revoked without prejudice to the effect of the certificate as respects any period before the revocation.
5 Moneylenders Act 1900, s. 6. Thus, a loan made for the purposes of the business of an issuing house is not governed by the Moneylenders Acts: *Frank H Wright (Constructions) Ltd v Frodoor* [1967] 1 All ER 433, [1967] 1 WLR 506. But it has been held that when a hire-purchase company made loans to dealers that were not linked to any hire-purchase transaction, the loans were governed by the Moneylenders Acts and as the provisions of these Acts had not been compiled with the loans were irrecoverable: *Premor Ltd v Shaw Bros* [1964] 2 All ER 583, [1964] 1 WLR 978, CA.

The Consumer Credit Act

15.03 The unwieldy definition above was aimed at catching only the transactions of the proverbial Shylock. However, the CCA has adopted a different approach, preferring to start by comprehending all persons who make a business of lending money, and then granting exemptions. This it does as follows: all loans to non-corporate borrowers within the upper financial limit are 'consumer credit agreements';[1] but they are not 'regulated agreements' if they are 'exempt',[2] and are saved from some provisions of the Act if they are 'non-commercial' or 'small' agreements.[3] Loans within the ambit of the CCA are further subject to the following (overlapping) classifications:

1. 'Restricted-use' (RU) or 'unrestricted-use' (UU) credit, depending on whether or not the debtor de facto acquires freedom to use the credit as he wishes;[4]
2. 'Debtor-creditor-supplier' (DCS) or 'debtor-creditor' (DC) agreement, depending on whether or not there is a pre-existing relationship between the financier and the supplier of the goods;[5]
3. 'credit-token' agreements, where, e.g. a credit card is used in connection with the provision of credit.[6]

Thus, the typical cash-loan which used to fall within the Moneylenders Acts will under the CCA be a DC agreement for UU credit. The types of control of such agreements under both the Moneylenders Acts and the CCA are as follows: (1) by way of licensing; and (2) transactional control.

1 See para. 14.14, ante.
2 CCA, s. 16: see para. 14.13, ante.

3 For 'non-commercial agreements', see s. 189 (1) of the CCA, and para. 14.13, ante. For 'small agreements', see s. 17 of the CCA, and para. 14.13, ante.
4 CCA, s. 11: see para. 14.15, ante.
5 CCA, ss. 12 and 13: see paras. 14.16–14.18, ante.
6 CCA, s. 14: see para. 14.15, ante.

2. Licensing

15.04   Both the Moneylenders Acts and the CCA—which has already replaced these Acts for this purpose—contained licensing provisions, but the CCA licensing provisions are wider in both the following respects:

1. A wider selection of those who make a business of lending money require a licence to do so; and
2. The CCA licensing system is administered centrally (as opposed to locally under the earlier Acts) by the Director General of Fair Trading (DG).[1]

In place of the unevenly administered Moneylenders Acts system, there is therefore an all-embracing, centrally and consistently administered CCA system.

1 See para. 14.19, ante.

The principles of the CCA licensing system

a) THE AMBIT OF THE SYSTEM
15.05   The principles of the licensing system are to be found in Part 3 of the CCA, apart from the special provisions for 'ancilliary credit businesses'.[1] Section 21 provides:

'(1) Subject to this section, a licence is required to carry on a consumer credit business or consumer hire business.
(2) A local authority does not need a licence to carry on a business.
(3) A body corporate empowered by a public general Act naming it to carry on a business does not need a licence to do so.'[2]

Leaving aside subsections (2) and (3), the ambit of the licensing system is thus restricted to those carrying on a consumer credit or consumer hire business, which is defined as any business so far as it comprises or relates to the provision of credit or hire under *regulated* 'consumer credit' or 'consumer hire' agreements.[3]

Accordingly, the licensing system is not applicable to creditors who:

1. provide credit only in excess of the financial limit stipulated in the Act and/or only to corporate borrowers; or
2. do not 'carry on a business' of the type referred to in s. 21, i.e., who only occasionally enter into transactions of that type.[4]

---

1 CCA, ss. 147–150. As to 'ancilliary credit businesses', see paras, 14.25 et seq., ante.
2 E.g. the Electricity Council or Gas Boards.
3 CCA, s. 189 (1), 'consumer credit business', 'consumer hire business'. For consumer credit and consumer hire agreements, see para. 14.14, ante.
4 CCA, s. 189 (2).

---

b) THE TYPES OF LICENCE

15.06 Where a business conducts activities which fall within the ambit of the licensing system, s. 22 (1) makes available the following two types of licence:

'(a) a standard licence, that is a licence, issued by the Director to a person named in the licence on an application made by him, which, during the prescribed period, covers such activities as are described in the licence, or
(b) a group licence, that is a licence, issued by the Director (whether on the application of any person or of his own motion), which, during such period as the Director thinks fit or, if he thinks fit, indefinitely, covers such persons and activities as are described in the licence'.

a) A standard licence The characteristics of a standard licence are as follows:

1. It is issued to a named person only. The licence does not authorise the licensee to carry on a business under any other than the specified name,[1] to do so being an offence.[2] In the case of a sole trader or registered company, the licence shall not be issued to more than one person;[3] and in the case of a partnership or other unincorporated body of persons, the licence shall be issued in the name of the partnership or body.[4]
2. It covers only the activities described. Where the licence is to carry on a particular type of business, it covers all lawful activities done in the course of that business, whether by the licensee or other persons on his behalf.[5] However, the Act allows that the licence may limit the activities it covers, whether by authorising the licensee to enter into certain types of agreement only, or in any other way;[6] and the DG has in fact specified seven different categories of business that may be applied for on a

driving-licence principle.[7] Additionally, there are the following limitations: first, whilst DC agreements may not be canvassed at all off trade premises,[8] DCS agreements may be so canvassed—but only if, and to the extent that, the licence specifically so provides;[9] and second, there is power by Regulation to specify other activities which may only be practised if covered by an express term of the licence.[10]

3. It is operative only for the prescribed period. It is envisaged that the normal standard licence will be granted for three years.[11]

b) A group licence   The Act lays down that:[12]

'the persons covered by a group licence may be described by general words, whether or not coupled with exclusion of named persons, or in any other way the Director thinks fit'.

Furthermore, a group licence differs from a standard licence in all the following ways: it does not *require* an individual application;[13] it cannot include a special licence to canvass DCS agreements off trade premises;[14] and it may be issued for an indefinite period of time. On issuing a group licence, the DG must give a 'general notice'.[15]

The Act envisages that a person may be covered by both a standard and a group licence, even in respect of the same activities.[16] Nevertheless the two types of licence are obviously designed for different sorts of situation; and it is clear that in the ordinary case a standard licence will be appropriate, for the Act provides that:[17]

'the Director may issue a group licence only if it appears to him that the public interest is better served by doing so than by obliging the persons concerned to apply separately for standard licences'.

Indeed, the group licence was designed as a sort of exemption category for these classes of persons or companies whose business activities occasionally came within the ambit of the Act, but where the DG felt it unnecessary to require every member of that class to have a standard licence. However, if a particular member of that class were engaged in a substantial amount of business within the Act, the DG could exclude him from the group licence and require him to apply for a standard licence. The point is this: the operation of the standard licence procedure will require considerable administrative effort; and by use of group licences the OFT will be able to reduce that burden, whilst leaving individuals within such groups still subject to the transactional controls.[18]

1 CCA, s. 24.
2 CCA, s. 39 (2); and see generally para. 14.19, ante.
3 CCA, s. 22 (3). Thus, even if operating under a franchise-name, each sole trader or company in the group requires a separate licence.
4 But where a change in the partnership results in a change in the partnership name, the licence shall cease to have effect: CCA, s. 36 (5).
5 CCA, s. 23 (1). E.g. servants or agents acting in the course of that business. But, where the debtor is introduced to the creditor by an unlicensed credit-broker, the agreement is enforceable against the debtor only where the DG so orders: ibid, s. 149 (1); and see para. 14.27, ante.
6 CCA, s. 23 (2).
7 The licence categories correspond to the categories of business as follows: (a) credit reference agency; (b) debt-collecting; (c) debt-adjusting; (d) debt-counselling; (e) consumer credit business; (f) consumer hire business; (g) credit brokerage.
8 CCA, s. 49: see para. 15.15, post.
9 CCA, s. 23 (2), i.e. knocker-men require a separate licence.
10 CCA, s. 23 (4).
11 For transitional provisions, see Sch. 3, para. 5 (2).
12 CCA, s. 22 (6). Group licences have been issued in respect of inter alia solicitors, liquidators, executors, administrators, trustees in bankruptcy, trustees, national CAB for all bureaux, Age Concern.
13 But if there is one, the licence shall be issued to that person: CCA, s. 22 (8).
14 CCA, s. 23 (3).
15 See the definition in CCA, s. 189 (1).
16 CCA, s. 22 (7).
17 CCA, s. 22 (5).
18 As to which, see paras. 15.13 et seq., post.

---

c) A TRADER'S RIGHTS AND DUTIES

15.07 Where a person carries on business activities which fall within the ambit of the licensing system and are not covered by a group licence, he is required to seek a standard licence in accordance with the rules discussed below.[1] However, the Act does not give him a right to a licence: s. 25 (1) stipulates that:

'A standard licence shall be granted on the application of any person if he satisfies the director that—
(a) he is a fit person to engage in activities covered by the licence and
(b) the name or names under which he applies to be licensed is or are not misleading or otherwise undesirable'.

Whilst the applicant who qualifies under these conditions[2] is expressed to have a *right* to a licence, this depends on his satisfying the DG that he does so: if the DG pronounces himself dissatisfied, this can probably only be attacked on the grounds that it is manifestly unreasonable.

The standard licence obtained by the successful applicant is clearly a very personal thing: it cannot be assigned, nor is it generally transmissible on death or in any other way;[3] but, whilst the licence generally terminates if the licensee dies, is adjudicated bankrupt or becomes a mental patient[4] regulations may be made to defer the termination for up to twelve months.[5]

---

1 See paras. 15.09 et seq., post.
2 Discussed para. 15.09, post.
3 CCA, s. 22 (2).
4 CCA, s. 37 (1). Or on the happening of some other event specified by Regulation: ibid, s. 37 (2).
5 CCA, s. 37 (3). Thus, there may be a 'holding period', during which the licensee's representative could himself apply for a standard licence should he wish to continue the business.

15.08   Where an unlicensed person carries on a business for which a group or standard licence is required, he commits an offence.[1] Furthermore, unless the DG orders to the contrary, most regulated agreements[2] made where the creditor or owner was unlicensed are unenforceable against the debtor or hirer;[3] that is, the contract still exists so that the capital sum cannot be claimed immediately, nor can the terms of the agreement be enforced.[4] A way out is offered to the unlicensed trader in that he (or his successors in title) may apply to the DG for an order that regulated agreements made by him during the unlicensed period are to be treated as if he had been licensed.[5] In considering such an application by an unlicensed trader, the DG is enjoined by the Act to consider, in addition to any other relevant factors:[6]

'(a) how far, if at all, debtors or hirers under regulated agreements made by the trader during that period were prejudiced by the trader's conduct,
(b) whether or not the Director would have been likely to grant a licence covering that period on an application by the trader, and
(c) the degree of culpability for the failure to obtain a licence'.

Nor is the DG limited simply to granting the requested order, being content to issue a warning, or to refuse an order[7] and prosecute: if he thinks fit, the DG may:[8]

'(a) limit the order to specified agreements, or agreements of a specified description or made at a specified time;
(b) make the order conditional on the doing of specified acts by the applicant'.

Where a person carrying on a business is licensed, the Act further provides for the control of the conduct of that business. Section 26 lays down that:[9]

'Regulations may be made as to the conduct by a licensee[10] of his business, and may in particular specify—

(a) the books and other records to be kept by him, and

(b) the information to be furnished by him to persons with whom he does business or seeks to do business, and the way it is to be furnished'.

---

1 S,. 49 (1); 147 (1); and see generally para. 14.19, ante.

2 Except 'non-commercial' agreements: as to which, see para. 14.13, ante.

3 CCA, s. 40 (1). Similary where the parties were introduced to one another by an unlicensed credit broker: ibid, s. 149. For credit brokers, see para. 14.27, ante.

4 A debtor or hirer may discover that his agreement is unenforceable via the publicity provisions considered, para. 15.12, post.

5 CCA, s. 40 (2).

6 CCA, s. 40 (4).

7 On refusal to grant an order, the usual appeal procedure is available (s. 40 (3)): see para. 15.11, post.

8 CCA, s. 40 (5).

9 See also CCA, s. 54: breach will be an offence (s. 167 (2)); and see further para. 14.19, ante. These regulations will overlap with the transactional controls on seeking business and entry into the agreement: as to which, see paras. 14.32, 14.33, ante.

10 Thus, an unlicensed trader cannot commit an offence hereunder.

The operation of the CCA licensing system

a) APPLICATIONS

15.09 Like any other application to the DG under the CCA, an application for a licence:[1]

'must be in writing, and in such form, and accompanied by such particulars, as the Director may specify by general notice, and must be accompanied by the specified fee'.

Furthermore, the DG has power to call for further and better particulars, and to require the information supplied to be verified,[2] and also to require the applicant to publicise details of his application:[3] the sanction is that:[4]

'An application to the Director under this Act is of no effect unless the requirements of this section are satisfied'.

As the Act stipulates that a standard licence may only be granted on application,[5] an invalid application[6] would therefore appear to invalidate the licence thereby obtained, so that the applicant will be operating as an unlicensed trader.

Once the DG has received a valid application, he shall only grant a licence if he is satisfied as to both the following matters:[7]

a) The applicant is a fit person   For this purpose, s. 25 (2) directs the DG to:

'have regard to any circumstances which appear to him to be relevant, and in particular to any evidence tending to show that the applicant, or any of the applicant's employees, agents or associates[8] (whether past or present) or, where the applicant is a body corporate, any person appearing to the Director to be a controller of the body corporate or an associate of any such person'

has engaged in any of the following activities: (a) offences of fraud or other dishonesty;[9] (b) contraventions of this or any other Act concerned with the provision of credit; (c) practised discrimination in his business; or (d) engaged in business practices appearing to the DG to be deceitful or oppressive, or otherwise unfair or improper (whether unlawful or not).[10]

b) The applicant's trading name is not misleading or undesirable[11]   Where the DG has received a valid application for a standard licence, he must record that application in the public register;[12] and he then has three choices: to grant the application as requested;[13] to refuse it absolutely; or to grant it in modified terms.[14] Unless the DG takes the first choice, the Act requires him to give reasons and invite representations.[15]

---

1 CCA, s. 6 (2).
2 CCA, s. 6 (3).
3 CCA, s. 6 (4).
4 CCA, s. 6 (1).
5 CCA, ss. 22 (1) (a); 25 (1).
6 E.g. by payment of the wrong fee.
7 CCA, s. 25 (1): set out para. 15.07, ante.
8 'Associate' includes 'business associate' (s. 25 (3)) and also the persons specified in the wide-ranging s. 184 of the CCA.
9 There is no restriction on how far back the DG can look for an offence.
10 E.g. persistently (a) selling credit to those who cannot afford it, (b) driving extortionate credit bargains, (c) using high-pressure sales techniques.
11 Cf. the Registration of Business Names Act 1916 (see para. 11.06 ante); s. 17 of the Companies Act 1948.
12 CCA, s. 35 (2).
13 Under CCA, s. 25 (1).
14 Under CCA, s. 27 (2). E.g. by way of the exercise of his powers under CCA, s. 23 (2) or (3): see para. 15.06, ante.
15 CCA, s. 27 (1). Similarly, where a named person is excluded from a group licence: ibid, s. 28.

---

b) RENEWAL, VARIATION ETC OF LICENCES

15.10   *a) Renewal*   Wherever a licence is granted for a limited period, application for its renewal may be made to the DG[1] by means of a valid application.[2] Generally speaking, all the previously discussed rules relating to first issue of a licence apply to renewals thereof.[3] Finally, in the event of an application for renewal not being granted:[4]

'the Director may give directions authorising a licensee to carry into effect agreements made by him before the expiry of the licence'.

b) Variation This may be made by request, or compulsorily. Where there is a valid application[2] to vary a standard licence, the DG may, if he thinks fit, grant the request;[5] and he has similar powers where an application to vary a group licence is made by the original applicant:[6] but on refusal, the disappointed applicant has similar rights to reasons and representations as on original application.[7] Alternatively, the DG is empowered to make a compulsory variation on the basis that:[8]

'if the licence had expired at that time, he would, on an application for its renewal or further renewal on the same terms (except as to expiry), have been minded to grant the application but on different terms'.

This power exists in relation to both standard[9] and group[10] licences; but such a compulsory variation shall not take effect before the end of the appeal period.[11] The DG has no power to validate agreements.

c) Suspension and revocation The DG has power to suspend or revoke any licence on the basis that he:[12]

'is of the opinion that if the licence had expired at that time he would have been minded not to renew it'.

Again there are safeguards similar to those on variation as to the period before the order takes effect,[13] but this time including a power to validate agreements.[14] The Act then makes some further provisions in respect of suspensions.[15]

---

1 CCA, s. 29 (1).
2 CCA, s. 6: see para. 15.09, ante. But the DG may also renew any group licence of his own motion: ibid, s. 29 (2).
3 CCA, s. 29 (3). But see ibid, s. 29 (4) and (6).
4 CCA, s. 29 (5).
5 CCA, s. 30 (1).
6 CCA, s. 30 (2), (3), (5).
7 CCA, s. 30 (4).
8 CCA, s. 31 (1).
9 CCA, s. 31 (2).
10 CCA, s. 31 (3), (4), (5), (6).
11 CCA, s. 31 (7): see further para. 15.11, post.
12 CCA, s. 32 (1).
13 CCA, s. 32 (2), (4), (6), (7).

14 CCA, s. 32 (5).
15 CCA, ss. 32 (8); 33.

c) APPEALS

15.11   Because the grant or refusal of a licence can affect a person's livelihood, the Act lays down a careful system of appeals, being especially lenient to persons already engaged in a business. Thus, in every case where the DG determines not to renew, to make a compulsory variation of, or to suspend or revoke a licence, the Act provides that the licence shall continue in force until the end of the 'appeal period';[1] but this is not the case where the application is to start a business.[2]

Where the DG indicates to the applicant/licensee that he is contemplating making a decision in regard to any of the foregoing matters that that person will not like,[3] s. 34 (1) provides that:

'the Director shall invite that person, within 21 days after the notice containing the invitation is given to him or published, or such longer period as the Director may allow—

(a) to submit his representations in writing to the Director, and

(b) to give notice to the Director, if he thinks fit, that he wishes to make representations orally'.

Taking into account those representations, the DG shall reach his determination,[4] and give notice thereof to the applicant/licensee.[5] Where that person is aggrieved by the final determination of the DG, he may appeal to the Secretary of State, the Act envisaging that the appeal will be heard by assessors on his behalf;[6] and in respect of points of law, a further appeal to the High Court is possible.[7]

The CCA is, however, silent on the participation of third parties, e.g. competitors or objectors, in this appellate process. Presumably, before he makes his final determination, the DG could invite or receive representations by third parties (possibly at an oral hearing); and on ordinary principles, a third party could apply to the High Court for a determination that the decision of the DG or Secretary of State was bad in law.[8] There is also the possibility of making an informal approach to the Secretary of State, requesting that he give 'specific directions' to the DG as to the carrying out of his functions.[9]

1 CCA, ss. 29 (4); 31 (7); 32 (7). For 'appeal period', see ibid, s. 189 (1).
2 For transitional provisions, see Sch. 3, para. 5 (2).
3 I.e. to refuse a standard licence in the terms of the application (CCA, s. 27 (1) (b)); to exclude any named person from a group licence (ibid, s. 28 (b)); to

refuse to renew a licence (ibid, s. 29 (3)); to make a compulsory variation (ibid, s. 31); to refuse an application to end a suspension (ibid, s. 33 (2) (b)), or by an unlicensed trader to enforce his agreements (ibid, ss. 29 (5), 32 (5)).
4 CCA, s. 34 (2).
5 CCA, s. 34 (3).
6 CCA, s. 41; and see S.I. 1976 No. 837.
7 CCA, s. 42.
8 See Goode *Consumer Credit Act 1974* ara. 5.61.
9 Under CCA, s. 2 (2).

d) PUBLICITY
15.12 To ensure adequate publicity for the administration of the licensing system, section 35 (1) provides as follows:

'The Director shall establish and maintain a register, in which he shall cause to be kept particulars of—
(a) applications not yet determined for the issue, variation or renewal of licences, or for ending the suspension of a licence;
(b) licences which are in force, or have at any time been suspended or revoked, with details of any variation of the terms of a licence;
(c) decisions given by him under this Act, and any appeal from those decisions; and
(d) such other matters (if any) as he thinks fit'.

As the Act requires traders to help the DG keep this register up to date,[1] it should provide a sort of current 'credit-driver's licence', available to the public.[2]

1 CCA, s. 36.
2 CCA, s. 35 (3).

3. Transactional control

15.13 Presently, the transactional control of moneylending contracts is to be found partly in the Moneylenders Acts 1900–27, and partly in the CCA; but, during the lifetime of this edition, the former should be completely superseded by the latter.[1] Many of the old Moneylenders Acts provisions are to be found (in new terminology[2]) in the CCA; and in such cases, the major change is likely to be that the provisions are applicable across a wider area.[3] Additionally, the CCA contains new provisions in respect of extortionate credit bargains and credit token agreements.[4]

1 See para. 14.11, ante. For transitional provisions, see the CCA Sch. 3. For the provisions and regulations for the time being in force, see para. 14.11, note 4, ante.
2 See paras. 14.13–14.28, ante.
3 See para. 15.03, ante.
4 See paras. 15.18, post, and 14.15, ante, respectively.

Restrictions on business

15.14 As a species of regulated consumer credit agreement,[1] the following types of provision of the CCA will, when in force, be applicable to moneylending contracts: as to cancellation;[2] preliminary notices;[3] death of the debtor;[4] misuse of credit facilities;[5] and security, whether by surety[6] or negotiable instrument.[7] Additionally, there are the old Moneylenders Acts' areas of control considered below.[8]

---

1 See para. 15.03, ante.
2 CCA, ss. 67–73: see para. 14.34, ante.
3 CCA, ss. 76, 87 (but not s. 98): see para. 14.37, ante.
4 CCA, s. 86 (2)—unsecured: see para. 14.38, ante.
5 CCA, ss. 83, 84.
6 CCA, ss. 105–113: see paras. 16.14 et seq., post.
7 CCA, ss. 123–125: see para. 14.42, ante.
8 Also still in force are: (a) the special rules as to limitation of actions (Moneylenders Act 1927, s. 13, as amended by the Limitation Act 1939, s. 34 (4)); and (b) the special rules for assignments of moneylenders' debts or security (Moneylenders Act 1927, ss. 8, 10, 17).

---

a) SEEKING BUSINESS

15.15 *a) Under the Moneylenders Acts* A moneylender must not issue any advertisement, circular or business letter which does not show his authorised name, or any document which implies that he carries on a banking business.[1] No person may send or deliver or cause to be sent or delivered any circular or other document to any person without his written request advertising the name, address or telephone number of a moneylender or containing an invitation to borrow money from a moneylender or to apply for information and advice as to so doing.[2] But newspaper advertisements and posters exhibited at an authorised address and limited to certain particulars are permitted.[3]

b) Under the CCA In due course, there will come into force the general provisions relating to the advertising of a consumer credit business which falls within s. 43,[4] and regulations may be made governing quotations, the display of information and the conduct of business.[5] However, already in force are the following provisions:

1) *Canvassing.* The CCA has replaced the previous prohibition on canvassing loans.[6] 'Canvassing' is carefully defined by s. 48 (1) as follows:

> 'An individual (the "canvasser") canvasses a regulated agreement off trade premises if he solicits the entry (as debtor or hirer) of another individual (the "consumer") into the agreement by making oral representations[7] to the consumer, or any other individual, during a visit by the canvasser to any place (not excluded by subsection (2)[8]) where the consumer, or that other individual, as the case may be, is, being a visit—
>
> (a) carried out for the purpose of making such oral representations to individuals who are at that place, but
>
> (b) not carried out in response to a request made on a previous occasion'.[9]

Section 49 (1) makes it an offence to canvass off trade premises any DC agreement other than an overdraft on an existing current account.[10] Moreover, even if the solicitation is 'carried out in response to a request made on a previous occasion', and therefore outside s. 49 (1), another offence is committed where the previous request was not in a signed writing.[11]

2) *Credit to minors.* Quite apart from the limitations contained in the law of contract on the making of loans to minors,[12] it was an offence to peddle loans to minors.[13] Section 50 (1) of the CCA now provides that:

> 'A person commits an offence who, with a view to financial gain, sends to a minor any document inviting him to—
>
> (a) borrow money, or
>
> (b) obtain goods on credit or hire,[14] or
>
> (c) obtain services on credit, or
>
> (d) apply for information or advice on borrowing money or otherwise obtaining credit, or hiring goods'.[14]

The offence here is *sending* a document;[15] but it is a defence for a person to prove that he did not know, and had no reasonable cause to suspect,[16] that the addressee was a minor.[17]

---

1 Moneylenders Act 1927, s. 4. This does not exempt the moneylender, if a company, from complying with s. 201 of the Companies Act 1948, or, if an individual or firm, with s. 18 of the Registration of Business Names Act 1916.

2 Moneylenders Act 1927, s. 5 (1).

3 Ibid, s. 5 (2).

4 See para. 14.32, ante.

5 CCA, ss. 52; 53; 54: breach will be an offence (s. 167 (2)); and see further para. 14.19, ante.
6 Moneylenders Act 1927, s. 5 (3).
7 'Representations' is widely defined by CCA, s. 189 (1).
8 S. 48 (2) excludes a place where a business is carried on (whether on a permanent or temporary basis) by (a) a creditor or owner, (b) a supplier, (c) the canvasser, his agent or employee, (d) the consumer.
9 E.g. a response to a reply-paid coupon, or to service an existing loan.
10 As determined by the DG: see further CCA, s. 49 (3) and (4).
11 CCA, s. 49 (2). For offences, see further para. 14.19, ante.
12 See para. 2.17, ante.
13 Under the Betting and Loans (Infants) Act 1892, ss. 2–4, now replaced by CCA, s. 50.
14 For consumer credit and consumer hire agreements, see para. 14.14, ante.
15 For offences, see para. 14.19, ante. *Handing over* a document to a minor is not such an offence, although it might be illegal canvassing.
16 He is deemed to have such reasonable cause if the document is knowingly sent by him at an educational establishment: CCA, s. 50 (3).
17 CCA, s. 50 (2).

---

b) ENTRY INTO THE AGREEMENT[1]

15.16 *a) Statement of interest rate* Under the Moneylenders Acts, if a document purports to indicate the terms of interest upon which a moneylender is willing to lend, it must either express the interest in terms of a rate per cent per annum, or show the rate per cent per annum represented by the interest proposed to be charged as calculated according to Schedule 1 of the 1927 Act:[2] a moneylending transaction brought about in contravention of this requirement is, generally speaking,[3] illegal, with the result that the loan cannot be enforced and any security must be restored.[4] Similar requirements may be embodied in regulations made under the CCA.[5]

b) Documentation Under the Moneylenders Acts, no money-lender's contract for repayment of money lent to a borrower or his agent or for payment of interest thereon and no security given by the borrower [6] or his agent in respect of such contract is enforceable unless:

1. A written memorandum of the contract is made and signed personally[7] by the borrower, and
2. A copy thereof is delivered to the borrower within seven days of the making of the contract.

The memorandum must contain all the terms of the contract, and must show the date when the money was lent, the amount of the principal,[8] and the interest charged[9] expressed in terms of a rate per cent per annum or the rate per cent per annum[10] represented by the interest charged as calculated by Schedule I of the 1927 Act.[11]

The omission or misstatement of a material term of the

contract will render it unenforceable;[12] but a composite document setting out all the terms of a contract may be a sufficient memorandum for this purpose, even though some of its provisions are obscure or ambiguous and require interpretation or construction by the court.[13] Moreover, even if the moneylending contract is unenforceable, the moneylender may still have some security: if, but only if,[14] it is a term of the loan agreement set out in the memorandum that the loan is to enable the borrower to extinguish a liability to a third party, the moneylender may be treated in equity as an assignee of that third party's rights against the borrower.[15]

If a loan is renewed by a substituted or varied agreement, which includes a promise by the borrower to pay the balance of the money previously lent to him, a memorandum of the new contract must be made and a copy sent to the borrower to render the transaction valid.[16] Where a contract is unenforceable against the borrower for non-compliance with s. 6 of the Moneylenders Act 1927, it is equally unenforceable against his surety.[16]

A memorandum is sufficient which merely contains a request to allocate a fresh advance to the settlement of an old loan;[17] but it is not sufficient if the memorandum does not state that payment of an old loan was a condition of the contract[18] or that a sum was paid out of a fresh advance to compensate the moneylender for an old loss which was only provable in the bankruptcy of the borrower.[19]

A bona fide compromise of a genuine dispute of fact whether or not a person is a moneylender is binding and enforceable.[20]

Similar requirements may be embodied in Regulations made under the CCA.[21]

c) Copies Without counter-part under the Moneylenders Acts, the CCA copies rules will be applicable.[22]

---

1 All the provisions of ss. 55–73 of the CCA dealt with in this paragraph are subject to s. 74 of the Act.
2 Moneylenders Act 1927, s. 5 (4).
3 But see ibid, s. 5 (6).
4 *Victorian Daylesford Syndicate Ltd v Dott* [1905] 2 Ch 624; *Bonnard v Dott* [1906] 1 Ch 740; and see generally para. 6.03, ante.
5 S. 55: see para. 14.33, ante.
6 *Argo Caribbean Group v Lewis* [1976] 2 Lloyd's Rep 289, CA; *Barclay v Prospect Mortgages* [1974] 2 All ER 672, [1974] 1 WLR 837.
7 If the borrower is a limited company, the memorandum may be signed on behalf of the company by any person acting under its authority and need not be under the seal of the company (*Re British Games Ltd* [1938] Ch. 240, [1938] 1 All ER 230).
8 I.e. the sum actually lent to the borrower.
9 See the 1927 Act, s. 15; and *Dunn Trust v Feetham* [1936] 1 KB 22, CA.

10 *London and Harrogate Securities v Pitts* [1976] 3 All ER 809. [1976] 1 WLR 1063, CA.
11 Moneylenders Act 1927, s. 6. The memorandum need not specify mere matters of machinery by which the terms are to be carried into effect: *Re 22 Albion Street, Westminster, Hanyet Securities Ltd v Mallet* [1968] 2 All ER 960, [1968] 1 WLR 18, CA.
12 *Orakpo v Manson Investments Ltd* [1978] AC 95, [1977] 3 All ER 1, HL.
13 *Holiday Credit v Erol* [1977] 2 All ER 696, [1977] 1 WLR 704, HL. See also *Reading Trust v Spero* [1930] 1 KB 492; *Mitchener v Equitable Investment Co* [1938] 2 KB 559, [1938] 1 All ER 303.
14 *Orakpo v Manson Investments Ltd* (above).
15 *Orakpo v Manson Investments Ltd* (above), obiter.
16 *Eldridge and Morris v Taylor*, [1931] 2 KB 416, CA; *Temperance Loan Fund v Rose* [1932] 2 KB 522, CA.
17 *Re BS Lyle Ltd v Chappell* [1932] 1 KB 691.
18 *Egan v Langham Investments* [1938] 1 KB 667, [1938] 1 All ER 193.
19 *Dunn Trust v Feetham* [1936] 1 KB 22.
20 *Binder v Alachouzos* [1972] 2 QB 151, [1972] 2 All ER 189, CA.
21 Ss. 60; 61: see para. 14.33, ante.
22 Ss. 62; 63; 180: see para. 14.33, ante.

---

c) DURING THE CURRENCY OF THE AGREEMENT

15.17 *a) Requirements as to information* A moneylender is bound on demand in writing by the borrower and tender of five pence for expenses, to supply information as to the state of the loan and also (if a reasonable sum is tendered for expenses) copies and documents relating thereto. If the moneylender fails without reasonable excuse to comply with such demand within a month he cannot, so long as the default continues, sue for any sum due under the contract and interest ceases to be chargeable in respect of the period of his default.[1]

Under the CCA are to be found rather more sophisticated requirements for the provision of information to the debtor under an agreement (unless non-commercial[2]) for fixed-sum or running-account credit.[3]

b) Prohibition of compound interest and certain charges It is illegal for a moneylender to charge compound interest, or for the rate or amount of interest to be increased by reason of any default in the payment of sums due under the contract; but he may charge simple interest on sums in respect of which default has been made at a rate not exceeding that payable on the principal apart from default.[4]

The CCA will likewise prohibit default interest;[5] but with regard to other interest rates it has a different approach.[6]

c) Fees Under the Moneylenders Acts, it is illegal for a moneylender to make any charge for negotiating or granting a loan, and if he does so the borrower or intending borrower may recover the amount charged as a debt, or set it off against the amount actually lent, which shall be deemed to be reduced accordingly.[7]

Where the apparent moneylender is in fact a broker, the CCA will severely limit his power to charge brokerage fees;[8] and where he is the actual lender, such amounts are likely to form part of the total charge for credit.[9]

---

1 Moneylenders Act 1927, s. 8.
2 See para. 14.13, ante.
3 Ss. 77; 78: see para. 14.35 A, ante. For running account and fixed sum credit, see para. 14.14, ante.
4 Moneylenders Act 1927, s. 7. In *Spector v Ageda* [1973] Ch 30, [1971] 3 All ER 417, it was *held* that a loan made by a solicitor to enable the borrower to discharge a debt incurred to a moneylender on which compound interest had been charged was itself illegal and irrecoverable. The solicitor knew the moneylender's loan was illegal.
5 S. 93. See further para. 15.18, note 11, post.
6 See para. 14.20, ante.
7 Moneylenders Act 1927, s. 12.
8 S. 155: see para. 14.27, ante.
9 Within the Regulations made under s. 20 of the CCA: see para. 14.20, ante.

Extortionate credit bargain

15.18   Since the abolition of the usury laws in 1854, moneylenders have been prima facie entitled to charge any rate of interest agreed upon. However, under the Moneylenders Acts it was provided that, if the interest charged exceeded a rate of 48% per annum, the transaction would be presumed harsh and unconscionable, and the court might reopen the transaction and give reasonable relief to the borrower. That protection has now been replaced and increased by the extortionate credit bargain provisions of the CCA (ss. 137– 140).

a) THE SCOPE OF THE PROVISIONS: CREDIT BARGAINS
According to s. 139 (1), the court may be invited to exercise its powers in this area in any of the following circumstances:

1. On an application made for the purpose by the debtor or any surety[1] in respect of a 'credit agreement';[2] or
2. At the instance of the debtor or surety[1] in respect of a 'credit agreement' in any proceedings to enforce that agreement or where the amounts due thereunder are relevant.

This power exists only in respect of 'credit agreements', which expression means;[3]

'any agreement between an individual (the "debtor") and any other person (the "creditor") by which the creditor provides the debtor with credit of any amount'.

It will therefore be noted that the extortionate credit provisions do not apply simply to agreements 'regulated' under the CCA: they do not apply at all to consumer hiring agreements;[4] but they do apply not only to all consumer credit agreements,[4] but also to those credit agreements made by non-corporate debtors where the credit-limit for that category is exceeded,[5] i.e. to all credit agreements of whatever value, and regardless of whether or not they are small or exempt agreements.[6]

However, in deciding whether to apply ss. 137–140, the court is allowed to look beyond the four corners of the 'credit agreement' to look at the whole of the 'credit bargain', this notion being defined as follows:[7]

'(i) where no transaction other than the credit agreement is to be taken into account in computing the total charge for credit,[8] means the credit agreement, or
(ii) where one or more other transactions are to be so taken into account,[8] means the credit agreement and those other transactions, taken together'.

This is primarily an anti-avoidance device: it prevents the creditor from avoiding ss. 137–140 by 'hiding' some of his charges in ancilliary agreements, e.g. maintenance or insurance contracts.

b) EXTORTIONATE CREDIT BARGAINS

Where any debtor or surety alleges that a credit bargain is 'extortionate', it is for the creditor to prove to the contrary.[9] According to s. 138 (1):

'A credit bargain is extortionate if it—
(a) requires the debtor or a relative[10] of his to make payments (whether unconditionally, or on certain contingencies[11]) which are grossly exorbitant, or
(b) otherwise grossly contravenes the ordinary principles of fair dealing'.

To help the court decide whether a credit bargain is grossly extortionate, the Act lays down a number of non-exhaustive[12] guidelines[13] as follows:

1. Interest rates prevailing at the time the credit bargain was made;[14]
2. The age, experience, business capacity and state of health of the debtor, together with the financial pressures on him;[15]
3. The degree of risk accepted by the creditor, his relationship

with the debtor, and whether a colourable cash price was quoted for any goods or services included in the credit bargain.[16]

c) THE NATURE OF THE RELIEF

If a court finds that a *credit bargain* is extortionate, it may re-open the *credit agreement* so as to do justice between the parties.[17] Whilst this process may not alter the effect of any judgment,[18] the court may:[19]

> 'for the purpose of relieving the debtor or a surety from payment of any sum in excess of that fairly due and reasonable,[20] by order—
> (a) direct accounts to be taken ... ,
> (b) set aside the whole or part of any obligation imposed on the debtor or a surety by the credit bargain or any related agreement,
> (c) require the creditor to repay the whole or part of any sum paid under the credit bargain or any related agreement by the debtor or a surety, whether paid to the creditor or any other person,
> (d) direct the return to the surety of any property provided for the purposes of the security, or
> (e) alter the terms of the credit agreement or any security instrument'.

Credit-token agreements

See para. 14.15, ante.

---

1 For sureties, see further chap. 16, post.
2 For the appropriate court to which application should be made, see CCA, s. 139 (5)–(7).
3 CCA, s. 137 (2) (a).
4 As to which, see para. 14.14, ante.
5 See s. 140.
6 For small and exempt agreements, see para. 14.13, ante.
7 S. 137 (2) (b).
8 For the computation of the total charge for credit, see para. 14.20, ante.
9 S. 171 (7)—however low the interest rate.
10 For the wide definition of 'relative', see s. 184.
11 E.g. including any provision for default interest: as to which, see s. 93; and para. 15.17, ante.
12 S. 138 (2) (c).
13 Most of these are based on decisions under the Moneylenders Acts.
14 S. 138 (2) (a). It would therefore appear safe to charge the prevailing market rate for a particular class of business.
15 S. 138 (2) (b), (3). For linked transactions, see s. 138 (5); and generally para. 14.15, ante.

16 S. 138 (2) (b), (4).
17 S. 137 (1).
18 S. 139 (4). This is to secure the finality of judgments, e.g. if there is a time order in force, application must be made for a variation thereof under s. 130 (6)—see para. 14.23, ante.
19 S. 139 (2).
20 Even where this places a burden on the creditor in respect of an unfair advantage enjoyed by another: s. 139 (3).

Part IV

Commercial securities

Chapter 16

Suretyship and guarantees

1. Nature and formation of the contract

16.01 A guarantee or contract of suretyship is an engagement to be collaterally answerable for the debt, default, or miscarriage of another person. A simple example is where, in consideration of B lending C £100, A agrees with B that if C does not repay the loan he (A) will repay it.

The assumption of *personal* liability is not an essential element of suretyship; one who merely charges his property to secure another's debt is a surety.[1] Such an agreement may be intended:

1. To secure the performance of something immediately connected with a business transaction, or
2. To secure the fidelity of a person about to be appointed to some employment, or
3. To secure one person from loss resulting from the torts of another;[2] or
4. To relate to numerous other matters.

In the present chapter it is proposed to deal with guarantees relating to business transactions only, where the guarantee will be given for consideration.[3] Unless the guarantee is given under seal, consideration will be required. However, as consideration need only move 'from the promisee' (B) and not necessarily 'to the promisor' (A),[4] the giving of credit to C will normally be sufficient consideration for A's promise.

---

1 *Re Conley* [1938] 2 All ER 127, where it was held that payment to a bank might amount to a fraudulent preference of a third person who had deposited documents of title to secure the overdraft.
2 See, e.g. *Kirkham v Marter* (1819) 2 B & Ald 613.
3 Entirely different principles may be applicable in respect of voluntary guarantees: see *Owen v Tate* [1976] QB 402, [1975] 2 All ER 129, CA.
4 See para. 4.01, n. 1, ante.

16.02   A contract to answer for the debt, default, or miscarriage of another is one within the unrepealed provisions of s. 4 of the Statute of Frauds, and is not enforceable by action unless it is evidenced by a written note or memorandum of the agreement signed by the party sought to be made liable under it.[1] The contents of a memorandum sufficient to satisfy the statute have been already stated;[2] and, whilst consideration is required, it is not necessary that the memorandum of a guarantee should contain any statement of that consideration.[3]

---

1 See para. 2.11, ante.
2 Paras. 2.12, 5.11, ante.
3 Mercantile Law Amendment Act 1856, s. 3.

16.03   At the outset, it should be borne in mind that the objectives achieved for a creditor by taking a guarantee may be similarly satisfied by the following other transactions:

a) Co-principals   Instead of making A guarantor of C's obligation to B, B may require that A become co-principal with C to the contract whereunder there arises the obligation to be 'guaranteed'. In such a case, the position is this: if it is genuinely intended that A be a co-principal, his obligations prima facie depend on the class of contract into which he has entered,[1] with the further issue of whether his liability is to be joint and/or several with C; but, if it was really intended that A sign as guarantor, then his liability will be that of a guarantor considered below.[2]

b) Indorsees   A form of transaction frequently used in commerce is that, instead of A entering a contract of guarantee, he is required to 'back' (indorse) a bill of exchange drawn by C in favour of B.[3] The effect of so doing is that A incurs the liabilities of an indorser to a holder in due course[4] or payee.[5] This form of transaction is particularly attractive to B in that he need not necessarily await payment, but may immediately negotiate C's bill—backed by A's signature—to a holder in due course (probably at a discount): whilst on normal principles, the holder in due course will take free of any equities which A or C may have against B,[6] this will not necessarily be the case where the bill was taken in discharge of a sum payable under a regulated agreement within the Consumer Credit Act 1974.[7]

c) Indemnifiers   Whilst as guarantor, A would only promise B to perform such obligations as C owes to B,[2] if A gives an indemnity he is promising to save B from loss, irrespective of the extent of C's liability;[8] and in the interpretation of such an indemnity, it has been decided that the courts will apply the same principles as they do to exclusion clauses.[9] The distinction between a guarantee and indemnity is important in law because, not only does the liability of A differ according to which he has given, but guarantees are within, whilst indemnities fall outside, the Statue of Frauds.[10] The issue of whether A's contract is one of guarantee or indemnity is also frequently a difficult one, turning on the intention of A and B.[11] However, where the agreement between B and C is a regulated one within the Consumer Credit Act 1974,[12] A's obligation to B will in all cases be treated as one of guarantee only.[13] Furthermore, the use of indemnities to limit product liability is restricted by the Unfair Contract Terms Act 1977, which provides that:[14]

'A person dealing as a consumer cannot by reference to any contract term be made to indemnify another person (whether a party to the contract or not) in respect of liability[15] that may be so incurred by the other for negligence or breach of contract, except in so far as the contract term satisfies the requirement or reasonableness'.

---

1 E.g. sale, hire, loan.
2 See para. 16.04, post.
3 For bills of exchange, see chap. 20. For payment by bill or cheque, see para. 7.16, ante.
4 Bills of Exchange Act 1882, s. 56: see para. 20.20, post.
5 *McDonald & Co v Nash & Co* [1924] AC 625, HL.
6 See para. 20.16, post.
7 Ss. 123–125: see para. 14.42, ante.
8 *Argo Caribbean Group v Lewis* [1976] 2 Lloyd's Rep 289, CA. Cf. contracts of insurance: see para. 26.02, post.
9 *Smith v South Wales Switchgear Ltd* [1978] 1 All ER 18, [1978] 1 WLR 165, HL(S). For the interpretation of exclusion clauses, see para. 3.16, ante.
10 For the Statute of Frauds, see para. 16.02, ante.
11 E.g. (a) indemnities—*Yeoman Credit Ltd v Latter* [1961] 2 All ER 294, [1961] 1 WLR 828, CA; *Goulston Discount Ltd v Clark* [1967] 2 QB 493, [1967] 1 All ER 61, CA; (b) guarantees—*Unity Finance Ltd v Woodcock* [1963] 2 All ER 270, [1963] 1 WLR 455, CA; *Western Credit Ltd v Alberry* [1964] 2 All ER 938, [1964] 1 WLR 945, CA.
12 As to which, see paras. 14.13–14.14, ante.
13 CCA, s. 113 (1): see para. 16.15 (v), post.
14 S. 4 (1). See generally para. 3.15, ante.
15 For that liability, see ibid, s. 4 (2).

The main features of a guarantee

16.04 The main features of a guarantee (as applied to business transactions) are as follows:
1) The contract of guarantee involves the existence of another

valid contract between B and C, one party to which (B) is a party to the contract of guarantee with A; and by that contract of guarantee, A guarantees to B that C will perform his obligations to B. Thus, prima facie[1] the liability of the guarantor (A) to B can be no greater than that of C to B. In *Coutts & Co v Browne-Lecky*:[2]

> A signed a guarantee in respect of the overdraft of his minor son. *Held:* the loan to the minor being void under the Infants Relief Act 1874 there was no debt which could be guaranteed and the guarantee was void.

Where a charge is provided by a company as security for a loan to finance the purchase of shares in the company and the company's obligations are guaranteed, since the charge is illegal under the Companies Act 1948, the guarantee is void too.[3]

2) If a contract is properly construed as a guarantee, the guarantor is under no liability whatsoever once the principal debtor has properly complied with all his obligations[4] or the contract is frustrated.

For this reason, in hire-purchase transactions, it is better from the finance company's point of view if the dealer who introduces a potential hirer agrees to indemnify the company against any loss the company may incur as a result of the hirer's default under the hire-purchase agreement rather than merely signs a contract of guarantee. Then, if the hirer exercises a contractual right to terminate the agreement, which may cause the finance company loss even when the payments the hirer has to make on exercising such right are taken into account, the loss can be recouped from the indemnifier.[5]

3) A guarantee contract is not a contract *uberrimae fidei* and, provided there is no undue influence[6] there is no obligation on the creditor to disclose material facts affecting the credit of the debtor or circumstances connected with the transaction which might make the guarantor's position more hazardous.[7] Thus, where a guarantee is given to secure an advance on a banking account, it is not incumbent on the banker, if he is not asked for information, to tell the surety that the account is already overdrawn.[8]

4) It is normally the surety's duty to see to it that the principal debtor pays or performs his own duty. In *Moschi v Lep Air Services Ltd*:[9]

> The appellant guaranteed performance by a company he controlled of its agreement to pay off its debts to the respondents by instalments. The company repudiated its agreement. The respondents accepted that repudiation and sued the appellant on his guarantee. *Held:* breach of the

debtor's obligations entailed a breach by the guarantor of his own contract as he was liable in damages to the same extent as the debtor—acceptance of the debtor's repudiation did not bring the guarantor's obligation to an end but transmuted it into an obligation to pay damages.

---

1 But see *First National Bank of Chicago v Moorgate Properties* [1975] CLY 1529, CA; *RD Harbottle (Mercantile) Ltd v National Westminster Bank* [1977] 2 All ER 862, [1977] 3 WLR 752.
2 [1947] KB 104, [1946] 2 All ER 207. Qy. whether the document might not have been construed as an indemnity and enforced as such as in *Yeoman Credit Ltd v Latter* [1961] 2 All ER 294; [1961] 1 WLR 828, CA.
3 *Heald v O'Connor* [1971] 2 All ER 1105, [1971] 1 WLR 497.
4 *Western Credit Ltd v Alberry* [1964] 2 All ER 938, [1964] 1 WLR 945, CA.
5 *Goulston Discount Co Ltd v Clark* [1967] 2 QB 493, [1967] 1 All ER 61, CA.
6 *Lloyds Bank v Bundy* [1975] QB 326, [1974] 3 All ER 757, CA: see further para. 5.16, ante.
7 *Trade Indemnity Co Ltd v Workington Harbour and Dock Board* [1937] AC 1, [1936] 1 All ER 454, HL; and see further *Chitty on Contract* (24th edn) vol II, para. 48.13. A fidelity guarantee contract is a contract *uberrimae fidei* so that failure by an employer to disclose to someone who gives a guarantee for the fidelity of a servant that the servant has been previously dishonest will entitle the guarantor to avoid liability; *London General Omnibus Co v Holloway* [1912] 2 KB 72, CA.
8 *Hamilton v Watson* (1885), 12 Cl & F 109, HL; *Cooper v National Provincial Bank Ltd* [1946] KB 1, [1945] 2 All ER 642.
9 [1973] AC 331, [1972] 2 All ER 393, HL.

Where writing not required

16.05 There are contracts for which no writing is required, which approach in characteristics closely to guarantees. The object of the contract must be regarded, and if the payment of another's debt is only involved as an incident of a larger purpose, that fact will not bring it within the Statute of Frauds.

Thus, if B sells goods to C, B generally has a right of lien over the goods, i.e. a right to retain possession of them until he is paid for them. Suppose C resells the goods to A and, in order to obtain possession of them, A orally promises B that if C does not pay for them he (A) will do so. A's promise is enforceable because made rather to protect his proprietary interest in the goods than to pay off another's debt.[1] Similarly, a *del credere* agent, an agent for sale who undertakes to pay if the buyer becomes insolvent, is liable on such undertaking even though it is not evidenced in writing.[2] On the other hand, a company shareholder who promises to pay off the company's debt in order to prevent the company's goods being taken in execution, he himself having no legal interest or charge over the goods, is only liable if there is evidence of his promise in writing.[3]

---

1 *Fitzgerald v Dressler* (1860) 7 CBNS 374.
2 *Sutton & Co v Grey* [1894] 1 QB 285, and para. 10.30, ante.
3 *Harburg India Rubber Comb Co v Martin* [1902] 1 KB 778.

---

2. Liability of the surety at common law

16.06 *The surety's liability* (which arises, as has been stated, only on the principal debtor's default) *is limited to the amount which the surety has undertaken to pay on such default.*

This may be the whole amount due to be paid by the principal debtor, or it may be something smaller beyond which it has been agreed that the surety's liability shall not extend.

If the guarantee is one which the surety has entered into jointly with others, he is still liable to pay the whole amount he has agreed to pay on the debtor's default, unless the wording of the guarantee otherwise provides. His right of contribution against co-sureties may be a partial indemnity, but he cannot, in the absence of agreement binding the creditor, compel the creditor to proceed against the other sureties.

It seems also that although the surety's liability arises only on the principal debtor's default,[1] the surety cannot insist that the creditor shall sue the debtor before resorting to him, even upon giving an indemnity against the cost and delay of such proceedings. The surety is not bound by any decision as to the liability of the debtor in actions to which he was not a party, and may insist (at his own risk as to costs) that the right of the creditor shall be proved against himself.[2]

Continuing Guarantee.[3] Upon the construction of the contract there is sometimes a question whether or not the guarantee is continuing, i.e. whether it is intended to continue until recalled, or whether it is to be confined to a single transaction or debt.

If A guarantees C to the extent of any goods he may purchase from B, not exceeding £150, he may mean to guarantee the money due on all C's purchases provided that the running account never exceeds £150;[4] or he may intend to guarantee C until he has obtained £150 worth of things, and then stop.[5]

Each case must be decided on the language of the document, and the presumed intention of the parties, for no definite rule can be drawn from the decisions.[6]

1 *Bache v Banque Vernes et Commerciale de Paris* (1973) 117 Sol Jo 483, CA ('conclusive evidence' clause).
2 *Re Kitchin Ex parte Young,* (1881) 17 ChD 668.
3 There are some special rules for discharge of a continuing guarantee: see para. 16.10 (6), post.
4 *Allnutt v Ashenden* (1843) 5 M & G 392.
5 *Wood v Priestner* (1867) LR 2 Ex Ch 66 at 282.
6 *Coles v Pack* (1870) LR 5 CP 65 at 70; *Wood v Priestner* (1867) LR 2 Exch 66 at 282.

3. Rights of the surety at common law

16.07 When he pays the debt he has the following rights:

A) *Against the principal debtor*

To recover, with interest,[1] from him all money properly paid when due[2] on account of the guarantee, provided, of course, that the debtor was a consenting party to the suretyship.[2]

Whether or not the costs of disputing the claim of the creditor can be recovered from the debtor, depends upon whether the expense of resistance to the claim was reasonably incurred; and it is advisable to inform the principal debtor of intended payment of the creditor's demand; this enables such defence to be set up as the debtor thinks fit, and prevents difficulties which might otherwise arise when the surety demands his indemnity from the principal.[3]

The surety is also entitled to enforce against the debtor the rights which the creditor enjoyed in regard to the debt in question.[4]

Moreover, a surety has the right *before* payment to compel the principal debtor to relieve him from liability by paying off the debt, if the debt is actually ascertained and due and the surety admits liability. In such a case it is not necessary to prove that the creditor has refused to exercise his rights to sue the principal debtor.[5]

1 *Petre v Duncombe* (1851) 20 LJQB 242.
2 *Exall v Partridge* (1799) 8 Term Rep at 310. The seizure and sale of the surety's property under execution for the debt will entitle the surety to sue the debtor (*Rodgers v Maw* (1846) 15 M & W 444).
3 *Duffield v Scott* (1789), 3 Term Rep 374.
4 See below. He may have larger rights than the creditor had. See *Badeley v Consolidated Bank* (1887) 34 ChD at 556.
5 *Ascherson v Tredegar Dry Dock etc Co Ltd* [1909] 2 Ch 401; *Thomas v Notts*

Incorporated Football Club Ltd [1972] Ch 596, [1972]1 All ER 1176; cf. *Morrison v Barking Chemicals Co Ltd* [1919] 2 Ch 325.

B) *Against the creditor*

16.08 To be placed in the position of the creditor as to all judgments,[1] securities given by the debtor, and other rights, e.g. rights of set off. If he is surety for part of the debt only, his rights to the securities also are but partial.[2] These may be used as against the debtor or co-sureties equally, but so that the latter can only be compelled to pay thereunder the proportionate shares to which they are liable.

As regards securities, Hall V-C in *Forbes v Jackson*,[3] said:

'The surety is entitled to have all the securities preserved for him, which were taken at the time of the suretyship, or, as I think it is now settled, subsequently. ... The principle is that the surety in effect bargains that the securities which the creditor takes shall be for him, if and when he shall be called upon to make any payment, and it is the duty of the creditor to keep the securities intact, not to give them up or to burden them with further advances.'

The creditor's priority, if he has any, passes also to the surety who pays the debt, e.g. a surety who paid a debt due to the Crown was held entitled to the Crown's priority, so far as was necessary for his indemnity.[4] By the Mercantile Law Amendment Act 1856, s. 5, the surety shall be entitled to have every judgment, deed or other security assigned to him, and shall be entitled to stand in the place of the creditor, and to use all the remedies,[5] including the name of the creditor, in any action against the debtor or any co-surety for the debt or a just proportion thereof[6] respectively.

---

1 *L.Lucas v Export Credits Guarantee Dept* [1974] 2 All ER 889, [1974] 1 WLR 909, HL (subject to the terms of the guarantee, see also para. 26.03, post). For export guarantees, see para. 13.44, ante.

2 *Goodwin v Gray (1874)* 22 WR 312. This right if the surety does not take from the creditor the right to surrender his security on the debtor's bankruptcy and prove as provided by the Bankruptcy Act 1914 (*Rainbow v Juggins* (1880) 5 QBD 138 at 122). A guarantor of a hire-purchase agreement does not acquire any interest in the property by payment (*Chatterton v Maclean* [1951] 1 All ER 761).

3 (1882) 19 ChD 615, 621. See also *Duncan, Fox & Co v North and South Wales Bank* (1881) 6 App Cas 1, HL.

4 *Re Lord Churchill* (1888) 39 ChD 174.

5 If the surety has not obtained an actual assignment of the judgment, he may still have the advantage of this section (*Re McMyn* (1886), 33 ChD 575).

6 He may sue or prove in bankruptcy for the total amount of the debt, but cannot actually get payment of more than his just proportion (*Re Parker* [1894] 3 Ch 400).

C) *Against co-sureties*

16.09 To contribution from them.[1] The right to contribution arises when two or more persons are sureties for the same principal and the same engagement although bound by different instruments, and although they became sureties in ignorance of the existence of another surety. If the principal makes default, all must contribute equally, if each is a surety to an equal amount, otherwise they must contribute in proportion to the amount for which each is a surety.[2] And in counting the number of sureties for this purpose, those unable to pay are not reckoned.[3] Thus:

> If A, B, and C are sureties for £1,200, and A pays the whole, he can claim £400 from B and £400 from C, or, according to equitable rules, if C is insolvent, A can claim £600 from B.

> But a surety who has paid cannot claim from his co-surety unless he has paid more than his proportion of the debt remaining due at the time of such payment, even though the co-surety has so far paid nothing; e.g.

> X owes a debt of £150 and this is guaranteed by four joint sureties; the liability of two sureties, A and B, is limited to £50 each and that of the other two sureties, C and D, is limited to £25 each. If £48 is due and payable and A pays the full £48 he is entitled to claim £16 from B and £8 each from C and D. But if A pays no more than £16 he has no claim to contribution from his co-sureties even if they pay nothing.[4]

Where there is one debt payable by instalments, a surety cannot call on a co-surety to contribute until he has paid more than his proportion of the entire debt, although he has paid more than his share of the part which has become due.[5]

The surety may (it seems) insist upon payment to the creditor of the co-surety's proportion, although he has not yet himself actually paid the creditor,[6] especially if judgment has been obtained against him.[7]

A co-surety is entitled to a share of every counter-security which has been delivered to any of the sureties, and such security must be brought into hotchpot in order that the ultimate burden may be equally divided.[8]

1 A surety is entitled to interest on the amount owing to him for contribution (*Hitchman v Stewart* (1855) 3 Drew. 271).
2 *Ellesmere Brewery Co v Cooper* [1896] 1 QB 75; 1 Com. Cas. 210.
3 *Re Snowdon* (1881) 17 ChD 44, CA; *Davies v Humphries* (1840) 6 M & W, at 168.
4 *Ellesmere Brewery Co v Cooper* [1896] 1 QB at 80; 1 Com Cas., at 212.
5 *Stirling v Burdett* [1911] 2 Ch 418.
6 Per James LJ in *Re Snowdon* (1881) 17 ChD at 47.
7 *Wolmershausen v Gullick* [1893] 2 Ch 514. For this purpose an admitted claim in an administration action is equivalent to judgment (ibid).
8 *Steel v Dixon* (1881) 17 ChD 825.

---

4. Discharge of the surety at common law

16.10 The surety will be discharged on any of the grounds which suffice to put an end to contracts in general,[1] and also on the following, which are peculiar to guarantees:[2]
1) If the creditor has altered the terms of the contract guaranteed without the assent of the surety. As Cotton LJ said in 1878:

> 'The true rule in my opinion is, that if there is any agreement between the principals with reference to the contract guaranteed, the surety ought to be consulted, and that if he has not consented to the alteration, although in cases where it is without inquiry evident that the alteration is unsubstantial, or that it cannot be otherwise than benefical to the surety, the surety may not be discharged; yet, that if it is not self-evident that the alteration is unsubstantial, or one which cannot be prejudicial to the surety, the court will not, in an action against the surety, go into an inquiry as to the effect of the alteration ... but will hold that in such a case the surety himself must be the sole judge whether or not he will consent to remain liable ... and that if he has not so consented he will be discharged.'[3]

In *Polak v Everett*,[4] Quain J said:

> 'The contract of the surety should not be altered without his consent, and the creditor should not undertake to alter the contract, and then say, "Although the contract has been altered, and I put it out of my power to carry it out by my voluntary act, I now offer you an equivalent." '

Acceptance by the creditor of the debtor's wrongful repudiation of his obligations is not in any sense a variation of the contract.[5]
2) Giving time to the principal debtor will, except in certain cases, release the surety, provided that there is a *binding contract* with the debtor (express or implied, written or verbal)

to give time, and not merely a forbearance by the creditor to enforce his rights.[6] Thus, in *Midland Motor Showrooms v Newman*:[7]

The parties to a hire-purchase agreement made a later agreement by which the hirer was given more time to pay off an instalment then due. *Held:* the guarantor of the hire-purchase agreement was discharged.

To this there is an important exception, since a surety is not released by an agreement to give time to the debtor if the creditor expressly reserves his rights against the surety. The reasons why the reservation by the creditor of his rights against the surety does not relearee the surety are that:

(i) it rebuts the implication that there was any intention to discharge the surety, and

(ii) the principal debtor, by consenting to this reservation, impliedly agrees that the surety shall have recourse against him; so that in effect the rights of the surety are not impaired, and he may, notwithstanding the agreement, pay the creditor and enforce his rights against the debtor.[8]

After the creditor has obtained judgment against both the principal and the surety, a binding agreement to give time to the former does not release the surety; the judgment creates a new liability in respect of which the judgment debtors are in the same postion.[9]

3) If the creditor gives up any security in respect of the debt or takes a new security from the debtor in lieu of the original security or of such kind as to operate by way of merger of the old security.[10]

4) A further ground of discharge is:

(i) the negligence[11] of the creditor in his dealings with the debtor,[12] or

(ii) misuse of securities held by him for the debt resulting in detriment to the surety, so that the surety's remedies are affected.

But mere passive acquiescence by the creditor in acts which are contrary to the conditions of a bond will not relieve the sureties.[13]

5) The absolute discharge of the principal is the discharge of the surety.[14] But a covenant entered into between debtor and creditor that the latter will not sue the former, with a reservation of rights against the surety, will not release the surety.[15] And an agreement which purports to release the debtor, but which reserves the rights against the sureties, will, in general, be construed merely as a covenant not to sue the debtor.[16]

When the creditor releases one of two or more sureties who

have contracted jointly or jointly and severally, the others are discharged because the creditor has broken his contract with them. But where a surety contracts severally he is discharged when the creditor releases another surety only if he can establish that he is thereby deprived of the equitable remedy of claiming contribution which even a several surety has against another surety.[17]

6) Death of a surety will, if the consideration be divisible, revoke a continuing guarantee, and his estate is not liable thereon for advances made subsequently to and with notice of the death,[18] but on a joint and several continuing guarantee, the death of one surety does not per se release his co-sureties.[19] Nor, if the consideration for the guarantee has been given once and for all, will the death of the surety release his estate from future liability under the guarantee;[20] and if any notice is required to revoke a continuing guarantee, mere knowledge of the surety's death is not sufficient to determine the liability.[21]

7) If the undertaking to become surety be entered into on the faith that another shall also become a surety, and that other refuses to, or for any other reason does not, join in the guarantee, those who have already executed it are entitled to consider their liability at an end.[22] Similarly, if a number of persons agree to be co-sureties for definite amounts and the creditor permits one surety to sign for a smaller amount without his co-sureties consenting, all the co-sureties (including the one who effected the alteration) are discharged.[23]

8) Whether a guarantee may be revoked by the surety depends upon circumstances, but speaking generally, it may be said that if the consideration for the guarantee has been given once and for all, the guarantee is irrevocable save by mutual consent;[23] if it be a continuing guarantee and the consideration is divisible, it may, as regards future transactions, be revoked by notice.[24]

Whether, in the absence of express stipulation, a guarantee given to secure the fidelity of a servant can be revoked, is open to question; it seems that in such a case the revocation cannot be immediate and probably a notice sufficient to enable the employment to be lawfully determined would at least be required.[25]

9) Prima facie, a continuing guarantee of a partnership is revoked as to the future by any change in the constitution of the firm.[26]

10) Neither the discharge in bankruptcy of the principal debtor, nor the acceptance of an arrangement by his creditors, will operate to discharge sureties for his debts.[27]

1 See chap. 8.
2 The contract of suretyship may, however, contain special clauses excluding the ordinary rights of a surety. See, for example, *Perry v National Provincial Bank of England* [1910] 1 Ch at 470.
3 *Holme v Brunskill* (1878) 3 QBD 495 at 505, followed in *National Bank of Nigeria Ltd v Oba M/S Awolesi* [1964] 1 WLR 1311.
4 (1876) 1 QBD 669 at 677. See also *In Re Darwen and Pearce* [1927] 1 Ch 176.
5 *Moschi v Lep Air Services Ltd* [1973] AC 331, [1972] 2 All ER 393, HL.
6 *Samuell v Howarth* (1817) 3 Mer. 272 at 278.
7 [1929] 2 KB 256, CA.
8 *Kearsley v Cole* (1847) 16 M & W 128 at 135.
9 *Re A Debtor* [1913] 3 KB 11.
10 *Boaler v Mayor* (1865) 19 CBNS 76; *Dowling v Ditanda* (1975) 236 Estates Gazette 485.
11 *Carter v White* (1884) 25 ChD at 670.
12 *Wulff and Billing v Jay* (1872) LR 7 QB 756.
13 *Mayor of Durham v Fowler* (1889) 22 QBD 394, where all the cases are considered; and see *Black v Ottoman Bank* (1862) 15 Moo PC 472.
14 *Commercial Bank of Tasmania v Jones*, [1893] AC at 316; cf. *Perry v National Provincial Bank of England* [1910] 1 Ch 464.
15 *Price v Barker* (1855) 4 E & B 760.
16 Lord Hatherley in *Green v Wynn* (1869), LR 4 Ch at 204, 206.
17 *Ward v National Bank of New Zealand* (1883) 8 App Cas 755.
18 *Coulthart v Clementson* (1880) 5 QBD 42.
19 *Beckett v Addyman* (1882) 9 QBD 783. For continuing guarantees generally see para. 16.06, ante; and for partnerships see infra.
20 *Lloyd's v Harper* (1881) 16 ChD 290.
21 *Re Crace* [1902] 1 Ch 733.
22 *Ward v National Bank of New Zealand* (1883) 8 App Cas 755; *Ellesmere Brewery Co v Cooper* [1896] 1 QB 75.
23 *Lloyd's v Harper* (1881) 16 ChD 290. See para. 8.01, ante.
24 *Coulthart v Clementson* (1880) 5 QBD 42. See para. 16.06, ante.
25 *Re Crace* [1902] 1 Ch 733.
26 Partnership Act 1890, s. 18: see para. 11.11, ante.
27 Bankruptcy Act 1914, ss. 16 (20), 28 (4): see generally paras. 33.11, 33.48, post.

Limitations of actions

16.11   Time begins to run in favour of the surety when the cause of action is complete. Generally where there is a present debt and an agreement to pay 'on demand', a request for payment is not a condition precedent to the right to sue;[1] but in the case of a surety, the debt is considered to be collateral, and if his promise is to pay on demand, no right of action accrues against him, until a demand for payment has been made.[2]

1 *Norton v Ellam* (1837) 2 M & W 461.
2 *Bradford Old Bank v Sutcliffe* [1918] 2 KB 833.

5. Instalment credit transactions

16.12 Where a contract of suretyship is entered into in respect of an instalment credit or moneylending contract[1] falling within the ambit of the legislation controlling such contracts in favour of consumers,[2] that legislation likewise takes steps to protect sureties of the consumer's obligations. As the object of these provisions is to prevent suppliers and financiers from avoiding the protections by having recourse to sureties who are relatives or friends of the consumer, the provisions are limited to sureties introduced by the consumer: trade sureties of instalment credit transactions remain outside these provisions and subject to the general rules previously considered.

---

1 For instalment credit contracts, see paras. 14.02–14.07, 15.03, ante.
2 For the ambit of the legislation, see paras. 14.13, 14.14, 15.03, ante.

The legislation presently in force[1]

16.13 Presently, the protections available for a surety introduced by the consumer depend on the classification of the consumer's contract. If that contract is a credit sale, conditional sale or h.p. agreement within the ambit of the Hire Purchase Acts, the surety enjoys the protection of those Acts.[2] Whereas if there is a moneylending contract within the Moneylenders Acts 1900–27, the surety must look to those Acts for his protection.[3]

---

1 For the dates when the relevant CCA provisions come into force, see para. 14.11, note 4, ante.
2 See para. 14.41, ante.
3 See para. 15.14, et seq., ante.

Consumer Credit Act 1974

16.14 The Act defines 'security' in very wide terms:[1]

'in relation to an actual or prospective consumer credit agreement[2] or consumer hire agreement,[2] or any linked transaction,[3] means a mortgage, charge, pledge, bond, debenture, indemnity, guarantee, bill, note or other right provided by the debtor or hirer, or at his request (express or implied), to secure the carrying out of the obligations of the debtor or hirer under the agreement'.

However, whilst Part VIII of the Consumer Credit Act (CCA) purports to deal with this very wide notion of security, its general effect is likely to be much narrower: leaving aside pledges,[4] it largely ignores real security;[5] and, apart from negotiable instruments,[6] it will have comparatively little effect on security provided by the debtor or hirer. Thus, in practice ss. 105–113 are chiefly concerned with guarantees and indemnities given at the express or implied request of the debtor or hirer under a regulated agreement.[7]

---

1 CCA, s. 189 (1).
2 See para. 14.14, ante.
3 See para. 14.15, ante.
4 CCA, ss. 114–122: see para. 17.04, post.
5 I.e. the granting of rights over property by way of security: see para. 17.01, post. It is envisaged that the granting of proprietary rights by way of security be the subject of a separate enactment: see para. 17.06, post.
6 CCA, ss. 123–125: see para. 14.42, ante.
7 See paras. 14.13, 14.14, ante.

16.15   The types of protection offered by the CCA are as follows:

i) Entry into the agreement
Section 105 requires that any security provided in relation to a regulated agreement[1] otherwise than by the debtor or hirer shall be in writing;[2] and the Act terms this a 'security agreement'.[3] The CCA then provides that security agreements must comply with the following requirements:
1) Regulations may prescribe the form and content of the security agreement in much the same manner as for the regulated agreement itself, contravention rendering the security instrument improperly executed;[4] and
2) a security agreement is not properly executed unless the surety is provided with a copy of *both* the regulated and security agreements.[5] The penalty for failure to comply with these rules is that the security, so far as provided in relation to a regulated agreement, is enforceable against a surety on an order of the court only;[6] and, where the court refuses such an order on other than technical grounds, it is an "ineffective security".[7] Generally speaking,[8] where there is an ineffective security, s. 106 provides that:

'(a) the security, so far as it is so provided, shall be treated as never having effect;

(b) any property lodged with the creditor or owner solely for the purposes of the security as so provided shall be returned by him forthwith;

(c) the creditor or owner shall take any necessary action to remove or cancel an entry in any register, so far as the entry relates to the security as so provided; and

(d) any amount received by the creditor or owner on realisation of the security shall, so far as it is referable to the agreement, be repaid to the surety'.

ii) During the currency of the agreement

The CCA gives the surety a right to obtain information from the creditor which is virtually identical with the rights of the debtor in this respect;[9] and it additionally entitles the debtor to call for a copy of the security agreement.[10] Furthermore, the surety can always take advantage of the extortionate credit bargain provisions.[11]

iii) Preliminary notices

Presumably so that the surety may have some hope of influencing events rather than being the prisoner of them, the CCA entitles the surety to receive a copy of any of the preliminary notices which the Act requires to be served on the debtor, breach making the security agreement enforceable on an order of the court only.[12]

iv) Realisation of securities

Subject to the special rules for pledges,[13] and land mortgages[14] and with the exception of non-commercial agreements,[15] s. 112 enables regulations to be made providing for:

'any matters relating to the sale or other realisation, by the creditor or owner, of property over which any right has been provided by way of security in relation to an actual or prospective regulated agreement'.

v) Evasion of the Act by use of security

Section 113 is designed to ensure that the creditor cannot, by enforcing any security, evade any of the restrictions imposed by the Act in favour of consumers: were it not for this section, the creditor could simply make full recovery under a contract of indemnity from a friend or relative of the debtor or hirer, leaving the friend or relative to have recourse on common law principles to the debtor or hirer.[16] Section 113 therefore imposes the following restrictions:

1) As a general principle:

'Where a security is provided in relation to an actual or prospective regulated agreement,[17] the security shall not be enforced so as to benefit the creditor or owner, directly or indirectly, to an extent greater (whether as respects the amount of any payment or the time or manner of its being made) than would be the case if the security were not provided and any obligations of the debtor or hirer, or his relative, under or in relation to the agreement were carried out to the extent (if any) to which they would be enforced under this Act'.

Thus, on termination of a regulated agreement by the consumer, the creditor cannot recover more from the surety than is allowable under s. 100.[18] The Act further states that, where a regulated agreement is enforceable only on an order of the court or the Director, any security is only enforceable where such an order has been made.[19] Moreover, by reason of the definition of 'security',[20] the general principle will prevent a creditor from obtaining greater rights under a contract of indemnity than he would have had under a contract of guarantee—the latter's liabilities being no greater than those of the debtor or hirer;[21] but, by way of exception, where the debtor or hirer is a minor or otherwise not of full capacity,[22] the surety agreement shall be treated as if it were a guarantee of a regulated agreement by a person of full capacity.[23]

2) Section 106 shall apply to render any security ineffective[24] in any of the following circumstances:[25]

a) The regulated agreement to which it relates is cancelled,[26] or is terminated after the creditor has repossessed protected goods[27]

b) On dismissal (except on technical grounds only) of any of the following applications: by an unlicensed trader to enforce a regulated agreement;[28] or where the creditor was introduced by an unlicensed credit-broker;[29] or where the agreement has been improperly executed;[30] or where a creditor or owner has wrongfully taken a negotiable instrument.[31]

c) The court makes a declaration in refusing an enforcement order.[32]

---

1 See paras. 14.13, 14.14, ante.
2 CCA, s. 105 (1), (6).
3 CCA, ss. 105 (2); 189 (1).
4 CCA, s. 105 (2), (3), (4). For the documentation rules in relation to regulated agreements, see para. 14.33, ante.
5 CCA, s. 105 (4) (d), (5). For the copies rules in relation to regulated agreements, see para. 14.33, ante.
6 CCA, s. 105 (7). For enforcement orders, see s. 127: see para. 14.22, ante.

7 CCA, s. 105 (8).
8 Except for registered charges on land: CCA, s. 177; and for mortgages of land, see paras. 12.09 et seq., ante.
9 CCA, ss. 107–109 (similarly, they do not apply to non-commercial agreements). For the rights of the debtor to information, see paras. 14.35 A, 15.17, ante.
10 CCA, s. 110.
11 CCA, ss. 137–140: see para. 15.18, ante.
12 CCA, s. 111. For enforcement orders, see s. 127: see para. 14.22, ante.
13 See para. 17.04, post.
14 CCA, s. 126: see para. 12.10, ante.
15 See para. 14.13, ante.
16 See para. 16.07, ante.
17 Or linked transaction: CCA, s. 113 (8). For linked transactions, see para. 14.15, ante.
18 See para. 14.36, ante.
19 CCA, s. 113 (2).
20 See para. 16.14, ante.
21 See para. 16.04, ante.
22 For contractual capacity, see paras. 2.15 et seq., ante.
23 CCA, s. 113 (7).
24 See supra.
25 CCA, s. 113 (3).
26 Under CCA, s. 69: see para. 14.34, ante. See also ibid, s. 113 (5).
27 CCA, s. 91: see para. 14.40, ante.
28 Under CCA, s. 40 (2): see para. 15.08, ante.
29 Under CCA, s. 149 (2): see para. 14.27, ante.
30 Under CCA, s. 65 (1): see para. 14.33, ante.
31 Under CCA, s. 124 (1): see para. 14.42, ante.
32 Under CCA, s. 142. But see ibid, s. 113 (4).

Chapter 17

Real security

17.01 Whereas chapter 16 was concerned with personal rights of action taken by way of security for the performance of contractual duties, the present chapter deals with real rights, i.e. rights against property, taken for this purpose. Such real rights broadly fall into three categories:

1. A *pledge*, under which the secured party is given possession of the security, plus a right to sell on default;[1]
2. A *mortgage* or *charge*, under which the secured party is given proprietary rights in the security, plus a right to sell on default;[1]
3. A *lien*, under which the secured party is given rights (usually possessory) by way of security.[2]

---

1 For the borderline between a pledge and a charge by way of mortgage, see *Dublin City Distillery Ltd v Doherty* [1914] AC 823, HL.
2 The rights granted to the lienholder are not possessory in respect of maritime and equitable liens: see paras. 17.13–17.14, post.

---

1. Pledge

17.02 This security transaction is a specialised form of bailment,[1] under which the debtor (the *pledgor*) delivers goods, or documents of title to goods,[2] to his creditor (the *pledgee*) as security for a debt, the pledgor retaining the general property in the goods whilst the pledgee acquires a special property in them.[3] The effect of a pledge is to transfer possession and consequent rights, and therefore the pledgee can bring an action for the return of the goods if they are taken from him; so also can the pledgor.[4] There is also an implied undertaking on the part of the pledgee to return the article when the debt is paid at the stated date, or if no time is stated, then whenever the pledgor pays or makes proper tender, and the pledgor impliedly undertakes that it is his property.[5] A man cannot ordinarily make an effective pledge of property which does not belong to him; but to this there are exceptions.[6]

Trust receipts In an international sale,[7] the buyer is frequently required to pay for the goods on presentation of the bill of lading either to himself, or to the confirming bank,[8] in circumstances where the buyer can only pay the price out of the proceeds of a sub-sale. Accordingly, the buyer will pledge the bill of lading (representing the goods) to his bank in return for an advance of the price he must pay for them. However, to complete the transaction, the buyer/pledgor needs to transfer possession of the documents of title to his sub-purchaser to obtain the price due under that contract.[9] As commercial necessity therefore requires that the bank hand back the bill of lading to the buyer/pledgor before reimbursement, the following precaution is frequently taken: the bill of lading is released by the bank to the buyer/ pledgor under a *trust receipt*, under which the buyer/pledgor takes possession of the bill of lading as trustee for his bank, undertaking to hold the goods, and sufficient of their proceeds in trust for the pledgee bank to redeem the pledge. The effect of a trust receipt is to protect the bank against the buyer's insolvency,[10] and sometimes as against a bona fide purchaser or further pledgee to whom the buyer/pledgor has disposed of the goods: if the bank has merely released the bill of lading to the buyer/pledgor so that he may obtain possession of the goods, he cannot normally transfer a good title free of the pledge;[11] but if the bank has assented to the sub-sale, it will lose its title to the goods under an exception to the nemo dat rule.[12]

---

1 For bailment, see generally para. 14.06, ante.
2 The transfer of documents of title to goods is in law regarded as a transfer of the goods; and the transfer of documents of title by way of pledge is sometimes termed 'hypothecation'. For documents of title to goods, see Factors Act 1889, s. 1 (4): see para. 10.20, ante.
3 For the concepts of the general and special property in goods, see the Sale of Goods Act 1893, s. 62 (1): para. 13.02, ante. The 1893 Act does not apply to pledges: ibid, s. 61 (4).
4 *Hyman v Nye* (1881) 6 QBD 685, and the Torts (Interference with Goods) Act 1977, s. 1. An express contractual term may exclude this implied term but the exclusion clause may not be effective if there has been a fundamental breach of contract: *Karsales (Harrow) Ltd v Wallis* [1956] 2 All ER 866, [1956] 1 WLR 936 and the Unfair Contract Terms Act 1977; and see paras. 3.15–3.16, ante.
5 *Cheesman v Exall* (1851) 6 Ex. 344.
6 See paras. 10.20–10.21, ante. Unless one of these exceptions apply receipt by way of pledge is an act of conversion: see Torts (Interference with Goods) Act 1977, s. 11 (2).
7 For international sales, see paras. 13.39 et seq., ante.
8 For confirmed letters of credit, see para. 13.43, ante.

9 Payment and delivery prima facie being concurrent terms: Sale of Goods Act 1893, s. 28: see para. 13.30, ante.

10 Because trust property will not fall into his bankruptcy: Bankruptcy Act 1914, s. 38: see para. 33.17, post. Nor do trust receipts require registration as bills of sale (see para. 17.08, post) or company charges (see para. 17.09, post).

11 *Mercantile Bank of India Ltd v Central Bank of India Ltd* [1938] AC 287, [1938] 1 All ER 52, PC. Contra if the buyer/pledgor is a mercantile agent: *Lloyds Bank Ltd v Bank of America National Trust and ˺Savings Association* [1938] 2 KB 147, [1938] 2 All ER 63, CA.

12 Sale of Goods Act 1893, ss. 21 (1) 1, 47 proviso: see paras. 13.12, 13.16, ante.

Rights and duties of pledgor and pledgee

17.03   The pledgee must use ordinary diligence in his care of the pledge; but if, notwithstanding such diligence, it is lost, he incurs no liability. If then the pledge is stolen, the pledgee must show that it was not lost for want of what an ordinarily prudent man would have done to ensure its safety; and, if notwithstanding it was taken by robbery, he is not bound to replace it.[1] He must not use goods pledged unless they are such as will not deteriorate by wear and even in such a case he uses them at his peril.[1]

He obtains a power of sale when default is made in payment of the debt at the stipulated time; or if no time is stipulated, then after a proper demand for payment has been made, and a reasonable time for performance has been allowed.[2] Any excess obtained by the sale beyond the amount necessary to liquidate the debt and expenses must be returned to the pledgor.

A pledgee usually loses his rights by parting with the possession of his pledge, but he may redeliver it to the pledgor under a trust receipt without losing such rights.[3]

---

1 *Coggs v Barnard* (1703) 2 Ld Raym. 909.
2 *Re Richardson* (1885) 30 ChD at 403, per Fry LJ.
3 *North Western Bank v Poynter* [1895] AC 56, HL (S).

Pawnbrokers

17.04   A pawnbroker is a person who carries on the business of taking goods in pawn. A specialised form of moneylending,[1] his business is currently governed by the Pawnbrokers Acts 1872 and 1960, but will eventually be regulated by the Consumer Credit Act, ss. 114–122.[2] Whilst both the old and the new legislation is restricted to those who make a business of taking goods in pawn,[3] the Consumer Credit Act (CCA) also expressly excludes pledges of documents of title.[4] Moreover, the CCA is much wider than the old Acts, applying to anyone who takes any article in pawn under a *regulated agreement*,[5] whereas the Pawnbrokers Acts do not generally apply to loans over £50.[6]

Among the provisions controlling pawnbroking are the following:

1. All pawnbrokers are now subject to the CCA licensing requirements, as they operate consumer credit businesses.[7]

2. The old Acts require the pawnbroker to give a pawn-ticket for the pledge;[8] and the CCA will similarly require a pawn-receipt in the prescribed form to be handed over.[9]

3. The CCA will forbid the taking of articles in pawn from persons who are, or appear to be, minors.[10]

4. All pledges are redeemable within six months of being made under both the old[11] and new[12] law.

5. The pledgee has a right of sale of unredeemed pledges as follows: under the Pawnbrokers Acts, pledges over £2 are to be sold by public aution on expiry of the six months, whilst pledges of £2 or less are then forfeit;[13] and the CCA will introduce an elaborate new system for the realisation of a pawnbroker's security.[14]

6. The pledgor has a right of redemption as follows: under the Pawnbrokers Acts, pledges over £2 are redeemable until sale;[15] and a similar right will be provided for all pledges under the CCA,[16] which will also forbid redemption charges[17] and lays down a redemption procedure.[18]

7. The extortionate credit bargain procedure is now available to the pledgor.[19]

8. When the CCA is fully in force, there will also be applicable to pledges its provisions as to copies[20] and time orders.[21]

---

1 Transactions within the Pawnbrokers Acts are wholly excluded from the Moneylenders Acts (see para. 15.02, ante); and whilst the transactional provisions of those Acts (see para. 15.13, et seq., ante) would prima facie apply to pawns outside the Pawnbrokers Acts, the Moneylenders Act 1927, ss. 6, 12 and 13, do not apply to a pawnbroker's loan if he complies with the substituted provisions of the 1927 Act, s. 14.

2 To be brought into force on a day to be appointed: CCA, Sch. 3, para. 39.

3 Pawnbrokers Act 1872, s. 5. The CCA provisions do not apply to 'non-commercial agreements': ibid, s. 114 (3) (b); and see para. 14.13, ante.

4 CCA, s. 114 (3) (a). For pledges of documents of title, see para. 17.02, ante.

5 CCA, s. 114 (1). For *regulated agreements*, see para. 14.13, ante.

6 Pawnbrokers Act 1872, s. 10; Pawnbrokers Act 1960, s. 1.

7 For licensing, see paras. 15.05, et seq., ante.

8 Pawnbrokers Act 1872, s. 14.

9 CCA, ss. 114 (1); 182.

10 CCA, s. 114 (2). Breach is an offence: see further para. 14.19, ante.
11 (Plus seven days grace): Pawnbrokers Act 1872, s. 16; Pawnbrokers Act 1960, s. 2. But where the pledge is for more than £50, the right of redemption can be cut down by agreement.
12 CCA, s. 116 (1), (2).
13 Pawnbrokers Act 1872, ss. 17, 19; and Pawnbrokers Act 1960, ss. 2, 3.
14 CCA, ss. 120, 121.
15 Pawnbrokers Act 1872, s. 18; and Pawnbrokers Act 1960, ss. 2, 3.
16 CCA, s. 116 (3).
17 CCA, s. 116 (4).
18 CCA, ss. 117–120.
19 CCA, ss. 137–140: see para. 15.18, ante.
20 CCA, s. 115. For the copies rules, see para. 14.33, ante.
21 For time orders, see CCA, s. 129; para. 14.23, ante. But note ibid, s. 130 (4).

2. Mortgage or charge

17.05 A mortgage or charge is the exact opposite of a pledge: under a mortgage of charge, the debtor ('mortgagor' or 'chargor') normally retains possession of the security for his loan, but grants to his creditor (the 'mortgagee' or 'chargee') proprietary rights over some of his property by way of security for the loan.[1] Treatment of the subject of mortgages and charges in English Law depends in the first instance on the nature of the property used as security:

1. Where an interest in land is mortgaged or charged, the matter is governed by the rules considered in chapter 12.
2. Where a chose in action is mortgaged or charged, the matter is governed by another set of rules.[2]
3. Where a chose in possession (goods) is mortgaged or charged, the matter is dealt with below.

Cutting across the above classification are the special rules applicable where the debtor is a registered company, irrespective of under which of the above three categories the security falls.[3]

With regard to mortgages or charges granted over goods, there is this clear dichotomy depending on the status of the borrower:[4] where the borrower is a registered company, the matter is governed by the Companies Acts 1948–76; whereas, if the borrower is an individual or unincorporated body, the matter falls within the Bills of Sale Acts 1878–82.

1 See para. 17.01, ante.
2 See paras. 4.08, et seq., ante.
3 See paras. 17.09–17.10, post.
4 For the position where the mortgagor is a minor, see para. 2.17, ante.

Bills of Sale Acts

17.06   A Bill of Sale is fundamentally a document evidencing the transfer of the property in goods either absolutely or by way of security. If the transferor of the goods, i.e. the *grantor* of the bill of sale, retains possession of the goods, the transaction is regulated by the following legislation:[1]

1. The Bills of Sale Act 1878, whose object is to prevent false credit being given to persons in apparent possession of goods which in reality belong to others; and

2. The Bills of Sale Act 1882,[2] whose object is to protect impecunious borrowers mortgaging or charging their goods as security for a loan.

The 1878 Act introduced an effective system for registering proprietary interests in goods in the possession of another. It was originally intended to apply to both absolute and mortgage transfers, but was immediately seized upon with enthusiasm by moneylenders as a device for registering mortgages or charges over the household effects of (largely working-class) borrowers. The consequent outcry led Parliament to contemplate the total prohibition of mortgage bills of sale, which prompted this counter-argument: if the rich man could raise money by mortgaging his real property, why should not the poor man be able to raise money by mortgaging his personal property? It was therefore decided to compromise in the 1882 Act as follows: all mortgages of goods were henceforth to be governed by the 1882 Act, which made such mortgages theoretically possible but commercially very difficult indeed. For instance, the 1882 Act totally invalidates all bills of sale which are not in strict compliance with the prescribed form set out in the Schedule, and also forbids all bills of sale in respect of after-acquired property, i.e. where the debtor grants security over property which he may thereafter acquire.

Whilst Parliament's original intention to forbid the mortgaging or charging by the debtor of his present property to secure loans was probably correct, it could obviously be achieved in a much simpler manner. Likewise far-sighted was the prohibition against mortgaging after-acquired property: such clauses are used as a matter of course in many North American sales on credit and have been the cause of much misery. However, an undesirable effect of the 1882 Act was to strike also at attempts to purchase goods on credit, granting proprietary rights therein to another by way of security for the payment of the price ('purchase-money loans'). Whilst it was eventually decided that the ordinary bona fide two-party hire-purchase agreement was not caught by the 1882 Act,[3] this Act caused considerable difficulty and uncertainty with regard to the financing of hire-purchase transactions.[4] Accordingly, the *Crowther Report on Consumer Credit*[5] recommended that the Bills of Sale Acts should be repealed and replaced by a new Lending and Security Act, which would provide a workable system of chattel mortgages by way of purchase-money security.[6]

Because the application of the provisions of the 1882 Act to transactions which unexpectedly fall within its ambit is usually fatal to the transaction, the key issue is normally whether a transaction falls within the ambit of the Act; that is, whether a document amounts to a *bill of sale* granted by way of security. Moreover, it is unusual for a party voluntarily to grant a bill of sale over his property in compliance with the Act, perhaps because it has come to be looked upon as an indicator of impending insolvency.[7] Accordingly, it is proposed to deal here only with the definition of a bill of sale, leaving the provisions of the Act to more specialised works.

---

1 An absolute bill of sale will fall within both the 1878 Act and the Sale of Goods Act 1893; as to the latter, see chap. 13, ante. A mortgage bill of sale will fall within the 1882 Act but outside the Sale of Goods Act 1893: see ibid, s. 61 (4).

2 Its full title is the Bills of Sale Act 1878 Amendment Act 1882.

3 *McEntire v Crossley Bros Ltd* [1895] AC 457, HL: see further para. 14.03, ante.

4 For instalment credit transactions, see paras. 14.08–14.10, ante. For some of the difficult cases see para. 17.08, note 15, post.

5 Cmnd. 4596 (1971): para. 14.11, ante.

6 The issue currently under debate is which of the following two sets of rules should be made applicable to such chattel mortgages: (a) the rules for mortgaging real property, suitably amended—see paras. 12.09–12.11, ante; or (b) an entirely new set of rules as the *Crowther Report* recommended, perhaps based on the US Art. 9 of the Uniform Commercial Code.

7 For some curious reason, the only areas where registered bills of sale appear at all popular are Newcastle upon Tyne and Bournemouth. For the most part, registration of a bill of sale against a trader tends to destroy his credit, whereas registration of a debenture against a company does not: see Gower *Company Law* (3rd edn) 79, n. 59.

Definition

17.07 The term 'bill of sale' is defined for both Acts by s. 4 of the 1878 Act. It includes not only:

1. Bills of sale strictly so called (i.e. assignments of personal chattels giving a title without delivery),

but also many other documents, viz.:

2. Assignments,

3. Transfers,
4. Declarations of trust without transfer,
5. Inventories of goods with receipt thereto attached or receipts for the purchase moneys of goods, and other assurances of personal chattels,
6. Licences to take possession of chattels as security for any debt, and also any agreement, whether intended or not to be followed by the execution of any other instrument, by which a right in equity to any personal chattels, or to any charge or security thereon, shall be conferred.[1]

Also any attornment or agreement, except a mining lease, whereby a power of distress is given, or agreed to be given, by way of security for any debt or advance and whereby any rent is reserved or made payable as a mode of providing for the payment of interest on such debt or advance, is to be deemed a bill of sale so far as distress is concerned. This does not apply to the mortgage of any land which the mortgagee in possession demises to the mortgagor as his tenant at a fair rent.[2]

---

1 Bills of Sale Act 1878, s. 4.
2 Ibid, s. 6; *Re Willis, Ex parte Kennedy* (1888) 21 QBD 384.

17.08 But the term 'bill of sale' is not to include:

1. Assignments for the benefit of creditors,[1]
2. Marriage settlements,[2]
3. Transfers of ships or shares therein,[3]
4. Transfers of goods in the ordinary course of trade,[4]
5. Bills of lading, or any documents used in the course of trade or business as proof of the possession or control of or authorising the possessor to transfer or receive goods,[5]
6. Assignments of fixtures, unless separately assigned,[6]
7. An agricultural charge on farming stock and other agricultural assets.[7]

The Act of 1882 does not apply to debentures issued by an incorporated company which require to be registered under the Companies Act 1948.[8] By the Industrial and Provident Societies Act 1967, a charge granted by a society registered under the Industrial and Provident Societies Act 1965 is outside the Bills of Sale Acts if application is made to register the charge in the Central Office of the Registry of Friendly Societies within the prescribed period.

Verbal contracts are not within the Acts, which strike at documents and not at transactions;[9] nor is any document which is merely ancillary and which does not give the transferee his title; hence, when property and possession pass under a verbal arrangement, a receipt for money payable in connection therewith given subsequently, will not be a bill of sale.[10] A pledge is not within the Acts.[11]

When goods have already passed out of the possession of the transferor, documents subsequently executed evidencing the transaction are not bills of sale;[12] for, as Cotton LJ said in *Marsden v Meadows*,[13] the document to be within the Act must be:

'one on which the title of the transferee of the goods depends, either as the actual transfer of the property, or an agreement to transfer, or as a muniment or document of title taken, to use an expression found in some of the cases, at the time as a record of the transaction.'

A constructive delivery is sufficient to constitute an actual transfer of possession; e.g.

handing over the keys of a locked room containing the chattels, and the transaction will not be rendered void by a written licence to enter and remove them being subsequently given.[14]

In considering whether a document, apparently not within this definition, is nevertheless covered by it, the court not only may but must inquire into the *real* nature of the transaction. Thus:

where the real agreement was one to lend money upon the security of goods in which the borrower had an interest, but took the form of a purchase of the goods by the lender, followed by a hire-purchase agreement with the borrower, the court held the latter agreement to be a bill of sale.[15]

But Russell LJ in *Snook v London and West Riding Investments Ltd*[16] said that a court will only hold such transaction to be intended to make a loan if it finds that *both* parties to the transaction so intended it.

Personal chattels   The Acts refer only to bills of sale of *personal chattels*, a term which will include fixtures and growing crops if assigned separately from the land to which they are attached; also trade machinery though attached to the land. But assignments of:

1. Stocks,
2. Shares,
3. Contracts,
4. Other choses in action,

are not assignments of personal chattels, and hence are not affected by these Acts.[17]

1 As to which, see para. 33.48, post. Though expressed to exclude creditors having notice of the deed, who do not come in within a given time (*Hadley v Beedom* [1895] 1 QB 646).

2 Including agreements to settle on marriage, even though informal and not under seal (*Wenman v Lyon* [1891] 2 QB 192).

3 As to which, see paras. 25.03, et seq., post.

4 This will protect a sale of growing crops, which are 'goods' (*Stephenson v Thompson* [1924] 2 KB 240), and trust receipts (*Re Hamilton, Young & Co, Ex parte Carter* [1905] 2 KB 772, CA.)

5 For bills of lading, see paras. 23.08, et seq., post.

6 Bills of Sale Act 1878, s. 4.

7 Agricultural Credits Act 1928, s. 8 (1).

8 Bills of Sale Act 1882, s. 17; *Re Standard Manufacturing Co* [1891] 1 Ch 627, CA.

9 *Manchester, Sheffield and Lincolnshire Rly Co v North Central Wagon Co* (1888) 13 App Cas 554, HL; *Newlove v Shrewsbury* (1888) 21 QBD 41, CA.

10 *Ramsay v Margrett* [1894] 2 QB 18.

11 *Waight v Waight and Walker* [1952] P 282, [1952] 2 All ER 290. For pledges, see paras. 17.02–17.04, ante.

12 *Charlesworth v Mills* [1892] AC 231.

13 (1881), 7 QBD at 84–85; and see *Re Hardwick, ex parte Hubbard* (1886) 17 QBD 690, contrasting it with *Re Townsend, ex parte Parsons* (1886) 16 QBD 532; *North Central Wagon Co v Manchester, Sheffield and Lincolnshire Rly Co* (1888), 13 App Cas 554.

14 *Wrightson v McArthur and Hutchisons* [1921] 2 KB 807.

15 *Beckett v Tower Assets Co* [1891] 1 QB 638, *Mellor v Maas* [1903] 1 KB 226, aff. in the House of Lords, sub nom *Maas v Pepper* [1905] AC 102, *Polsky v S and A Services Ltd* [1951] 1 All ER 185; affd. 1062 *n*, follwed in *North Central Wagon Finance Co v Brailsford* [1962] 1 All ER, 502, [1962] 1 WLR 1288.

16 [1967] 2 QB 786 at 804, [1967] 1 All ER 518 at 530, CA.

17 Bills of Sale Act 1878, s. 4.

Companies Acts

17.09   Where the debtor is a company registered under the Companies Acts, any charge (which expression includes mortgage[1]) granted over its property[2] to secure the loan is registrable under those Acts if, but only if,[3] it falls within any of the classes listed in s. 95 (2) of the 1948 Act as follows:

'(a) a charge for the purpose of securing any issue of debentures;[4]

(b) a charge on uncalled share capital of the company;[5]

(c) a charge created or evidenced by an instrument which, if executed by an individual, would require registration as a bill of sale;[6]

(d) a charge on land, wherever situate, or any other interest therein, but not including a charge for any rent or other periodical sum issuing out of land;[7]

(e) a charge on books debts of the company;[8]

(f) a floating charge on the undertaking or property of the company;[4]

(g) a charge on calls made but not paid;[5]

(h) a charge on a ship or any share in a ship;[9]

(i) a charge on goodwill, on a patent or a licence under a patent, on a trademark or on a copyright or a licence under a copyright.[10]

---

1 Companies Act 1948, s. 95 (10) (a).

2 The section is confined to proprietary rights granted by the company, and does not apply to those created by operation of law: *Brunton v Electrical Engineering Corpn* [1894] 1 Ch 434 (lien); *Re Overseas Aviation Engineering (GB) Ltd* [1963] Ch. 24, [1962] 3 All ER 12, CA (charging order).

3 *Aluminium Industrie Vaasen BV v Romalpa Aluminium Ltd* [1976] 2 All ER 552, [1976] 1 WLR 676, CA: set out in para. 14.02, ante.

4 A floating charge is one that is not initially fixed on specified assets, but floats over a class of assets, only crystallising when the creditor seeks to realise his security, and then fixing on all assets of that class at that moment owned by the company, e.g. stock-in-trade. A debenture is a loan to a company, normally secured by a fixed and/or floating charge.

5 Special forms of choses in action, they are uncommon nowadays.

6 See paras. 17.07–17.08, ante.

7 Specifically excluding leases (as to which see para. 12.01, ante), this requires land charges to be registered under this section. They must *also* be registered under the Land Charges Act 1972: see para. 12.11, ante.

8 Book debts are debts owing to a company which have arisen out of the normal carrying on of its business. They are a common form of chose in action, and are also governed by the rules considered para. 4.08, et seq., ante. S. 95 (2) (e) does not include trust receipts (*Re David Allester Ltd* [1922] Ch 211).

But note the case referred to in note 3 ante, whose effect is to enable the creation of a system of security outside s. 95, and thus possibly overturning the hitherto accepted order of priorities.

9 For mortgages of ships, see para. 25.05, post.

10 These are special types of chose in action. For goodwill, see para. 11.21, ante; for patents, see chap. 29; for trademarks, see chap. 30; for copyrights, see chap. 31.

17.10   Every charge falling within s. 95 (2) must be registered with the Registrar of Companies within twenty-one days.[1] Whilst the Act places on the company which grants such a charge over its property the duty of sending the prescribed particulars to the Registrar,[2] it allows registration to be effected on the application of any other person.[3] The Registrar is required to keep a public register of such charges,[4] and to grant a certificate of registration which shall be conclusive evidence of compliance with these registration requirements.[5] Having been submitted with the original appliction, the charge itself will be returned to the company, which is required to keep at its registered office a copy of every charge and its own register of charges.[6]

Failure to comply with the registration requirement leads not only to the liability of the company and its officers to fines,[7] but also destroys the validity of the charge as follows: the charge will, so far as any security on the company's assets is conferred thereby, be void as against the liquidator and any creditor of the company.[8] To reduce possible hardship on the chargee, the Act makes two concessions: first, the money secured thereby becomes immediately payable;[9] and second, the court is given power to extend the time for registration or rectify any error or omission.[10]

Thus, failure to register is not fatal so long as the debtor-company remains solvent. However, where the debtor-company becomes insolvent, the order of priority and validity of charges may become vital:[11] registered charges will prima facie [12] rank in order of registration,[9] whilst unregistered charges will reduce the holder to the status of an unsecured creditor.[9]

---

1 Companies Act 1948, s. 95 (1).
2 Ibid, ss. 96, 97.
3 Ibid, s. 96 (2).
4 Ibid, s. 98 (1). For up-dating and rectification of the register, see ibid, ss. 100–102.
5 Ibid, s. 98 (2). Even if inacurrate: see *Re Nye Ltd* [1971] Ch 442, [1970] 3 All ER 1061, CA.
6 Ibid, ss. 103, 104. Whilst the charge may be there inspected, the Act does not require a copy of the charge to be filed at the Companies Registry, which is probably a mistake.
7 Ibid, s. 96 (3).
8 Ibid, s. 95 (1). E.g. *Capital Finance Co Ltd v Stokes* [1969] 1 Ch 261, [1968] 3 All ER 625, CA.
9 Ibid, s. 95 (1).
10 Ibid, s. 101. Whilst the debtor-company remains solvent, this will normally be granted fairly freely, subject to the rights of creditors making loans to the company during the intervening time.
11 For the general position of secured creditors on insolvency, see para. 33.43, post.
12 Subject to the special rules for floating charges before crystalliation.

---

3. Lien

17.11 Liens are of various kinds:

1. Possessory,
2. Maritime,
3. Equitable.

Possessory liens

A possessory lien is one which appertains to a person who has possession of goods which belong to another, entitling him to retain them until the debt due to him has been paid. They are of two kinds:

a) Particular lien This is a right to retain the particular goods in connection with which the debt arose; e.g.

1. A carrier may retain goods given to him for carriage;[1] and
2. An innkeeper may retain his guest's goods,

until payment of charges due.
A particular lien may arise:

1. Out of express agreement or
2. By implication;

and the law will give an implied lien over goods which a person is compelled to receive; e.g. to an innkeeper over a guest's goods brought to the inn,[2] or to a common carrier over goods carried.[3] And when the debt has been incurred for labour or skill exercised upon a particular thing, the creditor has an implied lien upon that thing for his reward;[4] e.g. a shipwright has a lien on a vessel for the cost of repairs.

b) General lien This may arise from:

1. Custom (long existing, notorious, and reasonable) or
2. Contract;[5]

and it is a right of retaining goods not only for the debt incurred in connection with them, but for the general balance owing by their owner to the person exercising the right of lien.[5] Amongst trades or professions which have this lien may be mentioned factors,[6] bankers,[7] stockbrokers,[8] solicitors,[9] and sometimes insurance brokers.[10] Any right of lien implied from custom can be negatived by contract.[11] A possessory lien (as a rule) gives no right to sale,[12] nor in fact any right, except such as belongs to a possessor merely, as distinguished from an owner. It is lost by payment and by surrender of possession;[13] taking security may show an intention to abandon the lien.[14]

There are several instances where a right of lien can involve a right of resale. One example is the statutory right of resale given to an unpaid seller of goods.[15] A warehouseman or wharfinger may in certain events sell goods placed in his custody,[16] and innkeepers may under certain circumstances sell the goods of a guest.[17]

---

1 See para. 23.23, post.

2 An innkeeper's lien does not extend to motor cars or other vehicles or horses or other animals: Hotel Proprietors Act 1956, s. 2 (2).
3 See para. 22.03, post.
4 *Re Matthews, ex parte Ockenden* (1754) 1 Atk. 235.
5 *George Barker (Transport) v Eynon* [1974] 1 All ER 900, [1974] 1 WLR 462, CA.
6 *Cowell v Simpson* (1810) 16 Ves at 280. Cf. *Rolls Razor Ltd v Cox* [1967], 1 QB 552, [1967] 1 All ER 397, CA (mere agent to sell in the name of his principal *held* to have no lien on his principal's goods).
7 See para. 10.31, ante.
8 *Re London and Globe Finance Corpn* [1902] 2 Ch 416.
9 *Ex parte Sterling* (1810) 16 Ves 258. Likewise accountants: *Woodworth v Conroy* [1976] 1 QB 884, [1976] 1 All ER 107, CA.
10 See para. 10.29, note 11, ante.
11 *Rolls Razor Ltd v Cox* [1967] 1 QB 552, [1967] 1 All ER 397, CA.
12 *White v Spettigue* (1845) 13 M & M at 607.
13 *Kruger v Wilcox* (1755) Amb at 254.
14 *Cowell v Simpson* (1810) 16 Ves 275; *Re Taylor, Stileman and Underwood* [1891] 1 Ch 590; *Burston Finance v Spierway* [1974] 3 All ER 735, [1974] 1 WLR 1648.
15 Sale of Goods Act 1893, s. 39: see para. 13.38, ante.
16 Merchant Shipping Act 1894, s. 497.
17 Innkeepers Act 1878; see para. 13.12 (c), ante.

17.12   Under the Disposal of Uncollected Goods Act 1952, a limited class of bailee[1] of uncollected goods had been provided with a complicated right of sale. This right has now been replaced by the Torts (Intereference with Goods) Act 1977, which has granted a simplified right of sale to a wider range of bailees. Subject to the terms of any agreement between bailor and bailee,[2] the 1977 Act confers a power of sale on a bailee in possession or control of goods where:[3]

'(a) the bailor is in breach of an obligation to take delivery of the goods or, if the terms of the bailment so provide, to give directions as to their delivery, or
(b) the bailee could impose such an obligation by giving notice to the bailor, but is unable to trace or communicate with the bailor,[4] or
(c) the bailee can reasonably expect to be relieved of any duty to safeguard the goods on giving notice to the bailor, but is unable to trace or communicate with the bailor'.[4]

Where a bailee can bring himself within this provision, he will then have a statutory power of sale, provided that he *either*:

1. Gives notice to the bailee of his intention to sell the goods;[5] or
2. Shows that he has failed to trace or communicate with the bailor with a view to giving him such a notice, after having taken reasonable steps for the purpose; or
3. Applies for a court order for sale.[6]

Upon satisfaction of one of these conditions, the bailee will be entitled to sell the goods as against the bailor.[7] Such a sale by a bailee will give his buyer a good title as against the bailor;[8] but, if the bailor did not in fact own the goods, it will not give the buyer a good title as against the owner or a person claiming under him.[9] A bailee exercising such a power of sale shall be liable to account to the bailor for the proceeds of sale, less any costs of sale;[10] and:

'(a) the account shall be taken on the footing that the bailee should have adopted the best method of sale reasonably available in the circumstances, and

(b) [if the bailee has given a notice of intention to sell as per (1) above], any sum payable in respect of the goods by the bailor to the bailee which accrued due before the bailee gave notice ... shall be deductible from the proceeds of sale.'[11]

---

1 For the general rules of bailment, see para. 14.06, ante.
2 Torts (Interference with Goods) Act 1977, s. 12 (8). The expressions 'bailor' and 'bailee' include their respective successor in title: ibid, s. 12 (7) (a).
3 Ibid, s. 12 (1).
4 Ibid, s. 12 (2) and Sch. 1, Part 1.
5 As specified in Sch. 1, Part 2.
6 Under ibid, s. 13.
7 Ibid, ss. 12 (3); 13 (2).
8 Ibid, ss. 12 (6); 13 (2).
9 Ibid, s. 12 (4).
10 Ibid, s. 12 (5).
11 And see ibid, s. 12 (7) (b).

Maritime liens

17.13 A maritime lien is one which attaches to a thing in connection with some liability incurred in relation to a maritime adventure. It does not depend on the possession of the thing, but travels with it into whosoever's hands the thing may come. It is enforced by arrest and sale (unless security be given) through the medium of the Admiralty Court.[1]

Amongst maritime liens may be named:

1. The lien of a salvor;[2]
2. The lien of the seamen for their wages;[3]
3. The lien of the master for wages and disbursements;[4]
4. The lien over a colliding ship and freight of one whose property has been damaged by collision with a ship brought about by the default of that ship;
5. The lien of a bottomry bondholder.[4]

The order in which maritime liens are enforceable depends upon their nature and sometimes on equitable grounds which may be applicable to the circumstances of the case. The lien of a later salvor is preferred to that of an earlier salvor, and to a lien for prior damage,[5] because he has preserved the *res* for the benefit of the earlier liens. But this principle does not apply to the liens over a ship which has successively collided with two or more other vessels, nor do the claimants for damage rank in priority according to the dates of the respective collisions; if there is not sufficient to satisfy all the claims, the proceeds of the *res* must be divided rateably between all the claimants.[6] Where the conflict is between different classes of lien, the priorities depend upon varying circumstances and no single general rule can be laid down.

A maritime lien may come into conflict with a possessory lien. Thus, the possessory lien of a shipwright for the cost of repairs is subject to maritime liens which attached to the ship before it was taken into his yard; but the shipwright's possessory lien takes precedence of all maritime liens accruing after the commencement of his possession.[7]

It is doubtful whether a maritime lien is assignable with the debt, but a mere volunteer who pays the debt of a privileged claimant does not thereby acquire his lien.[8]

---

1 See *The Bold Buccleugh* (1851) Moo, PC 267 at 284. The Administration of Justice Act 1970, s. 2, created a separate Admiralty Court in the Queen's Bench Division of the High Court.
2 See para. 25.12, post.
3 See para. 25.16, post.
4 See para. 25.11, post.
5 *The Inna* [1938] P 148.
6 *The Stream Fisher* [1927] P 73.
7 *The Tergeste* [1903] P 26.
8 *The Petone* [1917] P 198.

Equitable liens

17.14 An equitable lien is nothing but the right to have a specific portion of property allocated to the payment of specific liabilities. The right of a partner on dissolution to have the firm's assets applied in payment of the firm's liabilities is a right of the class styled 'equitable liens'.[1]

---

1 See para. 11.16 (2), ante.

Part V

Consumer protection

Chapter 18

Trade descriptions

18.01 The Trade Descriptions Act 1968 grew out of, but is much wider than, the old Merchandise Marks Acts 1887–1953. Whereas the primary purpose of the Merchandise Marks Acts was to protect manufacturers and traders against the passing-off as theirs of the goods of others, the chief objective of the Trade Descriptions Act was the protection of consumers as against manufacturers and traders.[1] The law is now to be found in the Trade Descriptions Acts 1968–72.[2] The legislation is intended to deter the making of misleading statements in the supply of goods and services to consumers by making such statements criminal offences;[3] but it contains this major difference in treatment:[4] whereas there is strict criminal liability in relation to misstatements made in the supply of goods,[5] the criminal liability in respect of the supply of services depends on proof of mens rea.[6]

---

1 See the Report of the Molony Committee on Consumer Protection (Cmnd. 1781) (1961).
2 As amended. For suggestions for reform, see the Review of the 1968 Act in October 1976 (Cmnd. 6628).
3 For sanctions, responsibility defences and enforcement, see paras. 18.15, et seq., post.
4 It has been recommended that this distinction be removed by making them all offences of strict liability: Cmnd. 6628, paras. 49, 105.
5 See post.
6 See para. 18.14, post.

---

1. False statements as to goods

Prohibition of false trade descriptions

18.02 The principal offences to be found in the Trade Descriptions Act 1968 (TDA) are contained in s. 1 (1), which provides that:

'Any person who, in the course of a trade or business—
(a) applies a false trade description to any goods; or
(b) supplies or offers to supply any goods to which a false trade description is applied;
shall, subject to the provisions of this Act, be guilty of an offence'.

The offences are thus limited by the following requirements:
1) They must be committed 'in the course of a trade or business', so that private transactions are excluded.[1]
2) They comprehend only statements made in relation to 'goods', which expression is defined to include ships and aircraft, things attached to land and growing crops.[2] Whilst a false statement made in relation to the building of a house already amounts to an offence in so far as it relates to a supply of services,[3] it has been recommended that false statements about real property should themselves constitute an offence.[4]
3) The offences can only be committed in relation to the *supply* of goods. In *Wycombe Marsh Garages Ltd v Fowler*:[5]

A garage examined a car for the purposes of issuing a test certificate. The examination revealed tyre defects which were wrongly diagnosed and therefore a certificate was refused. A conviction on the basis that the incorrect diagnosis amounted to an application of a false trade description was quashed on the grounds that the diagnosis was not made in relation to a supplying of goods.

4) The prohibited acts involve statements made to induce the customer to enter into the transaction for the supply of the goods:[6] it is insufficient that the customer returns the goods, and the statement is then made to pacify him.[7] On the other hand, the offences can be committed by either transferor or transferee; in *Fletcher v Bugden*:[8]

In negotiating the purchase of a car from a private seller, a car dealer stated that the car was only fit for scrap. He was then able to buy it for £2, repair it, and sell at a large profit. *Held:* the car dealer commited an offence under s. 1.

---

1 For the special provision as to advertisements, see TDA, s. 39 (2): para. 18.04, post.
2 TDA, s. 39 (1). 'Ships' is itself defined ibid.
3 Under TDA, s. 14 (see para. 18.11, post): *Beckett v Cohen* [1973] 1 All ER 1210, [1972] 1 WLR 1593, DC.
4 Cmnd. 6628, para. 90.
5 [1972] 3 All ER 248, [1972] 1 WLR 1156, DC.
6 *Norman v Bennett* [1974] 3 All ER 351, [1974] 1 WLR 1229, DC.
7 *Wickens Motors (Gloucester) Ltd v Hall* [1972] 3 All ER 759, DC.
8 [1974] 2 All ER 1243, [1974] 1 WLR 1056, DC.

18.03   Where in the course of trade or business there is a *false trade description*[1] made in connection with the supply of goods, s. 1 creates two entirely separate offences of strict liability, the first[2] being the more heinous.

a) Applying a false trade description to goods   Section 4 provides:

'(1) A person applies a trade description to goods if he—
    (a) affixes or annexes it to or in any manner marks it on or incorporates it with—
        (i) the goods themselves, or
        (ii) anything in, on or with which the goods are supplied; or
    (b) places the goods in, on or with anything which the trade description has been affixed or annexed to, marked on or incorporated with, or places any such thing with the goods; or
    (c) uses the trade description in any manner likely to be taken as referring to the goods.
(2) An oral statement may amount to the use of a trade description.
(3) Where goods are supplied in pursuance of a request in which a trade description is used and the circumstances are such as to make it reasonable to infer that the goods are supplied as goods corresponding to that trade description, the person supplying the goods shall be deemed to have applied that trade description to the goods'.

Of particular significance is s. 4 (2): whilst the old Merchandise Marks Acts only applied to written misdescriptions, the TDA extends to oral misdescriptions. Nor need the speaker be a party to the contract for the supply of goods. Thus, in *Fletcher v Sledmore*:[3]

> D was a repairer of, and dealer in, cars. D sold a car to another dealer, X, on the basis that the car would remain on D's premises for repair. P, whom D knew to be a possible purchaser, was brought to D's premises to inspect the car; and D told P that the engine was all right. P, having purchased the car, found the engine to be defective. *Held:* D was guilty of the offence of applying by means of an oral statement a false trade description to the car.

b) Supplying goods to which a false trade description has been applied   The offence under s. 1 (1) (b) may be committed in either of two ways: (1) by supplying[4] goods; and (2) by offering to supply them. According to s. 6:

'A person exposing goods for supply or having goods in his possession for supply shall be deemed to offer to supply them'.

Thus, to facilitate enforcement, the Act has made it unnecessary to prove actual supply or exposure for supply, e.g. it is sufficient if the goods are in a stock-room. Note that the supplier of the goods does not himself need to apply the trade description to commit an offence under s. 1 (1) (b). Thus, a retailer commits such an offence in supplying goods to which another, e.g. the manufacturer, has applied the trade description, perhaps in an advertisement. In recognition that the retailer has here committed a less heinous offence than if he himself had applied the trade description, the Act allows him a wider range of defences[5] and it has been decided that the offence has only been committed where the supplier knows of the trade description,[6] though he does not need to be aware of its falsity.[7]

---

1 See paras. 18.05–18.07, post.
2 E.g. *Clode v Barnes* [1974] 1 All ER 1166, [1974] 1 WLR 544, DC (conviction of innocent partner with no knowledge or means of knowledge).
3 (1973) LGR 179, DC.
4 Includes sale, hire-purchase and simple hiring.
5 See para. 18.17 (ii), post.
6 *Cottee v Douglas Seaton (Used Cars) Ltd* [1972] 3 All ER 750, [1972] 1 WLR 1408, DC.
7 *Tarleton Engineering Co v Nattrass* [1973] 3 All ER 699, [1973] 1 WLR 1261, DC.

Advertisements

18.04 Where in an advertisement[1] a trade description is used in relation to any class of goods,[2] then for the purposes of both the above offences the trade description shall be taken as referring to all goods of the class, whether or not in existence at the time of the advertisement.[3] The effect of this provision is that the trade description used in the advertisement is then deemed to be used in relation to the goods,[3] and is hence applied to the goods by virtue of s. 4 (1) (c); but the Act makes it clear that this is restricted to advertisements, and does not extend to editorial material.[4] These advertisement provisions are widely drafted to catch both the following situations: (a) where the retailer advertises his own wares;[5] and (b) where a manufacturer advertises his wares to promote sales of them by retailers.

---

1 Includes catalogues, circulars and price lists: TDA, s. 39 (1).
2 In determining whether goods belong to such a class, the court is allowed to take account of a wide variety of matters: ibid, s. 5 (3).
3 TDA, s. 5 (2).

False trade descriptions

i) A trade description

18.05 The TDA continues the policy of the previous Acts in containing an exhaustive[1] list of those matters which are to be regarded as part of the trade description. Section 2 (1) provides:

'A trade description is an indication, direct or indirect, and by whatever means given, of any of the following matters with regard to any goods or part of goods, that is to say—
(a) quantity,[3] size or gauge;[4]
(b) method of manufacture, production, processing or reconditioning;
(c) composition;[5]
(d) fitness for purpose, strength, performance, behaviour or accuracy;[6]
(e) any physical characteristics not included in the preceding paragraphs;[5]
(f) testing by any person and results thereof;[7]
(g) approval by any person or conformity with a type approved by any person;[8]
(h) place or date of manufacture, production, processing or reconditioning;[9]
(i) person by whom manufactured, produced, processed or reconditioned;[10]
(j) other history, including previous ownership or use.'[11]

For the most part, the above list concentrates on matters of fact rather than opinion.[12] There is power to exempt from it goods sold for export;[13] and the Act also deals with the overlap between s. 2 and certain other statutes relating to specific trades.[14]

1 *Cadbury v Halliday* [1975] 2 All ER 226, [1975] 1 WLR 649, DC. But see TDA, s. 3 (3): para. 18.06, below.
2 In relation to livestock, see also TDA, s. 2 (2).
3 See further TDA, s. 2 (3).
4 E.g. 'all leather'; 'immaculate'; 'in excellent condition throughout'.
5 *British Gas Corpn v Lubbock* [1974] 1 All ER 188, [1974] 1 WLR 37, DC.
6 For civil liability for breach of the undertaking as to fitness, see paras. 13.22–13.23, ante.
7 E.g. 'MOT-tested'.
8 Overlaps with TDA, ss. 12, 13: see para. 18.08 (d), post.
9 For the power to make regulations as to country of origin, see TDA, s. 36.

This overlaps with the special provisions in relation to imported goods; see para. 18.08 (b), post.
10 May be a speedy alternative to a passing-off action: as to which, see para. 30.15, post.
11 E.g. 'new tv'; odometer reading; 'in perfect condition'.
12 See *R v Lloyd* [1976] CLY 2472.
13 TDA, s. 32.
14 TDA, s. 2 (4), (5).

ii) Falsity

18.06 It was not intended that every inaccurate statement should fall within the TDA, and s. 3 (1) therefore contains the basic rule that:

'A false trade description is a trade description which is false to a material degree'.

Frequently, the issue of falsity will turn on the exact words used;[1] and in this context any exclusion clause may be relevant.[2] The words 'material degree' were considered by the Court of Appeal in *R v Ford Motor Co Ltd*:[3]

A car manufactured by F was damaged whilst in the care of forwarding agents. It was repaired and supplied to the dealer as a 'new car'. *Held:* the damage was sufficiently limited and repairs sufficiently perfect for the car still to be a 'new car'.

Section 3 then seeks to plug three loopholes as follows:
1) The literally true but misleading statement. Section 3 (2) provides that:[4]

'A trade description which, though not false, is misleading, that is to say, likely to be taken for such an indication of any of the matters specified in section 2 of this Act as would be false to a material degree, shall be deemed to be a false trade description'.

Thus, to be effective any disclaimer must be as bold, precise and compelling as the trade description which is untrue.[5]
2) The wink to a blind donkey. According to s. 3 (3):

'Anything which, though not a trade description, is likely to be taken for an indication of any of those matters and, as such an indication, would be false to a material degree, shall be deemed to be a false trade description'.

3) False compliance or approval. Section 3 (4) enacts that:

'A false indication, or anything likely to be taken as an indication which would be false, that any goods comply with a standard specified or recognised by any person or implied by the approval of any person shall be deemed to be a false trade description, if there is no such person or no such standard so specified, recognised or implied'.

1 E.g. *Furniss v Scholes* [1974] RTR 133, DC.
2 See para. 18.07, post.
3 [1974] 3 All ER 489, [1974] 1 WLR 1220, CA. The court is not concerned with whether the bargain made was a fair one overall: *Furniss v Scholes* (ante).
4 E.g. *Robertson v Dicicco* [1972] RTR 431, DC ('beautiful car').
5 *Norman v Bennett* [1974] 3 All ER 351, [1974] 1 WLR 1229, DC.

Exclusion clauses

18.07 The issue under the TDA is not quite the same as with the exclusion of civil liability:[1] the issue under the TDA is whether the disclaimer is sufficiently compelling to neutralise the trade description.[2] The issue has most commonly arisen in connection with false odometer readings on motor vehicles. Thus, in *R v Hammertons Cars Ltd*:[3]

The dealer argued that, during negotiations prior to the sale, the purchaser had been orally informed that the odometer readings were not guaranteed; and he further relied upon a printed 'guarantee' supplied at the time of delivery which included an express disclaimer. *Held:* if the dealer wished to avoid conviction, he should have taken positive steps to negative the effect which such a reading might have upon the mind of the purchaser; and that neither a causal remark made in the course of oral negotiations nor the 'small print' in a contractual document were sufficient for this purpose.

1 As to which see para. 13.27, ante. Generally, there will be no civil liability arising simply by reason of a breach of this Act: see para. 18.15 post.
2 *Sawadski v Sleigh* [1975] RTR 113, DC.
3 [1976] 3 All ER 758, [1976] 1 WLR 1243, CA. See also *Waltham Forest LBC v TG Wheatley (Central Garage)* [1977] Crim LR 761, DC.

Other offences in connection with the supply of goods

18.08 *a) Definition and marking orders* The Government has power by order to assign definite meanings to expressions used in relation to goods and where such meaning is assigned to an expression it shall be deemed to have that meaning when used in a trade description or in such other circumstances as may be specified in the order.[1]

The Department of Trade also has power to require by order that goods be marked with or accompanied by any information (e.g. as to origin or contents), or instruction relating to the goods and to regulate or prohibit the supply of goods with respect to which the requirements are not complied with.[2] Similarly, an order may be made that an advertisement contain or refer to any information relating to the goods.[3]

b) Imported goods The 1968 Act prohibits the importation into the United Kingdom of any goods bearing a false indication of origin[4] and restricts the importation of goods bearing or infringing a trade mark.[5] Under the 1972 Act, if a UK name or mark is applied to goods manufactured outside the UK, the name or mark must be accompanied by an indication of the country where they were manufactured.[6]

c) False pricing (see below).

d) False claims as to approval, etc. In relation to the supply of *both* goods and services, it is an offence to give a false indication of royal approval or award,[7] or to make a false representation that they are of a kind supplied to any person.[8]

---

1 TDA, s. 7.
2 Ibid, s. 8.
3 Ibid, s. 9.
4 Ibid, s. 16.
5 Ibid, s. 17. For trade marks see chap. 30, post.
6 For the power to make regulations as to country of origin, see TDA 1968, s. 36. For an overlap, see ibid, s. 2 (1) (h): para. 18.05, ante.
7 TDA, s. 12.
8 Ibid, s. 13.

False or misleading pricing

18.09 Frankly experimental is s. 11 of the 1968 Act, which creates two new offences of strict liability in relation to false or misleading indications as to the price of goods supplied.[1] The offences may be committed even though the defendant was unaware of the falsity of the statement just so long as he was aware that the statement had been made.[2] The two offences are as follows:

a) False comparisons If any supplier of goods gives a false indication that the price at which they are being offered is equal to or less than either a price recommended by the manufacturer or the price at which the goods (or goods of the same description) were previously offered by him, he is guilty of an offence.[3] An indication that goods were previously offered at a higher price or at a particular price is treated as indicating that they were so offered within the previous six months for a continuous period of not less than twenty-eight days.[4]

b) Misleading pricing If any person offering to supply goods gives, by whatever means, any indication likely to be taken as an indication that the goods are being offered at a price less than that at which they are in fact being offered he commits an offence,[5] e.g. by omitting VAT from a price stated.[6] Whilst the provision does not say so, it has been assumed only to apply to price indications made in the course of a trade or business so that it did not extend to the internal transactions of a club.[7] In *Doble v David Greig Ltd*:[8]

> DG displayed in their self-service store bottles of fruit juice with a price label reading 5s 9d. The manufacturer's label on the bottle said that a 4d deposit was refundable on return of the bottle; but at the cash desk was a notice stating 'we do not accept the return of empty bottles. No deposit is charged'. *Held:* the shelf-display could equally mean that the 5s 9d price was inclusive or exclusive of the 4d deposit; and therefore an offence was committed at the display, the notice at the cash desk being irrelevant.

1 For suggestions as to reform, see Cmnd. 6628, paras. 211–234; and the OFT Consultative Document 'Bargain Offer Claims' (1975).
2 *Feiner v Barnes* (1973) 71 LGR 477, DC.
3 TDA, s. 11 (1).
4 TDA, s. 11 (3). But see *House of Holland v Brent London Borough Council* [1971] 2 QB 304, [1971] 2 All ER 296, DC. (The prosecution has the burden of proving that during the whole of the six months' period preceding the offer there was no offer at a higher price which continued for twenty-eight days.)
5 Ibid, s. 11 (2).
6 *Richards v Westminster Motors* (1975) 61 Crim App Rep. 228, DC.
7 *Whitehead v Collett* [1975] CLY 3064.
8 [1972] 2 All ER 195, [1972] 1 WLR 703, DC.

2. False statement as to services, etc.

18.10 Contrary to the recommendations of the Molony Report that the offences should be restricted to representations made in connection with the supply of goods,[1] s. 14 of the Act set out to regulate the supply of services;[2] but, in recognition that this was a new development, mens rea was required for this offence.[3]

1 Cmnd. 1781 (1961), para. 5.
2 For TDA, ss. 12 and 13, which apply to both goods and services, see para. 18.08 (d), ante.
3 See para. 18.14, post. It has now been recommended that the s. 14 offences be made ones of strict liability: Cmnd. 6628 (1976) para. 48.

Services, accommodation or facilities

18.11   Leaving aside for the moment the state of mind in which the representor makes his statement,[1] s. 14 (1) provides that:

'It shall be an offence for any person in the course of any trade or business [to make a false statement] ... as to any of the following matters, that is to say—
(i) the provision in the course of any trade or business of any services, accommodation or facilities;
(ii) the nature of any services, accommodation or facilities provided in the course of any trade or business;
(iii) the time at which, manner in which or persons by whom any services, accommodation or facilities are so provided;
(iv) the examination, approval or evaluation by any person of any services, accommodation or facilities so provided; or
(v) the location or amenities of any accommodation so provided'.

Where the statement within s. 14 (1) is made in a brochure, an offence will be committed every time it is communicated to a different reader.[2] Moreover, the offences under s. 14 are like those under s. 1 in all the following respects: the statements prohibited are those which are false to a material degree;[3] those statements must be made in the course of a trade or business;[4] and liability may be avoided by an adequate disclaimer.[5]

---

1 See para. 18.10, ante, n. 3.
2 *R v Thomson Holidays* [1974] QB 592, [1974] 1 All ER 823, CA.
3 TDA, s. 14 (4). Cf. para. 18.06, ante.
4 Cf. para. 18.02, ante.
5 *Edward A Savory and Associates Ltd v Noel Dawson* (1976) 26.2., DC. Cf. para., 18.07, ante.

Statements

18.12   Section 14 is primarily directed at 'statements', which expression is amplified by the following provision:[1]

'anything (whether or not a statement as to any of the matters specified in [s. 14 (1)]) likely to be taken for such a statement as to any of those matters as would be false shall be deemed to be a false statement as to that matter'.

The emphasis throughout is on statements of fact, so that promises prima facie fall outside the section.[2] This requirement has caused particular difficulty in relation to the advertising of holidays at hotels not then completed: forecasts as to what the

404

facilities at the hotel will be like when completed are not false trade descriptions;[3] but an offence is committed in so far as the brochure suggests an existing fact, e.g. that the hotel is already complete and conforming to those standards.[4]

1 TDA, s. 14 (2) (a). Cf. TDA, s. 3 (3).
2 *Beckett v Cohen* [1973] 1 All ER 120, [1972] 1 WLR 1593, DC; *British Airways Board v Taylor* [1976] 1 All ER 65, [1976] 1 WLR 13, HL.
3 *Sunair Holidays v Dodd* [1970] 2 All ER 410, [1970] 1 WLR 1037, DC. Cf. *British Airways Board v Taylor* (ante) (double-booking).
4 *R v Clarksons Holidays* (1972) 57 Crim. App. Rep. 38, CA.

As to services, etc.

18.13 The Act comprehends statements as to services,[1] accommodation and facilities, and empowers the Government to give designated meanings to these expressions.[2] The ambit of s. 14 is restricted in that it does not include anything done under a contract of service;[3] but it is extended by the provision that:[4]

'In relation to any services consisting of or including the application of any treatment or process or the carrying out of any repair, the matters specified in [s. 14 (1)] shall be taken to include the effect of the treatment, process or repair'.

1 See *Breed v Cluett* [1970] 2 QB 459, [1970] 2 All ER 662, DC (NHRBC guarantee); *R v Breeze* [1973] 2 All ER 1141, [1973] 1 WLR 994, CA (unqualified architect).
2 TDA, s. 15.
3 TDA, s. 14 (4), e.g. provision of services, etc., to employees.
4 TDA, s. 14 (3).

The representor's state of mind

18.14 According to s. 14 (1), it is an offence in the course of trade or business in relation to any of the matters there listed for a person:

'(a) to make a statement which he knows to be false; or
(b) recklessly to make a statement which is false'.

The Act further provides that:[1]

'a statement made regardless of whether it is true or false shall be deemed to be made recklessly, whether or not the person making it had reasons for believing that it might be false'.

Moreover, it would seem that a statement may be made 'recklessly' within s. 14 whether or not there is any dishonest intent. In *MFI Warehouses v Nattrass*:[2]

> D advertised the sale by mail order of louvre doors on fourteen days' free approval, after which price and carriage charges were payable. The advertisement also offered folding door gear on approval 'carriage free': D intended that the gear should be supplied only with the doors, and did not appreciate that the advertisement could be read so that gear might be taken to be offered separately. *Held:* in refusing to supply the door gear alone carriage free, D recklessly committed an offence under s. 14.

---

1 TDA, s. 14 (2) (b).
2 [1973] 1 All ER 307, [1973] 1 WLR 307, DC.

---

3. Sanctions, responsibility, defences and enforcement

Sanctions

i) Offences

18.15 A person guilty of an offence under this Act will usually be fined, but may be subjected to imprisonment on conviction on indictment.[1] Time-limits for prosecutions are laid down as follows:[2] the outside time-limit is three years from commission of the offence or one year from discovery, whichever is the earlier; but the usual six months limit is retained for offences committed by oral statement. There are complicated provisions to deal with the overlap of offences between this and certain other statutes.[3]

ii) Civil liability

The TDA does not itself purport to grant any civil rights of action. However, with the objective of not affecting the availability of civil rights under other rules of law one way or the other, s. 35 provides:

> 'A contract for the supply of any goods shall not be void or unenforceable by reason only of a contravention of any provision of this Act'.

Thus, on ordinary principles, an action may lie for breach of contract, e.g. for breach of an implied term,[4] or under the Misrepresentation Act 1967,[5] or in tort for deceit,[6] negligent misstatement,[7] or possibly for breach of statutory duty.[8] Moreover, prosecution to conviction before the institution of civil proceedings has the following advantages to any injured party: instead of civil proceedings, the convicting court may make a compensation order;[9] and in any event the conviction will provide prima facie evidence for the civil proceedings.[10]

---

1 TDA, s. 18. Prosecution will usually be summary, where there is a maximum fine. For the situations where imprisonment may be justified, see *R v Haesler* [1973] RTR 486, CA.
2 TDA, s. 19. For when time begins to run, see *Rees v Munday* [1974] 3 All ER 506, [1974] 1 WLR 1284, DC.
3 TDA, s. 22.
4 See paras. 13.19, et seq., ante.
5 See paras. 5.12–5.13, ante.
6 See paras. 5.10–5.11, ante.
7 See para. 5.12, ante.
8 Cf. *Square v Model Farm Dairies (Bournemouth) Ltd* [1939] 2 KB 365, [1939] 1 All ER 259, CA.
9 Powers of the Criminal Courts Act 1973, ss. 35, 43.
10 Civil Evidence Act 1968, s. 11.

Responsibility for offences

18.16 Not content with the imposition of (frequently strict) criminal liability in respect of the making of false statements, the TDA further introduces a measure of vicarious criminal liability.

a) Offences by corporations Recognising that a company is a figment of the legal imagination and is run by real people, the Act has sought to render those people vicariously liable. Section 20 (1) provides:

'Where an offence under this Act which has been committed by a body corporate[1] is proved to have been committed with the consent and connivance of, or to be attributable to any neglect on the part of, any director,[2] manager, secretary or other similar officer of the body corporate, or of any person who was purporting to act in any such capacity, he as well as the body corporate shall be guilty of that offence and shall be liable to be proceeded against and punished accordingly'.

The following two restrictions on the prosecution of an officer under s. 20 should be noted: first, he may only be convicted if the body corporate is guilty of an offence; second, that body's offence must be committed 'with his consent or connivance', or must be due to his 'neglect'.

b) Accessories to overseas offences Section 21 makes it an offence to act as an accessory within the UK to offences committed outside the UK.

c) Offences due to the default of another Section 23 provides as follows:

'Where the commission by any person of an offence under this Act is due to the act or default of some other person that other person shall be guilty of an offence, and a person may be charged with and convicted of the offence by virtue of this section whether or not proceedings are taken against the first mentioned person'.

Section 23 envisages that B be made criminally liable thereunder for offences committed by A. However, conviction of B requires the following: first, A must have committed an offence;[3] and second, A's offence must have been due to the act or default of B.[4] Given these requirements, s. 23 allows the prosecutor a discretion: he may proceed against either or both A and B. In *Nattrass v Timpson Shoes*:[5]

T, owners of multiple shoe shops issued to branch managers a warning against committing offences under the TDA and a procedure for re-pricing goods. In one of the shops where the manager re-dressed the window, one pair of shoes in the display was by mistake left displaying the old price. T was charged with an offence under s. 11 (2), and the manager with an offence under s. 23 on the grounds that it was due to his act or default. *Held:* T was rightly acquitted on the ground that the offence was due to the manager's default under s. 24 (1); but the manager's plea that it was due to the fault of his five assistants was rejected.

---

1 This has been held to include a Scottish partnership: *Douglas v Phoenix Motors* 1970 SLT 57. Quaere whether it applies to England.

2 'Director' is defined to include similar officers in nationalised industries: TDA, s. 20 (2).

3 *Coupe v Guyett* [1973] 2 All ER 1058, [1973] 1 WLR 669, DC; *Cottee v Douglas Seaton (Used Cars)* [1972] 3 All ER 750, [1972] 1 WLR 1408, DC.

4 *Tarleton Engineering Co Ltd v Nattrass* [1973] 3 All ER 699, [1973] 1 WLR 1261, DC.

5 [1973] Crim. LR 197, DC.

Defences

a) MISTAKE, ACCIDENT, ETC.

18.17 Section 24 sets out two such defences: (i) a general defence of limited scope; and (ii) a rather more generous defence in respect of offences under s. 1 (1) (b).

i) General defence

Section 24 (1) provides that in any proceedings for an offence under this Act it shall be a good defence for the defendant to prove:[1]

'(a) that the commission of the offence was due to a mistake or to reliance on information supplied to him or to the act or default of another person, an accident or some other cause beyond his control; and

(b) that he took all reasonable precautions and exercised all due diligence to avoid the commission of such an offence by himself or any person under his control'.

To succeed in this defence, a defendant must prove[1] *one* of the matters specified in paragraph (a) *and both* the matters specified in paragraph (b).

Paragraph (a) This envisages that the commission of the offence was due to:

1. A mistake, which must be that of the defendant;[2] or

2. Reliance on information supplied to him by another, e.g. an odometer reading,[3] but to rely on this ground the defendant may have to provide details in advance of the person on whom reliance was placed;[4] or

3. The act or default of another person, which expression includes the defendant's employee,[5] but to rely on this ground the defendant may have to provide details in advance of the person on whom reliance was placed;[4] or

4. An accident;[6] or

5. Some other cause beyond his control.[7]

Paragraph (b) Even assuming the defendant can prove one of the grounds listed above, the defendant must show that he *both*:

1. Took all reasonable precautions, e.g. if he cannot verify the facts, make an adequate disclaimer of them;[8] *and*

2. Exercised all due diligence.[9]

An early case set the defendant a high standard: he would be convicted unless he could show that there was no reasonable precaution, etc., which would have avoided commission of an offence;[10] but the effect of a House of Lords decision would appear to be that a corporate trader can only be convicted on proof of mens rea. In *Tesco Supermarkets Ltd v Nattrass*:[11]

T Ltd set up a careful and elaborate system of supervision of its employees to avoid the commission of offences under the TDA. Because a store manager failed to check the work of his staff in accordance with his duties, a 'special offer' poster was displayed at a time when no goods were available at the special price, so that a s. 11 (2) offence was committed. *Held*:

head office had set up a proper system of control and T Ltd should be acquitted because the offence had been committed through the default of another (their store manager).

ii) *Special defence to s. 1 (1) (b)*

Where the defendant had simply supplied goods to which another had applied a false trade description, Parliament took the view that the defendant was deserving of a somewhat more liberal defence. Accordingly, s. 24 (3) laid down that:

> 'it shall be a defence for the person charged to prove that he did not know, and could not with reasonable diligence have ascertained, that the goods did not conform to the description or that the description had been applied to the goods'.

Thus, it is a defence for the defendant to show that he did not know[12] and could not with reasonable diligence have ascertained[13] *either*

1. That the goods did not conform with the description, *or*
2. That the description had been applied to the goods.

---

1 *Whitehead v Collett* [1975] Crim. LR 53, DC.
2 *Birkenhead and District Co-Operative Society v Roberts* [1970] 3 All ER 391, [1970] 1 WLR 1497, DC; *Butler v Keenway Supermarkets* [1974] Crim. LR 560, DC.
3 *Simmons v Potter* [1975] RTR 347, DC.
4 TDA, s. 24 (2). See *McGuire v Sittingbourne Co-Operative Society* [1976] Crim. LR 268, DC.
5 *Tesco Supermarkets Ltd v Nattrass* [1972] AC 153, [1971] 2 All ER 127, HL.
6 E.g. notwithstanding that he acted as a diligent trader under para. (b), a 'pure' accident happened, i.e. his system does not need to be foolproof.
7 E.g. a practical joke by a member of the public.
8 See *Zawadski v Sleigh* [1975] RTR 113, DC; *Simmons v Potter* [1975] RTR 347, DC.
9 *Naish v Gore* [1971] 3 All ER 737, DC.
10 *Sherratt v Gerald's The American Jewellers* (1970) LGR 256, DC.
11 [1972] AC 153, [1971] 2 All ER 127, HL. But see the criticism in Cmnd. 6628, paras. 52–63.
12 *Furniss v Scott* [1973] RTR 314, DC.
13 *Naish v Gore* (ante); *Richmond-upon-Thames London Borough Council v Motor Sales (Hounslow)* [1971] RTR 116, DC.

---

b) INNOCENT PUBLICATION

18.18 To provide a special defence for owners of news media, s. 25 enacts as follows:

> 'In proceedings for an offence under this Act, committed by the publication of an advertisement[1] it shall be a defence for the person charged to prove that he is a person whose business

it is to publish or arrange for the publication of advertisements and that he received the advertisement for publication in the ordinary course of business and did not know and had no reason to suspect that its publication would amount to an offence under this Act'.

This section applies to the following offences: applying a false trade description to goods by publication of an advertisement;[2] contravening any regulations made under s. 9;[3] a misleading indication as to price;[4] a false representation of royal approval, etc.;[5] a false statement as to services.[6]

---

1 For 'advertisement', see TDA, s. 39 (1).
2 TDA, s. 5: see para. 18.04, ante.
3 See ante, para. 18.08 (a).
4 TDA, s. 11 (3) (d): see para. 18.09, ante.
5 TDA, ss. 12 and 13: see para. 18.08 (d), ante.
6 TDA, s. 14: see paras. 18.11, et seq., ante.

---

c) EXEMPTED EXPORTS, ETC.

18.19 Section 32 empowers the government by regulation to exempt goods sold for export from the strict rigours of a trade description.[1] Section 34 grants a limited exemption to certain registered trade marks.[2] Section 37 purports to exempt genuine market research experiments from the full rigours of the Act.

---

1 See TDA, s. 2: para. 18.05, ante.
2 They must be in existence on 30.5.68. For trade marks, see chap. 30.

Enforcement

i) Enforcing authorities

18.20 Section 26 envisages the following system of enforcement:

1. Local enforcement shall be in the hands of the Local Authorities, and it is their duty to enforce within their area the provisions of this Act.[1]
2. Central direction and supervision of the Local Authorities is envisaged,[2] and in practice these functions seem to have devolved on the Director General of Fair Trading.[3]

ii) Enforcement powers

In enforcing the Act, the Local Authority is given certain statutory powers:

1. To make test purchases.[4]

2. To enter premises and inspect goods[5]—where he can gain entry, the inspector can use this power to make 'spot checks'; but, where he does have reasonable suspicion of an offence, he may obtain a search warrant.[6]

3. If he has reasonable cause to believe that an offence has been committed under this Act, the local authority inspector may require the production of documents and make copies thereof,[7] seize suspected goods,[8] and also seize and detain evidence;[9] and he may enforce the foregoing by breaking open containers and vending machines.[10]

4. Whilst protecting solicitors' privileged communications[11] and seeking to guard against misuse of powers by local authority officers,[12] the Act makes it an offence wilfully to obstruct them in the course of their duties.[13]

iii) Duties of enforcing authorities

Whilst exercising the above enforcement powers, the local authorities are subject to the following duties:

1. To give notification of seizure of goods or documents, usually to the owner.[14]

2. To give notice of the results of any test to a person who is to be prosecuted.[15]

3. To give the Director General of Fair Trading 28 days' notice of intended prosecution before instituting proceedings.[16]

4. Unless the owner is convicted, to compensate him for all loss suffered by reason of the detention of goods.[17]

Finally, s. 31 empowers the govenment to make regulations as to the provision of evidence by certificate.

---

1 TDA, s. 26 (as amended).
2 TDA, ss. 26 (2)–(4); 30 (2).
3 See para. 19.01, post.
4 TDA, s. 27.
5 TDA, s. 28 (1) (a).
6 TDA, s. 28 (3).
7 TDA, s. 28 (1) (b).
8 TDA, s. 28 (1) (c).
9 TDA, s. 28 (1) (d).
10 TDA, s. 28 (1) (e).
11 TDA, s. 28 (7).
12 TDA, s. 28 (4)–(6).
13 TDA, s. 29.
14 TDA, s. 28 (2).
15 TDA, s. 30 (1).
16 Fair Trading Act 1973, s. 130: see para. 19.07, post.
17 TDA, s. 33.

Chapter 19

Fair trading

1. Introduction

19.01 The Fair Trading Act 1973 (FTA) has the following major objectives:

1. The promotion of increased economic efficiency through wide powers given to deal with monopolies, mergers and restrictive practices;[1] and
2. the protection of consumers against unfair trading practices.[2]

Central to the operation of the Act is the creation of the Office of Fair Trading (OFT), presided over by the Director General of Fair Trading (DG).[3] In relation to the second objective, the more important functions of the DG are as follows:[4]

a) To keep under review, and to collect, receive and collate information concerning, commercial activities in the United Kingdom affecting the interests of consumers.[5]

b) To make references, and give information and assistance, to the Consumer Protection Advisory Committee in respect of matters falling within Part 2 of the Act.[6]

c) To make recommendations to the Secretary of State as to what action to take in relation to matters within (a) or (b) above.[7]

d) To obtain undertakings and initiate court proceedings under Part 3 of the Act.[8]

e) To publish information and advice to consumers, and to encourage trade associations to prepare codes of practice for guidance in safeguarding and promoting the interests of UK consumers.[9]

f) To make annual and other reports to the Secretary of State in respect of matters falling within the scope of his duties under any enactment, such reports to be published and laid before Parliament.[10]

g) To act as the central enforcement agency for the Trade Descriptions Acts[11] and the Consumer Credit Act 1974.[12]

---

1 See chap. 28, post.
2 For pyramid selling, see Part XI of the FTA.
3 FTA, s. 1 and Sch. 1. For a summary of the functions of the DG, see the 1976 Annual Report, Appendix 5.
4 The DG is subject to the general control of the Secretary of State, as to whose powers, see FTA, s. 12.
5 FTA, ss. 2 (1), (2); 131.
6 FTA, s. 14 (4): see paras. 19.04, et seq., post.
7 FTA, s. 2 (3). For the power of the Secretary of State to make orders, see para. 19.07, post.
8 FTA, s. 2 (4): see paras. 19.09, et seq., post.
9 FTA, s. 124. The OFT has published a substantial number of leaflets and booklets.
10 FTA, s. 125. E.g. The Review of the Trade Description Act, Cmnd. 6628 (1976).
11 See para. 18.20, ante.
12 See para. 14.19, ante.

A 'consumer'

19.02 Clearly vital to this facet of the FTA is the concept of a 'consumer', which expression is defined by reference to the status of both the person supplying goods or services and the person to whom they are supplied:[1]

1) The supplier must supply in the course of a business,[1] which expression includes a foreign importer[2] and arrangements made in this country for the supply to be made abroad.[3] Where there is an instalment credit contract for the supply of goods,[4] both the suppliers of finance and goods are caught.[5]

2) The person to whom the supply is made does not receive them in the course of a business carried on by him.[1] This includes any surety for that person.[6]

This concept of a 'consumer' for the purposes of the FTA may be compared with the ambit of certain other statutory provisions designed to protect consumers, e.g. the Trade Descriptions Act 1968,[7] the Consumer Credit Act 1974,[8] the Unfair Contract Terms Act.[9]

---

1 FTA, ss. 137 (1); 138 (7).
2 FTA, s. 138 (2).
3 FTA, s. 138 (3).
4 For instalment credit contracts, see chap. 14, ante. But for FTA purposes, simple hiring is excluded.
5 FTA, s. 138 (4), (5). For vendor and lender credit, see paras. 14.09–14.10, ante.

6 FTA, s. 138 (6). For sureties, see chap. 16, ante.
7 See chap. 18, ante.
8 See paras. 14.12, et seq., ante.
9 See paras. 3.15, 13.27, ante.

19.03   Whereas the Acts just referred to themselves create a
substantial number of criminal offences and/or causes of action,
this is not the case with those Parts of the FTA which are
designed for the protection of the consumer, which instead
contain enabling provisions. If the DG discovers a business
activity which he considers to be detrimental to consumers, he is
given the following powers:

1. Where he considers that that type of conduct is not, but
should be, regulated, he may initiate the process under Part 2 of
the Act for the promulgation of a statutory order to deal with
that conduct.[1]
2. Where the business activity is already regulated by law, but a
particular business is finding it worthwhile to break that law
persistently, he may under Part 3 of the Act obtain a court order
requiring the cessation of that activity.[2]

---

1 See paras. 19.04, et seq., post.
2 See paras. 19.09, et seq., post.

---

2. Orders against unfair trade practices

19.04   The ambit of Part 2 of the FTA is restricted to 'consumer trade
practices', which expression means:[1]

'any practice which is for the time being carried on in
connection with the supply of goods (whether by way of sale
or otherwise) to consumers or in connection with the supply of
services for consumers and which relates—

(a) to the terms or conditions (whether as to price or
otherwise) on or subject to which goods or services are or
are sought to be supplied, or
(b) to the manner in which those terms or conditions are
communicated to persons to whom goods are or are sought
to be supplied or for whom services are or are sought to be
supplied, or
(c) to promotion (by advertising, labelling or marking of

415

goods, canvassing or otherwise) of the supply of goods or of the supply of services,[2] or

(d) to methods of salesmanship employed in dealing with consumers, or

(e) to the way in which goods are packed or otherwise got up for the purpose of being supplied, or

(f) to methods of demanding or securing payment for goods or services supplied'.[3]

Thus, the section does not insist that there be any contractual connection between the consumer and the supplier,[4] a matter likely to be of particular significance in relation to paragraphs (c), (d) and (e);[5] nor is it even restricted to persons in the chain of supply, so that it includes, e.g. advertising agencies. However, the list of practices is exhaustive for Part 2, and there is also specific exclusion of most professional services, e.g. legal or medical,[6] and of goods or services supplied by the nationalised industries.[7]

Where there is a consumer trade practice as above defined, the DG or Minister may refer to the Consumer Protection Advisory Committee (CPAC) the question of whether it 'adversely affects the economic interests of consumers in the United Kingdom'.[8] The CPAC has no powers of initiation itself, but just a very limited advisory role.

---

1 FTA, s. 13. For 'consumer', see para. 19.02, ante.
2 Many of these matters will also fall within the Trade Descriptions Acts: see chap. 18, ante.
3 Some of these may already amount to the unlawful harassment of debtors: Administration of Justice Act 1970, s. 40.
4 Including those by the suppliers of goods and suppliers of finance: see para. 19.02, ante.
5 E.g. to catch manufacturers.
6 FTA, s. 15 and Sch. 4.
7 FTA, s. 16 and Sch. 5.
8 FTA, s. 14 (1).

---

i) References to the CPAC

19.05 Section 14 merely imposes a general investigative role on the CPAC.[1] Unless the reference is also made under s. 17, there is no provision for action to be taken on the CPAC report.[2] The aim of s. 17 is to enable prompt action to be taken when new and unfair consumer trade practices come to light; and some idea of the types of practice which Parliament had in mind may be gathered both from the limitations spelt out in s. 17 and from the scope of the recommendations listed in Schedule 6. Section 17 is limited to:

1. consumer trade practices within s. 13, which
2. adversely affect the economic interests of U.K. consumers within s. 14, and also
3. appear to the DG to be likely to have the effect:[3]

'(a) of misleading consumers as to, or withholding from them adequate information as to, or an adequate record of, their rights and obligations under relevant consumer transactions, or
(b) of otherwise misleading or confusing consumers with respect to any matter in connection with relevant consumer transactions, or
(c) of subjecting consumers to undue pressure to enter into relevant consumer transactions, or
(d) of causing the terms or conditions, on or subject to which consumers enter into relevant consumer transactions, to be so adverse to them as to be inequitable'.

The reference to the CPAC must be in the stipulated form,[4] may include a draft statutory order,[5] and must be published in full.[6] The CPAC is required to take into account representations by persons having a substantial interest[7] and general directions from the Secretary of State,[8] but is otherwise free to determine its own procedure.[9]

---

1 For the CPAC, see s. 3 and Sch. 2.
2 Nor may the DG act under s. 17 except by making such a reference to the CPAC: FTA, s. 18.
3 FTA, s. 17 (2). 'Relevant consumer transaction' is defined ibid, s. 17 (5).
4 FTA, ss. 17 (3), 19 and Sch. 6.
5 FTA, s. 17 (2).
6 FTA, s. 17 (4).
7 FTA, s. 81 (1).
8 FTA, s. 81 (3), (4).
9 FTA, s. 81 (2).

---

ii) Reports by the CPAC

19.06 In order that the s. 17 procedure may be pursued, the following requirements must be fulfilled: a report by the CPAC must be made to the Secretary of State, generally within three months,[1] setting out in full the terms of reference[2] and their conclusions;[3] and it may also include reasoned dissents.[4] The whole report is absolutely privileged, but must attempt not to prejudice unduly the affairs of individuals.[5]

---

1 FTA, s. 20.
2 FTA, s. 21 (3).

3 FTA, s. 20 (1), (2).
4 FTA, s. 82 (3).
5 FTA, s. 82 (2), (1).

---

iii) Statutory orders in pursuance of CPAC reports

19.07 The Secretary of State is under a general duty to lay reports of the CPAC before Parliament,[1] but is then given a limited discretion as to whether to initiate a statutory order: provided the CPAC agree with the reference,[2] he may make a draft order giving effect to the proposals set out in the reference,[3] and lay it before Parliament.[4]

Contravention of the terms of such a statutory order is made an offence[5] with the usual time-limits;[6] but it is not to affect the civil rights of the parties.[7] Moreover, the FTA contains provisions with regard to the following matters which are virtually identical with those of the Trade Descriptions Acts:[8] offences by corporations;[9] offences due to the default of another;[10] defences;[11] enforcing authorities;[12] the powers to make test purchases,[13] and of entry, inspection and seizure;[14] and as to the duties of enforcing officers.[15]

---

1 FTA, s. 83.
2 FTA, s. 22 (1). There is allowance for modifications by the CPAC.
3 FTA, s. 22 (2), (3).
4 FTA, s. 22 (4).
5 FTA, s. 23. Cf. para. 18.15, ante.
6 FTA, s. 129. Cf. para. 18.15, ante.
7 FTA, s. 26. Cf. para. 18.15, ante.
8 Cf. also the Consumer Credit Act 1974: see para. 14.19, ante.
9 FTA, s. 132. Cf. para. 18.16 (a) ante.
10 FTA, s. 24. Cf. para. 18.16 (c), ante.
11 FTA, s. 25. Cf. para. 18.17, ante.
12 FTA, s. 27. Cf. para. 18.20 (*i*), ante.
13 FTA, s. 28. Cf. para. 18.20 (*ii*), ante.
14 FTA, ss. 29, 30. Cf. para. 18.20 (*ii*), ante.
15 FTA, ss. 31, 32, 130, 133. Cf. para. 18.20 (*iii*), ante.

19.08 This procedure under Part 2 has already been used to bring into force statutory instruments as follows:

a) Restrictions on statements Whilst clauses purporting to limit or exclude the terms implied in favour of a consumer in a sale or instalment credit contract are already avoided by statute,[1] nevertheless they have continued to appear and to mislead consumers as to their rights. It has therefore been made an offence for either the retailer or manufacturer to supply a statement which is either so avoided or is misleading as to the statutory implied terms.[2]

b) Business advertisements In contracts for the supply of goods, certain terms are implied only where the supply is made in the course of a business;[3] and the practice had developed of advertising goods for sale in such a manner that there appeared to be a private sale, and hence misleading the consumer into believing that his contract did not contain these implied terms. Such advertisements have now been made an offence.[4]

---

1 See paras. 13.27, 14.04, ante.
2 S.I. 1976 No. 1813.
3 See paras. 13.22–13.24, 14.04, ante.
4 S.I. 1977 No. 1918.

---

3. Persistent breaches of the law

19.09 According to s. 34 (1), the DG may exercise his powers under Part 3 of the FTA where it appears to him that a person carrying on a business[1] has in the course of that business persisted in a course of conduct[2] which satisfies *both* the following criteria:[3]

1. '[It] is detrimental to the interests of consumers[4] in the United Kingdom, whether those interests are economic interests or interests in respect of health, safety or other matters';[5] *and*
2. It is unfair to consumers,[3] in that it consists of *either:*

(a) 'contraventions of one or more enactments which impose duties, prohibitions or restrictions enforceable by criminal proceedings, whether any such duty, prohibition or restriction is imposed in relation to consumers[4] as such or not and whether the person carrying on the business has or has not been convicted of any offence in respect of any such contravention';[6] *or*

(b) 'things done, or omitted to be done, in the course of that business in breach of contract or in breach of a duty (other than a contractual duty) owed to any person by virtue of any enactment or rule of law and enforceable by civil proceedings, whether (in any such case) civil proceedings in respect of the breach of contract or breach of duty have been brought or not'.[7]

Where the above conditions are fulfilled, the DG will proceed as follows: he must first attempt to obtain suitable written undertakings to cease the practice; and, only if that attempt fails, or such undertakings are broken, may he apply for a court order.

1 See FTA, s. 137 (2).
2 For the ways in which the DG shall get evidence of this persistence, see s. 34 (4).
3 FTA, s. 34 (1).
4 For consumers, see para. 19.02, ante.
5 FTA, s. 34 (1). E.g. over-pricing; restricting supplies (inc. spares); goods and services which are dangerous.
6 FTA, s. 34 (2). E.g. offences under the Trade Descriptions Acts or Consumer Credit Act 1974.
7 FTA, s. 34 (3). E.g. breaches of implied terms in contracts for the supply of goods; manufacture of dangerous goods.

i) Written undertakings

19.10 Assuming the DG is satisfied that the above conditions exist, s. 34. directs him to:[1]

'use his best endeavours, by communication with that person or otherwise, to obtain from him a satisfactory written assurance that he will refrain from continuing that course of conduct and from carrying on any similar course of conduct in the course of that business'.

Nor can there be any hiding behind the device of incorporation. Where it appears to the DG that the conduct within s. 34 has been carried on by a body corporate 'with the consent or connivance' of what the Act terms an 'accessory', the DG may *also* proceed against that accessory.[2] A list of the undertakings so given is to be found in the OFT Annual Reports.

1 FTA, s. 34 (1).
2 FTA, s. 38.

ii) Court Orders

19.11 Where, but only where, he is unable to obtain satisfactory written assurances as above, or where such assurances are broken, the DG *may* bring proceedings before the Restrictive Practices Court.[1] In these proceedings, the DG will have to prove that the respondent's conduct is within s. 34, the decision of any court being prima facie evidence for this purpose.[2] The court then has a choice: it may accept any suitable offer from the respondent to refrain from that or any similar course of conduct;[3] or it may order that he do so.[4] Where the DG has additionally, or instead, brought an accessory before the court, the court has similar powers; and there are wide powers to prevent avoidance of the process by transferring business between companies in a group.[6] Legal aid is available in these proceedings,[7] and appeal on fact or law lies to the Court of

Appeal.[8] Breach of such an order will amount to a contempt of court.

---

1 FTA, s. 35. In respect of 'small traders', there is power instead to bring proceedings in the County Court: FTA, s. 41.
2 FTA, s. 36.
3 FTA, s. 37 (3).
4 FTA, s. 37 (2).
5 FTA, s. 39.
6 FTA, s. 40.
7 FTA, s. 43.
8 FTA, s. 42.

Part VI

Negotiable instruments

Chapter 20

Bills of exchange and other negotiable instruments

1. Introduction

20.01 A negotiable instrument was defined by Judge Willis, as

'one the property in which is acquired by any one who takes it bona fide, and for value, notwithstanding any defect of title in the person from whom he took it; from which it follows that an instrument cannot be negotiable unless it is such and in such a state that the true owner could transfer the contract or engagement contained therein by simple delivery of the instrument'.[1]

This definition involves the following characteristics of a negotiable instrument:

1. Property in it passes from hand to hand by mere delivery or delivery and indorsement;
2. The holder in due course, i.e. someone to whom it is thus transferred and who acquires it bona fide and for value, is not prejudiced by defects of title of his transferor or of previous holders;
3. He can sue in his own name;
4. He is not affected by certain defences which might be available against previous holders, e.g. fraud to which he is no party.[2]

This may be illustrated by examples:

A owes B £500; he gives a written recognition of the debt—say the shortened form of acknowledgment known as an IOU. The debt evidenced by this IOU can be *assigned* by B to C and such assignment will be effective under s. 136 of the Law of Property Act 1925 or in equity if certain conditions are satisfied[3] but any defence good against B, e.g. no consideration, will be good against C. However, if A gives B a bill of exchange payable to bearer for £500, then B can *negotiate* the bill to C simply by delivery of the bill and if C is a holder in due course, he is not liable to be defeated by any defence personal to B, e.g. fraud by B in obtaining the bill from A.

The character of negotiability does not attach itself to every instrument, but only to those which have acquired it either by mercantile custom or statute. Whether or not a document is negotiable is in many cases a question of fact to be proved by evidence; in some cases instruments are, as a matter of law, recognised as negotiable. The following are negotiable:

1. Bills of exchange.[4]
2. Promissory notes (including bank notes).[5]
3. Cheques.
4. Exchequer bills.
5. Circular notes.[6]
6. Dividend warrants.
7. Share warrants.[7]
8. Debentures payable to bearer.[8]
9. Certain bonds payable to bearer.
10 Scrip certificates, i.e., documents giving the bearer a right to shares after the instalments due upon the shares are duly paid.[9]
11. Bankers' drafts. These are often drawn by a branch on the head office or another branch.[10] As they embody the bank's own obligation to pay they are treated as the equivalent of cash and used in transactions where a very reliable means of payment is required as in the completion of the sale of real property.[11]

On the other hand, the following are not negotiable:

1. Postal orders and money orders.[12]
2. Share certificates and transfers.[13]

It is doubtful if travellers' cheques can be negotiable.[14] An IOU is not negotiable, nor is an ordinary letter of credit.[15]

The list of negotiable instruments may increase, as the law recognises instruments as negotiable when they are transferable by delivery and are regarded by custom as negotiable. As Cockburn CJ stated in *Goodwin v Robarts*, a contrary statement would be:

'founded on the view that the law merchant ... is fixed and stereotyped, and incapable of being expanded and enlarged so as to meet the wants and requirements of trade in the varying circumstances of commerce',[16]

and though the greater or less time during which a custom has existed may be material in determining how far it has generally prevailed, if a usage is once shown to be universal, effect will be given to it, though it may not have formed part of the law merchant as previously recognised and adopted by the courts.[17]

The decision of Kennedy J in *Bechuanaland Exploration Co v*

London Trading Bank,[18] shows that the class of negotiable instruments may be enlarged by the growth of mercantile custom. It was held in that case, upon proof by evidence adduced in court of recent usage in the mercantile world:

that debentures payable to bearer issued by an English company in England were negotiable instruments.

The court may later regard the custom as so well-known that special proof of it is not required but it is judicially noticed.[19]

---

1 *Willis on Negotiable Securities* (5th edn) 5, 6.
2 See per Bowen LJ in *Simmons v London Joint Stock Bank* [1891] Ch at 294.
3 See para. 4.09, ante.
4 See para. 20.03, post.
5 See chap. 21.
6 *Conflans Quarry Co v Parker* (1868) LR 3 CP 1.
7 *Webb, Hale & Co v Alexandria Water Co, Ltd* (1905) 21 TLR 572.
8 *Bechuanaland Exploration Co v London Trading Bank Ltd* [1898] 2 QB 658.
9 *Rumball v Metropolitan Bank* (1877) 2 QBD 194; *London Joint Stock Bank v Simmons* [1892] AC 201.
10 By the Bills of Exchange Act 1882, s. 5 (2) the holder may treat it either as a bill of exchange or promissory note. See para. 20.05, post.
11 See chap. 12.
12 *Fine Art Society v Union Bank of London* (1886) 17 QBD 705.
13 *Swan v North British Australasian Co* (1863) 32 LJ Exch at 278.
14 See *Chitty on Contracts* (24th edn) Vol. 2, 195–198.
15 See chap. 13.
16 *Goodwin v Robarts* (1875) LR 10 Ex. 346; 1 App Cas 476. The judgment of Cockburn CJ, in this case traces the origin and growth of negotiable instruments.
17 *Goodwin v Robarts* ante at 356.
18 [1898] 2 QB 658.
19 *Edelstein v Schuler* [1902] 2 KB 144.

Quasi-negotiability of bills of lading

20.02 According to the special verdict of the jury in *Lickbarrow v Mason,*[1] bills of lading, if drawn to order or assigns, are by the custom of merchants negotiable by delivery and indorsement for value, provided that the goods represented by the bills have been shipped and the voyage has not yet been completed nor delivery made; if the indorsement is in blank the holder is entitled to fill in the name, and thus put the bill of lading on a negotiable footing. This statement of custom has been adopted by the courts as law and if the bill of lading is not drawn to the order or assigns of the holder, it seems the bill is not negotiable.[2]

Nevertheless bills of lading, though drawn to order, are not negotiable as a bill of exchange is negotiable. They are not negotiable in the strict sense of the term, for the transferee, though bona fide, and though he has given value for the bill, cannot get a good title from a transferor whose title is defective. They are in effect only negotiable so as to defeat, in favour of a bona fide transferee for value, the lien of the unpaid vendor and his right to stop in transitu.[3]

1 (1793) 6 East 20n.
2 *Henderson v Comptoir D'Escompte de Paris* (1874) LR 5PC 253.
3 *Gurney v Behrend* (1854) 3 E & B at 633, 634, per Lord Campbell; *Schuster v McKellar* (1857) 7 E & B 704; and see observations of Selborne LC, and Lord Blackburn in *Sewell v Burdick* (1885) 10 App Cas 74.

2. Bills of exchange

20.03 The law relating to bills of exchange was put in the form of a code in the Bills of Exchange Act 1882, and in it will be found the chief law on the subject; but all rules of common law and the law merchant, relating to bills of exchange, promissory notes and cheques, remain in force except in so far as they are inconsistent with the Act.[1] The 1882 Act was mainly declaratory and made but few alterations in the law.[2]

1 Bills of Exchange Act 1882, s. 97 (2).
2 Lord Blackburn, in *McLean v Clydesdale Banking Co* (1884) 9 App Cas 105 at 106; cf. Lord Herschell, in *Bank of England v Vagliano Bros* [1891] AC at 145.

How a bill is used

20.04 The simplest way to understand a bill of exchange is to consider the position where A owes money to B, e.g. for goods sold to him, and requests C to pay his debt for him, C being, perhaps, an agent or financier whom A has put, or has agreed to put, in funds. A then draws a bill requiring C to pay the money to B or to B's order. A is the 'drawer', B is the 'payee' and C is the 'drawee'. C may not pay B immediately; he may 'accept' the bill by signing his name across the face of it (in which case he is referred to as the 'acceptor') or he may refuse to accept it or he may give a 'qualified acceptance'. It may be necessary for B to 'present' the bill to C in order to see whether C will accept it, e.g. if the money is not payable until C has had notice of the bill, in other words if it is payable so many days 'after sight'. Meanwhile B may have transferred his rights under the bill, i.e. negotiated the bill, and it may have passed through several hands. In order to back the bill with their credit other persons may have 'indorsed' it. The right of the holder of the bill to sue on it may be affected by the question whether he or a predecessor has given value for it and whether he was aware of any defects in the title to the bill of the person from whom he received it.

In due course the bill will normally be 'presented for payment' to the acceptor. If he fails to meet it, or has refused to accept it, the bill is said to be 'dishonoured'. It may be necessary or advisable to obtain formal evidence of dishonour and in this case the bill is 'protested'. The holder will then have rights against the other parties who have signed the bill. In certain cases he may be able to sue the drawer and indorsers without first presenting the bill for payment to the acceptor, for presentment is excused in some circumstances where it would serve no useful purpose or is not practicable.

A bill may be used in various ways. Thus, in order to make the buyer primarily liable on the bill, the seller might draw the bill payable to his own order. The buyer would then accept it and a third party might indorse it as guarantor.

Definition of a bill

20.05 Section 3 (1) of the Bills of Exchange Act 1882 gives the following definition of a bill of exchange:

> 'A bill of exchange is an unconditional order in writing, addressed by one person to another, signed by the person giving it, requiring the person to whom it is addressed to pay on demand, or at a fixed or determinable future time, a sum certain in money to or to the order of a specified person, or to bearer.'

From this it will be seen that what is required is:

1. A written instrument to which there are three parties.
2. The instrument must be an order to pay money, and
3. The order to pay must be unconditional.[1]

Thus, it may not order any act to be done, in addition to the payment of money;[2] nor must it order payment out of a particular fund, for this would not be unconditional;[3] but it may specify a fund out of which the payer may reimburse himself, or may specify a particular account to be debited with the amount.[3] The definition of a bill of exchange includes cheques,[4] and in *Bavins Junior and Sims v London and South Western Bank.*[5]

a document in the form of an ordinary cheque ordering a banker to pay a sum of money '*provided the receipt form at foot hereof is duly signed, stamped and dated,*' was held not to be unconditional, and therefore not a cheque within the meaning of the Act.

Some usual forms of bills are as follows:

(*I*)

£100.   London, [Date]

Two months after date pay C. D., or order, the sum of one hundred pounds sterling for value received.

To Mr. E. F.   A. B.
London.

(*II*)

£50.   Bristol, [Date]

Accepted, E. F.

On demand pay C. D. the sum of fifty pounds sterling for value received.

To E. F.   R. S.
York.

(*III*)

£70.   Newcastle, [Date]

Accepted payable at Coutt's Bank.
A. B. C.

Pay to X. Y. sixty days after sight seventy pounds sterling.

To A. B. C.   F. G.

(*IV*)

£100.   Newcastle, [Date]

Accepted payable at the National Westminster Bank Ltd. London only.
ARTHUR JAMES.

Pay James Brown or bearer on November 1st, 1978, the sum of one hundred pounds for value received.

To Mr. ARTHUR JAMES.   F. ROBERTS.

(*V*)

£150.   London, [Date]

Accepted payable at Coutts Bank.
HENRY BROWN.

Ten days after date pay to my order the sum of one hundred and fifty pounds for value received.

To HENRY BROWN.   JOHN SMITH.

The three parties are styled respectively in the case of Form I, the drawer A B, the payee C D, and the drawee (who, if he accepts, becomes acceptor) E F, but the bill is good if it is drawn payable to the drawer (see Form V above) or to the drawee.[6] If the drawer and drawee are the same person as in a banker's draft, the holder may at his option treat the instrument as a promissory note, thereby excusing himself from the duties of a holder of a bill of exchange.[7]

---

1 As to conditional acceptances and indorsements, see para. 2.11 and 13, post.
2 Bill of Exchange Act 1882, s. 3 (2). See *Dickie v Singh* 1974 SLT, (Notes) 3.
3 Ibid, s. 3 (3).
4 Post, chap. 21.
5 [1900] 1 QB 270; cf. *Nathan v Ogdens Ltd* (1905) 94 LT 126, where the document contained the words: 'the receipt at the back must be signed.' It was held that these words were addressed to the payee, not the drawee, the order on the drawee was therefore unconditional, and the document a valid bill of exchange.
6 Bills of Exchange Act 1882, s. 5 (1).
7 Ibid, s. 5 (2). So also if the drawee is a fictitious person or without contractual capacity: for contractual capacity, see para. 2.15, et seq., ante.

20.06   *Drawee*   The drawee must be named or indicated with reasonable certainty, and if the bill is not payable to bearer, the same will apply to the payee.[1] There may be several joint drawees, but alternative or successive drawees are not allowed;[2] a drawee or referee, in case of need, may be named who, after dishonour and protest for non-acceptance, may accept or pay the bill with the holder's assent.[3]

Payee   The payee is the bearer if the bill is expressed to be payable to bearer, or if the only or last indorsement is an indorsement in blank; it is payable to order if it is so expressed, or if it is expressed to be payable to a particular person, and does not contain words prohibiting transfer.[4] An instrument payable to 'cash' is not a bill of exchange as it is not payable either to a specified person or to bearer.[5] By s. 7 (3), 'where the payee is a fictitious or non-existing person, the bill may be treated as payable to bearer'. As will be seen more fully later, when the holder of a bill payable to a specified person (an order bill) claims payment on it, his claim will normally fail if one of the indorsements on which his title rests is forged or unauthorised.[6] However, any indorsements on a bearer bill are superfluous since a bearer bill is negotiable simply by delivery. In *Clutton v Attenborough & Son:*[7]

A clerk employed by the appellants falsely represented to them that work had been done on their account by one George Brett and persuaded them to draw cheques in Brett's favour. No one of that name was known to the appellants or had in fact done any work for them. The clerk indorsed the cheques in the name of 'George Brett' and negotiated them to the respondents who gave value for them in good faith. The House of Lords *held* that as the payee on the cheques was fictitious they could be treated as payable to bearer and the respondents' title did not depend on any forged indorsement as bearer cheques are negotiable without indorsement. The respondents had a good title to the cheques.

Contrast *Vinden v Hughes*.[8] In that case:

The plaintiff's clerk filled up cheques payable to the order of certain customers with the names of the customers and sums of money which were not in fact owing to them. The clerk obtained the plaintiff's signature as drawer, forged the indorsements and negotiated the cheques to the defendant, who took them in good faith and for value. It was *held* that the payees were not 'fictitious', because the drawer believed when signing the cheques that he owed the sums mentioned to the persons whose names appeared on the cheques. In consequence the bill was not payable to bearer and since the defendants claim was based on a forged indorsement the drawer was able to recover the amount of cheques which his bankers had paid to the defendant.

In an earlier case, *Bank of England v Vagliano Brothers*:[9]

the House of Lords *held* that the payee is 'fictitious' within the meaning of s. 7 (3) even though the name is that of an existing person if the name of the payee has been inserted by way of pretence, by whoever in fact signed the bill as drawer, without any intention that the person named as payee should ever receive payment.

In this case a fraudulent clerk did not intend the person designated as payee to receive payment, the clerk being treated as the drawer; in *Vinden v Hughes* the employer as drawer did intend the payees to receive payment though for fictitious reasons.

Date The date should be inserted, but if a bill is issued undated, the omission is not fatal,[10] and the holder may insert the true date; if by *bona fide* mistake he inserts the wrong date, and in every case where a wrong date is inserted and the bill comes into the hands of a holder in due course, the bill is payable as if the date inserted had been the true date.[11] An instrument to which the Act applies may be ante-dated, post-dated, or dated on a Sunday.[12]

It has been held, however, that when an instrument is payable 'on or before' a given date this is not 'a fixed or determinable' future time and imported an element of contingency so that the instrument could not be a promissory note.[13] Equally it would seem that such a document could not be a bill of exchange.

Amount payable The sum payable by a bill is 'certain',[12] although required to be paid:

1. With interest, or
2. By stated instalments, or
3. By stated instalments with a provision that, on default in payment of any instalments, the whole shall become due, or
4. According to an indicated rate of exchange to be ascertained as directed by the bill.[14]

If the words and figures differ, the amount payable is that expressed in words.[15]

The words 'value received' are usually inserted, but there is no necessity for this, as value is presumed until contradicted.[16] The place where the bill is drawn or payable need not be stated.[17]

The bill may be written on paper, or on parchment, or on anything except on a metallic substance,[18] and it may be written in pencil, or in ink, or may be partially or wholly printed. Stamp duty on bills of exchange and promissory notes has been abolished.[19]

---

1 Ibid, ss. 6 (1) and 7 (1). It is permitted to add the drawer's name after the acceptor's death (*Carter v White* (1884) 25 ChD 666).
2 Ibid, s. 6 (2). Cf. para. 21.10, post, for promissory notes.
3 Ibid, ss. 15, 67.
4 Ibid, s. 8 (3), (4). The effect of this is dealt with in para. 20.12, post.
5 *Cole v Milsome* [1951] 1 All ER 311; *Orbit Mining and Trading Co v Westminster Bank Ltd* [1963] 1 QB 794, [1962] 3 All ER 565, CA. It may, however, be a good order to a banker to make payment.
6 See para. 20.14, post.
7 [1897] AC 90.
8 [1905] 1 KB 795.
9 [1891] AC 107.
10 Bills of Exchange Act 1882, s. 3 (4) (a).
11 Ibid, s. 12. 'Holder in due course' is defined, post, para. 20.16.
12 Ibid, s. 13.
13 *Williamson v Rider* [1963] 1 QB 89, [1962] 2 All ER 268, CA. Contra *Burrows (John) Ltd v Subsurface Surveyors* (1968) 68 DLR (2d) 354; *Creative Press v Harman* [1973] IR 313.
14 See definition of a bill of exchange, ante, para. 20.05.
15 Bills of Exchange Act 1882, s. 9.
16 Ibid, s. 3 (4) (b).
17 Ibid, s. 3 (4) (c).

18 Coinage Act 1971, s. 9.
19 Finance Act 1970, s. 32.

---

3. Parties

20.07   The Act declares that capacity to incur liability on a bill is co-extensive with capacity to contract,[1] as to which see ante, chapter 2. But the following rules are peculiar to the present subject:

1) No person who has not signed as such can be liable as drawer, indorser, or acceptor, except that a trade signature, or signature under an assumed name, is the equivalent of signature in the signer's own name.[2]

The signature of the name of a firm is equivalent to the signature by a person so signing of the names of all persons liable as partners of that firm.[3]

2) A limited company incorporated for the purposes of trade or otherwise having capacity, may be a party to a bill, and will be bound if the bill is made, accepted, or indorsed in the name of, or by or on behalf or on account of the company by any person acting under its authority.[4] If the signature is by procuration, e.g. 'per pro', it operates as a notice that the agent has but limited authority to sign, and the principal is only bound if the agent was acting within the actual limits of his authority.[5] But where by the constitution of the company the person signing a bill on its behalf might have been so authorised, any one taking the bill as a holder in due course is entitled to assume that such person had authority in fact unless he is put upon inquiry by some unusual circumstance.[6] The name of the company must appear in legible letters, and the word 'limited' or 'Ltd.' after it; otherwise the officer who causes the signature to be attached is liable to a penalty and, unless the bill is duly paid by the company, he is also personally liable on the bill.[7]

3) Where a person signs a bill but adds words indicating that he signs *qua* agent merely he incurs no personal liability.[8] But it does not follow because a man signs his name with words describing himself as agent, manager, etc., that he will be relieved from liability; the point to be determined is whether the words used suffice to give notice that the signature was affixed in the capacity of agent, or whether they are words of description. Thus:

X accepts bills as 'X, manager'; he is liable.[9] But if he accepts 'For the A Co Ltd, X, manager,' he is not liable.[10]

Where it is not clear whether the signature is that of the principal or of the agent by whose hand it is written, the construction most favourable to the validity of the instrument must be adopted.[11] Thus:

a bill was addressed to the F Co Ltd. It was accepted 'A.B; C.D.; directors, F Co Ltd', and also indorsed 'F Co Ltd, A.B.; C.D.; directors.' The bill was held to be validly *accepted* by the company, but *indorsed* by the directors personally on the ground that if the company was to be treated as indorsing a bill on which they were already liable as acceptors nothing would be added to its value, and consequently it was most favourable to the validity of the bill to construe the indorsement as the personal indorsement of the directors.[12]

4) Where a bill is drawn or indorsed by a minor, or by a corporation having no capacity to incur liability on the bill, the holder may nevertheless enforce it against any other parties having power to contract;[13] i.e. the title to the bill is passed by the minor's signature, but is passed *sans recours* to him.[14]

---

1 Bills of Exchange Act 1882, s. 22 (1). A minor cannot bind himself by accepting a bill whether it is in respect of necessaries or not (*Re Soltykoff* [1891] 1 QB 413). See para. 2.17, ante.

2 Bills of Exchange Act 1882, s. 23.

3 Ibid, s. 23. See para. 11.10, ante.

4 Companies Act 1948, s. 33. See European Communities Act 1972, s. 9, for the validity of acts decided on by directors.

5 Bills of Exchange Act 1882, s. 25.

6 *Dey v Pullinger Engineering Co* [1921] 1 KB 77. See *Freeman and Lockyer v Buckhurst Park Properties (Mangal) Ltd* [1964] 2 QB 480, [1964] 1 All ER 630, CA, for a review of the cases.

7 Companies Act 1948, s. 108. However, where the holders of a bill had prepared it with the name of the company as drawee incorrectly stated, they were estopped from enforcing the personal liability under this section of the director of the company who had signed the bill on behalf of the company without ensuring that the company's name was correctly written out: *Durham Fancy Goods Ltd v Michael Jackson (Fancy Goods) Ltd* [1968] 2 QB 839, [1968] 2 All ER 987.

8 Bills of Exchange Act 1882, s. 26 (1).

9 *Liverpool Bank v Walker* (1859) 4 De G & J 24.

10 *Alexander v Sizer* (1869) LR 4 Ex. 102.

11 Bills of Exchange Act 1882, s. 26 (2).

12 *Elliott v Bax-Ironside* [1925] 2 KB 301.

13 Bills of Exchange Act 1 (82, s. 22 (2)).

14 See s. 16 and para. 20.19, post.

4. Acceptance

20.08 The liability of the drawee does not arise until he has accepted the bill, and this is done by writing his name across the face of it; sometimes the word 'accepted' is added, though this is not necessary. The Act defines acceptance as:

'the signification by the drawee of his assent to the order of the drawer;[1]

and it enacts that

1. The signature of the drawee must be written on the bill;
2. The acceptance must not stipulate for performance by any other means than the payment of money.[2]

The bill may be accepted though it has not yet been signed by the drawer or is otherwise incomplete, or though already dishonoured, or though overdue;[3] but no signature will be binding and irrevocable against any person until after unconditional delivery of the instrument, in order to give effect thereto. An acceptance becomes irrevocable if the drawee gives notice to or according to the directions of the person entitled to the bill that he has accepted it.[4]

Only the person to whom the bill is addressed can accept it, unless he accepts *suprà protest* for the honour of a party liable on the bill.[5] The holder has no rights on the bill against the drawee if he does not accept it. Refusal to accept amounts to dishonour.[6]

Delivery

Every contract on a bill is incomplete and revocable until delivery of the instrument to give effect to the contract.[7] Delivery means transfer of possession, actual or constructive, from one person to another.[8]

Delivery between immediate parties and any remote party who is not a holder in due course may be shown to have been conditional only; but a valid delivery of the bill by all parties prior to him is conclusively presumed in favour of a holder in due course.[9] A valid delivery is also presumed to have taken place where the bill is no longer in the possession of a party who has signed it as drawer, acceptor, or indorser, but this presumption may be rebutted.[10]

---

1 Ibid, s. 17 (1).
2 Bills of Exchange Act 1882, s. 17 (2).
3 Ibid, s. 18.

4 Ibid, s. 21 (1). An acceptance should normally be unconditional. As to qualified acceptances see para. 20.11, post.

5 *Jackson v Hudson* (1810) 2 Camp. 447; para. 20.10, post.

6 See para. 20.20, post.

7 Bills of Exchange Act 1882, s. 21 (1).

8 Ibid, s. 21 (1). Constructive transfer takes place when an agent 'attorns' or agrees to hold a bill for a different principal.

9 Ibid, s. 21 (2).

10 Ibid, s. 21 (3).

Presentment for Acceptance

20.09 It is always advisable to present the bill for acceptance, for if it is refused, the parties, other than the drawee, become immediately liable, though the bill has not yet matured;[1] and it is sometimes necessary, e.g. where a bill is payable after sight to fix the maturity of the instrument; and when it is payable at a place other than the place of residence or business of the drawee, or when it is expressly stipulated that presentment shall be made, it must be presented for acceptance before it can be presented for payment.[2]

The holder must present a bill payable after sight for acceptance, or negotiate it, within a reasonable time; what is a reasonable time depending upon usage and the facts of the particular case.[3] Thus, in *Fry v Hill*:

> On Friday a person received at Windsor a bill drawn on a person in London, and the bill being payable after sight it had to be presented for acceptance; the holder presented it on Tuesday, and the jury, considering the fact that there was no post on Saturday, thought the time reasonable.[4]

The effect of failing to comply with this requirement as to a bill payable after sight is to discharge the drawer and all prior indorsers.[5]

The following rules as to presentment for acceptance are given in s. 41 of the Act:

> '(a) The presentment must be made by or on behalf of the holder to the drawee or to some person authorised to accept or refuse acceptance on his behalf at a reasonable hour on a business day and before the bill is overdue:
>
> (b) Where a bill is addressed to two or more drawees, who are not partners, presentment must be made to them all, unless one has authority to accept for all, then presentment may be made to him only:

(c) Where the drawee is dead, presentment may be made to his personal representative:

(d) Where the drawee is bankrupt, presentment may be made to him or to his trustee:

(e) Where authorised by agreement or usage, a presentment through the post office is sufficient.'

Presentment, though otherwise necessary, is excused in the following cases, and the holder may treat the bill as though acceptance had been refused, i.e. may (in fact, must if he desires to hold his remedies against the drawer and the indorsers)[6] treat the bill as dishonoured for non-acceptance:

'(a) Where the drawee is dead or bankrupt, or is a fictitious person or a person not having capacity to contract by bill:

(b) Where, after the exercise of reasonable diligence, such presentment cannot be effected:

(c) Where, although the presentment has been irregular, acceptance has been refused on some other ground.[7]

The fact that the holder has reason to believe that the bill, on presentment, will be dishonoured does not excuse presentment'.[8]

---

1 Ibid, s. 43 (2).
2 Ibid, s. 39: unless the holder has not time to present for acceptance before presenting for payment (ibid, s. 39 (4)).
3 Bills of Exchange Act 1882, s. 40 (3).
4 (1817) 7 Taunt. 398; and see *Shute v Robins* (1828) Moo & M 133; 3 C & P 80.
5 Bills of Exchange Act 1882, s. 40 (2).
6 See ibid, s. 43 (1) (b).
7 Bills of Exchange Act 1882, s. 41 (2).
8 Ibid, s. 41 (3).

Acceptance for honour suprà protest

20.10 If the drawee does not accept upon presentment, it is the duty of the holder at once to treat the bill as dishonoured,[1] and he may, if he thinks fit, note and protest[2] the bill for non-acceptance. In that case, if the bill is not overdue, and if the holder consents, any person not being a party already liable on the bill may accept it for the whole or part of the sum drawn,[3] and such person is styled an *acceptor for honour suprà protest*. He must sign the bill, and indicate thereon that his acceptance is for honour, and it is presumed to be an acceptance for the honour of the drawer, unless it states some other party for whose honour it has been made. Usually the acceptance for honour is attested by a notarial 'act of honour' recording the process, but this may not be necessary.[4]

The holder of a bill dishonoured by non-acceptance, who has an offer of an acceptance for honour should first cause the bill to be protested, and then to be accepted *suprà protest*. At maturity he should again present it to the drawee for payment, in case in the meantime he has been put in funds by the drawer for the purpose. If payment is refused the bill should be protested a second time for non-payment, and then presented for payment to the acceptor for honour.[5]

---

1 Ibid, s. 48.
2 See para. 20.25, post.
3 Ibid, s. 65. This may be done if the acceptor is insolvent or bankrupt, and the bill is protested for better security (ibid, s. 51 (5)).
4 See para. 20.20, post.
5 Bills of Exchange Act 1882, s. 67.

Qualified acceptances

20.11 The following are qualified acceptances:

1. Conditional, i.e. which make the bill payable on a condition therein stated;
2. Partial, i.e. which limit the agreement to pay to a named portion of the amount for which the bill is drawn;
3. Qualified as to time;
4. Acceptance by some, but not all, of the drawees;
5. Local qualification, e.g. 'accepted payable at the National Westminster Bank, Ltd., Lothbury only' (as in Form III, para. 20.05, ante). But an acceptance to pay at a particular place is unqualified, and payment may be demanded anywhere, unless it states that the payment is to be made at a particular place only, and not elsewhere.[1] An acceptance will not be treated as qualified unless the words used clearly make it so.[2]

The holder is not bound to take a qualified acceptance, and if the drawee refuses any other, the bill may be treated as dishonoured by non-acceptance;[3] and except in the case of a partial acceptance of which due notice has been given, if the holder without the express or implied authority or subsequent assent of the drawer or any indorser, takes a qualified acceptance, he will release those who have not authorised it or assented to it.[4]

1 Bills of Exchange Act 1882, s. 19.
2 *Decroix v Meyer*, per Bowen LJ (1890) 25 QBD at 349; [1891] AC 520, HL.
3 Bills of Exchange Act 1882, s. 44 (1).
4 Ibid, s. 44 (2), (3).

5. Negotiation and indorsement

Negotiation

20.12   A bill may contain words prohibiting transfer or indicating an intention that it should not be transferable, and if it contains such words, although valid between the parties, it is not negotiable; but the intention to prohibit negotiation must be clearly expressed.[1] The words 'not negotiable' written across an ordinary bill prohibit transfer, although in the case of cheques which are crossed 'not negotiable', the words have a special and restricted meaning which does not prohibit transfer altogether.[2]

The characteristics of negotiability have already been pointed out, and it now remains only to show in what manner the instrument is put in circulation. The Act says that a bill is negotiated when it is so transferred as to make the transferee the holder of the bill.[3] In the case of bills payable to bearer, this is done by mere delivery.[4] In the case of those payable to order, indorsement, in addition to delivery, is required;[5] and transfer, though for value, without indorsement gives only such rights as the transferor had in the bill, with a right to require indorsement.[6] Thus:

> If A has a bill payable to bearer, and he gives it in due course to B, B holds it with all A's rights of suit on it, and without A's defects of title; if it be payable to order, B may require A to indorse it, but until this is done he holds it subject to any defence which could be raised against A; such indorsement operates as a negotiation, but will not cure any defect of the transferor's title of which the indorsee had notice before the indorsement was obtained.[7]

1 Ibid, s. 8 (1); *National Bank v Silke* [1891] 1 QB 435.
2 *Hibernian Bank Ltd v Gysin and Hanson* [1939] 1 KB 483, [1939] 1 All ER 166. The bill in this case was made payable to the order of a particular person only. As to cheques, see para. 21.04, post.
3 Bills of Exchange Act 1882, s. 31 (1).
4 Ibid, s. 31 (2).
5 Ibid, s. 31 (3).
6 Ibid, s. 31 (4).
7 *Whistler v Forster* (1863) 14 CBNS at 257, 258.

Indorsements

20.13 An indorsement must be written on the bill, and signed by the indorser (in general, the signature alone is placed on the back, or, if there be not sufficient room on the bill, then on an annexed paper styled an 'allonge', and this is sufficient);[1] if his name is misspelt, he may sign according to the misspelling, and then add his correct name.[2] Indeed, the indorsement should always correspond with the drawing. Thus, a cheque payable to A B per X, must be indorsed 'A B per X'; and not simply 'X'. X must show that he indorses as agent for A B.[3]

A partial indorsement, i.e., a purported transfer of part only of the amount, is useless as a negotiation;[4] so would be the signature of one of several parties (not being partners) to whose joint order the bill is payable, unless such party is authorised by the others to act in this matter for them.[5]

An indorsement may be made in blank or special:

1. *In blank*, when the signature of the indorser is written without any direction as to whom or to whose order the bill is to be payable; the bill is then payable to bearer.
2. *Special*, when the indorsement specifies the indorsee.[6]

Thus:

If A indorses a bill 'Pay to B & Co or order,' this operates as a special indorsement, and if B & Co desire to negotiate the bill they must themselves indorse it; this they may do either in blank or specially.

It is always at the option of a holder to convert a blank into a special indorsement: he does so by writing above the indorser's signature a direction to pay the bill to, or to order of himself or of some other person.[7]

Indorsements are sometimes:

Conditional, e.g. 'Pay D on his obtaining a degree'.[8] A particular form of conditional indorsement is the *restrictive indorsement*.

A *restrictive indorsement* may be a mere authority to deal with the bill as directed, or it may be an indorsement prohibiting further negotiation; e.g.

'Pay D only',
'Pay D or order for collection',
'Pay to A B or order for my use'.

Such an indorsement gives the indorsee the right to receive payment of the bill and to sue any party that his indorser could have sued, but he cannot transfer his rights as indorsee unless it expressly authorises him to do so. If the restrictive indorsement authorises further transfer, all subsequent indorsees take the bill with the same rights and subject to the same liabilities as the first indorsee under the restrictive indorsement.[9]

---

1 Bills of Exchange Act 1882, s. 32 (1).
2 Ibid, s. 32 (4).
3 *Slingsby v District Bank Ltd* [1931] 2 KB 588; affd. [1932] 1 KB 544. (See further, para. 20.33, post.)
4 Bills of Exchange Act 1882, s. 32 (2).
5 Ibid, s. 32 (3).
6 Ibid, s. 34.
7 Ibid, s. 34 (4).
8 The acceptor may pay the indorsee on maturity though the condition has not yet been fulfilled (ibid, s. 33).
9 Bills of Exchange Act 1882, s. 35 (3).

Forged and unauthorised signatures

20.14 A forged or unauthorised indorsement is wholly inoperative and anyone taking the bill after such an indorsement has no title to it, or right to sue it, even though he may have no knowledge that the indorsement is forged or unauthorised.[1] The only proviso to this statutory rule is if the party against whom it is sought to retain or enforce payment of the bill is precluded (i.e. estopped) from setting up the forgery or want of authority.[2] An unauthorised signature may be ratified unless it amounts to a forged signature which would be the case if put on for a fraudulent purpose. A party may however be estopped from alleging forgery.[3] An estoppel arises when a person represents a signature to be genuine and the representee acts on this to his detriment. Silence will amount to a representation when there is a duty to disclose[4] but it has been held that a banker by paying a cheque does not thus impliedly represent the drawer's signature to be genuine so as to be precluded from recovering the money paid.[5] A forged signature may also be disregarded when an instrument is treated as payable to bearer because the payee is fictitious.[6]

Although anyone taking the bill after a forged or unauthorised signature has no right to sue on the bill, he will have claim against anyone who indorsed the bill after the forged or unauthorised signature. This is because an indorser is precluded from denying to his immediate or a subsequent indorsee that the bill was at the time of his indorsement a valid and subsisting bill and that he then had a good title thereto.[7]

1 Bills of Exchange Act 1882, s. 24. He may be liable in conversion to the owner.
2 Ibid, s. 24, *Greenwood v Martins Bank Ltd* [1933] AC 51; para. 21.01, post.
3 *Leach v Buchanan* (1802) 4 Esp. 226. For the common law doctrine of estoppel, see generally para. 2.05, ante.
4 *Greenwood v Martins Bank Ltd* [1933] AC 51, HL; para. 21.01, post; *Brown v Westminster Bank* [1964] 2 Lloyd's Rep 187.
5 *National Westminster Bank Ltd v Barclays Bank International* [1975] QB 654, [1974] 3 All ER 834.
6 See para. 20.06, ante.
7 Bills of Exchange Act 1882, s. 55 (2).

Transferor by delivery

20.15   A holder who negotiates a bill payable to bearer by delivery without indorsement is styled a transferor by delivery; he incurs no liability on the instrument. However, such transferor by delivery does warrant to his immediate transferee being a holder for value:

1. That the bill is what it purports to be;
2. That he has a right to transfer it;
3. That at the time of the transfer he is not aware of any fact which renders it valueless.[1]

---

1 Bills of Exchange Act 1882, s. 58.

---

6. Rights and liabilities

Rights of the holder

20.16   The holder is defined as the payee or indorsee of a bill or note who is in possession of it, or the bearer.[1] Holders fall into one of two divisions, viz.:

1. Those who are holders in due course, and
2. Those who are not.

1) A *holder in due course* is one who has taken a bill,
   (i) complete and regular on the face of it;[2]
   (ii) before it was overdue, and without notice that it had been previously dishonoured, if such was the fact;
   (iii) in good faith and for value; and
   (iv) without notice of any defect in the title of the person who negotiated it.
All four are requisite.[3]

The rights of the holder in due course are to sue in his own name any or all of the parties to the bill, and to do so free of any defence depending upon any defect of title or any mere personal defence available to prior parties amongst themselves.[4]

The original payee of a bill cannot be a holder in due course; the bill is not negotiated to him.[5]

2) A holder who had not obtained the bill in due course may sue on it in his own name if he is simply a holder for value but he is liable to be defeated by some defect of title in his predecessors or by defences of a personal nature available against them, other than set-off.[6] He may, however, indorse it to a holder in due course, in which case the latter obtains a good and complete title; he may also receive payment in due course, and may give the payer a valid discharge for the bill.[7] Section 29 (3) enacts:

'A holder (whether for value or not), who derives his title to a bill through a holder in due course, and who is not himself a party to any fraud or illegality affecting it, has all the rights of that holder in due course as regards the acceptor and all parties to the bill prior to that holder'.[8]

From the above it is clear that a holder cannot be 'in due course', unless he is ignorant of any fraud or illegality in connection with the bill on the part of the person who negotiated the bill to him, *and* unless he has given value for it.

The defects of title specially mentioned in the Act, which afford an answer to an action on the bill by any party with notice of the defects are:

1. Fraud,
2. Duress [force and fear],
3. Other unlawful means,
4. Illegal consideration, and
5. Negotiation in breach of faith, or under circumstances amounting to a fraud.[9]

Though actual notice of these defects is, of course, sufficient to invalidate the title of a person claiming to be a holder, notice will be imputed to him if it can be shown that he received information which cast upon him the duty of making further inquiries, and that he abstained from doing so because they might injure his title. However:

'It is not enough to show that there was carelessness, negligence or foolishness in not suspecting that the bill was wrong, when there were circumstances that might have led a man to suspect that. All these are matters which tend to show that there was dishonesty in not doing it, but they do not, in themselves, make a defence to an action upon a bill of exchange'.[10]

Negligence will not affect the title of the holder if his conduct is, in fact, honest.[10]

---

1 Bills of Exchange Act 1882, s. 2.
2 The face includes the back (*Arab Bank Ltd v Ross* [1952] 2 QB 216 at 226, [1952] 1 All ER 709 at 715). An indorsement is irregular if it raises any doubt whether it is the indorsement of the named payee or indorsee (ibid.).
3 Bills of Exchange Act 1882, s. 29. As to what constitutes a defective title, see below. A forger's title is not defective—he has no title at all. See para. 20.14, ante.
4 Bills of Exchange Act 1882, s. 38.
5 *R. E. Jones v Waring and Gillow* [1926] AC 670.
6 Bills of Exchange Act 1882, s. 38; *Ex parte Swan* (1868) LR 6 Eq. 344.
7 Ibid, s. 38 (3).
8 Ibid, s. 29 (3). See *Jade International Steel v Robert Nicholas* (1978) The Times, March 8 (drawer discounts bill which is later dishonoured. Drawer entitled to sue, having received the bill from a holder in due course, the discounter).
9 Bills of Exchange Act 1882, s. 29 (2). These are not exhaustive; 'force and fear' is a technical term of Scottish law, inserted because the Act applies to Scotland.
10 *Jones v Gordon* (1877) 2 App Cas at 628, per Lord Blackburn; *Miller v Race* (1758), 1 Burr. 452. Bills of Exchange Act 1882, s. 90.

20.17 '*Valuable consideration*' in connection with bills of exchange means any consideration necessary to support a simply contract[1] or an antecedent debt or liability;[2] and where value has at any time been given for a bill, the holder for the time being is deemed to be a holder for value, as regards the acceptor, and all parties who became such prior to the time when value was given.[3] And as the law does not inquire into the adequacy of a consideration, taking a bill at a considerable undervalue is not of itself sufficient to affect a holder's title,[4] though in the circumstances of any particular case it may be evidence that he was not acting honestly.[5]

Where the holder of a bill has a lien on it, he is deemed to be a holder for value to the extent of the lien.[6] Thus, if the payee of a cheque for £100 asks his bank to collect payment for him and he has a £75 overdraft at the bank, the bank has a lien on the cheque for £75. The bank will be holders for value to the full amount of a cheque if that is less than the payee's overdraft.[7]

'*Accommodation party*' Sometimes a bill is signed by a person as drawer, acceptor, or indorser without consideration for the purpose of lending his name to some other person. The person so signing is an 'accommodation party' to the bill, and is in substance a surety for the person accommodated; but a holder for value may sue the accommodation party, although he knew him to be such when he took the bill.[8]

Presumption in favour of holder It often becomes important to decide on whom lies the burden of proof of showing bona fides and the giving of value. The ordinary rule is this:

> When it is shown that the acceptance, issue, or negotiation of the bill is affected with fraud, duress, or illegality, the holder (unless he is the person to whom,the bill was originally delivered[9]) must prove that after the alleged fraud, etc., value has in good faith been given for the instrument.[10] But until such defect is shown a holder is deemed to be a holder in due course.[11]

1 See as to the common law, para. 3.18, ante.
2 Bills of Exchange Act 1882, s. 27. If a cheque is paid into a bank on the footing that the amount may be at once drawn on, the bank is a holder for value (*Ex parte Richdale* (1882) 19 ChD 409). Where the antecedent debt is not owed by the giver of the bill but by some third party, the recipient of the bill must provide consideration by forbearing to sue the debtor. *Oliver v Davis* [1949] 2 KB 727, [1949] 2 All ER 353, CA; *Hasan v Willson* [1977] 1 Lloyd's Rep 431.
3 Ibid, s. 27. It is not necessary that the holder should have given value *to* someone a party to the bill: *Diamond v Graham* [1968] 2 All ER 909, [1968] 1 WLR 1061, CA. If there is a failure of consideration a cheque may be countermanded. *Hasan v Willson* [1977] 1 Lloyd's Rep 431.
4 In *Pollway v Abdullah* [1974] 2 All ER 381, [1974] 1 WLR 493, CA, the consideration for a cheque for £555 was either an auctioneers' warranty that he was entitled to accept cheques for the price or the acceptance of the cheque instead of legal tender. For auctioneers, see further para. 10.32, ante.
5 *Jones v Gordon* (1877) 2 App Cas 616.
6 Bills of Exchange Act 1882, s. 27 (3).
7 *Barclays Bank v Astley Industrial Trust* [1970] 2 QB 527, [1970] 1 All ER 719; *Re Keever a bankrupt, Ex parte Trustee of Property of Bankrupt v Midland Bank* [1966] Ch 182, [1966] 3 All ER 631.
8 Bills of Exchange Act 1882, s. 28. See para. 20.19, post.
9 *Talbot v Von Boris* [1911] 1 KB 854.
10 Bills of Exchange Act 1882, s. 30 (2); and see *Hall v Featherstone* (1858) 3 H & H 284; *Tatam v Haslar* (1889) 23 QBD 345.
11 Bills of Exchange Act 1882, s. 30.

20.18 *Overdue bills* It has already been said that to constitute a 'holder in due course', he must have acquired the bill before it was overdue, for a bill which is negotiated after that date is taken subject to any defect of title affecting it at maturity, and henceforth none can give a better title than they themselves have.[1] A bill payable on demand is overdue when it appears on the face of it to have been in circulation for an unreasonable time;[2] the maturity of other bills depends upon their date and wording.[3] Payment before maturity will not discharge the bill, and if it is put in circulation afterwards such payment will be no answer to a holder in due course.[4] Where a bill, which is not overdue, has been dishonoured by non-acceptance, any person who takes it with notice of the dishonour takes it subject to any defects of title attaching to it at the time of dishonour.[5]

Lost bill If the bill is lost before it is overdue, the drawer may be compelled to give another bill of the same tenor, at the request of the person who was the holder; the latter giving security against the claims of any person who may become possessed of the lost instrument.[6]

Negotiation back to holder A case of some peculiarity arises when the bill is negotiated back to a holder, who has previously signed it as an acceptor, drawer or indorser, e.g.:

A draws a bill in favour of C; C indorses it to D, D to E, and E to A. In this case A cannot enforce the bill against any intervening party, for they themselves have an exactly corresponding right against him (see next paragraph). He is said to be precluded from suing on the ground of 'circuity of action'; but he may reissue the bill.[7]

However, if, owing to the circumstances, the holder would not have been liable to the particular indorser whom he is suing, then his own previous signature is no answer in the action. For instance:

A bought goods of B, and C was to be surety for the price; B drew bills on A, indorsed them to C, who reindorsed them to B, and it was decided that as in this case there was a state of facts negativing the intention of reserving in C a right of action against B, 'circuity of action' would not avail as a defence in an action by B against C.[8]

---

1 Bills of Exchange Act 1882, s. 36 (2).
2 Ibid, s. 36 (3). This is not so with promissory notes. See para. 21.10, post.
3 See para. 20.28, post.
4 *Burbridge v Manners* (1812) 3 Camp. 193.
5 Bills of Exchange Act 1882, s. 36 (5).
6 Bills of Exchange Act 1882, s. 69. And the court may in any proceeding upon a bill (even against some other party than the drawer) order that the loss of it shall not be set up, provided an indemnity be given against the claims of any other person upon the instrument (ibid, s. 70).
7 Ibid, s. 37.
8 *Wilkinson & Co v Unwin* (1881) 7 QBD 636.

Rights of parties other than the holder

20.19 Each of the indorsers of the bill is liable to the holder, and to any subsequent indorser who pays the bill at maturity. Correlatively each party who has put his name to the bill may claim against any who previously have signed it, whether by way of acceptance, drawing, or indorsement; e.g. the drawer may fall back on the acceptor for compensation; the first indorser has his remedy against the acceptor and the drawer, and so forth. Any party but the acceptor may sign the bill *sans recours*, i.e. may put his name on the bill, expressly and on the instrument itself disclaiming any personal liability, and any party taking after this is bound by the disclaimer.[1]

It will be seen from the above that a bill with several names attached is a form of contract of suretyship;[2] the acceptor being the principal debtor, the other parties being sureties with regard to him, but generally not in regard to each other;[3] they have no right of contribution *inter se*: but any indorser who pays is entitled to claim in full against prior indorsers. The indorser who pays a holder is entitled, as a surety who pays the creditor would be, to any securities held by the holder in respect of the bill.[4] So if the holder agrees to give time to the acceptor after maturity, the indorsers who do not assent are discharged.[5] If the bill has been accepted for the accommodation of the drawer, the acceptor is liable to the holder, but he has a right of indemnity against the drawer, and the rights of a surety in connection therewith.[6]

---

1 Bills of Exchange Act 1882, s. 16. For the liabilities of a transferor by delivery see para. 20.15, ante, s. 58.
2 See *Jones v Broadhurst* (1850) 9 CB 173.
3 *Macdonald v Whitfield* (1883) 8 App Cas 733, 744.
4 *Duncan, Fox & Co v North and South Wales Bank* (1881) 6 App Cas 1.
5 *Tindal v Brown* (1786) 1 Term Rep 167. See further, chap. 16, ante.
6 *Bechervaise v Lewis* (1872) LR 7 CP at 377.

Liabilities

20.20 *Liability of the acceptor* The drawee is not obliged to accept the bill, and in the event of refusal is under no liability on it.[1] If he does accept, he engages to pay according to the tenor of his acceptance.[2] By accepting he is precluded from denying to a holder in due course:

1. The existence of the drawer,

2. The genuineness of the drawer's signature,
3. The drawer's capacity, and
4. His authority to draw,
and if the bill is payable to the drawer's order:
5. The drawer's then capacity to indorse.

Further, if the bill is payable to the order of a third person, the acceptor admits:

1. The existence of the payee, and
2. His then capacity to indorse.

But these admissions do not include the genuineness or validity of the indorsements.[3]

If he has given his acceptance for honour, '*suprà protest*', the liability is not absolute, but accrues only if the drawee does not pay, and then only when the bill has been duly presented for payment and dishonoured, and has been again protested (the protest on non-acceptance is of itself insufficient), and of these facts he is entitled to notice.[4] His liability, when it attaches, is to the holder and to all parties subsequent to the party for whose honour the bill was accepted.[5]

Liability of the drawer   He must pay the bill if it is dishonoured by non-acceptance or by non-payment on the part of the drawee if due notice of dishonour is given.[6] He may not deny to a holder in due course the existence of the payee, and his then capacity to indorse.[7]

Liability of the indorser   He engages, if the bill is duly presented and dishonoured, to compensate the holder or any subsequent indorser, provided he has the requisite notice of dishonour.[8] He must be taken to admit to a holder in due course the genuineness of the signatures of the drawer and of the previous indorsers; and he may not deny to a subsequent indorsee the validity of the bill, and that he had a good title to it at the time of indorsement.[9]

A person who signs a bill otherwise than as drawer or acceptor thereby incurs the liability of an indorser to a holder in due course.[10] Suppose that A sells goods to B Co Ltd, and it is arranged that A will draw a bill of exchange on B Co Ltd in favour of A, that B Co Ltd. will accept it and, because A does not consider that the liability of the company itself is sufficient security, that one of the directors of the company should also sign the bill in his personal capacity. If the bill is drawn and signed by the various parties as arranged, the director's personal indorsement of the bill will render him liable to a holder in due course under s. 56. The director is said to be a quasi-indorser of the bill and to have 'backed' it.

As has been stated above, each indorser may be called on to pay, by way of indemnity, the whole amount (unless he protected himself against this by the form of his indorsement[11]) paid on the bill by a subsequent indorser, and the liabilities of indorsers *inter se* will ordinarily be determined according to this rule. But any special circumstances may be considered, in order to ascertain the true relations of the parties. Thus:

> When A, B, and C, directors of a company, mutually agreed with each other to become sureties to a bank for a certain debt of the company, and in pursuance of that agreement indorsed three promissory notes of the company, it was decided that the first of the three indorsers need not indemnify the others, but that each was liable in a proportionate amount.[12]

The rule is that indorsements are presumed to have been made in the order in which they appear on the bill; but this presumption may be displaced by evidence.[13]

---

1 Bills of Exchange Act 1882, s. 53 (1).
2 Ibid, s. 54 (1). The 'tenor' means the terms of acceptance.
3 Bills of Exchange Act 1882, s. 54 (2).
4 Ibid, s. 66 (1).
5 Ibid, s. 66 (2).
6 Ibid, s. 55 (1).
7 Ibid, s. 55 (1).
8 Ibid, s. 55 (2).
9 Ibid.
10 Ibid, s. 56.
11 See s. 16, para. 20.19, ante.
12 *Macdonald v Whitfield* (1883) 8 App Cas 733 at 734.
13 Bills of Exchange Act 1882, s. 32 (5).

Inchoate Bills

20.21 A signature on blank paper, e.g. what is commonly known as a blank cheque, may be delivered[1] by the signer for the purpose of being converted into a bill, and such delivery operates as a prima facie authority to fill it up as a complete bill for any amount. Such an instrument after completion cannot be enforced against any person who became a party to it before completion, unless it was filled up within a reasonable time, and strictly in accordance with the authority given;[2] except where after completion it is negotiated to a holder in due course.[3] Thus, if A signs a cheque form as drawer but does not complete the cheque and delivers it to someone to fill up for, say, the purchase price of a television set, prima facie A is not liable on the cheque unless it is filled up within a reasonable time and according to A's instructions. But, if after it has been completed the cheque comes into the hands of a holder in due course who has no knowledge that it has been filled up contrary to instructions A is liable on it to such holder in due course for the amount now on the cheque.

The original holder of a bill cannot be a holder in due course,[4] but he may be able to rely on the doctrine of estoppel: Thus, in *Lloyds Bank Ltd v Cooke*:[5]

> Where the defendant signed his name on a blank stamped piece of paper and handed it to a customer of the plaintiffs with authority to fill it up as a promissory note for a certain sum payable to the plaintiffs and deliver it to the plaintiffs as security for an advance to be made by them, and the customer fraudulently filled in a larger amount and obtained that amount from the plaintiffs, who did not know of the fraud, it was held that the defendant was estopped from denying the validity of the note as between himself and the plaintiffs. The plaintiffs could not have relied on s. 20, Bills of Exchange Act, because the note had not been negotiated to them—they were the original payees.

In *Smith v Prosser*:

> Where the defendant signed blank forms of promissory notes and handed them to an agent for safe custody, it was held that the defendant was not liable to a bona fide indorsee for value to whom the agent had fraudulently negotiated them: for having handed the notes to his agent as custodian only and not for completion, he was not estopped from denying their validity.[6]

The distinction is that in the first case but not in the second the paper was delivered to the person who filled it up for the purpose of completion.

---

1 For delivery see para. 20.08, ante.
2 A precaution frequently adopted by drawers of blank cheques is to write not over £?' as an indication that authority is limited.
3 Bills of Exchange Act 1882, s. 20. The Finance Act 1970 Sch. 8, Part V repealed references to the signed paper being 'stamped'. This was to give effect to the abolition of stamp duty for bills and cheques.
4 *R. E. Jones v Waring and Gillow* [1926] AC 670.
5 [1907] 1 KB 794; cf. *Wilson and Meeson v Pickering* [1946] KB 422, [1946] 1 All ER 394.
6 [1907] 2 KB 735.

7. Presentment for payment and notice of dishonour

Presentment for payment

20.22   *Presentment for payment* is necessary (except in the cases mentioned below), and without it there is no right to enforce payment against the drawer and indorsers of the bill,[1] but if the bill be accepted generally no presentment is required to render the acceptor liable.[2]

The time of presentment is determined as follows:

If the bill is payable on demand it must (to affect the drawer) be presented within a reasonable time after its issue, and (to affect an indorser) within a reasonable time after its indorsement; if payable otherwise, then it must be presented on the day on which the bill falls due.[3]

The place of presentment is determined by the terms of the acceptance. If accepted payable at a particular place, presentment must be made at the place named; if the acceptor's address is on the bill, this (if no other place is specified) will demonstrate the proper place; if no place is specified and no address given, it should be presented to the acceptor at his place of business if known, and if not, at his ordinary residence; otherwise it may be presented to the acceptor at his last-known place of business or residence, or to himself wherever he may be found.[4] In *Yeoman Credit Ltd v Gregory*,[5] a bill, accepted payable at the N.P. Bank, fell due for payment on December 9, 1959. The bill was not presented there until December 10. *Held:* the defendant indorser was discharged from liability.

The presentment must be made by the holder or by some person authorised to receive payment on his behalf at a reasonable hour on a business day. It must be made to the person designated by the bill as payer or to some person authorised by him to pay or to refuse payment, if such can be found. If there are several designated payers and no place of payment is specified, then to all of them, unless they are partners. If the drawee or acceptor is dead, presentment must be· made, if possible, to his personal representative. Agreement or usage may authorise presentment through the post office.[4]

Delay in making presentment is excused by circumstances beyond the control of the holder and not imputable to his default, misconduct or negligence. Presentment will be dispensed with:

1. Where after the exercise of reasonable diligence it cannot be effected;
2. Where the drawee is a fictitious person;[6]

3. As regards the drawer, where the drawee or acceptor is not bound, as between himself and the drawer, to accept or pay the bill, and the drawer has no reason to believe that the bill would be paid if presented;[7]

4. As regards an indorser, where the bill was accepted or made for the accommodation of that indorser, and he has no reason to expect that the bill would be paid if presented;

5. If it is waived, expressly or by implication.[8]

The holder must, on presentment, exhibit the bill to the person from whom payment is demanded and when it is paid deliver it to the party paying it.[9]

---

1 Bills of Exchange Act 1882, s. 45.
2 Ibid, s. 52 (1).
3 Ibid, s. 45. The acceptor cannot always demand the exact carrying out of this duty. See s. 52 (2).
4 Bills of Exchange Act 1882, s. 45.
5 [1963] 1 All ER 245, [1963] 1 WLR 343.
6 See para. 20.06, ante.
7 E.g. if as between them it is an accommodation bill.
8 Bills of Exchange Act 1882, s. 46.
9 Bills of Exchange Act 1882, s. 52 (4).

Notice of dishonour

20.23 When a bill has been dishonoured either by non-acceptance or by non-payment, there is, in the former case, an immediate right of recourse against the drawer and indorsers, and in the latter against the acceptor, the drawer, and the successive indorsers; but these have, in general, a right to notice of dishonour, and those who receive no notice when such is requisite are freed from liability.[1] The acceptor is not entitled to notice of dishonour.[2]

The notice must be given within a reasonable time after dishonour, and, in the absence of special circumstances, these rules apply:

Time The following points should be noted:

1. Where the parties who are to give and receive notice respectively, reside in the same place, it should be sent in such time as to reach the person to whom it is sent on the day after dishonour;

2. Where they live in different places it should be sent on the day after dishonour, or if there be no post at a convenient hour on that day, then by the next post thereafter.[3]

Notice of dishonour *posted before* the bill is dishonoured can be effective if the notice is received or is deemed to have been received after the dishonour.[4] If the bill when dishonoured is in the hands of an agent, he has a similar time allowed him wherein to communicate with his principal, and then the principal in turn has a similar allowance; the agent may, however, give notice direct to the parties interested;[5] and each person who receives notice has a similar time after receipt of notice wherein to communicate with prior parties.[6]

Delay in giving notice of dishonour is excused if it is caused by circumstances beyond the control of the party giving notice, and is not imputable to his negligence.[7]

TO AND BY WHOM TO BE GIVEN

1. It should be given by the holder, or by an indorser who is himself liable on the bill, or by an agent acting on behalf of either;[8]
2. It must be given to the person entitled to it, or to his agent in that behalf;[9] or (if the drawer or indorser entitled to notice is dead, and the holder knows it) to his personal representative, if there be one, and he can be found with reasonable diligence;[10] or (if he is bankrupt) either to the party himself or to his trustee in bankruptcy.[11]

Where there are two or more drawers or indorsers, not being partners, notice must be given to each, unless one of them has authority to receive notice for the others.[12] When a bill drawn or indorsed by partners is dishonoured after the dissolution of the firm, notice to one partner is sufficient.[13]

No form of notice No particular form is required; writing or oral communication, or partly one and partly the other, will suffice, provided that the identity of the bill and its dishonour by non-acceptance or non-payment is sufficiently indicated; so also will return of the dishonoured bill to the drawer or indorser.[14] When given by the holder it enures for the benefit of all subsequent holders, and of all prior indorsers who have a right against the party to whom it has been given; and notice given by an indorser enures for the benefit of the holder and all indorsers subsequent to the party who has received notice.[15]

Notice is required in the generality of cases, and that this should be so is clearly equitable. A man may have indorsed a bill, value £100, due on September 3; if he hears nothing about it, by, say, September 12, his remedies against parties liable to him might become less valuable or be lost by his being unable to enforce them promptly. If afterwards he is asked to pay, great hardship might be inflicted upon him: hence the necessity for notice of dishonour. But in the following cases either this would not apply, or else a greater hardship would be inflicted on the holder by requiring him to give notice.

Thus, an omission to give notice of dishonour will not operate as a discharge:

1. Where the bill is dishonoured by non-acceptance, and notice of dishonour is not given, the rights of a holder in due course subsequent to the omission will not be prejudiced, or

2. Where due notice of dishonour is given on non-acceptance, and no acceptance is in the meantime given, notice of subsequent dishonour by non-payment is unnecessary.[16]

---

1 Bills of Exchange Act 1882, ss. 43, 47 and 48.
2 Ibid, s. 52 (3).
3 Ibid, s. 49 (12). *Hamilton Finance v Coverley Westray Walbaum and Tosetti and Portland Finance Co* [1969] 1 Lloyd's Rep 53. (West End and City of London 'same place' for this purpose). When the letter is duly addressed and posted, subsequent miscarriage will not affect the party's rights (ibid, s. 49 (15)).
4 *Eaglehill Ltd v J Needham, Builders, Ltd* [1973] AC 992, [1972] 3 All ER 895, HL.
5 Ibid, s. 49 (13). *Lombard Banking Ltd v Central Garage and Engineering Co Ltd* [1963] 1 QB 220, [1962] 2 All ER 949. This case drew a distinction between a warning which did not affect the timetable and notice which would do so.
6 Ibid, s. 49 (14).
7 Ibid, s. 50 (1).
8 Bills of Exchange Act 1882, s. 49 (1), (2).
9 Ibid, s. 49 (8).
10 Ibid, s. 49 (9).
11 Ibid, s. 49 (10).
12 Ibid, s. 49 (11).
13 *Goldfarb v Bartlett and Kremer* [1920] 1 KB 639.
14 Bills of Exchange Act 1882, s. 49 (5)–(7).
15 Ibid, s. 49 (3), (4).
16 Bills of Exchange Act 1882, s. 48.

20.24 *Excuses for non-notice* Notice of dishonour is dispensed with in the following cases:[1]

1. Where reasonable diligence is used, but notice is impossible, or does not reach the person sought to be charged;
2. Where notice is waived by the party entitled to it;[2]
3. As regards *the drawer* when:
  (i) drawer and drawee are the same person;
  (ii) where the drawee is a fictitious person or a person having no capacity to contract;

(iii) where the drawer is the person to whom the bill is presented for payment;

(iv) where the drawee or acceptor is as between himself and the drawer under no obligation to accept or pay the bill;[3]

(v) where the drawer has countermanded payment;

4. As regards the *indorser*:

(i) where the bill was accepted or made for his accommodation;

(ii) where the indorser is the person to whom the bill is presented for payment;

(iii) where the drawee is a fictitious person or person not having capacity to contract, to the knowledge of the indorser at the time of indorsement. The meaning of 'fictitious' has been examined already.[4]

---

1 Ibid, s. 50 (2).
2 *Lombard Banking Ltd v Central Garage and Engineering Co Ltd* [1963] 1 QB 220, [1962] 2 All ER 949.
3 For instance, where a banker has no funds to meet a cheque, or the bill was accepted for the accommodation of the drawer.
4 Para. 20.06, ante.

Noting and Protesting

20.25 In the case of an inland bill,[1] protest, though sometimes useful, is optional, save where acceptance or payment for honour is desired.[2] But in the case of a foreign bill,[1] appearing on the face of it to be such, the drawer and indorsers are discharged if, in the event of non-acceptance, the bill is not protested; and protest is necessary also, if a foreign bill which was not dishonoured by non-aaceptance is dishonoured by non-payment.[3] Protest may be excused under circumstances similar to those mentioned above in the case of notice of dishonour.[4]

Form of protest Protest of a foreign bill after it has been dishonoured (or more accurately, noting and protesting such a bill) involves handing the bill to a notary public who again formally presents the bill for acceptance or payment. Upon redishonour, the notary makes a memorandum on the bill of his initials, his charges, the date and a reference to his register where the details are entered and he attaches a slip to the bill giving the 'answer he receives', That is the 'noting' and the 'protest', strictly so called, is the formal document recording the fact of dishonour. A protest must:

1. Contain a copy of the bill;

2. Be signed by the notary making it;
3. Must specify the person at whose request the bill is protested;
4. The place and date of protest;
5. The cause or reason for protesting the bill;
6. The demand made and the answer given, if any, or the fact that the drawee or acceptor cannot be found.[5]

If the services of a notary cannot be obtained, any householder or substantial resident of the place may, in the presence of two witnesses, give a certificate, signed by them, attesting the dishonour of the bill, and the certificate will in all respects operate as a formal protest.[6]

Time for protest The bill should be protested on the day of dishonour, but if noted on that day, or not later than the next succeeding business day,[7] it may be protested afterwards as of that day,[8] delay is excused if caused by circumstances beyond the control of the holder, not imputable to his default, misconduct, or negligence.[9]

Place of protest A bill must be protested at the place where it is dishonoured, save that:

1. When a bill is presented through and returned dishonoured through the post, it may be protested at the place to which it is returned, and
2. If the bill is drawn payable at some place of business or residence other than that of the drawee, and is dishonoured by non-acceptance, it must be protested at the place where it is expressed to be payable.[10]

---

1 Para. 20.35, post.
2 Bills of Exchange Act 1882, s. 51 (1). For acceptance and payment for honour see para. 20.10, ante, and para. 20.29, post.
3 Bills of Exchange Act 1882, s. 51 (2).
4 Ibid, s. 51 (9).
5 Bills of Exchange Act 1882, s. 51 (7). If the bill is lost or destroyed or is wrongfully detained from the person entitled to hold it, protest may be made on a copy or written particulars thereof (ibid, s. 51 (8)).
6 Ibid, s. 94. A special form is given in the Schedule to the Act.
7 Ibid, s. 51 (4); Bills of Exchange (Time of Noting) Act 1917, s. 1.
8 Bills of Exchange Act 1882, s. 93. 'Noting' is the minute made by the notary on which the formal notarial certificate—the protest—is based.
9 Ibid, s. 51 (9).
10 Ibid, s. 51 (6).

Measure of damages on a dishonoured bill

20.26 This differs in the case of a bill dishonoured in the British Isles and one dishonoured abroad. The measure of damages on a bill dishonoured at home is:

1. The amount of the bill; added to
2. Interest from the date of maturity, or if the bill is payable on demand, of presentment for payment; added to
3. The expenses of noting, and of any necessary protest.[1]

On a bill dishonoured abroad the measure was, the amount of the re-exchange with interest till the time of payment.[2] This provision has now, however, been repealed by the Administration of Justice Act 1977.[3]

If justice requires it, the interest may be withheld whether the bill be an inland or a foreign bill.[4]

---

1 Ibid, s. 57 (1). See para. 20.25, ante.
2 Bills of Exchange Act 1882, s. 57 (2).
3 S. 4.
4 Bills of Exchange Act 1882, s. 57 (3).

---

8. Discharge of the bill

20.27 The grounds of discharge are these:

1. Payment in due course,
2. Waiver,
3. Cancellation,
4. Merger,
5. Alteration.

In addition certain parties may be discharged by want of notice of dishonour or by omission to duly present the bill.

1. Payment in due course

20.28 In order to operate as a discharge, this must be made by the proper person and in due course. Payment by or on behalf of the acceptor at or after maturity will always operate as a discharge if made bona fide to the holder without notice of any defect there may be in his title.[1] An accommodation bill is discharged if paid by the party accommodated[2] but with other bills payment by the drawer or an indorser does not discharge the bill but merely discharges subsequent indorsers from liability.[11] The drawer may sue the acceptor if the drawer pays and the indorser who pays may sue the drawer and prior indorsers on the bill. Where a bill payable to the order of a third party is paid by the drawer, the drawer may enforce payment against the acceptor but not reissue the bill. On the other hand, where a bill payable to the drawer's order is paid by the drawer, or where any bill is paid by an indorser, the party paying may strike out his own and subsequent indorsements and again negotiate the bill.[3]

To whom Payment must be made to the party entitled,[4] and it is on this account that the payee must be in the first instance a person named or indicated with reasonable certainty, though a bill may be made payable to several payees jointly, or alternatively to one of them, or to the holder of an office for the time being,[5] and it may be made payable to bearer. If a fictitious[6] or non-existing person is named as payee the bill may be treated as payable to bearer.[7]

Amount payable The amount paid must be the correct amount, which, therefore, must be a sum certain.[8] If interest has been agreed, then the amount payable is the amount due plus interest and such interest runs from the date of the bill, or (if it be undated) from date of issue, unless the bill otherwise provides;[9] a partial acceptance makes the acceptor liable only to the amount for which he has accepted. When the drawer pays part of the amount, is the acceptor to that extent freed from liability to the holder or can he be sued for the whole, the holder being then liable to the drawer for the excess recovered?[10] In an action by a holder against the acceptor, payment by the drawer or an indorser of any part is no answer,[11] unless the bill is an accommodation bill, given for the accommodation of the drawer.[12]

When The bill is payable at maturity. It is payable on demand, if it is so expressed, or if no time for payment is named, or if it is stated to be payable at sight or on presentation; also if it is accepted or indorsed when overdue, it is, as regards such acceptor or indorser, deemed to be payable on demand.[13] If it is payable at a fixed period after date or sight or on or after a fixed period after any specified event which is certain to happen, the date is determined according to the tenor.[14]

A demand bill is payable on the day of demand, but in other cases the bill is due and payable on the last day of the time of payment as fixed by the bill,[15] or if that is non-business day,[16] on the succeeding business day.

The whole day is available for payment, i.e. in general the whole of the business hours of the day.[17] Payment may be made before it is due, but it will not then operate as a discharge except

459

between the parties to the payment, and will be no answer to a holder in due course.[18]

When a bill is paid the holder may be compelled to deliver it up to the party paying it.[19]

---

1 Bills of Exchange Act 1882, s. 59.
2 Ibid, s. 59 (3).
3 Ibid, s. 59 (2).
4 But see para. 21.05, post, as to payment by a banker of a demand draft bearing a forged indorsement.
5 Bills of Exchange Act 1882, s. 7.
6 See *Bank of England v Vagliano Bros* para. 20.06, ante.
7 Bills of Exchange Act 1882, s. 7 (3). See para. 20.06, ante.
8 Para. 20.06, ante.
9 Bills of Exchange Act 1882, s. 9 (3).
10 See *Byles on Bills* (23rd edn) 117.
11 Bills of Exchange Act 1882, s. 59 (2).
12 *Lazarus v Cowie* [1842] 3 QB 459; *Cook v Lister* (1863) 32 LJCB 121 (ibid, s. 59 (3)).
13 Bills of Exchange Act 1882, s. 10.
14 Ibid, s. 11. It must be observed, however, that an instrument drawn payable on a contingency cannot be a valid bill of exchange. In *Williamson v Rider* [1963] 1 QB 89, [1962] 2 All ER 268, it was held that an instrument drawn payable 'on or before December 31, 1956' created an uncertainty and a contingency in the time of payment; and see s. 12, as regards filling up the date when the instrument has been issued undated, para. 20.06, ante.
15 Ibid, s. 14 as amended by the Banking and Financial Dealings Act 1971, s. 3.
16 Non-business days mean Saturday, Sunday, Good Friday, Christmas Day, a bank holiday and a day appointed by Royal proclamation as a public fast or thanksgiving day: Bills of Exchange Act 1882 s. 92 as amended by the Banking and Financial Dealings Act 1971, s. 3.
17 *Kennedy v Thomas* [1894] 2 QB 759.
18 Bills of Exchange Act 1882, s. 59 (2).
19 Ibid, s. 52 (4).

---

2. Payment for honour

20.29 If a bill is not paid at maturity it becomes dishonoured by non-payment, and the holder immediately acquires his consequent rights against the parties. If it has been protested for non-payment, any person may intervene and pay it for the honour of any party liable thereon or for whose account the bill is drawn;[1] the intervention is then called 'payment for honour', and the payer steps into the place of the holder, to the extent of his rights against the defaulter and those who were liable to him; parties subsequent to the party for whose honour the bill is paid are discharged;[2] this 'payment for honour *suprà protest*' must be attested by a notarial act of honour, which may be appended to the protest.[3]

---

1 Bills of Exchange Act 1882, s. 68 (1).
2 Ibid, s. 68 (5).
3 Ibid, s. 68 (3).

---

3. Renunciation

20.30 When the holder of a bill *at* or *after* maturity absolutely and unconditionally renounces his rights against the acceptor, the bill is discharged. The renunciation must be in writing unless the bill is delivered up to the acceptor.[1] If *in like manner* a holder renounces his rights against a particular indorser of the bill *before, at* or *after* maturity, that indorser will be discharged. If a holder renounces his rights against a party before maturity and then negotiates the bill to a holder in due course who is ignorant of the renunciation, the holder in due course is not affected by the renunciation.[2] At common law accord without satisfaction does not operate to discharge a party from liability, unless a release under seal is given;[3] the law merchant did not adopt this principle and permitted the holder of a bill to discharge the acceptor without consideration; and, subject to the conditions above mentioned, the Act has recognised this peculiar rule of the law merchant.

---

1 Ibid, s. 62 (1).
2 Ibid, s. 62 (2).
3 See para. 8.01, ante.

---

4. Cancellation[1]

20.31 Cancellation discharges the person whose name is cancelled, and also all indorsers who would have a right of recourse against him, unless

    (i) the cancellation was not intentional; or
    (ii) was made without the holder's consent; or
    (iii) was made by mistake; burden of proving that the cancellation took place under these conditions is on the party seeking to support the bill.

If the bill as a whole is thus cancelled, all parties are discharged.

1 Bills of Exchange Act 1882, s. 63.

5. Merger

20.32 Under some circumstances this will discharge the bill, e.g. when the acceptor becomes holder of the bill in his own right, at or after maturity.[1] The acceptor must, however, receive back the bill with a right good against the world and not subject to that of any other person, so that if it is transferred to him without consideration in fraud of a previous holder in due course, he will still remain liable on it.[2]

1 Ibid, s. 61.
2 *Nash v De Freville* [1900] 2 QB 72.

6. Alteration

20.33 Material alteration of the bill or acceptance without the assent of all parties liable, avoids the bill, except as against a party who has made, authorised, or assented to the alteration and except as against subsequent indorsers. If, however, the alteration is not apparent, the holder in due course may sue for the amount of the bill as it stood before alteration.[1] Material alterations are, inter alia, alterations of date, amount, time and place of payment, or the addition of a particular place of payment, where the original acceptance was general.[2]

So also, the alteration of the place of drawing of a completed bill which converts the instrument from an inland into a foreign bill is material;[3] but such an alteration is not material if made by the drawer before the bill is completed.[4] A bill is not avoided by an alteration which is not material. In *Garrard v Lewis*:[5]

> Defendant signed an acceptance, the amount being left in blank, but the figures in the margin were £14 0s 6d; the drawer filled up the bill for £164 0s 6d, and altered the figures to make them correspond, and it was decided that the marginal figures not being a material part of the bill, the alteration was no defence to an action by a bona fide holder.[6]

But s. 64 does not apply to alterations resulting from mutilation. Thus, where the note of a bank was accidentally torn into fragments and then pieced together so as to contain all the elements necessary to render it valid and effectual as a negotiable instrument and establish its identity as a note of the bank, but not so as to show the number of the note, the holder was held entitled to recover from the bank the amount for which the note has been issued.[7]

---

1 See *Scholfield v Earl of Londesborough* [1896] AC 514.
2 Bills of Exchange Act 1882, s. 64. See also *Slingsby v District Bank*, para. 20.13, ante, where an alteration in the name of the payee was held to be material.
3 *Koch v Dicks*, [1933] 1 KB 307.
4 *Foster v Driscoll* [1929] 1 KB at 494.
5 (1883) 10 QBD 30.
6 These rules do not apply to Bank of England notes. See para. 21.13, post.
7 *Hong Kong, etc, Banking Corpn v Lo Lee Shi* [1928] AC 181. *Semble*, even a material part of the instrument might be supplied by clear verbal evidence of its destruction (*Hong Kong, etc, Banking Corp v Lo Lee Shi*, ante).

---

9. Bill in a set

20.34 Bills are sometimes drawn in a set,[1] e.g. two, three, or more parts, and if they are numbered and refer one to the other, the whole of the parts constitute one bill. The drawee should accept one part only, and, if he accepts more than one he will be liable on each part as though it were a separate bill, save where all get into the hands of one holder; he should not pay unless the accepted part is produced to him, for if he does so, and that part is eventually presented by a holder in due course, he must pay again.

If a holder of a set indorses different parts to different persons, he is liable on each part for the full amount, and so will be all subsequent indorsers on the parts they indorse. Subject to the above, payment of one part discharges the set. Where two or more parts of a set are negotiated to different holders in due course, the holder whose title first accrues is as between such holders deemed the true owner of the bill; but this must not prejudicially affect the position of a person who in due course accepts or pays the first part presented to him.

---

1 Bills of Exchange Act 1882, s. 71.

10. Foreign bills

20.35 An inland bill is one which is or purports on the face of it to be both drawn and payable within the British Islands[1], or to be drawn within them, upon some person resident therein. Any other bill is a foreign bill. Unless the contrary appear on the face of it, a bill may be treated by the holder as an inland bill.[2] When a foreign bill is dishonoured, protest is necessary save as against the acceptor; in the case of an inland bill it is optional.[3]

It is a matter of some difficulty to decide what law governs a foreign bill, whether the law of the place of draft, or of the place of payment. The rules relating to this are to be found in s. 72 of the Bills of Exchange Act 1882; their main result seems to be that the law of the place where the act is done is to be the law governing the validity in form and the interpretation of that act, e.g. a bill drawn in England, accepted in France, payable in Holland; here English law governs the drawing, French law the acceptance, Dutch law the payment. Thus, where a foreign bill drawn on an English acceptor payable to the order of a named payee was indorsed in France with the authority of the payee by an agent *in his own name* simpliciter, then, that indorsement being valid by French law, although it would not be recognised by the law of England as a good indorsement of an inland bill, was sufficient to entitle the indorsee to sue the English acceptor.[4]

---

1 This does not include the Republic of Ireland. See *Byles on Bills* (23rd edn) 34.
2 Bills of Exchange Act 1882, s. 4.
3 Ibid, ss. 51, 52 (3).
4 *Koechlin et Cie v Kestenbaum Bros* [1927] 1 KB 889. S. 72 (4) of the Bills of Exchange Act 1882, which dealt with the calculation of the amount of a bill expressed in a foreign currency, has been repealed by the Administration of Justice Act 1977, s. 4.

Chapter 21

Cheques, promissory notes and bank notes

1. Cheques

21.00 The present law relating to cheques is contained in the Bills of Exchange Act 1882 and the Cheques Act 1957. Section 73 of the Bills of Exchange Act defines cheques as bills of exchange drawn on a banker, payable on demand; the definition of a bill of exchange given in the Act applies to cheques, and so generally do all provisions of the Act applicable to bills payable on demand, except as otherwise provided in Part III of the Bills of Exchange Act (ss. 73—81).

Duties of a banker

21.01 When a cheque is presented, the banker must pay it if he has funds in his hands belonging to the drawer available for the purpose; otherwise he becomes liable to an action at the suit of the customer for wrongfully dishonouring the cheque. If the customer is not a trader he will only receive nominal damages unless the damage he has suffered is alleged and proved as special damage[1] but if a trader's cheque is wrongfully dishonoured, the customer can recover substantial damages without giving evidence of having sustained any special loss.[2]

The other main responsibility that the banker has to his customer is to make payment out of the customer's account only on the customer's signature and only according to the customer's direction. Prima facie, therefore, the banker has no right to debit his customer's account for the amount of a cheque on which the customer's signature has been forged[3] and, if the banker pays someone whose title rests on a forged indorsement the banker is not entitled to debit the customer's account. However, there are statutory provisions to be considered shortly which protect a banker in some circumstances. Further, where the banker's error is occasioned by the customer's breach of his duty to draw his cheques properly the bank is also protected. A customer does owe a duty to take reasonable precautions against forgery and if he carelessly draws a cheque with spaces which can be utilised to alter fraudulently the amount of the cheque and this is in fact done, the customer must bear the loss caused by payment of the cheque as altered.[4] It has, however, been held not to be a breach of duty to leave a blank space after the payee's name on a cheque payable to order.[5]

In the case of a company account (or the account of any incorporated or unincorporated body), the bank will be authorised to pay only on a cheque which is signed by specifically authorised persons. Moreover, as the paying bank owes a duty of care to its customer, even where a cheque contains the authorised signatures, if the bank knows or ought to know that the cheque has been drawn for an unauthorised purpose (e.g. purchase of the company's own shares), it will be liable to its customer should it pay out on the cheque.[6]

If a banker by mistake credits money to a customer's account and this is drawn upon by the customer the banker will not be estopped from recovering the money if the customer knew of the mistake and was not misled into changing his position.[7] It is otherwise if the customer did not know and was misled.[8]

---

1 *Gibbons v Westminster Bank* [1939] 2 KB 882, [1939] 3 All ER 577.
2 *Fleming v Bank of New Zealand* [1900] AC 577. These cases apply to an action for breach of contract. Traders or non-traders may also be able to recover in an action for defamation arising from wrongful dishonour. *Jayson v Midland Bank* [1968] 1 Lloyd's Rep 409.
3 Bills of Exchange Act 1882, s. 24. See para. 20.14, ante. But the customer may be estopped by conduct from questioning the banker's payment of the cheque—e.g. if he has delayed informing the bank of the forgery after he has become aware of it. *Greenwood v Martins Bank* [1933] AC 51. *Brown v Westminster Bank* [1964] 2 Lloyd's Rep 187. For the doctrine of common law estoppel, see para. 2.05, ante.
4 *London Joint Stock Bank v Macmillan* [1918] AC 777.
5 *Slingsby v District Bank Ltd* [1932] 1 KB 544.
6 *Selangor United Rubber Estates Ltd v Cradock (No. 3)* [1968] 2 All ER 1073, [1968] 1 WLR 1555; *Karak Rubber Co Ltd v Burden (No. 2)* [1972] 1 All ER 1210, [1972] 1 WLR 602.
7 *United Overseas Bank v Jiwani* [1977] 1 All ER 733, [1976] 1 WLR 964.
8 *Holt v Markham* [1923] 1 KB 504.

Duty of a holder

21.02 The holder of a cheque should present it for payment within a reasonable time of its issue.[1] If the drawer is entitled at the time of such presentment as between himself and the banker to have the cheque paid, and if owing to non-presentment within a reasonable time he is damnified (e.g. by the insolvency of the banker), he is discharged to the amount of the damage suffered; in such a case, the holder may obtain judgment for the amount against the banker.[2]

1 Bills of Exchange Act 1882, s. 74 (2).
2 Bills of Exchange Act 1882, s. 74 (1), (3).

Revocation of banker's authority

21.03 A banker's authority to pay a customer's cheque is revoked:

1. By countermand of payment;[1]
2. By notice of the customer's death;[1] and
3. By notice of the presentation of a bankruptcy petition by or against a customer, and in any case, by the making of a receiving order against him.[2]

He must refuse to pay a cheque on an account which is the subject of a garnishee order;[3] and the common form of order will apply to the 'client account' kept by a solicitor unless the order is modified so as not to affect such an account.[4]

A cheque is not an equitable assignment of the drawer's balance, and accordingly a third party has no right of action against a banker for refusing to honour it.[5]

1 Bills of Exchange Act 1882, s. 75. The banker is not bound to act on an unauthenticated telegram (*Curtice v London, City and Midland Bank* [1908] 1 KB 293).
2 Bankruptcy Act 1914, ss. 45, 46 and *Re Dalton (a bankrupt), Ex parte Herrington & Carmichael (a firm) v Trustee of Property of Bankrupt* [1963] Ch 336. [1962] 2 All ER 499. But where payment has been made to a third party in ignorance of a receiving order and before it is gazetted, the trustee must endeavour if practicable to seek to recover the sum from the payee of the cheque: Bankruptcy (Amendment) Act 1926, s. 4.
3 *Rogers v Whiteley* [1892] AC 118. A garnishee order directs one who owes money to a judgment debtor to make payment to the judgment creditor.
4 *Plunkett v Barclay's Bank* [1936] 2 KB 107.
5 *Schroeder v Central Bank of London* (1876) 34 LT 735. See also Bills of Exchange Act 1882, s. 53.

Crossed cheques

21.04   A cheque, across the face of which two parallel lines are drawn (between which the words 'and Company', or any abbreviation of them, may be placed), is styled a crossed cheque. A cheque crossed generally contains the above only; a cheque crossed specially contains the name of a banker in addition, and then is said to be crossed to the banker.[1]

This crossing (which is a material part of the cheque[2]) may be added to an uncrossed cheque by the drawer or the holder, and either may turn a general into a special crossing.[3] A banker may convert:

1. An uncrossed cheque into a crossed one, or
2. A general crossing into a special crossing to himself.[3]

He may

3. Re-cross a specially crossed cheque to another banker for collection.[4]

In no other case may a specially crossed cheque be crossed to more than one banker, and if it is so crossed, the duty of the banker to whom it is presented is to refuse payment.[5]

When a cheque is crossed generally it must be paid to a banker, and if it is crossed specially, to the banker whose name is on it.[6] For safety's sake the words '*not negotiable*' are often added, and although they do not affect the transferability of the cheque, they limit its negotiable character, rendering a transferee liable to have set up against him the defects of title available against a previous holder. In the words of the Act:

> 'he shall not have and shall not be capable of giving a better title to the cheque than that which the person from whom he took it had'.[7]

Thus, if A draws a bearer cheque crossed 'not negotiable' and the cheque is stolen from the bearer, C may take a transfer of that cheque in good faith and for value but he cannot obtain a good title to the cheque.

Frequently the cheque is further crossed 'account payee', which, as shown below, seems to put the collecting banker under a greater duty of care than his ordinary duty of care.[8]

---

1 Bills of Exchange Act 1882, s. 76.
2 Ibid, s. 78.
3 Ibid, s. 77.
4 Ibid, s. 77.
5 Ibid, s. 79 (1).
6 Ibid, s. 79 (2). Otherwise the banker will be liable to the true owner.

7 Ibid, s. 81. See para. 20.12, ante, as to the meaning of the words 'not negotiable' when written on an ordinary bil. of exchange.

8 See para. 21.08, post.

The paying banker

21.05 A banker who pays a cheque drawn on him otherwise than according to the crossing is liable to the true owner[1] for any loss he may sustain by such payment.[2] If the crossing is obliterated, or if the cheque appears not to be crossed, and not to have been added to, or altered otherwise than in accordance with the Act, then if the banker acts in good faith and without negligence, he is not responsible if he treats the cheque as uncrossed.[3]

Further statutory protection is provided for the paying banker by s. 60 and s. 80 of the Bills of Exchange Act and by s. 1 of the Cheques Act.

a) Section 80 of the Bills of Exchange Act If the banker pays in conformity with the crossing in good faith and without negligence, he is placed in the same position as if he had paid the true owner, and if the cheque has reached the payee, the drawer is entitled to the same protection. It follows that if a crossed order cheque is stolen from the payee and the thief forges the payee's indorsement, then so long as the paying bank pays according to the crossing in good faith and without negligence, it is entitled to debit the drawer's account with the amount and the drawer is in no way liable to the payee.

b) Section 60 of the Bills of Exchange Act This provides wider protection as it applies to uncrossed as well as to crossed cheques and the paying banker is deemed to have paid a cheque in due course despite the existence of a forged indorsement on the cheque provided the paying banker has acted in good faith and 'in the ordinary course of business'.

c) Section 1 of the Cheques Act The main purpose of the Cheques Act 1957 was to make it unnecessary for the payee of a cheque or a subsequent indorsee to indorse the cheque before paying it into his own bank account. Indorsement remains necessary to effect the negotiation of an order cheque. By s. 1 of the Act, if a banker in good faith and 'in the ordinary course of business' pays a cheque which is not indorsed or is irregularly indorsed he is deemed to have paid it in due course. Thus, if an order cheque is stolen from the payee and the thief opens a bank account in the name of the payee, the bank on which the cheque is drawn may pay the amount to the bank at which the thief has opened this account and if it does so it may be able to rely on the protection of this section.

A banker who pays a cheque on which the drawer's signature has been forged is not taken impliedly to represent that the signature is genuine so as to be estopped from recovering the money from the recipient.[4]

---

1 As to who is 'true owner', see *Marquess of Bute v Barclays Bank Ltd* [1955] 1 QB 202 at 211, 212, [1954] 3 All ER 365 at 368, 369.
2 Bills of Exchange Act 1882, s. 79 (2).
3 Ibid, s. 79 (2).
4 *National Westminster Bank v Barclays Bank International* [1975] QB 654, [1974] 3 All ER 834.

The collecting banker

21.06 At common law, if a banker collected a cheque for his customer and that customer had no rightful title to it, he would be liable in conversion to the true owner. However, by statutory provision, where a banker in good faith and without negligence receives payment of a cheque, whether crossed or not, or having credited a customer's account with the amount of a cheque receives payment for himself, he does not incur any liability to the true owner by reason only of having received payment even if the customer has no title or a defective title to the cheque.[1] The banker need not concern himself with the absence of, or irregularity in, indorsement of the cheque.[2]

Who is a 'customer'?—Lord Dunedin in *Taxation Commissioners v English, Scottish and Australian Bank*, said:

> 'The word "customer" signifies a relationship in which duration is not of the essence. A person whose money has been accepted by a bank on the footing that they undertake to honour cheques up to the amount standing to his credit is a customer of the bank in the sense of the statute, irrespective of whether his connection is of short or long standing. The contrast is not between an habitué and a newcomer, but between a person for whom the bank performs a casual service, such as, for instance, cashing a cheque for a person introduced by one of their customers, and a person who has an account of his own at the bank'.[3]

The meaning so given to the words 'customer' is of importance because it sometimes happens that a person opens an account for the purpose only of clearing cheques to which he has no title, and if this is not coupled with circumstances which ought to put the banker on inquiry, the protection of the section is not lost.

A bank collecting cheques for another banker does so for a 'customer'.[4]

---

1 Cheques Act 1957, s. 4, superseding Bills of Exchange Act 1882, s. 82 (as amended), which only applied to *crossed* cheques. Formerly in the case of an *uncrossed* cheque the bank had to prove that it was a holder for value to avoid liability for conversion of the cheque.

2 Cheques Act 1957, s. 4 (3). It seems clear, however, that a bank collecting for someone other than the payee must ensure that there are indorsements on the back of the cheque linking the payee with the present holder and that they are not irregular. Breach of that duty would amount to negligence.

3 [1920] AC 683 at 687. See also *Great Western Rly Co v London and County Banking Co* [1901] AC 414.

4 *Importers Co v Westminster Bank* [1927] 2 KB 297.

21.07 *What is negligence?*—Negligence must be considered with reference to an implied duty to use due care to protect the true owner of the cheque; and the onus of proving absence of negligence lies on the banker.[1] Negligence must be connected with a particular cheque, and, coupled with the circumstances antecedent and present, must involve a departure from the standard of care required by the practice of bankers.[2] Examples are as follows:

> Where a cheque drawn payable to the order of or indorsed by a public official is paid into a private account, as the transaction is quite out of the ordinary course of business, the banker cannot safely collect the cheque without inquiry into his customer's title.[3]

So, again:

> Where an official of a limited company, even though he be the sole director of a one-man company, pays into his private account cheques drawn in favour of the company, the banker must make proper business inquiries into the reason justifying the collection of such cheques for the personal account of a servant or agent of the company.[4]

Contrast:

> Where W and E were jointly authorised to sign cheques on the plaintiff company's account and W left some blank cheques, signed by himself on the company's behalf, in E's possession. E drew the cheques 'Pay cash or order', added his own signature and the defendant bank collected the amount for E's private account. *Held:* the defendant bank was not negligent

because E's signature on the instruments was not legible and it did not know of E's connection with the plaintiff company whose name appeared on them. It made no difference that being drawn 'Pay cash' the instruments were not strictly cheques as s. 4 (2) of the Cheques Act gives a collecting bank protection in the case of 'Pay cash' documents, bankers' drafts, etc., as well as cheques.[5]

And:

A cheque for £3,000 was signed on behalf of a company in favour of E. K, calling himself E, sought to open an account at a branch of the Midland Bank in the name of E. The bank agreed to do this and obtained a reference from A who knew K as E and had been a valued customer of the bank for six years. The bank collected the cheque for K (known as E) and after a few weeks K withdrew all the money from his account and left the country. *Held:* the bank acted according to the current practice of bankers and, relying on A's reference, was not negligent in failing to ask for identification or inquire as to K's employment.[6]

Where cheques are paid in at one branch for the account of a customer at another branch, the branch which first receives and clears the cheques, which are not seen by the crediting branch, ought to inform the latter of the names of the drawers of the cheques: otherwise a dishonest servant or agent might pay into his private account his employer's or principal's cheques without the risk of detection he would run by delivering the cheques to the branch at which his account was kept which is more likely to know the name of his employer.[7]

If a collecting bank is held not to be protected by s. 4 of the Cheques Act because of negligence, the damages it must pay in conversion to the true owner will not be reduced by the contributory negligence of the owner,[8] since the Torts (Interference with Goods) Act 1977 now provides that contributory negligence is not to be a defence to conversion.[8]

In exceptional circumstances, where there is an established course of business or where the needs of business clearly indicate such a course, it may not be negligent for a bank to collect for an agent or employee cheques drawn in favour of the principal or employer.[9] In such a case the court may find an implied authority for the agent or employee to pay such cheques into his own account.

But where cheques were drawn in the form 'R by T his attorney', and paid by T into his own *overdrawn* banking account, his bankers, having notice by the form of the cheques that the money was not T's money, were held to have been negligent by omitting to ask to see T's power of attorney or to make any inquiry as to T's authority to pay the moneys into his own account.[10]

---

1 *Lloyd's Bank v Savory & Co* [1933] AC 201, *Midland Bank v Reckitt* [1933] AC 1.
2 *Bissell & Co v Fox* (1884), 51 LTNS 663; on appeal (1885), 53 LTNS 193; *Taxation Comr v English, Scottish and Australian Bank* [1920], AC 683; *Lloyds Bank v Chartered Bank of India, etc,* [1929] 1 KB 40.
3 *Ross v London County Westminster and Parr's Bank* [1919] 1 KB 678.
4 *A L Underwood Ltd v Bank of Liverpool* [1924] 1 KB 755. See also *Marquess of Bute v Barclays Bank Ltd* [1955] 1 QB 202, [1954] 3 All ER 365.
5 *Orbit Mining and Trading Co Ltd v Westminster Bank Ltd* [1963] 1 QB 794, [1962] 3 All ER 565.
6 *Marfani & Co Ltd v Midland Bank Ltd* [1968] 2 All ER 573, [1968] 1 WLR 956, CA.
7 *Lloyds Bank v Savory & Co* [1933] AC 201.
8 S. 11 (see generally, para. 1.03, ante).
9 *Australia and New Zealand Bank v Ateliers etc de Charleroi* [1967] 1 AC 86.
10 *Midland Bank v Reckitt* [1933] AC 1.

21.08 *'Account payee' crossing* If a cheque is marked 'account payee' the collecting banker is under a duty to make inquiry to see that he collects for the payee named on the cheque or that his customer has the payee's authority. It does not restrict the negotiability of the cheque,[1] but if the banker does not make such inquiry, he will be liable in conversion if he collects for someone other than its true owner. If such a cheque is being collected for *another banker*, as the collecting bank cannot control the ultimate destination of the money, it is sufficient for it to hand the proceeds to the proper receiving banker and leave it to him to comply with the direction.[2]

---

1 Paget *Law of Banking* (8th edn) 256–257.
2 *Importers Co v Westminster Bank* [1927] 2 KB 297.

21.09 *Collecting banker as holder for value or holder in due course.*[1] Value is deemed to have been given by a collecting bank to the customer who asks it to collect payment on a cheque if (i) there is an express or implied agreement to apply the cheque in reduction of an overdraft, or to allow him to draw against it before it is cleared, or (ii) if in fact, it gives him cash at once for the cheque or allows it to be drawn against before the proceeds have been cleared, or (iii) if the bank has a lien on the cheque—where the customer is overdrawn the bank has a lien on any cheque paid in up to the amount of the overdraft.[2]

By s. 2 of the Cheques Act, a collecting banker, who gives value for or has a lien on an order cheque given to him for collection without any indorsement on it, is a holder for value of the cheque despite the lack of indorsement. Thus, where the payee of an order cheque gives no value for it and therefore could not sue upon it, hands the cheque in to a bank (with or without his indorsement) for collection for his account (or even for someone else's account) the bank is able to enforce payment provided it can show it is a holder for value.[3]

If the bank has not only given value but fulfils all the particulars of the definition of a holder in due course, by reason inter alia of being in good faith and having no knowledge of any defect in the title of its customer, it has a good defence to any claim in conversion even if it could not, by reason of negligence, claim the protection of s. 4 of the Cheques Act. Of course, the collecting bank cannot claim to be a holder in due course of a cheque if its title rests on a forged indorsement.

Cheque as a receipt

By s. 3 of the Cheques Act, 'an unindorsed cheque which appears to have been paid by the banker on whom it is drawn is evidence of receipt by the payee of the sum payable by the cheque'.

---

1 For the meanings of a holder for value and a holder in due course, see para. 20.16, ante.
2 See *Barclays Bank v Astley Industrial Trust* [1970] 2 QB 527, [1970] 1 All ER 791, *Re Keever a Bankrupt, Ex parte Trustee of Property of Bankrupt v Midland Bank Ltd* [1967] Ch 182, [1966] 3 All ER 631, and para. 20.17, ante.
3 *Midland Bank Ltd v RV Harris Ltd* [1963] 2 All ER 685, [1963] 1 WLR 1021; *Westminster Bank Ltd v Zang* [1966] AC 182, [1966] 1 All ER 114, HL.

---

2. Promissory notes

21.10 A promissory note is defined by the Act to be:[1]

'an unconditional promise in writing made by one person to another signed by the maker, engaging to pay, on demand or at a fixed or determinable future time, a sum certain in money, to, or to the order of, a specified person or to bearer.'

An instrument in the form of a note payable to maker's order is not a note until indorsed by the maker. If on the face of the note it purports to be both made and payable within the British Isles, it is an inland note; any other is a foreign note.[2] The usual form of a promissory note is as follows:

£50.   *York*, [Date]

[Three] months after date [or on demand] I promise to pay

A B or order [or bearer] fifty pounds.

A. F. G.

Here A F G is the maker and A B the payee; when A B puts his name on the back he becomes an indorser. The differences between a note and a bill are manifest; a bill has three original parties, a note has but two.

The contract of the maker is to pay the note according to its tenor, and he may not deny to a holder in due course the existence of the payee, and his then capacity to indorse.[3] This liability may be:

1. Joint, or
2. Joint and several,

according to the number of makers—for any number many jointly make a note—and their liability depends upon the tenor of the note. Thus:

1. 'I promise to pay', etc., signed by more than one person, is a joint and several promise;[4]
2. 'We jointly agree', etc., is a joint promise.

There is no liability till delivery of the note, for until then the instrument is incomplete.[5]

A holder of a demand note is treated as the holder in due course of it although more than a reasonable time has elapsed between its issue and its negotiation to him—it is not deemed to be overdue as a promissory note is treated as a continuing security; in this respect the law relating to bills and to notes differs.[6]

---

1 Bills of Exchange Act 1882, s. 83.
2 See para. 20.35, ante, for the somewhat different definition of a foreign *bill*.
3 Bills of Exchange Act 1882, s. 88.
4 Ibid, s. 85.

5 Ibid, s. 84.
6 Ibid, s. 86 (3); *Glasscock v Balls* (1890) 24 QBD 13.

Presentment for payment

21.11 Where a note is in the body of it made payable at a particular place it must be presented for payment at that place; in any other case presentment for payment is not necessary to make the maker liable; but presentment (within a reasonable time of the indorsement in the case of a demand note or on the day it falls due in the case of time notes) is always necessary to make the indorser liable. Further, presentment must be at the place specified in the body of the note, if any, to make the indorser liable.[1] A note is only made payable 'in the body of it' if the stipulation is part of the actual terms of the contract made by the maker of the note; a memorandum indicating a place of payment is not sufficient to render presentation for payment necessary to render the maker liable.

In cases where presentment for payment is necessary, the Limitation Act will not commence to run until that has taken place.[2]

---

1 Ibid, s. 87.
2 *Re British Trade Corpn* [1932] 2 Ch 1. and see para. 8.08, ante.

Generally

21.12 Subject to the necessary modifications, the provisions of the Act as to bills apply to notes,[1] except as above, and except those relating to:

1. Presentment for acceptance;
2. Acceptance;
3. Acceptance *suprà protest*;
4. Bills in a set.

And protest of a foreign note on dishonour is not necessary.

In applying such provisions to notes, the maker of the note corresponds to the acceptor of a bill, and the first indorser of a note corresponds to the drawer of an accepted bill payable to drawer's order.[2]

1 See chap. 20, ante.
2 Bills of Exchange Act 1882, s. 89 (2).

---

3. Bank notes

21.13 These are promissory notes issued by a banker, payable to bearer on demand. Their properties were considered in the leading case of *Miller v Race,*[1] where Lord Mansfield recognised them as negotiable instruments:

> 'They are not goods, nor securities, nor documents for debts, nor are so esteemed; but are treated as money, as cash, in the ordinary course and transaction of business, by the general consent of mankind; which gives them the credit and currency of money, to all intents and purposes.'

In a later case,[2] Denman J said that Bank of England notes differ from ordinary promissory notes and notes of other banks in two important characteristics, viz., they are always payable to bearer without indorsement, and they are legal tender for the amounts represented by them. He did not consider that the ordinary rules relating to bills would of necessity relate to bank notes, though they do relate to promissory notes generally. For example, any alteration of a bank note makes it void as against the issuing bank irrespective of whether the alteration is apparent or not.

So also, in *Suffell v Bank of England,*[3] Jessel MR said:

> 'A Bank of England note is not an ordinary commercial contract to pay money. It is, in one sense, a promissory note in terms, but no one can describe it as simply a promissory note. It is part of the currency of the country. It has long been made so by Act of Parliament'.[4]

Consumer Credit Act 1974 This Act contains provisions restricting the use of negotiable instruments in connection with 'regulated agreements' as defined in the Act.[5] A creditor or owner must not take a negotiable instrument other than a bank note or cheque in discharge of any sum payable under such an agreement.[6] A cheque must be negotiated to a banker within the meaning of the Bills of Exchange Act 1882. No negotiable instrument of any kind may be taken as a security. This occurs when payment is primarily intended to be made in some other way and the instrument is only to be presented for payment if that other means fails. These provisions are not to apply to non-commercial agreements or, subject to order made by the Secretary of State, when the agreement is connected with another country. If there is a breach of these provisions the agreement can only be enforced by court order and if the application is dismissed on non-technical grounds the agreement is nullified.[7] A person who takes a negotiable instrument in contravention of s. 123 cannot be a holder in due course and negotiation in contravention of the section will be a defect of title. A holder in due course can, however, enforce such an instrument against the debtor who is then give a right of indemnity against the creditor or owner.[8]

---

1 (1758) 1 Burr. 452.
2 *Leeds Bank v Wallker* (1883) 11 QBD 84.
3 (1882) 9 QBD 555.
4 At 563; and see remarks of Brett LJ at 567. A Bank of England note is now legal tender for any amount, see para. 7.16, ante.
5 Consumer Credit Act 1974, ss. 189, 8, 9 and 15. See chap. 14 for full treatment of this Act.
6 Ibid, s. 123: see further, para. 14.42, ante.
7 Ibid, s. 124 and 106.
8 Ibid, s. 125.

Part VII

Carriage and shipping

Chapter 22

Carriage on land

1. Introductory

Carriers at common law

22.01 The common law recognises two classes of carrier, common carriers and private carriers, the distinction being that the former holds himself out as being ready to carry goods or passengers or both[1] for *anyone* who wishes to engage him, and a private carrier is one whose practice is to pick and choose his customers or who undertakes carriage only as a casual occupation. The importance of this division lies in the fact that a common carrier is under a duty to carry passengers and goods of the class which he professes to carry and cannot refuse custom except on certain well-defined grounds. His liability in respect of passengers depends on negligence, but his liability in respect of goods is that of an 'insurer', i.e. he is strictly liable for all loss or damage irrespective of negligence subject to express contractual terms excluding or limiting such liability.[2] The position of a private carrier on the other hand is that, subject to the terms of the contract in which he has entered, he is liable in respect of passengers and goods only for such injury, loss or damage as is caused by his negligence[3] though in respect of goods the burden of proof is on the carrier.[4] A person who reserves the right of accepting or rejecting offers of goods for carriage is not a common carrier.[5]

---

1 *Clarke v West Ham Corpn* [1909] 2 KB 858.
2 For exclusion of liability see paras. 22.05, et seq., post.
3 *Joseph Travers & Sons Ltd v Cooper* [1915] 1 KB 73.
4 *Houghland v Low (Luxury Coaches) Ltd* [1962] 1 QB 694, [1962] 2 All ER 159, CA.
5 *Belfast Ropework Co Ltd v Bushell* [1918] 1 KB 210.

Statutory modifications

22.02 The position of land carriers has been considerably modified by various statutory provisions, all of which directly or indirectly affect the terms and conditions upon which goods or passengers are carried.

The chief of these are the following:

1. The Carriers Act 1830 limits the liability of the common carrier in respect of loss or damage to certain types of goods;[1]

2. Railway companies before the Transport Act 1947 were controlled by a number of statutory provisions the underlying objects of which were to secure that:

(a) reasonable facilities were provided for the public; and

(b) no undue preference was shown to any individual.

3. The Transport Act 1947 created a new public corporation known as the British Transport Commission to which was given a monopoly in rail transport.

4. The Transport Act 1962 divided the functions of the Commission into various Boards of which the British Railways Board is the most important.[2] The Boards are not common carriers.

5. The Carriage of Goods by Road Act 1965 (which came into effect in June 1967) enacts the Geneva Convention for the International Carriage of Goods by Road (1956) which governs all contracts where the place of taking over the goods and the place designated for delivery are situated in two different countries, at least one of which is a party to the Convention. The provisions of the Convention, covering *inter alia* liability for loss, damage and delay are set out in the Schedule to the Act and cannot be excluded by contract.[3]

6. The Transport Act 1968 created the National Freight Corporation which took over the Freight Liner division of British Rail[4] and the various road haulage companies, already publicly owned, such as British Road Services Ltd; The Corporation is not a common carrier, and has adopted British Rail's General Conditions for the Carriage of Goods.[5]

The Unfair Contract Terms Act 1977 applies to contracts of carriage.[6]

---

1 Para. 22.06, post.

2 The others are the British Transport Docks Board, the British Waterways Board and the London Transport Board (replaced by the London Transport Executive by the Transport (London) Act 1969).

3 See *James Buchanan & Co Ltd v Babco Forwarding and Shipping (UK) Ltd* [1977] 3 All ER 1048, [1977] 3 WLR 907, HL. (English text to be given broad interpretation to produce, if possible, conformity amongst contracting States but decisions of foreign courts not to be used).

4 This has now been returned to British Rail.
5 See para. 22.08, post.
6 See para. 3.14, ante.

---

2. Rights and duties at common law

Common Carriers of goods

22.03 At common law a common carrier of goods must carry the goods
of the class he professes to carry of anybody who delivers them
to him, and who offers to pay reasonable hire.[1] He may claim
payment in advance, i.e. before he carries, but not before he
receives the goods.[2] This duty of taking anybody's goods is that
which makes him a common carrier, i.e. a carrier common to all.
He should:

1. Carry the goods by his ordinary route, not of necessity the
shortest, but without unnecessary deviation or delay;[3]
2. Deliver them to the consignee, at the place (if any) designated
by the consignor; unless the consignee requires the goods to be
delivered at another place, in which case he may deliver them
according to the orders of the consignee;[4] and if as between the
consignor and the consignee there was a right in the former to
change the destination of the goods, the carrier, on receiving due
notice, must take the goods to the new destination if it is within
the area of his operations.[5]

He cannot be compelled to take the goods:[6]

1. If his vehicle is already full;
2. If the goods are such as he cannot, or does not profess to
convey;
3. If they are of a nature such as to subject him to extraordinary
risk.[7]
4. If they are inadequately packed.[8]

A consignor who delivers goods of a dangerous character to a
common carrier (although the consignor may be ignorant of the
danger) impliedly warrants that the goods are fit to be carried
with safety. This implied warranty does not arise in cases where
the carrier knows of the danger. Thus, in *Bamfield v Goole and
Sheffield Transport Co*:[9]

> The defendants, who were forwarding agents, delivered
> 'ferro-silicon' in casks to a common carrier under the descrip-
> tion of 'general cargo,' but did not inform him that it was
> ferro-silicon, although they were aware of the fact. The

ferro-silicon during carriage gave off poisonous gases, which caused the death of the carrier.

The judge found on the evidence that ferro-silicon was liable under certain conditions to be dangerous, that neither the defendants nor the carrier knew this, and that the defendants were not guilty of negligence in not knowing the dangerous character of the goods. The defendants were held liable in damages for causing the death of the carrier.

The common carrier has a lien for his charges on the goods carried in respect of which the claim arises, but it is a particular and not a general lien.[10]

1 *Garton v Bristol and Exeter Rly Co* (1861) 1 B & S 112 at 162.
2 *Pickfords v Grand Junction Rly Co* (1841) 8 M & W 372.
3 *Briddon v Great Northern Rly Co* (1859) 28 LJ Ex. 51; *Myers v London and South Western Rly Co* (1870) LR 5 CP 1.
4 *London and North Western Rly Co v Bartlett* (1861) 7 H & N 400.
5 *Scothorn v South Staffordshire Rly Co* (1853) 8 Exch 341.
6 *Batson v Donovan* (1820) 4 B & A at 32.
7 *Edwards v Sherratt* (1801) 1 East 604.
8 *Sutcliffe v Great Western Rly Co* [1910] 1 KB 478 at 503.
9 [1910] 2 KB 94. The warranty also applies to goods delivered to a private carrier (*Great Northern Rly Co v LEP Transport and Depository*, [1922] 2 KB 742).
10 *Rushforth v Hadfield* (1805) 6 East 519, (1806), 7 East 224. See para. 17.11, ante.

Liability for loss or damage

22.04   At common law, the common carrier of goods must make good any loss or damage whether or not it is caused by his negligence, for his agreement is to carry safely and securely, unless the loss or damage is caused by:

1. An act of God.[1] This is some unforeseen accident occasioned by the elementary forces of nature unconnected with the agency of man or other cause the occurrence of which could not have been reasonably foreseen and the consequence of which could not have been prevented by reasonable precautions.[2]
2. The Queen's enemies.

He is, in fact, in the 'nature of an insurer' in regard to the carriage of goods whereas one who carries goods, not being a common carrier, is bound only to carry with due care.[3] The exceptions to the common carrier's liability, whether those mentioned above or whether fixed by contact, do not avail him if the loss or damage to the goods is contributed to by his negligence, or if he does not provide a proper vehicle.[4]

He is responsible for the safety of the goods so long as they are in his custody; i.e. during transit and (as his duty is usually to deliver as well as to carry) after transit for a reasonable time, varying with circumstances. After the lapse of such time he becomes a mere bailee, and is liable only for negligence, unless otherwise agreed.[5]

If the consignee refuses to take the goods, the carrier must do what, in all the circumstances, is reasonable,[6] and may recover expenses properly incurred in consequence of the refusal to accept delivery.[7] It will be safer for him to give notice of the refusal to the consignor, though this may not be always necessary.[8]

A carrier is not liable for damage or loss to goods which has arisen owing:

1. To an inherent vice in or natural deterioration of the goods delivered to be carried; or
2. To the neglect of the owner, without negligence on the part of the carrier; or
3. If the packing is defective, although that fact is known to him at the time when the goods are received.[9]

And if from any cause (e.g. the nature of the goods) special care is required, the carrier is entitled to be informed of this, otherwise he will not be liable for damage which but for such cause would not have occurred.

In *Baldwin v London, Chatham and Dover Rly Co*:[10]

Rags were sent for transit to the company, and by mistake the company failed to send them in proper time to their destination; the rags were packed wet, and were in consequence spoilt by the delay, but had they been dry, no damage would have been suffered.

The court decided that in the absence of notice of the state of the rags to the carriers, they were not liable for the loss, and that nominal damages would suffice to meet the damage suffered through their default.

---

1 *Forward v Pittard* (1785) 1 Term Rep 27.
2 *Nugent v Smith* (1876) 1 CPD 423.
3 *Coggs v Bernard* (1703) 2 Ld Raym 909.
4 *The Xantho* (1887) 12 App Cas at 510; and see per Bowen, LJ, in *Steinman & Co v Angier Line* [1891] 1 QB at 624.
5 Per Cockburn CJ in *Chapman v Great Western Rly Co* (1880) 5 QBD at 281, 282; *Mitchell v Lancashire and Yorkshire Rly Co* (1875) LR 10 QB 256.

6 *Crouch v Great Western Rly Co* (1857) 2 H &N 491 affd., 3 H & N 183.
7 *Great Northern Rly Co v Swaffield* (1874) LR 9 Exch 132.
8 *Hudson v Baxendale* (1857) 2 H & N 575.
9 *Gould v South Eastern and Chatham Rly Co* [1920] 2 KB 186. But being aware of the facts the carrier must do what is reasonable to prevent further loss (*Beck v Evans* (1812) 16 East 244 at 247).
10 (1882) 9 QBD 582.

Exclusion and limitation of liability of common and private carriers of goods

22.05 Even at common law, a common carrier (and of course a private carrier) could agree with his customer that his liability should be excluded or limited. Thus, if the owner of goods received a ticket, on which was a notice limiting the carrier's liability, this would be strong evidence that he agreed to the terms so that the owner was bound by the condition though not actually aware of it if the carrier had taken all reasonable steps to bring it to his notice.[1]

Those carriers who are members of the Road Haulage Association normally contract on the basis of the Association's Conditions of Carriage which were revised in 1967 and 1971. Clause 2 states that 'the carrier is not a common carrier and will accept goods for carriage only on these conditions'. Clause10 provides time limits for claims and by Clause 11 it is provided that there is no liability for loss, misdelivery or damage which has arisen from Act of God, war, seizure under legal process, act or omission of the trader, inherent vice, insufficient packing or labelling, or riots. Otherwise, Clause 12 provides for liability on the carrier subject to financial limits.

A contractual clause excluding or limiting the carrier's liability will now be subject to the provisions of the Unfair Contract Terms Act 1977.[2]

COMMON CARRIERS OF PASSENGERS

A common carrier of passengers must carry any passenger, not being an objectionable person, who offers himself and is willing to pay the fare, provided that there is accommodation.[3] He is not an 'insurer' of his passengers but is bound to exercise due care for their safety.[4]

Any contract for the conveyance of passengers in a public service vehicle is void in so far as it purports to restrict liability in respect of the death of or personal injury to a passenger while being carried in, entering or alighting from the vehicle.[5]

COMMON CARRIERS TODAY

Most road hauliers reserve the right to accept or reject offers of goods for carriage and are therefore not common carriers, or, as in the case of those contracting on the basis of the Road Haulage Association's Conditions of Carriage, expressly state that they are not common carriers. However, a bus or coach running as part of a regular transport service (and known in law as a public service vehicle) is still a common carrier of any passenger's luggage that it carries.[6]

---

1 See per Blackburn J in *Peek v North Staffordshire Rly Co* (1863) 10 HL Cas at 494; and see para. 3.12, ante.

2 See para. 3.15, ante.

3 *Clarke v West Ham Corpn* [1909] 2 KB 258.

4 *Barkway v South Wales Transport Co* [1950] AC 185, [1950] 1 All ER 392.

5 Road Traffic Act 1960, s. 151. Even a condition to like effect on a free pass may be ineffective: *Gore v Van der Lann* [1967] 2 QB 31, [1967] 1 All ER 360, CA. The pass was regarded as a contract. See also Transport Act 1962, s. 43.

6 For a recent case in which a road haulier was held to be a common carrier see *A Siohn & Co and Academy Garments (Wigan) Ltd v RH Hagland & Sons (Transport) Ltd* [1976] 2 Lloyd's Rep 428.

---

3. The Carriers Act 1830

22.06 *Protection of carriers* By the Carriers Act 1830,[1] it is enacted:

1. That no common carrier by land[1] for hire shall be liable for loss or injury to certain articles when the value exceeds £10, unless at time of delivery the value and nature of the property shall have been declared, and an increased charge paid or agreed to be paid.[2] Such notice must be express. Amongst the articles mentioned are:

(i) gold, (ii) jewellery, (iii) watches, (iv) negotiable paper, (v) pictures, (vi) china, (vii) furs, and (viii) silks.

The amount is the aggregate value of the parcel.

2. All common carriers may demand on such packages an increased charge, but the amount per scale must be notified in legible characters in some conspicuous part of the office where the parcels are received. Such notice will bind those sending goods, without proof that it was brought to their knowledge.[3]

The exemption from the common law liability is given only where this notification and demand have been made, or when the declaration of value has not been given.

3. Except as provided for by the Act, no public notice shall be allowed to limit the liability of carriers.[4]

The carrier's exemption applies only in the case where there is loss[5] or injury to the goods; he is therefore liable as before the Act for damage caused by delay.

Most road hauliers today (as well as British Rail) are not common carriers and, therefore, the significance of the Carriers Act 1830 is now small. It still applies to the carriage of passenger's luggage on buses and coaches running as public service vehicles.[6]

---

1 This is applicable where the transit is *partly* by sea, if the loss occurs on land (*Le Conteur v London and South Western Rly Co* (1866) LR 1 QB 54).
2 Carriers Act 1830, s. 1.
3 Carriers Act 1830, s. 2.
4 Carriers Act 1830, s. 4, and see Unfair Contract Terms Act 1977: para. 3.15, ante.
5 This includes a temporary loss (*Millen v Brasch* (1883) 10 QBD 142).
6 See *Chitty on Contracts* (24th edn) Vol 2, 328. As to the meaning of 'luggage' see ibid at 352–358 and *Macrow v Great Western Rly Co* (1871) LR 6 QB 612 at 622. It may be for personal use or convenience and either for immediate necessities or for the ultimate purpose of the journey.

---

4. Rail transport

22.07 The railways were taken into public ownership by the Transport Act 1947, and a public corporation, the British Railways Board, now manages the railways.

The British Railways Board have power to demand such charges as they think fit, and are not subject to any control as regards charges by the Transport Tribunal. The Board are under no duty to provide reasonable facilities to the public for receiving forwarding and delivering goods and are not common carriers of goods or passengers.[1] Because the Board are not common carriers, the Carriers Act 1830 no longer has any application to goods carried on the railways.

International aspects of carriage by rail are governed by the Carriage by Railway Act 1972.

---

1 Transport Act 1962, s. 43 (6).

Conditions of carriage of goods

22.08 The Board enjoy complete freedom to make the use of their services and facilities 'subject to such terms and conditions as they think fit'.[1] The Board have issued sets of conditions on the basis of which they are prepared to carry goods. The principal set contains 'General Conditions for the Carriage of Goods (other than Goods for which Conditions are specially provided)'. Under these conditions when the goods are carried at the Board's risk the Board are liable for any loss, or misdelivery of, or damage to, merchandise during transit, unless the Board can prove it has arisen from act of God, war, seizure under legal process, act or omission of the trader, inherent vice, insufficient or improper packing, labelling or addressing, riot or strikes, or the consignee not taking delivery within a reasonable time.

However, liability is limited in respect of loss of the whole consignment to £800 per ton, and in respect of a partial loss to such proportion of £800 per ton as the value of the part lost bears to the whole consignment. The Board is not liable where the consignor or consignee is fraudulent.

With regard to goods carried at Owner's Risk (in which case, the charges are lower), the Board's only liability for loss, damage, misdelivery, delay, or detention is where wilful misconduct on the part of the Board or their servants can be proved. However, there is liability without proof of wilful misconduct where there has been a misdelivery of the whole consignment or of a separate package forming part of a consignment. Board's risk defences then apply.

In the case of damageable goods not properly protected by packing the Board are generally liable only for wilful misconduct. However, the Board are also liable if it can be proved that the damage would still have been suffered even if properly packed.

Written notice of any claim must be made within three days of the transit terminating, and the claim itself must be made within seven days. These times give way to longer periods of twenty-eight days and forty-two days where the claim is in respect of non-delivery of the whole consignment or of a separate package forming part of a consignment.

---

1 Ibid., s. 43 (3).

Carriage of passengers

22.09 The Board's liability for injury to a passenger depends on proof of negligence. By s. 43 (7) of the Transport Act 1962, the Board was not allowed to exclude or limit their liability to a passenger by rail other than one travelling on a free pass. This section has now been repealed by the Unfair Contract Terms Act 1977 of which s. 2 (1) makes general provision for avoiding terms excluding or restricting liability in negligence for death or personal injury.[1]

---

1 See Unfair Contract Terms Act 1977, Sch. 4. See also s. 28 for temporary provisions for certain contracts for the sea carriage of passengers. For the Act see generally para. 3.15, ante.

Chapter 23

Carriage of goods by sea

1. Introduction

23.01 A contract for the carriage of goods by sea is also known as a contract of affreightment, the consideration being called 'freight'.[1] It is found in two forms:—

1. A charter-party, which provides for the hiring of the ship itself;[2]
2. A contract for the conveyance of goods in a general ship, the terms of which are evidenced by a bill of lading. A bill of lading also operates as a receipt for the goods shipped on board and as a document of title to the goods.[3]

These two contracts have many incidents in common. Sometimes the charterer (i.e. the person who hires the ship from the shipowner) uses the ship as a general ship, carrying goods of third parties under bills of lading. Alternatively, the charterer may find the cargo himself in which case there may well be a bill of lading as well as a charter-party because the charterer may wish to use the bill of lading as a document of title to transfer the cargo while it is still in transit—the charter-party, not the bill of lading, will comprise the contract between the shipowner and the charterer. However, as regards assignees of the bill of lading, the bill of lading contains the terms of the contract of carriage made with the shipowners, and unless the bill of lading refers to and incorporates with itself any or all of the terms of the charter-party in clear terms, the assignee is not affected by the charter-party. If the bill of lading contains a statement:

'freight and all other conditions as per charter-party,'

the terms of the charter-party govern the payment of freight and all other conditions which would have to be performed by the recipient of the goods, so far as these are not in conflict with any express stipulations of the bill of lading; but conditions of the charter-party which are not to be performed by the consignee of the goods are not incorporated.[4]

---

1 See para. 23.22, post. Much shipping business is arranged on the Baltic Exchange in London.
2 See para. 23.02, post.
3 See further as to bill of lading, para. 23.08, et seq., post. A 'general ship' is one used to carry the goods of a number of persons.
4 *Serraino v Campbell* [1891] 1 QB 283.

---

2. Charter-parties

23.02 'When the agreement is to carry a complete cargo of goods or to furnish a ship for that purpose, the contract of affreightment is almost always contained in a document called a *charter-party*, the *shipowner* letting the ship for the purpose of carrying, or undertaking to carry, the *charterer* hiring the ship for such purpose, or undertaking to provide a full cargo'.[1]

The charter-party may, but need not, be under seal. It may amount to a complete demise of the ship; that is to say, it may put the vessel altogether out of the power and control of the owner, and vest that power and control in the charterer, so that during the hiring the master and crew are servants of the charterer and the shipowner is under no liability with regard to the cargo carried during the demise.[2] However, a charter-party by demise is uncommon[3] and generally the ship remains in the possession of the owner, the charterer acquiring the right only to put his goods on the vessel, and to have them carried.[4] It is a matter of construction whether the charter-party is one by demise or not, but the most common types of charter-party are (i) a *voyage charter-party*, where the ship is chartered for a particular voyage, and (ii) a *time charter-party*, where the ship is chartered for a particular period of time.

It would seem that the charterer's right to the use of the ship can be disregarded by a person who purchases the ship even with notice of the terms of the charter-party. For he is no party to the contract and although in equity certain convenants run with the land, there is no similar doctrine applicable to chattels.[5] Of course, if the owner sold the ship during the currency of a charter-party the owner would be liable to the charterer for breach of contract.

---

1 *Scrutton on Charter-parties and Bills of Lading* (18th edn) 2–3, Art. 3 and

also p. 1 which lists a number of documents used as contracts of affreightment which are neither charter parties nor bills of lading.

2 *Baumwoll, Manufactur Von Carl Scheiber v Furness* [1893] AC 8, HL.

3 *Sea and Land Securities Ltd v Dickinson & Co Ltd* [1942] 2 KB 65, 69, [1942] 1 All ER 503. See, however, Payne and Ivamy *Carriage of Goods by Sea* (10th edn) 10.

4 *Sandeman v Scurr* (1867) LR 1 QB 86 at 96.

5 *Port Line Ltd v Ben Line Steamers Ltd* [1958] 2 QB 146, [1958] 1 All ER 787, not following the Privy Council decision in *Lord Strathcona S S Co v Dominion Coal Co* [1926] AC 108. For the principle that a contract is not binding on third parties, see para. 4.02, ante. See also *Cheshire and Fifoot on Contract* (9th edn) 446–450.

Voyage charter-parties

23.03 An example is given below of the *express* terms commonly found in a voyage charter-party. There are, however, a number of terms that are *implied* by law. It has earlier been pointed out that the introduction of an implied term into a contract can be justified only when it is not inconsistent with an express term of the contract, and where the implied term is necessary to give business efficacy to the contract.[1] There is a wealth of judicial precedent establishing the following three terms as implied obligations of the shipowners in a voyage charter-party—the first one mentioned is also an implied obligation of the shipowners in a time charter-parter:

(i) that the ship is seaworthy at the time of sailing from the port of loading;

(ii) that the voyage will be commenced and carried out without unreasonable delay; and

(iii) that there shall be no unwarranted deviation from the route.

The charterer is under an implied obligation not to ship goods which involve the risk of unusual danger or delay to the ship. This applies to both voyage and time charters.

Any of these implied obligations can be excluded or varied by an express term in the charter-party provided this is done by clear unambiguous language.[2]

1 Para. 7.05, ante.

2 *Nelson Line Liverpool) Ltd v James Nelson & Sons Ltd* [1908] AC 16. The Hague Rules which are imported into bills of lading by the Carriage of Goods by Sea Act 1971 do not automatically apply to charter-parties but may be incorporated by agreement. See para. 23.18, post, and 23.20, post, for Unfair Contract Terms Act 1977.

Implied obligations of shipowner

23.04 a) *Seaworthiness* In the case of both voyage and time charter-parties, there is implied by law an obligation on the part of the shipowner that the ship is seaworthy and fit to receive cargo at the time of sailing from the port of loading. This means that the ship is fit to encounter the ordinary perils of navigation and that the ship, its furniture, and equipment are fit to carry the cargo.[1] It is not enough that the shipowner does his best to make the ship fit—it must in fact be fit. There is thus an absolute twofold obligation on the shipowner as to seaworthiness at the time of sailing from the port of loading and as to the ship's fitness to receive the particular cargo at the time of loading. If the ship is seaworthy and fit to receive cargo at these times, defects arising subsequently do not amount to breach of this obligation but if the voyage is of necessity divided into stages, e.g. to take in coal, the vessel must be made seaworthy at the commencement of each stage.[2]

Bad stowage will amount to unseaworthiness only if it endangers the safety of the ship as distinct from merely the safety of the cargo.[3]

If the shipowner is in breach of his implied undertaking of seaworthiness, this does not automatically discharge the contract of affreightment. The charterer is entitled, of course, to sue for damages and where he learns of the unseaworthiness before the journey begins he is entitled to repudiate the contract if the ship cannot be rendered seaworthy within a reasonable time[4] but the charterer is not entitled to repudiate for a trifling breach. As Diplock LJ said in a leading case,[5] the shipowner's undertaking to deliver a seaworthy ship is neither a 'condition' nor a 'warranty':

'but one of that large class of contractual undertakings one breach of which may have the same effect as that ascribed to a breach of "condition" under the Sale of Goods Act 1893 and a different breach of which may only have the same effect as that ascribed to a breach of "warranty" under that Act.'

If the ship is unseaworthy at the start of the voyage, the shipowner is liable for damage to cargo which would not have occurred but for the unseaworthiness, even if other causes contribute to the loss.[6] Where, however, unseaworthiness at the start of the voyage does not cause some subsequent damage to cargo, the shipowner's liability will depend on whether the damage is due to an 'excepted peril', i.e. is covered by a term in the charter-party exempting the shipowner from liability in the circumstances that have occurred.[7]

b) Reasonable despatch   There is an implied obligation on the shipowner under a voyage charter-party that the voyage will be commenced and carried out without unreasonable delay.[8] If the breach is so serious that the commercial purpose of the charterer is substantially defeated, he may repudiate the contract but otherwise he is confined to a remedy in damages.

c) No unwarranted deviation   The shipowner is under an implied obligation to ensure that there is no unnecessary or unwarranted deviation of the ship from its proper course. The route may be specified in the contract but otherwise the proper course is either the shortest geographical route or the usual route.[9]

Voluntary unwarranted deviation renders the contract of affreightment voidable so that, at the charterer's option, a voyage charter-party may be avoided as from the beginning of the voyage, no matter when or where the deviation took place. Moreover, if loss or damage to cargo occurs, the shipowner cannot rely on the excepted perils clause in the charter-party even though the loss or damage to cargo was not caused by the deviation.[10] In *James Morrison & Co v Shaw, Savill & Co.*[11]

A ship was torpedoed by an enemy submarine during an unwarranted deviation. *Held*: the shipowners could not rely on the excepted perils clause; nor could they rely on the exceptions available to common carriers at Common Law that the loss was caused by the King's enemies unless they could prove that the loss would have occurred if the ship had been on her proper course. Clearly the shipowners could not prove this here.

Breach of the obligation also entitles the charterers to claim damages for any loss resulting.

Deviation is permissible where it is necessary for the safety of the ship or crew even though this necessity was caused by unseaworthiness or was due to some culpable act on the part of the ship's master. If, therefore, the ship is in peril the master is not faced by the alternative of having to choose between the safety of his ship and crew and the loss of the contract of affreightment.[12] Furthermore, there is a general right to deviate in order to save life, e.g. the crew of another ship in distress, but not to save property.[13]

The contract may of course contain an express term allowing the ship to call at ports that are not on the usual route or to make other deviations not warranted at Common Law.[14]

---

1 *Steel v State Line SS Co* (1878) 3 App Cas 72; *McFadden v Blue Star Line* [1905] 1 KB 697.

2 *The Vortigern* [1899] P. 140.
3 *Elder Dempster & Co v Paterson Zochonis & Co* [1924] AC 522.
4 *Stanton v Richardson* (1874) LR 9 CP 390.
5 *Hong Kong Fir Shipping Co Ltd v Kawasaki Kisen Kaisha Ltd* [1962] 2 QB 26, 41, [1962] 1 All ER 474, 488.
6 *Smith, Hogg & Co Ltd v Black Sea and Baltic Insurance Co* [1940] AC 997, [1940] 3 All ER 405; see also *Monarch SS Co v Karlshamns Oljefabriker (A/B)* [1949] AC 196, [1949] 1 All ER 1.
7 *The Europa* [1908] P. 84.
8 *McAndrew v Adams* (1834) 1 Bing NC 29.
9 *Reardon Smith Lines Ltd v Black Sea and Baltic Lines Insurance Co Ltd, The Indian City,* [1939] AC 562, [1939] 3 All ER 444.
10 *Joseph Thorley Ltd v Orchis Co Ltd* [1907] 1 KB 405.
11 [1916] 2 KB 783 (a bill of lading case, but the same principle applies to charter-parties).
12 *Kish v Taylor* [1912] AC 604.
13 *Scaramanga v Stamp* (1880) 5 CPD 295. But in bills of lading governed by the Carriage of Goods by Sea Act 1971, deviation to save property is permissible. See para. 23.19, post.
14 See Clause 10 of the form of charter-party set out in para. 23.06, post.

Implied Obligation of Charterer

23.05 In both voyage and time charter-parties, the charterer is under an implied obligation not to ship goods which involve the risk of unusual danger or delay to the ship, e.g. goods which the charterers know cannot be discharged at the port of discharge without violating the law prevailing at that port.[1]

---

1 *Mitchell, Cotts & Co v Steel Bros & Co Ltd* [1916] 2 KB 610. Under a time charter-party, the charterer is also under an implied obligation to use only good and safe ports.

FORM OF CHARTER-PARTY

23.06 While a charter-party may be in any form, a shipowner and charterer will normally employ one of the various standard forms originating in agreement between the Chamber of Shipping of the United Kingdom and the Baltic and International Maritime Conference whose membership comprises shipowners, ship-brokers and chartering agents. These standard contracts are known by various code names such as 'Gencon', 'Nubaltwood', 'Austwheat' etc. The following is the 'Gencon' form reproduced by kind permission of the Baltic and International Maritime Conference. It is used the world over and considered particularly suitable for cargoes of grain, fertilisers, salt, scrap iron, bricks, cattle and several other types of cargo.

PART A   Place and date:

1) IT IS THIS DAY MUTUALLY AGREED between
                                         Owners of the steamer
or motor-vessel
                         of   tons gross/net Register
and carrying about   tons of deadweight cargo, now[1]
and expected ready to load under this Charter about   and
Messrs.   of   as Charterers.
     That the said vessel shall proceed to[2]
                         or so near thereto as she may safely get
and lie always afloat,[3] and there load a full and complete cargo[4] if
shipment of deck cargo agreed same to be at Charterers' risk) of

(Charterers to provide all mats and/or wood for dunnage and any
separations required, the Owners allowing the use of any dunnage
wood on board if required) which the Charterers bind themselves
to ship,[5] and being so loaded the vessel shall proceed to
                         as ordered on signing Bills of Lading
or so near thereto as she may safely get and lie always afloat and
there deliver the cargo on being paid freight—on delivered/intaken
quantity—as follows:[6]

2) The freight to be paid in cash[7] without discount on delivery of the
cargo at mean rate of exchange ruling on day or days of payment,
the receivers of the cargo being bound to pay freight on account
during delivery, if required by Captain or Owners.
     Cash for vessel's ordinary disbursements at port of loading to be
advanced by Charterers if required at highest current rate of
exchange, subject to two per cent. to cover insurance and other
expenses.

3) Cargo to be brought alongside in such a manner as to enable vessel
to take the goods with her own tackle and to load
                         the full cargo in
running working days.[8] Charterers to procure and pay the necessary
men on shore or on board the lighters to do the work there, vessel
only heaving the cargo on board.
     If the loading takes place by elevator cargo to be put free in
vessel's holds, Owners only paying trimming expenses.
     Any pieces and/or packages of cargo over two tons weight, shall
be loaded, stowed and discharged by Charterers at their risk and
expense.
     Time to commence at 1 p.m. if notice of readiness to load is given
before noon and at 6 a.m. next working day if notice given during
office hours after noon.
     The notice to be given to the Shippers, Messrs.

Time lost in waiting for berth to count as loading time.

4) Cargo to be received by Merchants at their risk and expense along-side the vessel not beyond the reach of her tackle and to be discharged in   running working days.[9] Time to commence at 1 p.m. if notice of readiness to discharge is given before noon, and at 6 a.m. next working day if notice given during office hours after noon.

Time lost in waiting for berth to count as discharging time.

5) Ten running days on demurrage at the rate of   per day or pro rata for any part of a day, payable day by day, to be allowed Merchants altogether at ports of loading and discharging.

6) Should the vessel not be ready to load (whether in berth or not) on or before the   Charterers have the option of cancelling this contract, such option to be declared, if demanded, at least 48 hours before vessel's expected arrival at port of loading. Should the vessel be delayed on account of average[10] or otherwise, Charterers to be informed as soon as possible, and if the vessel is delayed for more than 10 days after the day she is stated to be expected ready to load, Charterers have the option of cancelling this contract, unless a cancelling date has been agreed upon.

7) In every case the Owner shall appoint his own Broker or Agent both at the port of loading and the port of discharge.

8)   brokerage on the freight earned is due to

In case of non-execution at least 1/3 of the brokerage on the estimated amount of freight and dead-freight to be paid by the Owners to the Brokers as indemnity for the latter's expenses and work. In case of more voyages the amount of indemnity to be mutually agreed.

9–15): as in part B, which constitutes a part of this Charter as though fully set forth herein.

PART B

9) Owners are to be responsible for loss of or damage to the goods[11] or for delay in delivery of the goods only in case the loss, damage or delay has been caused by the improper or negligent stowage of the goods (unless stowage performed by shippers or their stevedores or servants) or by personal want of due diligence on the part of the Owners or their Manager to make the vessel in all respects sea-worthy and secure that she is properly manned, equipped and supplied or by the personal act or default of the Owners or their Manager.

And the Owners are responsible for no loss or damage or delay arising from any other cause whatsoever, even from the neglect or default of the Captain or crew or some other person employed by the Owners on board or ashore for whose acts they would, but for this clause, be responsible, or from unseaworthiness of the vessel on loading or commencement of the voyage or at any time whatsoever.

Damage caused by contact with or leakage, smell or evaporation from other goods or by the inflammable or explosive nature or insufficient package of other goods not to be considered as caused by improper or negligent stowage, even if in fact so caused.

10) The vessel has liberty to call at any port or ports in any order, for any purpose, to sail without pilots, to tow and or assist vessels in all situations, and also to deviate for the purpose of saving life and/or property.[12]

11) Owners shall have a lien on the[13] cargo for freight, dead-freight, demurrage and damages for detention. Charterers shall remain responsible for dead-freight and demurrage (including damages for detention), incurred at port of loading. Charterers shall also remain responsible for freight and demurrage (including damages for detention) incurred at port of discharge, but only to such extent as the Owners have been unable to obtain payment thereof by exercising the lien on the cargo.

12) The Captain to sign Bills of Lading at such rate of freight as presented without prejudice to this Charterparty, but should the freight by Bills of Lading amount to less than the total chartered freight the difference to be paid to the Captain in cash on signing Bills of Lading.

13) General average to be settled according to York–Antwerp Rules,[14] 1950, Proprietors of cargo to pay the cargo's share in the general expenses even if same have been necessitated through neglect or default of the Owner's servants (see clause 9).

14) Indemnity for non-performance of this Charterparty, proved damages, not exceeding estimated amount of freight.

15) **Strike-Clause, War-Clause and Ice-Clause as below.**

GENERAL STRIKE CLAUSE
Neither Charterers nor Owners shall be responsible for the consequences of any strikes or lock-outs preventing or delaying the fulfilment of any obligations under this contract.

If there is a strike or lock-out affecting the loading of the cargo, or any part of it, when vessel is ready to proceed from her last port or at any time during the voyage to the port or ports of loading or after her arrival there, Captain or Owners may ask Charterers to declare, that they agree to reckon the laydays as if there were no strike or lock-out. Unless Charterers have given such declaration in writing (by telegram, if necessary) within 24 hours, Owners shall have the option of cancelling this contract. If part cargo has already been loaded, Owners must proceed with same (freight payable on loaded quantity only), having liberty to complete with other cargo on the way for their own account.

If there is a strike or lock-out[15] affecting the discharge of the cargo on or after vessel's arrival at or off port of discharge and same has not been settled within 48 hours, Receivers shall have the option of keeping vessel waiting until such strike or lock-out is at an end against paying half demurrage after expiration of the time provided for discharging, or of ordering the vessel to a safe port where she can safely discharge without risk of being detained by strike or lock-out. Such orders to be given within 48 hours after Captain or Owners have given notice to Charterers of the strike or lock-out affecting the discharge. On delivery of the cargo at such port, all conditions of this Charter-party and of the Bill of Lading shall apply and vessel shall receive the same freight as if she had discharged at the original port of destination, except that if the distance of the substituted port exceeds 100 nautical miles, the freight on the cargo delivered at the substituted port to be increased in proportion.

GENERAL WAR CLAUSE

If the nation under whose flag the vessel sails should be engaged in war and the safe navigation of the vessel should thereby be endangered either party to have the option of cancelling this contract, and if so cancelled, cargo already shipped shall be discharged either at the port of loading or, if the vessel has commenced the voyage, at the nearest safe place at the risk and expense of the Charterers or Cargo-Owners.

If owing to outbreak of hostilities the goods loaded or to be loaded under this contract or part of them become contraband of war whether absolute or conditional or liable to confiscation or detention according to international law or the proclamation of any of the belligerent powers each party to have the option of cancelling this contract as far as such goods are concerned, and contraband goods already loaded to be then discharged either at the port of loading, or if the voyage has already commenced, at the nearest safe place at the expense of the Cargo-Owners. Owners to have the right to fill up with other goods instead of the contraband.

Should any port where the vessel has to load under this Charter be blockaded the contract to be null and void with regard to the goods to be shipped at such port.

No Bills of Lading to be signed for any blockaded port, and if the port of destination be declared blockaded after Bills of Lading have been signed, Owners shall discharge the cargo either at the port of loading, against payment of the expenses of discharge, if the ship has not sailed thence, or, if sailed at any safe port on the way as ordered by Shippers or if no order is given at the nearest safe place against payment of full freight.

GENERAL ICE CLAUSE

a) In the event of the loading port being inaccessible by reason of ice when vessel is ready to proceed from her last port or at any time during the voyage or on vessel's arrival or in case frost sets in after vessel's arrival, the Captain for fear of being frozen in is at liberty to leave without cargo, and this Charter shall be null and void.

b) If during loading the Captain, for fear of vessel being frozen in, deems it advisable to leave, he has liberty to do so with what cargo he has on board and to proceed to any other port or ports with option of completing cargo for Owner's benefit for any port or ports including port of discharge. Any part cargo thus loaded under this Charter to be forwarded to destination at vessel's expense but against payment of freight, provided that no extra expenses be thereby caused to the Receivers, freight being paid on quantity delivered (in proportion if lump sum), all other conditions as per Charter.

c) In case of more than one loading port, and if one or more of the ports are closed by ice, the Captain or Owners to be at liberty either to load the part cargo at the open port and fill up elsewhere for their own account as under section *b* or to declare the Charter null and void unless Charterers agree to load full cargo at the open port.

d) This Ice Clause not to apply in the Spring.

a) Should ice (except in the Spring) prevent vessel from reaching port of discharge Receivers shall have the option of keeping vessel waiting until the re-opening of navigation and paying demurrage, or of ordering the vessel to a safe and immediately accessible port where she can safely discharge without risk of detention by ice. Such orders to be given within 48 hours after Captain or Owners have given notice to Charterers of the impossibility of reaching port of destination.

b) If during discharging the Captain for fear of vessel being frozen in deems it advisable to leave, he has liberty to do so with what cargo he has on board and to proceed to the nearest accessible port where she can safely discharge.

c) On delivery of the cargo at such port, all conditions of the Bill of Lading shall apply and vessel shall receive the same freight as if she had discharged at the original port of destination, except that if the distance of the substituted port exceeds 100 nautical miles, the freight on the cargo delivered at the substituted port to be increased in proportion.

1 See para. 23.07 (1), post.
2 See para. 23.07 (2), post.
3 See para. 23.07 (3), post.
4 See para. 23.07 (4), post.
5 See para. 23.07 (5), post.
6 See para. 23.07 (6), post.
7 See para. 23.22, post.
8 See para. 23.07 (8), post.
9 Ibid.
10 See para. 23.24, post.
11 See para. 23.07 (9), post.
12 See para. 23.07 (10), post.
13 See para. 23.23.
14 See para. 23.27, post.
15 See para. 23.07 (1), post.

Notes on the form of charter-party

23.07 1) *Now ...* This is to indicate the position of the ship at the date of the charter-party. A statement as to where the ship is will generally be construed as a condition precedent, the falsity of which entitled the charterers to rescind.[1]

2) *Shall proceed to ...* The owner must bring the ship to the agreed place of loading at the port where the voyage is to commence within a reasonable time.

3) *Or so near thereto as she may safely get and lie always afloat.* If the ship cannot safely reach the place named, the shipowner complies with his obligation by taking the ship as near to that place as is safe. The first part of this phrase entitles the shipowner to demand that the cargo be loaded at some place other than at the named place if she is prevented from getting there by some permanent obstacle, e.g. ice or a blockade in wartime, which cannot be overcome by the shipowner within such time as according to all the circumstances of the case may reasonably be allowed.[2] The phrase 'always afloat' means that if the ship cannot load without touching ground at the named port, the master is entitled to load at the nearest safe port. If, however, the ship can safely lie at the named port in order to load for a certain time only, the master is bound to load there.[3] A port is not safe if the exercise of ordinary care and skill would not prevent the vessel being exposed to danger and, even if a port is safe within its geographical limits, it is not safe if an ordinary prudent and skilful master could not reach it in safety.[4]

4) *A full and complete cargo* But for this provision, a shipowner paid at a rate per ton of the cargo might find that owing to waste of space his freight has not come up to what he

had contemplated. If the ship is described in the earlier part of the document as—'of 340 tons or thereabouts' and the words—'full and complete cargo' are unqualified, the charterer does not fulfil his obligation by putting on board a cargo of 340 tons, if in fact the ship will take more; he must pay freight not only on the 340 tons shipped but also 'dead' freight, i.e. damages for failing to provide a full and complete cargo.[5] The charterer is of course not liable for putting less than 340 tons on board if the ship cannot take that quantity.

Sometimes the charter-party runs thus:

'a full and complete cargo, say [about 1,100] tons';

in such a case the charterer is not bound to load the ship up to her actual capacity, but his obligation will be satisfied if he loads to about three per cent. in excess of the 1,100 tons, though the ship's capacity is over 1,200 tons.[6] But the word 'cargo' alone, in the absence of anything in the charter-party to qualify it, means the entire load of the vessel, and therefore the omission of the words 'full and complete' is often immaterial.[7]

On the other hand, subject to the stipulations of the charter-party, it is an implied condition that the shipowner shall not use the ship in a manner prejudicial to the charterer, e.g. he cannot load bunker coal intended for a future voyage so as to prevent the charterer having full advantage of the ship.[8]

Where the charter-party provides for a cargo of 'lawful merchandise', the cargo must be such that it not only can be loaded without breach of the law in force at the port of loading, but also can be lawfully discharged at the port of destination.[9]

5) *Which the Charterers bind themselves to ship* When the charterer has notice that the ship is ready to load, he must bring the cargo alongside the ship and deliver it to the master of the ship.[10]

In the absence of express stipulation in the charter-party, the charterer is liable for not producing a cargo, even if he is not personally at fault in failing to do so.[11] As a rule the shipowner is responsible for proper stowage[12] but the exceptions are numerous.[13]

6) *The vessel shall proceed to ... or so near thereto as she may safely get and lie always afloat and there deliver the cargo* The phrases 'so near thereto as she may safely get' and 'always afloat' have already been explained.

In *Nelson v Dahl*, Brett LJ stated that:

'The liability of the shipowner as to the commencement of the unloading is to use all reasonable dispatch to bring the ship to the named place where the carrying voyage is to end, unless prevented by excepted perils, and when the ship is there arrived, to have her ready with all reasonable dispatch to discharge in the usual or stipulated manner'.[14]

The shipowner is not, in the absence of express provision, under an obligation to give notice that he is ready to unload. The consignee or charterer must be ready without any such notice to take the cargo from alongside, and for that purpose provide the proper appliances for taking delivery there;[15] the shipowner should put the cargo over the rail of the ship, and in such a position that the consignee can take it.

The shipowner must deliver the goods to the consignee or charterer or an agent thereof unless by custom or contract some mode of delivery other than personal delivery is permissible. Normally the goods must be delivered only against production of the bill of lading.[16]

Under the Merchant Shipping Act 1894, the master of a ship has certain statutory powers of landing goods in the United Kingdom where the owner of goods imported into the United Kingdom fails to take delivery of them. If such owner fails to land or take delivery of the goods at the time agreed (or if no time is agreed, within seventy-two hours, exclusive of a Sunday or holiday), from the time of the report of the ship (required by the Customs laws) the shipowner may land or unship the goods and place them at certain places according to circumstances. The shipowner may, by giving written notice to the person in whose custody the goods are placed, retain his lien for freight on the same, and then, subject to certain conditions, the person with whom the goods are deposited may, and if required by the shipowner shall, if the lien is not discharged as provided by the Merchant Shipping Act 1894, at the expiration of ninety days from the time when the goods were placed in his custody (or earlier if they are perishable), sell by public auction sufficient of the goods to satisfy the Customs dues, the expenses, and the freight.[17]

7) *On being paid freight*   Freight is dealt with later; see para. 23.22, post.

8) *Running working days and Demurrage*[18]   Normally, a charter-party specifies the number of 'lay days', i.e. the number of days allowed for loading and discharging the cargo. Where they are referred to as 'running working days' as in clause 3 (for loading) and clause 4 (for discharging), this means days on which work is usually done in the port. Lay days commence when the ship arrives at the place agreed on in the charter-party, and the charterer has notice that she is ready to load (no notice is required that she is ready to discharge). The days run

continuously, each day being counted from midnight to midnight and not periods of twenty-four hours.[19]

If a port only is named without, e.g., any particular dock or mooring being specified, the ship is deemed to be an 'arrived' ship when she comes within the commercial area of the port even though no berth is available for her.[20] Dispatch money may be payable to the charterers if the loading or discharging is completed early.[21] However, charterers are entitled to use the whole of the lay time for loading and need not hurry to suit the convenience of the owners.[22]

'*Demurrage*' properly signified the agreed additional payment, generally per day (i.e. agreed damages) for delay beyond the 'lay days'. This is the strict meaning of demurrage and the freighter who agrees to pay demurrage for detention beyond the lay days will have to pay so long as the ship is in such condition that she cannot be handed back to the use of the shipowner, even if the delay is not caused by the freighter's default.[23]

The House of Lords has held[24] that the shipowner's claim is confined to the amount of demurrage agreed even though, because of the extent of the charterer's delays, the charterer is guilty of a fundamental breach of contract and the shipowner is therefore entitled to repudiate the contract. The shipowner cannot claim instead unliquidated damages based, e.g. on loss of profit through the ship being able to make fewer voyages during the period of the charter.

The word 'demurrage' is also used to mean compensation by way of unliquidated damages for undue detention when the agreement has not specially provided for agreed damages.[25] Thus, if no lay days are mentioned, the charterer is liable to pay damages if he detains the ship beyond what, in the actual circumstances, is a reasonable time.[26] But in either case, the charterer is not liable to pay if the delay is due to the default of the owner or of those for whom the owner is responsible or if the contract clearly specifies.

Demurrage in the sense of unliquidated damages is only damages for the detention of the ship. It does not preclude damages under a totally different head.[27]

9) *Owners are to be responsible for loss of or damage to the goods* ... There is some doubt as to the Common Law liability of a carrier of goods by sea, but invariably the matter is provided for by the terms of the contract. Thus the effect of this clause is to confine the shipowner's liability for loss of or damage to the cargo or for delay in delivery of the goods to cases where such loss, damage or delay is caused by improper or negligent stowage where stowage has been by or on behalf of the shipowner, or by personal want of due diligence on the part of the owner or his

manager to make the ship seaworthy and see that she is properly manned, equipped and supplied. The clause makes it clear that the owners are responsible for no loss or damage or delay 'arising from any other cause whatsoever'. It is thus much broader in exempting the owner from liability than a charter-party which sets out a number of specific excepted perils such as act of God and perils of the sea and leaves the owner liable for any damage not caused by one of the excepted perils mentioned.

10) *The vessel has liberty ... to deviate for the purpose of saving life and/or property* As was said in discussing the implied obligation of the shipowner that there shall be no unwarranted deviation from the route, there is a general right in order to save life but not to save property.[28] The terms of this clause do entitle the ship to deviate to save property.

11) *Receivers shall have the option of keeping the vessel waiting until such strike ... is at an end against paying half demurrage after expiration of the time provided for discharging* Where a strike continued beyond the lay days, but goods were discharged on the strike ending and the ship was delayed through congestion at another port, it has been held that half demurrage only was payable both for the period from the end of the lay days to the end of the strike and for the period from then until the end of discharging at the last port.[29]

---

1 *Behn v Burness* (1863) 3 B & S 751. *The Mihalis Angelos* [1971] 1 QB 164, [1970] 3 All ER 125, CA.

2 Brett LJ in *Nelson v Dahl* (1879) 12 ChD at 592.

3 *Carlton SS Co v Castle Mail Packets Co* [1898] AC 486.

4 *The Polyglory* [1977] 2 Lloyd's Rep 353.

5 *Hunter v Fry* (1819) 2 B & Ald 421; *Morris v Levison* (1876), 1 CPD 155. However, the *de minimis* rule applies in determining whether 'a full and complete cargo' has been loaded: *Margaronis Navigation Agency Ltd v Henry W Peabody & Co of London Ltd* [1965] 2 QB 430, [1964] 3 All ER 333, CA.

6 *Morris v Levison*, ante; cf. *Miller v Borner* [1900] 1 QB 691; where the charterer contracted only to load a 'cargo of ore, say about 2,800 tons,' not a 'full and complete cargo'.

7 *Borrowman v Drayton* (1877) 2 Ex D 15; *Jardine, Matheson & Co v Clyde Shipping Co* [1910] 1 KB 627; cf. *Miller v Borner* [1900] 1 QB 691, where on the construction of the particular charter-party the omission of the words 'full and complete' was held to be material.

8 *Darling v Raeburn* [1906] 1 KB 572, affd. [1907] 1 KB 846.

9 *Leolga Compagnia de Navigacion v John Glynn & Son Ltd* [1953] 2 QB 375, [1953] 2 All ER 327.

10 Per Selborne LC in *Grant v Coverdale* (1884) 9 App Cas at 475. See also *The Angelia* [1973] 2 All ER 144, [1973] 1 WLR 210.

11 *Grant v Coverdale* (1884) 9 App Cas 470 is a good example.

12 *Blaikie v Stembridge* (1859) 6CB, NS 894. See *Ismail v Polish Ocean Lines* [1976] QB 893, [1976] 1 All ER 902, (charterer through agent accepted responsibility).

13 E.g. *Canadian Transport Co Ltd v Court Line Ltd* [1940] AC 934, [1940] 3 All ER 112.
14 (1879) 12 ChD at 584.
15 *Dahl v Nelson Donkin & Co* (1881) 6 App Cas, per Lord Blackburn, at 43.
16 *Sze Hai Tong Bank Ltd v Rambler Cycle Co* [1959] AC 576, [1959] 3 All ER 182, PC.
17 Merchant Shipping Act 1894, ss. 492–501.
18 For a survey of the cases see Payne and Ivamy *Carriage of Goods by Sea* (10th edn) chap. 10.
19 *The Katy* [1895] P. 56.
20 *Oldenorff, EL Oldenorff & Co GmbH v Tradex Export SA* [1974] AC 479, [1973] 3 All ER 148, HL (giving a wide meaning to port); *The Maratha Envoy* [1978] AC 1, [1977] 2 All ER 849, HL. Once the ship has arrived lay-time provisions in a Gencon charter-party prevail over lost time provisions: *The Darrah* [1977] AC 157, [1976] 2 All ER 963, HL.
21 See e.g. *Alma Shipping Co SA v VM Salgeances e Irmaos Ltd* [1954] 2 QB 94, [1954] 2 All ER 92.
22 *Margaronis Navigation Agency v Henry W Peabody & Co of London Ltd* [1965] 2 QB 430, [1964] 3 All ER 333.
23 Esher MR in *Budgett & Co v Binnington* [1891] 1 QB 35 at 38, CA; App Cas 599 at 608, *Postlethwaite v Freeland* (1879) 5.
24 *Suisse Atlantique Sociéte d'Armement Maritime SA v Rotterdamsche Kolen Centrale* [1967] 1 AC 361, [1966] 2 All ER 61, HL.
25 Bowen LJ in *Clink v Radford* [1891] 1 QB at 630.
26 *Hick v Raymond* [1891] 2 QB 626, CA, Affd., [1893] AC 22, HL.
27 *Aktieselskabet Reider v Arcos Ltd* [1926] All ER Rep 140; [1927] 1 KB 352, CA.
28 See para. 23.04, ante.
29 *The Onisilos* [1971] 2 QB 500, [1971] 2 All ER 497, CA.

---

3. Bills of lading

23.08 A bill of lading is a document acknowledging the shipment of goods, signed by or on behalf of the carrier.[1] It is, secondly, excellent evidence of the contract for the carriage of goods but is not in itself the contract of carriage and evidence may be given that a contract was made before the bill of lading was signed and that the contract differs in some respect from the provisions of the bill of lading.[2] Its third function is as a document of title and this aspect is considered below.[3]

A bill of lading is generally used when the ship is chartered. If the charterer finds the cargo himself, the bill of lading is usually, but not always, a mere receipt for the goods given by the master and a document of title but does not contain the contractual terms of the carriage. The form of a bill of lading varies much according to the practice of the parties and the various shipping conferences.

Many matters already mentioned in connection with charter-parties apply equally to bills of lading. There is, however, this difference: a shipowner, when the contract is contained in a charter-party, may have duties to perform before the time of shipment of the goods; this is not so often the case when the contract is evidenced by a bill of lading only.

1 *Caldwell v Ball* (1786) 1 TR 216. A document acknowledging the receipt of goods 'for shipment' was held to be a bill of lading by the Privy Council in *'Marlborough Hill' (Ship) v Cowan & Sons* [1921] 1 AC 444, but in the subsequent case of *Diamond Alkali Export Corpn v Fl. Bourgeois*, [1921] 3 KB 443, McCardie J refused to treat such a document tendered by the sellers under a CIF contract as a good bill of lading. See *Scrutton on Charter-parties* (18th edn) 377, where it is suggested that 'received for shipment' bills of lading, 'through' bills of lading and combined transport bills of lading would now be regarded as by custom transferable documents of title. Combined transport bills of lading are used for container traffic. See also *Benjamin's Sale of Goods*, para. 18.40.
2 *The Ardennes* [1951] 1 KB 55, [1950] 2 All ER 517.
3 See para. 23.12, post.

Bill of Lading and Mate's Receipt

23.09   The bill of lading is generally signed by the master (or nowadays by the shipowner's loading broker) though in practice, where the goods are shipped, the acknowledgment first given is a less formal receipt ('*mate's receipt*'—not a document of title), which is afterwards exchanged for a bill of lading. But there is nothing to prevent the giving of a bill of lading without production of the mate's receipt, if the goods are on board, and if there is no interest in them known to the master except that of the shipper.[1]

By local custom a mate's receipt may be a document of title but it must not contain a term inconsistent with such a function.[2] If the mate's receipt and the bill of lading get into different hands the goods must be delivered to the holder of the bills.[3]

1 *Hathesing v Laing* (1874) LR 17 Eq. 92.
2 *Kum v Wah Tat Bank Ltd* [1971] 1 Lloyd's Rep 439 at 443.
3 *Baumwoll, etc v Furness* [1893] AC 8, HL.

Whose agent is the master or loading broker

23.10   The master, or loading broker, when he signs, affixes his signature as agent of the owners of the vessel; except that when a vessel has been chartered, and the charterers put up the vessel as a general ship, then the master may be agent of the charterer and not of the owner, the decision in each case depending upon the facts. If the ship has been demised[1] to the charterer, the master is generally the charterer's agent,[2] but the mere fact that the charter-party provides that the master shall be the agent of the charterer does not of itself bind those who deal with the ship without actual notice of this clause.[3] The law on this subject may be stated in the words of Cockburn CJ in *Sandeman v Scurr*:[4]

> 'where a party allows another to appear before the world as his agent in any given capacity, he must be liable to any party who contracts with such apparent agent in a matter within the scope of such agency. The master of a vessel has by law authority to sign bills of lading on behalf of his owners. A person shipping goods on board a vessel, unaware that the vessel has been chartered to another, is warranted in assuming that the master is acting by virtue of his ordinary authority, and therefore acting for his owners in signing bills of lading.'

In this case:

> The charterers put up a vessel as a general ship, and the plaintiff put on board wine, and received bills of lading in ordinary form signed by the master, and the owners were held liable for loss by leakage arising from improper stowage, it being questioned whether an action would not lie also against the charterers.

An indorsee of the bill of lading, who takes it bona fide, and for value, and without notice of the charter-party, may hold the shipowner to the terms of the bill of lading; but if this indorsee was aware of the charter-party when he took the bill, the shipowner will not be bound if the bill of lading was signed without the shipowner's authority.[5]

---

1 See ante, para. 23.02, ante.
2 *Baumwoll Manufactur Von Carl Scheiber v Furness* [1893] AC at 14.
3 *Manchester Trust v Furness* [1895] 2 QB 539.
4 (1866) LR 2 QB 86 at 97.
5 *The Patria* (1872) LR 3 A & E 436. See also n. 2 under para. 23.11, post.

Effect of master's signature

23.11   The master has no authority to sign a bill of lading for goods not actually received on board,[1] and if he does so, the shipowners are not liable[2] to the shippers of the goods, but the master's signature is prima facie evidence against the shipowners that the goods were shipped, and it lies on the shipowners to rebut this evidence if they allege that the goods never were on board.[3] This applies both to partial and total failure to ship goods.

By express stipulation the bill of lading may be made conclusive evidence against the shipowners of the quantity shipped.[4]

As regard the *master's personal liability*, by section 3 of the Bills of Lading Act 1855:

'every bill of lading in the hands of a consignee or indorsee for valuable consideration, representing goods to have been shipped on board a vessel, shall be *conclusive evidence* of such shipment as against the master or other person signing the same, notwithstanding that such goods or some part thereof may not have been so shipped.'

But even the master will not be liable if:

1. The holder of the bill at the time of receiving it is aware that the goods have not been actually shipped; or
2. The misrepresentation in the bill was caused by the fraud of the shipper, the holder, or of some person under whom the holder claims.[5]

Those provisions of the Act apply only to the liability of the master. The shipowner or carrier (who may be a charterer) will not be liable to the original shipper but will be liable under the Hague Rules to a transferee in good faith of the bill of lading if the goods have not been shipped. When goods have been shipped the master, signing as agent for the shipowner or carrier, will bind them. Their liabilities are discussed later.[6]

---

1 *McLean v Fleming* (1872) LR 2 HL Sc. 128; *Grant v Norway* (1851) 10 CB 665.
2 Under the Carriage of Goods by Sea Act 1971 which now applies amended Hague Rules to very many bills of lading there will be liability to a transferee in good faith of the bill of lading. Art. III 4. See *Scrutton on Charterparties* (18th edn) 459–460.
3 *Smith & Co v Bedouin Steam Navigation Co* [1896] AC 70, HL.
4 *Lishman v Christie* (1887) 19 QBD 333.
5 Bills of Lading Act 1855, s. 3. See also Carriage of Goods by Sea Act 1971 Sch. Hague Rules Art. IV 5 (h) which provides that neither the carrier nor the shipowner shall be responsible for loss or damage to the goods if their nature or value has been knowingly misstated by the shipper in the bill of lading.
6 See para. 23.15, post: 'Duty of the shipowner or carrier'; and para. 23.17, post: 'Carriage of Goods by Sea Act 1971'.

Transfer of bill of lading

23.12 A bill of lading is not only a document containing the terms of a contract of carriage, it is in addition a document of title; it is the symbol of goods at sea, and remains so until the goods have come to the hands of a person entitled under the bill of lading to the possession of them.[1]

The person to whom the bill is made out may transfer his rights under it; if the bill is drawn to order, he does so by indorsing the bill and delivering it to the assignee; and if it is drawn to bearer he may transfer his rights under it by mere delivery. Where the bill is indorsed, it may be indorsed in blank (i.e. the mere signature of the transferor on the back of the bill) or be specially indorsed (i.e. on indication of the transferee's name together with the transferor's signature). Where a bill of lading is transferred by indorsement and delivery or by delivery, the transferee is entitled to demand possession of the goods as owner or pledgee according to the nature of the transaction.[2]

The transfer of a bill of lading drawn to order, though it passed the goods, did not until 1855 transfer the right to sue on the contract or the obligations under the contract. But by the Bills of Lading Act 1855, s. 1, it was provided that

> 'every consignee of goods named in a bill of lading, and every indorsee of a bill of lading, to whom the property in the goods therein mentioned shall pass, upon or by reason of such consignment or indorsement, shall have transferred to and vested in him all rights of suit, and be subject to the same liabilities in respect of such goods as if the contract contained in the bill of lading had been made with himself.'

When the property in the goods passes to the consignee or indorsee by reason of consignment or indorsement the right to sue the shipowner passes to the consignee and the consignor may not sue even though the consignor made the contract.[3]

It has been decided that the pledge of a bill of lading does not per se pass the property within the meaning of this section, so that the pledgee is not liable to pay the freight; but the case is otherwise if the pledgee exercises his right to take possession of the goods.[2]

---

1 *Barber v Meyerstein* (1870) LR 4 HL 317; *Barclays Bank v Comrs Customs and Excise* [1963] 1 Lloyd's Rep 81.
2 *Sewell v Burdick* (1885) 10 App Cas 74. It should be noted that s. 2 of the Bills of Lading Act enables the shipowner alternatively to claim the freight direct from the original shipper even after he has assigned the bill of lading.
3 *The Albazero: The Albacruz,* [1977] AC 774, [1976] 3 All ER 129, HL.

Delivery of goods

23.13   The master must deliver the goods to the consignee upon payment of freight; or if the bill of lading has been properly assigned, then he should deliver to the holder. Sometimes the bill of lading is executed in duplicate or triplicate, and the different parts may get into the hands of different persons; in such case the first transferee for value of the bill is entitled to the goods.[1]

But the master who, acting *bona fide* and without notice of conflicting claims, delivers to a holder who presents any of the parts of the bill of lading to him, is not liable if it should prove that that holder is not the first transferee.[2] This is a consequence of the clause found in bills of lading drawn in a set:

'one of these bills of lading accomplished, the other shall stand void.'

If the master has notice of conflicting claims, it is his duty to interplead.

If the bill of lading is drawn to a specified person without the addition of the words 'or order or assigns' the bill cannot be transferred. Where the bill can be transferred the transferee cannot normally obtain a better title than the transferor as a bill of lading is not a negotiable instrument. However, a bill of lading is often said to be quasi-negotiable because the rights of a bona fide transferee for value of a bill of lading can prevail over the lien of an unpaid seller of goods and over his right to stop the goods in the course of transit.[3] If the master delivers to a person who does not produce a bill of lading he will be in fundamental breach of contract and the carrier will not be able to rely on exemption clauses, but an indemnity given to the master to induce him to make the delivery will be enforceable.[4]

---

1 *Barber v Meyerstein* (1870) LR 4 HL 317. Sale of Goods Act 1893, s. 19 (1) provides that if a bill of lading is made out to the seller's order he is deemed to reserve a right of disposal and s. 19 (3) provides that if a bill of exchange is sent to the buyer for acceptance with the bill of lading the buyer must return the bill of lading if he does not accept the bill of exchange, and if he retain the bill of lading no property passes to him: see para. 13.10, ante. S. 25 (2) provides that the transfer of a bill of lading by a buyer in possession before the property has passed to him will give a good title to a bona fide buyer or pledgee of the bill and s. 47 provides that such a transferee may override the seller's right of lien or stoppage in transitu. See para. 13.16, ante.
2 *Glyn, Mills & Co v East and West India Docks* (1882) 7 App Cas 591.
3 Para. 13.16, ante.
4 *Sze Hai Tong Bank Ltd v Rambler Cycle Co* [1959] AC 576, [1959] 3 All ER 182.

Duty of shipper or consignor

23.14 The shipper is under an implied obligation not to ship goods which involve the risk of unusual danger or delay to the ship unless the shipowner is aware or ought to be aware of this fact as a result of notice from the shipper or otherwise. The Merchant Shipping Act 1894 imposes penalties for shipping certain dangerous goods if notice is not given to the master or owner. Such goods may be thrown overboard or forfeited by the court.[1]

---

1 Merchant Shipping Act 1894, ss. 446–450. See to the like effect Carriage of Goods by Sea Act 1971, Sch. Hague Rules Art. IV 6.

Duty of shipowner or carrier

23.15 Like the obligations of a shipowner implied in a charter-party, the shipowner impliedly undertakes in a bill of lading that the ship is seaworthy,[1] that she will proceed with reasonable despatch, and that she shall proceed without any unwarranted deviation.[2] The meaning of these terms was considered in the discussion of Charter-parties but the freedom with which these obligations were at one time modified or excluded in bills of lading by carriers led to shipping interests agreeing at a conference held at The Hague in 1921 on a set of rules (known as the 'Hague Rules') to be incorporated in bills of lading. These rules governed the scope of the carriers' obligations and it was not possible to exclude or restrict them. The Carriage of Goods by Sea Act 1924 applied the rules to bills of lading for shipments from this country and other maritime nations enacted similar legislation. The original Hague Rules were amended by a protocol agreed on at a conference in Brussels in 1968. The Carriage of Goods by Sea Act 1971 was enacted to give effect to the Rules as amended and has recently come into force. Its provisions and the Rules themselves are considered in the following section.

---

1 There is no absolute undertaking of seaworthiness in contracts to which the Carriage of Goods by Sea Act 1971 applies. See s. 3 and Sch. Hague Rules Art. III 1. For the undertaking as to seaworthiness in a charter-party, see para. 23.04, ante.
2 For permissible deviation see now Carriage of Goods by Sea Act 1971, Sch. Hague Rules Art. IV 4, and para. 23.19, post.

23.16 When the bill states that the goods are shipped:
'in good order and condition',

it is called a *clean* bill of lading. These words refer to the apparent and external condition. They operate as prima facie evidence in favour of the shipper and as conclusive evidence in favour of the indorsee of the bill of lading. If the words are untrue, the shipowner will be liable in damages to an indorsee of the bill of lading who suffers loss by acting on the faith of the representation.[1] This statement is not sufficiently qualified by adding the words 'condition unknown' so as to convey to a transferee of the bill of lading notice that the goods are or may be in a damaged state.[2] If the master signs a clean bill of lading knowing that the goods shipped are not in good order and condition in return for an indemnity by the shipper, such indemnity is illegal and unenforceable.[3]

---

1 *Silver v Ocean SS Co Ltd* [1930] 1 KB 416; *Brandt v Liverpool, etc, Steam Navigation Co* [1924] 1 KB 575; and see amended Hague Rules Art. III 4, post, para. 23.18; *Cremer v General Carriers SA* [1974] 1 All ER 1, [1974] 1 WLR 341.

2 *The Skarp* [1935] P. 134. But see *Canada and Dominion Sugar Co Ltd v Canadian National SS Ltd* [1947] AC 46.

3 *Brown, Jenkinson & Co v Percy Dalton (London) Ltd* [1957] 2 QB 621, [1957] 2 All ER 844, CA.

---

4. Limitations on liability of sea carriers

The Carriage of Goods by Sea Act 1971[1]

23.17 By this Act, which replaces with amendments the original Hague Rules scheduled to the Carriage of Goods by Sea Act 1924, the responsibilities, liabilities, rights and immunities attaching to carriers under *bills of lading*[2] are governed by the Hague Rules (amended) which are set out in the Schedule to the 1971 Act. The Rules apply to the carriage of goods[3] by sea in ships carrying goods from any port in Great Britain or Northern Ireland to any other port whether in or outside Great Britain or Northern Ireland[4] and also where the bill of lading is issued in another contracting state or the port of shipment is in such a state. In these two cases the voyage must be from a port in one state to a port in another state. The Hague Rules also apply when the contract contained in or evidenced by a bill of lading expressly provides they are to apply and similarly when a non-negotiable receipt makes such provision. The Act applies not only to bills of lading but also to 'any similar document of title'.[5] The Act applies to the coastal trade.[6]

As Lord Hodson said of the 1924 Act, it was 'not passed for the relief of shipowners but to standardise within certain limits the rights of the holder of every bill of lading against the shipowner'.[7] 'Carriage of goods' covers the time from when the goods are loaded on to the time they are discharged from the ship.[8]

---

1 The Act came into force on June 23 1977 and gives effect to amendments in the Hague Rules agreed on at a conference in Brussels in 1968.

2 S. 1 (4) of the Act provides that subject to s. 1 (6) (which provides for the Rules to apply when the parties expressly agree to their application and for them to apply to non-negotiable receipts) the Rules are not applied to any contract for the carriage of goods by sea unless it expressly or impliedly provides for the issue of a bill of lading or similar document of title.

3 'Goods' does not include live animals and cargo which by the contract or carriage is stated as being carried on deck and is so carried (Carriage of Goods by Sea Act 1971, Sch. Art. I (c)); s. 1 (7) of the Act, however, applies the Rules to such carriage. If bills of lading are issued in the case of a ship under charter-party, they must comply with the Rules: see Art. V.

4 Carriage of Goods by Sea Act 1971, s. 1. This Act, where it applies, does not exclude the limitations on liability provided by the Merchant Shipping Act 1894. See Carriage of Goods by Sea Act 1971, s. 6 (4). It should be noted that most contracts for the carriage of goods by sea are governed by the Hague Rules because many other countries have in fact adopted them.

5 Art. X and s. 1 (6) and see para. 23.08, ante, n. 1. *Scrutton on Charterparties* (18th edn) 1.

6 S. 1 (3).

7 *Riverstone Meat Co v Lancashire Shipping Co* [1961] AC 807 at 879, [1961] 1 All ER 495 at 528.

8 Art. I (e). Art VII allows liability before loading and after discharge to be governed by contractual terms to which the Rules do not apply.

In cases to which the Rules apply,[1] the position is as set out in the next two paragraphs.

23.18 1) The undertaking to provide a seaworthy ship is not absolute; but the carrier is bound, before and at the beginning of the voyage, to exercise due diligence to make the ship seaworthy. The phrase 'before and at the beginning of the voyage' means that the obligation is a continuing one from at least the beginning of loading until the ship starts on her voyage.[2] Where the voyage is in stages, the carrier must exercise due diligence before and at the beginning of the voyage to have the vessel adequately bunkered for the first part of the voyage and to arrange for adequate bunkers at intermediate ports.[3] He must also use due diligence properly to man, equip and supply the ship and to make all parts of the ship in which goods are carried fit and safe for their reception, carriage and preservation.[4] The burden of proving due diligence is on the carrier, but if due diligence has been exercised neither the carrier nor the shipowner is liable for loss or damage arising from unseaworthiness.[5] The diligence required of the carrier to make the ship seaworthy and fit for the carriage of goods is not limited to his personal diligence; his responsibility extends to the acts of his servants and agents. If the ship has been built for him or bought by him and is defective, he is not liable if he has taken all reasonable and proper precautions to satisfy himself that the ship is fit for service,[6] but if he has delegated the work of repairing the ship to an independent contractor the carrier is liable for negligence on the part of such contractor.[7] Breach of this statutory obligation disentitles the shipowner from relying on the 'excepted perils' set out in the Act and listed in para. 5 below.

2) The carrier must properly and carefully load, handle, stow, carry, keep, care for and discharge the goods carried.[8]

The carrier will not be liable if damage to the cargo was caused by negligence in the *management of the ship*, but that expression does not include an act done solely in relation to the cargo, and not directly or indirectly in relation to the management of the ship as such.[9] Thus, a distinction is drawn between want of care of the cargo and want of care of the vessel indirectly affecting the cargo. It follows that the carrier will not be protected if cargo is damaged by want of care in the management of the refrigerating machinery.[10]

3) The carrier must, on demand of the shipper,[11] issue a bill of lading showing:

i) The leading marks necessary for identification of the goods[12] as furnished in writing by the shipper, and clearly stamped or otherwise shown on the goods or on their cases or coverings in such a manner as would ordinarily remain legible until the end of the voyage.

ii) The number of packages or pieces, or the quantity or weight as furnished in writing by the shipper.[13]

iii) The apparent order and condition of the goods.

The carrier is not bound to state any mark number, quantity or weight which he has reasonable ground for suspecting does not accurately represent the goods, or which he has no reasonable means of checking.

The bill of lading need not now contain an express statement that it is subject to the Hague Rules as applied by the Act (the old Paramount Clause), and it is prima facie evidence of the receipt of the goods as described therein.[14] Proof to the contrary is not admissible when the bill of lading has been transferred to a third party who took it in good faith.[15]

4) Unless written notice of loss or damage stating the general nature thereof is given to the carrier at the port of discharge before or at the time of the removal of the goods into the custody of the person entitled to them, or if the loss or damage be not apparent, within three days, such removal shall be prima facie evidence of the delivery by the carrier of goods as described in the bill of lading. The notice need not be given if the state of the, goods has at the time of their receipt been the subject of joint survey or inspection. In any event the carrier and the ship shall be discharged from all liability in respect of loss or damage unless suit is brought within one year after delivery of the goods or the date when the goods should have been delivered.[16] The period has been extended by British shipowners to two years under the British Maritime Law Agreement 1950. An action for an indemnity against a third person may be brought even after the expiration of the year if allowed by the law of the court seised of the case. At least three further months must be allowed for such an action.[17]

---

1 Where the Rules are incorporated into a *charter-party*, though designed only for bills of lading, the owner's liability to the charter is limited as provided by the Rules: *Adamastos Shipping Co Ltd v Anglo-Saxon Petroleum Co Ltd* [1959] AC 133, [1958] 1 All ER 725.

2 *Maxime Footwear Co Ltd v Canadian Government Merchant Marine Ltd* [1959] AC 589, [1959] 2 All ER 740.

3 *The Makedonia* [1962] P. 190, [1962] 2 All ER 614.

4 Carriage of Goods by Sea Act 1971, s. 3; Sch. Art. III, para. 1.

5 Ibid, Sch. Arts. I, IV, para. 1.

6 *W Angliss & Co v P and O Steam Navigation* [1927] 2 KB 456.

7 *Riverstone Meat Co v Lancashire Shipping Co* [1961] AC 807, [1961] 1 All ER 495.

8 Carriage of Goods by Sea Act 1971, Sch. Art. III, para. 2.

9 Ibid, Sch. Art. IV, para. 2; *Gosse Milierd v Canadian Government Merchant Marine* [1929] AC 223.

10 *Foreman and Ellams v Federal Steam Navigation Co* [1928] 2 KB 424.

11 Art. III 3.

12 See para. 23.17, n.

13 The shipper is deemed to guarantee the accuracy of these particulars, and must indemnify the carrier against loss resulting from inaccuracies (Carriage of Goods by Sea Act 1971, Sch. Art. III, para. 5).

14 Sch. Art. III, para. 4.

15 Carriage of Goods by Sea Act 1971, Sch. Art. III 4; see para. 23.15, ante, as to effect of a clean bill of lading at common law.

16 Carriage of Goods by Sea Act 1971, Sch. Art. III, para. 6. For the effect of this on a general average claim, see *Goulandris Bros Ltd v B Goldman & Sons Ltd* [1958] 1 QB 74, [1957] 3 All ER 100: see para. 23.24, post. The requirement of bringing an action within one year is not satisfied by the same plaintiff bringing an action relating to the same subject-matter against the

same defendants in another jurisdiction within the one year: *Compania Colombiana de Seguros v Pacific Steam Navigation Co* [1965] 1 QB 101, [1964] 1 All ER 216.

17 Art. III 6 bis.

23.19   5) The exemptions from liability conferred on the carrier by the Act are very extensive. Thus, neither the carrier nor the ship shall be responsible for loss or damage arising or resulting from:

' a) Act, neglect, or default of the master, mariner, pilot or the servants of the carrier in the navigation or in the management of the ship.[1]

b) Fire, unless caused by the actual fault or privity of the carrier.

c) Perils, dangers and accidents of the sea or other navigable waters.

d) Act of God.

e) Act of war.

f) Act of public enemies.

g) Arrest or restraint of princes, rulers or people, or seizure under legal process.

h) Quarantine restrictions.

i) Act or omission of the shipper or owner of the goods, his agent or representative.

j) Strikes or lock-outs or stoppage or restraint of labour from whatever cause, whether partial or general.

k) Riots and civil commotions.

l) Saving or attempting to save life or property at sea.

m) Wastage in bulk or weight or any other loss or damage arising from inherent defect, quality, or vice of the goods.

n) Insufficiency of packing.

o) Insufficiency or inadequacy of marks.

p) Latent defects not discoverable by due diligence.

q) Any other cause arising without the actual fault or privity of the carrier, or without the fault or neglect of the agents or servants of the carrier, but the burden of proof shall be on the person claiming the benefit of this exception to show that neither the actual fault or privity of the carrier nor the fault or neglect of the agents or servants of the carrier contributed to the loss or damage.[2]

A case where the shipowner was able to rely on para (q) is *Leesh River Tea Co v British Indian Steam Navigation Co:*[3]

Tea carried under a bill of lading incorporating the Hague Rules was damaged by water getting into the hold through a storm valve. This occurred because the brass cover of the valve had been stolen by stevedores at an intermediate port which made the ship unseaworthy but the theft could not reasonably have been detected. *Held:* the shipowner was exempt from liability by para. (q) as while stealing the cover the stevedores were not the shipowner's servants or agents because it was unconnected with the cargo they were engaged to unload.

The 'excepted perils' cannot be relied on if the shipowner is in breach of his obligation to exercise due diligence to make the ship seaworthy and this breach causes the damage.

Where the carrier is not exempted from liability, his liability is nevertheless limited. He is not liable for any loss or damage to goods exceeding 10,000 gold francs per package or unit or 30 francs per kilo of gross weight, whichever is the higher, unless the nature and value of the goods have been declared by the shipper before shipment and inserted in the bill of lading.[4] Where a container is used to consolidate goods, if the number of packages or units is enumerated in the bill of lading this number shall be deemed to be the number of packages or units. There is no limitation of liability if it is proved that the damage to the goods arose from an act or omission of the carrier done with intent to cause damage or recklessly and with knowledge that damage would result.[5] Neither the carrier nor the ship shall be responsible if the nature or value of the goods has been knowingly misstated by the shipper in the bill of lading.[6]

6) *Deviation for the purpose of saving life or property* is expressly permitted; so also is any 'reasonable deviation'.[7] This has been defined by Lord Buckmaster as meaning 'a deviation which, where every circumstance has been duly weighed, commends itself to the common sense and sound understanding of sensible men'.[8] Lord Atkin in the same case gave as examples where some person on board is a fugitive from justice or the presence of someone on board was urgently needed on a matter of national importance.

Unwarranted deviation disentitles the shipowner from relying on any of the excepted perils listed in para. 5.

7) Inflammable, explosive or dangerous goods shipped without the knowledge of the carrier may be landed, destroyed or rendered innocuous without liability on the part of the carrier and the shipper will be liable for all resulting damages and expenses. Even if such goods were shipped with the carrier's knowledge they may be disposed of in the same manner if they become a danger to the ship or cargo without liability on the part of the carrier, except to general average, if any.[9]

8) The carrier may surrender rights and immunities and increase his responsibilities, if such surrender or increase is embodied in the bill of lading.[10] But, in general, the extent of the

immunity given to a carrier by the Act cannot be increased and *any contractual clause purporting to relieve him of his statutory liability is void.*[11]

The carrier and shipper may make any special conditions with regard to particular goods[12] if instead of a bill of lading a non-negotiable receipt is issued, provided the circumstances, terms and conditions under which the carriage is to be performed reasonably justify a special agreement.[13]

A servant or agent of the carrier, but not an independent contractor, shall be entitled to avail himself of the defences and limits of liability which the carrier is entitled to under the Rules. He is not so entitled if it is proved that damage resulted from an act or omission of the servant or agent done with intent to cause damage or recklessly and with knowledge that damage would probably result.[14]

---

1 As to the meaning of 'management of the ship', see para. 23.18 (2), ante.
2 Carriage of Goods by Sea Act 1971, Sch. Art. IV, para. 2. For the relation of this clause to an express clause in the bill of lading, see *GH Renton & Co Ltd v Palmyra Trading Corpn of Panama* [1957] AC 149, [1956] 3 All ER 957, HL.
3 [1967] 2 QB 250, [1966] 3 All ER 593.
4 Carriage of Goods by Sea Act 1971, Sch. Art. IV 5 (a).
5 Art. IV 5 (c), (e).
6 Art. IV, para. 5.
7 Ibid, Sch. Art. IV, para. 4.
8 *Stag Line Ltd v Foscolo, Mango & Co* [1932] AC at 336, HL.
9 Ibid, Sch. Art. IV, para. 6. For general average see para. 23.24, post.
10 Ibid, Sch. Art. V.
11 Ibid, Art. III 8.
12 These will not include ordinary commercial shipments made in the ordinary course of trade and it has been said that the proviso applies only where the carrier has to perform some service apart from his usual duties as a carrier: Payne and Ivamy *Carriage of Goods by Sea* (10th edn) 74–75, 81.
13 Ibid, Sch. Art. VI.
14 Ibid, Sch. Art. IV.

Unfair Contract Terms Act 1977

23.20 Under the Unfair Contract Terms Act 1977 it is not possible by means of a contract term or notice to exclude liability in negligence for death or personal injury in any charter-party of a ship or hovercraft and in any contract for the carriage of goods by ship or hovercraft, but certain other provisions of the Act do not extend to such contracts except in favour of a person dealing as a consumer. These include the subjection of terms excluding liability in negligence for loss or damage other than personal injury to a test of reasonableness, provisions relating to contractual liability and provisions relating to miscellaneous contracts (e.g. work and materials) under which goods pass.[1] Where goods are carried by ship or hovercraft under a contract which provides that they are to be the means of carriage over part of the journey, or makes no provision as to the means but does not exclude ship or hovercraft, the position is the same except that the provisions of the Act relating to miscellaneous contracts under which goods pass then have their full effect.[2]

---

1 Unfair Contract Terms Act 1977, s. 1 and Sch. 1, para. 2 (b), (c). See also ss. 2–4, 7. See generally para. 3.15, ante.
2 Ibid, s. 7 has full effect.

The Merchant Shipping Act 1894

23.21 The Merchant Shipping Act 1894, as amended, gives protection to the 'owner' of a *British ship*[1] and the term 'owner' now covers 'any charterer and any person interested in or in the possession of the ship and, in particular, any manager or operator of the ship', when certain kinds of damage occur to goods without any actual fault or privity on his part.[2]

Where a claim arises from the act or omission of any person in his capacity as master or member of the crew or as servant of the owners, charterers, etc., similar protection is given to employer and employee alike.

No liability at all arises in the following cases unless there is actual fault or privity on the part of the 'owner':

1. When goods or other things on board are lost or damaged by reason of fire on board the ship.[3] Where fire has been caused by unseaworthiness of the ship that does not deprive the shipowner of the statutory exception[4] but the onus is upon the shipowner to prove that the loss happened without his fault; if the owner knew or had the means of knowing of the danger, but gave no special instructions and took no proper steps to prevent injurious consequences arising, he will not be entitled to protection. A corporate body can be made liable if the negligence was that of its head or brain, or central or governing management, and the faulty decision falls within the purview of that authority.[5] A shipowner is, however, not liable merely because of the fault or privity of his servants.

2. When gold, silver, diamonds, watches, jewels, or precious stones are lost or damaged by reason of any robbery,

embezzlement, making away with or secreting thereof, and when the shipowner or master had not at the time of shipment received a written declaration of their true nature and value.[6]

By s. 503[7] *liability is limited* in the cases mentioned below if the misfortune has occurred without his actual fault or privity, *irrespective of whether the ship is British or foreign.*

1. Where any loss of life or personal injury is caused to any person being carried in the ship;
2. Where any damage or loss is caused to any goods, merchandise, or other things on board;
3. Where any loss of life or injury is caused to any person not carried on the ship or any damage is caused to any property not on the ship or any rights are infringed by improper navigation of the ship, or by acts or omission of any person in loading carriage or discharge of its cargo or embarkation carriage or disembarkation of its passengers.[8] Failure of owners to take steps to ensure that the master used radar in a proper manner may constitute 'actual fault', disentitling them to limit their liability.[9]

It is the duty of the owner to give instructions to the master where an owner knows that owing to the special construction of the vessel particular precautions of an unusual character require to be taken to keep her seaworthy, and the facts are such that a competent and experienced master might not be aware of the danger to be guarded against. An omission by the owners to give such instructions amounts to 'actual fault or privity', and they are not entitled to have their liability limited.[10]

The limit in respect of loss of life or personal injury (with or without damage to vessels or goods) is an aggregate amount equivalent to 3,100 gold francs for each ton of the ship's tonnage,[11] and in respect of damage to vessels or goods (with or without loss of life or personal injury) an aggregate amount not exceeding 1,000 gold francs.[12] If there are claims in respect of loss of life and goods exceeding the fund for the ship, the claims for loss of life will be entitled to 2,100 gold francs per ton, and the balance of the claims for loss of life and the claims for goods will rank equally against the remaining 1,000 gold francs.[13] The limits of liability apply to the aggregate of such liabilities which are incurred on any distinct occasion.[14] The fault of one part owner does not take away the right of another part owner to limit his liability.[15]

---

1 See chap. 25.
2 Merchant Shipping Act 1894, s. 503; Merchant Shipping (Liability of Shipowners and Others) Act 1958, s. 3. A master who is also owner of a ship is entitled to this protection: *The Annie Hay* [1968] 1 All ER 657.

3 This includes damage done by smoke, or water used in putting out the fire (*The Diamond* [1906] P. 282).

4 *Dreyfus (Louis) & Co v Tempus Shipping Co Ltd* [1931] AC 726.

5 *Lennard's Carrying Co v Asiatic Petroleum Co* [1915] AC 705. As to the shipowner's right to recover a general average contribution, where he is relieved from liability by the section, see paras. 23.25, et seq., post.

6 Merchant Shipping Act 1894, s. 502. Protection is not now confined to sea-going ships: Merchant Shipping (Liability of Shipowners and Others) Act 1958, s. 8 (1). S. 502 is expressly saved by the Carriage of Goods by Sea Act 1971, s. 6.

7 Ibid, s. 503, as amended by the Merchant Shipping (Liability of Shipowners and Others) Act 1958, s. 2.

8 See *The Bramley Moore* [1964] P. 200, [1964] 1 All ER 105.

9 *The Lady Gwendolen* [1965] P. 294, [1964] 3 All ER 447.

10 *Standard Oil Co of New York v Clan Line Steamers Ltd* [1924] AC 100 (turret ship lost through master emptying water ballast tanks).

11 Where the tonnage is less than 300 tons the sum is multiplied by 300. The Department of Trade may specify the equivalent of gold francs and the conversion rate applicable at the date of judgment prevails: *The Abadesa* [1968] P 656, [1968] 2 All ER 726; *The Mecca* [1968] P. 665, [1968] 2 All ER 731.

12 Merchant Shipping Act 1894, s. 503, as amended by Merchant Shipping (Liability of Shipowners and Others) Act 1958, s. 1, and s. 69 of the Merchant Shipping Act 1906. There are special provisions for calculating the tonnage for this purpose. Statutory instruments provide sterling equivalents.

13 *The Victoria* (1888) 13 PD 125.

14 Merchant Shipping Act 1894, s. 503 (3), as substituted by Merchant Shipping (Liability of Shipowners and Others) Act 1958, s. 8 (2).

15 *The Obey* (1886) LR 1 A & E 102.

5. Freight

23.22 Freight is the name given to the reward paid to the shipowner for the carriage of goods. It is not unless otherwise agreed payable until the voyage has been completed and on delivery of the goods, except when non-delivery is caused by the fault of the shipper alone. Even when inability to deliver arises because of one of the excepted perils, the shipowner is not entitled to freight.[1] Nor in the absence of contrary agreement is freight payable if the goods delivered are for business purposes not of the same nature as the goods shipped.[2] Freight is, however, payable where the goods are merely damaged though the charterer would have a cross-claim in respect of the damage.[3] A claim in respect of short delivery of cargo cannot be set up by way of defence or set-off to a claim for freight.[4]

If the shipowner abandons his vessel without any intention to retake possession, even if he does so under stress of weather,[5] the cargo owner can treat the contract of affreightment as at an end, and if the cargo is subsequently salved he can take possession of it without paying freight. But where ship and cargo had been abandoned by the master and crew on being attacked by an enemy submarine, and the ship was for a time erroneously believed to have been sunk, but ship and cargo were subsequently salved, the House of Lords *held* there had been no such abandonment of the ship as to entitle the cargo owners to claim possession of the cargo without paying freight.[6] The shipowner is not disentitled to freight on the ground that he has overloaded the ship contrary to Merchant Shipping (Safety and Load Line Conventions) Act 1932.[7]

'Advance freight'

If payable, is due at the moment of starting, unless otherwise agreed and if the ship is lost there is no right to recover the freight;[8] even if not paid it can be recovered by the shipowner from the charterer upon the loss of the ship.[9] But if any goods are destroyed before the ship sails so as to make it impossible that any freight could be earned on them, advance freight will not be payable on the portion of the cargo destroyed.[10] Each case depends upon its own circumstances, and to these it is necessary to look to determine whether a given payment is intended as freight in advance, or as a loan; and though it be called 'freight in advance', it by no means follows as of course that it is such.[11]

'Dead freight'

If the charterer fails to load a full cargo according to agreement, he is liable in damages; such damages are styled 'dead freight'.[12]

Lump sum freight

This is an entire sum to be paid for the hire of the ship for one entire service.[13] If the whole cargo is lost, no freight will be earned, but if a substantial portion is delivered and the residue has been lost by excepted perils, although the ship does not arrive, the whole freight will be recoverable.[14]

Freight pro rata

This is the term given to a payment which is sometimes made for carriage of goods when the contract has been performed in part only. If the original contract has not been performed no claim can arise under it, but if there is a *voluntary* acceptance of the goods at a point short of their destination in such circumstances that the shipowner was able and willing to carry the goods to their destination, a new contract will be implied to pay freight for that part of the voyage actually performed.

But where owing to the outbreak of war a ship was compelled to discharge its cargo at an intermediate port because further prosecution of the voyage was illegal, the shipowners could not recover the freight in whole or in part—no fresh agreement by the cargo owners to pay freight *pro rata* was inferred from the fact of their taking possession of the goods.[15]

Under the Bills of Lading Act 1855 consignees named in bills of lading and indorsees to whom the property in the goods passes are liable to pay freight but this does not relieve the original shipper of liability.[16]

---

1 *Liddard v Lopes* (1809) 10 East 526. If the vessel is wrecked, the shipowner may tranship the goods to earn freight (*Hunter v Prinsep,* ibid, 378; and see lump sum freight, post.

2 *Asfar & Co v Blundell* [1896] 1 QB 123 (dates under water for two days and impregnated with sewage).

3 *Dakin v Oxley* (1864) 15 CBNS 646.

4 *Aries Tanker Corpn v Total Transport Ltd* [1977] 1 All ER 398, [1977] 1 WLR 185, HL; *The Alfa Nord* [1977] 2 Lloyd's Rep 434. But equitable set-off in respect of time is available: *The Teno* [1977] 2 Lloyd's Rep 289.

5 *The Cito* (1881) 7 PD 5, CA.

6 *Bradley v H Newsum Sons & Co* [1919] AC 16.

7 *St John Shipping Corporation v Joseph Rank Ltd* [1957] 1 QB 267, [1956] 3 All ER 683.

8 *De Silvale v Kendall* (1815) 4 M & S 37.

9 *Byrne v Schiller* (1871) LR 6 Exch 319; and per Esher MR in *Smith & Co v Pyman & Co* [1891] 1 QB at 744.

10 *Weir & Co v Girvin & Co* [1900] 1 QB 45.

11 *Allison v Bristol Marine Insurance Co* (1876) 1 App Cas 209 at 217, 233.

12 *McLean v Fleming* (1872) LR 2 HL Sc. 128. *The Ionian Skipper* [1977] 2 Lloyd's Rep 273.

13 *Robinson v Knights* (1873) LR 8 CP 465.

14 *Thomas v Harrowing SS Co* [1915] AC 58, where cargo was delivered from a ship wrecked outside the port of discharge.

15 *St Enoch Shipping Co v Phosphate Mining Co* [1916] 2 KB 624.

16 Ss. 1, 2.

Shipowner's lien

23.23 The shipowner possesses a lien[1] upon the goods which he carries, until he has received payment of freight; it ceases upon delivery of the goods. The lien extends to all the property consigned on the same voyage under the same contract by the person from whom the freight is due so that delivery of a part does not defeat the lien on the remainder. At common law it does not apply to advance freight, dead freight or freight payable after delivery.

In many cases it may be inconvenient to retain the goods on board, and yet if landed the lien upon them would be in danger of being lost; this difficulty is provided for by certain sections of the Merchant Shipping Act 1894.[2] The shipowner has a possessory lien for general average[3] contributions, and also for expenses incurred in protecting the goods.[4]

---

1 See para. 17.11, ante.
2 See para. 23.07 (6) ante.
3 See below.
4 *Hingston v Wendt* (1876) 1 QBD 367.

---

6. Average

23.24   Average is of two kinds:

1. Particular average

This arises whenever any damage is done to the property of an individual by accident or otherwise, which is not suffered for the general benefit, e.g.

(i) Loss of an anchor,
(ii) Damage by water to cargo.

These losses remain where they fall, and no extraordinary compensation is granted in respect of them.

2. General average

A general average loss is caused by or directly consequential on a general average act, which occurs where any extraordinary sacrifice or expenditure is voluntarily and reasonably made or incurred in time of peril for the purpose of preserving the property imperilled in the common adventure. The loss must be borne rateably by all interested.[1]

---

1 Marine Insurance Act 1906, s. 66 (1), (2), (3).

23.25   Extraordinary expenditure must be connected with an extraordinary occasion, and hence it was held the expense of hiring a tug to accelerate the voyage in time of war so as to minimise the risk of destruction by enemy submarines is not a general average act, because the risk of being attacked by the Queen's enemies during war is not an extraordinary or abnormal peril.[1]

The essentials of a general average sacrifice are:

(i) that is was incurred to avoid a danger which was real and not just imagined by the master and which was common to all interests;[2]

(ii) that it was necessary to incur some sacrifice;[3]

(iii) that it was voluntary;[4]

(iv) that it was

'a real sacrifice and not a mere destruction or casting off of that which had become already lost and consequently of no value'.[5]

(v) that the ship, cargo, or some portion have actually been preserved;[3]

(vi) the danger must not be one which arises through the default of the person demanding a general average contribution which fault might result in legal liability.[6]

Thus:

Where coal shipped without any negligence, caught fire owing to its liability to spontaneous combustion, and water was poured into the holds to extinguish the fire, the owners of the coal were held entitled in respect of damage done by water to the coal which was not ignited, to a general average contribution from the ship.[7]

Again, if a fire on board gives rise to a general average loss, the fact that the fire was caused by the general unseaworthiness of the ship, but without the actual fault or privity of the shipowner, will not deprive him of his right to a general average contribution from the cargo; because the shipowner is relieved from liability for damage resulting from the fire by s. 502 of the Merchant Shipping Act 1894.[8]

On the other hand:

Where the circumstance giving rise to a general average loss is the shipowner's failure to use due diligence to make the ship seaworthy, his claim for general average can be met by a corresponding cross claim in damages which can be set up as a defence.[9]

Examples of general average sacrifices

Ordinary cases of loss which amount to a general average loss are:

    (i) jettison of cargo;[10]
    (ii) voluntary stranding to avoid wreck;
    (iii) damage to cargo by scuttling the ship to extinguish fire;
    (iv) expenses of putting into a port of refuge for the preservation of ship and cargo.[11]

---

1 *Société Nouvelle d'Armement v Spillers and Bakers* [1917] 1 KB 865.
2 *Joseph Watson & Sons Ltd v Fireman's Fund* [1922] 2 KB 355.
3 *Pirie v Middle Dock Co* (1881) 44 LT 426.
4 *Shepherd v Kottgen* (1877) 2 CPD 585; cf. *Athel Line Ltd v Liverpool and London War Risks Insurance Association Ltd* [1944] KB 87, [1944] 1 All ER 46; where the master obeyed the orders of the commodore of a convoy.
5 Per Williams J in *Pirie v Middle Dock Co* (1881) 44 LT at 430; *Iredale v China Traders' Insurance Co* affd. [1900] 2 QB 515, CA.
6 *Strang v Scott* (1889) 14 App Cas 601.
7 *Greenshields, Cowie & Co v Stephens & Sons Ltd* [1908] AC 431, HL.
8 *Louis Dreyfus & Co v Tempus Shipping Co* [1931] AC 726, and see para. 23.21, ante.
9 *Goulandris Bros Ltd v B Goldman & Sons Ltd* [1958] 1 QB 74, [1957] 3 All ER 100.
10 If cargo stowed on deck is jettisoned, there is no right of general average contribution from the other interest, unless deck stowage is allowed by express agreement or by custom of the trade or port.
11 See *The Corinthian Glory* [1977] 2 Lloyd's Rep 280.

Interests liable to contribute

23.26 Whatever comes under the head of general average loss must be shared by those who have been in a position to be benefited by the sacrifice, e.g. the owners of the ship and the freight, and

'all merchandise put on board for the benefit of traffic must contribute';

but the wages and effects of the seamen and passengers' luggage are not affected.

The position of cargo owners who are liable to contribute to general average expenditure is not one of insurers of the shipowners. General average expenditure is incurred on behalf of all concerned. Thus in *Morrison SS Co Ltd v Greystoke Castle (Cargo Owners)*:[1]

A collision occurred between two ships the *Cheldale* and the *Greystoke Castle*. The *Cheldale* was held to be partly to blame. The *Greystoke Castle* had to put into port and incurred general average expenditure. It was held that owners of cargo in the *Greystoke Castle* had a direct right of action against the owners of the *Cheldale* in respect of their contributions. Had they been merely liable to indemnify the owners of the *Greystoke Castle*, only the latter could have sued.

Where the general average act involves a voluntary injury to the property of third person, e.g. to the pier of a dock, those benefited must contribute their share of the damages payable, although they may be in the position of joint tortfeasors.[2]

Cargo which had been landed to ensure its safety and not for the purpose of lightening the ship, is not liable to contribute in respect of a general average loss subsequently incurred; such cargo was not then at risk, and derived no benefit from the sacrifice.[3] It is the duty of the master to retain the cargo until he has been paid the amount due in respect of it for general average.

23.27 The rules relating to the amounts to be made good vary in different countries. In the absence of agreement, adjustment of the amounts to be contributed in respect of general average will take place at and according to the law of the port of discharge, i.e. in general, the place to which the vessel is destined, unless the voyage is justifiably terminated at an intermediate port.[4] But a temporary suspension of the voyage at a port of refuge does not justify an average adjustment there.[5]

It frequently happens that, in marine insurance policies, the underwriter agrees to be liable for general average 'as per foreign statement'; this binds him as to the correctness of the statements of the foreign average statement, and to accept as general average whatever is such according to the law of any foreign place at which the adjustment is properly made.[6] A set of rules intended to be the basis of a uniform practice in all countries was adopted in 1877. The present rules known as the York-Antwerp Rules 1974 are frequently adopted in contracts of affreightment and marine insurance, and provide a complete code governing the law of general average for those who are parties to the contract.[7]

1 [1947] AC 265, [1946] 2 All ER 696.
2 *Austin Friars SS Co v Spillers and Bakers Ltd* [1915] 3 KB 586. The common law doctrine that there cannot be contribution between joint tortfeasors was held in this case not to apply to a contribution in general average. This doctrine was abolished by the Law Reform (Married Women and Tortfeasors) Act 1935, s. 6.

3 *Royal Mail Steam Packet Co v English Bank of Rio de Janeiro* (1887) 19 QBD 362.
4 *Simonds v White* (1824) 2 B & C 805.
5 *Hill v Wilson* (1879) 4 CPD 329.
6 *Mavro v Ocean Marine Insurance Co* (1875) LR 10 CP 414.
7 *Vlassopoulos v British and Foreign Marine Insurance Co* [1929] 1 KB 187.

Chapter 24

Carriage by air

24.01 A virtual monopoly of civil aviation was given by the Civil
Aviation Act 1946, to three corporations, the British Overseas
Airways Corporation, the British South American Airways
Corporation and the British European Airways Corporation. The
first two of these corporations were amalgamated in 1949 and
their monopoly was ended in 1960 since when private airline
operators have been permitted to run scheduled flights as well as
charter flights. By the Civil Aviation Act 1971 two bodies were
established with important functions for the regulation of civil
aviation. The Civil Aviation Authority, appointed by the
Secretary of State for Trade and Industry, is given the function
of securing that British airlines provide adequate air transport
services. Any aircraft operator must obtain a licence from the
Authority if the aircraft is registered in the United Kingdom or
if the flight begins or ends in the United Kingdom. The other
body is the British Airways Board, also appointed by the
Secretary of State for Trade and Industry. The Board took over
the activities and property of BOAC and BEA in 1974 and these
corporations were dissolved.[1]

---

1 See British Airways Board Act 1977.

24.02 The development of international air transport gave rise to
special codes of rules agreed on at international Conventions.
The principal Convention, the Warsaw Convention of 1929, laid
the foundation of the present law and was given statutory force
in this country by the Carriage by Air Act 1932. The Warsaw
Convention was amended at The Hague in 1955 and the
Carriage by Air Act 1961 enabled the Government to ratify the
Hague Protocol which it eventually did in 1967.[1] The purposes of
these Conventions was to unify the rules relating to international
carriage by air so that the same rules would govern the

contractual requirements and the liability of an airline for passengers and goods, irrespective of the nationality of the airline or persons concerned or the route being travelled. However, since each Convention binds only those countries that have acceded to it, the ideal has not entirely been achieved.

The Warsaw Convention as amended by the Hague Protocol applies to all journeys between the countries adhering to both the Convention and the Protocol and the following are the rules governing such journeys. It should, however, be appreciated that many countries that acceded to the Warsaw Convention have not acceded to the Hague Protocol and in respect of, e.g. a journey between Britain and such a country, the unamended Warsaw Convention (set out in Schedule I of the repealed Carriage by Air Act 1932) continues to apply.

The amended Convention (which is set out in the First Schedule to the Carriage by Air Act 1961) applies to 'international carriage' as therein defined[2] but power was reserved by s. 10 of the Act to apply it to non-international carriage by air (i.e., carriage between two points within the UK, or between the UK and a country that has not acceded to the Warsaw Convention) and in fact the Convention has been applied with modifications (shown in footnotes hereafter) to non-international carriage by air.[3]

---

1 See also the Guadalajara Convention 1961, now given effect by the Carriage by Air (Supplementary Provisions) Act 1962 which came into force in 1964. This deals with sub-contracted carriage.

2 'any carriage in which ... the place of departure and the place of destination ... are situated either within the territories of two High Contracting Parties or within the territory of a single High Contracting Party if there is an agreed stopping place within the the territory of another State, even if that State is not a High Contracting Party': Carriage by Air Act 1961, Sch. I, Art. 1. The Crown may certify what states are party to the Convention; s. 2 and Carriage by Air (Parties to Convention) Orders 1975–77.

3 Carriage by Air Acts (Application of Provisions) Order 1967 (S.I. 1967 No. 480).

24.03 The principal provisions of the amended Convention are considered in the remainder of this chapter.

a) *Passenger Ticket* The carrier must deliver to the passenger a passenger ticket containing prescribed particulars. The ticket is prima facie evidence of the conditions of the contract of carriage. The absence, irregularity or loss of the ticket does not affect the existence or validity of the contract but, if the carrier accepts a passenger without delivering the ticket, the carrier is not entitled to rely on Article 22 (to be referred to) which entitles the carrier to limit his liability.[1]

b) *Baggage Check* In respect of the carriage of registered baggage, (not hand baggage), a baggage check must be delivered (containing prescribed particulars unless combined with or incorporated in a passenger ticket complying with the requirements of Article 3). The baggage check is prima facie evidence of the conditions of the contract of carriage. The absence, irregularity or loss of the check does not affect the existence or validity of the contract of carriage but if the carrier accepts baggage without delivering the check, the carrier is not entitled to rely on Article 22 (to be referred to) which entitles the carrier to limit his liability.[2]

c) *Air Waybill* Every carrier of cargo has a right to require that the consignor make out and hand over to him an 'air waybill' (air consignment note) and the consignor has the right to require the carrier to accept this document. Its absence, irregularity or loss does not affect the existence or validity of the contract of carriage.[3] The air waybill must contain certain particulars[4] and, if all the particulars required by the Convention are not given, the carrier is not entitled to limit his liability in accordance with the provisions of Article 22.[5]

It appears that the air waybill is neither a negotiable instrument nor a document of title to the goods.[6] The amended Convention provides that it does not prevent the issue of a negotiable air waybill.

---

1 Carriage by Air Act 1961, Sch. 1, Art. 3.
2 Ibid, Art. 4.
3 Ibid, Art. 5.
4 Ibid, Art. 8.
5 Ibid, Art. 9; Neither a passenger ticket nor baggage check nor air waybill are required in the case of non-international carriage.
6 See Benjamin *Sale of Goods*, paras. 1810–1816.

24.04 d) *Consignor's Rights* Subject to his liability to carry out all his obligations under the contract of carriage the consignor may dispose of the goods by withdrawing them at the aerodrome of departure or destination, or by stopping them in the course of the journey on any landing, or by calling for them to be delivered at the place of destination or in the course of the journey to a person other than the named consignee, or by requiring them to be returned to the aerodrome of departure. These rights cease when the consignee becomes entitled to delivery.[1]

1 Carriage by Air Act 1961, Sch. 1, Art. 12.

24.05   *e) Consignee's Rights*   Unless the consignor has stopped the goods the consignee is entitled to have them delivered to him on payment of the charges due and on complying with the conditions set out in the air consignment note.

Unless otherwise agreed the carrier must give notice to the consignee as soon as the goods arrive; but if the carrier admits the loss of the goods, or if they have not arrived at the expiration of seven days after the due date the consignee is entitled to put in force against the carrier the rights which flow from the contract of carriage.[1]

---

1 Carriage by Air Act 1961, Sch. I, Art. 13.

24.06   *f) Liability re death or injury and re loss or damage of goods*   Subject to certain exemptions, the carrier is liable:

(i) For the death of or personal injury caused to a passenger by any accident which takes place on board the aircraft or in the course of the operations of embarking or disembarking.[1] This liability is limited to 250,000 francs[2] for each passenger but the carrier and the passenger may by special contract agree to a higher limit of liability.[3]

(ii) The carrier is liable for the loss of or damage to any registered baggage or any cargo which occurs during the carriage by air, i.e. while the baggage or cargo are in charge of the carrier, whether in an aerodrome or on board an aircraft, but not during any carriage by land, sea or river outside an aerodrome[4] unless there has been a landing outside an aerodrome. This liability is limited to 250 francs per kilogram unless the passenger or consignor has at the time of handing over the package to the carrier made a special declaration of value and has paid an additional charge if required. In that case the carrier will be liable to pay a sum not exceeding that declared unless he proves that this sum is greater than the actual value to the consignor at destination.[5] As regards objects of which the passenger himself takes charge the liability is limited to 5,000 francs per passenger.[6]

(iii) The carrier is liable for delay in the carriage by air of passengers, baggage or cargo.[7]

Any provision tending to relieve the carrier of liability or fix a lower limit than that which is laid down in the Convention is null and void but this does not involve nullity of the whole contract which remains subject to the provisions of the Convention.[8] The limits of liability specified in Article 22 do not apply if it is proved that the damage resulted from an act or omission of the carrier, his servants or agents, done with intent to cause damage or recklessly and with knowledge that damage would probably result.[9] If an employee of the carrier is sued in respect of the death or injury of a passenger or for loss or damage to goods, he is entitled to the same limitation of liability as the carrier himself.[10] By the Carriage of Air (Supplementary Provisions) Act 1962, where the contract of carriage is entered into with one carrier and another carrier, with authority from the first carrier, performs all or part of the carriage, both may be liable to the passenger or consignor, subject to the same statutory exceptions and limits. The aggregate of the amounts recovered in personal injury cases must not exceed the highest amount which could have been recovered from one alone.

---

1 Carriage by Air Act 1961, Sch. I, Art. 17.

2 This refers to the French franc consisting of 65½ milligrams of gold of millesimal fineness 900 (ibid, Art. 22).

3 Ibid, Art. 22 (1). For journeys which originate from or terminate in or have an agreed stopping place in the United States, most of the world's airlines have agreed to a limit of $75,000 (Montreal Agreement). British Airways voluntarily accepted these limits for European flights, but for journeys governed by the unamended Warsaw Convention (e.g., between Britain and a country that accedes to the Warsaw Convention but not to the Hague Protocol) the limit is only 125,000 francs: Carriage by Air Acts (Application of Provisions) Order 1967 (S.I. 1967 No. 480). Since October 1975 the Civil Aviation Authority has made the acceptance of a limit (originally £25,000) a condition of the grant of an air transport licence.

4 Carriage by Air Act 1961, Sch. I, Art. 18.

5 Ibid, Art. 22 (2).

6 Ibid, Art. 22 (3).

7 Ibid, Art. 19.

8 Ibid, Art. 23.

9 Ibid, Art. 25. *Rustenburg Platinum Mines Ltd v South African Airways and Pan-American World Airways Inc* [1977] 1 Lloyd's Rep 564.

10 Ibid, Art. 25a.

24.07 *g) Defences of the Carrier* The Carriage by Air Act 1961 exempts the carrier from liability in the following circumstances:

(i) If he can prove that his servants or agents have taken all necessary measures to avoid the damage or it was impossible for them to take such measures.[1]

(ii) If the damage was caused by or contributed to by the negligence of the injured person, the Court may, in accordance with the provisions of its own law, exonerate the carrier wholly or partly from liability.[2]

(iii) Where baggage or cargo are damaged, a complaint in writing must be made to the carrier at latest in the case of baggage within seven days and in the case of cargo within fourteen days of the receipt thereof respectively. In the case of delay the complaint must be made at the latest within twenty-one days. If no complaint has been made in accordance with these provisions, no action will lie against the carrier unless there is fraud on his part.[3] A claim for loss of the contents of baggage is not a claim in respect of 'damage' to baggage and hence does not require to be notified within seven days.[4]

(iv) The right to recover damages is extinguished if an action is not brought within two years from the date on which the aircraft arrived or ought to have arrived at its destination or from the date on which carriage stopped.[5]

---

1 Carriage by Air Act 1961, Sch. I, Art. 20. In respect of journeys which originate from or terminate in or have an agreed stopping place in the United States, most of the world's airlines have agreed to waive this defence. So, too, has the European Division of British Airways. But see *Rustenburg Platinum Mines v South African Airways and Pan American World Airways Inc* [1977] 1 Lloyds Rep 654.
2 Ibid, Art. 21. This in England is subject to the Law Reform (Contributory Negligence) Act 1945 which entitles a Court to apportion the damages.
3 Carriage by Air Act 1961, Art. 26.
4 *Fothergill v Monarch Airlines* [1977] 3 All ER 616.
5 Ibid, Sch. I, Art. 29.

24.08   *h) Jurisdiction*   Actions for damages must be brought at the option of the plaintiff in the territory of one of the High Contracting Parties, before the court having jurisdiction either:

i) Where the carrier is ordinarily resident; or
ii) Has his principal place of business; or
iii) Has an establishment by which the contract was made; or
iv) At the place of destination.[1]

The Hovercraft Act 1968 provides for the application by Order in Council of legislation relating both to shipping and to air transport to carriage by hovercraft.[2]

---

1 Carriage by Air Act 1961, Art. 28. These provisions do not apply to non-international carriage.
2 Hovercraft (Civil Liability) Order 1971; Hovercraft (Application of Enactments) Order 1972.

Chapter 25

Shipping

1. Registration of a British ship

25.01 A British ship[1] is one which is owned wholly by those qualifed to be owners of a British ship. These are:[2]

1. British subjects.
2. Bodies corporate, established under, and subject to the laws of some part of Her Majesty's Dominions and having their principal place of business in those Dominions.

With certain exceptions, every British ship must be registered or she will not be recognised as a British ship and will not be entitled to the benefits of British ownership or the use of the British flag.[3] Before registration these requisites must be satisfied:

1. The name of the ship[4] must be marked as prescribed on the bows, and her name and the name of her port of registry on the stern;
2. The official number and tonnage must be cut on her main beam, and a scale of feet denoting her draught of water in Roman letters or figures must be painted on the stem and stern post.[5]

Before registry, the ship must be surveyed and measured and the *certificate of survey* must be produced, giving the tonnage and build of the vessel, and generally identifying her;[6] also on the occasion of the first registry, a *builder's certificate*, giving particulars as to the build and tonnage of the ship, and of the sale of the vessel to the person desiring to be registered as owner.[7]

The *owner* must then make a declaration of ownership, stating:

1. His qualification to hold a British ship;
2. The number of shares he holds in the ship;

3. A denial that, as he knows, any unqualified person is entitled to any interest in her;

4. The name of the master;

5. When and where the ship was built.[8]

A body corporate makes this declaration through its secretary or other proper officer.

Application for registry should be made by:

1. Those requiring to be registered as owners or some of them, or

2. By their duly authorised agent appointed by individuals in writing, or

3. By a corporation's duly authorised agent appointed under the common seal of the corporation;[9]

and the registration is then performed by the chief officer of customs of the port, if it be in the United Kingdom, or by certain specified officers if it be in the colonies.[10] An entry of the particulars contained in the certificate of survey and in the declaration of ownership is made in the *register book*,[11] and a *certificate of registry*[12] is given, which must contain the particulars relating to the ship entered in the register book with the name of the owner. The certificate may, if lost, be renewed on following out the procedure prescribed by the Act;[13] and it may not be detained for any lien or other such purpose—it is for use in navigation only.[14]

If the ownership changes hands, an indorsement to this effect must be placed on the certificate at the port of registry if the vessel is there; if not, on her first arrival there, or the indorsement may be made at another port if the registrar at the port of registry advises the registrar of the latter port.[15] If a ship is lost, or ceases to be a British ship, the certificate of registry must be given up.[16]

---

1 'Ship' includes every description of vessel used in navigation not propelled by oars (Merchant Shipping Act 1894, s. 742).

2 Merchant Shipping Act 1894, s. 1, as amended by the British Nationality Act 1948, s. 31, Sch. IV, which ended the preferred position of a natural-born British subject. The administration of this Act is committed to the Department of Trade.

3 Merchant Shipping Act 1894, ss. 2 and 72.

4 The Minister may refuse to register any ship by a name already belonging to a registered British ship or so similar as to be calculated to deceive (Merchant Shipping Act 1906, s. 50). Change of name requires the previous written consent of the Minister (Merchant Shipping Act 1894, s. 47).

5 Merchant Shipping Act 1894, s. 7.

6 Ibid, s. 6.

7 Ibid, s. 10.

8 Ibid, s. 9.

9 Ibid, s. 8.
10 Ibid, s. 4.
11 Ibid, s. 11.
12 Ibid, s. 14.
13 Ibid, s. 18.
14 Ibid, s. 15.
15 Ibid, s. 20.
16 Ibid, s. 21. Section 52 of the Merchant Shipping Act 1906, contains provisions for the protection of mortgagees of ships sold to aliens.

Property in a British ship[1]

25.02 The property in a British ship is divided into sixty-four shares, and no more than sixty-four persons may be registered at the same time as owners of the ship. But any share may be held in joint ownership, and the joint owners, not exceeding five in number, may be registered and shall be considered as constituting one person, and any number of persons may have a beneficial title in a single share, the registering owner representing them; a company or corporation may be registered by its corporate name. No person may be registered as owner of a fraction of a share. Most ships are now in fact owned by companies who are bodies corporate.

1 Merchant Shipping Act 1894, s. 5.

2. Transfers, transmissions, and mortgages

A) *Sale of ship or shares*

25.03 A sale will pass a registered ship or any share in her if the professing owner is in a position to give a good title, and if the proper formalities are observed. The method of passing the property is by bill of sale, which must:

  i) be in the form set forth in the Act of 1894,
  ii) be executed before and attested by one or more witnesses, and
  iii) must contain an identifying description, generally the same as is contained in the surveyor's certificate.[1]

The transferee must make a declaration (called a *'declaration of transfer'* stating that he (or his corporation, if he be an officer of a corporation) is in a position to hold a British ship, and that to the best of his knowledge and belief no unqualified person has any interest, legal or beneficial, in the ship, or in any share of her.[2] The bill of sale and the declaration are then produced to the registrar, and the transaction is recorded in the register book, and a statement of the entry indorsed upon the bill of sale itself.[3]

---

1 Merchant Shipping Act 1894, s. 24. The Bills of Sale Acts do not apply. The Sale of Goods Act 1893 and the Supply of Goods (Implied Terms) Act 1973 do, however apply with qualifications. See Benjamin *Sale of Goods*, para. 74; *Lloyd del Pacifico v Board of Trade* (1929) 35 Ll. LR 217; *Behnke v Bede Shipping Co Ltd* [1927] 1 KB 649.

2 Merchant Shipping Act 1894, s. 25.

3 Ibid, s. 26.

B) *Transmission by operation of law*

25.04 Ownership in a British ship or of shares in her may be transmitted:

    i) by death to the executor or administrator of a deceased owner, or

    ii) on bankruptcy to the owner's trustee in bankruptcy.

In every case the person to whom the share is transmitted must be one capable of owning a British ship, and he must make and sign a declaration (called a '*declaration of transmission*') identifying the ship, with the requisite particulars, and stating the mode of transmission, and must produce the proper documentary proof of his right to represent the former owner; whereupon the registrar will make the requisite entries in the register book.[1]

If the transmission is to one not qualified to be the holder of a British ship, there is power in the High Court to hold a sale at such person's request if application is made within four weeks of the transmission; the money is paid to such person as the court may direct. The time for making this application may be extended to one year, but if not made within the time limited, the ship or share is subject to forfeiture.[2]

---

1 Merchant Shipping Act 1894, s. 27.

2 Ibid, s. 28.

C) *Mortgages*

25.05   A registered ship, or any share therein, may be mortgaged in two ways:

> i) by a direct mortgage with registration;
> ii) by a mortgage under a mortgage certificate.[1]

A direct mortgage must be in the form prescribed, and must, upon the production of the necessary instruments, be recorded by the registrar in the register book.[2] Upon the order in the register book will depend the priority of mortgages inter se.[3]

It must be noted that the mortgage will not transfer the ownership of the vessel,[4] but, subject to the rights of prior mortgagees, it confers a power of sale[5] on non-payment of the debt.

When a mortgage is discharged, the mortgage deed with a receipt for the mortgage money, indorsed, duly signed, and attested, should be produced to the registrar, and an entry recording the matter must be made by him in the register book.[6] Any transfer of the mortgage must also be in a prescribed form and recorded by the registrar.[7] The court has inherent jurisdiction to expunge the entry of an invalid mortgage from the register.[8]

Certificates of sale or mortgage   Difficulties might arise in selling or mortgaging ships which, at the time, are out of the country or colony where the port of registry is situated. To obviate these, the Act in such cases gives power to registrars to give *certificates of sale or mortgage* enabling certain persons to sell or mortgage the ship wherever she may be, but in accordance with the conditions of the certificate. The owner must in applying for the certificate give particulars to the registrar as to:

> i) who is to exercise the power;
> ii) the minimum price of sale, if a minimum is to be fixed, or the maximum amount to be raised on the ship, if a maximum is intended to be fixed;
> iii) the place where the power is intended to be exercised or a declaration that it is intended to be exercised anywhere;
> iv) the time within which it is to be exercised.

These particulars are to be entered into the register book.[9] The power is not to be used in the United Kingdom, nor in any British possession, if the port of registry is situated within it.[10]

The certificate must give the particulars from the register book which have to be entered therein on the application for the certificate, and must enumerate any registered mortgages or certificates of sale or mortgage affecting the ship.[11] Rules are laid down with respect to certificates of sale amongst which is a rule that no certificate of sale can be granted except for the sale of an entire ship. Certificates of mortgage may be given to allow the mortgage of a share in a vessel.[12]

When a ship is mortgaged in accordance with the powers given in the certificate, the mortgage must be registered by indorsement on the certificate of mortgage by a British consular officer.

In the case of sale, the certificate and the bill of sale must be produced to the registrar of the port where the sale takes place, as also the certificate of original registry; the certificates of sale and registry are then forwarded to the original port of registry, the registration of which closes the original registry, except so far as relates to unsatisfied mortgages or certificates of mortgages entered therein and these will be entered also in the new registry to be opened at the port of transfer.

A certificate not used must be re-delivered to the registrar by whom it was granted.[13] The registered owner may cause the registrar to give notice of revocation to the registrar of the port where the power of sale or mortgage is to be exercised, and after such notice has been recorded the certificate will then be revoked, save in so far as transactions under it have already taken place.[13]

Rights of mortgagee A mortgagee is entitled to possession if money becomes due under the mortgage, or the mortgagor is doing something to impair the security;[14] and on taking possession he becomes entitled to the accruing freight,[15] but not to unpaid freight which became due before he took possession.[16]

---

1 See below.
2 Merchant Shipping Act 1894, s. 31. If a ship is owned by a company a mortgage should also be registered under s. 95 of the Companies Act 1948 to preserve priorities against the company's creditors. See para. 17.09, ante, and Pennington *Company Law* (3rd edn) 420.
3 Merchant Shipping Act 1894, s. 33.
4 Ibid, s. 34.
5 Ibid, s. 35.
6 Ibid, s. 32.
7 Ibid, s. 37.
8 *Brond v Bromhall* [1906] 1 KB 571.
9 Merchant Shipping Act 1894, s. 40.
10 Ibid, s. 41.
11 Ibid, s. 42.
12 Ibid, ss. 43, 44.
13 Ibid, s. 46.
14 *Law Guarantee and Trust Society v Russian Bank* [1905] 1 KB 815; *The Manor* [1907] P. 339.
15 *Keith v Burrows* (1877) 2 App Cas 636.
16 *Shillito v Biggart* [1903] 1 KB 683.

D) Equitable interests

25.06 No notice of any trust, express, implied, or constructive, can be entered on the register book, and subject to any limitations appearing on the register book, itself, the registered owner of a ship or a share in her has absolute power to dispose of his ship or share; but, subject to this, beneficial interests (including those arising under contracts and other equitable interests) may be enforced by and against owners or mortgagees of ships just as they could against owners of any other personal property.[1] Thus in *Black v Williams*,[2]

> The holders of floating debentures given an equitable charge on certain steamships were postponed to persons having a subsequent registered legal mortgage on the same ships, though the latter had notice of the debentures when they took the mortgages; but though the trust for the debenture holders could not be recognised as against the registered mortgagees, it remained valid and enforceable for other purposes.

An unqualifed person cannot hold a share in a British ship, even as a beneficial owner.[3]

1 Merchant Shipping Act 1894, ss. 56, 57.
2 [1895] 1 Ch 408.
3 Merchant Shipping Act 1894, ss. 1, 25, 57.

E) Ship's papers

25.07 A ship must carry the proper papers, and is bound to show them to (inter alia) any:

1. Naval commissioned officer of any of Her Majesty's ships,
2. Officer of the Department of Trade,
3. Chief officer of customs,
4. Mercantile marine office superintendent,
5. British consular officer, or
6. Registrar-general of seamen or his assistant.[1]

Those usually carried are:

1. The certificate of registry;[2]
2. The crew agreement;[3]
3. The charter-party and the bills of lading;[4]
4. The bill of health;
5. Invoices containing the particulars of the cargo;
6. The official log book.[5]

Regulations may prescribe the particulars to be entered in the log book and the persons by whom such entries are to be made.[6]

---

1 Merchant Shipping Act 1894, s. 723.
2 See para, 25.01, ante.
3 See para. 25.14, post.
4 See para. 23.02, et seq., and 23.08, et seq.
5 See para. 25.10, post.
6 Merchant Shipping Act 1970, s. 68.

---

3. Position of owners

25.08 The possession of the ship is prima facie evidence of ownership,[1] so also is the certificate of registry.[2] The owner must appoint a proper master and crew, with a view to the general safety; therefore, a contract to sell a vessel, one condition being the appointment of a particular person as master, was held illegal.[3] His liability at common law and under legislation for the safety of all goods delivered to him to be carried has been mentioned.[4]

The registered owners are prima facie liable to pay for all repairs and necessaries, the term 'necessaries' including anchors, cables, coals, and indeed:

> 'all that is fit and proper for the service in which the ship is engaged, and that the owner, as a prudent man, would have ordered if present'.[5]

But the evidence is prima facie only, for ownership does not per se carry with it the liability to pay for repairs, etc. If the owner gave the orders himself, or expressly or impliedly authorised another to do it for him, he is liable to pay the cost of the fulfilment of these orders; a master usually has such authority, but not:

> 'where the owner can himself personally interfere, as in the home port, or in a port which he has beforehand appointed an agent who can personally interfere to do the thing required'.[6]

Co-owners are not of necessity partners,[7] but in many cases are tenants in common, and it depends upon all the circumstances taken together, whether they are the one or the other. If merely tenants in common, each may transfer his share without consulting the others; they are not, in the absence of contract, agents for one another, nor do they bind each other by admissions.

Sometimes one owner is appointed by the others, or by some of them, to manage the employment of the ship and to do what is necessary in order to make her a profitable speculation;[8] such an owner, termed a *managing owner,*[9] can bind such of his co-owners as have given him authority, express or implied, to do so,[10] and he has implied authority to do what is necessary in the ordinary course to carry out on shore all that concerns the employment of the ship,[11] i.e.

1. He may take charter-parties;[12]
2. He may not cancel them;[13]
3. He may employ a shipbroker and make the consequent payments.[14]

If an owner is liable to a creditor for work done to the ship, he may be made to pay the whole, and must rely for contribution on any right he may have against his co-owners.

---

1 *Robertson v French* (1803) 4 East 130.
2 Merchant Shipping Act 1894, s. 695.
3 *Card v Hope* (1824) 2 B & C 661.
4 See paras. 23.07, 23.15, 23.17–19, 23.21.
5 *The Riga* (1872) LR 3 A & E 516.
6 Lord Abinger in *Arthur v Barton* (1840) 6 M & W at 143; and see *Gunn v Roberts* (1874) LR 9 CP 331.
7 The name and address of the person to whom the management is entrusted must be registered (Merchant Shipping Act 1894, s. 59). For partnership see para. 11.04, ante.
8 *The Huntsman* [1894] P. 214. See Temperley *Merchant Shipping Acts* (7th edn) para. 11.
9 If the manager is not a co-owner, he is styled the *'ship's husband.'*
10 *Hibbs v Ross* (1866) LR 1 QB 534; *Frazer v Cuthbertson* (1880) 6 QBD 93 at 97.
11 *The Huntsman* [1894] P. 214.
12 See paras. 23.01, 23.02.
13 *Thomas v Lewis* (1879) 4 Ex D 18.
14 *Williamson v Hine* [1891] 1 Ch 390.

Control of ship

25.09 Disputes may arise between co-owners as to the destination and details of an intended voyage. These are settled in the Admiralty Court (now a separate court in the Queen's Bench Division of the High Court), which has jurisdiction in disputes concerning possession, earnings, etc. If the majority of owners desire to send the vessel on a particular voyage, but this is objected to by the minority, the court will, at the instance of the latter, arrest the vessel till the majority have entered into a bond to an amount equivalent to the value of the shares held by the minority, to return the vessel safe, and to answer judgment in an action.[1] The dissentient who thus gets security for his share has no claim to any freight earned on the voyage in question, nor is he liable for any of the expenses.[2]

Part-owners of a ship may be partners but they are not necessarily so, and the mere fact that a person is registered as part-owner of a ship does not give his co-owner authority to pledge his credit for necessary repairs. There must be some evidence of express or implied authority or holding-out.[3]

---

1 *Re Blanshard* (1822) 2 B & C at 248.
2 *The Vindobala* (1888) 13 PD 42; on appeal 14 PD 50, CA; *The England* (1887) 12 PD 32.
3 *Brodie v Howard* (1855) 17 CB 109.

---

4. Position of the master

25.10 *The master* The master (who must be duly certificated) must start on the voyage in time, and must take care to have a proper crew and equipment. He should manage the vessel, and navigate her in the agreed-upon manner, employing a pilot, where such is the custom of the port. He must keep an official log, and this, with the ship's papers, he must guard and show to the proper officer when required to do so.

He must take the cargo as quickly as possible, must store it properly and must sign the bill of lading for all he has taken on board.[1] He should deliver the cargo, on arrival at the destination, to the proper person, subject to his lien for freight.[2]

He is, of course, answerable for any fraudulent or illegal conduct of which he is guilty affecting the owner's interest, such conduct being, in his case, styled *barratry*.

He has the same rights as a seaman, including a maritime lien, for the recovery of his wages, and for such disbursements or liabilities as he may properly make or incur on account of the ship.[3]

---

1 See paras. 23.08, et seq. The bill of lading is now often signed by the loading broker. See Singh and Colinvaux, *Shipowners* 292, 302.
2 Para. 23.23, ante.
3 Merchant Shipping Act 1970, s. 18; *The Castlegate* [1893] AC 38; *The Orienta* [1895] P. 49; and cf. *The Ripon City* [1897] P. 226. For seamen's rights see paras. 25.13 et seq.

25.11 Among his powers are:

1. Hypothecation. The master may, in case of necessity in order to raise money, assign the ship or the ship and cargo by what is known as a *bottomry bond*, the master thereby binding himself to repay the principal and interest of the loan on safe arrival of the ship at the end of her voyage.[1] If the cargo alone is hypothecated, the document is called a *respondentia bond*. Both types of instrument are obsolete.[2]

2. Sale, where this course is necessary, and the best course, and communication with the owner in time is impossible;

3. Transhipment, in cases where it is desirable in the interest of his owners;

4. Disciplinary powers over those on board the vessel;[3]

5. Jettison, i.e. throwing goods overboard to lighten the ship;

6. In the absence of the owners, and if communication is impossible in time, he may bind them by contracts for the supply of necessaries, or may borrow money on their credit to pay for necessaries to be supplied, but not for those already supplied.[4]

---

1 The bottomry bondholder also has a maritime lien over the ship: see para. 17.13, ante.

2 Halsbury's *Laws of England* (3rd edn) Vol. 35, 137.

3 He can arrest anyone on board if he has reasonable cause to believe that it is necessary for the preservation of the ship or safety of the passengers: Merchant Shipping Act 1970. s. 79. See also ss. 34–38 esp. s. 36 providing for the setting up of ship's disciplinary committees.

4 *Arthur v Barton* (1840) 6 M & W 129. 'The master's authority has declined considerably in the last hundred years.' Halsbury's *Laws of England* (3rd edn) Vol. 35, 132 (s). This is partly because of radio, partly because shipowners appoint foreign agents from whom the master can take instructions. All the older authorities are to be read in the light of this. For agency of necessity see para. 10.05, ante.

---

5. Salvage

25.12 This is a reward allowed to persons who save or assist in saving[1] a ship, apparel and cargo, or what had formed part of these, or freight or the lives of persons belonging to any vessel from shipwreck, capture, or similar jeopardy.[2] The right to salvage may, but does not necessarily, arise out of contract.[3] To support the claim the salvor must show:

1. That the services rendered were voluntary. This means the services must not be such as would be called for under a pre-existing contract; but if a tug has agreed to tow a vessel and circumstances have arisen which justify the tug in abandoning that contract, she may recover salvage for further services which

are outside the scope of the contract of towage.[4] There is no right to recover salvage if the salvor has acted in pursuance of a special statutory duty other than the general obligations to render assistance and save life.[5]

2. That there was skill and peril, and some enterprise shown in the performance of the work.[6]

3. That the services were beneficial. Actual benefit is not essential where the services are rendered at the request of the vessel in distress. The acceptance of the offer of a particular ship to come to assistance in response to a radio call entitles that ship to a salvage award, although little or no benefit is conferred, if the disabled ship is ultimately saved; but a mere response to an s.o.s. call does not of itself give a right to salvage remuneration.[7]

Although 'no cure, no pay' is of the essence of salvage, an agreement to pay the salvor some remuneration in the event of failure is enforceable.[8]

The owner of a salving ship can recover for services rendered by him to a ship damaged through the fault of a vessel of which the salvor was also the owner. The maxim that 'no man can profit by his own wrong' does not apply to such a case.[9]

The salvor has a maritime lien, extending to ship, freight and cargo upon the property salved, the lien ranking first, above all other liens which have already previously attached to the property. The cargo owners are liable for salvage, and in proportion to its value rateably with the other property salved.[10]

The amount payable for salvage is generally assessed by the court, but it is quite competent for the masters of the vessels concerned to enter into an agreement before assistance is rendered fixing the amount to be paid. The master of the salving vessel can bind his owners and crew by such an agreement if it is fair and honest;[11] but the agreement will be set aside if it is inequitable. An agreement to pay an exorbitant sum coupled with the fact that the master about to be salved is acting under the stress of circumstances, will be treated as inequitable.[12]

The salvage money is apportioned between the owners, master, officers and crew of the salving vessel. Except in the case of a seaman belonging to a ship employed on salvage service, a seaman cannot agree to abandon any right that he may have or obtain in the nature of salvage.[13]

Salvors who are guilty of or are privy to the theft of salved property forfeit all claim to salvage; and those who by negligence or lack of supervision fail to prevent or detect such theft are liable to forfeiture or diminution of the award according to the view taken by the Court of their conduct.[14] There is no rule of maritime law that a successful salvor is free from liability for negligence.[15]

The Crown is liable in respect of salvage services in assisting any of Her Majesty's ships or aircraft or in saving life therefrom, or in saving cargo belonging to the Crown.[16] The Crown may claim salvage to the same extent as any other salvor.[17]

At common law there was no payment for life salvage unless property was also saved but by statute life salvage may be claimed and if the property saved is insufficient payment may be made from the Mercantile Marine Fund.[18]

Under the Unfair Contract Terms Act 1977 it is not possible by means of a contract term or notice to exclude liability in negligence for death or personal injury in a salvage or towage contract, but certain other provisions of the Act do not extend to such contracts except in favour of a person dealing as a consumer. These include the subjection of terms excluding liability in negligence for loss or damage other than personal injury to a test of reasonableness, provisions relating to contractual liability and provisions relating to miscellaneous contracts (e.g. work and materials) under which goods pass.[19]

---

1 For the distinction between salvage and towage, see *The Troilus* [1951] AC 820.

2 *Wells v Owners of Gas Float Whitton* [1897] AC, at 344. Salvage also applies to aircraft. Civil Aviation Act 1949, s. 51 (1).

3 *Five Steel Barges* (1890) 15 PD 142; per Hannen P at 146.

4 See *The Leon Blum* [1915] P. 90; affd. [1915] P. 290, CA.

5 *The Gregerso* [1973] 1 QB 274, [1971] 1 All ER 961.

6 *The Golden Sands* [1975] 2 Lloyd's Rep 166 (services not particularly difficult).

7 *The Stiklestad* [1926] P. 205.

8 *Admiralty Coms v Valverda* [1938] AC 173 at 187, 197, 202; [1938] 1 All ER 162 at 169, 176, 178.

9 *The Beaverford v The Kafiristan* [1938] AC 136, [1937] 3 All ER 747.

10 *The Longford* (1881) 6 PD 60. Devaluation of the pound between the date of the termination of the salvage services and the date of the award might not properly be taken into account in fixing the amount of the award: *The Teh Hu* [1970] P. 106, [1969] 3 All ER 1200, CA. For liens see chap. 17, ante.

11 *The Nasmyth* (1885) 10 PD 41.

12 *The Medina* (1877) 2 PD 5; *The Rialto* [1891] P. 175; *The Port Caledonia* [1903] P. 184.

13 Merchant Shipping Act 1970, s. 16.

14 *The Clan Sutherland* [1918] P. 332; *The Kenora* [1921] P. 90.

15 *The Tojo Maru* [1972] AC 242, [1971] 1 All ER 1110, HL.

16 Crown Proceedings Act 1947, s. 8 (1).

17 Ibid, s. 8 (2).

18 Merchant Shipping Act 1894, s. 544.

19 Unfair Contract Terms Act 1977, s. 1 and Sch. 1, para. 2 (a). See generally para. 3.15, ante.

6. Employment of seamen

25.13 Following the Report of a Court of Inquiry into the shipping industry, under the chairmanship of Lord Pearson,[1] the provisions of the Merchant Shipping Acts 1894 to 1967 relating to the conditions of service, discipline and general welfare of merchant seamen have been replaced by the Merchant Shipping Act 1970.

1 Cmnd. 3211 (1967).

Crew agreements

25.14 With certain exceptions, an agreement in writing must be made between each person employed as a seaman in a ship registered in the United Kingdom and the persons employing him and must be signed both by him and by or on behalf of them.[1] The agreements made with the several persons employed in a ship are to be contained in one document—a crew agreement—subject to exceptions approved by the Department of Trade. The Department must approve the provisions and form of a crew agreement and normally the crew agreement must be carried on the ship to which it relates whenever it is at sea. Both the employer and the master of the ship are liable for failure to comply with these provisions. Department of Trade Regulations may provide for notice to be given to a superintendent or proper officer before a crew agreement is made and for requiring copies or extracts of crew agreements to be supplied to members of the crew demanding them.[2]

1 Merchant Shipping Act 1970, s. 1.
2 Ibid, s. 2.

Discharge of seamen

25.15 Department of Trade Regulations may prescribe the procedure to be followed in connection with the discharge of seamen from ships registered in the United Kingdom. In particular Regulations may require notice of a discharge to be given to the superintendent or proper officer.[1] Regulations may prescribe that a seaman be not discharged outside the United Kingdom from a ship registered in the United Kingdom without the consent of the proper officer.

---

1 Merchant Shipping Act 1970, s. 3. 'Proper officer' means a consular officer appointed by HM Government.

Wages

25.16 Wages due to a seaman under a crew agreement must normally be paid to him in full when he leaves the ship on being discharged from it.[1] If the amount shown in the account (which must also be delivered to him[2]) exceeds £50, not less than £50 or less than one-quarter of the amount shown must be paid to him at that time and the balance within seven days of that time. So long as any amount due is not paid the seaman is entitled to wages for a period of up to fifty-six days after his discharge and thereafter all moneys due carry interest at the rate of 20% p.a. The penalties for failure to pay have no application if due to a mistake or a reasonable dispute as to liability.

Regulations may provide for deductions to be made from wages due to a seaman where he has broken his obligations under the crew agreement.[3] Any dispute as to the amount payable may be submitted by the parties to the superintendent or proper officer whose decision is final.[4]

A seaman's wages are not subject to attachment and any assignment of such wages before they have accrued is not binding on the seaman.[5] However, a seaman may, by means of an allotment note, allot to any person or persons part of the wages to which he will become entitled.[6] The person named in the allotment note has the right to recover in his own name that part of the seaman's wages alloted to him.[7]

If a ship registered in the United Kingdom is wrecked or lost a seaman whose employment in the ship is thereby terminated is entitled to wages for every day on which he is unemployed in the two months following the date of the wreck or loss unless it is proved he did not make reasonable efforts to save the ship and persons and property carried in it.[8] Similarly, where a ship is sold outside the United Kingdom and a seaman's employment is thereby terminated, he is entitled to wages for every day on which he is unemployed in the two months following the date of the sale.[9]

A seaman's lien,[10] his remedies for the recovery of his wages, his right to wages in case of the wreck of loss of the ship, and any right he may have or obtain in the nature of salvage are not capable of being renounced by any agreement.[11] This does not affect terms of any agreement made with the seamen belonging to a ship which is to be employed on salvage service as provide for the remuneration to be paid to them for salvage services rendered by that ship.

If expenses are incurred by Government Departments or a local authority for the benefit of any dependants of a seaman and are expenses provided for by regulations, the persons employing the seaman may be required to retain a proportion of the seaman's net wages.[12] A magistrates' court may make an order for such sum to be paid to the authority concerned.

1 Merchant Shipping Act 1970, s. 7.
2 Ibid, s. 8.
3 Ibid, s. 9.
4 Ibid, s. 10.
5 Ibid, s. 11. For attachment of earnings see para. 32.14, post.
6 Ibid, s. 13.
7 Ibid, s. 14.
8 Ibid, s. 15 (1).
9 Ibid, s. 15 (2).
10 Claims for pension contributions have the priority of a lien for wages: *The Halcyon Skies* [1977] QB 14, [1976] 1 All ER 856.
11 Ibid, s. 16.
12 Ibid, s. 17.

Safety, health and welfare

25.17   The Act makes provision for regulations to secure safe working conditions and means of access, adequate crew accommodation, provisions, water and medical stores and for the submission of complaints by seamen and for medical treatment.[1]

1 Merchant Shipping Act 1970, ss. 19–26.

Offences by seamen

25.18   Various *criminal* offences specified in the Merchant Shipping Act 1970 include misconduct endangering the ship or persons on board the ship, drunkenness on duty, wilful disobedience to lawful commands, continued or concerted disobedience or neglect of duty and absence without leave at the time of sailing.[1]

Regulations may specify any misconduct on board as a *disciplinary* offence and enable the master or other officer to impose fines on seamen committing disciplinary offences.[2] The amount of the fine may not exceed £20. Provision is made for appeal against the imposition of a fine to a superintendent or proper officer.[3] Regulations may provide for the setting up of a ship's disciplinary committee to exercise the powers of the master in dealing with disciplinary offences. The amount of any fine imposed on a seaman for disciplinary offence may be deducted from his wages or otherwise recovered by the persons employing him and paid by them to a superintendent or proper officer.[5]

1 Merchant Shipping Act 1970, ss. 27–30; Merchant Shipping Act 1974, s. 19.
2 Merchant Shipping Act 1970, s. 34.
3 Ibid, s. 35.
4 Ibid, s. 36.
5 Ibid, s. 38.

Civil liability of seamen

25.19 A seaman is liable in damages for breach of contract if he is absent from his ship at a time when he is required by his contract of employment to be on board unless he proves his absence was due to an accident or mistake or some other cause beyond his control and that he took all reasonable precautions to avoid being absent.[1] Damages are limited to £10 unless special damages are claimed when the limit is £100.

If a seaman is found in civil proceedings in the United Kingdom to have committed an act of smuggling he is liable to make good any expense that the act has caused to any other person.[2]

1 Merchant Shipping Act 1970, s. 39.
2 Ibid, s. 40.

Relief and repatriation of seamen left behind

25.20 Where a seaman in a ship registered in the United Kingdom is left behind in a country outside the United Kingdom or is taken to such a country on being shipwrecked, the persons who last employed him as a seaman must make such provision for his return and for his relief and maintenance until his return as regulations may require.[1] This also applies to persons employed outside the United Kingdom but left there or taken there after shipwreck.

---

1 Merchant Shipping Act 1970, s. 62.

Part VIII

Insurance

Chapter 26

Insurance other than Marine

1. Introduction

26.01 A contract of insurance is a contract either to indemnify against a loss which may arise upon the happening of some event, or to pay, on the happening of some event, a definite sum of money or equivalent benefit in services[1] to the person insured. The instrument containing the contract to insure is called a *policy of insurance*, the person insured is called the *assured* or *insured*, and the persons who insure are called the *insurers* or, in the case of insurance provided by members of Lloyd's,[2] *underwriters*.

There are many forms of this contract, for a man may agree to insure anything in which he has an insurable interest, from a pane of glass to his own life: but three forms of considerable importance are:

1. Life Insurance,
2. Fire Insurance, and
3. Marine Insurance.

These will be considered separately.

Distinguish wagers
In *Carter v Boehm*[3] Lord Mansfield said:

'Insurance is a contract on speculation';

and this being the case, it is frequently hard to distinguish a contract to insure from an ordinary wager.[4] In *Godsall v Boldero*,[5] Lord Ellenborough said that insurance was in its nature a contract of indemnity, as distinguished from a contract by way of gaming or wagering. This means that it is not an agreement to pay money on the mere happening of a certain event, but to compensate the insured for any damage suffered owing to its occurrence. This statement, though true of marine and fire insurance, does not accurately describe the contract of life insurance; the latter is an engagement to pay a certain sum of money on the death of a person, and when once fixed it is constant and invariable.[6]

Insurable interest

Another distinction suggested is, that in the case of a wager, there is no interest except the interest provided by the stake, whereas in all insurance contracts such an interest must exist, i.e. there must be what is styled an *insurable interest.* There is no generally accepted definition of insurable interest,[7] but apart from the interest that a person has in their own life or the life of their spouse,[8] it means in general that they must stand to suffer financial loss through loss of or damage to their property or through the non-fulfilment or the incurring of a legal liability. An equitable or joint or defeasible or limited interest in property is enough but not a merely sentimental interest or one founded on honour alone.[9] Nor, apart from marine insurance, does the expectation of an interest suffice.[10] Financial loss through loss of property is not enough if the insured had no legally recognised interest in the property. Thus the majority shareholder in a company has no insurable interest in the property of the company[11] but a shareholder does have an insurable interest in his own shares.[12]

---

1 *Department of Trade and Industry v St Christopher Motorists Association* [1974] 1 All ER 395, [1974] 1 WLR 99 (transport for disqualified motorists).
2 An association of underwriters in London, dating from the eighteenth century and incorporated in 1871. Its members operate in a way analagous to members of the Stock Exchange.
3 (1766) 3 Burr. 1905, 1909.
4 For wagering contracts see paras. 6.06, et seq., ante.
5 (1807) 9 East 72, 81.
6 *Dalby v India and London Life Assurance Co* (1854) 15 CB 365.
7 *Lucena v Crauford* (1806) 2 Bos. & PNR 269 at 302; *Macaura v Northern Assurance Co* [1925] AC 619 at 627; *Stockdale v Dunlop* (1840) 6 M & W 224.
8 For life insurance see paras. 26.07, et seq., post.
9 *Lucena v Crauford*, ante.
10 For marine insurance see para. 27.03, post.
11 *Macaura v Northern Assurance Co* [1925] AC 619.
12 *Wilson v Jones* (1867) LR 2 Exch 139.

Principle of indemnity

26.02 Apart from contracts of life assurance and accident or sickness insurances, all contracts of insurance are contracts of *indemnity*, e.g.:

> A insures a house against fire for £10,000; in course of time suppose the house to be burnt down; if £5,000 will restore it, that amount, and that amount only, can be obtained.

Brett LJ said:

> 'The very foundation, in my opinion, of every rule which has been promulgated and acted on by the courts with regard to insurance law is this, viz., that the contract of insurance contained in a marine or fire policy is a contract of indemnity, and of indemnity only, and that this contract means that the assured, in case of a loss against which the policy has been made, shall be fully indemnified, but shall never be more than fully indemnified.[1]

Thus:

> A agreed to sell a house to B for £3,100, and had insured the premises against fire. Before completion of the contract to sell, the house was burnt, and the insurance company not having been informed of the contract of sale, paid the amount of damage; subsequently the purchase was completed, and the vendor obtained the full value agreed, and it was decided that the amount of the insurance money must be refunded to the company.[2]

In giving judgment, Bowen LJ said:

> 'What is really the interest of the vendors, the assured? Their insurable interest is this—they had insured against fire, and they had then contracted with the purchasers for the sale of the house, and, after the contract, but before completion, the fire occurred. Their interest, therefore, is that at law they are the legal owners, but their beneficial interest is that of vendors, with a lien for the unpaid purchase-money. That was decided in the case of *Collingridge v Royal Exchange Assurance Corpn*;[3] but can they keep the whole, having lost only half? Surely it would be monstrous to say that they could keep the whole, having lost only half. ... They would be getting a windfall by the fire, their contract of insurance would not be a contract against loss, it would be a speculation for gain'.[4]

In short in indemnity insurance the assured is only entitled to the amount of his actual loss or what is deemed to be his actual loss if the policy is a valued one.[5]

---

1 *Castellain v Preston* (1883) 11 QBD 380 at 386.
2 *Castellain v Preston*, ante. But see now the Law of Property Act 1925, s. 47 (para. 26.15, post), as to the right of a purchaser in such cases to receive the insurance money on completion. This change in the law does not affect the principle illustrated in the text.
3 (1877) 3 QBD 173.
4 *Castellain v Preston* (1883) 11 QBD at 401.
5 For valued policies see para. 26.12 n. 9, post.

SUBROGATION

26.03   In an indemnity contract, the insurer is entitled to every right of the assured, or, as Brett LJ says:

'As between the underwriter, and the assured, the underwriter is entitled to the advantage of every right of the assured, whether such right consist in contract, fulfilled or unfulfilled, or in remedy for tort capable of being insisted on or already insisted on, or in any other right, whether by way of condition or otherwise, legal or equitable, which can be, or has been, exercised or has accrued, and whether such right could or could not be enforced by the insurer in the name of the assured by the exercise or acquiring of which right or condition the loss against which the assured is insured can be, or has been, diminished.[1]

This is called the *doctrine of subrogation*. It entitles the insurer who pays the insured not only to the value of any benefit received by the latter by way of compensation for actual loss, but also to the value of any rights or remedies the insured may have against third parties in respect of the damage.[2] The doctrine applies not only to fire policies but to all indemnity policies. Thus:

If A's servant negligently drives A's vehicle and injures B, A's insurers after paying B can sue A's servant for damages for breach of the contract of service.[3]

If the insured renounces or in any way compromises rights to which the insurer would be subrogated, he is bound to make up the amount to the insurer. Policies are usually made voidable on such an event. The doctrine does not apply to non-indemnity insurance, e.g. life assurance and personal accident insurance.

DOUBLE INSURANCE

An assured may take out many policies with different insurers against the same risk exceeding the amount of his interest though once he has received an indemnity he cannot claim further against the insurers.[4] When one insurer pays in full he may under the principle of contribution claim proportionate amounts from the other insurers. These problems are now usually dealt with by express terms in policies.

---

1 *Castellain v Preston* (1883) 11 QBD at 388. For subrogation in marine insurance, see para. 27.30, post.

2 In *Lucas v Export Credits Guarantee Department* [1974] 2 All ER 889, [1974] 1 WLR 909, HL, subrogation was not applied to a benefit resulting from the repayment of a debt in dollars after the devaluation of sterling. See also para. 16.08, ante.

3 *Lister v Romford Ice and Cold Storage Co Ltd* [1957] AC 555, [1957] 1 All ER 125. There is an agreement amongst insurers that they will normally waive this right against an employee. See *Chitty on Contracts* (24th edn) Vol. 2, 565–566. The court may also imply a term excluding subrogation in such a case: *Morris v Ford Motor Co Ltd* [1973] QB 792, [1973] 2 All ER 1084. See also *Street on Torts* (6th edn) 480–481.

4 In the case of policies on lives and buildings within the Life Assurance Act 1774 any cover further than the full extent of his interest may be illegal and void.

Uberrima fides

26.04 Contracts of insurance are *uberrimae fidei*, that is the insured owes a duty to disclose before the contract is made every material fact of which he knows or ought to know. If a material fact is not so disclosed, the insurers have the right at any time to avoid the contract. Lord Mansfield said:

> 'Good faith forbids either party, by concealing what he privately knows, to draw the other into a bargain from his ignorance of that fact and his believing the contrary,[1]

and in insurance contracts the rule is strictly enforced, as the facts are generally within the knowledge of the insured alone. Life insurance stands on the same footing. In the case of *London Assurance Co v Mansel,*[2] Jessel MR said:

> 'As regards the general principle, I am not prepared to lay down the law as making any difference in substance between one contract of assurance and another. Whether it is life, or fire, or marine insurance, I take it good faith is required in all cases, and though there may be certain circumstances, from the peculiar nature of marine insurance, which require to be

disclosed, and which do not apply to other contracts of insurance, that is rather, in my opinion, an illustration of the application of the principle, than a distinction in principle.'

It has now been settled that this principle applies to all contracts of insurance, e.g. a policy which covers the risk of a debtor becoming insolvent.[3]

At common law every material fact known to the assured must be revealed, whether or not he believed it to be material but there is no duty to reveal unknown facts.[4] A fact is material if it would influence the judgment of a prudent insurer in deciding whether to accept the risk, and if so, at what premium. A material fact need not necessarily relate exclusively to the particular kind of risk. Thus, a fire policy may be avoided for non-disclosure of a previous refusal of motor-car insurance on grounds which affected the moral integrity of the proposer.[5]

The duty to disclose continues up to the conclusion of the contract and covers any material alteration in the character of the risk which may take place between proposal and acceptance.[6]

Insurers are also entitled to avoid liability under a policy where the insured, in the course of negotiations or in the proposal form for insurance, has made any fraudulent misstatement or has made an innocent misstatement of a material fact.[7] Moreover, if the policy contains a declaration that the proposal form constitutes the 'basis of the contract', the insurers are entitled to avoid liability if any answer in the proposal form is incorrect, irrespective of whether the insured made the answer fraudulently or innocently and irrespective of whether the answer relates to a material fact. Thus, in *Dawsons Ltd v Bonnin*:[8]

> The proposal form for the insurance of a lorry against fire required the proposer to state the full address at which the lorry would be garaged, and inadvertently the wrong address was inserted. A claim was made under the policy when the lorry was lost by fire. The House of Lords *held* that as the proposal form was clearly expressed by the terms of the policy to be 'the basis of the contract', the answer in the proposal form amounted to a contractual promise as to its accuracy. Since the answer was not accurate the insurers had a right to avoid the policy for breach of warranty. It made no difference that the answer was not material, i.e. the premium would have been no different had the correct address been shown, nor that the inaccuracy was inadvertent.

---

1 Lord Mansfield, in *Carter v Boehm* (1766) 3 Burr. 1905 at 1909.

2 (1879) 11 ChD 363; and see *Lindenau v Desborough* (1828) 8 B & C, 586 at 592.

3 *Seaton v Heath* [1899] 1 QB 782, revsd. on the facts, sub nom *Seaton v Burnand* [1900] AC 135. It may, however, be difficult to distinguish such a contract from a contract of suretyship where the duty of disclosure is less strict.

4 *London Assurance v Mansel* (1879) 11 ChD 363; *Joel v Law Union and Crown Insurance Co* [1908] 2 KB 863 at 884. The latter case shows that a policy may by its terms be invalidated for the non-disclosure of unknown facts.

5 *Locker and Woolf Ltd v West Australian Insurance Co Ltd* [1936] 1 KB 408, and see *March Cabaret Club v London Assurance* [1975] 2 Lloyd's Rep 169; *Lambert v Co-operative Insurance Society* [1975] 2 Lloyd's Rep 485 (failure to disclose convictions); *Arterial Caravans Ltd v Yorkshire Insurance Co* [1973] 1 Lloyd's Rep 169 (failure to disclose fire suffered by another company under the same management).

6 *Canning v Farquhar* (1886) 16 QBD 727; *Looker v Law Union etc Insurance Co* [1928] 1 KB 554.

7 *London Assurance v Mansel* (1879) 11 ChD 363; *Kumar v Life Assurance of India* [1974] 1 Lloyd's Rep 147.

8 [1922] 2 AC 413.

---

2. Liability insurance

26.05 One common type of insurance is against the liability which one may incur to third parties. A statutory obligation exists to take out such insurance in relation to the liability that may arise from the negligent driving of a motor vehicle and in respect of an employer's liability for injury to his employees but these are not the only kinds of liability insurance. It is, however, contrary to public policy for a claim to be allowed under a liability policy in respect of a deliberate unlawful act by the insured. In *Gray v Barr*:[1]

> B shot and killed G in a struggle. B was acquitted of murder and manslaughter but G's personal representatives sued B under the Fatal Accidents Acts and B sought an indemnity, in respect of such damages as he might be required to pay, under his accident liability policy. *Held:* B was not entitled to claim under the policy.

Where any person is entitled to claim from insurers in respect of liabilities which he may incur to third parties,[2] then:

> If either before or after the events mentioned below any such liability is incurred by the person insured, his rights against the insurer are transferred to and vest in the third party to whom the liability was incurred.

Such transfer of rights comes into operation:

> i) if the person insured is an individual: when he becomes bankrupt, or makes a composition or arrangement with his creditors;

ii) if the person insured is a company: when it goes into liquidation,[3] or holders of any debentures secured by a floating charge appoint a receiver or manager of the company's business.

Thus, suppose a company has an insurance policy that covers its liability in negligence to members of the public up to £5,000 and someone injured by the company's negligence obtains judgment against the company for £8,000. If, before or after judgment, the company has gone into liquidation, the injured party can claim direct against the insurers for the amount of the policy, £5,000.[4] The insurers may rely on any defence which they could have raised against the insured, such as breach of a condition to give prompt notice of a claim[5] but may not claim a set-off in respect of premiums due under the policy.[6]

---

1 [1971] 2 QB 554, [1971] 2 All ER 949, CA.
2 Third Parties (Rights against Insurers) Act 1930.
3 This does not include voluntary liquation merely for the purposes of reconstruction or amalgamation with another company.
4 No such claim could be made by the injured party against the insurers until the *liability* of the company has been established, either in litigation or by arbitration or by agreement: *Post Office v Norwich Union Fire Insurance Society Ltd* [1967] 2 QB 363, [1967] 1 All ER 577, CA.
5 *Farrell v Federated Employers Insurance Association* [1970] 3 All ER 632, [1970] 1 WLR 1400, CA.
6 *Murray v Legal and General Assurance Society* [1970] 2 QB 495, [1969] 3 All ER 794.

26.06 **The Road Traffic Act 1972** This Act compels users of motor vehicles to insure against any liability which may be incurred in respect of the death or bodily injury of any persons arising out of the use of the vehicle on the road. Insurers issuing policies to comply with such requirements of the Act must indemnify the persons or classes of persons specified in the policy (e.g. persons using the vehicle with the owner's consent) in respect of any liability which the policy purports to cover in the case of those persons or classes of persons.[1] Such persons have a direct right to sue the insurers notwithstanding the common law rule that only parties to a contract can enforce it.[2]

Judgments against persons insured against such third-party risks covered by the terms of the policy must be satisfied by the insurer direct to the person(s) entitled to the benefit of the judgment but this liability does not attach to the insurer unless before or within seven days after the commencement of the proceedings in which judgment was given he had notice of the bringing of the proceedings.[3]

The rights so conferred on third parties are not effective unless and until the insurer has delivered a 'certificate of insurance' to the assured.[4]

If the policy is by its terms limited to the user of the vehicle in a particular way (e.g. user for private purposes only), then, if an accident happens while the vehicle is not being used in a manner permitted by the policy, a third party who is injured cannot recover damages against the insurer. However, certain restrictions contained in a motor vehicle policy are of no effect as regards a person killed or injured, liability to whom is compulsorily insurable under the Road Traffic Act. Such restrictions include restrictions as to the age or physical or mental condition of the driver, the condition of the vehicle and the number of persons carried.[5] Similarly any condition in the policy relieving the insurers of liability, in the event of some specified thing being done or not being done *after* the accident, is of no effect as regards a person killed or injured, liability to whom is compulsorily insurable under the Act.[6]

Sometimes a judgment is obtained against a motorist in respect of a liability required by the Road Traffic Act to be covered by a policy of insurance, but the judgment is unsatisfied. This may happen, for example, because no insurance policy was taken out or because the insurers have gone into liquidation. To meet these eventualities, the Motor Insurers' Bureau was set up in 1946 by the motor vehicle insurers who undertake to keep it in funds. By agreement with the Department of the Environment (the current agreement was made in 1971 and is published by HMSO) the Bureau will meet any such unsatisfied judgment provided that, where there is no insurance policy notice of proceedings is given to the Bureau before or within twenty-one days after the commencement of the proceedings. The Bureau will, however, not meet an unsatisfied judgment against a motorist unless it is in respect of a risk which was compulsorily insurable. The Court of Appeal held in *Hardy v Motor Insurers Bureau*[7] that the Bureau was liable to indemnify a man who had been deliberately injured by being dragged along the ground by the driver of an uninsured van. Insurance is compulsory in respect of 'any liability' whether arising out of deliberate or negligent action.

Employers' Liability (Compulsory Insurance) Act 1969 This Act compels employers to insure against liability for bodily injury or disease sustained by his employees and arising in the course of their employment.

---

1 Road Traffic Act 1972, ss. 143, 148 (4). This Act consolidates earlier

legislation. Compulsory insurance in respect of liability to third parties other than passengers has existed since 1930. The Motor Vehicles (Passenger Insurance) Act 1971 extended compulsory cover to passengers.

2 *Tattersall v Drysdale* [1935] 2 KB 174. For the common law rule of privity of contract, see para. 4.01, ante.

3 Road Traffic Act 1972, s. 149. In certain cases and subject to certain conditions the insurer may be relieved from liability when he has avoided or cancelled, or is entitled to avoid the policy (ibid.).

4 Ibid, s. 147.

5 Ibid, s. 148.

6 Ibid, s. 206 (2).

7 [1964] 2 QB 745, [1964] 2 All ER 742, CA.

---

3. Life assurance

26.07 Life assurance is:

'a contract by which the insurer, in consideration of a certain premium, either in a gross sum, or by annual payments, undertakes to pay to the person for whose benefit the insurance is made, a certain sum of money or annuity on the death of the person whose life is insured'.[1]

To prevent gambling in these transactions, the Life Assurance Act 1774 was passed. This enacts that:

1. No insurance shall be made by any person or persons, bodies politic or corporate, on the life or lives of any other person or persons, wherein the persons for whose use, benefit, or on whose account such policies shall be made, shall have no interest (which means pecuniary interest) or by way of gaming or wagering; and every insurance made contrary to the true intent and meaning hereof shall be null and void to all intents and purposes;[2]

2. The name of the person so interested, or for whose benefit the policy is made, shall be inserted in the policy;[3]

3. In all cases where the insured has such an interest, no greater sum shall be recovered than the value of the interest at the date of the policy.[4] If, in the meantime, his interest ceases, he may yet recover at the death, it only being essential that he should have his interest at the date of the making of the policy.[5]

It should further be observed that an assignee of a valid policy need not have an interest.[6]

A person who has effected a policy on the life of another in which he has no insurable interest cannot as a rule repudiate the policy and recover the premiums paid;[7] but he may do so if he was induced by the fraud of the insurers to believe that he was effecting a valid and legal policy, because in such case the parties are not *in pari delicto.*[8]

1 *Smith's Mercantile Law* (13th edn) 514.
2 Life Assurance Act 1774, s. 1.
3 Ibid, s. 2. These requirements do not apply to an insurance against third-party risks under the Road Traffic Act 1972.
4 Life Assurance Act 1774, s. 3.
5 *Dalby v India and London Life Assurance* (1854) 1 5CB 365.
6 *Ashley v Ashley* (1829) 3 Sim 149. For assignment see para. 26.11 post.
7 *Harse v Pearl Life Assurance Co* [1940] 1 KB 558.
8 *Hughes v Liverpool Victoria etc Society* [1916] 2 KB 482.

Insurable interest in lives

26.08 What is an insurable interest? It is difficult to describe, but the following illustrations will show what has been the opinion of the courts:[1]

1. A creditor may insure the life of his debtor to the extent of his debt;[2]
2. Employer and employee may insure each others lives;[3]
3. A wife may insure her husband;[4]
4. A husband may insure his wife;[5] and
5. A man may insure himself;

but a father has not necessarily an insurable interest in the life of his son.[6]

1 See generally para. 26.01, ante; and for insurable interest in marine insurance, see paras. 27.03, et seq., post.
2 *Dalby v India and London Life Assurance Co* (1854) 15 CB 365.
3 *Hebdon v West* (1863) 3 B & S 579; *Turnbull & Co v Scottish Provident* 1896 34 SLR 146.
4 *Reed v Royal Exchange Assurance Co* (1795) Peake, Add. Ca 70.
5 *Griffiths v Fleming* [1909] 1 KB 805.
6 *Halford v Kymer* (1830) 10 B & C 724.

Alien enemies and suicide

26.09 *Alien enemies* Where a policy has been effected on the life of a person who subsequently becomes an alien enemy, the policy does not become void and the continued payment and receipt of premiums does not involve unlawful intercourse with an alien enemy, but in the event of the death of the assured the right of his executors to demand payment of the policy moneys is suspended during the war.[1]

Suicide In *Beresford v Royal Insurance Co*,[2] a life policy expressly provided that it would be invalidated if the assured should die by his own hand whether sane or insane within one year from the date of the policy. The assured committed suicide while sane *after* one year had elapsed from the date of the policy. By implication from the express terms of the policy the policy moneys were payable but the House of Lords held that, since committing suicide while sane was a criminal offence, it was contrary to public policy to allow the moneys to be recovered. Since the Suicide Act 1961, sane suicide is no longer a criminal offence but on the general principal of insurance law that no claim may be made on a policy when the assured deliberately brings about the event insured against, if similar facts occurred today the policy moneys may still not be recoverable. However an express term providing clearly that the moneys are payable even on a sane suicide would presumably prevail over the general principle though it might be avoided as contrary to public policy.

---

1 *Seligman v Eagle Insurance Co* [1917] 1 Ch 519.
2 [1938] AC 586, [1938] 2 All ER 602.

Married women

26.10   By the Married Women's Property Act 1882, s. 11, it is provided that a married woman may effect a policy upon her own life, or upon the life of her husband, for her own benefit. Further, it provides that if a man or a married woman effect a policy[1] upon his or her own life, or on each other's lives, and the policy is expressed to be for the benefit of the other or for the benefit of the children, this shall create a trust,[2] which, so long as any object of the trust remains unperformed, shall not form part of the insured's estate, nor be subject to the insured's debts. A policy effected by a husband simpliciter for the benefit of a named wife creates an immediate vested interest, and if the wife pre-deceases her husband the policy will pass to her executors as part of her estate;[3] but the husband is entitled to a lien on the policy moneys for premiums paid by him since his wife's death as being money expended by a trustee to preserve the property of a certain given trust.[4] If it be proved that the policy was effected, and the premiums paid to defraud the creditors of the insured, these will be entitled out of the moneys payable under the policy to a sum equal to the premiums paid.

1 This includes a policy providing for payment of money upon death by accident (*Re Gladitz* [1937] Ch 588, [1937] 3 All ER 173).
2 Apart from the statute the person named as beneficiary would have no rights (*Cleaver v Mutual Reserve Fund Life Association* [1892] 1 QB 147). See para. 4.01, ante.
3 *Cousins v Sun Life Assurance Society* [1933] 1 Ch 126.
4 *Re Smith's Estate,* [1937] Ch 636, [1937] 3 All ER 472.

Assignment of the policy

26.11 The Policies of Assurance Act 1867 provided for the legal assignment of a life policy before legal assignments of choses in action generally became possible under the Judicature Act 1873. The assignment must be in writing, either by endorsement on the policy or by a separate instrument, but:

1. The assigneee is liable to be defeated by defences which would have been good against the assignor;[1]
2. He should give written notice to the insurance company, for in the event of a second or further assignment, the priorities will depend upon the date of this notice; and further, any bona fide payment made by the company previous to such notice will be valid in favour of the company.[2]

The company must specify on the policy the place of business at which such notices may be given, and upon receiving notice it must upon a written request and payment of a fee not exceeding 25p. acknowledge the receipt of it in writing.[3] An assignment is also effective at law if it complies with the provisions of the Law of Property Act, s. 136.[4]

1 Policies of Assurance Act 1867, s. 2.
2 Ibid, s. 3.
3 Policies of Assurance Act 1867, ss. 4, 6.
4 See para. 4.09, ante.

4. Fire insurance

26.12 Fire insurance is a contract, one party to which undertakes to indemnify the other against the consequence of a fire[1] happening within an agreed upon period, in return for the payment of money in a lump sum or by instalments. The insured must have an insurable interest in the premises or goods insured at the time of the loss,[2] i.e. he must be in such a position that he incurs loss by the burning; thus

1. A creditor may insure a house over which he has a mortgage;[3]
2. A bailee may insure his customer's goods for the full value and, if loss occurs, he may retain so much of the policy moneys as would cover his own interest while being trustee for the owners in respect of the rest.[4] Alternatively a bailee may take out a policy which covers merely his own liability as bailee and it is a matter of construction which type of policy has been taken out.

But a shareholder of an incorporated company, even though he may hold all the shares, has no insurable interest in the company's property; nor has an unsecured creditor such an interest.[5] A shareholder may, however, insure against resultant loss in the value of his shares.[6]

A contract of fire insurance made by an agent without authority cannot be ratified by the principal after and with knowledge of the loss by fire of the subject-matter insured.[7]

The contract being one of indemnity, only the amount of loss actually suffered can be recovered; this Bowen LJ calls 'the infallible rule'.[8] But the parties may agree beforehand the value of the premises or goods insured. And in the absence of fraud the agreement will be binding. Thus in *Elcock v Thomson:*[9]

Premises were insured in 1940 and it was agreed that £106,850 was the true value and that in the event of loss the property would be assumed to be of such value and would be assessed accordingly. A fire occurred in 1947 and it was found that immediately before the fire the real value of the premises was £18,000 and immediately after the fire it was £12,600.

It was held that estimate was binding on the insurers and, as the real value of the premises had been depreciated by 30 per cent (£18,000 down to £12,600), the insurers were liable to pay 30 per cent of £106,850.

---

1 'Fire' is not confined to fires started accidentally. The policy covers loss through accidentally putting articles into the grate (*Harris v Poland* [1941] 1 KB 462). There is a distinction between fire and an explosion although the latter involves combustion of gas which may have been ignited by a flash (*Boiler Inspection and Insurance Co of Canada v Sherwin-Williams Co of Canada Ltd* [1951] AC 319, PC at 338).
2 The Life Assurance Act 1774 (see para. 26.07, ante) applies to insurances on buildings but not to insurances of 'ships, goods or merchandise.' It follows that an insurance on a building is only legal under the Act if the insured has an insurable interest in the building at the time of the contract *and*, by virtue of the principle of indemnity, at the time of the loss.

3 *Westminster Fire Office v Glasgow Provident Investment Society* (1888) 13 App Cas 699.

4 *Waters v Monarch Assurance Co* (1856) 5 E & B 870; and *Hepburn v A Tomlinson (Hauliers) Ltd* [1966] AC 451, [1966] 1 All ER 418, HL.

5 *Macaura v Northern Assurance Co* [1925] AC 619.

6 *Wilson v Jones* (1867) LR 2 Exch 139.

7 *Grover and Grover v Matthews* [1910] 2 KB 401. This rule does not apply to contracts of marine insurance. See para. 27.03, post.

8 *Castellain v Preston* (1883) 11 QBD at 401. See also para. 26.02, ante, where the facts of the cases are set out and the application of this principle generally to contracts of insurance is discussed.

9 [1949] 2 KB 755, [1949] 2 All ER 381. Such a policy is known as a 'valued policy.'

'Subject to average' clause

26.13 Where fire causes only partial loss to premises or goods, the general rule is that the insured is entitled to the full cost of repairs, provided that comes within the total amount covered by the policy. However, if the policy contains a 'subject to average' clause and the property is under-insured, the insurers are only liable for that proportion of the actual loss which the sum insured bears to the value of the property.[1]

1 *Acme Wood Flooring Co Ltd v Marten* (1904) 90 LT 313.

Reinstatement

26.14 By the Fires Prevention (Metropolis) Act 1774, s. 83, it is provided that any interested person may procure that the insurance money shall be laid out in rebuilding the premises, but a clear and unambiguous request to the insurance company to rebuild should be made. This right is of general and not merely of local application to the Metropolis, and a judgment creditor of the person insured who seeks to attach the insurance moneys cannot deprive a person interested of his right to have the moneys expended in rebuilding.[1] Instead of rebuilding the place themselves, the insurers may permit the parties claiming the money to do so upon sufficient security being given that the money shall be laid out in such rebuilding.[2]

1 *Sinnott v Bowden* [1912] 2 Ch 414.

2 See *Westminster Fire Office v Glasgow Provident Investment Society* (1888) 13 App Cas 699.

Assignment and transferability of policies

26.15 The right to receive the proceeds under a fire policy (or any other policy) is assignable, but in the case of a fire policy, being an indemnity policy, the assignee may only claim if the insured still has an insurable interest in the property at the time of loss.

Although the right to receive the proceeds under a fire policy is assignable, the policy cannot itself be transferred so that it attaches to different property or so that there is a different insured person *unless* the insurers consent. If, therefore, A sells property to B, any purported transfer by A to B of his fire policy on the premises can only be effective if the insurers consent. However, if insurance money becomes payable to a vendor in respect of damage to or destruction of property between the date of the contract of sale and the completion of the purchase, the money when received by the vendor must be paid to the purchaser on or after completion, subject to any stipulation to the contrary and any requisite consent of the insurers. The purchaser must pay the proportionate part of the premium from the date of the contract.[1]

---

1 Law of Property Act 1925, s. 47. Apart from the section the benefit of the insurance does not run with the property. See *Rayner v Preston* (1881) 18 ChD 1, and para. 26.02, ante. A purchaser may be able to require reinstatement.

Exclusion clauses

26.16 Those sections of the Unfair Contract Terms Act 1977 which govern negligence liability, liability arising out of contract and unreasonable indemnity clauses do not apply to contracts of insurance including a contract to pay an annuity on a human life.[1]

---

1 Unfair Contract Terms Act 1977, s. 1 and Sch. 1, para. 1 (a); and see generally para. 3.15, ante.

Policyholders Protection Act 1975

26.17 This Act set up the Policyholders' Protection Board to protect the interests of policyholders who are prejudiced by the failure of an authorised insurance company to meet its liabilities. The

Board is financed by levies on insurance companies and will pay a full indemnity in respect of a compulsory insurance policy and ninety per cent in respect of other policies. The protection of the Act is confined to United Kingdom policies.

Re-insurance

26.18 An insurer has an insurable interest in his prospective liability under the policies he issues and may re-insure this. A policy of re-insurance is governed by the same rules as apply to the policy re-insured. An agreement to re-insure a class of policies or a defined amount of the other insurer's risk is known as a 're-insurance treaty' and is also a contract of insurance.[1]

1 See further para. 27.19, post.

Chapter 27

Marine Insurance

1. Introduction

27.01 The law relating to marine insurance was codified by the Marine Insurance Act 1906. It is unnecessary, therefore, to cite earlier cases as authorities for propositions of law laid down in the Act but some are referred to for purposes of illustration where the scope and meaning of a section in the Act are not at first sight apparent.

Marine insurance is a contract whereby the insurer undertakes to indemnify the assured in the manner and to the extent thereby agreed, against marine losses, that is to say, the losses incident to marine adventure.[1] The person who is indemnified is called the *'assured'*, or the *'insured'*, the other party being styled the *'insurer'* or the *'underwriter'*.

The policy may be so extended as to protect the assured against losses on inland waters or on any land risk which may be incidental to a sea voyage.[2]

The contract is generally entered into through the agency of brokers, who are responsible to the underwriters for the premium, and the mode of contracting and the various details are largely determined by the custom of the different associations whose members are engaged in this particular kind of transaction.

All persons who have insurable interests may be insured, unless they are alien enemies,[3] and any companies or persons not under disability may be insurers.

Amongst subject-matters of marine insurance may be named the ship, the goods connected therewith, the cargo, freight, money lent on bottomry,[4] etc.; but as in other contracts, so in marine insurance, there can be no valid agreements with regard to illegal trading.

---

1 Marine Insurance Act 1906, s. 1. See para. 27.03, post, for the statutory definition of a 'marine adventure'.

2 Ibid, s. 2 (1).
3 *Brandon v Nesbitt* (1794) 6 Term Rep 23.
4 A form of mortgage of a ship by the master. Now obsolete. See para. 25.11, ante.

Assignment of policy

27.02 When a person has insured his interest in any vessel, cargo, or freight, he may assign his policy to another, unless the terms of the policy forbid it, and that other may sue in his own name, but is liable to be met by the same defences as would have been valid against the original assured; e.g.

that the policy is void through the non-disclosure of material facts by the assignor.[1]

The policy may be assigned either before or after loss.[2] An assured who has no interest cannot assign; but this rule does not affect the assignment of a policy after loss.[3] An assigment can be made by indorsement, or in other customary manner.[2]

1 *W Pickersgill & Sons v London and Provincial etc Insurance Co* [1912] 3 KB 614.
2 Marine Insurance Act 1906, s. 50.
3 Ibid, s. 51. If an assured at one time had an interest the fact that it may have been lost does not prevent him assigning.

2. Insurable interest

27.03 A person has an insurable interest when he is interested in a marine adventure, and in particular where he stands in any legal or equitable relation to the adventure or to any insurable property[1] at risk therein, in consequence of which he may benefit by the safety or due arrival of insurable property, or may be prejudiced by its loss, damage, or detention, or may incur liability in respect thereof.[2]

There is a *marine adventure* where insurable property[1] is exposed to maritime perils, or where the earning of freight, etc., or the security for advances is endangered by the exposure of insurable property to maritime perils, or where any liability is incurred by a person interested in or responsible for insurable property, by reason of maritime perils. *Maritime perils* means the perils consequent on, or incidental to, the navigation of the sea, that is to say, perils of the sea, fire, war perils, pirates, rovers, thieves, captures, seizures, restraints and detainments of princes and peoples, jettison,[3] barratry,[4] and any other perils, either of the like kind or which may be designated by the policy.[5]

The assured must be interested in the subject-matter insured at the time of the loss though he need not have more than an expectation of an interest when the insurance is effected and if the goods are insured, 'lost or not lost', the policy is valid although the property may already be lost at the time the policy is effected, unless at the time of effecting the insurance, the assured was aware of the loss and the insurer was not.[6] Defeasible and contingent interests are insurable, and so is a partial interest of any nature.[7]

The following are examples of persons having an insurable interest:

1. Shipowners and owners of goods—to the extent of the value of their interest.[8]
2. A mortgagee—to the extent of the sum due to him.[9]
3. A mortgagor—to the full value of the property.[9]
4. An insurer—who may reinsure to the extent of his liability.[10]
5. A bottomry bondholder—to the extent of the amount payable to him under the bond.[11]
6. A person who has advanced money for the ship's necessaries.[12]
7. A person advancing freight—if such freight is not repayable in case of loss.[13]
8. The master and crew may insure their wages.[14]

An assignment of the interest of the assured in the subject-matter insured, does not, in the absence of express or implied agreement, transfer the rights of the assured under the policy.[15]

---

1 Ship, goods or other movables (Marine Insurance Act 1906, s. 3 (2) (a)). For insurable interest generally, see paras. 26.01, 26.08, ante.
2 Ibid, s. 5.
3 See para. 25.11, ante.
4 See para. 27.15, post.
5 Ibid, s. 3 (2). See for list of perils in policy, paras. 27.08, 27.15, post.
6 Ibid, s. 6.
7 Ibid, ss. 7, 8.
8 Ibid, s. 14 (3). On a sale 'ex ship' the purchaser has no insurable interest 'upon goods' until they have been delivered to him (*Yangtze Insurance Association v Lukmanjee* [1918] AC 585). See para. 13.42, ante.
9 Ibid, s. 14 (1).
10 Ibid, s. 9.
11 Ibid, s. 10. Bottomry is a mortgage of the ship or the ship and cargo. See para. 25.11, ante.
12 *Moran & Co v Uzielli* [1905] 2 KB 555.
13 Marine Insurance Act 1906, s. 12.

14 Ibid, s. 11.
15 Ibid, s. 15.

Gambling policies

27.04   Where the assured has no insurable interest and no expectation of acquiring such an interest at the time of the contract, the policy is void. So are policies made:

1. 'Interest or no interest', or
2. 'Without further proof of interest than the policy itself', or
3. Policies made 'without benefit of salvage to the insurer', except in cases where there is no possibility of salvage.[1]

A policy containing a PPI clause (policy proof of interest) is rendered void by s. 4 (2) (b), even though the assured had an insurable interest when the policy was signed and issued.[2] A piece of paper attached to a policy containing such a clause, which the assured is expressly permitted to detach and which he does detach, remains none the less part of the policy and makes it void.[3]

Gambling on loss by maritime perils is an offence punishable by fine or imprisonment. The prohibition extends to:[4]

1. Contracts made by a person without having any bona fide interest in the safe arrival of the ship or the safety of the subject-matter insured, or a bona fide expectation of acquiring such an interest, and
2. To contracts made by any person in the employment of the shipowner (not being a part owner) where the contract is made:

    i) 'Interest or no interest', or
    ii) 'Without further proof of interest than the policy itself', or
    iii) 'Without benefit of salvage to the insurer', or
    iv) Subject to any like term.

Any broker through whom and any insurer with whom such a contract has been effected is also guilty of an offence, if he knew the nature of the contract.[4]

---

1 Marine Insurance Act 1906, s. 4.
2 *Cheshire & Co v Vaughan Bros & Co* [1920] 3 KB 240; *John Edwards & Co v Motor Union Assurance Co* [1922] 2 KB 249. PPI means no proof of interest other than the policy is required.
3 *Re London County Commercial Re-insurance Office* [1922] 2 Ch 67.
4 Marine Insurance (Gambling Policies) Act 1909.

3. Disclosure and representations

27.05   A contract of marine insurance requires the utmost good faith, and if that be not observed by either party, the other party may avoid the contract.[1]

It is the duty of the person intending to insure to communicate to the insurer every circumstance known to him or which in the ordinary course of business he ought to know, which is material to the risk, that is, every circumstance which would influence the judgment of a prudent insurer in fixing the premium, or determining whether he will take the risk.[2]

The obligation to disclose extends to communications made to, or information received by, the assured.[2] Thus:

1. He must communicate news tending to show that a vessel is overdue,
2. That it is damaged,
3. That it is lost,[3]
4. That goods have already been in peril of damage so as to increase the risk.[4]

But there is no need to communicate circumstances which the underwriters are likely to know, such as:

1. General trade customs,
2. Speculations as to war,
3. Tempest, etc.,

nor need the intending assured disclose his opinion on matters relating to the adventure;[5] or any circumstance as to which information is waived by the insurer[6] or which diminishes the risk.[7]

A principal is deemed also to know, and to be bound by the non-communication of, circumstances within the knowledge, or which in the ordinary course of business ought to be within the knowledge of his agent.[8] Lindley LJ said:

> 'It is a condition of the contract that there is no misrepresentation or concealment, either by the assured or by any one who ought as a matter of business and fair dealing to have stated or disclosed the facts to him, or to the underwriter for him'.[9]

But this must not be carried too far. Lord Watson says:[10]

> 'The responsibility of an innocent insured for the non-communication of facts which happen to be within the private knowledge of persons whom he merely employs to obtain an insurance upon a particular risk, ought not to be carried beyond the person who actually makes the contract on his behalf.'

Similarly, every material representation made by the assured or his agent during the negotiations for, and before the conclusion of, the contract must be true, or the insurer may avoid the policy. A representation may be of fact, of expectation, or of belief. It is sufficient if a representation of fact be substantially correct, and if a representation of expectation or belief be made in good faith.[11]

---

1 Marine Insurance Act 1906, s. 17.
2 Ibid, s. 18; and see *Associated Oil Carriers Ltd v Union Insurance Society* [1917] 2 KB 184.
3 *Gladstone v King* (1813) 1 M & S 35. This applies even if it is ultimately lost by another peril, e.g. captured instead of sunk *Seaman v Fonereau* (1743) 2 Stra. 1183.
4 *Greenhill v Federal Insurance Co* [1927] 1 KB 65. See also s. 18.
5 *Carter v Boehm* (1766), 3 Burr. 1905.
6 See *Mann Macneal and Steeves Ltd v General Marine Underwriters Ltd* [1921] 2 KB 300.
7 Marine Insurance Act 1906, s. 18 (3).
8 Ibid, s. 19.
9 *Blackburn v Vigors* (1886) 17 QBD 578.
10 *Blackburn v Vigors* (1887) 12 App Cas 531, where the point was fully considered; and see *Blackburn v Haslam* (1888) 21 QBD 144.
11 Marine Insurance Act 1906, s. 20.

---

4. The policy

27.06 A marine policy must be signed by or on behalf of the insurer and it must specify the name of the assured or of some person who effects the policy on his behalf. Where the insurer is a corporation, the policy *may* be under seal.[1]

The slip It is customary to draw up a memorandum of the terms, which is initialled by the underwriters before the execution of the formal policy, and the general practice of the commercial community is to recognise this memorandum (called *The Slip*) as though it were the contract; reference may be made to the slip for the purpose of showing when the proposal was accepted, that being the date when the contract is deemed to be concluded.[2] The initialling of the slip creates a contract to enter into a policy,[3] but the contract is not admissible in evidence unless and until it is embodied in a marine policy.[4]

---

1 Marine Insurance Act 1906, ss. 22, 23, 24.
2 Ibid, ss. 21 (as amended by Finance Act 1959, s. 37, Sch. VIII), 89.
3 *Fisher v Liverpool Marine Insurance Co* (1874) LR 9 QB 418. This will not

apply to the case of a fire policy where the slip can be enforced as a policy (*Thompson v Adams* (1889) 23 QBD 361).
4 Marine Insurance Act 1906, s. 22.

Kinds of Marine Policies

27.07 Among the most important divisions is that into:

1. *Valued policies* which specify the agreed value of the subject-matter insured.[1]
2. *Unvalued policies*, which do not state the value of the subject-matter of the insurance; hence, after a loss, the amount to be paid by the underwriter remains a matter of assessment, subject to the limit of the sum insured.[2]

Policies may also be divided into:

3. *Voyage policies*, which cover the subject-matter 'at and from' or from one place to another or others.
4. *Time policies* covering the subject-matter during a specified period.[3]
5. *Mixed policies.* A time policy in which the voyage also is specified, is styled a mixed policy, e.g. A to X for six months.[4]
6. *Floating policies*, which describe the insurance in general terms, and leave the name of the ship or ships and other particulars to be defined by subsequent declaration.[5]

As a general rule, the name of the ship must be stated accurately in the policy, but when cargo is insured under a floating policy and the ship in which it is to go is at the time of insuring not yet determined, the name of the ship may be communicated later by indorsement on the policy or in other customary manner. In such cases the insured should declare the shipment and the value of it as soon as he knows of it, and the policy attaches to the goods in the order in which they are shipped. Unless otherwise agreed, where a declaration of value is not made until after notice of loss or arrival, the policy must be treated as unvalued.

---

1 Marine Insurance Act 1906, s. 27. See para. 27.10, post.
2 Ibid, s. 28. See *Berger and Light Diffusers Pty Ltd v Pollock* [1973] 2 Lloyd's Rep 442.
3 Time limits on such policies were removed by Finance Act 1959, ss. 30, 37, Sch. VIII.
4 Marine Insurance Act 1906, s. 25.
5 Ibid, s. 29.

Form of Marine Policy

27.08 The policy may be in print or writing, or partly written and partly printed. The form set out below is known as Lloyd's S. G. policy, and is the form of policy scheduled to the Marine Insurance Act 1906. The notes which follow will, it is hoped, elucidate it. It should be noted that the words or clauses appearing in black type in the following form are those commented upon hereafter.

S. G.[1]

£——

BE IT KNOWN THAT *A and or as Agent* **as well in** *his* **own name** as for and in the name and names of all and every other person or persons to whom the same doth, may, or shall appertain, in part or in all doth make assurance and cause *himself* and them, and every of them, to be insured (1), **lost or not lost** (2) **at and from** (3) *London*. Upon any kind of goods and merchandises, and also upon the body, tackle, apparel, ordnance, munition, artillery, boat, and other furniture, of and in the good ship or vessel called the *Mary*, whereof is master under God, for this present voyage, *John Smith*, or whosoever else shall go for master in the said ship, or by whatsoever other name or names the said ship, or the master thereof, is or shall be named or called; **beginning the adventure upon the said goods** and merchandises from the loading thereof aboard the said ship (3)   upon the said ship, etc. and so shall continue and endure, during her abode there, upon the said ship, etc.; and further, until the said ship, with all her ordnance, tackle, apparel, etc., and goods and merchandises whatsoever shall be arrived at *Melbourne* upon the said ship, etc., **until she hath moored** at anchor twenty-four hours in good safety (4); and upon the goods and merchandises, **until the same be there discharged** and safely landed (5). And it shall be lawful for the said ship, etc., in this voyage, **to proceed and sail to and touch and stay** (6) at any ports or places whatsoever *on the West Coast of Africa* without prejudice to this insurance. The said ship, etc., goods and merchandises, etc., for so much as concerns the assured, by agreement between the assured and assurers in this policy, are and **shall be valued at** (7).

Touching the adventure and **perils** which we, the assurers, are contented to bear and do take upon us in this voyage: they are **of the seas** (8), men of war, **fire** (9), enemies, **pirates** (10), rovers, **thieves** (11), **jettisons** (12), letters of mart and countermart, surprisals, **takings at sea, arrests, restraints, and**

detainments of all kings, princes, and people (13) of what nation, condition, or quality soever, **barratry (14) of the master and mariners,** and of **all other perils** (15), losses, and misfortunes, that have or shall come to the hurt, detriment, or damage of the said goods and merchandises and ship, etc., or any part thereof; And **in case of any loss or misfortune** it shall be lawful to the assured, their factors, servants and assigns, to sue, labour, and travel for, in and about the defence, safeguards, and recovery of the said goods and merchandises, and ship, etc., or any part thereof, without prejudice to this insurance; to the charges whereof we, the assurers, will contribute each one according to the rate and quantity of his sum herein assured (16). And it is especially declared and agreed that no acts of the insurer or insured in recovering, saving or preserving the property insured, shall be considered as a **waiver, or acceptance of abandonment** (16). And it is agreed by us, the insurers, that this writing or policy of assurance shall be of as much force and effect as the surest writing or policy of assurance heretofore made in Lombard Street, or in the Royal Exchange, or elsewhere in London. **And so we, the assurers,** are contented, and do hereby promise and bind ourselves, each one for his own part, our heirs, executors, and goods to the assured, their executors, administrators, and assigns, for the true performance of the premises (17), **confessing ourselves paid** the consideration (18) due unto us for this assurance by the assured, at and after the rate of

IN WITNESS whereof we, the assurers, have subscribed our names and sums assured in *London.*

N.B.—Corn, fish, salt, fruit, flour, and seed are warranted free from average, unless general, or the ship be stranded; sugar, tobacco, hemp, flax, hides, and skins are warranted free from average under five pounds per cent; and all other goods, also the ship and freight, are warranted free from average, under three pounds per cent, unless general, or the ship be stranded (19).

---

1 These indicate it is a ship and goods policy.

Notes on the above Form of Policy

27.09 *1. 'As well in his own name',* etc.   The words of the policy are sufficient to protect all persons who possessed an insurable interest at the time of the insurance or acquire one during the risk; and under them a person interested, who did not authorise an insurance to be effected for him, may subsequently, even after the loss, adopt and claim the benefit of the insurance.[1]

But it is not enough that the person claiming the benefit of the policy should be within the description of those insured, if the person effecting the policy did not in fact intend to insure on his behalf.[2]

2. *'Lost or not lost'* The words cover the assured, although the subject-matter of the insurance has been partially or entirely lost at the conclusion of the contract of insurance unless the assured was aware of the loss and the insurer was not.[3] They also entitle the underwriter to his premium although the subject-matter has actually arrived safely at the time when the contract was concluded unless at such time the insurer knew of the safe arrival.[4]

3. *'At and from'. 'Beginning the adventure on the said goods',* etc. These are the words which determine the time from which the insurer is at risk. If the ship is insured 'from' a place, the insurer's risk dates from the time when she starts on the voyage insured;[5] if she is insured 'at and from', the risk dates from the time when the contract is concluded, if at that time she is in safety at that place; otherwise, the risk commences from the time she arrives in good safety at that place.[6] If freight is insured the risk, under the words 'at and from', attaches immediately the ship is in good safety at that place, provided that the freight is chartered freight, otherwise it usually attaches pro rata as the cargo is loaded.[7]

Whether the ship is insured "at" or "at and from" it is an implied condition that she shall commence the venture within a reasonable time unless the delay was caused by circumstances known to the insurer before the conclusion of the contract, or the insurer has waived the condition.[8] If a place of departure is mentioned, no risk will attach to the underwriter if the ship does not sail from that place.[9]

The insurer's risk on goods insured "from the loading thereof" does not attach until they are on board, the risk during transit from shore to the ship is on their owner.[10] To meet this and the case of loss whilst unloading, a clause is often put in the margin of the policy to the following effect:

'including all risk of craft to and from the vessel.'

4. and 5. *'Until she hath moored',* etc. *'Until the same be there discharged',* etc. These words are intended to fix the date of cessation of the insurer's risk. Where the risk on goods continues until they are "safely landed", they must be landed in the customary manner and within a reasonable time after arrival at

the port of discharge, and if they are not so landed the risk ceases.[11] So, if it is customary at the port to land the goods by means of lighters, the risk continues until the goods are safely landed after transport in the lighters.[12]

---

1 Marine Insurance Act 1906, s. 86.
2 *Boston Fruit Co v British and Marine Insurance Co* [1906] AC 336.
3 Marine Insurance Act 1906, Sch. I, r. 1.
4 Ibid, s. 84 (3) (b).
5 Ibid, Sch. I, r. 2.
6 Ibid, Sch. I, r. 3 (a), (b).
7 Ibid, Sch. I, r. 3 (c), (d).
8 Ibid, s. 42.
9 Ibid, s. 43.
10 Ibid, Sch. I, r. 4.
11 Ibid, Sch. I, r. 5.
12 *Hurry v Royal Exchange Co* (1801) 2 Bos. & P. 430.

27.10   6. *'To proceed and sail to and touch and stay',* etc.   It is the duty of the assured not to deviate, that is to say, not to go out of the proper course, as agreed or as prescribed by custom, between the termini of the voyage.

Deviation, without lawful excuse, entitles the underwriter to avoid the policy, even though the ship has regained her course before any loss occurs, and the risk was not increased by such deviation.[1] But a mere intention to deviate which is not carried into effect will not discharge the insurer from his liability.[2]

Deviation is excused if:

i) specially authorised by the policy, or
ii) if caused by circumstances beyond the control of the master or his employer, or
iii) if reasonably necessary to comply with a warranty; or
iv) to ensure the safety of the ship, or
v) to save human life; or
vi) to obtain medical or surgical aid for any person on board, or
vii) if caused by barratrous conduct of master or crew, if barratry be a peril insured against.[3]

But a deviation for the mere purpose of saving property is not justifiable.[4]

The words quoted at the head of this note authorise the subject of insurance to proceed to and stay at certain ports mentioned in the policy, but not even to stay at such ports may the ship deviate from the voyage; she may touch and stay at them in the course of the voyage from the port of departure to the port of destination.[5] Thus, liberty given to a ship insured on a voyage from London to Plymouth to touch at any port in the English Channel will not excuse a call at Penzance, this last-named port being beyond the voyage in question, but it would allow a call at Newhaven in Sussex.

If after the commencement of the risk the destination of the ship is voluntarily changed from that contemplated by the policy there is said to be a change of voyage, and not a mere deviation, and is not authorised by the clause now being considered.[6] Where there is a change of voyage, the insurer is discharged from the time when the determination to change is manifested, even though the ship be lost before she has actually changed the course of the voyage for which the insurance was effected.[7]

Where the destination is specified and the ship sails for a different destination, the risk does not attach.[8]

The voyage must be prosecuted with reasonable diligence, and unjustifiable delay will discharge the insurer.[9] The reason is that:

'the voyage commenced after an unreasonable interval of time would have become a voyage at a different period of the year, at a more advanced age of the ship, and, in short, a different voyage than if it had been prosecuted with proper and ordinary diligence; that is, the risk would have been altered from that which was intended'.[10]

Circumstances which excuse deviation will also excuse delay.[11]

7. *'Shall be valued at'*, etc. The value of the subject-matter as stated is accepted for the purposes of assessing compensation when a loss has happened as the true value, and is conclusive between the insurers and the assured except for the purpose of determining whether there has been a constructive total loss;[12] unless there is evidence that the amount fixed was fraudulently stated, or intended by both parties as a mere wager. It has been stated that:

'An exorbitant valuation may be evidence of fraud, but when the valuation is *bona fide*, the valuation agreed upon is binding'.[13]

The effect of a valued policy may be illustrated by the case of *Balmoral Company (SS) v Marten*:[14]

The defendant in that case insured a ship valued in the policy at £33,000. The ship incurred salvage expenses and a general average loss. In the salvage action the real value of the ship was proved to be £40,000, and in the average statement the rights of the parties were adjusted upon the footing that £40,000 was the contributory value of the ship. The insurers were held liable to make good to the owners only 33-40ths of the salvage and general average losses; that is, to pay in the proportion of the insured value to the contributory or salvage value.

---

1 Marine Insurance Act 1906, s. 46.
2 Ibid, s. 46 (3).
3 Ibid, s. 49. 'Barratry' includes every wrongful act wilfully committed by the master or crew to the prejudice of the owner, or as the case may be, the charterer: ibid, Sch. I, r. 11.
4 *Scaramanga v Stamp* (1880) 5 CPD 295. But see the Carriage of Goods by Sea Act 1971, see para. 23.19 (6), ante.
5 Marine Insurance Act 1906, Sch. I, r. 6.
6 Ibid, s. 45 (1).
7 Ibid, s. 45 (2).
8 Ibid, s. 44.
9 Ibid, s. 48.
10 *Mount v Larkins* (1832), 8 Bing 122, per Tindal CJ.
11 Marine Insurance Act 1906, s. 49. See para. 27.10 n., ante.
12 Ibid, s. 27.
13 Bovill CJ in *Barker v Janson* (1868) LR 3 CP 306. See also *The Main* [1894] P. 320. *Berger and Light Diffusers Pty Ltd v Pollock* [1973] 2 Lloyd's Rep 442.
14 [1902] AC 511.

27.11 8. *'Perils ... of the seas'* The clause in which these words occur defines the various dangers against loss in connection with which the insurers agree to indemnify the assured. The term 'perils of the seas' refers only to fortuitous accidents or casualties of the seas, and does not include the ordinary action of the winds and waves.[1] The indemnity is against accidents which may happen, not against events which must happen; nor need the loss be occasioned by extraordinary violence of the winds or waves. If a vessel strikes upon a sunken rock in fair weather and sinks, this is a loss by perils of the sea. And a loss by foundering, owing to a vessel coming into collision with another vessel, even when the collision results from the negligence of that other vessel, falls within the same category.[2]

A loss brought about by negligent navigation will be covered, if that which immediately caused the loss was a peril of the sea, even if the negligence is that of the assured himself, so long as it does not amount to wilful misconduct.[3] Damage done by rats to a vessel which prevents her from sailing is not a peril of the sea; but if in consequence of the ravages of rats sea water enters the ship and damages the cargo, there is a loss by a peril of the seas.[4] The burden of proving, on a balance of probabilities, that loss has occurred by perils of the sea lies on the assured.[5]

The case of *The Inchmaree*[6] should be noted.

In that case a vessel was lying at anchor off the shore, about to proceed on her voyage; the boilers were being filled by means of a donkey-engine; owing to a failure on the part of somebody on board to see that a certain valve was open, the valve remained closed, and consequently, in the operation of pumping, water was forced back, split the air chamber, and disabled the pump.

The House of Lords decided that the damage was not caused by 'perils of the seas', nor by any cause similar to 'perils of the seas', and that the insurers were not liable on the policy.

In consequence of this decision a special clause—styled *The Inchmaree* clause—is now usually added to the policy. It now covers (amongst other things):

i) certain losses caused by the negligence of master, mariners, engineers and pilots, or

ii) through explosions, etc., or

iii) any latent defect in the machinery or hull.

iv) contact with aircraft and land conveyances, or

v) bursting of boilers and breakage of shafts, or

vi) accidents to nuclear installations,

vii) earthquake, volcanic eruption or lightning provided the loss has not resulted from want of due diligence on the part of the assured, owners or managers.

But the operation of the clause must be confined to the specific causes of loss enumerated, and not extended to matters *ejusdem generis*.

Thus, the clause has been held not to cover damage caused to the hull of a ship by a boiler falling into the hold while it was being lowered by a floating steam crane of which the tackle was defective.[7]

---

1 Marine Insurance Act 1906, Sch. I, r. 7. Under perils of the seas are comprehended winds, waves, lightning, rocks, shoals, collisions, and in general all causes of loss and damage to the property insured, arising from the elements, and inevitable accidents, other than those of capture and detention. See *The Stranna* [1938] P. 69, where the meaning of the term was fully considered.

2 *The Xantho* (1887) 12 App Cas at 509, per Lord Herschell.

3 *Trinder & Co v Thames etc Marine Insurance Co* [1898] 2 QB 114.

4 *Hamilton v Pandorf* (1887) 12 App Cas 518; cf. *E. D. Sasson v Western Assurance Co* [1912] AC 561.

5 *Compania Naviera Santi SA v Indemnity Marine Insurance Co Ltd* [1960] 2 Lloyd's Rep 469.

6 *Thames and Mersey Marine Insurance Co v Hamilton, Fraser & Co* (1887) 12 App Cas 484.

7 *Stott (Baltic) Steamers Ltd v Marten* [1916] 1 AC 304. This is now covered by additional words in the clause referring to 'loading, discharge or handling cargo.'

27.12 *9. 'Fire'* The peril insured against is not merely unintentional burning; for instance, a fire voluntarily caused in order to avoid capture by an enemy is covered by the policy;[1] or a fire intentionally caused by a person other than the assured.[2] Of course, no claim may be made in respect of a fire wrongfully caused by the assured, but once it is shown that the loss has been cause by fire, the plaintiff has made out a prima facie case and the onus lies upon the defendant to show on a balance of probabilities that the fire was caused by or connived at by the plaintiff. If the court determines that the loss is equally consistent with arson as it is with an accidental fire, the plaintiff would win on that issue.[3] A policy on goods will not cover any loss caused by a fire resulting from the condition in which they were shipped.[4]

10. 'Pirates' The term includes passengers who mutiny and rioters who attack the ship from the shore.[5] But the expression must be construed in its popular sense as meaning persons who plunder indiscriminately for private gain and not persons who seize property for some public political end.[6]

11. 'Thieves' Clandestine theft, or theft committed by any of the crew or passengers, is not included in the term 'thieves' as used in this clause of the policy.[7]

12. 'Jettisons' This means the throwing overboard of tackle or cargo to lighten the ship bona fide and in an emergency. As a rule the insurer is not liable to indemnify the owner of the goods if they were being carried on deck or in deck houses; but custom of the trade or express agreement may throw the loss on the insurer.[8]

---

1 *Gordon v Rimmington* (1807) 1 Camp. 123.
2 *Midland Insurance Co v Smith* (1881) 6 QBD 561.
3 *Slattery v Mance* [1962] 1 QB 676, [1962] 1 All ER 525.
4 *Boyd v Dubois* (1811) 3 Camp. 133. It follows that generally it is not necessary for the insured to disclose information relating to their condition. However, the previous history or condition of goods may in certain circumstances be a material fact which ought to be disclosed: *Greenhill v Federal Insurance Co* [1927] 1 KB 65, disapproving a dictum of Lord Ellenborough in *Boyd v Dubois*.
5 Marine Insurance Act 1906, Sch. I, r. 8.
6 *Republic of Bolivia v Indemnity Mutual Marine Assurance Co* [1909] 1 KB 785.
7 Marine Insurance Act 1906, Sch. I, r. 9.
8 *Milward v Hibbert* (1842) 3 QB 120.

27.13 *13. 'Takings at Sea, Arrests, restraints, etc. ... of kings, princes, and people'* This includes political or executive acts, such as capture in time of war by an enemy, stoppage of neutral vessels suspected of carrying enemy goods, embargo in time of peace, etc.[1] A declaration of war by Her Majesty which renders the further prosecution of a voyage to an enemy port unlawful is a restraint of princes, although the assured may voluntarily abandon the adventure.[2] Thus in *Rickards v Forestal Land, Timber and Rail Co*:[3]

> British subjects shipped goods in German vessels to various ports. The goods were insured by the appellants. Shortly before the outbreak of war the German government ordered all German vessels to put in at a neutral port and, if possible, to return to Germany. The ship tried to get back to Germany but when intercepted was scuttled by her crew. It was held that this was a 'restraint of princes' as the order was carried out on behalf of the German government.

But this principle does not apply merely because the captain of the ship voluntarily puts into a neutral port of refuge to avoid the risk of capture, before the peril has actually begun to operate.[4] There must be an actual restraint in existence; a reasonable apprehension that a restraint will be imposed, though justified by the event, does not excuse the abandonment of the voyage.[5]

'Takings at sea' covers not only capture and seizure but where, for example, the master on instructions from the owner of the ship, assumes a dominion over the cargo inconsistent with the cargo owner's rights—this is a taking at sea of the cargo.[6]

The operation of a muncipal law preventing the delivery of goods at their destination (e.g. the landing the cattle suffering from disease) is a 'restraint of people'.[7]

The property of an alien enemy cannot of course be insured against capture during war with this country; but if such property were insured and seized by the Government of the assured before an actual state of war existed, the subsequent breaking out of war would not invalidate the contract of insurance, although the right to recover would be suspended during the continuance of hostilities.[8] The insurer is not liable under this heading for loss occasioned by riot, or by ordinary judicial process.[9]

---

1 Marine Insurance Act 1906, Sch. I, r. 10.
2 *British and Foreign Marine Insurance Co v Sanday & Co* [1916] 1 AC 650; and see para. 27.14, post.
3 [1942] AC 50, [1941] 3 All ER 62. Cf. *Czarnikow Ltd v Java Sea and Fire Insurance Co Ltd* [1941] 3 All ER 256.
4 *Becker, Gray & Co v London Assurance Corpn* [1918] AC 101.
5 *Watts, Watts & Co v Mitsui & Co* [1917] AC 227; but see *Atlantic Maritime Co Inc v Gibbon* [1954] 1 QB 105, [1953] 2 All ER 1086, CA.

6 *Nishina Trading Co Ltd v Chiyoda Fire and Marine Insurance Co* [1969] 2 QB 449, [1969] 2 All ER 776, CA.

7 *Miller v Law Accident Insurance Co* [1903] 1 KB 712.

8 *Janson v Driefontein Consolidated Mines* [1902] AC 484.

9 Marine Insurance Act 1906, Sch. I, r. 10.

27.14   *F. C. & S. Clause*   It is not unusual for insurers to stipulate by a special clause in the policy that they shall not be liable for loss caused by capture or seizure. This clause is known as the F. C. & S. clause (free of capture and seizure), and since the Second World War runs as follows:

'Warranted free of capture, seizure, arrest, restraint or detainment, and the consequences thereof or of any attempt thereat; also from the consequences of hostilities or warlike operations, whether there be a declaration of war or not; but this warranty shall not exclude collision, contact with any fixed or floating object (other than a mine or torpedo), stranding, heavy weather or fire unless caused directly (and independently of the nature of the voyage or service which the vessel concerned or, in the case of collision, any other vessel involved therein, is performing) by a hostile act by or against a belligerent power; and for the purpose of this warranty "power" includes any authority maintaining naval, military or air forces in association with a power.

Further warranted free from the consequences of civil war, revolution, rebellion, insurrection, or civil strife arising therefrom, or piracy.'

It withdraws from the protection of the policy certain risks which would otherwise be covered. For instance:

Where in anticipation of war the Government of the South African Republic seized gold belonging to its own subject, it was held that there was a seizure within the meaning of the warranty and that the insurers were not liable on the policy.[1]

But if a loss occurs the court, in the absence of specific evidence must consider the probabilities and decide as well as it can whether that loss will fall upon the marine underwriters or the war risk insurers.[2]

When the policy contains a warranty of freedom from capture, the insurer's liability ceases on capture of the vessel. Thus:

In a policy against total loss by perils of the sea, containing the F. C. & S. clause, a neutral ship carrying contraband during the Russo-Japanese war, was captured by the Japanese. While being navigated towards a Court of Prize, the ship was wrecked and became a total loss. She was afterwards condemned in the prize Court. On a claim by the owners under the policy, it was held that when the ship was first seized there was a total loss by a capture, the lawfulness of which was authoritatively determined by a subsequent decision of the Prize Court and that the *captors* and not the *assured* had lost the vessel by shipwreck. Accordingly, the owners failed to recover.[3]

---

1 *Robinson Gold Mining Co v Alliance Insurance Co* [1902] 2 KB 489; [1904] AC 359.
2 *Munro Brice & Co v Marten* [1920] 3 KB 94.
3 *Anderson v Marten* [1908] AC 334.

27.15 *14. 'Barratry of the master and mariners'* The term 'barratry' includes every wrongful act wilfully committed by the master or crew to the prejudice of the owner or charterer.[1] For example, setting fire to or scuttling a ship or employing it for smuggling[2] are barratrous acts.

15. 'All other perils' This means all other perils of a nature similar to those which have already been enumerated in the policy.[3] Thus:

it does not include the scuttling of a ship with the connivance of the owner.[4]

16. 'In case of any loss or misfortune ... waiver or acceptance of abandonment' This is styled the 'sue and labour clause'. The object is to encourage the insurer and the assured to do work to preserve after an accident the property covered by the policy, and to make the best of a bad state of affairs. Should they do so, the clause provides that their respective rights shall be in no wise prejudiced by any acts done in pursuance of such object, and that the assured shall be entitled to obtain his expenses consequent on the work from the insurers.

But for this clause an assured might abstain from any attempt to safeguard wrecked property for fear that such conduct might be deemed a waiver of his right to abandon; under such a clause it is his duty to take reasonable measures to avert or minimise loss.[5] General average losses and contributions and salvage charges are not recoverable under the clause, nor are expenses incurred to avert loss not covered by the policy.[6] Moreover, if the insurer incurs expenses which, if they had been incurred by the assured, would have been recoverable from the insurer under the clause, the insurer cannot recover them from the assured.[7]

17. 'And so we the assurers', etc. This clause requires modification to adapt it to the needs of an underwriting limited liability company. Each insurer who signs, signs on his own behalf only, and agrees to indemnify the assured to an amount not exceeding the sum he places next his name. Where there is a loss recoverable under the policy, each insurer, if there are several, is liable for such proportion of the loss as the amount of his subscription bears to the value or assessed amount of the loss; one insurer is not liable for another's default unless it is expressly so agreed.[8]

18. *'Confessing ourselves paid', etc.* This recital is sometimes varied by stating that the persons negotiating the policy have agreed to pay: in either case, unless otherwise agreed, the broker is directly responsible to the insurer for the premium. The custom making the broker and not the assured liable to the insurer for the premium extends also to a 'company's policy', which contains a promise by the assured to pay. Even this does not make the assured directly liable to the insurer, for payment must be made according to the custom, i.e. by the broker.[9] In the absence of fraud, an acknowledgment on the policy of the receipt of the premium is conclusive as between the insurer and the assured, but not as between the former and the broker.[10]

---

1 Marine Insurance Act 1906, Sch. I, r. 11; and see *Earle v Rowcroft* (1806) 8 East 126.
2 *Cory v Burr* (1883) 8 App Cas 393.
3 Marine Insurance Act 1906, Sch. I, r. 12.
4 *P Samuel & Co v Dumas* [1924] AC 431.
5 Marine Insurance Act 1906, s. 78 (4).
6 Ibid, s. 78 (2), (3).
7 *Crouan v Stanier* [1904] 1 KB 87.
8 CF. *Tyser v Shipowners' Syndicate (Reassured)* [1896] 1 QB 135.
9 *Universo Insurance Co of Milan v Merchants' Marine Insurance Co* [1897] 2 QB 93; 2 Com. Cas. 28 at 180.
10 Marine Insurance Act 1906, s. 54.

27.16   19. *'N.B.' etc.* This clause is styled the 'memorandum'; its object is to prevent the insurers from being liable for loss on certain goods peculiarly liable to damage on a sea voyage, or for certain small losses which must almost necessarily occur, but which might increase the liability of the insurer beyond what he could calculate on.

The meaning of the clause has been much considered, and it is believed that the result of the cases may be summarised thus:

i) the insurer is not liable to indemnify against a partial loss or damage to the first group of goods (viz., corn, fish, etc.) unless the loss is a general average loss,[1] or unless the ship is stranded;[2]

ii) he is not liable to indemnify against a partial loss or damage to the second group (viz., sugar, etc.) unless the damage amounts to five per cent. of the value of the thing damaged.

iii) he is not bound to indemnify against partial loss or damage to the ship, freight, or any goods other than the above, unless the loss amounts to three per cent. of the value of the thing lost or damaged, or unless it is a general average loss, or unless the ship is stranded.

It should be noted that a general average loss may not be added to a particular average loss to make up the specified percentage;[3] but in a voyage policy successive losses, though from different perils, may be added together for this purpose, and in a time policy successive losses occurring on the same voyage may be added together, but not losses occuring on distinct and separate voyages.[4]

The meaning of 'stranding' in this memorandum is not always very clear; it means that the ship has by some accident, or (at any rate) out of ordinary course,[5] touched the sea bottom or something in immediate contact with it, and has thereby been retarded on her course for an appreciable length of time. The fact that the stranding has taken place renders the insurer liable (save to goods in class (ii)) for all losses on the goods, though happening before or after the stranding, and not attributable to it;[6] but the goods must be actually on board at the time of the stranding.[6]

The words 'sunk or burnt' are sometimes added at the end of the memorandum. In such case a ship is not 'burnt' within the meaning of the policy, unless the injury by fire is such as to constitute a substantial burning of the ship as a whole.[7]

---

1 See paras. 23.24, et seq., ante.
2 The term 'average unless general,' means a partial loss of the subject-matter insured, other than a general average loss, and does not include 'particular charges.' Marine Insurance Act 1906, Sch. I, r. 13, 14.
3 Marine Insurance Act 1906, s. 76 (3).
4 *Stewart v Merchants' Marine Insurance Co* (1886) 16 QBD 619.
5 *Kingsford v Marshall* (1832) 8 Bing at 463.
6 Marine Insurance Act 1906, Sch. I, r. 14.
7 *The Glenlivet*, [1894] P. 48.

The F P A Clause

27.17 Another clause, being an additional limitation of the insurer's liability, is of frequent occurrence; it is styled the F P A (free of particular average) clause, and begins thus:

'Warranted free from particular average unless the vessel or craft be stranded, sunk, or burnt, ...'

It goes on to provide that the underwriters are to pay for any packages totally lost in loading, transhipment or discharge and also for any loss or damage to the interest insured which may be attributed to fire, explosion, collision or contact with anything external to the ship including ice but not water. They are also to be liable for unloading at a port of distress or special charges at a port of call or refuge for which they would be liable under a standard English policy with average.

Except for the matters specially referred to in this clause, the warranty 'free from particular average' prevents the assured from recovering for a loss of part other than a loss incurred by a general average sacrifice;[1] but if the policy covers parcels separately valued, or when by usage the contract is apportionable, the risk for loss of an apportionable part is on the insurer.[2] This warranty does not exonerate the insurer from salvage charges or from liability under the suing and labouring clause, if expense is incurred to save the subject-matter of insurance from a loss for which the insurers would have been liable.[3] Such expenses are termed 'particular charges'.[4]

---

1 See on general and particular average paras. 23.24, et seq., ante.
2 Marine Insurance Act 1906, s. 76 (1). See *Fabrique de Produits Chimiques v Large* [1923] 1 KB 203.
3 Ibid, s. 76 (2).
4 Ibid, s. 64 (2).

The Running Down Clause

27.18 A further clause, which is either printed in the body of the policy, or put in the margin, or otherwise attached to the policy, is the *Running Down Clause*, the object of which is to cover the shipowner from loss in the nature of damages payable by him by way of compensation for collisions between his and other ships caused by the default of those in charge of his ship. The collision need not be directly between the insured ship and the vessel entitled to compensation, and where, owing to the negligent navigation of the insured ship, a third vessel is run down by a ship which has been forced into it through being struck by the insured ship, the damages payable to the third vessel will be covered by this clause.[1]

---

1 *W France Fenwick & Co v Merchants' Marine Insurance Co* [1915] 3 KB 290.

---

5. Re-insurance and double insurance

Re-insurance

27.19 Re-insurance occurs when one insurer insures the risk he has undertaken with another insurer. An agreement to re-insure is a policy of "sea insurance" which must comply with the statutory requirements affecting an original policy.[1]

The law applicable is in the main the same as that which governs an original insurance. The contract of re-insurance is also a contract of indemnity, and if the original insurer enters into a compromise with the original assured, paying less than he was liable for, the re-insurer is entitled to the benefit of that compromise.[2] The re-insurer usually undertakes, with regard to the original policy, "to pay as may be paid thereon". These words do not create any liability unless the re-insured actually became bound to pay under the original policy; it is not sufficient that he has paid in good faith in the belief that he was liable.[3]

A re-insurer need not give the notice of abandonment that is usually necessary in the case of constructive total loss.[4] The doctrine of subrogation applies to re-insurance, and the re-insurer is entitled to his proper proportion of any money which has been or could be recovered by enforcing a right that would diminish the loss of the original insurer.[6]

---

1 *Imperial Marine v Fire Insurance Corpn Ltd* (1879) 4 CPD 166; *English Insurance Co v National Benefit Assurance Co* [1929] AC 114; *Genforsikrings Aktieselskabet v Da Costa* [1911] 1 KB 137, and see para. 27.06, ante. Some of the statutory requirements were removed by Finance Act 1959, ss. 30, 37, Sch. VIII.
2 *British Dominions General Insurance Co v Duder* [1915] 2 KB 394.
3 *Chippendale v Holt* (1895) 1 Com Cas 197.
4 Marine Insurance Act 1906, s. 62 (9); and see para. 27.24, post.
5 See paras. 26.03 ante, and 27.30, post.
6 *Assicurezioni Generali de Trieste v Empress Assurance Corpn* [1907] 2 KB 814.

Double insurance

27.20 A double insurance occurs when the assured effects two or more policies on the same interest and adventure. If the two together cause an over-insurance the excess cannot be recovered, but the assured may sue on whichever policy he desires, and may recover the whole sum to which he is entitled by way of indemnity.[1]

Where the policy is a valued policy, the assured must give credit as against the valuation for any sum received by him under any other policy without regard to the actual value of the subject-matter insured;[2] and where the policy is unvalued, he must give the like credit as against the full insurable value.[3]

As between the insurers each is liable to contribute rateably his proportionate part,[4] the assured holding any excess he may have received in trust for such of the insurers as are inter se entitled to it.[5] Any insurer who pays more than his proportion of the loss is entitled to contribution from the other insurers in the same way as a surety who has paid more than his proportion of the debt.[6]

---

1 Marine Insurance Act 1906, s. 32 (2) (a).
2 Ibid, s. 32 (2) (b).
3 Ibid, s. 32 (2) (c). For the mode of ascertaining insurable value, see ibid, s. 16.
4 Ibid, s. 80 (1).
5 Ibid, s. 32 (2) (d).
6 Ibid, s. 80 (1) and (2).

---

6. Alteration of a policy

27.21 In accordance with the general principles of insurance contracts an unauthorised alteration in a policy has the effect of making it void as against all who were not parties to the alteration. A material alteration by consent is usually made by indorsement signed by the parties.

7. Losses

27.22 Except where otherwise agreed, the insurer is liable for any loss proximately caused by a peril insured against, even though the loss would not have occurred but for the negligence or misconduct of the master or crew. The rule that the loss must be traced to a 'proximate cause' has always been rigorously applied in insurance cases.[1] The cause which is truly proximate is that which is proximate in efficiency. That efficiency may have been preserved although other causes may have meantime sprung up which have not yet destroyed it, or truly impaired it, and it may culminate in a result of which it still remains the real efficient cause to which the event can be ascribed.[2] Thus:

> If a ship insured against all consequences of hostilities runs upon the sunken wreck of a vessel torpedoed by an enemy submarine, the act of hostility is not the proximate cause of the loss; but it would be otherwise if the enemy had deliberately sunk a vessel in a narrow and shallow entrance to a port for the purpose of damaging vessels trying to make the port.[3]

But the insurer is not liable for ordinary wear and tear, nor for loss caused by inherent vice of the subject-matter insured, or by rats or vermin.[4]

Losses are of two kinds:

Partial, where the subject-matter of the insurance is only partially damaged, or where there is only an obligation to contribute to general average, and

Total, where the subject-matter is wholly destroyed, or has become so damaged that the owner is justified in abandoning it. These are subdivided into

1. Actual total losses, and
2. Constructive total losses.

---

1 See per Lord Sumner in *Becker, Gray & Co v London Assurance Corpn* [1918] AC at 112 et seq.
2 *Leyland Shipping Co v Norwich Union Fire Insurance Co* [1918] AC 350, per Lord Shaw of Dunfermline at 369.
3 *France Fenwick & Co v North of England etc Association* [1917] 2 KB 522.
4 Marine Insurance Act 1906, s. 55. Subject to agreement, salvage charges incurred in preventing a loss by perils insured against, may be recovered as a loss by those perils (ibid, s. 65).

---

1. Actual total loss

27.23   This occurs:

i) when the subject-matter is actually destroyed, or irreparably damaged or

ii) where the assured is irretrievably deprived of it;[1] e.g. when a ship ceases any longer to be a ship, and becomes a mere bundle of planks; or

iii) when goods are so damaged as to have ceased to exist in such condition or form as to answer the denomination under which they were insured;[2] or

iv) when lost to the owner by an adverse valid decree of a court of competent jurisdiction in consequence of a peril insured against.[3]

But possession restored after action brought does not disentitle the owners to recover as for a total loss.[4]

Where the ship concerned is missing, her actual total loss may be presumed, if no news be received after the lapse of a reasonable time.

---

1 Marine Insurance Act 1906, s. 57 (1). *Berger and Light Oil Diffusers Pty Ltd v Pollock* [1973] 2 Lloyd's Rep 442.
2 *Asfar v Blundell* [1896] 1 QB 123, CA. But see Chalmers *Marine Insurance* (8th edn) 84.
3 E.g. sale by the Court of Admiralty (*Cossman v West* (1888) 13 App Cas 160).
4 *Ruys v Royal Exchange Assurance Corpn* [1897] 2 QB 135.

---

2. Constructive total loss

27.24 This occurs:

i) where the subject-matter insured is reasonably abandoned[1] on account of its actual loss appearing to be unavoidable, or
ii) because it could not be preserved from actual loss without an expenditure which would exceed its value when the expenditure had been incurred.[2]

In particular, there is a constructive total loss:

i) where a vessel has sunk in deep water and cannot be raised without incurring an expense greater than her value,[3] or
ii) when a ship has been so damaged that the cost of repair would exceed her value when repaired.[4]

The insurers cannot by gratuitously intervening and incurring an expense which a prudent uninsured owner would not have done, convert a constructive total loss into a partial one; e.g.

by raising a vessel which has been sunk in deep water and abandoned by the assured.[5]

Again, there is a constructive total loss where the assured is deprived of his ships or goods by a peril insured against and it is *unlikely* that he can recover them; but if at the date of the commencement of the action on the true facts as then existing the recovery of the vessel or goods is a matter of uncertainty and the assured cannot show that on the balance of probability the ship or goods will not be recovered his claim will fail.[6]

When goods are insured at and from a port of loading to a port of destination, there is a loss if the adventure is frustrated by a peril insured against, although the goods themselves may continue in existence uninjured and be under the control of the owner. The subject-matter of the insurance is primarily the physical safety of the merchandise; but it is also an insurance of its safe arrival at the designated port. Accordingly, although in possession of the goods, the owner may in such case, on giving due notice of abandonment, recover for a constructive total loss.[7]

Where goods were insured and the policy contained a clause 'warranted free of any claim based upon loss of, or frustration of, the insured voyage or adventure' and both the goods and the adventure were lost to the owners as a result of restraint of princes, it was held that the exception did not apply, for it was confined to a case where the goods were not physically lost, but became a constructive total loss by reason of the frustration of the adventure.[8] In other words the 'frustration clause' as it is called confines the insurance to the safety of the goods and excludes the right of the insured to claim merely because it has not been possible to convey them to their destination owing to a peril insured against.

Notice of abandonment In cases of constructive total loss, notice of abandonment must generally be given; otherwise—unless notice is waived by the insurer—the loss will be considered as partial.[9] A notice of abandonment must indicate the intention of the assured to abandon his insured interest unconditionally,[10] e.g. an owner cannot abandon part of a ship. The notice must be given with reasonable diligence after the receipt of reliable information, a reasonable time for inquiry being allowed where the information is of doubtful character,[11] i.e. at the earliest opportunity consistent with making inquiry as to the circumstances; and it must be given by the owner or a properly authorised agent. It need not be in writing.[12]

Where notice of abandonment is properly given the assured is not prejudiced by the refusal of the insurer to accept it, but the notice is irrevocable after acceptance, express or implied, and acceptance is a conclusive admission of liability for the loss.[13]

When an insurer receives valid notice of abandonment, he is entitled to stand in the place of the assured as to the subject-matter of the policy;[14] hence, the effect of a proper notice of abandonment is to transfer the rights (including the right to any freight earned subsequently to the accident) formerly possessed by the assured to the insurer, and such transfer dates back to the time of the accident.[15] If a ship is carrying the owner's goods, the insurer is entitled to reasonable remuneration for the carriage of the goods subsequent to the casualty causing the loss.[16]

If after payment of the loss the vessel arrives safe, she is treated as having been abandoned, and becomes the property of the insurers.[17]

Total loss of freight   Different considerations apply to a total loss of chartered freight. On a claim against underwriters for such a loss it is sufficient for the shipowner to show that before loading or in the course of the contemplated voyage the ship has sustained damage which prevents it from commencing or continuing the voyage, and that a prudent owner, uninsured, would not incur the cost even of such temporary repairs as might be necessary to complete the voyage and earn the freight.[18]

---

1 'Abandoned' here means simply 'given up for lost,' not formally surrendered to the underwriters: *Court Line Ltd v R, The Lavington Court* [1945] 2 All ER 357.
2 Marine Insurance Act 1906, s. 60 (1).
3 Ibid, s. 60 (2) (i); *Kemp v Halliday* (1866) LR 1 QB 520.
4 As to taking general average contributions into account, see s. 60 (2) (ii); *Kemp v Halliday*, ante.
5 *Sailing Ship Blairmore Co v Macredie* [1898] AC 593.
6 Marine Insurance Act 1906, s. 60 (2); *Polurrian SS Co v Young* [1915] 1 KB 922 (capture of neutral ship by belligerent); *Marstrand Fishing Co v Beer* [1937] 1 All ER 158 (barratrous seizure of ship).
7 *British and Foreign Marine Insurance Co Ltd v Samuel Sanday & Co* [1916] 1 AC 650, HL.
8 *Rickards v Forestal Land, Timber and Rly Co* [1942] AC 50, [1941] 3 All ER 62. For the facts, see para. 27.13, ante.
9 Marine Insurance Act 1906, s. 62 (1), (8). Notice of abandonment is also unnecessary where, at the time when the assured receives notice of the loss, the insurer could not possibly benefit if notice were given to him (ibid, s. 62 (7)). See also *Roura and Forgas v Townend* [1919] 1 KB 189.
10 Marine Insurance Act 1906, s. 62 (2).
11 Ibid, s. 62 (3).
12 Ibid, s. 62 (2).
13 Ibid, s. 62 (4)–(6).
14 Ibid, s. 63.
15 Ibid. See *Barclay v Stirling* (1816) 5 M & S 6.
16 Ibid, s. 63 (2).
17 *Houstman v Thornton* (1816) Holt, NP 242.
18 *Carras v London and Scottish Assurance Corpn* [1936] 1 KB 291; *Kulukundis v Norwich Union Insurance Society* [1937] 1 KB 1, [1936] 2 All ER 242.

Adjustment of Losses

27.25   The settlement between the assured and the insurer is styled the adjustment, and is usually settled on behalf of the parties by their brokers. If an insurer settles with the broker, the former is, according to Lloyd's rules, discharged as against the claims of the assured; but at law this rule has not been fully recognised, nor, unless it can be shown that the assured was aware of the custom, is it likely that in future the courts will act on it.[1]

---

1 *Todd v Reid* (1821) 4 B & Ald 210; *Bartlett v Pentland* (1830) 10 B & C 760; but see *Stewart v Aberdein* (1838) 4 M & W 211.

27.26 *On ship* As to the amounts allowed (in the absence of express provision in the policy):

1. In the case of *partial loss* to the ship, the insurers will have to pay the cost of repairs less customary deductions,[1] which once meant that they would pay two-thirds of the expenditure on the repairs, the other third being an arbitrary amount supposed to be equivalent to the gain obtained by the owner by the substitution of new materials and work for old. But on a first voyage they usually had to pay the whole. If the ship is not repaired, or only partially repaired, the assured is entitled to indemnity for the reasonable depreciation arising from the unrepaired damage; but he cannot recover more than if the ship had been repaired.[2]

2. In the case of a *total loss*, if the policy is a valued policy, the amount payable is fixed in the policy. If the policy is unvalued, the amount payable is the full insurable value of the ship at the commencement of the risk;[3] which includes outfit, stores, provisions, money advanced for seamen's wages, together with the cost of insurance.[4] In the case of a steamer, "ship" includes machinery, boilers and coals, etc.[4]

---

1 Marine Insurance Act 1906, s. 69 (1).

2 Ibid, s. 69 (2), (3).

3 Ibid, s. 68. The sum recoverable is called the measure of indemnity, each insurer being liable for such proportion of the measure of indemnity as the amount of his subscription bears to the value fixed by the policy or to the insurable value (ibid, s. 67).

4 Ibid, s. 16 (1); Sch. I, r. 15.

27.27 *On goods*[1] In the case of:

1. A total loss of goods, when the policy is:

   i) unvalued, the assured may recover the insurable value, i.e. the prime cost of the goods, plus expenses of shipping and insurance charges;[2]

   ii) if valued, then the amount agreed.

2. A *partial* loss, subject to any agreement, where part of the goods is totally lost and the policy is valued, the sum recoverable is such proportion of the sum fixed by the policy as the insurable value of the part lost bears to the insurable value of the whole, ascertained as in the case of an unvalued policy.[3] Where part of the goods is lost and the policy is unvalued, the sum recoverable is the insurable value of the part lost.[4]

Where all or part of the goods arrive damaged, the assured is entitled to such proportion of the sum fixed (in the case of a valued policy), or of the insurable value (in the case of an unvalued policy), as the difference between the gross sound and damaged values at the place of arrival bears to the gross sound value.[5]

---

1 The term 'goods' means goods in the nature of merchandise, and does not include personal effects or provisions and stores for use on board. In the absence of any usage to the contrary, deck cargo and living animals must be insured specifically and not under the general denomination of goods (Marine Insurance Act 1906, Sch. I, r. 17).

2 Ibid, s. 16 (3).

3 Ibid, s. 71 (1).

4 Ibid, s. 71 (2).

5 Ibid, s. 71 (3). As to the meaning of 'gross value,' see ibid, s. 71 (4).

27.28 *General average loss* Unless the policy expressly provides to the contrary, where the assured has incurred a general average[1] expenditure or suffered a general average sacrifice, he may recover from the insurer without enforcing his rights of contribution.[2]

Again, if the assured has paid or is liable for any general average contribution, he is, subject to any special terms of the policy and to the limit of the sum insured, entitled to be indemnified to the full amount of his general average contribution or to a proportionate part, depending on whether the subject-matter liable to contribution is or is not insured for its full contributory value.[3] The same rule obtains where the assured is owner of the different interests, although in such a case there could be no contribution in fact.[4]

In the absence of express stipulation, the insurer is not liable for any general average loss or contribution, which was not incurred for the purpose of avoiding a peril insured against.[5]

---

1 See paras. 23.25, et seq., ante, where the meaning of 'general average' is given.

2 Marine Insurance Act 1906, s. 66 (4).

3 Ibid, s. 73. The insurer's liability for salvage charges must be determined on

the like principle Ibid). See para. 27.10 (7), as to mode of assessing amount
payable under a valued policy for a general average loss.
4 Ibid, s. 66 (7).
5 Ibid, s. 66 (6).

27.29 *Successive losses* Unless the policy otherwise provides, an
insurer is liable for successive losses, even though the total
amount may exceed the sum insured; but a partial loss, not made
good, followed by a total loss under the same policy, can only be
treated as a total loss.[1] The same rule applies where the
subsequent total loss is not covered by the policy, because
payment for the previous partial loss would involve indemni-
fication for an expenditure which could never be made.[2]

---

1 Marine Insurance Act 1906, s. 77.
2 *British and Foreign Insurance Co v Wilson Shipping Co* [1921] 1 AC 188.

---

8. Subrogation

27.30 Where the insurer pays for a total loss either of the whole or in
the case of goods of any apportionable part, he becomes entitled
to the interest of the assured in the subject-matter insured, *and* is
subrogated to all his rights and remedies therein. Where an
insurer pays for a partial loss, he acquires no title to the
subject-matter insured, or such part of it as may remain, but is
subrogated to the assured's rights and remedies therein, in so far
as the assured has been indemnified by payment.[1] However, in
Yorkshire Insurance Co Ltd v Nisbet Shipping Co Ltd,[2] it was
held that where insurers paid the assured the full value of a ship
at the time of the loss and subsequently the assured brought
proceedings against the Canadian Government and received an
agreed sum which exceeded that paid by the insurers owing to
the devaluation of the pound against the dollar, the insurers
could not recover under s. 79 anything more than they had paid.

Thus, the insurer is subrogated to the rights of the assured
only to the extent to which he has insured, the assured being
entitled to benefit to the extent to which he has left himself
uninsured. The following case will serve as an illustration:

The owners of a schooner insured her for £1,000 under a
policy stating her value to be £1,350. The schooner was totally
lost in a collision with a steamship, and the insurers, having
paid the £1,000, sued the steamship owners and recovered
£1,000, which was found to be the value of the schooner in the

action. *Held:* that the owners of the schooner were entitled to be treated as their own insurers for £350, and, therefore, the £1,000 must be divided between them and the insurers in the proportion of their respective interests, viz., $\dfrac{350}{1350}$ and $\dfrac{1000}{1350}$.[3]

On the other hand, if the ship is valued in the policy at less than the real value, and a proportion of the loss is recovered by the assured from the owners of another vessel in a collision action in which both ships were held to blame, and such proportion is based on the real or higher value, the underwriters who have paid a *total* loss will be entitled to the whole sum recovered, up to the amount paid by them on the policy.[4] The same principle applies where underwriters are liable for a *partial* loss under a valued policy; they are entitled to deduct the full amount recovered by the assured from third persons in respect of that loss.[5]

Where property is insured for its full value and a subsequent and subsidiary 'increased value' policy is taken out with other insurers and both policies are paid in full on a total loss occuring, the whole of the salvage, if it does not exceed the amount covered by the primary policy, belongs to the original insurers. It might be different if by the terms of the primary policy the assured had reserved a right to effect a further insurance for increased value.[6]

---

1 Marine Insurance Act 1906, s. 79. See further as to subrogation, para. 26.03, ante.
2 [1962] 2 QB 330, [1961] 2 All ER 487. But where insurers, having paid out the assured, are given an assignment of the assured's rights against third parties, the insurers are entitled to bring such action in their own name and may recover more than 100 per cent. of their loss: *Compania Colombiana de Seguros v Pacific Steam Navigation Co* [1964] 1 All ER 216, [1965] 1 QB 101. Cf. *Lucas v Export Credits Guarantee Department* [1974] 2 All ER 889, [1974] 1 WLR 909, HL; see para. 26.03, ante.
3 *The Commonwealth* [1907] P. 216; and see s. 81.
4 *Thames and Mersey Marine Insurance Co v British and Chilian SS Co* [1915] 2 KB 214; affd. [1916] 1 KB 30, CA.
5 *Goole etc Towing Co v Ocean Marine Insurance Co* [1928] 1 KB 589.
6 *Boag v Standard Marine Insurance Co* [1937] 2 KB 113, [1937] 1 All ER 714. See para. 27.20, ante, as to contribution between insurers in cases of double insurance.

---

9. Return of the premium

27.31   In the absence of fraud or illegality on the part of the assured or his agents:

1. Where the consideration for the payment of the premium totally fails the premium becomes returnable to him;

2. Where the consideration partially fails, a proportionate part is returnable, but only if the premium is apportionable and there is a total failure of any apportionable part of the consideration.[1]

Thus the premium, or a part of it, is returnable:

1. If the policy is void or is avoided by the insurer from the commencement of the risk;[2]

2. If the subject-matter insured, or an apportionable part of it, is never subjected to the risk;[3]

3. If the assured had no insurable interest at any time during the currency of the risk unless the policy was a contract of wagering.[4]

When the assured:

1. Over-insures on an unvalued policy, a proportionate part of the premium is returnable.[5]

2. Over-insures by double insurance a proportionate part of the several premiums is returnable, except when the double insurance is effected knowingly by the assured.

When the policies have been effected at different times, no premium is returnable in respect of any earlier policy which has borne the entire risk, or on which a claim has been paid in respect of the full sum insured.[6]

---

1 Marine Insurance Act 1906, s. 84 (1), (2).
2 Ibid, s. 84 (3) (a).
3 Ibid, s. 84 (3) (b). But if insured 'lost or not lost,' the fact that, unknown to the insurer, the ship had in fact arrived in safety at the date of the conclusion of the contract to insure, does not entitle the assured to a return of premium (ibid).
4 Ibid, s. 84 (3) (c). The expectation of acquiring an interest will prevent the policy being a wager in marine insurance. See s. 4 (2) (a).
5 Ibid, s. 84 (3) (e).
6 Ibid, s. 84 (3) (f).

---

10. Warranties

27.32 By a warranty the assured undertakes that some particular thing shall or shall not be done, or that some condition shall be fulfilled, or he affirms or negatives the existence of a particular state of facts.[1] Lord Mansfield has stated:

'A warranty in a policy of insurance is a condition or contingency, and unless that be performed there is no contract; it is perfectly immaterial for what purpose a warranty is introduced, but being inserted the contract does not exist, unless it is literally complied with'.[2]

A warranty, therefore, when once introduced must be exactly complied with, whether it be material to the risk or not, otherwise, subject to any express provision in the policy, the insurer will be discharged from the date of the breach of warranty, though the loss had nothing whatever to do with it,[3] and though the breach of warranty arose owing to events beyond the control of the warrantor.[4] A warranty may be:

1. Express, or
2. Implied.

If express, it must be inserted in or incorporated by reference into the contract.[5]

If, owing to a change of circumstances, the warranty no longer applies to the circumstances of the contract, or if it is rendered unlawful by legislation, a non-compliance with it is excused.[6] Where a warranty has been broken, it is of no avail for the assured to remedy the breach and comply with the warranty before loss; but the breach may be waived by the insurer.[6]

A representation is a statement by the assured to the insurer regarding the proposed risk, but it is not an integral part of the contract itself. If made, and if material, it must be substantially complied with.[7] It seems then to differ in effect from a warranty in this, that whereas a misrepresentation if untrue entitles the insurer to avoid the policy only if it is material, a warranty avoids the contract under any circumstances; and further, that whereas substantial compliance is sufficient in the case of a representation, strict compliance is needed for a warranty.[8]

---

1 Marine Insurance Act 1906, s. 33.
2 *De Hahn v Hartley* (1786), 1 TR 343 at 345.
3 Marine Insurance Act 1906, s. 33.
4 *Hore v Whitmore* (1778) 2 Cowp. 784.
5 Marine Insurance Act 1906, ss. 33 and 35.
6 Ibid, s. 34.
7 *De Hahn v Hartley* (1786) 1 TR 343 at 345.
8 The word 'warranty' has not in insurance law the meaning it bears in general contract law. See para. 7.08, ante.

27.33 *The more usual express warranties are—*

1. To sail on a given day;
2. That the vessel is safe on a particular day. This is complied with if the vessel is safe at any time on that day, though at the hour when the policy is signed she has been lost;[1]

3. To sail with convoy;

4. That the ship is neutral. This implies a condition that she shall be neutral at the commencement of the risk, and that, as far as the assured can control the matter, she will remain neutral during the risk, and will carry the proper papers;[2]

5. That the goods are neutral; which implies that they are neutral owned, and, so far as the assured can control the matter, that they will be carried to a neutral destination by a neutral ship.[2]

---

1 Marine Insurance Act 1906, s. 38.
2 Ibid, s. 36.

27.34   *The implied warranties are—*

1. In a voyage policy, that at the commencement of the voyage the ship shall be seaworthy for the purpose of the particular adventure.[1] If the policy contemplates a voyage in different stages, involving different or varied risks, it will suffice if, at the commencement of each distinct stage, she is seaworthy in view of the risks to be encountered on the next stage.[2] In a time policy there is no implied warranty of seaworthiness at any stage of the adventure;[3] but where, with the privity of the assured, the ship is sent to sea in an unseaworthy state, the insurer is not liable for any loss attributable to unseaworthiness. This means, however, the particular unseaworthiness of which the assured had knowledge, and if a ship is unseaworthy in two respects, to one only of which the assured was privy, he can recover for a loss caused by the other.[4]

2. In a voyage policy attaching whilst a ship is in port, an implied warranty that she is reasonably fit, at the commencement of the risk, to encounter the ordinary perils of that port.[5]

3. In a voyage policy on goods, there is an implied warranty that at the commencement of the voyage the ship is not only seaworthy as a ship, but also that she is reasonably fit to carry the goods. But in a policy on goods or other movables, there is no implied warranty that the goods or movables are seaworthy.[6]

4. That the venture is a lawful one, and will, so far as the assured can control it, be carried out in a lawful manner.[7]

There is no implied warranty as to the nationality of a ship, or that her nationality shall not be changed during the risk;[8] but if a ship is expressly warranted neutral there is an implied condition that, so far as the assured can control the matter, she shall be properly documented.[9]

Those sections of the Unfair Contract Terms Act 1977 which

govern negligence liability, liability arising out of contract and unreasonable indemnity clauses do not apply to contracts of insurance.[10]

---

1 Marine Insurance Act 1906, s. 39 (1). A ship is seaworthy if she is reasonably fit to encounter the ordinary perils of the seas in view of the adventure insured (ibid), s. 39 (4)). Cf. Carriage of Goods by Sea Act 1924, para. 23.18, ante.

2 Marine Insurance Act 1906, s. 39 (3); and see *Greenock SS Co v Maritime Insurance Co* [1903] 2 KB 657. See also para. 23.04, ante.

3 Marine Insurance Act 1906, s. 39 (5).

4 *Thomas v Tyne and Wear SS Freight Insurance Association* [1917] 1 KB 938.

5 Marine Insurance Act 1906, s. 39 (2).

6 Ibid, s. 40. See *Daniels v Harris* (1875) LR 10 CP 1.

7 Ibid, s. 41.

8 Ibid, s. 37.

9 Ibid, s. 36 (2).

10 Unfair Contract Terms Act 1977, s. 1 and Sch. 1, para. 1 (a). See generally para. 3.15, ante.

Part IX

Competition

Chapter 28

Monopolies and restrictive trade practices

1. The common law

28.01 The attitude of the common law to monopolies and restrictive trade practices has varied from time to time. Attempts by the Crown since the time of Edward III to claim the right to grant monopolies were challenged by the Courts [1] and the Statute of Monopolies[2] confined the Crown's prerogative of granting monopolies to letters patent in favour of inventors.

Contracts tending to create a monopoly by eliminating competition, restricting output and regulating prices and wages have in certain cases been held to be in illegal restraint of trade and void, particularly where they purported to be unrestricted in point of time and did not reserve a right to the parties to withdraw.[3] But the growing reluctance of the courts to declare contracts void on grounds of public policy had the effect that few agreements were upset on this ground. In *A-G of Australia v Adelaide Steamship Company*,[4] Lord Parker said:

> 'It is clear that the onus of showing that any contract is calculated to produce a monopoly or enhance prices to an unreasonable extent will lie on the party alleging it, and that if the Court is satisfied that the restraint is reasonable as between the parties, this onus will be no light one.'

It was thus held that a price-maintenance agreement between producers was not necessarily in unreasonable restraint of trade[5] and a similar agreement between manufacturers and a retailer could be enforced either directly by action[6] or by the use of 'stop-lists' and other forms of coercion.[7] On the other hand a manufacturer could not enforce resale price conditions by action against anyone with whom he had not directly contracted.[8]

---

1 *Case of Monopolies* (1602) 11 Co Rep. 84b.
2 (1624) 21 Jac. 1, c. 3. See para. 29.01, post.
3 *Hilton v Eckersley* (1856) 6 E & B 47; *Evans v Heathcote* [1918] 1 KB 418;

Kores Manufacturing Co Ltd v Kolok Manufacturing Co Ltd [1959] Ch 108, [1958] 2 All ER 65. As to restraint of trade, see para. 6.10, ante.
4 [1913] AC 781, 796. See also *North Western Salt Co v Electrolytic Alkali Co* [1914] AC 461.
5 *English Hop Growers, Ltd v Dering* [1928] 2 KB 174.
6 *Palmolive Co of England Ltd v Freedman* [1928] Ch 264.
7 *Thorne v Motor Trade Association* [1937] AC 797. Cf. *Mogul SS Co Ltd v McGregor Gow & Co* [1892] AC 25.
8 *Dunlop Pneumatic Tyre Co Ltd v Selfridge & Co Ltd* [1915] AC 847. See para. 4.03, ante.

2. The Monopolies and Mergers Commission

Appointment of Commission

28.02   The Monopolies and Restrictive Practices (Inquiry and Control) Act 1948, the first of a series of 'anti-trust laws,' established the Monopolies and Restrictive Practices Commission, now known as the Monopolies and Mergers Commission,[1] consisting of not less than ten and not more than twenty-seven members.[2] The Department of Prices and Consumer Protection appoints one of the members Chairman.[3] The general duty of the Commission is to investigate and report upon matters referred to it by the Department. The 1948 Act applied only to monopoly in the supply of goods but by the Monopolies and Mergers Act 1965, the Commission's jurisdiction was extended to cover the supply of services and proposed mergers of companies that may lead to monopoly.

1 Fair Trading Act 1973, s. 4 and Sch. 3.
2 Ibid, s. 4, as amended by the Monopolies and Mergers Commission (Increase in Membership) Order 1977, S.I. 1977 No. 2081.
3 Fair Trading Act 1973, Sch. 3.

Monopoly references

28.03   The Fair Trading Act 1973 created the new office of Director General of Fair Trading.[1] One of the Director's duties is to review commercial activities and bring to the attention of the Department monopoly situations and uncompetitive practices.[2] Either the Director or the Secretary of State may make a monopoly reference if it appears to them that a monopoly position exists[3] as respects:

a) the supply of goods of any description; or

b) the supply of services; or

c) the export of goods of any description from the United Kingdom either generally or to any particular market.

The Commission may then investigate and report unless the monopoly arises from an agreement registrable under the Restrictive Trade Practices Act 1976.[4]

---

1 See generally para. 19.01, ante.
2 Fair Trading Act 1973, s. 2.
3 Ibid, ss. 50 and 51.
4 Ibid, s. 10 (2), as amended by the Restrictive Trade Practices Act 1976, s. 44, Sch. 5.

Conditions of monopoly

28.04 The conditions to which the Act applies are deemed to prevail:

a) in relation to the supply of goods, if *either* at least one-quarter of all the goods of that description which are supplied in the United Kingdom or any part thereof are supplied by or to any one person (or by or to two or more persons if they are interconnected bodies corporate or so conduct their affairs whether by agreement or not as to prevent, restrict or distort competition), *or* any agreements or arrangements (whether legally enforceable or not) have the result that goods of that description are not supplied at all in the United Kingdom or any part thereof;[1]

b) in relation to the supply of services of any description, if *either* the supply of services of that description in the United Kingdom or any part thereof is, to the extent of at least one-quarter, by or for any one person (or by or for any two or more persons being interconnected bodies corporate or who so conduct their affairs whether by agreement or not so as to prevent, restrict or distort competition), *or* any agreements or arrangements (whether legally enforceable or not) are in operation the result of which is that in the United Kingdom or any part thereof services of that description are not supplied at all;[2]

c) in relation to exports, if:

i) at least one-quarter of the goods of the description in question which are produced in the United Kingdom are produced by one person or group of interconnected companies; or

ii) agreements affecting at least one-quarter of the goods of that description which are produced in the United Kingdom prevent, restrict or distort export from the United Kingdom or prevent, restrict or distort competition in relation to such export; or

iii) agreements affecting at least one-quarter of the goods of that description which are produced in the United Kingdom prevent, restrict or distort supply of goods of that description (whether from the United Kingdom or not) to a particular market or prevent, restrict or distort competition in relation thereto.[3]

In deciding whether one-quarter of all goods or services of a certain description is supplied or produced by a monopoly group the Department and the Commission are to apply such criterion (value, cost, price, etc.) as they think fit.[4]

---

1 Fair Trading Act 1973, ss. 6 and 9.
2 Ibid, ss. 7 and 9.
3 Ibid, s. 8.
4 Ibid, s. 10 (6) and (7).

Scope of references

28.05 The Commission may be required simply to investigate and report on the facts, viz. whether conditions of monopoly do in fact prevail, and if so in what manner and to what extent, and what is done by the parties concerned as a result of, or for the purpose of preserving those conditions. It may also be asked to report further whether the conditions or any of the things done operate or may be expected to operate against the public interest.[1] The reference may confine the investigation to specified practices of the parties, or to specified parts of the United Kingdom.[2] References may be varied.[3]

The Commission may be required to submit a report (i) on the general effect on the public interest either of practices of a specified class commonly adopted to preserve monopoly conditions or of any specified practices which may prevent, restrict or distort competition, or (ii) on the desirability of action to remedy mischiefs which result from monopoly conditions or conditions preventing or restricting competition.[4]

In deciding what is in the public interest all relevant matters are to be taken into account, particularly the need for maintaining and promoting effective competition in the United Kingdom, promoting the interest of consumers, purchasers and users of goods and services in the United Kingdom both in regard to price and variety, promoting the reduction of costs and the development of new techniques and products and facilitating the entry of new competitors into existing markets. Regard is also to be had to the balanced distribution of industry and employment in the United Kingdom and the need for promoting competition in markets outside the United Kingdom amongst producers of goods and services in the United Kingdom.[5]

1 Fair Trading Act 1973, ss. 48 and 49.
2 Ibid, s. 47.
3 Ibid, s. 52.
4 Ibid, s. 54.
5 Ibid, s. 84.

Proceedings and Reports of Commission

28.06 The Commission can require the attendance of witnesses and administer oaths. It can require the production of documents, estimates, returns or other information but not evidence which could not be required in ordinary civil proceedings.[1] After completing its investigations it submits its Report which must deal with the question referred to it and give reasons and a survey of the general position to facilitate a proper understanding of the matter. Where the reference is not confined to fact-finding it must consider whether any and if so what action is needed to remedy any mischief which it finds.[2] In the case of an equality of votes the Chairman has a casting vote.[3] A dissenting member can require a statement of his dissent and the reason for it to be included in the report.[4] The Department of Prices and Consumer Protection must lay the report before each House of Parliament unless it is contrary to the public interest to publish any part of it.[5] The Commission in reporting must consider how far it is practicable to exclude any matter which relates to the private affairs of an individual or specifically to the affairs of a body of persons when publication might seriously and prejudicially affect their interests.[6]

A monopoly reference must specify a time limit for making the report and if this is not observed the reference lapses. Extensions may be allowed.[7]

1 Fair Trading Act 1973, s. 85. See also s. 81.
2 Ibid, s. 54.
3 Ibid, Sch. 3, Part II, para. 19.

4 Ibid, s. 82 (3).
5 Ibid, s. 83. It is doubtful if the whole report can now be suppressed.
6 Ibid, s. 82 (1).
7 Ibid, s. 55.

Action on reports

28.07   Before any action can be taken there must have been a reference not limited to investigation and report on the facts; the report must have been laid before Parliament, with or without omissions; and it must contain a finding that conditions of monopoly exist and that they or things done as a result of them or to preserve them operate or may be expected to operate against the public interest.[1] When these conditions are satisfied, power is given to the Department to make orders to remedy the mischief found to exist by the Commission and requiring existing agreements not to be carried out.[2] The Director General of Fair Trading may obtain undertakings from relevant parties to remedy or prevent adverse effects of monopoly.[3] The order may prohibit the withholding of, or threats to withhold, supplies or services, or the attaching of conditions to the supply of goods or services.

The order may also (i) declare it to be unlawful to discriminate in prices to be charged or to give other preferences; (ii) publish price lists or other information; (iii) regulate prices to be charged when the Department considers the prices charged to be against the public interest; (iv) forbid the acquisition of another person's business; (v) require the division of any trade or business.[4]

Contraventions of such an order do not give rise to criminal proceedings, but the Crown can bring civil proceedings for an injunction or for any other appropriate relief. And the absence of criminal liability is not to limit the right of private persons to bring civil proceedings in respect of any contravention or apprehended contravention.[5]

When the Director-General of Fair Trading obtains from relevant parties undertakings to desist from practices regarded by the Commission as having adverse effects, he is to keep under review the carrying out of the undertaking, to consider whether it requires to be varied or superseded and, if it is not being fulfilled, to give appropriate advice to the Department.[6]

1 Fair Trading Act 1973, s. 56.
2 Ibid, s. 90.

3 Ibid, s. 88.
4 Ibid, Sch. 8, Parts I and II.
5 Ibid, s. 93.
6 Ibid, s. 88.

Mergers

28.08   The Monopolies and Mergers Act 1965 contained provisions to refer proposed mergers of companies to the Monopolies Commission and special provision was made for proposed newspaper mergers. The law is now embodied in Part V of the Fair Trading Act 1973.

If as a result of the merger of two or more enterprises, *either* (i) monopoly conditions (as defined above) will prevail or will be strengthened, *or* (ii) the value of the assets taken over will exceed £5 million, the Department of Prices and Consumer Protection may refer the matter to the Commission for investigation and report.[1] If the Commission find that the merger will operate against the public interest, the Commission must consider what action ought to be taken and may include recommendations as to such action in their report.[2] The Commission's report must be made within such period not exceeding six months as may be specified by the Department or within such further time not exceeding three months, as the Department may allow.[3] If the Commission reports that a proposed merger operates against the public interest, the Department may order inter alia that it is unlawful to carry out the merger and, in order to prevent action being taken which might prejudice the making of such an order, the Secretary of State may require that the merger be held up pending the Commission's report.[4]

1 Fair Trading Act 1973, s. 64. The conditions must prevail in a 'substantial' part of the United Kingdom.
2 Ibid, s. 72.
3 Ibid, s. 70.
4 S. 73, Sch. 8 and s. 74.

28.09   *Newspaper Mergers*   The transfer of a newspaper or of newspaper assets to a newspaper proprietor whose newspapers have an average circulation per day of publication amounting, with that of the newspaper concerned, to 500,000 or more copies, is unlawful and void unless the Secretary of State consents.[1] The Secretary of State must refer such a proposed transfer to the Commission (within one month of application for consent to transfer) except where he is satisfied that the newspaper concerned has an average circulation of less than 25,000 copies per day of publication or is satisfied that the newspaper is not economic as a going concern and *either* (i) that it is not to continue as a separate newspaper *or* (ii) that if it is, the case is one of urgency.

Where a reference is made to the Commission, the Commission must report (within three months or within such further time not exceeding three months as the Secretary of State may allow) whether or not the transfer may operate against the public interest 'having regard (amongst other things) to the need for accurate presentation of news and free expression of opinion'.[2] For the purposes of a reference to the Commission of a proposed newspaper merger, the Secretary of State may appoint three to five additional members to the Commission from a special panel maintained by the Secretary of State.[3]

---

1 Fair Trading Act 1973, s. 58.
2 Ibid, ss. 59 and 60.
3 Ibid, Sch. 3, para. 22.

---

3. Restrictive trade practices

The Restrictive Trade Practices Act 1956

28.10 This Act provided for the appointment of a Registrar of Restrictive Trading Agreements and the setting up of a Restrictive Practices Court. Certain agreements were made registrable and the Restrictive Practices Court could inquire into registered agreements and decide whether restrictions contained in them were contrary to the public interest. If it so found the agreement was void as regards those restrictions and the Court could make certain consequential orders. The office of Registrar was abolished by the Fair Trading Act 1973[1] and its functions transferred to the Director General of Fair Trading. The 1956 Act has been almost wholly superseded by the Restrictive Trade Practices Act 1976 and the Restrictive Practices Court Act 1976, which re-enact most of its provisions.

---

1 Fair Trading Act 1973, s. 94.

The Director General and the Court

28.11   The Director General is appointed by the Secretary of State and holds office for a term not exceeding five years but may be re-appointed. He is charged (inter alia) with the duty of compiling and maintaining a register of agreements made registrable by the 1976 Act and of taking proceedings before the Court in respect of registered agreements.[1]

The Director General determines where the Register is to be kept and its form. There must be a special section for information, publication of which would be contrary to the public interest and information as to secret processes. The rest of the register is open to inspection by the public who may obtain certified copies.[2]

---

1 Fair Trading Act 1973, ss. 1 and 94; Restrictive Trade Practices Act 1976, s. 1.
2 Ibid, s. 23.

28.12   The Court consists of five judges and not more than ten other members. The judges are three judges of the High Court nominated by the Lord Chancellor, one of the Court of Session, nominated by Lord President of the Court, and one of the Supreme Court of Northern Ireland nominated by the Lord Chief Justice of Northern Ireland. The nominated judges must give priority to the work of the Court which is a superior court of record. In the case of temporary absence or inability to act, other judges may be nominated.[1] The other members are appointed by the Crown on the nomination of the Lord Chancellor being persons with knowledge of or experience in industry, commerce or public affairs. Their appointment is for not less than three years and is renewable. They may resign at any time or may be removed by the Lord Chancellor for inability or misbehaviour or on the ground of any employment or interest incompatible with their functions.[2]

The number of members of the court, whether judges or other members, may be increased.[3]

The Court may sit anywhere in the United Kingdom, but its central office is in London.[4] It may sit as a single court or in divisions and either in private or in open court. For a hearing there must be a presiding judge and at least two other members, except that in a case involving only issues of law a judge alone may sit.[5] The opinion of the judge or judges sitting as members prevails on a point of law; otherwise decisions are by a majority of all members, the presiding judge having a casting vote. The judgment is delivered by the presiding judge.[6] The Lord Chancellor can make rules of procedure covering in particular the persons to be made respondents,[7] the place where the Court is to sit and the evidence which may be required or admitted. The rules can provide inter alia for preliminary statements, discovery of documents, and the administration of interrogatories. In regard to the attendance and examination of witnesses, production and inspection of documents and the enforcement of its orders the Court has all the powers of the High Court or Court of Session.[8] The Court proceeds as far as possible on documentary evidence, the proofs of witnesses and memoranda being exchanged and submitted to the Court before the hearing.[9]

The decision of the Court on questions of fact is final except in regard to proceedings under Part III of the Fair Trading Act 1973[10] but an appeal by way of case stated lies to the Court of Appeal on questions of law.[11]

---

1 Restrictive Practices Court Act 1976, ss. 1, 2 and 4.
2 Ibid, s. 3.
3 Ibid, s. 4.
4 Ibid, s. 6.
5 Ibid, s. 7.
6 Ibid.
7 Every person who has the right of audience at the trial of an action in the High Court or in the Court of Session has the like right at the hearing of an application to the Court whether sitting in England, Wales or Scotland: Restrictive Practices Court Act 1976, s. 8.
8 Ibid, s. 9.
9 *Re Chemist's Federation Agreement* [1958] 3 All ER 448; LR 1 RP 43.
10 See paras. 19.09–19.11, ante.
11 Restrictive Practices Court Act 1976, s. 10.

Registration of agreements

28.13 Subject to exceptions later referred to, all agreements[1] are registrable if (1) they are made between two or more persons carrying on business in the United Kingdom[2] in the production or supply of goods or in the application to goods of any process of manufacture; and (2) restrictions[3] are accepted by two or more parties in respect of:

a) the prices to be charged, quoted or paid for goods supplied, offered or acquired, or for the application of any process of manufacture to goods;

b) the prices to be recommended or suggested as the prices to be charged or quoted on resale;

c) the terms or conditions on or subject to which goods are to be supplied or acquired or any such process is to be applied to goods;

d) the quantities or descriptions of goods to be produced, supplied or acquired;

e) the process of manufacture to be applied to any goods, or the quantities or descriptions of goods to which any such process is to be applied; or

f) the persons or classes of person, to, for, or from whom, or the areas or places in or from which, goods are to be supplied or acquired, or any such process applied.[4]

By statutory instrument, the Secretary of State may apply the registration provisions of the 1976 Act to any class of 'information agreement'.[5] An 'information agreement' is an agreement for the furnishing of information on prices charged, prices to be recommended, terms of supply, costs, quantities or descriptions of goods, processes of manufacture, or persons or places supplied.

---

1 This includes arrangements not intended to be enforceable: Restrictive Trade Practices Act 1976, s. 43 (1). And see *Re British Basic Slag Ltd's Agreements* [1963] 2 All ER 807, CA, where Diplock LJ followed the words of Cross J: '... all that is required to constitute an arrangement is that the parties to it shall have communicated with one another in some way and that as a result of the communication each has intentionally aroused in the other an expectation that he will act in a certain way.'

2 The addition of other parties does not affect the position. Where a trade association is a party, the agreement is treated as if it were made between or restrictions accepted by all the members: Restrictive Trade Practices Act 1976, s. 8. If specific recommendations are made by a trade association to its members, the agreement for the constitution of the association is deemed to include a term that members will comply with them: s. 8 (2) and (3). See *National Federation of Retail Newagents Booksellers and Stationers v Registrar of Restrictive Trading Agreements* [1972] 2 All ER 1269, [1972] 1 WLR 1162, HL.

3 An agreement which confers privileges only on those complying with conditions is equivalent to acceptance of restrictions: Restrictive Trade Practices Act 1976, s. 6 (3).

4 Restrictive Trade Practices Act 1976, s. 6.

5 Ibid, s. 7.

Excepted matters

28.14 In determining whether agreements are registrable certain restrictions are to be disregarded under section 9 and certain agreements are excepted from registration under section 28. The most important exceptions and exemptions are:

1. In agreements for the supply of goods or for the application of any process of manufacture, terms relating exclusively to the goods supplied or processed are to be disregarded. But this does not apply where two or more suppliers or processors or two or more customers accept restrictions, unless this is done in pursuance of a registered agreement or is exempt from registration.[1]

2. An agreement for the supply of goods or information between two persons neither of whom is a trade association is exempt from registration if no other person is a party and the only restrictions accepted or provision for the furnishing of information are:

    a) by the party supplying the goods, in respect of the supply of goods of the same description to other persons; or

    b) by the party acquiring the goods, in respect of the sale or acquisition for sale of other goods of the same description.[2]

In *Re Austin Motor Co Ltd's Agreement*,[3] it was held that where a manufacturer enters into a series of identical bipartite agreements with each distributor and dealer, these are exempt from registration unless there is evidence of an agreement or 'gentlemen's agreement' that the distributors and dealers will all be treated alike.

Other disregarded restrictions and excepted agreements include terms as to complying with British Standards or as to conditions of employment, agreements made under certain statutes or relating to patents, designs and the use of trade marks, agreements for exchange of information as to processes and agreements relating exclusively to exports or trade outside the United Kingdom.[4]

The Secretary of State may make an order exempting from registration certain agreements of importance to the national economy and any of a number of Ministers may make an order exempting from registration agreements designed to prevent or restrict price increases or to secure reductions in prices.[5]

It seems that the Acts have no application to agreements conferring rights or interests on the Crown which might be affected by registration.[6]

---

1 Restrictive Trade Practices Act 1976, s. 9 (3) and (4). See *Re Cadbury Schweppes Agreement* [1975] 2 All ER 307, [1975] 1 WLR 1018.

2 Restrictive Trade Practices Act 1976, Sch. 3, para. 2.

3 [1958] Ch 61, [1957] 3 All ER 62. This is now doubtful. The court can look at all the circumstances. *Schweppes Agreement* [1965] 1 All ER 95, [1965] 1 WLR 157; *Automatic Telephone and Electric Co Ltd v Registrar of Restrictive Trading Agreements* [1965] 1 All ER 206, [1965] 1 WLR 174 CA;

Re Crane Makers Association's Agreement [1965] 2 All ER 561, [1965] 1
WLR 917.
4 Restrictive Trade Practices Act 1976, s. 28 and Sch. 3. Also s. 18.
5 Ibid, ss. 29 and 30.
6 *Re Automatic Telephone and Electric Co Ltd's Application* [1963] 2 All ER
302, [1963] 1 WLR 463, CA.

Registration procedure

28.15 The particulars to be furnished are the names and addresses of
the parties and the whole of the terms of the agreement, but
regulations may provide for excluding certain matters of detail.[1]
An agreement which has become registrable remains so
notwithstanding subsequent variation or determination and
particulars of the variation or determination must be furnished
to the Registrar.[2]

Where the agreement in question is in writing the original or a
true copy must be furnished, otherwise a memorandum must be
produced.[3] The time within which registration must be effected
is normally before the date on which any relevant restriction
accepted under the agreement takes effect and in any case within
three months of the agreement.[4]

The Restrictive Practices Court has power to order the
register to be rectified by the variation or removal of particulars
and may also declare whether an agreement is registrable or
not.[5]

1 Restrictive Trade Practices Act 1976, ss. 24 and 27.
2 Ibid, Sch. 2.
3 Ibid, para. 3.
4 Ibid, para. 5.
5 Ibid, s. 26.

Enforcement of registration

28.16 The Director General may give notice to persons or trade
associations who he has ground to suppose are or may be parties
to a registrable agreement requiring them to say whether they
are parties and if so to register particulars.[1] After giving such
notice he may apply to the Restrictive Practices Court for an
order that the person (or an officer of the body corporate) attend
and be examined on oath.[2] There are penalties for failure to
comply with a notice and for furnishing false particulars

knowingly or recklessly or wilfully altering, suppressing or destroying documents.[3] If particulars of a registrable agreement are not duly furnished, the agreement is void in respect of all relevant restrictions accepted thereunder, and it is unlawful for any party to the agreement carrying on business in the United Kingdom to enforce it in respect of such restrictions. The Restrictive Practices Court, on application by the Director General, may make an order restraining a party from enforcing the agreement in respect of any relevant restrictions.[4]

---

1 Restrictive Trade Practices Act 1976, s. 36.
2 Ibid, s. 37.
3 Ibid, s. 38.
4 Ibid, s. 35.

Investigation by Restrictive Practices Court

28.17 The function of the Court is to declare whether or not any of the restrictions which make an agreement registrable are contrary to the public interest.[1] Application is made by the Director General. A party against whom an Order has been made by the High Court can also apply after two years.[2] Where the restrictions are found to be contrary to public policy they are void and the Court may make an order restraining the parties from giving effect to or enforcing or purporting to enforce the agreement in respect of those restrictions or from making any other agreement to the like effect.[3] The Court may discharge any previous declaration or order and make a new one. Applications to discharge can only be brought by leave which will not be given unless the Court is satisfied of prima facie evidence of a change of circumstances.[4] The House of Lords in *Associated Newspapers v Registrar of Restrictive Trading Agreements*,[5] held that all agreements entered on the register, whether subsisting or determined, are referable to and justifiable by the Restrictive Practices Court. But, if a registered agreement has been determined in respect of all relevant restrictions before proceedings have been taken, the Director General at his discretion may decline to take such proceedings. Moreover, on the representation of the Director General, the Secretary of State may discharge the Director General from taking proceedings where the relevant restrictions accepted under a registered agreement are 'not of such significance as to call for investigation' by the Restrictive Practices Court. The Director General may also refrain from taking proceedings if he thinks it proper to do so having regard to any directly applicable EEC provision and any authorisation or exemption granted in connection with it.[6]

---

1 Restrictive Trade Practices Act 1976, s. 1 (3).
2 Ibid, Sch. 4, para. 5.
3 Ibid, s. 2 (2). By s. 5, the Court may decline or postpone the exercise of its powers having regard to the operation of Article 85 of the Treaty of Rome or exemptions granted under that Article. Generally, s. 5 makes it clear that all the requirements of the 1976 Act continue to apply irrespective of the operation of Article 85 which prohibits practices affecting trade between EEC countries which distort competition within the EEC. For an outline of EEC competition law see *Chitty on Contracts* (24th edn) Vol. 2, 836–855.
4 Restrictive Trade Practices Act 1976, s. 4 (4).
5 [1964] 1 All ER 55, [1964] 1 WLR 31, HL.
6 Restrictive Trade Practices Act 1976, s. 21.

Public interest

28.18 There is a presumption that any restriction is contrary to the public interest. To rebut it the Court must be satisfied of one or more of the following circumstances:[1]

a) That it is reasonably necessary to protect the public against injury;

b) That the removal of the restriction would deny to the public as purchasers, consumers or users of goods, other substantial benefits;

c) That it is reasonably necessary to counteract restrictive action by any one person not a party to the agreement;

d) That it is reasonably necessary to enable the parties to negotiate fair terms with a monopolistic supplier or customer;

e) That its removal would be likely to have a serious and persistently adverse effect on the general level of unemployment in an area;

f) That export business might be substantially affected;

g) That the restriction is reasonably required to maintain another restriction which is found not to be contrary to public policy;

h) That the restriction does not restrict or discourage competition to any material degree and is not likely to do so.

The Court must first of all be satisfied that the restriction can be brought within one or more of these subsections. Then it must also be satisfied that the restriction is not unreasonable, having regard to the balance between those circumstances and any detriment to the public which may result from the operation of the restrictions.

---

1 Restrictive Trade Practices Act 1976, s. 10.

28.19 1) *Protection of public against injury.* The first ground on which a restrictive agreement may be justified was considered in *Re Chemists' Federation Agreement (No. 2).*[1]

> The objects of the Federation were that proprietary medicines should be sold to the public only through registered pharmacists. The main arguments in support of this policy were that without the restriction some retail chemists might be driven out of business and that some injury to the public might result from sale by other retailers. It was *held* that the protection which the restriction was supposed to afford was not reasonably necessary and that the removal of the restriction would not deprive the public of substantial benefit or enjoyment. Accordingly the restrictions were declared contrary to public policy.

Delivering the judgment of the Court, Devlin J said this as to what was 'reasonably necessary':

> 'We have to ask ourselves whether a reasonable and prudent man who is concerned to protect the public against injury would enforce this restriction if he could. He would not do so unless he was satisfied, first, that the restriction afforded an adequate protection and, secondly, that the risk of injury was sufficiently great to warrant it. ... We find that the protection which the existence of this restriction is supposed to afford is not reasonably necessary because the risk of injury is too slight to justify so wide a restriction and because, if the risk were greater than we think it is, the restriction affords no real protection against it.'

2) *Denial to the public of substantial benefits.* This ground has been the one most frequently relied on in many of the cases that have been contested before the Restrictive Practices Court. For example, in *Associated Newspapers Ltd v Registrar of Restrictive Trading Agreements:*[2]

> Restrictions were imposed on new entrants into the newsagency trade. It was said that if the restrictions were discontinued, the influx of new entrants would cause existing newsagents to lose profits and to restrict delivery services. The argument was rejected as a 'gloomy prophecy' and the agreement declared void.

A successful attempt to rely on the same ground was made in *Re Net Book Agreement, 1957*:[3]

> Publishers agreed not to permit the retailing of 'net books' below their published prices. The court accepted that if the agreement was abolished, resale price maintenance in such books would cease, and the public would suffer because it would lead to fewer stockholding booksellers, higher overall prices, and fewer new titles. The agreement was upheld.

In few price-fixing agreements has the court been convinced by the argument that termination would lead to substantial deterioration in quality or to a curtailment of research and development.[4] But while the court has several times stated as a general view that a free market is preferable to price stabilisation, a price-fixing agreement was upheld in *Re Black Bolt and Nut Association's Agreement*:[5]

> The Association's members manufactured 90 per cent. of the black bolts and nuts, carriage bolts and nuts and railway fastenings used in the UK, in some 3,000 standard sizes. The Association recommended prices at which members would sell their products, subject to certain discounts and rebates. The court upheld the restrictions, mainly because the prices recommended were reasonable, also because purchasers were saved the expense of 'going shopping,' i.e. enquiring of several manufacturers to find out the lowest price.

3) *To counteract restrictive action by others.* This paragraph has not yet been pleaded.

4) *To negotiate fair terms with a monopoly.* This has been pleaded in two cases where the preponderant purchaser was the Central Electricity Generating Board—*Re Water-tube Boiler-makers' Association's Agreement*[6] and *Re Associated Transformer Manufacturers' Agreement.*[7] In neither case were the restrictions as to minimum tenders held to be justified. In the latter case, the court said that in order to justify restrictions on this ground, it must be shown that without them they would be unable to obtain terms comparable with those paid or charged by other buyers or sellers who had not got preponderant bargaining power. In a later case, *Re National Sulphuric Acid Association's Agreement*,[8] UK manufacturers formed a joint buying organisation, agreeing not to buy sulphur otherwise than through this body. The members relied for a large part of their supplies of sulphur on one American supplier who had in the past forced up the price of sulphur. The restrictions accepted by the association's members were held by the court to be justified.

5) *Avoidance of unemployment.* This was relied on in *Re Yarn Spinners' Agreement*:[9]

The members of the Yarn Spinners' Association agreed not to sell yarn at prices lower than those fixed in the agreement. The court accepted that the effect of ending the scheme would be to raise the level of unemployment. However, there were countervailing detriments to the public in the maintenance of a higher price for yarn. High prices were a handicap in the export trade and they encouraged an excess of capacity. Although the agreement was justified under s. 21 (1) (e), of the 1956 Act (s. 10 (1) (e) of the 1976 Act), this was outweighed by detriment to the public of higher prices; and the agreement was held to be void.

6) *The protection of exports.* This ground has been relied on in several cases but was only successfully relied on in *Re Watertube Boilermakers' Association's Agreement:*[10]

7) *Restrictions necessary for the maintenance of other proper restrictions.* If parties have justified a price-fixing agreement under, say, para. (b), this para. may enable them to justify reasonable uniform conditions of sale.[11]

8) *Restrictions not discouraging competition to a material degree.* This was a new ground introduced by the Restrictive Trade Practices Act 1968.[12]

---

1 [1958] 3 All ER 448, LR 1 RP 75. See also *Re Motor Vehicle Distribution Scheme Agreement* [1961] 1 All ER 161, [1961] 1 WLR 92; and *Re Tyre Trade Register Agreement* [1963] 1 All ER 890, [1963] 1 WLR 367.
2 [1961] 3 All ER 428, [1961] 1 WLR 1149.
3 [1962] 3 All ER 751, [1962] 1 WLR 1347.
4 But see *Re Permanent Magnet Association's Agreement* [1962] 2 All ER 775, [1962] 1 WLR 781, where the court held that the provisions in the Association's rules for establishing a minimum tender price were essential for the continuation of joint research, which had already shown beneficial results. See also *Re Distant Water Vessels Development Scheme* [1966] 3 All ER 897, [1967] 1 WLR 203.
5 [1960] 3 All ER 122, [1960] 1 WLR 884; followed in *Re Cement Makers' Federation Agreement* [1961] 2 All ER 75, [1961] 1 WLR 581; and see *Re Standard Metal Window Group's Agreement* [1962] 3 All ER 210, [1962] 1 WLR 1020.
6 [1959] 3 All ER 257, [1959] 1 WLR 1118.
7 [1961] 2 All ER 233, [1961] 1 WLR 660.
8 [1963] 3 All ER 73, LR 4 RP 169.
9 [1959] 1 All ER 299, [1959] 1 WLR 154.
10 [1959] 3 All ER 257, [1959] 1 WLR 1118.
11 *Re Black Bolt and Nut Association's Agreement* [1960] 3 All ER 122, [1960] 1 WLR 884.
12 S. 7.

4. Services

28.20 The Fair Trading Act 1973 made provision for bringing restrictive agreements relating to services and information agreements relating to services within the restrictive practices legislation and these provisions have now been re-enacted in Part III of the Restrictive Trade Practices Act 1976.[1] 'Services' do not include the application to goods of any process of manufacture or services under an employment contract but do include engagements whether professional or not, which for gain or reward are undertaken and performed other than for the production and supply of goods.[2] The Secretary of State may by statutory instrument order that the Act shall apply to agreements and information agreements relating to restrictions on or information about charges for, terms and conditions of supply, extent and scale of supply, form and manner of supply of services and the persons or classes of persons to be supplied with services.[3] In the case of a services supply association, agreements will be regarded as having been made between the members.[4] No account is to be taken of any term which relates exclusively to services supplied under the agreement containing the term nor is account to be taken of terms by which parties agree to observe standards approved by the British Standards Institution or prescribed or adopted by some other body approved by the Secretary of State. As with goods, restrictive agreements and information agreements relating to services are deemed to be contrary to the public interest unless the Restrictive Practices Court find that they satisfy a set of criteria which reproduce those prescribed by s. 10 for goods.[5] The Restrictive Trade Practices Act 1977 is designed to ensure that agreements between banks and financial institutions for the provision of loans and credit are exempt from registrations so long as restrictions accepted under them are directed to the maintenance of the security. Information agreements are similarly exempted.

---

1 Restrictive Trade Practices Act 1976, ss. 11–20.
2 Ibid, s. 20.
3 Ibid, ss. 11, 12 and 17. Most commercial service agreements have been brought within the Act. Many professional services are exempt by Sch. 1 of the Act. Sch. 3 excepts other services. See also *Re Ravenseft Properties Ltd's Application* [1978] 1 QB 52, [1977] 1 All ER 47 (covenants in leases rarely restrictions on services).
4 Ibid, s. 16.
5 Ibid, s. 19. See para. 28.18, ante.

5. Resale price maintenance

Collective enforcement prohibited

28.21 It is unlawful for two or more[1] suppliers to make any agreement or arrangement to withhold supplies from dealers who do not observe resale[2] price conditions;[3] or to offer them supplies only on less favourable terms than those applicable to other dealers; or to deal only with wholesalers who undertake to operate such restrictions. Similarly it is unlawful for dealers to agree to withhold orders from or discriminate against suppliers who do not enforce resale price maintenance.[4] An agreement for the exaction of penalties is likewise unlawful.[5] These provisions do not affect an agreement between seller and buyer to which no third person is a party where the undertakings are confined as regards the buyer to the goods sold and as regards the seller to goods of the same description.[6] The sanction for these sections is not criminal proceedings but a civil action. The Crown can sue for an injunction or other appropriate relief.[7]

---

1 Interconnected bodies corporate or partners count as one: Resale Prices Act 1976, s. 8 (2).
2 Selling includes letting on hire-purchase: ibid, s. 7 and Sch. 1, para. 1 (2).
3 This includes conditions as to discount and allowances in part exchange: ibid, s. 6.
4 Ibid, ss. 1, 2 (1).
5 Ibid, s. 2 (2). A recommendation by one dealer or supplier to others is as unlawful as if there were an agreement: s. 3. An association is in the same position as an individual for this purpose: s. 4.
6 Ibid, s. 5.
7 Ibid, s. 25.

Individual enforcement

28.22 Subject to restrictions considered below where goods are sold by a supplier subject to a resale price condition, the condition can be enforced by the supplier against any person not party to the sale who has notice of the condition as if he had been party thereto.[1] This right does not apply against a person who did not buy the goods for resale in the course of business or against one who derives title from such a person. Nor does it apply to sales pursuant to an order of a court or by way of execution or distress. Nor does this provision permit the enforcement of restrictions which have been declared by the Restrictive Practices Court to be contrary to the public interest.[2] An injunction granted under the section can extend to any goods of the supplier concerned and not merely goods of the same description.[3]

---

1 Resale Prices Act 1976, s. 26 (2). If the dealer has 'notice' of the existence of the restriction, it is not necessary that he should know all its terms: *Goodyear Tyre and Rubber Co (Great Britain) Ltd v Lancashire Batteries Ltd* [1958] 3 All ER 7, LR 1 RP 22. Contra common law: see para. 4.03, ante.
2 Resale Prices Act 1976, s. 26 (4).
3 Ibid, s. 26 (5).

Resale Prices Act 1976

28.23 The Resale Prices Act 1964 imposed restrictions on contractual and other means of maintaining minimum resale prices. The 1964 Act was repealed but re-enacted in substance and consolidated with other legislation in the Resale Prices Act 1976. Subject to a claim for exemption and powers given to the Restrictive Practices Court by the Act, any term of a contract for the sale of goods by a supplier to a dealer, or relating to such a sale, is void so far as it provides for the establishment of minimum prices to be charged on the resale of goods in the UK.[1] This prohibition applies to patented goods as it applies to other goods.[2] Moreover, subject to the exemption provisions of the Act, it is made unlawful for supplies to be withheld from a dealer or for there to be discrimination against a dealer on the ground that he has sold or is likely to sell such goods below their recommended resale price.[3] Withholding goods is, however, permitted if the dealer has been using such goods as 'loss leaders'.[4] Breach of the Act gives rise not to criminal proceedings, but to civil proceedings at the instance either of a dealer or of the Crown.[5]

---

1 Resale Prices Act 1976, s.9.
2 Ibid, s. 10.
3 Ibid, s. 11.
4 Ibid, s. 13.
5 Ibid, s. 25.

28.24 Upon an application made by the Director, a supplier of goods in question or a trade association of such suppliers, the Court may grant exemption on one or other of the grounds specified in the Act. There are five gateways through one or other of which the class of goods must pass for the Court to be able to grant exemption. An exemption order may be made if it appears to the

Court that in default of a system of maintained minimum resale prices applicable to the goods:

a) the quality of goods available for sale, or the varieties of the goods so available, would be substantially reduced to the detriment of the public as consumers or users of those goods; or

b) the number of establishments in which the goods are sold by retail would be substantially reduced to the detriment of the public as such consumers or users; or

c) the prices at which the goods are sold by retail would in general and in the long run be increased to the detriment of the public as such consumers or users; or

d) the goods would be sold by retail under conditions likely to cause danger to health in consequence of their misuse by the public as such consumers or users; or

e) any necessary services actually provided in connection with or after the sale of the goods by retail would cease to be so provided or would be substantially reduced to the detriment of the public as such consumers or users;

and in any case that the resulting detriment to the public as consumers or users of the goods in question would outweight any detriment to them as such consumers or users (whether by the restriction of competition or otherwise) resulting from the maintenance of minimum resale prices in respect of the goods.[1]

In *Re Chocolate and Sugar Confectionery Reference*[2] the manufacturers' application for exemption from the general ban on resale price maintenance was dismissed on the ground that the evidence did not show there was likely to be a substantial shift of trade to supermarkets and self-service grocers with a consequent closure of a large number of small confectionery shops. However, the Restrictive Practices Court has declared that ethical and proprietary drugs are exempted goods under the Resale Prices Act 1964.[3] The Court considered that removal of r.p.m. would cause a substantial reduction in the services provided by pharmaceutical wholesalers and a reduction in the number of chemists' shops. The Registrar did not oppose an exemption order in favour of books.

---

1 Resale Prices Act 1976, s. 14.
2 [1967] 3 All ER 261, [1967] 1 WLR 1175.
3 *Re Medicaments Reference (No. 2)* [1971] 1 All ER 12, [1970] 1 WLR 1339.

Chapter 29

Patents and designs

1. Introduction

29.01 There is a common law right inherent in the Crown to grant a subject the monopoly of a trade or manufacture. This right was restricted by the Statute of Monopolies 1623–4[1] but the prerogative of the Crown to grant letters patent for the sole working of new trades or manufactures to the true inventor for a period of fourteen years or under[2] was preserved by s. 6 of that Act which enacted as follows:

> 'Provided also that any declaration before mentioned shall not extend to any letters-patent and grants of privilege for the term of fourteen years or under, hereafter to be made, for the sole working or making of any manner of new manufactures within this realm, to the true and first inventor and inventors of such manufactures, which others at the time of making such letters-patent and grants shall not use, so as also they be not contrary to the law nor mischievous to the state, by raising prices of commodities at home, or hurt of trade, or generally inconvenient; the said fourteen years to be accounted from the date of the first letters-patent or grants of such privilege hereafter to be made; but that the same shall be of such force as they should be if this Act had never been made, and of none other.'

This section of the Statute of Monopolies which formed the basis of all modern grants of letters-patent sustained no alteration in principle during the intervening three hundred years. To be patentable an invention must be machinery, an industrial process or a product. A patent is essentially an agreement between the State and an inventor by which the State confers a monopoly of exploitation on the inventor for a limited period in exchange for the inventor making full disclosure of the invention. An inventor may, if he wishes, keep an invention secret but then the only protection given by the law is an action for breach of confidentiality against anyone who has broken an express or implied agreement to maintain secrecy.[3] The various statutory provisions dealing with the machinery of patent practice were consolidated in two enactments, the Patents Act 1949 and the Registered Designs Act 1949.

1 21 Jac. I, c. 3.
2 Later sixteen years or more; now twenty years.
3 See *Yates Circuit Foil Co v Electrofoils Ltd* [1976] FSR 345.

2. Patents

29.02 The Patents Act 1949 remains in force for patents granted before the commencement of the Patents Act 1977[1] which introduces a new framework for patent law, in large part designed to fulfill international obligations.

1 Patents Act 1977, Sch. 1.

New domestic law

29.03 This is embodied in Part I of the Patents Act 1977. A patent may be granted for an invention which is new, involves an inventive step and is capable of industrial application.[1]
Novelty An invention is new if it does not form part of 'the state of the art.'[2] This comprises all matter available to the public at any time before the priority date of the invention.[3] It also includes matter published in an application for another patent on or after the priority date if that other patent has an earlier priority date. Disclosure within six months before the filing of the application is to be disregarded if it was obtained unlawfully or made in breach of confidence or resulted from display at an international exhibition. If an invention is a substance for use in the treatment or diagnosis of humans or animals the fact that the substance itself is part of the art will not deprive it of novelty if the use of the substance does not form part of the state of the art.[4]
Inventive step This is present if the invention is not obvious to anyone skilled in the art. For this purpose the contents of other patent applications after the priority date are to be disregarded.[5]
Industrial application This is present if the invention can be

made or used in any kind of industry, including agriculture. A method of treatment or diagnosis for humans or animals is not regarded as capable of industrial application but a substance for use in such procedures can be capable of industrial application.[6]

---

1 Patents Act 1977, s. 1.
2 Ibid, s. 2.
3 This is normally the date of filing the application, ibid, s. 5. See also s. 15 and para. 29.06, post.
4 Ibid, s. 2.
5 Ibid, s. 6.
6 Ibid, s. 4.

29.04 *Matters excluded* A discovery, scientific theory, mathematical method, literary, dramatic, musical, artistic work, any other aesthetic creation, any scheme, rule, method for performing a mental act, playing a game, or doing business, a computer programme and the presentation of information are not inventions and cannot be patented. An invention involving such excluded matter can, however, be patented except in so far as it relates to excluded matter. Patents may not be granted for inventions the publication or exploitation of which would encourage offensive, immoral or anti-social behaviour nor for any variety of animal or plant nor for any biological process other than a micro-biological process.[1]

---

1 Patents Act 1977, s. 1. Some of these can be protected as registered designs or copyright if in suitable form, under the Plant Varieties and Seeds Act 1964 or under the law of confidence.

29.05 *Right to apply for and obtain a patent* A patent may be granted to the inventor or joint inventors or to anyone entitled under any rule of law, domestic or foreign, or treaty or enforceable agreement to the whole of the property in the invention or to successors in title. The inventor means the actual devisor of the invention.[1] Questions relating to entitlement to patents may be determined before or after grant by the comptroller of patents.[2]

The inventor has a right to be mentioned in every patent or published application for a patent.[3]

An invention made by an employee shall be taken to belong to the employer if it was made in the course of the employee's normal duties or of special duties assigned to him and such an invention might reasonably be expected to result or it was made in the course of duty and the employee's duties and responsibilities imposed a special obligation to further the interests of the employer's undertaking. Any other invention made by an employee will normally belong to the employee.[4] When an invention made by an employee belongs to the employer and is of outstanding benefit to him the employee may be compensated.[5] Any term in a contract which diminishes an employee's patent rights is to that extent unenforceable against him but this is not to affect any obligation of confidentiality.[6]

---

1 Patents Act 1977, s. 7.
2 Ibid, ss. 8, 9, 37, 38. Appeals from the comptroller to the Patents Court are governed by s. 97.
3 Ibid, s. 13.
4 Ibid, s. 39.
5 Ibid, ss. 40, 41.
6 Ibid, s. 42.

29.06 *Application for a patent* Every application must be in prescribed form, must be filed at the Patent Office and must contain a request for a patent, a specification describing the invention, a claim or claims and an abstract. The specification must disclose the invention sufficiently clearly and completely for it to be performed by anyone skilled in the art. The claims must define the matter for which protection is sought, must be clear and concise, must be supported by the description and must relate to one invention or several inventions so related as to form one inventive concept. The abstract is to give technical information, its publication does not form part of the art and the comptroller may reframe it if it is not adequate. Rules may prevent an applicant from restricting the availability or use of a micro-organism required for the performance of an invention. An application may be withdrawn before grant but a withdrawal may not be revoked.[1] An application may, however, be amended at any time before grant.[2]

The date of filing is normally the earliest date on which documents filed at the Patent Office indicate that a patent is sought, identify the applicants and describe the invention and the filing fee is paid.[3]

Subject to security considerations, the comptroller will after a prescribed[4] period publish the application unless it has already failed, omitting any disparaging, offensive, immoral or antisocial matter.[5] The comptroller will, on request, refer the application for preliminary and substantive examinations and searches to determine whether the application complies with the

Act.[6] Third parties may make written observation on applications to the comptroller.[7] The comptroller may prohibit or restrict the publication of information prejudicial to the defence of the realm or the safety of the public, and United Kingdom residents are forbidden to apply for a patent abroad unless they have applied for a patent in the United Kingdom and within six weeks no restrictive security directions have been given.[8]

If a decision that the application complies with the Act has not been given before the end of the prescribed period the application must be treated as refused.[9] Appeal lies to the Patents Court established by the Act within the Chancery Division.[10]

1 Patents Act 1977, s. 14. See s. 26 (para. 29.07, post) for patents not to be impugned for lack of unity.
2 Ibid, s. 19.
3 Ibid, s. 15.
4 Ibid, s. 123.
5 Ibid, ss. 16 and 22.
6 Ibid, ss. 17 and 18.
7 Ibid, s. 21.
8 Ibid, ss. 22, 23.
9 Ibid, s. 20.
10 Ibid, ss. 96, 97, 99.

29.07   *Grant and term of patent*   After grant the comptroller shall publish in the journal[1] a notice and also the specification, the names of the proprietor, inventor and any other matter he thinks proper. The term of a patent begins with the publication of the notice and lasts for twenty years unless renewed.[2] There is provision for the restoration of lapsed patents if application is made within one year after lapse, a general power to apply to amend the specification after grant and the comptroller may himself amend to acknowledge a registered trade mark. No one may impugn a patent on the ground that it lacks unity in that it contains more than one invention not so linked as to form one inventive concept. The proprietor of a patent may at any time by notice to the comptroller offer to surrender it.[3]

1 Patents Act 1977, ss. 24, 123.
2 Ibid, ss. 24, 25.
3 Ibid, s. 26–29.

29.08   *Property in patents and registration*   A patent or application for a patent is personal property and may be assigned, mortgaged, vested by operation of law and may be vested by the assent of personal representatives. Licences to work the invention may also be granted. All these transactions are void unless they are in writing signed by the parties, or in the case of a corporation signed on its behalf or sealed.[1] A register of patents is to be kept at the Patent Office to record the grant and other transactions relating to patents. Its contents are prima facie evidence but the register may be rectified. As between contending claimants to the property in or licence to work a patent the later claimant is entitled as against an earlier whose transaction is unregistered or for which no application for registration has been made.[2] Patents may be held in co-ownership and the comptroller may determine disputes as to ownership.[3] Restrictive conditions which purport to require a person supplied with a patented product or a licensee of a patent to acquire other things only from the supplier or licensor or to prevent them from being acquired elsewhere or which forbid the use of other products or processes are generally void. Supply contracts and licences relating to expired patents may be determined by three months written notice on either side.[4]

---

1 Patents Act 1977, s. 30.
2 Ibid, ss. 32–35.
3 Ibid, s. 36.
4 Ibid, ss. 44, 45.

29.09 *Licences as of right, compulsory licences and Crown use* At any time after the grant of a patent the proprietor may ask the comptroller to make an entry on the register that licences are to be as of right. Thereafter any person shall be entitled as of right to a licence on terms settled by agreement or failing that, by the comptroller. A licensee as of right may ask the proprietor to take steps to prevent infringement and, if he fails to do so, may take proceedings himself to make the proprietor a defendant.[1] At any time after three years from the grant any person may apply to the comptroller for a licence or for an entry that licences are to be as of right or if the applicant is a government department for the grant of a licence to a specified person. The grounds for such an application are either:

1. That the invention is not being commercially worked to the fullest extent that is reasonably practicable in the United Kingdom; or
2. That the demand for it is not being met on reasonable terms or is being met by importation; or

3. That its commercial working in the United Kingdom is being hindered by importation; or

4. That because of a refusal to grant licences an export market is not being supplied or that working of another invention which makes a substantial contribution to the art is hindered in the United Kingdom or that the development of industrial and commercial activity in the United Kingdom is unfairly prejudiced; or

5. That because of restrictions in licences already granted the manufacture, use or disposal of materials not within the patent is unfairly prejudiced.

If the comptroller is satisfied under any of these heads he may grant the application according to its terms. He may also adjourn the application when he thinks there has been insufficient time for commercial exploitation.[2] The powers of the comptroller are to be so exercised as to ensure that a patent is worked commercially to the fullest extent reasonably practicable in the United Kingdom, that the proprietor or inventor shall be reasonably remunerated and that anyone working or developing a patent in the United Kingdom is not unfairly prejudiced. He must take into account the nature of the invention, the length of time since the grant, the steps already taken to make use of it, the ability of a prospective licensee to work it to the public advantage and the financial risks involved.[3] In cases of monopoly or merger which involve patented products, on application by the Crown relief may be granted by the comptroller directing that an entry be made in the register that licences are to be as of right.[4] Any government department may use or authorise, without the consent of the proprietor of the patent, the use of any patented invention for the service of the Crown and there are special provisions for Crown use in a period of emergency.[5]

---

1 Patents Act 1977, s. 46.
2 Ibid, s. 48.
3 Ibid, s. 50.
4 Ibid, s. 51.
5 Ibid, ss. 55–59.

29.10   *Infringement*   This occurs when any person in the United Kingdom without the consent of the proprietor makes, disposes of, offers to dispose of, keeps for disposal, uses or imports a patented product. It is also infringement to use or offer for use a patented process when he knows or reasonably should know that its use would be an infringement. Moreover, there is infringement if a person offers to supply in the United Kingdom to a person other than a licensee or other entitled person any of the means, relating to an essential element of the invention, for working the invention when he knows or should know these means are suitable and intended for putting the invention into effect in the United Kingdom.

29.11   There is no infringement if what is done:

1. Is done privately;
2. For experiment;
3. In the extemporaneous preparation of a medicine for an individual in accordance with a medical or dental prescription;
4. Consists in the use of a product or process for the needs of a ship, aircraft hovercraft or vehicle which is temporarily or accidentally in the United Kingdom, its internal or territorial waters or airspace. The various means of transport must belong to some country other than the United Kingdom, that other country being a party to the 1883 Paris Convention for the Protection of Industrial Property.
5. Is the use of an aircraft exempted from seizure for patent claims by the Civil Aviation Act 1949 when the aircraft has lawfully entered the United Kingdom.[1]

---

1 Patents Act 1977, s. 60.

29.12   Civil proceedings for infringement may be brought in the High Court or by agreement of the parties before the comptroller. These may result in an injunction restraining apprehended infringement, an order to deliver up or destroy an infringing article, damages, an account of profits and a declaration. Damages and an account are not to be awarded for the same infringement. No damages are to be awarded or account ordered against a defendant who proves that he did not know and had no reasonable grounds for supposing that a patent existed. The fact that the word 'patented' or any similar word is on an article is not enough to give reasonable grounds unless the patent number appears also. When a patent is partially valid that part may be protected. Where a person makes serious and effective pre-parations to do an otherwise infringing act before the priority date (filing of application) he may do or continue to do that act and transmit his right to do so. The court or comptroller may certify that a patent was found to be valid in contested proceedings and in any subsequent proceedings if the party relying on validity is successful he will be entitled to heavier (solicitor and own client) costs. One co-owner or an exclusive licensee may bring infringement proceedings but an unregistered proprietor is not entitled to damages or an account unless the transaction or event under which he claims is registered within six months or it is shown that it was not practicable to register.[1] Where an application for a patent is published an applicant has the same right to damages for infringement as if the patent had been granted. Where a person makes groundless threats of infringement proceedings the person threatened may claim an injunction, a declaration and damages for any loss he has suffered. No action will lie for threats to bring proceedings for alleged infringement which is said to consist in making or importing a product for disposal or of using a process. Merely notifying the existence of a patent does not amount to a threat. Where a person has applied in writing to a proprietor for an acknowledgment that proposed action is not infringement and the proprietor has not replied the court or comptroller can make a declaration of non-infringement.[2]

1 Patents Act 1977, ss. 61–68.
2 Ibid, ss. 69–71.

29.13 *Revocation* The court or the comptroller may on application revoke a patent either unconditionally or where it is only partly invalid subject to it not being amended within a limited time. The grounds on which revocation may be ordered are:

1. The invention was not patentable;
2. The patent was not granted to the only person or persons entitled;
3. The specification did not disclose the invention sufficiently clearly and completely;
4. The matter disclosed in the specification extends beyond what is disclosed in the application;
5. The protection of the patent was extended by an amendment which should not have been allowed.

The comptroller may on his own initiative revoke a patent when it appears that it formed part of the state of the art or when a patent under domestic law and a European patent exist in respect of the same invention he may revoke the domestic patent.

In any revocation or infringement proceedings the comptroller may allow the specification to be amended but no amendment to an application or patent is to include added matter.[1]

1 Patents Act 1977, ss. 72, 73, 75, 76.

Provisions about International Conventions

29.14 These are embodied in Part II of the Patents Act 1977. They cover European Patents (UK) granted by the European Patent Office under the European Patent Convention and Community Patents also granted by the European Patent Office under the EEC Patent Convention.

European Patent (UK) A European Patent (UK) is in general treated as if it had been granted under domestic patent law ('patents under this Act') and the proprietor has the same rights and remedies as a domestic patentee. Amendments and revocations under the convention are to be treated as if made under the Act. There are special provisions for the authentic text to be that of the language in which proceedings were conducted in the European Patent Office and for translations. In certain circumstances an application for a European patent (UK) may be treated as an application for a domestic patent. The jurisdiction of the court or the comptroller to determine questions as to the right to a patent is subject to conditions as to residence of the parties, location of place of business or employment and agreement to accept or exclude jurisdiction which in turn may be subject to the rules of the relevant proper law.[1] There is provision for staying proceedings in United Kingdom courts when they have also been commenced in the courts of another contracting state and for the recognition of final decisions of competent authorities in other states unless the applicant shows that he was not notified of the proceedings or the decision is in conflict with one between the same parties in another contracting state.

No one is to carry on for gain the business of acting as a patent agent in relation to European patents unless their names are on the European list of agents.[2]

1 Patents Act 1977, ss. 77–83.
2 Ibid, s. 84.

29.15 *Community patents* All rights, powers, liabilities, obligations and restrictions created or arising under the Community Patent Convention shall have the force of law in the United Kingdom and there is power for the Secretary of State to make regulations to give effect to this. Any question as to the meaning or effect of the Convention or of any instrument made under it shall be treated as a question of law. There are complex provisions as to residence for the purpose of jurisdiction.[1]

---

1 Patents Act 1977, ss. 86–88.

29.16 *International applications for patents* An international application for a patent under the Patent Cooperation treaty is to be treated for many purposes as if it were an application for a domestic patent ('patent under this Act'). This ceases to be the case if the application is withdrawn or the United Kingdom designation is withdrawn except by error on the part of the Patent Office or other treaty institution or when the application is received late by the International Bureau owing to circumstances outside the applicant's control. Provision is made for countries to be declared 'Convention countries' by Order in Council.[1]

---

1 Patents Act 1977, ss. 89, 90.

29.17 *Patent agents* These carry on the business of acting for others in applying for patents. They must reside or have a place of business in the United Kingdom. They must be registered as such and if in partnership all members of the firm must be registered. In the case of companies formed after November 17th 1917 every director or managing member must be so registered. They do not commit offences under the Solicitors Act 1974 merely in carrying on proceedings before the comptroller or appeals under the Patents Acts.[1] A person must not act for gain in applying for European patents unless they are on the European list and European patent attorneys do not commit offences under the Solicitors Acts merely by so describing themselves.[2] The comptroller may refuse to deal as agents with persons whose names have been struck off the register, who have been suspended from practice, who have committed certain offences or who are acting without proper qualification.[3]

---

1 Patents Act 1977, s. 114.
2 Ibid, ss. 84, 85.
3 Ibid, s. 115.

Plant varieties

29.18 The Plant Varieties and Seeds Act 1964 grants breeders' rights for periods of fifteen to twenty-five years to the discoverer or breeder of a new plant variety. The Act is administered by a Controller with appeal to a Plant Variety Rights Tribunal.

3. Registered designs

29.19 *Design* means:

> 'features of shape, configuration, pattern, or ornament applied to any article by any industrial process or means, being features which in the finished article appeal to and are judged solely by the eye, but does not include a method or principle of construction, or features of shape or configuration which are dictated solely by the function which the article ... has to perform'.[1]

Designs are thus essentially ornamental.

Before a design can be registered, it must be new or original.[2] The effect of registration is to give the proprietor copyright in the registered design for five years from the date of registration. The proprietor is entitled to two extensions of five years each.[3] Damages cannot be awarded against innocent infringers.[4] To protect the proprietor the registered number of the design must be marked on the article.[4] A claim for a compulsory licence may be made at any time.[5] Government departments have rights similar to those relating to patents.[6] Applications made in convention countries give priority similar to that accorded to applications for patents.[7]

Statutory provision is made for the interrelation of registered designs and copyright.[8]

---

1 Registered Designs Act 1949, s. 1 (3).
2 Ibid, s. 1 (2).
3 Ibid, ss. 7, 8.
4 Ibid, s. 9.
5 Ibid, s. 10.
6 Ibid, s. 12, Sch. I.
7 Ibid, ss. 13–16.
8 Copyright Act 1956, s. 10; Design Copyright Act 1968. For Copyright see chap. 31, post.

4. Exclusion clauses

29.20 Those sections of the Unfair Contract Terms Act 1977 which govern negligence liability, liability arising out of contract and unreasonable indemnity clauses do not apply to any contract in so far as it relates to the creation or transfer or termination of any right in a patent, trade mark, copyright, registered design, technical or commercial information or other intellectual property.[1]

---

1 Unfair Contract Terms Act 1977, s. 1 and Sch. 1, para. 1 (c). See generally para. 3.15, ante.

Chapter 30

Trade marks, passing-off and trade libel

1. Introduction

30.01   At common law there is a right of action against any person for 'passing off' goods as those of another person; the usual method of 'passing off' is to adopt or to imitate the 'mark' which that other person generally applies to his goods for the purpose of identifying them. Trade marks have been protected by legislation which is now embodied in the Trade Marks Act 1938 and the general effect of the Act is that if a trade mark is *registered*, unauthorised use of the mark is conclusive evidence that the tort of 'passing-off' has been committed. This does not affect the common law with regard to other forms of passing-off and, therefore, the owner of an unregistered trade mark may still succeed in a claim for damages in a passing-off action even though not protected by the Act.[1]

---

1 Trade Marks Act 1938, s. 2.

---

2. Trade marks

30.02   A trade mark means 'a mark used or proposed to be used in relation to goods for the purpose of indicating, or so as to indicate, a connection in the course of trade between the goods and some person having the right either as proprietor or as registered user to use the mark, whether with or without any indication of the identity of that person'.[1] This definition does not apply to a 'certification trade mark' which means a mark registered or deemed to be registered under s. 37.[2]

A trade mark which is equally apt to describe the goods of other firms does not fulfil the definition and will not be registered.[3] Thus in *Re Wheatcroft Bros' Trade Marks*:[4]

the respondents had registered eleven variety names in respect of roses. The name was intended to be used not only for instances of the variety raised by the respondents but for all instances of the variety. *Held:* the register must be rectified by removal of the marks.

1 Trade Marks Act 1938, s. 68.
2 See para. 30.10, post.
3 *Yorkshire Copper Works Ltd v Registrar of Trade Marks* [1954] 1 All ER 570, [1954] 1 WLR 554, HL.
4 [1954] Ch 210, [1954] 1 All ER 110. See now Plant Varieties and Seeds Act 1964, under which such names are registrable (see para. 29.18, ante). See also *Ogen Trade Mark* [1977] RPC 529.

Registration

30.03 The main object of the Act is to fix the proprietorship of a trade mark; the registration of a person under the Act as proprietor of a trade mark gives him the exclusive right to the use of the trade mark upon or in connection with the goods for which it is registered and consequently if another person adopts this mark or an imitation of it, upon the same or analogous goods, the registered proprietor has a right of action for infringement, and in an action of 'passing off' (the two actions are usually combined) the adoption of a registered trade mark is conclusive evidence against the defendant. The underlying idea is that goods of different qualities but of apparent similarity should be clearly distinguished from one another in the interest both of the manufacturer and of the purchasing public. It differs thus from 'design' in that the trade mark is intended to indicate the origin of the merchandise whereas the design is primarily an artistic feature in the goods themselves.[1]

The register of trade marks is kept at the Patent Office under the control of the Comptroller-General of Patents, Designs and Trade Marks (referred to in the Act as the Registrar) and is divided into two parts: Part A and Part B.[2]

1 See para. 29.19, ante.
2 Trade Marks Act 1938, s. 1.

30.04 *Class A* A trade mark (other than a certification trade mark) can only be registered in respect of particular goods or classes of goods,[1] and to be registrable in class A must contain or consist of at least one of the following essential particulars:

1. The name of a company, individual or firm represented in a special or particular manner;
2. The signature of the applicant for registration or some predecessor in his business;
3. An invented word or invented words;
4. A word or words having no direct reference to the character or quality of the goods, and not being according to its ordinary signification a geographical name or a surname;[2]
5. Any other distinctive mark; but a name, signature, or word other than such as fall within (1), (2), (3) or (4) is not registrable except upon evidence of its distinctiveness.[3]

A colour scheme may be a trade mark.[4]

Registration in Part A gives the proprietor an exclusive right to use the trade mark.[5] After seven years the registration is presumed to be valid unless the registration was obtained by fraud, the mark is scandalous or likely to deceive or is contrary to law.[6]

---

1 Trade Marks Act 1938, s. 3. Thus it cannot be registered in respect of a repairing process (*Aristoc Ltd v Rysta Ltd* [1945] AC 68, [1945] 1 All ER 34).
2 An application to register 'Tastee Freez' as a trade mark for ice cream was refused as it was directly descriptive of the character and quality of the goods: *Re Tastee Freez International's Application* [1960] RPC 255. See also *Re Soflens Trade Mark* [1976] RPC 694; *Re Must Trade Mark* [1976] RPC 712.
3 Trade Marks Act 1938, s. 9 (1) (e).
4 *Smith, Kline and French Laboratories Ltd v Sterling-Winthrop Group* [1975] 2 All ER 578, [1975] 1 WLR 914.
5 Ibid, s. 4.
6 Ibid, ss. 11 and 13.

30.05 *Class B* A trade mark may be registered in Part B where it is capable, in relation to the goods in respect of which it is registered, of distinguishing goods with which the proprietor of the trade mark is or may be connected in the course of trade from goods in the case of which no such connection subsists, either generally or, where the trade mark is registered or proposed to be registered subject to limitations, in relation to use within the extent of the registration.[1]

The protection afforded by registration in class B is not so complete as that given by class A; and in any action for infringement, no relief of any kind will be granted if the infringer proves to the satisfaction of the court that the user complained of is not likely to deceive, or cause confusion, or to be taken as indicating a connection in the course of trade between the goods and some person entitled as proprietor or as registered user to use the mark.[2] There is no presumed validity after seven years in the case of class B.

---

1 Trade Marks Act 1938, s. 10 (1).
2 Ibid, s. 5.

30.06 *Prohibited marks* A trade mark which is likely to deceive or cause confusion, whether by reason of similarity to another mark or otherwise, or which is contrary to law or morality, cannot be registered; nor can any scandalous design.[1]

---

1 Trade Marks Act 1938, s. 11. See *Bass, Ratcliff and Gretton Ltd v Nicholson & Sons Ltd* [1932] AC 130, HL; *Re Smith Hayden & Co Ltd* (1945) 63 RPC 97; *Re Stredóceska Fruta Narodni Podnik's' Application* [1968] 2 All ER 913, [1969] 1 WLR 36; *Re Hallelujah Trade Mark* [1976] RPC 605; *Re Zing Trade Mark* [1978] RPC 47.

30.07 *Registered users* A person who is not the proprietor of a trade mark may, on the joint application of himself and the proprietor, be registered as a registered user thereof in relation to goods with which he is connected in the course of trade.[1]

---

1 Trade Marks Act 1938, s. 28.

30.08 *Disclaimers* If a trade mark (a) contains any part not separately registered by the proprietor as a trade mark; or (b) contains matter common to the trade or otherwise of a non-distinctive character, the Registrar or the Department of Trade or the Court, in deciding whether the trade mark shall be entered or remain on the register may require as a condition of its being on the register that the proprietor disclaim any right to the exclusive use of any part of the trade mark or to the exclusive use of any such matter or that the proprietor shall make any such other disclaimer as is considered necessary.[1]

---

1 Trade Marks Act 1938, s. 14.

30.09 *Associated trade marks* The same proprietor may have what are called associated trade marks, viz., identical or similar marks for certain classes of goods;[1] he may also split up a mark, using its component parts as separate trade marks, or have a series of marks for a number of similar goods.[2]

---

1 Trade Marks Act 1938, s. 23 (2).
2 Ibid, s. 21.

30.10 *Certification trade marks* Where goods are certified by any person in respect of origin, material, mode of manufacture, quality or other characteristics, to distinguish them from other goods, a certification trade mark may be registered with the consent of the Department of Trade.[1] Accordingly, associations which examine or test particular kinds of goods and certify the result of their examination by marking the goods may register their marks as trade marks. Lloyds' Register (LR) on ship-building materials is an example of this. The privileges of the Cutlers' Company in relation to Sheffield goods are incorporated into the Act;[2] their register forms part of the general register; a similar arrangement is made for Manchester cotton goods, the marks of which are registered at 'The Manchester Branch'.[3]

---

1 Trade Marks Act 1938, s. 37, Sch. I.
2 Ibid, s. 38.
3 Ibid, s. 39.

30.11 *Defensive marks* Where a well-known trade mark, consisting of an invented word or words, is registered in respect of any goods, a defensive trade mark may be registered (notwithstanding that it is not used or proposed to be used) to prevent its user in relation to other goods, if such user is likely to be taken as indicating a connection in the course of trade between those other goods and the person entitled to use the mark in relation to the first-mentioned goods.[1]

---

1 Trade Marks Act 1938, s. 27; and see *Re Eastex Manufacturing Co Ltd's Application* [1947] 2 All ER 55, for the principles to be applied.

Procedure on registration

30.12 Any person claiming to be the proprietor of a trade mark who is desirous of registering the same must apply in writing to the registrar. There is a right of appeal from the decision of the registrar either to the Department of Trade or to the court at the option of the applicant.[1] After the application has been accepted, it is advertised by the registrar. Any person may within one month from the date of the advertisement give notice to the registrar of opposition to the registration of the mark stating the grounds of opposition. Thus, he may object that it resembles an existing trade mark or is not sufficiently distinctive.[2] The matter is decided by the registrar subject to appeal to the court.[2]

When the time for opposition has expired the trade mark is registered by the registrar as of the date of the application for registration, and a certificate is issued to the applicant.[3] The duration of registration of a trade mark is seven years but the registration may be renewed from time to time for fourteen years at a time on payment of the prescribed fees.[4]

If the proprietor does not use his trade mark for five years, unless such non-user is due to special circumstances in the trade, any one who is aggrieved may apply to the court to have it removed from the register.[5]

1 Trade Marks Act 1938, s. 17.
2 Ibid, s. 18.
3 Ibid, s. 19.
4 Ibid, s. 20.
5 Ibid, s. 26. As to special circumstances, see *Aktiebolaget Manus v RJ Pulwood and Bland Ltd* [1949] Ch 208, [1949] 1 All ER 205, CA.

Assignment

30.13 Subject to certain exceptions, registered trade marks (and some unregistered trade marks) are assignable and transmissible either in connection with the goodwill of a business or not, and in respect of all or some of the goods in respect of which it was registered.[1] The effect of transfer of a mark without the goodwill of a business will be that thenceforth the mark will be applied to goods of a different origin and perhaps made by a different process.[2] For this reason the registrar has power to direct advertisements and it may be that if as a result the trade mark would be deceptive, the assignment would not be valid.[3] The assignee of a trade mark is entitled to be registered as the proprietor.[4] A registered user cannot assign or transmit his right to use a trade mark.[5]

1 Trade Marks Act 1938, s. 22.

2 See *RJ Reuter & Co Ltd v Mulhens* [1954] Ch 50, [1953] 2 All ER 1160, CA (No. 4711 eau-de-Cologne).
3 Ibid at 1176. The use of the trade mark may also amount to a false trade description under the Trade Description Act 1968, s. 34. See para. 18.05, ante.
4 Ibid, s. 25.
5 Ibid, s. 28 (12).

Rectification

30.14 The register may be rectified by the registrar or by the court, either at the request of the proprietor or on the application of a person aggrieved.[1] In *Berlei (UK) v Bali Brassiere Co*:[2]

> The House of Lords agreed that a trade mark should be removed from the Register on the ground that it was likely to deceive or cause confusion and it was not necessary for the aggrieved persons to prove they had a reasonable chance of success in a passing-off action.

A fine may be imposed on a person for falsely representing a trade mark as registered[3] and any one authorised to use the Royal Arms in connection with his trade may take proceedings against a person in a similar trade using them without authority.[4]

Those sections of the Unfair Contract Terms Act 1977 which govern negligence liability, liability arising out of contract and unreasonable indemnity clauses do not apply to any contract in so far as it relates to the creation or transfer or termination of any right in a trade mark.[5]

The hallmarking of articles of gold, silver and platinum is governed by the Hallmarking Act 1973.

1 Trade Marks Act 1938, ss. 32–34.
2 [1969] 2 All ER 812, [1969] 1 WLR 1306, HL. But the House of Lords *held* in *General Electric Co v General Electric Co Ltd* [1972] 2 All ER 507, [1972] 1 WLR 729, HL, that a trade mark liable to cause confusion will not be expunged from the Register unless the likelihood of confusion existed before the original registration or arose subsequently as a result of blameworthy conduct by the registered proprietor.
3 Ibid, s. 60.
4 Ibid, s. 61; Patents Act 1949, s. 92, also imposes penalties. See also Trade Descriptions Act 1968, ss. 12, 13, para. 18.08 (d), ante.
5 Unfair Contract Terms Act 1977, s. 1 and Sch. 1, para. 1 (c). See generally para. 3.15, ante.

3. Trade names and passing-off

30.15   A person who uses a name or mark, even one which is not a registered trade mark, has at common law the right to prevent others from using the same or a similar name or mark in such a way as to deceive the public into thinking that the business carried on by those persons or the goods sold by them are his.[1] In general a man may trade under his own name unless he has a fraudulent purpose or the name has become identified with a well-known business. Certainly, he must not use abbreviations likely to deceive:

> Thus it was held that not only could the makers of the well-known 'Wrights Coal Tar Soap' prevent Mr. W. F. Wright from selling toilet preparations under styles such as 'Wrights Baby Powder' but an injunction would also be granted restraining him from *carrying on business* under any name of which 'Wright' or 'Wrights' formed part without clearly distinguishing his business from that of the plaintiffs.[2]

Similarly a word in common use may become so much connected in the public's mind with goods of a particular trader as to entitle that trader to protection. The burden is on the trader claiming protection to show that a descriptive term has acquired a secondary meaning so as to mean his goods and not merely goods of a class. In *Bollinger v Costa Brava Wine Co*:[3]

> Injunctions were granted preventing the defendant company from passing off Spanish wine as wine made in the Champagne district and from selling such wine under any name or description, including the word 'champagne'. The word 'champagne', though not associated with one producer only, was associated with a wine produced in the Champagne district of France.

The burden is less if the word in question is one which he has invented.[4] But even an invented word may lose its distinctive character.[5]

> Another method of 'passing-off' is by imitation of a distinctive get-up which a trader has used for his goods.[6] The question is whether a purchaser looking fairly at the goods without concealment of the marks would be likely to be deceived.[7]
>
> If there is no common field of activity and hence no possibility of confusion between two businesses there will be no passing-off.[8] A business carried on abroad may have a goodwill entitled to protection in this country, especially if it is carried on in a Common Market country.[9]

1 *Reddaway v Banham* [1896] AC 199. An injunction will be granted without proof of fraud.
2 *Wright, Layman and Umney Ltd v Wright* (1949) 66 RPC 149, CA. Cf. *Baume & Co v A. H. Moore* [1958] Ch 907, [1958] 2 All ER 113.
3 [1961] 1 All ER 561, [1961] 1 WLR 277. Followed in *John Walker & Sons v Henry Ost & Co Ltd* [1970] 2 All ER 106, [1970] 1 WLR 917. See also *University of Oxford v Pergamon Press Ltd* (1977) *Times*, October 19.
4 *Cellular Clothing Co v Maxton and Murray* [1899] AC 326, 343.
5 *Havana Cigar and Tobacco Factories Ltd v Oddenino* [1924] 1 Ch 179.
6 *White Hudson & Co v Asian Organisation* [1965] 1 All ER 1040, [1964] 1 WLR 1466.
7 *Payton & Co v Snelling, Lampard & Co* [1901] AC 308.
8 *Wombles v Wombles Skips* [1975] FSR 488.
9 *Maxim's Ltd v Dye* [1977] 1 WLR 1155.

4. Trade libel

30.16 Akin to passing-off are cases where one trader (orally or in writing) injures another trader by disparaging his property without using words defamatory of the trader himself. This is known as the tort of trade libel or injurious falsehood. Such statements are actionable if the plaintiff can prove:

1. That the statements are false and made to some person other than the plaintiff;
2. That they were published with malice; and
3. That they were calculated to produce and did produce actual damage.[1] But it is not necessary to prove actual damage if the words are calculated to cause pecuniary damage and either are published in writing or other permanent form,[2] or are calculated to damage the plaintiff in a trade or business carried on by him at the time of the publication.[3]

Similarly a false statement that a trader has ceased to carry on business is actionable if it is published maliciously and causes damage.[4]

In *Wilts United Dairies Ltd v Thomas Robinson Son and Co Ltd*:[5]

The defendants sold tinned milk manufactured by the plaintiffs, knowing that it was old and would have deteriorated. It was *held* that by so doing they were falsely representing that it was suitable for resale and the plaintiffs were entitled to damages.

1 *Ratcliffe v Evans* [1892] 2 QB 524.
2 E.g. broadcasting (Defamation Act 1952, ss. 1, 3 (2)).
3 Ibid, s. 3 (1).
4 *Joyce v Motor Surveys Ltd* [1948] Ch 252.
5 [1958] RPC 94.

Chapter 31

Copyright

1. Introduction

Copyright Act 1956

31.01 Copyright in new works is governed mainly by the Copyright Act 1956 which made substantial changes in the law. As regards works existing before the Act it may also be necessary to refer to earlier legislation, particularly the Copyright Act 1911.

Nature of copyright

31.02 Copyright is primarily 'the right to multiply copies' and, as a corollary, the right to prevent unauthorised persons from doing so.[1] But it means in fact much more for there are many ways in which one man may use the original work of another for his own advantage. Thus:

> A book may be dramatised; a drama may be performed in public; the performance of a musical work may be broadcast or recorded; the record in turn may be played in public; an architect's plans may be used to build a house; or a cartoon character may be reproduced as a toy.

Copyright is given in respect of literary, dramatic, musical and artistic works. A 'literary work' need not have any literary merit. A compilation is sufficient if it involves skill and painstaking labour.[2]

Protection is given not only to the author of original works but to the producers of sound recordings, cinematograph films, broadcasts, etc.

There can be no copyrights in immoral, scandalous, obscene or libellous works.[3]

---

1 *Walter v Lane* [1900] AC 539. There is no copyright in a live performance:

Apple Corps Ltd v Lingasong Ltd [1977] FSR 345. Lectures may be protected by an express or implied obligation of confidence: *Caird v Sime* (1887) 12 App Cas 326.

2 See e.g. *Football League Ltd v Littlewoods Pools Ltd* [1959] Ch 637, [1959] 2 All ER 546 (league fixtures used for football pools), and *Ladbroke (Football) Ltd v William Hill (Football) Ltd* [1964] 1 All ER 465, [1964] 1 WLR 273, HL (fixed odds betting coupons arranged in a certain general form).

3 *Glynn v Western Feature Film Co* [1916] 1 Ch 261.

Definition

31.03 The scheme of the Act is to define precisely what acts constitute infringement of copyright in different cases and copyright in relation to a work is defined as:

'the exclusive right, by virtue and subject to the provisions of this Act, to do, and to authorise other persons to do, certain acts in relation to that work in the United Kingdom or in any other country to which the relevant provision of this Act extends'.[1]

Various sections of the Act enumerate 'the acts restricted by the copyright' in a work of the description dealt with in the section.

Infringement thus consists of doing or authorising another to do any of the restricted acts without the licence of the owner.[2]

1 Copyright Act 1956, s. 1 (1); this definition is applied to copyright in sound recordings, etc., by s. 1 (4). 'Relevant provision' means the subsection conferring copyright: s. 1 (3).

2 Ibid, s. 1 (2).

Qualified persons

31.04 Copyright is given to individuals who are British subjects, British protected persons, citizens of the Republic of Ireland and to persons domiciled or resident in the United Kingdom or in other countries to which the relevant provision extends. It is also given to corporate bodies incorporated under the laws of any part of the United Kingdom or of another country to which the relevant provision extends.[1] Thus copyright generally does not depend upon where the work originated but upon the status of the person claiming it. Provision was made in the Act to extend it by Order in Council to the Isle of Man, the Channel Islands, colonies and dependencies and for applying it to countries which by a

Convention agree to afford similar treatment to works protected in this country.[2] Copyright may also be extended to works of international organisations such as the United Nations Organisation.[3]

There is Crown copyright in government publications.[4]

---

1 Copyright Act 1956, s. 1 (5).
2 Ibid, ss. 31, 32, 35. Thus, Copyright (International Convention) Orders apply the Act to countries that are members of the Berne Copyright Union or parties to the Universal Copyright Convention.
3 Copyright Act 1956, s. 33, and Orders made thereunder.
4 Copyright Act 1956, s. 39.

Ownership of copyright

31.05 Subject to contrary agreement the author of original literary, dramatic, musical and artistic works is entitled to the copyright. But where the work is made in the course of the author's employment under a contract of service or apprenticeship the employer is the person entitled. There are, however, two special rules:

i) Where the author is employed by a newspaper, magazine or periodical the proprietor is only entitled to copyright so far as it relates to publication in newspapers, etc.; in all other respects the author has the copyright;

ii) Where a photograph, a portrait, or an engraving is commissioned for money or money's worth the person commissioning it is entitled to the copyright.[1]

Anonymous works, pseudonymous works and works of joint authorship are subject to special rules.[2] Copyright is also given to the publisher of every published edition of any one or more literary, dramatic or musical works to prevent imitation of his typography.[3]

---

1 Copyright Act 1956, s. 4.
2 Ibid, s. 11, Sch. II, III.
3 Ibid, s. 15. This copyright lasts for only twenty-five years, as against the usual fifty years.

2. Original works

Literary, dramatic and musical works

31.06   Copyright is given in respect of every original literary, dramatic or musical work which is *unpublished* if the author was a qualified person at the time when it was made or for a substantial part of the time while it was being made.[1] If the work is *published*, copyright subsists in it or continues to subsist if, but only if:

i) it was first published in the United Kingdom or a country to which the section extends; or

ii) the author was a 'qualified person' when the work was first published; or

iii) the author had died before that time, but was a qualified person immediately before his death.[2]

Publication   A work is published if reproductions have been issued to the public. Performance is not publication nor is the issue of records, the exhibition of an artistic work, construction of a work of architecture or the issue of photographs or engravings of a work of architecture or of a sculpture. Except in so far as it may constitute an infringement of copyright, a publication which is merely colourable and not intended to satisfy the reasonable requirements of the public is to be disregarded.[3] No account is to be taken of any unauthorised publication.[4]

Duration   Copyright continues to subsist in a work for fifty years after the calendar year in which the author died. But if, before the death of the author, the work has not been published, performed in public, offered for sale in the form of records or broadcast, the period does not begin till the end of the calendar year when first one of these things is done to the work or an adaptation of it.[5]

Acts restricted   The acts[6] restricted by the copyright in a literary, dramatic or musical work are:

i) reproducing the work in any material form;

ii) publishing the work;

iii) performing the work in public;

iv) broadcasting the work;

v) causing the work to be transmitted to subscribers to a diffusion service;

vi) making an adaptation of the work;[7]

vii) doing in relation to an adaptation any of the acts specified in (i) to (v) above.[8]

Importation, sale and other dealings with offending articles also constitute infringements.[9]

---

1 Copyright Act 1956, s. 2 (1).
2 Ibid, s. 2 (2).
3 Ibid, s. 49 (2). 'Reproduction' is defined in s. 48 (1).
4 Ibid, s. 49 (3).
5 Ibid, s. 2 (3), (4).
6 Ibid, s. 2 (5). Acts in relation to a substantial part of a work are included: ibid, s. 49 (1). As to what is 'substantial,' see *Hawkes & Son (London) Ltd v Paramount Film Service Ltd* [1934] Ch 593 (a few bars of music substantial). But fair dealing for the purposes of reporting current events would not now be an infringement: Copyright Act 1956, s. 6 (3).
7 'Adaptation' means turning a non-dramatic work into a dramatic one or vice versa, translating a work or producing it in picture strips, or arranging or transcribing a musical work: Copyright Act 1956, s. 2 (6). Arranging or transcribing presupposes a conscious and deliberate process. Reproduction, however, by subconscious copying may be an infringement if the composer of the work was in fact familiar with the original work and there was some causal connection between the two works: *Francis, Day and Hunter Ltd v Bron* [1963] Ch 587, [1963] 2 All ER 16.
8 Ibid, s. 2 (5).
9 Ibid, s. 5.

Artistic works[1]

31.07 These include paintings, sculptures, drawings, engravings and photographs, irrespective of artistic quality; works of architecture including models for buildings; and other works of artistic craftsmanship.[2] Copyright subsists in published and unpublished works in similar circumstances to those affecting literary, dramatic and musical works. The duration is again fifty years from the end of the year of the author's death, but

i) in the case of an *engraving* not published before the death time runs from first publication;
ii) in the case of a *photograph* time runs in any case from first publication.

The acts restricted are:
i) reproducing the work in any material form;[3]
ii) publishing the work;
iii) including the work in a television broadcast;
iv) causing a television programme which includes the work to be transmitted to subscribers on a rediffusion service.

---

1 Copyright Act 1956, s. 3.
2 This does not include a suite of furniture: *George Hensher v Restawhile* [1976]

AC 64; but engineering drawings may be artistic works *LB (Plastics) Ltd v Swish Products Ltd* [1977] FSR 87.

3 Ibid, s. 3 (5). E.g. *King Features Syndicate (Incorporated) v O and M Kleeman Ltd* [1941] 2 All ER 403, [1941] AC 417 (dolls reproducing cartoon figure); *Dorling v Honnor Marine Ltd* [1965] Ch 1, [1964] 1 All ER 241, CA (boats and kits of boat parts designed from plans comprising the artistic work); *Merchant Adventurers v M Grew & Co* [1972] Ch 242, [1971] 2 All ER 657 (three-dimensional reproductions of drawings of electric light fittings). See also *Krisarts v Briarfine* [1977] FSR 557 (in a painting of a well known subject copyright consists in choice of viewpoint, balance of foreground, features in middle ground and figures).

Exempted dealings

31.08 Fair dealing with a literary, dramatic or musical work is permitted if it is for research or private study, or for purposes of criticism or review or for the purpose of reporting current events in a newspaper or periodical, accompanied by a suitable acknowledgment, or by means of broadcasting or in a film.[1] Reproduction for the purposes of a judicial proceeding (or a report thereof) is no infringement.[2] Recitation by one person in public of a literary or dramatic work accompanied by a suitable acknowledgment is not an infringement.[3] Nor is inclusion of a short passage in a collection for use in schools, provided certain conditions are fulfilled.[4] Where by virtue of an assignment or licence there is a right to broadcast a literary, dramatic or musical work, a reproduction in the form of a record or film may be made for the purpose of that broadcast. Such reproductions must be destroyed within twenty-eight days of their first use for broadcasting.[5]

Somewhat similar exemptions apply in relation to artistic works.[6] Painting, drawing, making an engraving of or photographing a sculpture, etc., which is permanently situated in a public place is no infringement, and works of architecture can be similarly treated.[7] An artistic work may be included in a film or television broadcast if it is only by way of background.[8] The author of an artistic work (who may not own the copyright) may reproduce parts of his earlier work as long as he does not repeat or imitate the main design.[9] Reconstruction of a building is not an infringement of copyright.[10]

Special exemptions cover copying by certain libraries.[11] Where records of a musical work have been made or imported for retail sale any manufacturer can make records for retail sale or for supply to a retailer on giving notice and paying a royalty fixed under the Act.[12] Double protection under this Act and the

Registered Designs Act 1949[1] is avoided.[13] Use of copyright material by teachers or in examination papers is protected.[14]

There is no royal prerogative to print or authorise others to print any material the printing of which would be a breach of copyright. In *Oxford University and Cambridge University v Eyre and Spottiswoode Ltd*:[15]

> Defendants, as Queen's printers, published the 'New English Bible: Gospel according to John,' which was admittedly a copy of the same gospel in the 'New English Bible,' published earlier by the plaintiffs. Defendants claimed the right to publish by virtue of a patent from the Crown which under the prerogative had the exclusive right to publish certain books including the Bible. *Held:* the prerogative right to grant exclusive rights to publish certain books was not a right to expropriate private copyright. The defendants had no right to publish 'New English Bible: Gospel according to John.'

---

1 Copyright Act 1956, s. 6 (1)–(13). The defence of 'fair dealing' is not confined to criticising a plaintiff's literary work but also covers criticism of the philosophy underlying the plaintiff's work: *Hubbard v Vosper* [1972] 2 QB 84, [1972] 1 All ER 1023, CA.
2 Ibid, s. 6 (4).
3 Ibid, s. 6 (5).
4 Ibid, s. 6 (6).
5 Ibid, s. 6 (7). These are known as 'ephemeral recordings.'
6 Ibid, s. 9.
7 Ibid, s. 9 (3), (4).
8 Ibid, s. 9 (5).
9 Ibid, s. 9 (9).
10 Ibid, s. 9 (10). As to the separate copyright in plans and buildings, see *Meikle v Maufe* [1941] 3 All ER 144.
11 Ibid, s. 7.
12 Ibid, s. 8. See *Chappell & Co Ltd v Nestlé & Co Ltd* [1960] AC 87, [1959] 2 All ER 701.
13 Ibid, s. 10, as amended by the Design Copyright Act 1968.
14 Ibid, s. 41.
15 [1964] Ch 736, [1963] 3 All ER 289.

---

3. Sound recordings, films and broadcasts

Copyright

31.09 Copyright is given in respect of sound recordings, films and broadcasts.[1] In relation to *records* the acts restricted are making a record embodying the recording, causing the recording to be heard in public or broadcasting the recording.[2] But causing it to be heard in public in a residential hotel or holiday camp (unless a special charge is made for admission to the part where the recording is to be heard) or in certain non-profit making clubs (unless a charge is made and the proceeds are not applied to the purpose of the club) is no infringement.[3] As regards films,[4] the acts restricted are making a copy of the film, causing it to be seen or heard in public, broadcasting it or causing it to be transmitted to subscribers to a diffusion service.[5] The copyright belongs to the 'maker,' that is the person by whom the arrangements necessary for the making of the film are undertaken.[6] As regards *television and sound broadcasts* copyright subsists where they are made by the British Broadcasting Corporation or the Independent Broadcasting Authority from a place in the United Kingdom or in any other country to which this provision extends. The copyright belongs to the Authority concerned.[7] The acts restricted are, as regards visual images, making, otherwise than for private purposes,[8] a film or copy of a film;[9] as regards sounds making a recording of them otherwise than for private purposes; causing them to be seen or heard in public by a paying audience;[10] or re-broadcasting them.[11]

The period of copyright in these cases is fifty years from the end of the calendar year when the recording or film is first published or the broadcast first made.[12] When the copyright in a film has expired, to show it in public is not an infringement of the copyright in the work on which it was based.[13]

Use of films and broadcasts for purposes of judicial proceedings is protected.[14]

---

1 Copyright Act 1956, ss. 12–14.
2 Ibid, s. 12 (5). Copyright is lost if records have been issued to the public without a label on the records or their containers indicating the year of first publication: s. 12 (6).
3 Ibid, s. 12 (7); *Phonographic Performance Ltd v Pontin's Ltd* [1968] Ch 290, [1967] 2 All ER 736 (holiday camp).
4 Film includes the sound-track: ibid, s. 13 (9).
5 Ibid, s. 13 (5).
6 Ibid, s. 13 (4), (10).
7 Ibid, s. 14 (1), (2). It can be extended to any new authority: s. 34.
8 A 'still' is not an infringement, but any sequence of images sufficient to be seen as a moving picture is: s. 14 (6).
9 See s. 14 (7).
10 For the definition of 'paying audience,' see Copyright Act 1956, s. 14 (8).
11 Ibid, s. 14 (4).
12 Ibid, ss. 12 (3), 13 (3), 14 (2). As regards news films and other registrable films under part II of the Films Act 1960, the fifty years run from the year of registration: s. 13 (3) (a). It is no infringement to show news films more than fifty years after the year when the principal events depicted occurred: s. 13 (8). Repetition of a broadcast does not increase the length of a copyright: s. 14 (3).

13 Ibid, s. 13 (7).
14 Ibid, ss. 13 (6), 14 (9).

---

4. Enforcement of copyright

Civil remedies

31.10 The owner of copyright may sue for damages and for an injunction to restrain infringement. As an alternative to damages he may claim an account of profits.[1] Further, he may treat infringing copies or plates used to make them as if they were his own property and claim delivery up of those in the defendant's possession and damages for those which have been sold.[2] However, he cannot claim damages for infringement or conversion against an innocent infringer, that is, one who was not aware and had no reasonable grounds for suspecting that copyright subsisted in the work, or had reasonable grounds for believing that the copies or plates in question were not infringing copies used or to be used for making infringing copies.[3]

Additional damages in respect of flagrancy or benefit may be awarded if the circumstances warrant them.[4] An injunction will not be granted for infringement of copyright in respect of the construction of a building after construction has been begun either so as to prevent its completion or to have it demolished.[5] The Commissioners of Customs and Excise may be required to prohibit the import of infringing copies.[6]

False attribution of ownership of a copyright work or passing off an altered artistic work as an unaltered one gives rise to an action for damages.[7]

---

1 Copyright Act 1956, s. 17 (1).
2 Ibid, s. 18 (1). When suing in respect of infringing copy it is not necessary to show that the defendant acquired the copy with knowledge of the infringement. *WEA Records v Benson King (Sales)* [1974] 3 All ER 81, [1975] 1 WLR 44.
3 Ibid, ss. 17 (2), 18 (2). The onus of establishing this defence is a heavy one: see, e.g., *John Lane, The Bodley Head Ltd v Associated Newspapers Ltd* [1936] 1 KB 715.
4 Ibid, s. 17 (3). See, for example, *Williams v Settle* [1960] 2 All ER 806, [1960] 1 WLR 1072, CA.
5 Ibid, s. 17 (4).
6 Ibid, s. 22.
7 Ibid, s. 43. Such right of action is not limited to professional authors: *Moore v News of the World* [1972] 1 QB 441, [1972] 1 All ER 915, CA.

Evidence

31.11   Certain presumptions are made in copyright actions. Copyright is presumed to subsist in the work and the plaintiff is presumed to be the owner if he so claims unless these matters are put in issue by the defence.[1] Where a work bears the name of an author, the person named is presumed to be the author and owner of the copyright.[2] If no author is named but the publisher is, he is presumed to be the owner.[3] Where the author is dead the burden is put on the defence to show that the work is not original and to disprove any allegation as to first publication.[4] Similar presumptions apply in relation to anonymous or pseudonymous works.[5] And it is for the defence to disprove certain statements on labels borne by records at the time of issue.[6]

---

1 Copyright Act 1956, s. 20 (1).
2 Ibid, s. 20 (2). And see s. 20 (3) as to joint authors.
3 Ibid, s. 20 (4); *Warwick Film Productions Ltd v Eisinger* [1969] Ch 508, [1967] 3 All ER 367.
4 Ibid, s. 20 (5).
5 Ibid, s. 20 (6).
6 Ibid, s. 20 (7).

Criminal offences

31.12   Deliberate infringements of copyright are also offences punishable by a court of summary jurisdiction.[1] And it is an offence knowingly to make records, films or broadcasts of the performance of a dramatic or musical work unless written consent has been given by or on behalf of the performers.[2]

---

1 Copyright Act 1956, s. 21.
2 Dramatic and Musical Performers' Protection Act 1958 and Performers' Protection Act 1963.

---

5. Assignments and licences

Dealings with copyright

31.13   Copyright may be assigned, bequeathed[1] or transmitted by operation of law. Assignments may be limited so as to apply to only some of the acts restricted by the copyright or they may be limited as regards the country or countries in relation to which the owner has exclusive rights or so as to apply to part only of the period of copyright. These limitations may be combined. Any assignment must be in writing signed by or on behalf of the assignor.[2] Where a work has not yet been produced, future copyright can be assigned and it will automatically vest in the assignee when produced.[3]

Apart from assignments, licences may be granted and they are binding on successors in title except purchasers in good faith for valuable consideration without notice (actual or constructive) of the licence.[4] The grantee of an *exclusive* licence (which has to be granted in writing) can bring proceedings for infringement in his own name as if he were an assignee. The licensee may make substantial alterations in the work unless the licence expressly or by implication restricts that right.[5]

---

1 A bequest of the manuscript of an unpublished work carries the copyright unless a contrary intention is shown: Copyright Act 1956, s. 38.
2 Ibid, s. 36 (1)–(3).
3 Ibid, s. 37.
4 Ibid, s. 36 (4).
5 *Frisby v British Broadcasting Corpn* [1967] Ch 932, [1967] 2 All ER 106.

Bankruptcy

31.14 By s. 60 of the Bankruptcy Act 1914, where copyright is vested in a bankrupt and he is liable to pay royalties to the author of the work the trustee in bankruptcy cannot sell or authorise the sale of any copies of the work except on the terms of paying to the author the same royalties as would have been payable by the bankrupt; nor can the trustee, without the consent of the author or the court, assign the copyright, except upon terms which will secure to the author payments by way of royalty at a rate not less than that which the bankrupt was liable to pay.[1]

---

1 This section is not applicable in company liquidations: *Re Health Promotion Ltd* [1932] 1 Ch 65.

Performing right tribunal

31.15 To assist composers and publishers of musical works and makers of records to collect royalties from dance halls and other places of entertainment, societies have been formed which negotiate with the proprietors, collect royalties and distribute them according to their rules. The most important perhaps is the Performing Right Society.

To determine disputes between these licensing bodies and persons requiring licences or organisations representing them, the Act establishes the Performing Right Tribunal.[1] It can deal with licence schemes referred to it or with applications by persons requiring a licence either in accordance with a licence scheme or in a case not covered by a licence scheme.[2] If a licence scheme is in operation an individual may complain of the refusal or failure of the licensing body to grant him a licence under the scheme. If no scheme is in operation he may apply if he can show that licence has been unreasonably refused or if the terms offered were unreasonable. The tribunal may declare him to be entitled to a licence on proper terms.[3] Acts authorised by an order made on reference of a scheme or on the application of an individual are not infringements of copyright if all the conditions are complied with.[4] The Copyright (Amendment) Act 1971 provides for reference back and review by the Tribunal of any proceeding under s. 27 of the Copyright Act 1956.

1 Copyright Act 1956, s. 23.
2 Ibid, s. 24 (1). For the procedure, see ss. 25, 26. Questions of law can be referred to the High Court: s. 30.
3 Ibid, s. 27.
4 Ibid, s. 29.

Crown Copyright

31.16   This exists in literary, dramatic, musical or artistic work made by or under the direction of the Crown or a government department. It exists whilst the work is unpublished and for fifty years from the end of the year in which it was first published.[1]

1 Copyright Act 1956, s. 39. It will not generally be enforced in respect of legislation. See GEN 75/10. 1976 CLY 358.

Exclusion clauses

31.17   Those sections of the Unfair Contract Terms Act 1977 which govern negligence liability, liability arising out of a contract and unreasonable indemnity clauses do not apply to any contract in so far as it relates to the creation or transfer or termination of any right in a patent, trade mark, copyright, registered design, technical or commercial information or other intellectual property.[1]

---

1 Unfair Contract Terms Act 1977, s. 1 and Sch. 1, para. 1 (a). See generally para. 3.15, ante.

Part X

Employment

Chapter 32

Contracts of employment

32.01 Lord Denning has pointed out that the master-servant relationship, that is, the relationship that exists between an employer and an employee under a contract of service, is easier to recognise than to define.[1] A chauffeur, for example, is employed under a *contract of service*, but a taxicab driver is not employed under a contract of service with the person who hires him for a journey. The taxicab driver is engaged under a *contract of services*, and is an independent contractor, rather than a servant. The usual test once cited for determining whether a master-servant relationship existed was to ask if there was a right in the employer to say not only what work was to be done for him but how it was to be done.[2] It was sometimes an artificial test because in many cases of skilled servants, the master could not in practice control how he did his work, but if the right of control existed, the contract was one of service.[3] In any case, the test was not an exclusive one.[4]

One solution has been to reinterpret the control test so that the court asks not whether the work itself is controlled but whether its incidental features such as time and locality are subject to managerial control.[5] This may be linked with the 'scope of organisation' test propounded by Lord Denning in the case above.[6] He went on to say that the common feature in service contracts is that 'a man is employed as part of the business, and his work is done as an integral part of the business; whereas under a contract for services, his work, although done for the business, is not integrated into it but is only accessory to it.'

If the relationship of master and servant does exist, then not only is the master vicariously liable for any torts committed by the servant while acting in the course of his employment, but certain terms are implied by law in every contract of service which do not necessarily apply to contracts for services. It should also be noted that the Contracts of Employment Act 1972, whose provisions are considered below,[7] applies only to persons employed under a contract of service or apprenticeship.

---

1 *Stevenson, Jordan and Harrison Ltd v MacDonald and Evans* [1952] 1 TLR 101 at 111.
2 *Performing Right Society v Mitchell and Booker Ltd* [1924] 1 KB 762.
3 *Cassidy v Minister of Health* [1951] 2 KB 343, [1951] 1 All ER 574.
4 *Amalgamated Engineering Union v Minister of Pensions and National Insurance* [1963] 1 All ER 864, [1963] 1 WLR 441; *Morren v Swinton and Pendlebury Borough Council* [1965] 2 All ER 349; *Ready Mixed Concrete (South East) v Minister of Pensions* [1968] 2 QB 497, [1968] 1 All ER 433.
5 Atiyah *Vicarious Liability*, p. 47.
6 See note 1 above.
7 Para. 32.02, post.

Formation of the contract

32.02 The rules as to capacity are the same as for the general law of contract.[1] It follows that if a minor enters into a contract of employment of apprenticeship, it is binding on him if the contract, looked at as a whole, is beneficial to him.[2]

At common law, a contract of service may be in writing or oral and there is no special requirement as to form. However, the Merchant Shipping Act 1970 requires written contracts with each member of the crew,[3] and contracts of apprenticeship must be in writing. Furthermore, the Contracts of Employment Act 1972 requires employers (with certain exceptions) to give employees written particulars of the terms of their employment not later than thirteen weeks after the beginning of a period of employment.[4] The statement must identify the parties, specify the date when the employment began, state whether any employment with a previous employer counts as part of a period of continuous employment and the date on which it began, and give the following particulars of the terms of employment as at a specified date not more than one week before the statement is given:

i) the scale or rate of remuneration, or the method of calculating remuneration,
ii) the intervals at which remuneration is paid (e.g. weekly or monthly),
iii) any terms and conditions relating to hours of work,
iv) any terms and conditions relating to holidays and holiday pay, incapacity for work due to sickness or injury (including any provision for sick pay), and pensions and pension schemes,

v) the length of notice the employee is obliged to give and entitled to receive to determine the contract,

vi) the title of the job which the employee is employed to do, and

vii) whether a contracting out certificate is in force under the Social Security Pensions Act 1975.

In addition, the statement must include a note (a) specifying any disciplinary rules or referring to a reasonably accessible document which specifies these rules; (b) a person to whom the employee can apply if he is dissatisfied with any disciplinary decision; (c) specifying a person to whom the employee can apply for the redress of any grievance relating to his employment; (d) explaining any further steps or referring to an explanatory document. These (b–d) do not apply to discipline relating to health and safety at work.

Where there are no particulars to be entered under any of those heads, that fact must be stated.[5] If the contract is for a fixed term, the date when the contract expires must be stated.[6] Where there is a change in the terms, the employer must, not more than one month after the change, inform the employee of the nature of the change by a written statement, and if he does not leave a copy of the statement with the employee, he must ensure that the employee has reasonable opportunities of reading it or that it is made reasonably accessible to him in some way.[7] Any of the particulars specified may be given by referring the employee to a copy of his contract of employment or some document which the employee has reasonable opportunities of reading or which is made reasonably accessible to him.[8]

Failure on the part of an employer to comply with the Contracts of Employment Act 1972 entitles the employee to require a reference to be made to an Industrial Tribunal. If the Tribunal determines that certain particulars which ought to have been given to the employee have not been given, then 'the employer shall be deemed to have given to the employee a statement in which these particulars were included ... as specified in the decision of the tribunal'.[9] The requirements do not apply to any employee who has a written contract of service containing terms affording the same particulars as specified above and a copy of the contract has been given to him, or he has reasonable opportunities of reading such copy or such copy is made reasonably accessible to him in some other way.[10] Nor do the requirements apply to any employee whose hours of work are normally less that sixteen hours (or eight in some cases) a week[11] or to certain excepted classes of employees, namely registered dock workers, some seamen, or an employee who is the husband or wife, of the employer, or to a person employed on a task not expected to last for more than twelve weeks.[12] Nor does it apply to Crown servants or to work wholly or mainly outside Great Britain unless the employee normally works in Britain and his work abroad is for the same employer.[13]

---

1 Paras. 2.15, et seq., ante.
2 *Doyle v White City Stadium Ltd* [1935] 1 KB 110.
3 Para. 25.14, ante.
4 Contracts of Employment Act 1972, s. 4, as amended by Employment Protection Act 1975, s. 125, and Sch. 16, Part II.
5 Ibid, s. 4 (3).
6 Ibid, s. 4 (4).
7 Ibid, s. 5.
8 Ibid, s. 6.
9 Contracts of Employment Act 1972, s. 8.
10 Ibid, s. 6.
11 Ibid, s. 4 (7) and Employment Protection Act 1975, Sch. 16, Part II, paras. 7 and 8.
12 Ibid, s. 9 and Employment Protection Act 1975, Sch. 16, Part II, para. 10.
13 Contracts of Employment Act 1972, s. 12

Termination of contract

32.03 At common law where the contract specifies that it is to endure for a certain fixed period, clearly the contract terminates at the end of such period. If no such fixed period is specified but the terms lay down certain grounds on which the contract may be terminated by the employer, these grounds may be construed as exhaustive, so that if no such ground exists, a dismissal even on reasonable notice would not be valid.[1]

The general rule of common law where the contract is for an indefinite term is that the contract may be determined by either party giving reasonable notice to the other. What is 'reasonable' depends on the nature of the employment, and the more responsible or specialised the work of the employee the longer will be the notice that must be given.[2] Under the Contracts of Employment Act 1972 certain *minimum* periods of notice are specified, depending on the time served by the employee. Thus, an employee who has been employed for a continuous period of at least four weeks is entitled to a minimum notice of one week if the continuous period is less than two years, of one week for each year of continuous employment if the period of continuous employment is more than two but less than twelve years, and not less than twelve weeks if the period of continuous employment is more than twelve years.[3] The notice required to be given by an employee, who has been continuously employed for four weeks or more, must be not less than one week.[4]

Any provision for shorter notice in any contract with a person who has been continuously employed for four weeks or more has effect subject to these statutory provisions, but either party may waive his right to notice on any occasion and may accept a payment in lieu of notice.[5] It should be emphasised, however, that if under the express terms of a contract or by virtue of the Common Law, a longer period of notice must be given, such express term or terms implied by Common Law prevails. The Act specifies only *minimum* periods of notice.

---

1 *McClelland v Northern Ireland General Health Services Board* [1957] 2 All ER 129, [1957] 1 WLR 594.
2 Cf. *Savage v British India Steam Navigation Co* (1930) 46 TLR 294; *Manubens v Leon* [1919] 1 KB 208.
3 Contracts of Employment Act 1972, s. 1, as amended by the Employment Protection Act 1975, s. 125 and Sch. 16, Part II.
4 Ibid, s. 1 (2). Continuity of employment is preserved during weeks when there is absence because of a strike or lock-out but the weeks do not count to a total period: ibid, Sch. 1, paras. 6 and 7.
5 Ibid, s. 1 (3).

32.04   A breach of contract only brings about termination if the breach amounts to a repudiation of the contract or a breach of condition and the other party elects to treat the contract as at an end. A contract of employment may be terminated by frustration, for example, by the death[1] or serious illness of either party.[2] It may also be terminated by dissolution of a partnership,[3] by bankruptcy of the employer,[4] and by the winding up of an employing company.[5]

---

1 Legislative provisions preserve many of the rights of an employee on the death of an employer: Redundancy Payments Act 1965, s. 23; Employment Protection Act 1975, s. 110 and Sch. 12; Contracts of Employment Act 1972, Sch. 1, para. 9 (4).
2 *Poussard v Spiers and Pond* (1876) 1 QBD 410; *Bettini v Gye* (1876) 1 QBD 183; *Marshall v Harland and Wolff Ltd* [1972] 2 All ER 715, {1972] 1 WLR 899 (illness not such as to frustrate contract); *Egg Stores v Leibovici* [1976] IRLR 376.
3 *Brace v Calder* [1895] 2 QB 253.
4 See Bankruptcy Act 1914, s. 34 (apprentice). But not generally: *Thomas v Williams* (1834) 1 Ad & E 685. Contracts of a personal character may not pass to the trustee: *Lucas v Moncrieff* (1905) 21 TLR 683. See also Employment Protection Act 1975, ss. 63 to 69.
5 *Reid v Explosives Co Ltd* (1887) 19 QBD 264.

32.05   At Common Law, provided a contract of employment for an indefinite term was terminated by the employer giving 'reasonable' notice the termination was not a wrongful dismissal and the employee had no remedy. However, by the Trade Union and Labour Relations Act 1974[1] as amended by the Employment Protection Act 1975,[2] if an employee is 'unfairly' dismissed he is entitled to claim compensation. Unfair dismissal is administered by Industrial Tribunals with appeal on law to the Employment Appeal Tribunal. In considering whether the dismissal is fair or unfair, the employer must show (a) the reason or reasons for the dismissal and (b) that the reason related to the capability or qualifications of the employee or his conduct or that he was redundant or that to have retained him would have contravened an enactment or some other substantial reason justifying dismissal. The dismissal is unfair unless the employer also acted reasonably.[3] Statute provides that certain reasons are unfair. These include dismissal for joining or taking part in the activities of an independent trade union, dismissal for refusing to join a non-independent trade union or, subject to conditions, pregnancy.[4] On the other hand, dismissal for refusing, except on religious grounds, to join a trade union when there is a closed shop or dismissal during a strike or lock-out, except when there is discrimination in dismissal or re-engagement, are fair. Moreover redundancy may, subject to conditions, render a dismissal fair.

If the complainant agrees, the tribunal may make order for reinstatement or re-engagement.[5] The employer may be liable to pay additional compensation if he does not re-employ the complainant. In a case where these orders are not made compensation may be awarded, consisting of a 'basic award', calculated on the same basis as a redundancy payment and available when there is no redundancy payment and a compensatory award.[6] This latter is not to exceed £5,200. There is provision for interim relief pending a hearing.[7] Compensation for unfair dismissal must take into account the employee's duty to mitigate.

Any attempt to contract out of the unfair dismissal procedures is normally void. There are exceptions for fixed term contracts of two years or more, dismissal procedure agreements approved by the Department of Employment and agreements relating to a dismissal which has taken place.[8] Unfair dismissal need not be a breach of contract and hence need not necessarily be wrongful dismissal which continues as a separate ground of liability.[9] The unfair dismissal provisions do not apply where the employer is the husband or wife of the employee, to employment as a registered dock worker, to share-fishermen or when the employee under his contract of employment normally works outside Britain.[10]

The Rehabilitation of Offenders Act 1974,[11] the Sex Discrimination Act 1975,[12] and the Race Relations Act 1976[13] contain provisions relating to dismissals which contravene their provisions.

---

1 Sch. 1, Part II.
2 Ss. 70–80.
3 Trade Union and Labour Relations Act 1974, Sch. 1, Part II.
4 Employment Protection Act 1975, s. 34.
5 Ibid, ss. 71–72.
6 Ibid, ss. 73–77.
7 Ibid, ss. 78–80.
8 Trade Union and Labour Relations Act 1974, Sch. 1, Part II and Employment Protection Act 1975, Sch. 16, Part III.
9 For wrongful dismissal see para. 32.11, post.
10 Ibid.
11 S. 4 (3). There is no specific enforcement machinery but such a dismissal may be unfair.
12 S. 6 (2). Complaint lies to an Industrial Tribunal (s. 63) and the Employment Protection Act 1975, s. 77, excludes any double compensation on the basis of ordinary unfair dismissal. The Equal Opportunities Commission may investigate and take proceedings also: Sex Discrimination Act 1975, ss. 57, 67 and 71.
13 S. 4 (2). Complaint lies to an Industrial Tribunal (s. 54). The Commission for Racial Equality has functions similar to those of the Equal Opportunities Commission: Race Relations Act 1976, ss. 48, 58, 62–64.

Implied duties of an employee

32.06 Subject to any express terms of the contract,[1] the following duties are implied from the master-servant relationship.

1. *To attend the place of work* unless there is reasonable excuse, such as illness. The Employment Protection Act 1975 provides for time to be allowed for trade union activities, public service and seeking work or training in the event of redundancy.[2] The Act also makes provision for absence because of maternity and a right to return to work.[3]

2. *To obey lawful orders.* All orders within the scope of the servant's employment must be obeyed unless to do so would imperil the servant's life or limb or would amount to an unlawful act. However, disobedience does not entitle the employer to dismiss unless the servant's conduct evinces a clear intention to flout the essential conditions of the contract.[4]

3. *To exercise due care and skill.* An employee not only undertakes possession of the skill necessary to carry out his job

properly but also that he will exercise that skill with reasonable care. In *Lister v Romford Ice and Cold Storage Co Ltd*:[5]

A lorry driver employed by the company injured his father, who was a fellow-employee, while backing a lorry. The company was made liable vicariously for the driver's negligence. *Held:* the company was entitled to an indemnity against the driver who was in breach of the duty of care implied in his contract of employment.

4. *To conduct himself properly.* Insolence, persistent laziness, bad timekeeping, and drunkenness are examples of breach of this duty. Whether such misconduct justifies dismissal is a matter of degree,[6] but dishonesty always justifies dismissal.[7]

5. *To observe good faith.* It is a breach of this duty for an employee to take a secret commission[8] or to solicit the employer's customers with a view to transferring their custom to him when he leaves his present employment.[9] Working in his spare-time for a rival employer may also be a breach of the employee's duty of fidelity.[10]

When an employee makes an invention in the course of his duties it may belong to his employer but the employee may be compensated if it is of outstanding benefit to the employer. Any term in a contract which diminishes an employee's patent rights is to that extent unenforceable against him but this is not to affect any obligation of confidentiality.[11]

It is part of the employee's duty of good faith to perform the employment contract in such a way that it does not frustrate the commercial object of the contract and in consequence an employee is in breach if he 'works to rule' in a wholly unreasonable way so that the employer's work is disrupted.[12]

The implied duty of fidelity survives the termination of the contract in that an ex-employee may be restrained from disclosing his former employer's trade secrets[13] or from using for his own purpose lists of his employer's customers that he has drawn up.[14] But, unless there is an express restrictive covenant he is free to compete with his former employer, to solicit his former employer's customers, and to advertise that he formerly worked for that employer.[15]

---

1 The contract may often incorporate, expressly or impliedly, the terms of a collective agreement.
2 Ss. 57–62.
3 Ss. 34–52.
4 *Laws v London Chronicle Ltd* [1959] 2 All ER 285, [1959] 1 WLR 698.
5 [1957] AC 555, [1957] 1 All ER 125. Insurers have agreed not to enforce this against a servant unless there is collusion or wilful misconduct. See Gardiner (1959) 22 MLR 652, and the courts may also exclude this in an industrial

context. *Morris v Ford Motor Co* [1973] QB 792, [1973] 2 All ER 1084. See *Street on Torts* (6th edn) 481.

6 *Clouston & Co Ltd v Corry* [1906] AC 122; *Pepper v Webb* [1969] 2 All ER 216, [1969] 1 WLR 514, CA.
7 *Cunningham v Fonblanque* (1833) 6 C & P 44.
8 *Boston Deep Sea Fishing and Ice Co v Ansell* (1888) 39 ChD 339.
9 *Wessex Dairies Ltd v Smith* [1935] 2 KB 80, followed in *Sanders v Parry* [1967] 2 All ER 803, [1967] 1 WLR 753.
10 *Hivac Ltd v Park Royal Scientific Instruments Ltd* [1946] Ch 169, [1946] 1 All ER 350.
11 Patents Act 1977, ss. 39–43. See para. 29.05, ante.
12 *Secretary of State for Employment v Associated Society of Locomotive Engineers and Firemen (No. 2)* [1972] 2 QB 455, [1972] 2 All ER 949, CA.
13 Unless disclosure is justified in the public interest as where, for example, the employer has engaged in illegal practices: *Initial Services Ltd v Putterill* [1968] 1 QB 396, [1967] 3 All ER 145, CA.
14 *Robb v Green* [1895] 2 QB 315.
15 *National Provincial Bank of England v Marshall* (1888) 40 ChD 49. For covenants in restraint of trade, see para. 6.10, ante.

Implied duties of the employer

32.07 1. *To retain the employee for agreed period.* While the employer is bound to retain the employee for the period agreed unless the contract permits it to be terminated earlier, there is in general no duty to provide the employee with work.[1] However, exceptionally, there is a duty to provide work in the case of apprentices, and wherever payment is wholly or partly on a commission basis.[2] Similarly, if, as with an actor, the opportunity of work is of the essence of the contract, work giving the actor the chance of enhancing his reputation, there is a breach of contract if the work agreed is not provided even though the employer has complied with his obligation to pay the agreed remuneration.[3]

1 *Turner v Sawdon* [1901] 2 KB 653, but see *Breach v Epsylon Industries* [1976] ICR 316.
2 *Bauman v Hulton Press* [1952] 2 All ER 1121.
3 *Herbert Clayton and Jack Waller Ltd v Oliver* [1930] AC 209.

32.08 2. *To pay agreed remuneration.* Where an employee is away from work because of illness but the illness is not sufficiently serious to cause frustration of the contract, it is presumed that he is still entitled to be paid his wages. This presumption applies where the written terms are silent and the employer is unable to establish an implied term to the effect that wages are not paid during illness.[1]

By the Equal Pay Act 1970,[2] women must be given equal treatment as regards terms and conditions of employment with men in the same employment.

The Employment Protection Act 1975 provides that employees are entitled to certain guaranteed minimum payments when they cannot be provided with work to earn wages, to similar payments when they are suspended on medical grounds, to maternity pay, to paid time off for trade union duties and to payments under protective awards when the employer fails to consult with unions on redundancies.[3] Employees are also entitled in the event of redundancy to paid time off to look for work or training.[4]

The Apportionment Act 1870 provides that payments in the nature of income shall be deemed to arise from day to day. Hence when an employee is through no fault of his own unable to complete his contract he is entitled to a proportionate part of his remuneration since it has been held that the Act applies to wages and salaries.[5] It has not yet been determined whether the Act applies in a case where an employee is properly dismissed.[6]

---

1 *Orman v Saville Sportswear Ltd;* [1960] 3 All ER 105, [1960] 1 WLR 1055.
2 As now amended by Sex Discrimination Act 1975, Sch. 1, Part II.
3 Ss. 22–28, 29–33, 34–43, 57, 101.
4 S. 61.
5 *Moriarty v Regents Garage Co* [1921] 1 KB 423.
6 *Chitty on Contracts* (24th ed) Vol. 2, 620.

32.09 3. *To take reasonable care for servant's safety.* It was held by the House of Lords in *Wilsons and Clyde Coal Co v English*[1] that an employer owes a personal duty to use due care to provide a competent staff of men, adequate material, a safe system of work and adequate supervision. These are all aspects of the employer's duty to take reasonable care for the servant's safety. Whether or not the duty has been broken is essentially a question of fact, and decisions on fact should not be treated as binding authorities.[2] An employer may be liable for breach even where the employee is working on premises not in the employer's occupation,[3] and in determining whether the employer has taken reasonable care, it is relevant that he is aware that a particular employee is susceptible to certain risks.[4] If the employer is in breach and could have foreseen the risk of some kind of injury, the employer is liable for all physical harm to the employee directly resulting from the injury, including injury that could not itself be reasonably foreseen.[5]

By the Employer's Liability (Defective Equipment) Act 1969, if an employee suffers personal injury because of a defect in equipment provided by his employer and the defect is attributable wholly or partly to the fault of a third party (e.g. the manufacturers), the employer is liable. Any agreement purporting to exclude or limit this liability is void.

All employers are required to insure against their liability for damages for personal injuries to their employees by the Employers' Liability (Compulsory Insurance) Act 1969.

One defence that an employer may have when being sued for breach of his implied duty of care is that the servant has voluntarily accepted the particular risk which caused the injury, but it is not enough that the servant knew of the risk. The defence is *volenti non fit injuria* not *scienti non fit injuria.*[6] Another possible defence is that the injury was caused in fact by the servant's own lack of care for his safety. If this is established, a court has power to apportion by reducing the plaintiff's damages in accordance with his degree of fault under the Law Reform (Contributory Negligence) Act 1945.[7]

Apart from the Common Law duty of care implied in every contract of employment, the employer may be liable in damages for breach of statutory duties, for example those imposed by the Factories Act 1961.[8]

---

1 [1938] AC 57, [1937] 3 All ER 628.
2 *Qualcast (Wolverhampton) Ltd v Haynes* [1959] AC 743, [1959] 2 All ER 38.
3 *General Cleaning Contractors Ltd v Christmas* [1953] AC 180, [1952] 2 All ER 1110. See Salmond *Torts* (17th edn) 481–482 and cases cited.
5 *Paris v Stepney Borough Council* [1951] AC 367, [1951] 1 All ER 42.
5 *Smith v Leech, Brain Co Ltd* [1962] 2 QB 405, [1961] 3 All ER 1159.
6 *Smith v Baker & Sons* [1891] AC 325. The defence will rarely succeed in an employment case but see *Imperial Chemical Industries v Shatwell* [1965] AC 656, [1964] 2 All ER 999, HL.
7 For contributory negligence in employment see *Flower v Ebbw Vale Steel, Iron and Coal Co Ltd* [1934] 2 KB 132 at 140, but *Staveley Iron and Chemical Co Ltd v Jones* [1956] AC 627, [1956] 1 All ER 403, HL; *Mullard v Ben Line Steamers* [1970] 1 WLR 1414, CA.
8 See now Health and Safety at Work etc. Act 1974, s. 47 (2), which preserves the right of action for damages for breach of statutory safety duties unless it is excluded.

32.10   4. *To make redundancy payments.* By the Redundancy Payments Act 1965 as amended by the Employment Protection Act 1975, an employer is bound to make a redundancy payment to any employee who has been continuously employed for two years or more and is dismissed on the ground of redundancy or is laid off or kept on short-time for certain periods. The Act does not apply to certain excluded cases as where the employee has attained the age of sixty-five if a man or sixty if a woman, nor where the employee has been properly dismissed for misconduct, nor where the employee has unreasonably refused an offer by his employer to provide suitable employment. There is now provision for a trial period of at least four weeks for an employee to decide whether he considers new employment to be suitable or whether he wishes to continue his employment after a change in the ownership of the business employing him.[1] The amount of any redundancy payment payable is calculated in accordance with the First Schedule to the 1965 Act and the Employment Protection Act 1975.[2] On payment the employer is entitled to claim a rebate from the Redundancy Fund.[3] Disputes under the Act are determined by the Industrial Tribunals.

Employers are now obliged to consult recognised trade unions about certain proposed redundancies and also to notify them to the Department of Trade.[4]

---

1 Employment Protection Act 1975, Sch. 16, Part I, para. 3.
2 Ibid, Schs. 4 and 16.
3 Redundancy Rebates Act 1977.
4 Employment Protection Act 1975, Part IV, ss. 99–107.

Remedies of employer and employee

32.11 1. *Employer.* While an employer may always dismiss an employee instantly if he has been dishonest, in all other cases of breach of duty on the employee's part, it is a matter of degree whether the breach justifies dismissal. If the employer was not aware of any good grounds until after the date of the dismissal he still has a good defence to an action for wrongful dismissal at common law if, in fact, good grounds did exist.[1]

When an employee with twenty-six weeks or more continuous service is dismissed he is entitled to a written statement of the reasons for his dismissals from his employer. This statement must be given within fourteen days of the employee's request for it and is admissible in evidence. If no statement is provided or the employee considers one provided to be inadequate or untrue he may complain to an industrial tribunal.[2]

Where the employee's breach is not sufficiently serious as to justify dismissal, the employer's only remedy against him is a claim for damages. Specific performance is never awarded of a contract for personal services.

---

1 *Boston Deep Sea Fishing and Ice Co Ltd v Ansell* (1888) 39 ChD 339. This

does not apply to unfair dismissal: *W Devis & Sons Ltd v Atkins* [1977] AC 931, [1977] 2 All ER 321, HL, though the amount of compensation may be affected, but this case may not be binding in respect of the Employment Protection Act 1975.

2 Ibid, s. 70.

32.12   2. *Employee*. An employee has the right to leave without giving notice only if the employer's breach amounts to a repudiation of the essential conditions of the contract. In these circumstances, the employee is freed from all the obligations of the contract, including any covenants in restraint of trade.[1]

Where a servant is working under a statutory scheme of employment he may, in the discretion of the court, obtain a declaratory judgment to the effect that he has been wrongfully dismissed.[2] A declaration will not normally be granted if it is an ordinary contract of employment.[3] However, the rule is not inflexible and in special circumstances a declaration may be granted and even an injunction to prevent wrongful dismissal.[4]

The usual remedy for wrongful dismissal is an action for wages accrued due, remuneration for the broken period of employment and damages.[5] The principal measure of damages, where it is a contract for a fixed period, is the amount of wages or salary that would have been paid during the remainder of that period, and if it is a contract terminable by notice, the wages or salary that would have been paid in the period of such notice. However, this amount will be reduced if the employee has failed in his duty to mitigate damages.[6] More significant, in so far as the total loss of wages or salary is not more than £5,000, is that the tax that would have been paid on the earnings must be allowed for in the award of damages. Any sum in excess of £5,000 is taxable in the plaintiff's hands under the Income and Corporation Taxes Act 1970[7] and hence no deduction will be made from it.

Damages for breach of an apprenticeship contract may cover not only pecuniary loss but also loss of future training and diminution of future prospects.[8]

3. Where an employer becomes bankrupt or a company is wound up as insolvent the wages or salary of employees not exceeding £800 for the four months preceeding the relevant date rank as preferential debts.[9] The Employment Protection Act 1975[10] also provides that various claims arising under it shall enjoy similar priority and the Secretary of State may make a direct payment out of the Redundancy Fund to an employee when the employer is insolvent.[11] The Employment Protection Act 1975 makes similar provision for a number of debts which may be due to employees.[12]

1 *General Billposting Co Ltd v Atkinson* [1909] AC 118.
2 *Vine v National Dock Labour Board* [1957] AC 488, [1956] 3 All ER 939. And see *Ridge v Baldwin* [1964] AC 40, [1963] 2 All ER 66.
3 *Francis v Municipal Councillors of Kuala Lumpur* [1962] 3 All ER 633, [1962] 1 WLR 1411; *Taylor v National Union of Seamen* [1967] 1 All ER 767, [1967] 1 WLR 532. See also *Denmark Productions Ltd v Boscobel Productions Ltd* [1969] 1 QB 699, [1968] 3 All ER 513, CA.
4 *Hill v CA Parsons & Co Ltd* [1972] 1 Ch 305, [1971] 3 All ER 1345, CA.
5 As to damages in contract generally see para. 7.27, et seq., ante.
6 *Bruce v Calder* [1895] 2 QB 253, CA.
7 Ss. 187, 188. *Parsons v BNM Laboratories Ltd* [1964] 1 QB 95, [1963] 2 All ER 658; *Bold v Brough, Nicholson and Hall Ltd* [1963] 3 All ER 849, [1964] 1 WLR 201, decided on Finance Act 1960.
8 *Dunk v George Waller & Son* [1970] 2 QB 163, [1970] 2 All ER 630, CA.
9 Insolvency Act 1976, Sch. I, Part I.
10 Ss. 63–69.
11 Redundancy Payments Act 1965, s. 32.
12 Employment Protection Act 1975, s. 64.

The Truck Acts

32.13 As a general rule, by virtue of the Truck Acts 1831–1940, all 'workmen' must be paid their wages in full in cash. A 'workman' means a labourer, servant in husbandry, journeyman, artificer, handicraftsman, miner, or someone otherwise engaged in manual labour not being a domestic or menial servant.[1]

Under the provisions of the Truck Acts, any contract to pay a workman wages otherwise than in cash is illegal. Moreover, any contractual provision directing the workman as to how or where to spend his wages is illegal. If payment is made otherwise than in cash the workman can claim the full wages without any set-off for the goods supplied in lieu of wages. It is not contrary to the Truck Acts for an employee to be paid less than the usual rate if, for example, the contract impliedly permits a deduction to be made for bad workmanship in the calculation of wages due.[2]

The Acts have been modified to some extent by the Payment of Wages Act 1960. This Act provides that if the workman requests in writing, and the employer agrees, he may have his wages or part of them paid by crediting his bank account with the amount due, or by postal order, money order, or cheque. An arrangement to pay wages by one of these methods may be terminated by either party giving not less than four weeks' written notice and may be terminated at any time by written agreement. A special provision in the Act provides that wages may be paid by postal or money order where the workman is absent from his usual place of employment, either on account of illness or injury or on duty, without any request by the workman or agreement with him, unless the workman notifies his employer in writing that he does not wish his wages to be so paid in such circumstances.[3]

Under provisions in the Truck Acts themselves, certain deductions are permitted. For example, if the workman has signed a written agreement, his employer may deduct up to the real value of (i) any medicine or medical treatment, (ii) fuel, (iii) materials, tools or implements used by a workman who is employed in mines, (iv) hay, corn or provender to be consumed by a beast of burden, (v) rent of living accommodation, or (vi) food prepared and consumed on the employer's premises.[4] A resonable fine in respect of some conduct likely to cause damage or loss to the employer may be deducted, provided there is either a written contract signed by the workman or a notice conspicuously displayed, specifying the acts or omissions for which fines may be imposed.[5] With the workman's agreement, his employer may deduct the amount of any debt due from the workman to a third party,[6] but not the amount of any debt owed by the workman to the employer himself.[7]

1 Employers and Workmen Act 1875.
2 *Sagar v H Ridehalgh & Son Ltd* [1931] 1 Ch 310.
3 Payment of Wages Act 1960, s. 4.
4 Truck Act 1831, s. 23.
5 Truck Act 1896, s. 2.
6 *Hewlett v Allen & Sons* [1894] AC 383, HL: *Williams v Butlers Ltd* [1975] 2 All ER 889, [1975] 1 WLR 946 (union dues).
7 *Williams v North's Navigation Collieries (1889) Ltd* [1906] AC 136.

32.14 The Health and Safety at Work etc. Act 1974 forbids an employer to levy any charge on an employee in respect of things done or provided to comply with relevant statutory provisions relating to health and safety.[1] Under the Attachment of Earnings Act 1971 an employer may be directed by a court to make deductions from the earnings of an employee against whom an attachment of earnings order has been made. These sums must be paid to an officer of the court but the employer is himself entitled to make a small deduction to cover administrative expenses.[2]

1 Ss. 9 and 53 (1).
2 Ss. 1, 6, 7.

Exclusion clauses

32.15 Provisions of the Unfair Contract Terms Act 1977 which avoid terms in contracts or notices purporting to restrict or exclude liability in negligence for death or personal injury and which render exclusion terms relating to other loss or damage subject to a test of reasonableness do not extend to contracts of employment except in favour of an employee. The employee may exclude such liability but the employer is subject to the limits imposed by the Act. There is also special provision for the coal industry.[1]

---

1 Unfair Contract Terms Act 1977, s. 1 and Sch. 1, paras. 4, 5. See generally para. 3.15, ante.

Part XI

Bankruptcy

Chapter 33

Bankruptcy

Introductory

33.00 The earliest bankruptcy statutes date back to the time of Henry VIII, and of Elizabeth and James I. Before 1861 the advantages of bankruptcy belonged only to those who came under the category of traders, but in an Act of that year non-traders were included amongst those who could be made bankrupt. The objects of modern bankruptcy legislation are:

1. To ensure the fair distribution of the property of an insolvent debtor among his creditors.
2. To allow the debtor to relieve himself of the burden of his debts and start afresh.
3. To prevent abuses of the process.

The principal statute governing bankruptcy law today is the Bankruptcy Act 1914.

2. Who may be made bankrupt

33.01 In order that a court may make an adjudication of bankruptcy it is necessary that a 'debtor' has committed 'an act of bankruptcy.' Section 1 of the Act lists a number of acts as 'acts of bankruptcy' and these are examined below.[1] A 'debtor' is defined[2] to include any person, whether a British subject or not, who at the time when any act of bankruptcy was done or suffered by him:

a) was personally present in England; or
b) ordinarily resided or had a place of business in England; or
c) was carrying on business in England personally or by means of an agent or manager;[3] or
d) was a member of a firm or partnership which carried on business in England.

The position of various special classes of persons is as follows:

1. *Minors.* A minor can be made a bankrupt in respect of debts legally binding on him, e.g. if the debt on which the bankruptcy is founded was incurred for necessaries, or is a judgment debt founded on a tort,[4] but if there is no debt legally enforceable against him, he cannot be made a bankrupt even on his own petition.[5] When a plea of minority would have been a defence to an action the court of bankruptcy will give effect to it although judgment has been obtained.[6]

2. *Married women.* Since 1935, a married woman has been subject to bankruptcy law as if she were a feme sole.[7]

3. *Aliens.* An alien who commits an act of bankruptcy comes within the definition of a 'debtor' and is, therefore, subject to English bankruptcy law if he is either personally present in England at the time of the act of bankruptcy or satisfies any of the other conditions listed above in the meaning given by the Act to a 'debtor' and may be made bankrupt on his own petition. However, any creditor, whether or not an alien, may only present a petition against a debtor, whether an alien debtor or not, in the more limited circumstances referred to later.[8]

4. *Mentally disordered persons.* Mentally disordered persons perhaps cannot commit an act of bankruptcy involving *intent*, e.g. fraudulent preference; they can be adjudged bankrupt even without the consent of the Court of Protection where the act of bankruptcy was committed before the debtor came under that court's jurisdiction, but it seems that even if the act of bankruptcy takes place before a receiver of the patient's estate is appointed, the trustee in bankruptcy will not be entitled to the debtor's property to the exclusion of the Court of Protection at any rate if that court asserts its control before the receiving order in bankruptcy.[9]

5. *Partnerships.* A partnership may be made bankrupt.[10] A receiving order against the firm is equivalent to a receiving order against each of the general partners.

6. *Deceased persons.* A deceased person cannot be made bankrupt on proceedings instituted after his death, but his estate may be administered in bankruptcy.[11] Where a debtor dies after presentation of the petition the proceedings will, unless the court otherwise orders, be continued as if he were alive.[12]

7. *Registered companies.* No corporation or registered company can be made bankrupt.[13] The winding-up of a company under the Companies Act 1948 is the equivalent of bankruptcy in the case of an individual.

---

1 Para. 33.03, post.

2 Bankruptcy Act 1914, s. 1 (2).
3 A foreigner who had ceased to trade in England but left debts unpaid in England was treated as still carrying on his business in England (*Theophile v Solicitor-General*, [1950] AC 186, [1950] 1 All ER 405, HL).
4 *Re Debtor (No. 564 of 1949)* [1950] Ch 282, [1950] 1 All ER 308.
5 *Re A and M* [1926] Ch 274; and *Re Davenport Ex parte Bankrupt v Eric Street Properties Ltd*, [1963] 2 All ER 850, [1963] 1 WLR 817, CA.
6 *Ex parte Kibble* (1875) LR 10 Ch 373.
7 Law Reform (Married Women, and Tortfeasors) Act 1935, s. 1 (d).
8 Para. 33.04, post.
9 *Re Debtor (No. 1 of 1941)* [1941] Ch 487, [1941] 3 All ER 11. See para. 2.21, ante.
10 Including limited partnerships; see para. 11.22, ante.
11 See para. 33.51, post.
12 Bankruptcy Act 1914, s. 112.
13 Ibid, s. 126.

---

3. Procedure

33.02 To proceed against a person in bankruptcy, it is necessary:

1. That a bankruptcy petition should be presented either by the debtor or by a creditor,[1] and
2. In accordance with this petition, that a receiving order should be made.[2]

This cannot be done unless an act of bankruptcy has been committed by the debtor. There is one exception to this statement:

> If a judgment summons is taken out against a debtor, the court may, instead of exercising the jurisdiction to commit, with the creditor's assent, make a receiving order against the debtor; in such case, however, the debtor is deemed to have committed an act of bankruptcy at the time the order is made.[3]

The court, however, cannot make a receiving order unless there is evidence of means which would have justified the making of a committal order.[4]

---

1 See para. 33.04, post.
2 See para. 33.06, post.
3 Ibid, s. 107 (4). See now Administration of Justice Act 1970, s. 11.
4 *Re A Debtor* [1905] 1 KB 374.

Acts of bankruptcy

33.03   By section 1 (1) of the Act, a 'debtor' commits an act of
bankruptcy in each of the following cases:

> 1. 'If in England or elsewhere he makes a conveyance or
> assignment of his property to a trustee or trustees for the
> benefit of his creditors generally.'

An assignment to one or more particular creditors is not an
act of bankruptcy under this head, nor is an assignment of his
property by a debtor for the benefit of his trade creditors only:
the act of bankruptcy here meant is a conveyance of all or
substantially all a debtor's property to a trustee, who is to
represent all the creditors.[1]

An assignment executed by a foreigner resident abroad but
trading in England and intended to operate according to the law
of his domicil is not an act of bankruptcy.[2]

A creditor who has acquiesced in a deed of assignment or has
recognised the title of the trustee thereunder, e.g. by trading with
him as such, cannot rely on the assignment as an act of
bankruptcy, although he may not have assented to the deed so as
to be bound thereby.[3] But such a creditor may present a petition
founded on an independent act of bankruptcy.[4] Moreover, a
creditor whose assent to a deed of assignment has been obtained
by fraud or misrepresentation is not precluded from relying upon
the execution of the deed as an act of bankruptcy;[5] and a creditor
who has assented to a *proposed* deed of assignment may revoke
his assent before the execution of the deed, and then rely on any
act of bankruptcy connected with the proposed assignment.[6]

> 2. 'If in England or elsewhere he makes a fraudulent con-
> veyance, gift, delivery, or transfer of his property, or of any
> part thereof.'

Section 172 of the Law of Property Act 1925 provides that
any conveyance of property made with intent to defraud
creditors is voidable at the instance of anyone prejudiced by it
though a bona fide transferee for value is protected. The
Bankruptcy Act provision, quoted here, does not refer to any
specific intent but a 'fraudulent' conveyance, etc., by the debtor
does mean one which is fraudulent as against his creditors or
some of them and the Court is entitled to infer fraud in this sense
from the circumstances. Thus, if a debtor assigns all his property
for the benefit of one or several creditors to the exclusion of
others, this is 'fraudulent.' On the other hand, if he sells or
mortgages his property in the ordinary course of business, this is
not necessarily 'fraudulent.' Similarly, if the debtor assigns his

property partly in consideration of a past debt and partly as security for a further advance, then if the lender intended to enable the debtor to carry on his business, the assignment is not 'fraudulent'; contra, if the advance were a mere device for securing payment of or security for an earlier debt.[7]

A bona fide purchaser for value without notice of the property fraudulently transferred cannot retain it against a trustee in bankruptcy, if the transaction of purchase took place within the period of relation back, i.e. three months before presentation of the bankruptcy petition.[8]

3. 'If in England or elsewhere he makes any conveyance or transfer of his property or any part thereof, or creates any charge thereon which would under this or any other Act be void as a fraudulent preference if he were adjudged bankrupt'.[9]

It should be observed that in both these subsections the fraudulent conveyance is the cause of its being made an act of bankruptcy; a bona fide conveyance or gift may be set aside, but it will not ground a petition.

4. 'If with intent to defeat or delay his creditors he does any of the following things, namely, departs out of England, or being out of England remains out of England, or departs from his dwelling-house, or otherwise absents himself, or begins to keep house.'

In this case there is no act of bankruptcy unless there is an intention to defeat or delay creditors; a mere staying at home, or going abroad, though in fact followed by delay in payment, will not be an act of bankruptcy;[10] but, of course, all the circumstances will be looked to, and the court will find the intention from the facts. Leaving a place of business without paying creditors or notifying the change of address is an act of bankruptcy within this sub-section.[11]

5. 'If execution against him has been levied by seizure of his goods under process in an action in any court, or in any civil proceeding in the High Court, and the goods have been either sold or held by the sheriff for twenty-one days.[12] Provided that, where an interpleader summons has been taken out in regard to the goods seized, the time elapsing between the date at which summons is taken out and the date at which the proceedings on such summons are finally disposed of, settled, or abandoned, shall not be taken into account in calculating such period of twenty-one days.'

6. 'If he files in the court a declaration of his inability to pay his debts or presents a bankruptcy petition against himself.'

7. 'If a creditor has obtained a final judgment, or final order[13] against him for any amount, and execution thereon not having been stayed,[14] has served on him in England, or, by leave of the court, elsewhere, a *bankruptcy notice* under this Act, and he does not, within ten days[15] after service of the notice, in case the service is effected in England, and in case the service is effected elsewhere, then within the time limited in that behalf by the order giving leave to effect the service, either comply with the requirements of the notice,[16] or satisfy the court that he has a counter-claim set off or cross-demand which equals or exceeds the amount of the judgment debt, or sum ordered to be paid, and which he could not set up in the action in which the judgment was obtained, or the proceedings in which the order was obtained.'

A bankruptcy notice in the prescribed form requires the debtor to pay the judgment debt or sum ordered to be paid in accordance with the terms of the judgment or order, or to secure or compound for it to the satisfaction of the creditor or the court.[17]

It should be noted that the judgment debt may be of any amount, and that there are but three ways of avoiding committing the act of bankruptcy when a bankruptcy notice has been served, viz.:

i) paying; or
ii) giving satisfactory security; or
iii) showing a cross-claim equal to or exceeding the judgment debt, which could not have been set up in the action in which judgment was obtained.[18]

Bankruptcy notices are strictly construed and any irregularity which might in any way mislead or embarrass the debtor will render the notice void.[19]

8. 'If the debtor gives notice[20] to any of his creditors that he has suspended, or that he is about to suspend, payment of his debts.'

9. Where a criminal bankruptcy order is made against a person he shall be treated as having committed an act of bankruptcy, on the date on which the order was made.[21]

10. Where a person fails to make any payment which is required by an administration order and the court revokes that order and makes a receiving order he shall be deemed to have committed an act of bankruptcy when the receiving order is made.[22]

1 *Re Phillips* [1900] 2 QB 329. See Deeds of Arrangement Act 1914, para. 33.49, post.
2 *Re Debtors (No. 836 of 1935)* [1936] Ch 622 [1936] 1 All ER 875.
3 *Ex parte Stray* (1867) LR 2 Ch 374; *Re Brindley* [1906] 1 KB 377.
4 *Re Mills* [1906] 1 KB 389.
5 *Re Tanenberg & Sons* (1889) 6 Morr. 49.
6 *Re Jones Bros* [1912] 2 KB 234.
7 *Re Sinclair, Ex parte Chaplin* (1884) 26 ChD 319.
8 *Re Gunsbourg* [1920] 2 KB 426. See para. 33.17, post. As to protected transactions, see para. 33.19, post.
9 See para. 33.24, post.
10 *Ex parte Brandon* (1884) 25 ChD 500; *Re A Debtor (No 360 of 1951)* [1952] 1 All ER 519, n., CA.
11 *Re Worsley* [1901] 1 QB 309. The section includes a foreigner who leaves business debts in England (*Theophile v Solicitor-General* [1950] AC 186, [1950] 1 All ER 405, HL).
12 It was held in *Re Dalton (a Bankrupt), Ex parte Herrington and Carmichael (a Firm) v Trustee of Property of Bankrupt* [1963] Ch 336, [1962] 2 All ER 499, that a sheriff does 'hold' goods although, after seizure, the debtor is allowed under a 'walking possession' agreement between him and the sheriff to trade in the goods seized provided any goods sold were replaced.
13 This includes any person for the time being entitled to enforce a final judgment or order (Bankruptcy Act 1914, s. 1 (g)).
14 This would include a case where leave to issue execution was necessary and had not been obtained. See *Re Ide, Ex parte Ide* (1886) 17 QBD 755.
15 Insolvency Act 1976, s. 4 substituting ten days for the former period of seven days.
16 If the debtor gives a promissory note, which is taken, even conditionally, the creditor cannot get a receiving order on the notice: *Re Matthew (Ex parte Matthew* (1884) 12 QBD 506).
17 Bankruptcy Act 1914, s. 2.
18 As to the time limits for setting up payment or a cross-demand, see *Re a Debtor (No. 30 of 1956)* [1957] Ch 381, and *Re a Debtor (No. 991 of 1962) Ex parte Debtor v Tousson* [1963] 1 All ER 85, [1963] 1 WLR 51, CA.
19 *Re a Debtor (No. 21 of 1950)* [1951] Ch 313, [1950] 2 All ER 1129 (wrong county court named); *Re a Debtor (No. 41 of 1951)* [1952] Ch 192, [1952] 1 All ER 107 (proceedings in name of liquidator instead of company).
20 This notice need not be in writing; it suffices if the language used be such as to lead any reasonable person to suppose that the debtor intended to suspend payment (*Crook v Morley* [1891] AC 316. See also *Re a Debtor* [1929] 1 Ch 362, and cf. *Clough v Samuel* [1905] AC 442.
21 Powers of Criminal Courts Act 1973, s. 39 and Sch. 2, Part I, para. 1.
22 Insolvency Act 1976, s. 11 (1), (5).

The petition

33.04 This may be presented either by the debtor or by a creditor, or several creditors may join in presenting the petition.

A Creditor's Petition The following are the conditions on which a creditor may petition:[1]

1. The debt[2] due to him or, if more than one join in the petition,

the aggregate amount of the debts, must amount to £200 or more.[3]

2. It must be liquidated and payable immediately or at a certain future time. The debt must be liquidated *before* the act of bankruptcy on which the petition is founded and at the hearing the creditor will have to show that the debt continued to exist at the time of presentation of the petition and at the hearing.

3. The act of bankruptcy on which the petition is grounded must have occurred within three months before the presentation of the petition.

4. The debtor is (a) domiciled in England, or (b) has ordinarily resided in, or had a dwelling-house or place of business in England, within a year before presentation of the petition, or (c) has carried on business in England, personally or by an agent, or is, or has been within the said period a member of a firm which has carried on business by a partner or agent.[4]

The references to 'business' do not apply to anyone who is domiciled, nor to a firm having its principal place of business, in Scotland or Northern Ireland.

5. If the creditor is secured, he must in his petition, either state that he is prepared to surrender his security, or give an estimate of its value, and in the latter case there must be a balance of at least £200 owing to him after deducting from his debt the estimated value of it.[5]

If the petition states the wrong figure as the debt owing, but the correct figure would have been sufficient to support the petition, the receiving order will not be rescinded. But if the creditor fails to disclose a security, the order will be rescinded unless there are circumstances to justify leave being given to amend the petition.[6]

A Debtor's Petition If the petition is that of the debtor, he must allege in it his inability to pay his debt. Presentation of a petition by the debtor is deemed to be an act of bankruptcy without the previous filing by him of any declaration of inability to pay his debt and 'the court shall thereupon make a receiving order'.[7] A debtor's petition cannot be withdrawn without leave of the court.

---

1 Bankruptcy Act 1914, s. 4. The conditions are cumulative.

2 Rates are a sufficient debt although only recoverable by distress (*Re McGreavy Ex parte McGreavey v Benfleet UDC* [1950] Ch 269, [1950] 1 All ER 442, CA). Water rates are now recoverable as a civil debt and a magistrates' court judgment for them can ground a bankruptcy petition: see *Re A Debtor (No. 48 of 1952)* [1953] Ch 335, [1953] 1 All ER 545, CA.

3 Insolvency Act 1976, s. 1 and Sch. 1, Part I.

4 See *Re Brauch (A Debtor), ex parte Britannic Securities and Investments Ltd* [1978] 1 All ER 1004, [1977] 3 WLR 354, CA.

5 Bankruptcy Act 1914, s. 4 (2). As to the trustee's right to redeem, see para. 33.43, *post*. Where execution has not been completed by the appointment of a receiver the creditor is not secured. *Re a Debtor (No. 39 of 1974) ex parte Okill v Gething* [1977] 3 All ER 489, [1977] 1 WLR 1308.

6 *Re A Debtor (No. 6 of 1941)* [1943] Ch 213, [1943] 1 All ER 553.

7 Bankruptcy Act 1914, s. 6. In *Re A Debtor (No. 17 of 1966)* [1967] Ch 590, [1967] 1 All ER 668, a judgment of £2,400 damages was required to be paid by weekly instalments of 25*s.* and the judgment debtor filed a petition for his own bankruptcy. *Held:* an adjudication based on this petition must be annulled as the debtor was able to pay the instalments as they became due though not the whole of the judgment at once.

33.05   *The place of presentation* is:

1. The High Court of Justice, where the debtor:

i) has carried on business or has resided in the London bankruptcy district during the greater part of the six months before the presentation of the petition, or

ii) for a longer period thereof than in the district of any county court, or

iii) when he is not resident in England, or

iv) when his residence cannot be ascertained.

2. In any other case in the county court (not comprised in the London bankruptcy district) within whose district the debtor has resided or carried on business during the greater part of the said six months.[1]

Preference is to be given to his 'business' over his 'residential' district.[2]

---

1 Bankruptcy Act 1914, ss. 98, 99. As to transfers, see ibid, s. 100.

2 Bankruptcy Rules 1952, r. 145 (2).

The receiving order

33.06   This may be made at any time after the presentation of the petition, but, in the case of a creditor's petition, not until after the hearing. If, on a creditor's petition, the court is not satisfied with the proof of any of the matters required to be shown (i.e. the petitioning creditor's debt, the act of bankruptcy and the service of the petition) or is satisfied by the debtor that he is able to pay his debts or if there is other 'sufficient cause,' it will dismiss the petition.[1] Examples of sufficient cause are:

1. That the debtor's only asset is a life interest which will be forfeited on bankruptcy;[2]

2. That there are no assets *and no reasonable probability of any;*[3]

3. That the petition is brought for some collateral end or to extort more than is due.[4]

The effect of a receiving order is to constitute the official receiver—an officer appointed by the Department of Trade[5]—receiver of the property of the debtor, and thereafter no creditor has any remedy against the debtor or his property or may commence an action against the debtor without leave of the court. Creditors not subject to this rule are:

1. Secured creditors;[6]
2. Creditors whose debts are not provable in bankruptcy;[7] and
3. To a certain extent, the landlord.[8]

Even before a receiving order is made, at any time after the petition is presented, the court may, if this is shown to be necessary for the protection of the estate, appoint the official receiver to be interim receiver of the debtor's property.[9]

Any proceedings (e.g. action, execution) may be stayed by the court when a petition has been presented, though a receiving order has not yet been made.[10]

Notice of every receiving order stating the name, address and description of the debtor, the date of the order, the court by which the order is made, and the date of the petition, must be advertised in the *London Gazette* and in a local paper.[11]

The court has a general discretion under s. 108 to rescind its orders, and can therefore rescind a receiving order. In exercising this discretion the court is not confined to the grounds on which an order of adjudication can be annulled.[12] Thus, the court may rescind a receiving order not only where it thinks the order was wrongly made or where there has been payment in full (these being the statutory grounds of annulment) but also if it thinks rescission would be for the benefit of creditors and not detrimental to the public. In *Re Izod*,[13] a receiving order was rescinded when the debtor's father paid the creditors ten shillings in the pound and they withdrew their proofs and released the debtor. But even if the creditors are paid in full and support the debtor's application for rescission of the receiving order, it may be refused if the official receiver considers the debtor's conduct should be subjected to a public examination.[14] If the receiving order is obtained by the presentation of a petition under circumstances which amount to an abuse of the process of the court, it will, of course, be rescinded.[15]

Every receiving order must be registered by the official receiver with the chief land registrar if any part of the debtor's property consists of land, but a purchaser is not protected against an unregistered receiving order unless he acquires a legal estate in good faith for money or money's worth without notice of an available act of bankruptcy.[16]

---

1 Bankruptcy Act 1914, s. 5 (3).
2 *Re Otway, Ex parte Otway* (1851) 1 QB 812.
3 *Re Betts* [1897] 1 QB 50. The court will not refuse to make an order on the ground of want of assets when the only evidence is that of the debtor. *Re Field (A Debtor)* [1977] 3 WLR 937.
4 *Re Shaw* (1901) 83 LT 754; cf. *Re Sunderland* [1911] 2 KB 658; *Re A Debtor (No. 883 of 1927)* [1928] Ch 199; *Re A Judgment Summons (No. 25 of 1952)* [1953] Ch 195, [1953] 1 All ER 424, CA; *Re Majory A Debtor, Ex parte Debtor v FA Dumont* [1955] Ch 600, [1955] 2 All ER 65.
5 Para. 33.27, post.
6 Bankruptcy Act 1914, s. 7.
7 Para. 33.39, post, and s. 30. See *James v James* [1964] P. 303, [1963] 2 All ER 465.
8 Para. 33.42, post.
9 Bankruptcy Act 1914, s. 8.
10 Ibid, s. 9.
11 Ibid, s. 11.
12 See para. 33.10, post.
13 [1898] 1 QB 241. This decision was distinguished in *Re a Debtor (No. 12 of 1970) Ex parte Official Receiver v the Debtor* [1971] 2 All ER 1494, [1971] 1 WLR 1212, CA.
14 *Re Leslie, Ex parte Leslie* (1887) 18 QBD 619. By s. 12 of the Act a receiving order may be rescinded if a majority of the creditors in number and value are resident in Scotland or Northern Ireland.
15 *Re Betts* [1901] 2 KB 39. In this case the debtor repeatedly presented petitions against himself for the purpose of avoiding the effect of orders for his committal. But in a proper case the debtor may relieve himself from such pressure by seeking the protection of the bankruptcy court: *Re Harry Dunn* [1949] Ch 640, [1949] 2 All ER 338, CA.
16 Land Charges Act 1972, ss. 6, 8.

Normal course of proceedings after receiving order

33.07 The debtor will attend a *private interview* with the Official Receiver, where he will receive instructions as to preparing his *statement of affairs*. This gives full particulars as to his assets, debts, creditors, securities held by them, etc. It must be verified by affidavit, and made within three or seven days after the receiving order according to whether the petition was presented by himself or by a creditor.[1] If necessary, the official receiver will allow the debtor skilled assistance in the preparation of his statement. If he fails to submit a statement, without reasonable excuse, he may be adjudged bankrupt on the application of the official receiver or of any creditor. He must also attend the *first* *meeting of creditors* at which he should present any proposals he may have for a composition.[2] The creditors will decide whether a composition is to be accepted. The debtor must also attend a *public examination* which must not be concluded until after the first meeting of creditors has been held.[3] In default of the creditors accepting a composition, an *adjudication order* will be made in due course and a trustee in bankruptcy will be appointed.[4] His property will vest in the trustee who will realise it and distribute it among the creditors in accordance with the Act.[5] At any date after being adjudged bankrupt the debtor may apply for his *discharge.*[6] He may also be discharged on the application of the official receiver or automatically discharged under provisions of the Insolvency Act 1976.[7]

---

1 Bankruptcy Act 1914, s. 14. By the Bankruptcy Rules 1952, s. 329, the Official Receiver may require the debtor to furnish him with a trading and profit and loss accounts and a cash and goods account for any period not exceeding two years before the date of the receiving order.
2 See para. 33.48, post.
3 See para. 33.09, post.
4 See para. 33.10, post.
5 See paras. 33.37, et seq., post.
6 See para. 33.11, post.
7 Ss. 7, 8.

Creditors' meetings

33.08 The first meeting is generally the most important, and is often the last. On this occasion the chief business consists of the determination whether a proposal for a composition or scheme of arrangement shall be entertained, or whether it is desirable to have the debtor adjudicated bankrupt, and if bankruptcy is resolved upon, the appointment of a trustee and a committee of inspection.[1] This meeting may be adjourned or any particular question may be left to a subsequent meeting. The debtor must attend and submit to such examination and give such information as the meeting may require.[2]

---

1 See paras. 33.26–33.31, post.
2 Bankruptcy Act 1914, s. 22.

Public examination[1]

33.09 As soon as convenient after the expiration of time for the submission by the debtor of his statement of affairs, he must undergo an examination in open court[2] touching his conduct, dealings and property. It is the duty of the official receiver to apply to the court for the appointment of a time and place for the examination, to give notice to the creditors and to the debtor, and to publish it in the London Gazette and in a local paper.[3] The object of the examination is the protection of the public as well as of the interests of the creditors. He must therefore answer questions put to him even if they may incriminate him.[4]

The debtor is put upon his oath, and may be examined:

1. By the court,
2. The official receiver,
3. The trustee, if appointed before the conclusion of the examination, or
4. By any creditor who has tendered a proof or his representative authorised in writing.

Notes are taken, which must be signed by the debtor after being read over to or by him and may thereafter be used in evidence against him. The court may adjourn the examination if it sees fit; and, if it thinks the debtor is not making a full and true disclosure of his affairs or, without good reason, has failed to attend or comply with any order of the court, may do so *sine die*;[5] this makes it necessary for the debtor, when he desires to have his examination continued, to get a fresh appointment and to bear personally the expense of advertising. Alternatively the registrar may report the matter to the judge who can commit the debtor for contempt of court.[6]

If the debtor makes default in attending his public examination, a warrant may be issued for his arrest.[7]

The court may, if it thinks fit having regard to all the circumstances, including whether or not the debtor has made a full disclosure, whether he has been previously adjudged bankrupt, the number and nature of his debts and whether the bankruptcy might be a matter of public concern, dispense with the public examination. An application for such an order may only be made by the official receiver, but an application for review of such an order may be made either by the official receiver, the debtor, a creditor or the trustee.[8]

---

1 Bankruptcy Act 1914, s. 15, and Insolvency Act 1976, s. 6.
2 When the debtor cannot, from incapacity, attend the court, an order may be made dispensing with the examination, or directing that it be held at such

place and in such manner as the court thinks expedient (Bankruptcy Act 1914, s. 15 (10)).
3 Bankruptcy Rules 1952, rr. 188 and 189.
4 *Re Paget*, [1927] 2 Ch 85.
5 Bankruptcy Rules 1952, r. 192.
6 Bankruptcy Act 1914, s. 102 (4); Bankruptcy Rules 1952, r. 83.
7 Bankruptcy Rules 1952, r. 190.
8 Insolvency Act 1976, s. 6.

Adjudication[1]

33.10 The debtor may, at his own request, be adjudged bankrupt at the time of the receiving order or at any time thereafter.[2] Otherwise, any creditor or the official receiver (usually the latter) may apply to the court to adjudge the debtor bankrupt. The court has power to make such adjudication on any of the following grounds:

1. An ordinary[3] resolution of the creditors in favour of adjudication;
2. That no resolution of any kind has been passed;
3. That the creditors have not met;
4. That a scheme has not been approved within fourteen days after the public examination;[4]
5. That the debtor has failed to pay any instalment due under a composition;[5]
6. That the debtor has failed without reasonable cause to give a proper account of his affairs;[6]
7. That the public examination has been adjourned sine die.[7]

Notice of the adjudication must be advertised in the London Gazette and in a local paper.[8]

Effect The effect of adjudication is to vest the bankrupt's property[9] in the trustee whose position is examined below.[10] If an undischarged bankrupt obtains credit to the extent of £50 or more or trades under a different name from that under which he was adjudged bankrupt, without informing his intended creditor that he is an undischarged bankrupt, or without disclosing the name under which he was adjudged bankrupt, he will be liable to imprisonment.[11] An undischarged bankrupt cannot be a director or take part in the management of a company except with the consent of the court.[12]

An adjudication may be *annulled*:

1. If the court thinks that the debtor ought not to have been made bankrupt;[13] or

2. If the debts are paid in full or, in the case of disputed debts, secured to the satisfaction of the court;[13] or

3. If a scheme is accepted after adjudication and the court approves the scheme.[14]

Even when the debts have been paid in full, the court has discretion to refuse an order of annulment. Thus:

> Where the bankrupt had been guilty of a falsification of his statement of affairs, and of a substantial concealment of assets, the court refused to annul the adjudication.[15] But, where a minor had been adjudicated bankrupt and there were no debts legally enforceable against him at all, the court did exercise its discretion to annul the order.[16]

An unconditional release given to the bankrupt is not equivalent to payment in full.[17]

On annulment the property of the bankrupt will be vested in him, or in such other person as the court may appoint.[18] And if on annulment under a composition, which is paid, the court makes no special order, the property of the bankrupt will revest in him.[19]

Notice of the order annulling an adjudication must be advertised in the London Gazette and in a local paper.

---

1 Bankruptcy Act 1914, s. 18.
2 Bankruptcy Rules 1952, r. 217.
3 An ordinary resolution is one carried by a majority in *value* of the creditors present and voting in person or by proxy (Bankruptcy Act 1914, s. 167).
4 Ibid, s. 18 (1).
5 Bankruptcy Act 1914, s. 16 (16).
6 Ibid, s. 14 (3); Bankruptcy Rules 1952, r. 219; as to the validity of this Rule, see *Re Fletcher, a Debtor Ex parte Fletcher v Official Receiver* [1956] Ch 28, [1955] 2 All ER 592.
7 Bankruptcy Rules 1952, r. 220.
8 Bankruptcy Act 1914, s. 18 (2).
9 See para. 33.16, post.
10 See para. 33.29, post.
11 Bankruptcy Act 1914, s. 155. See *R v Doubleday* (1964) 49 Cr. App. Rep. 62, CCA. Insolvency Act 1976, s. 1 and Sch. 1, Part I, raised the amount from £10 to £50. See also *R v Miller* [1977] 3 All ER 986, [1977] 1 WLR 1129, CA.
12 Companies Act 1948, s. 187.
13 Bankruptcy Act 1914, s. 29. 'Debts' means proved debts, and if a bankruptcy is annulled, the right of a creditor, who did not prove, to sue the debtor is revived: *More v More* [1962] Ch 424, [1962] 1 All ER 125.
14 Ibid, s. 21 (2). See para. 33.48, post.
15 *Re Taylor* [1901] 1 QB 744.
16 *Re Davenport, Ex parte Bankrupt v Eric Street Properties Ltd* [1963] 2 All ER 850, [1963] 1 WLR 817, CA. See *Re Noble (a Bankrupt), ex parte Bankrupt v Official Receiver* [1964] 2 All ER 522, CA, [1965] Ch 129.
17 *Re Keet* [1905] 2 KB 666.

18 Bankruptcy Act 1914, ss. 21 (2), 29 (2).
19 *Flower v Lyme Regis Corpn* [1921] 1 KB 488.

Discharge of bankrupt[1]

33.11 The discharge is the order of the court granting the bankrupt a release,[2] and removing from him the status of bankruptcy.

A bankrupt may apply at any time after being adjudged bankrupt for an order of discharge, and the court will appoint some day subsequent to the conclusion of the public examination on which to hear the application. This is heard in open court after fourteen days' notice to the creditors; and the trustee, the creditors, and the official receiver may all oppose. The official receiver's report on the debtor's conduct and affairs, a copy of which must be sent to the bankrupt not less than seven days before the hearing, is read in court and if he intends to dispute any statement contained in it he must give appropriate notice to the official receiver not less than two days before the hearing.[3] The court may put such questions to the debtor and receive such evidence as it thinks fit and, in its discretion, may grant a discharge.

The discharge is either:

1. *Unconditional*, which frees the bankrupt at once as from the date of the order.
2. *Conditional*, having the same effect, but subject to conditions as to any future earnings or income or after-acquired property.
3. *Suspensive*, which stays the operation of the order till the expiration of a certain time.
4. *Conditional and suspensive.*

1 Bankruptcy Act 1914, s. 26, as amended by s. 1 of the Bankruptcy (Amendment) Act 1926. Insolvency Act 1976, ss. 7 and 8.
2 See para. 33.15, post.
3 Bankruptcy Rules 1952, rr. 229 and 230.

33.12 *Cases where court's discretion is limited* Where the bankrupt has committed an offence under the Act,[1] or any other offence connected with his bankruptcy, or where any of the facts mentioned below are proved, the court cannot grant an unconditional discharge. The discharge must either be:

1. Refused, or
2. Suspended for such period as the court thinks proper, or

3. Suspended until the bankrupt has paid a dividend of 50p. in the £ to the creditors, or

4. Granted, subject to the condition of judgment being entered against the debtor for any part of the unpaid provable debts, such amount to be paid out of future earnings or after-acquired property on such conditions as the court may direct.

In *addition* to one of these four alternatives, the court may include any other conditions which it could impose under the general powers of s. 26, e.g. the court may suspend the order for two years *and* then make it conditional on the debtor paying a periodic sum out of future earnings until a particular dividend has been paid.[2]

---

1 Bankruptcy Act 1914, ss. 154 et seq.
2 *Re Tabrisky, Ex parte Board of Trade*, [1947] Ch 565, [1947] 2 All ER 182; *Re Mills, Ex parte Bankrupt v Official Receiver* [1966] 1 All ER 516, [1967] 1 WLR 580.

33.13   The facts requiring the court to refuse an immediate unconditional order are as follows:

i) When the bankrupt's assets are not of a value equal to 50p. in the £ on his unsecured liabilities, unless this has arisen from circumstances for which he cannot justly be held responsible.

ii) When the bankrupt has omitted to keep such books of account as are usual and proper in the business carried on by him,[1] and as sufficiently disclose his business transactions and financial position[2] within the three years immediately preceding his bankruptcy.[3]

iii) When he has continued to trade after knowing himself to be insolvent.

iv) If he has contracted any debt provable in bankruptcy without having at the time of contracting it any reasonable or probable ground of expectation (proof whereof shall lie on him) of being able to pay it.

v) If he fails to account satisfactorily for any loss of assets, or deficiency of assets to meet his liabilities.

vi) If he has brought on or contributed to his bankruptcy by rash and hazardous speculations, or unjustifiable extravagance in living, or by gambling, or by culpable neglect of his business affairs.

vii) If he has put any of his creditors to unnecessary expense by a frivolous or vexatious defence to any action properly brought against him.

viii) If he has brought on or contributed to his bankruptcy by incurring unjustifiable expense in bringing any frivolous or vexatious action.

ix) If he has a within three months before the date of the receiving order, when unable to pay his debts as they become due, given an undue preference[4] to any of his creditors.

x) If within three months before the receiving order, he incurred liabilities with the view of making his assets equal to 50p. in the £ on his unsecured liabilities.

xi) If on any previous occasion he has been adjudged bankrupt, or has made a composition or arrangement with his creditors.

xii) If he has been guilty of any fraud or fraudulent breach of trust.[5]

---

1 This is strictly construed and will not apply to speculations outside the business (*Re Mutton* (1887) 19 QBD 102), or to isolated transactions without continuity of trading.

2 And this without the need of long and skilled investigation (*Re Reed and Bowen Ex parte Reed and Bowen* (1886) 17 QBD 244).

3 In certain cases where a person has been previously adjudged bankrupt, the failure to keep proper books is an offence. S. 158, as amended by s. 7 of the Bankruptcy (Amendment) Act 1926.

4 Not necessarily a 'fraudulent' preference (*Re Bryant* [1895] 1 QB 420).

5 The making of an ante-nuptial marriage settlement, which is unjustifiable having regard to the state of the settlor's affairs at the time of making it is equivalent to fraud for the purpose of the bankrupt's discharge (Bankruptcy Act 1914, s. 27).

33.14 *Certificate of misfortune* When a person's bankruptcy has been caused by misfortune without any misconduct on his part, the court may grant the discharge with a certificate to that effect, and this frees the bankrupt from certain statutory disqualifications which otherwise prevent him from taking part in a number of public affairs, e.g. membership of either House of Parliament, for five years from the date of his discharge.[1] A bankrupt who initiates litigation when he has no prospects of paying the costs if he loses his cases and whose assets are not equal to 50p. in the £ on his unsecured liabilities is not entitled to an immediate discharge from bankruptcy nor to a certificate of misfortune.[2]

Two further methods of discharge are now provided by the Insolvency Act 1976. Where the court makes an order that the public examination has been concluded or may be dispensed with it may also make an order that the debtor is in any event to be discharged five years after adjudication. Such an order may be rescinded on the application of the official receiver or the trustee before the expiry of the five years. This is known as automatic discharge.[3] Provision is also made for discharge on the application of the official receiver in cases where the debtor has not applied for discharge or the adjudication has not been annulled and no order for automatic discharge was made.[4] Such an application must be made in the sixth year after adjudication and the court may grant the application unconditionally, conditionally or suspensively or refuse it. Suspension may be for such period as the court thinks fit or until the debtor pays a dividend of not less than 50p. in the pound. It may be a condition that the bankrupt submit to judgment for any balance not satisfied at the discharge, such balance to be paid out of future earnings or after-acquired property as the court may direct.

1 Bankruptcy Act 1914, s. 26 (4); Bankruptcy Act 1883, s. 32; Bankruptcy Act 1890, s. 9; Local Government Act 1972, ss. 80, 81. Should the debtor wish to appeal against refusal of a certificate of misfortune, he must make the official receiver a respondent: *Re Joyce, Ex parte Joyce* [1955] 2 All ER 747, [1955] 1 WLR 800.
2 *Re Wenlock* (1968) 112 Sol Jo 722.
3 Insolvency Act 1976, s. 7.
4 Ibid, s. 8.

33.15 *Effect of discharge* The effect of discharge is to release the bankrupt (but not his partner, or his surety) from every provable debt, except in the following cases:

1. A debt due on a recognisance or to the Crown;[1]
2. Debts incurred for offences against the revenue;[1]
3. Debts incurred through fraud, or fraudulent breach of trust;
4. Liabilities under an affiliation order, except to such extent as the court expressly orders.[2]

It will not protect him from criminal proceedings.

1 Unless the Treasury gives its consent in writing.
2 Bankruptcy Act 1914, s. 28.

4. What property is available for the creditors

33.16 Subject to a number of exceptions, all property belonging to the debtor vests on adjudication in the trustee and is therefore available for distribution to the creditors. Also available, again subject to exceptions, is all property that may be acquired by or devolve on the bankrupt before his discharge.[1] A fuller examination of the statutory provisions must now be given.

---

1 Bankruptcy Act 1914, s. 38.

---

1. *All property belonging to the bankrupt at the commencement of the bankruptcy*

33.17 I.e. the date when he committed the act of bankruptcy on which the receiving order was made or, if he is proved to have committed more than one act of bankruptcy, the date of the first of the acts of bankruptcy proved to have been committed within three months of the presentation of the petition. The bankruptcy and the trustee's title are said to *relate back* to such act of bankruptcy.[1]

This category of property divisible amongst creditors includes payments to any creditor since that date and the right to bring actions both in contract and in tort. The following limits are suggested:[2]

i) A right of action arising or a tort resulting immediately in injury to the person, reputation or feelings of the bankrupt, will not pass to the trustee; nor will a right of action for breach of contract with similar results (e.g. to cure him).

ii) If the estate is *directly* affected together with the person, the cause of action will be split, and so much of it as relates to the estate will pass to the trustee.[3]

iii) If a bankrupt has been wrongfully dismissed from his employment *after* adjudication, the right to sue for damages remains in him and does not vest in his trustee.[4]

iv) The trustee may assign choses in action, including a right to sue, to the bankrupt on proper terms.[5]

The trustee is, under the bankruptcy laws, only statutory assignee of the bankrupt's choses in action, and therefore takes them subject to all equities existing at the date of the commencement of the bankruptcy. Thus, except where the Act expressly allows it, he obtains no better title than the bankrupt had. For example:

If a building contract provides that the building owner may in certain circumstances pay sub-contractors direct, or if the sub-contracts contain an equitable assignment of part of the moneys payable under the main contract, the rights of the trustee of the main contractor are subject to these provisions.[6]

Exceptions The following property is not available for creditors:[7]

i) Tools of a bankrupt's trade, and the necessary wearing apparel and bedding of himself, his wife and children, to a value, all included, of not more than £250;

ii) Property held on trust for others, if it can be distinguished from the bulk of the bankrupt's property, i.e. if it is ear-marked.[8]

Special Rules must be noted in connection with (*a*) the rights of execution creditors; (*b*) protected transactions.

---

1 Bankruptcy Act 1914, s. 37, and see *Re Burrows, Ex parte Official Receiver v Steel* [1944] Ch 49 (continuing act of bankruptcy).
2 Williams (18th edn) 321–322.
3 *Rose v Buckett* [1901] 2 KB 449, CA; *Re Kavanagh, Ex parte The Bankrupt v Jackson (Trustee)* [1950] 1 All ER 39, CA, n. (prima facie a lump sum recovered in a compromise will be divided fifty-fifty).
4 *Bailey v Thurston* [1903] 1 KB 137.
5 *Ramsey v Hartley* [1977] 2 All ER 673, [1977] 1 WLR 686, CA.
6 *Re Tout and Finch Ltd* [1954] 1 All ER 127, [1954] 1 WLR 178.
7 Bankruptcy Act 1914, s. 38 (1), (2). The Insolvency Act 1976, s. 1, and Sch. 1, Part I, raised the amount from £20 to £250.
8 *Re Hallett & Co Ex parte Blane* [1894] 2 QB 237.

33.18 *a) The rights of execution creditors.* When execution has issued against the land, goods, or debts of the bankrupt, the execution creditor is not entitled to retain the *benefit of the execution* or attachment unless it is completed by:

i) the seizure and sale of the goods, or

ii) seizure or appointment of receiver over the land, or

iii) the receipt of the debt,[1]

and this before the date of the receiving order and before the execution creditor has notice of any bankruptcy petition or any available act of bankruptcy.[2]

In relation to an execution against goods, 'the benefit of the execution refers to the charge on the debtor's goods obtained by the execution creditor by the issue of his writ, and does not include any moneys actually received by the creditor in whole or partial satisfaction of his debt, whether under or in consequence of an execution or not. If part of the debt has been discharged by sale or payment, and the execution is still subsisting, a supervening bankruptcy will deprive the creditor of the benefit of the execution in respect of the unpaid balance'.[3]

The Act imposes certain duties on a sheriff in relation to goods taken in execution. If previous to sale or completion of the execution by the receipt or recovery of the full amount of the levy, notice is served on the sheriff that a receiving order has been made against the debtor, he must hand over the goods, and any money received in part satisfaction, to the trustee or official receiver on request.[4]

Where goods are seized in respect of a judgment exceeding £250, the sheriff must deduct the expenses of execution and retain the balance of the proceeds of the sale or of money paid to avoid it,[5] for fourteen days; if during that time he is served with notice of a bankruptcy petition and a receiving order is made against the debtor thereon or on any other petition of which the sheriff has notice, the sheriff must pay the balance to the official receiver or trustee who is entitled to retain it as against the execution creditor.[6]

---

1 An order for payment out of court is not sufficient (*George v Tompson's Trustee* [1949] Ch 322, [1949] 1 All ER 554); nor receipt by the creditor's solicitor as stakeholder (*Re Lupkovics* [1954] 2 All ER 125, [1954] WLR 1234).

2 Bankruptcy Act 1914, s. 40. An execution may be completed by a partial levy followed by a return of nulla bona to a subsequent levy (*Re Fairley* [1922] 2 Ch 791); or 'by the receipt or recovery of the full amount of the levy,'s. 41. An execution levied by seizure and sale of the goods of a debtor is not invalid by reason of it being an act of bankruptcy and a person who purchases the goods in good faith under a sale by the sheriff shall acquire a good title to them against the trustee in bankruptcy (s. 40 (3)).

3 *Re Andrew, Ex parte Official Receiver (Trustee) (No. 2)* [1937] Ch 122, [1936] 3 All ER 450; *Re Love* [1952] Ch 138, [1951] 2 All ER 1016.

4 Bankruptcy Act 1914, s. 41 (1).

5 The sale must be public unless the court otherwise orders (Bankruptcy Act 1883, s. 145); this also applies to sales by the registrar of a county court (County Courts Act 1959, s. 132).

6 Bankruptcy Act 1914, s. 41 (2). Insolvency Act 1976, s. 1 and Sch. 1, Part I, raised the amount from £20 to £250. See *Marley Tile Co v Burrows* [1978] 1 All ER 657, [1977] 3 WLR 641, CA (money paid to avoid sale goes to execution creditor when fourteen days expire without notice of bankruptcy).

33.19 *b) Protected transactions* Subject to the foregoing provisions of the Act as to the effect of bankruptcy on an execution or attachment, and to the provisions to be examined later with respect to the avoidance of certain settlements, assignments and preferences, any payment by the bankrupt to any of his creditors, any payment or delivery to the bankrupt, and any conveyance by or contract with him for valuable consideration will hold good, provided the transaction takes place before the date of the receiving order, and before any notice to the person dealing with the bankrupt of any 'available act of bankruptcy'.[1]

A payment made to or for the bankrupt after the date of the

receiving order is not protected, although the person making the payment had no knowledge of the receiving order and could not by any reasonable means have ascertained that it had been made.[2] But the hardship imposed by the above rule on agents and other persons, e.g. bankers, in possession of money or property of a bankrupt has to some extent been mitigated. Where such person has paid or transferred the money or property to another person on or after the date of the receiving order without knowledge that it had been made and before it has been gazetted, then, if the transaction is void, the trustee's right to recover from the innocent payer or transferor cannot be enforced except where and so far as the court is satisfied that it is not reasonably practicable to recover from the person to whom the money or property was paid or transferred.[3]

A payment of money or delivery of property (e.g. on the redemption of securities) to a person who is subsequently adjudged bankrupt is a good discharge, although made with notice of an available act of bankruptcy, if made before the actual date of the receiving order in the ordinary course of business or otherwise bona fide. Such payment or delivery of property cannot, however, be safely made after notice of the presentation of a bankruptcy petition.[4] This provision enables, e.g., a bank to pay the debtor money it holds on his behalf although the bank know he has committed an act of bankruptcy and thereby may enable the debtor to pay his debts and avert the presentation of a petition.[5]

---

1 Bankruptcy Act 1914, s. 45. A past debt may be good consideration for a conveyance by a bankrupt, but if a creditor takes over substantially the whole of a debtor's property in satisfaction for a past debt, knowing that there are other creditors, the transaction will not be protected: *Re Jukes* [1902] 2 KB 58.

2 *Re Wigzell* [1921] 2 KB 835. If, however, a receiving order is made on appeal from the dismissal of a petition and *antedated* to the date when the petition was wrongly dismissed, the 'date of the receiving order' for the purposes of s. 45, ibid, is the date on which it was actually made and not the date appearing on the order. Where a debtor has benefited from transactions after the receiving order the court may refuse to allow the trustee to enforce his right to recover payments made to a supplier who acted in ignorance of the order. *Re Clark (a Bankrupt) Ex parte Trustee of Property of Bankrupt v Texaco* [1975] 1 All ER 453, [1975] 1 WLR 559.

3 Bankruptcy (Amendment) Act 1926, s. 4.

4 Bankruptcy Act 1914, s. 46. See *Re Dalton (a Bankrupt) Ex parte Herrington and Carmichael (a Firm) v The Trustee* [1963] Ch 336, [1962] 2 All ER 499.

5 Williams on Bankruptcy (18th edn) 401.

2. *All property acquired by or devolving on the bankrupt before his discharge*

33.20 But (a) it is important to appreciate that the trustee may only enforce his rights to such property if he intervenes before the bankrupt disposes of it to a bona fide transferee for value. All transactions by a bankrupt with anyone dealing with him bona fide and for value, in respect of real or personal property, acquired after adjudication are valid against the trustee if completed before the trustee intervenes.[1] It makes no difference that the transferee knows of the bankruptcy.

Ordinary dealings between banker and customer after adjudication are to be deemed transactions for value. But where a banker ascertains that his customer is an undischarged bankrupt he must forthwith inform the trustee or Department of Trade of the existence of the account, and thereafter he must not make any payments out of it except under an order of the court or in accordance with the instructions of the trustee, unless by the expiration of one month from the date of giving the information no instructions have been received from the trustee.[2]

b) The trustee has no right to such part of the bankrupt's personal earnings as is necessary for the support of himself and his family.[3] If a bankrupt dies leaving savings out of his personal earnings, the trustee is entitled to the money only subject to the payment of creditors for necessaries supplied since the adjudication and payment to the creditors for funeral expenses after adjudication.[4]

c) With regard to certain property, the trustee is only entitled to such part of it as may be allotted to him under the provisions of ss. 50 and 51:

i) The benefit of a clergyman's stipend does not go to the trustee, but it may be sequestrated.[5] In this event, an amount to be fixed by the bishop must be allowed to the clergyman; and the curate's stipend for services rendered during four months before the date of the receiving order, to an extent not exceeding £800, is payable in priority in full.

ii) So much of the salary of an officer[6] or civil servant of the state is obtainable by the trustee in bankruptcy, as the court, with the written consent of the chief officer of the department, may direct, and will be paid to the trustee.

iii) Where a bankrupt is in receipt of a salary or income, i.e. of some income payable at a fixed time, or is entitled to half pay or pension, the court may make an order that such salary or part of it be paid to the trustee.[7]

Where a bankrupt wife is in receipt of maintenance under an

order of the divorce court, it is salary or income within this section.[8]

The expression 'income' points to some definite annual payments coming to the bankrupt.[9] Accordingly, it will include sums payable for maintenance to a former wife under an order of the divorce court;[10] but the prospective and contingent earnings of a professional man are not such income, and no part of those earnings can be ordered to be set aside for the benefit of his creditors.[11]

---

1 Bankruptcy Act 1914, s. 47 (1). The value given need not augment the bankrupt's estate; a settlement on marriage of after-acquired property will be good (*Re Behrend's Trust* [1911] 1 Ch 687).

2 Bankruptcy Act 1914, s. 47 (2).

3 *Re Roberts* [1900] 1 QB 122. The trustee may be entitled to the debtor's share in a jointly owned matrimonial home and this may be sold to give effect to the trustee's claims. *Re Bailey (a Bankrupt) Ex parte Bailey v Trustee of Property of Bankrupt* [1977] 2 All ER 26, [1977] 1 WLR 278.

4 *Re Walter* [1929] 1 Ch 647.

5 Bankruptcy Act 1914, s. 50. Insolvency Act 1976, and Sch. 1, Part I, raised the amount for the curates stipend from £50 to £800.

6 Bankruptcy Act 1914, s. 51 (1). An order under this section may be continued on discharge (*Re Gardner, Ex parte Official Receiver v Gardner* [1942] Ch 50, [1941] 3 All ER 289).

7 Bankruptcy Act 1914, s. 51 (2). See *Re Cohen* [1961] Ch. 246, [1961] 1 All ER 646, CA. It was held that income from the life interest of a bankrupt under his father's will did not come within the word 'income.' An order under s. 51 (2) was not necessary as the income vested automatically in the trustee in bankruptcy along with the bankrupt's other assets. And see *Re Duckett* [1964] Ch 398, [1964] 1 All ER 19, CA.

8 *Re Tennant's Application* [1956] 2 All ER 753, [1956] 1 WLR 874.

9 See, further, as to the meaning of salary or income (*Re Shine* [1892] 1 QB 522; *Re Hutton, Ex parte Benwell* (1884) 14 QBD 301; *Re Landau* [1934] Ch 549).

10 *Re Landau*, ante.

11 *Re Hutton, Ex parte Benwell*, ante.

33.21 3. *The capacity to exercise all powers in respect of property which the bankrupt might have exercised for his own benefit*

4. *All goods being, at the commencement of the bankruptcy, in the possession, order, or disposition of the bankrupt, in his trade or business, by the consent and permission of the true owner, under such circumstances that he is the reputed owner thereof*

33.22 Choses in action, other than debts due or growing due to the bankrupt in the course of his trade or business, are not 'goods' within this section.[1]

The reputation of ownership may be excluded by a well-known custom, e.g.

hotel furniture is not in the reputed ownership of the bankrupt, since it is well known that such furniture is frequently hired.[2]

Where goods are taken by the trustee under this clause, the true owner is entitled to prove for their value.[3] Goods subject to hire purchase conditional sale or some other agreement may be within reputed ownership but this may be negatived by the service of a default notice.[4] Because of the widespread prevalence of customs excluding its operation reputed ownership is now of limited practical importance.

---

1 Bankruptcy Act 1914, s. 38 (2) (c), which is usually referred to as the 'reputed ownership' clause. Bills of sale, if absolute and properly registered, are not within this section: Bills of Sale Act 1878, s. 20 Contra bills given by way of security: Bills of Sale Act 1882, s. 15. See generally para. 17.06, ante.
2 *Re Parker ex parte Turquand* [1885] 14 QBD 636.
3 *Re Button* [1907] 2 KB 180.
4 Bankruptcy Act 1914, s. 38 A (i), inserted by Consumer Credit Act 1974, Sch. 4, Part I, para. 6.

---

5. *Property comprised in certain settlements*

33.23 a) *Voluntary settlements made before commencement of bankruptcy.*[1] If a voluntary settlement is not fraudulent and more than ten years have elapsed from the making of it, it is unimpeachable.

If less than ten years but more than two have elapsed, the settlement is voidable[2] by the trustee, unless those claiming under it show:

i) that the settlor was solvent at the making of the settlement without the aid of the property comprised in it; and
ii) that the interest of the settlor passed to the trustee of the settlement on the execution thereof.

If it was executed within two years of the commencement of the bankruptcy it is void as against the creditors.
Thus:

Less than two months before the commencement of his bankruptcy, a man paid part of the price of a house which his wife contracted for in her own name and mortgaged in her sole name to raise the rest of the price. The conveyance was also in her sole name. *Held:* the conveyance to the wife was void as against the man's trustee in bankruptcy under s. 42.[3]

A gift of personal property—e.g. jewellery—will be a settlement within this section, if although there is no restriction on the donee's power of alienation, yet the intention was that the donee should use or retain the property for an indefinite time;[4] but a gift of money which is not intended to be retained, but to be employed in a business, not itself settled, cannot be avoided as a 'settlement,' if the money has been so employed or spent.[5] A transaction by which two parties acquire joint ownership of property, one paying less than half the purchase price is a settlement within s. 42.[6] Again where a wife in good faith took a transfer of property from her husband agreeing to indemnify him against all liabilities in connection with the property she was not 'a purchaser for valuable consideration' within s. 42 since there was no commercial return and the settlement was void against the trustee.[7]

The following settlements are excepted from the operation of s. 42 (1); viz.:

i) a settlement made before and in consideration of marriage;

ii) a settlement made in favour of a bona fide purchaser or incumbrancer for value; or

iii) a post-nuptial settlement on a wife or children of property which has accrued to the settlor in right of his wife. This includes property to which a husband becomes entitled on the death of his wife intestate, so that a settlement, within two years of his bankruptcy, of such property on a child of the marriage is valid.[8]

b) Contracts for future settlements. A covenant made in consideration of the settlor's marriage for the benefit of his spouse or children for the future payment of money or settlement of property in which at the date of the marriage the settlor had no interest is void against the trustee if the settlor is adjudged bankrupt, unless the covenant has been executed before the commencement of bankruptcy. Further, transfers under any covenant to make future payments or a settlement will be void unless:

i) made more than two years before the bankruptcy, or

ii) at a time when the settlor was able to pay his debts without the aid of the money paid or property transferred, or

iii) the payment or transfer was made in pursuance of a covenant to pay or transfer money or property expected to come from a person named in the covenant and was made within three months after it comes into the possession of the settlor.[9]

c) Assignments of book debts. A general assignment of book debts by a person engaged in trade or business is void against the trustee as to any debts not paid at the commencement of the bankruptcy, unless it has been registered as if it were a bill of sale.[10] This provision does not apply to debts due from specific debtors or growing due under specific contracts, or to book debts included in a transfer of a business made bona fide and for value, or to debts included in any assignment for the benefit of creditors generally.[11]

---

1 Bankruptcy Act 1914, s. 42 (1). The word 'settlement' includes a conveyance of property, and, indeed, any disposition, verbal or not, which is in the nature of a settlement (*Re Vansittart* [1893] 1 QB 181). This section does not apply to the administration of the estate of deceased insolvents (*Re Gould* (1887) 19 QBD 92).

2 *Re Brall* [1893] 2 QB 381; approved *Re Carter and Kenderdine's Contract* [1897] 1 Ch 776. As to the deferred right to prove, see para. 33.45 (6), post.

3 *Re a Debtor, Ex parte Official Receiver, Trustee of the Property of the Debtor v Morrison* [1965] 3 All ER 453, [1965] 1 WLR 1498.

4 *Re Tankard* [1899] 2 QB 57.

5 *Re Plummer* [1900] 2 QB 790.

6 *Re Densham (a Bankrupt), ex parte Trustee of Bankrupt v Densham* [1975] 3 All ER 726, [1975] 1 WLR 1519.

7 *Re Windle (a Bankrupt), ex parte Trustee of Bankrupt v Windle* [1975] 3 All ER 987, [1975] 1 WLR 1628.

8 *Re Bower Williams* [1927] 1 Ch 441. It may be that there is now no property which accrues to a husband in right of his wife, *Williams Bankruptcy* (18th edn) 366.

9 Bankruptcy Act 1914, s. 42 (2), (3).

10 As to which, see para. 17.06, et seq., ante.

11 Ibid, s. 43. As to assignment generally see paras. 4.07, et seq., ante.

---

6. *Property used to give a fraudulent preference to any creditor*

33.24 If a person unable to pay his debts when they become due within *six* months[1] before the presentation of a bankruptcy petition upon which he is adjudged bankrupt, with a *view to prefer* a creditor, or any surety for the debt due to such creditor,[2] transfers property to that creditor, pays the debt, or allows his property to be taken for the debt, he has made a fraudulent preference, which is void against the trustee in bankruptcy, to whom the creditor must return the property or money. Preference must be the 'dominant' intention[3] and 'with a view to prefer' means with the intention of preferring though the intention can be inferred from the circumstances.[4]

The word 'preference' implies an act of free will, and therefore any facts showing that the advantage given to the creditor was not voluntary will be entitled to great weight. Thus:

i) Pressure by the creditor, especially where it involves a threat of legal proceedings, has been held to negative a fraudulent preference.[5]

ii) A mistaken apprehension that legal proceedings would be taken negatives a fraudulent preference.[6]

iii) So also if the debtor's object was to shield himself against the possibility of criminal proceedings for breach of trust.[7]

iv) And even a desire upon the debtor's part to repair a wrong that he has committed (e.g. a breach of trust), though the breach was at the time only known to himself, has been treated as warranting the conclusion that there was no view to prefer.[8]

An example of the facts from which the intent to prefer may be inferred is *Re Kushler (M) Ltd:*[9]

A director had guaranteed the overdraft of a private company. He was advised that it was insolvent. From then on payments were made to the bank till the overdraft was cleared off. No substantial trade creditor had been paid during that period. The bank had not been pressing, though a creditor had. The fact that the overdraft was guaranteed by the director was concealed at a meeting of creditors. It was held that the intention to prefer the director was proved.

The rights of a third person who for value and bona fide has obtained the bankrupt's property from such creditor, are not affected.

Fraudulent Transfer of Property By s. 172 of the Law of Property Act 1925, already referred to, a transfer of property made with intent to defraud creditors to the knowledge of all parties concerned in the transaction can be set aside at the instance of anyone thereby prejudiced.

---

1 Bankruptcy Act 1914, s. 44 (1) as amended by the Companies Act 1947, s. 115 (3).

2 A person who merely deposits documents to secure another's debt without assuming any liability to pay the debt is a 'surety' within the meaning of the section (*Re Conley* [1938] 2 All ER 127).

3 *Peat v Gresham Trust Ltd* [1934] AC 252.

4 *Re Eric Holmes (Property)* [1965] Ch 1052, [1965] 2 All ER 333.

5 *Ex parte Taylor* (1886) 18 QBD 295.

6 *Thompson v Freeman* (1786) 1 TR 155.

7 *Sharp v Jackson* [1899] AC 419.

---

5. Control over the property and person of the debtor

33.25   After a receiving order has been made the court may, on the application of the official receiver or the trustee, order any of the following to come before it and be examined on oath concerning the debtor, his dealings, or property:

1. The debtor,[1]
2. His wife,
3. Any person known or suspected to have in his possession property of the debtor, or supposed to be indebted to him; or
4. Any person deemed capable of giving information respecting the debtor, his dealings or property.[2]

These persons may be required to produce any relevant documents in their custody or power. If any person on examination admits that he is indebted to the debtor or in possession of property belonging to him, an immediate order may be made for payment of the debt or delivery up of the property.

The debtor must give such inventory of his property, such lists of his creditors and debtors, and generally do all such acts in relation to his property and the distribution of the proceeds as may reasonably be required by the official receiver or trustee.[3] The purpose of the private examination under s. 25 is to enable the trustee to discover assets and this justifies the practice of keeping depositions off the file of the court with a 'stop order' where publication would prejudice the chief purpose. The fact that a third party is involved in proceedings for libel is not a sufficient 'special circumstance' to warrant any lifting of the order to allow inspection of the depositions.[4]

The Debtors Act of 1869 abolished imprisonment for debt, except in certain cases;[5] but under the law of bankruptcy the court may order arrest of the debtor and seizure of his books and papers, if a bankruptcy notice has been issued,[6] or if a petition has been filed, and if there is reason to believe that the debtor has absconded or is about to abscond, with the view:

1. Of avoiding payment, or
2. Of avoiding service of or appearance to any petition, or
3. Of avoiding examination as to his affairs, or
4. Of otherwise avoiding, embarrassing, or delaying bankruptcy proceedings against him.[7]

He may also be arrested:

5. If, after presentation of a bankruptcy petition, there is probable ground for believing that he intends to remove, conceal, or destroy his papers or property;[8] or

6. If after service of a bankruptcy petition he removes any goods above the value of £60, without the leave of the trustee or of the official receiver;[9] or

7. If he fails without good cause to attend any examination ordered by the court.[10]

---

1 A bankrupt may be examined even after his discharge has become effective *Re Coulson* [1934] 1 Ch 45); *Re a Debtor (No. 12 of 1958) Re Ex parte Trustee of Property and the Debtor v Clegg* [1968] 2 All ER 425, (personal representatives may be examined after the discharge and death of the debtor).

2 Bankruptcy Act 1914, s. 25.

3 Ibid, s. 22.

4 *Re Poulson (a Bankrupt) Ex parte Granada Television v Maudling* [1976] 2 All ER 1020, [1976] 1 WLR 1023.

5 See the Debtors Act 1869, ss. 4, 5; County Courts Act 1959, s. 144 and Adminstration of Justice Act 1970, s. 11.

6 The notice must be served before or at the time of the arrest (Bankruptcy Act 1914, s. 23).

7 Ibid, s. 23 (1) (a).

8 Ibid, s. 23 (1) (b).

9 Ibid, s. 23 (1) (c). Insolvency Act 1976, s. 1 and Sch. 1, Part I, raised the value from £5 to £60.

10 Bankruptcy Act 1914, s. 23 (1) (d).

---

6. Officers

33.26 The administration of the estates of bankrupts is now under the control of the court and Department of Trade, and subject to such control there are several classes of officers; e.g.

1. Official receivers.
2. Special managers.
3. Trustees.

I. *The official Receiver*

33.27 *Appointment.* He is an official appointed by the Department of Trade but is also an officer of the court to which he is attached. On the making of the receiving order it becomes his duty to receive the bankrupt's property until the appointment of a trustee. It is not usual to nominate a separate receiver for each estate, the practice being to appoint a receiver, who acts in all bankruptices within a given district. The Department of Trade may at any time appoint a deputy or a temporary receiver, and it has power to remove any person whom it has appointed.[1]

His duties are

1. With regard to the debtor's conduct, to report thereon, stating whether anything has occurred which should guide the court as to making an order on the debtor's application for discharge. He should take part in the public examination;[2]

2. As regards the property, he must see that the proper statement of affairs is made;

3. He must act as trustee[3] during any vacancy in the office of trustee;

4. He must summon and preside at the first meeting of creditors, and must issue forms of proxy;

5. He may appoint a special manager, and may remove him;

6. He must advertise the receiving order, the date of the creditors' first meeting and of the debtor's public examination;

7. He must report to the creditors on any proposal made by the debtor to liquidate his affairs.

8. He makes applications in connection with new forms of discharge introduced by the Insolvency Act 1976[4]

His powers as receiver are such as are possessed by a receiver and manager appointed by the High Court.[5]

---

1 Bankruptcy Act 1914, ss. 70, 71.
2 Ibid, s. 73.
3 And as such can sell the property (*Turquand v Board of Trade* (1886) 11 App Cas 286, HL).
4 Ss. 7 and 8. See para. 33.14, ante.
5 Bankruptcy Act 1914, s. 74 (2).

II. *Special Manager*[1]

33.28 A special manager is a person whose duty it is to manage the business until a trustee is appointed. The appointment is made by the official receiver if he is satisfied that the nature of the bankrupt's business requires it and if asked to do so by any creditor. Such manager must give security to the satisfaction of the Department of Trade, and he may receive remuneration at such rate as the creditors by ordinary resolution may fix, or in default of this as the Department of Trade may determine. His powers are such as are entrusted to him by the official receiver to whom he accounts. He may be removed if the official receiver considers his services unnecessary and he must be removed if the creditors pass a special resolution.

---

1 Bankruptcy Act 1914, s. 10; Bankruptcy Rules 1952, rr. 319, 353, 354.

III. *The Trustee*

33.29 *Appointment.* He may be appointed:

1. By the creditors by ordinary resolution[1] at any of their meetings,[2] after the debtor has been adjudged bankrupt, or the creditors have resolved that he be so;

2. By the committee of inspection[3] after the debtor has been adjudged bankrupt, and the creditors decide to leave the choice to that body;

3. By the Department of Trade, if the creditors do not appoint within four weeks of the adjudication, or within seven days of the failure of negotiations relating to a composition, or within three weeks of a vacancy. But the trustee chosen by the Department ceases to hold office if the creditors subsequently take a trustee of their own choosing.[4]

The official receiver must not be trustee except in the following cases:[5]

1. Where there is a vacancy in the trusteeship, then he acts until a new trustee is appointed;[6]

2. Where the value of the estate is not likely to exceed £4000;[7]

3. Where the estate is that of a deceased insolvent.[8]

Certificate of appointment   The appointment of a trustee is not complete until the Department of Trade has given a certificate of appointment, and this is not obtained until the trustee has given security for the due performance of his duties.[9] The security must be given to some person appointed by the Department of Trade, which fixes the amount and nature of such security, and may from time to time increase or diminish the amount.

When that has been given, the certificate of appointment will, unless there is ground for objecting to the trustee, be granted, and the appointment takes effect as from that date;[11] the certificate is conclusive evidence of the appointment.[12] The Department may refuse the certificate if:

1. The trustee was not elected bona fide;

2. If he is unfit to act, e.g. if he has been previously removed from the office of trustee of a bankrupt's property for misconduct;

3. If his connection with the bankrupt or his estate, or any creditor, makes it difficult for him to be impartial.[13]

If the certificate is refused the Department must, on the demand of a majority in value of creditors, signify the fact and the grounds thereof to the High Court and the validity of the refusal may be then tried.[14]

The appointment must be advertised in the *London Gazette* and in a local paper; the cost is payable by the trustee, but he may recoup himself out of the estate.[15]

Any number of trustees may be appointed,[16] but it is usual to select one person only, who may be a creditor or not, as may seem best.

Determination of the appointment

The trustee will cease to be such in the following cases:

1. If he resigns. He should call a meeting of the creditors, and give seven days' notice of the meeting to the official receiver.[17] The meeting has power to accept or refuse the resignation.

2. If he is removed. This may be at the instance of the creditors; to obtain the removal, a meeting, of which seven days' notice should be given, must, at the request of one-sixth in value of the creditors, be specially called by a member of the committee of inspection, or by the official receiver (on a deposit of costs), and an ordinary resolution for removal must be carried.[18]

The Department of Trade also has power to remove a trustee if of the opinion:

i) that he is guilty of misconduct or fails to perform his duties, or

ii) that the trusteeship is being needlessly protracted without probable advantage to creditors, or

iii) that by reason of mental disorder, continued sickness, or absence he is incapable of performing his duties, or

iv) that through his connection with or relation to the bankrupt, the bankrupt's estate or a particular creditor, it might be difficult for him to act impartially.

or where in any other matter he has been removed from office, but if the creditors by ordinary resolution disapprove of his removal, he or they may appeal to the High Court.[19]

3. If a receiving order in bankruptcy has been made against him.[20]

4. If he has been released by the Department of Trade.[21] When the estate has been fully realised, or on resignation, or removal, a trustee may, if he wishes, apply for his *release*. This is granted by the Department after a proper investigation has been made into his accounts, and after due notice has been given to the debtor

and creditors. Its effect is to free the trustee with regard to all matters done during his trusteeship in his official capacity; but it is revocable on proof of fraud or of material concealment.[22] Appeal against refusal of release lies to the High Court.

---

1 I.e. a majority in value of those present, and voting either in person or by proxy.
2 Bankruptcy Act 1914, s. 19 (1).
3 Para, 33.30, post, and s. 19 (1).
4 Bankruptcy Act 1914, ss. 19 (6), (7), 78.
5 Ibid, s. 19 (5).
6 Ibid, ss. 53 (1), 74 (1) (g), 78 (4).
7 Ibid, s. 129 (1). The Insolvency Act 1976 raised the figure for summary administration from £300 to £4000.
8 Ibid, s. 130 (4).
9 Ibid, s. 19 (2), (4).
10 Bankruptcy Rules 1952, r. 355.
11 Bankruptcy Act 1914, s. 19 (4).
12 Ibid, s. 143.
13 Ibid, s. 19 (1), (2).
14 Ibid, s. 19 (3).
15 Bankruptcy Rules 1952, r. 331.
16 Bankruptcy Act 1914, s. 77.
17 Bankruptcy Rules, 1952, r. 340.
18 Bankruptcy Act 1914, s. 95 (1); Bankruptcy Rules 1952, r. 345.
19 Bankruptcy Act 1914, s. 95 (2).
20 Ibid, s. 94.
21 Ibid, s. 93 (5). The Board of Trade may also remove the trustee for failure to keep up his security (Bankruptcy Rules 1952, r. 338).
22 Bankruptcy Act 1914, s. 93; Bankruptcy Rules 1952, rr. 341–345.

The committee of inspection

33.30 This is a committee, consisting of from three to five persons, appointed by the creditors at the first or a subsequent meeting from amongst the creditors qualified to vote or persons who hold general proxies or powers of attorney from such creditors, or to whom a creditor intends to give a general proxy or power of attorney;[1] but no creditor or holder of general proxy or power of attorney can act as a member of the committee until the creditor has proved his debt and the proof has been admitted.

A member of the committee is in a fiduciary position, and like any other trustee, he must not purchase any part of the estate or derive any profit from any transaction arising out of the bankruptcy, except by leave of the court.[2]

The Committee's duty is to supervise the trustee, and to superintend the general administration of the estate. For certain acts the trustee requires its approval.[3] It audits his books.[4] It may act by a majority of the members present at a meeting, and a majority of its members forms a quorum.

It is not necessary that a committee should be appointed, and if there is none, the trustee may obtain sanction from the Department of Trade for the exercise of the powers in respect of which he is required to get the permission of the committee.[5]

---

1 These persons cannot *act* until they hold the proxy or power of attorney (Bankruptcy Act 1914, s. 20 (2) (b)).
2 Bankruptcy Rules 1952, rr. 349, 350 (2); *Re Bulmer, Ex parte Greaves* [1937] Ch 499, [1937] 1 All ER 323, CA.
3 See para 33.33, post.
4 See para. 33.35 (n.).
5 Bankruptcy Act 1914, s. 20 (10).

Duties of a trustee

33.31 From the date of the adjudication and until the appointment of a trustee, and during any vacancy in the trusteeship, the official receiver is trustee for the purposes of the Act. The trustee when appointed takes the property and when there are resignations and new appointments it passes from trustee to trustee. No conveyance is necessary; the certificate of appointment is sufficient evidence of ownership.[1] In general terms, the trustee's duty is:

1. To realise the estate to the best advantage, and to distribute it as quickly as possible;

2. To have regard to the resolutions of the creditors, and to the orders of the Department of Trade; and

3. To make no profit in any way except what may be specially allowed him as remuneration.

With regard to the bankrupt's property:

1. The trustee must not directly or indirectly purchase the estate, nor may he make a profit out of it.

2. The trustee must collect debts and take possession of the estate, real and personal.

3. He may transfer choses in action, stock, shares in ships, and shares and property of the like nature to the same extent as the bankrupt might have done.[2]

---

1 Bankruptcy Act 1914, s. 53.
2 Ibid, s. 48.

Disclaimer of onerous property[1]

33.32 This is the formal notification by the trustee of his refusal to accept the ownership of onerous property. With regard to any property consisting of land burdened with onerous covenants, unprofitable contracts, shares or stock in companies, or of any other property unsaleable or saleable only with difficulty owing to its burdens, the trustee may disclaim the property; but:

1. The disclaimer must be in writing and signed by the trustee. It need not be made by deed.[2]

2. It must take place within twelve months after the first appointment of a trustee; or, if he has no knowledge of the property within a month of his appointment, then within twelve months of his acquiring the knowledge.[3]

3. If the property consists of leaseholds he must obtain leave of the court, unless the property has not been sublet or mortgaged; and either:

    i) its value is under £20 per annum; or

    ii) the estate is being administered summarily; or

    iii) the lessor does not bring the matter before the court within seven days of being served with notice of the trustee's intention to disclaim.

If the property has been sublet or mortgaged he must apply to the court for leave to disclaim, unless notice having been served on the lessor, mortgagee, or sub-lessee, none of them within fourteen days requires the matter to be brought before the court.[4]

A person interested may make written application to the trustee, requiring him to decide whether he will disclaim or not, and in the event of no disclaimer within twenty-eights days the right is gone, and the trustee may in consequence become personally liable in respect of the property.[5]

Effect The effect of the disclaimer is to release the bankrupt and the estate from any liability in respect of the property from the date of the disclaimer, and to discharge the trustee from personal liability, notwithstanding previous acts of ownership;[6] but it will not release a trustee from personal liability to pay rates incurred by his voluntary occupation of the premises disclaimed.[7]

A trustee is bound specifically to perform a contract for the sale of real estate for valuable consideration to the same extent as the bankrupt could have been compelled to carry it out.[8] He cannot disclaim the contract so as to defeat the equitable interest vested in the purchaser under the contract.[9]

Persons injured by disclaimer If they have an interest in the property, they may apply to the court, and get an order vesting it in themselves. If the person is an underlessee or a mortgagee by demise of a lease, the order will make the person taking it subject to the bankrupt's liabilities in connection with the property, or if in the particular case the court thinks fit, subject to the liabilities of an assignee of the bankrupt's interest therein. If the underlessee or mortgagee declines to take a vesting order upon the terms offered by the court, he will be excluded from all interest in the property.[10] In any case, a loss caused by disclaimer is a provable debt.[11]

Rescission of contracts Any person who is, against the trustee, entitled to the benefit or subject to the burden of a contract made with the bankrupt, may apply to the court for its rescission and the court may rescind such contract on such terms as it thinks equitable. Damages may be awarded to either party and the creditor may prove for these against the estate.[12]

---

1 Bankruptcy Act 1914, s. 54.
2 Law of Property Act 1925, s. 52 (1), (2) (b).
3 Bankruptcy Act 1914, s. 54 (1). The Official Receiver acting as trustee during a vacancy has an independent right to disclaim even if the trustee's time has expired: s. 54 (7). The court can extend the time of a trustee but not of the official receiver *(Re A Debtor (No. 416 of 1940)* [1950] Ch 423, [1950] 1 All ER 1085, CA).
4 Bankruptcy Act 1914, s. 54 (3) and Bankruptcy Rules 1952, r. 278.
5 Bankruptcy Act 1914, s. 54 (4).
6 Ibid, s. 54 (2).
7 *Re Lister* [1926] Ch 149.
8 *Re Scheibler, ex parte Holthausen* (1874) 9 Ch App 722.
9 *Pearce v Bastables Trustee in Bankruptcy* [1901] 2 KB 518.
10 Bankruptcy Act 1914, s. 54 (6); and see *Re Carter and Ellis, Ex parte Savill Bros* [1905] 1 KB 735.
11 Ibid, s. 54 (8).
12 Ibid, s. 54 (5).

Powers of the trustee

33.33 On his own responsibility the trustee may do the following:

1. Sell all or any of the bankrupt's property by public or private sale, and may transfer the portions sold to the purchaser; and the trustee is not personally liable for selling goods which are on the debtor's premises, or in his possession, if he does so without negligence and without notice that the goods belong to a third person;[1]

2. Give receipts which effectually discharge the person paying;

3. Prove for and draw dividends to which the bankrupt is entitled;

4. Exercise any power given him by the Act, and execute instruments necessary for carrying it out;

5. Deal with property of which the bankrupt is tenant-in-tail, just as could the bankrupt himself.[2]

With the permission of the commitee of inspection (or if none, the Department of Trade[3]), he may exercise more extended powers; viz. he may:

1. Carry on the business, so far as is necessary for the beneficial winding up of the estate;

2. Bring or defend actions relating to the property;

3. Employ a solicitor or agent to do any particular act;

4. Agree to accept a future payment for property sold, subject to such security as the committee think fit;

5. Mortgage or pledge the property to raise money for the payment of debts;

6. Compromise claims, whether by or against the bankrupt, and refer disputes to arbitration;

7. Divide in its existing form amongst creditors such property as from its nature is not readily or advantageously capable of sale.

In no case must the permission be general; it is requisite for each particular act desired to be done.[4]

8. Appoint the bankrupt to carry on his trade for the benefit of his creditors;[5]

9. Make an allowance to the bankrupt out of his property for the support of himself and his family or in consideration of services if engaged in winding-up his estate, but any such allowance may be reduced by the court.[6]

In every case the wishes of the general body of creditors must be regarded, when such wish is properly and regularly expressed.[7] It must be remembered that the assistance of the court may always be invoked against a trustee who is exceeding his powers, or who is exercising them improperly.

---

1 Bankruptcy Act 1914, s. 61.
2 Ibid, s. 55.
3 Ibid, s. 20 (10).
4 Ibid, s. 56.
5 Ibid, s. 57.
6 Ibid, s. 58.
7 Ibid, s. 79 (1).

Appeal against acts of trustee

33.34 If the bankrupt or any of the creditors or any other person is aggrieved by any act or decision of the trustee he may apply to the court which may make such order as it thinks just.[1] The bankrupt himself can only apply to the court if he can show that there will or might be a surplus. Nor can he in the absence of fraud interfere in the day to day administration of the estate or question the exercise by the trustee in good faith of his discretion. Thus if a trustee in good faith decides to admit a disputed claim by a creditor, the bankrupt has no right to object.[2]

---

1 Bankruptcy Act 1914, s. 80.
2 *Re A Debtor (No. 400 of 1940), ex parte The Debtor v Dodwell (Trustee)* [1949] Ch 236, [1949] 1 All ER 510.

Trustee's obligation to account

33.35 1. *List of creditors.* If required by any creditor to do so, the trustee must furnish a list of creditors showing the amount of the debt of each creditor.[1]

2. *Statement of accounts.* If required by one-sixth of the creditors, the trustee must furnish a statement of accounts up to the date of such notice.[2]

3. *Books to be kept.* The trustee must keep the following books:[3]

   a) A record book. This will contain an account of all proceedings and information necessary to furnish an accurate record of his administration, e.g. resolutions of creditors.[4]

   b) A cash book. This must contain the receipts and payments as made from day to day, except those falling under the next head.[5]

   c) A trading account book where the trustee is carrying on the debtor's business.

4. *Submission to audit.* The accounts are audited by two separate bodies, by the committee of inspection, and by the Department of Trade. The committee must see all books and vouchers at least once in every three months, but it may require them at any time; at the close of each audit, it must enter and sign a dated certificate in the Cash Book.[6]

   The Department of Trade inspects and may audit the accounts every six months from the date of the receiving order until the debtor's release.[7]

5. *Annual statement.* At least once a year the trustee must submit a statement to the Department of Trade showing the proceedings in the bankruptcy up to the date of statement.[8]

6. *Receipt and payment of money.* The trustee must not pay any sums received by him as trustee into his private banking account,[9] and if he retains for more than ten days a sum exceeding £100 without the authority of the Department of Trade, he makes himself liable to severe penalties.[10] It should be paid into the Insolvency Services Account kept by the Department of Trade at the Bank of England and a receipt from the Department of Trade should be obtained by the trustee.[11] Any balance in the Insolvency Services Account which the Department considers is not required for the purposes of bankrupts' estates is transferred, under the Insolvency Act 1976, to the Insolvency Services Investments Account and dealt with according to the provisions of this Act.[12]

In some cases money may be left at a local bank. Thus, when a debtor has an account at any bank, it is usually kept open for seven days after the first meeting of creditors; and the general funds of the estate may be paid into and out of a local bank, if the trustee, on the application of the committee of inspection, gets permission from the Department of Trade; or where there is no committee, if the Department of Trade for special reasons authorises the trustee to keep a local banking account. All moneys received should be at once paid into this account; all payments out must be made by cheques to order.

---

1 Bankruptcy Act 1914, s. 84.
2 Ibid, s. 85.
3 Ibid, s. 86.
4 Bankruptcy Rules 1952, r. 362.
5 Ibid, r. 363.
6 Ibid, rr. 367, 368.
7 By the Insolvency Act 1976, s. 2, the Secretary of State is given a discretion to audit and the obligation imposed by the Bankruptcy Act 1914, s. 92 (3), has been abrogated. Vouchers and information may still be called for even if no audit is to take place.
8 Bankruptcy Act 1914, s. 87.
9 Ibid, s. 88.
10 Ibid, s. 89 (5). Insolvency Act 1976, s. 1, Sch. 1, Part I, raised the amount from £50 to £100.
11 Ibid, s. 89 (2).
12 Insolvency Act 1976, s. 3.

Trustee's remuneration

33.36 This is settled by the creditors, or by the committee of inspection, if the creditors so resolve. In three cases the Department of Trade will fix the amount, viz.:

1. When a fourth in value or number of the creditors dissent from the amount fixed by the others,
2. When the bankrupt satisfies the Department that the remuneration given is unreasonably large,[1] or
3. When the trustee was appointed by the Department of Trade.

The trustee must not under any circumstances make an arrangement to accept remuneration from the bankrupt, or any solicitor, or other person employed about the bankruptcy, nor may he make any arrangement for sharing his remuneration with such persons.[2] An agreement with creditors under which the latter are to receive part of the trustee's remuneration in augmentation of their dividends is a fraud upon the bankruptcy laws and illegal.[3]

---

1 Bankruptcy Act 1914, s. 82 (1), (2).
2 Ibid, s 82 (5).
3 *Farmer's Mart Ltd v Milne* [1915] AC 106.

---

7. Distribution of the property

33.37 Generally speaking, a trustee's duty under this head is to pay various costs and charges and then to distribute what is left among the creditors who prove their debts. As will be seen, some creditors are preferred over others, and before any creditor can be paid he must *prove* his debt as soon as possible after the making of the receiving order by sending particulars of the debt to the trustee. An unsworn claim may be delivered or sent by post unless the official receiver or trustee requires it to be verified by affidavit.[1] The form of proof and the duties of the trustee when he receives it are examined below.

---

1 Insolvency Act 1976, s. 5.

Costs and charges[1]

33.38 These are payable in a certain order, each being entitled to payment in full in the order in which they are listed. Amongst the more ordinary expenses, grouped as they are entitled to payment, are:

1. Actual expense of the official receiver incurred in protecting the assets of the debtor, or incurred by him or by his authority in carrying on the business, including the costs of shorthand notes taken at the instance of the official receiver;
2. Certain fees, percentages and charges payable under the Scale of Fees;
3. The petitioning creditor's deposit;
4. The remuneration of the special manager (if any);
5. The taxed costs of the petitioner;
6. Subsistence allowance made to the debtor by the official receiver;[2]
7. Trustee's disbursements;
8. Allowance to the debtor by the trustee;[3]
9. Trustee's remuneration;
10. Necessary out-of-pocket expenses of the committee of inspection subject to the approval of the Department of Trade.

---

1 Bankruptcy Rules 1952, rr. 115, 116.
2 Ibid, r. 313, giving the official receiver this power is supplementary to the power conferred on the trustee by the Bankruptcy Act 1914, s. 58.
3 Bankruptcy Act 1914, s. 58.

Provable debts

33.39 A creditor may prove for all debts and liabilities, present or future, certain or contingent, to which the debtor is subject at the date of the receiving order, or to which he may become subject before his discharge by reason of any obligation incurred before the date of the receiving order.[1] Thus, in *Hardy v Fothergill*:[2]

> *Held* that the future contingent liability of the assignee of a lease on a covenant to indemnify the lessee is provable unless the lessee obtains a court order that it is a liability incapable of estimation.

A contingent claim must be estimated by the trustee (subject to appeal to the court). If no estimate is possible, the court may on application declare the debt not provable.[3]

The following debts are not provable:[4]

1. Demands in the nature of unliquidated damages not arising from a contract, promise, or breach of trust—claims for damages in tort are therefore excluded;

2. Debts contracted by the debtor after knowledge by the creditor of an available act of bankruptcy;

3. Debts contracted after the receiving order;

4. Debts the value of which cannot fairly be estimated. Arrears under a maintenace order have been held to be in this category as the court has a discretion whether or not to enforce them.[5]

---

1 Bankruptcy Act 1914, s. 30 (3).
2 (1888) 1 App Cas 351.
3 Bankruptcy Act 1914, s. 30 (4), (5), (6).
4 Ibid, s. 30 (1), (2), (6).
5 *James v James* [1964] P. 303, [1963] 2 All ER 465. In consequence, the wife may take proceedings before the magistrates to compel payment without leave of the bankruptcy court. The liability of the bankrupt continues in respect of all debts not provable in bankruptcy.

Preferential debts

33.40   The following debts are given priority in bankruptcy:[1]

i) Local rates due within the year preceding the date of the receiving order and assessed taxes, and income tax assessed up to April 5th preceding the same date, but not exceeding the amount due for one year. Sums due within the year preceding the relevant date from a bankrupt employer who has deducted PAYE but not paid these sums to the Inland Revenue are also preferred.[2]

ii) Wages or salary of any clerk or servant,[3] workman or labourer not exceeding £800,[4] for services rendered during four months before the receiving order. This includes guarantee payments, medical suspension payments, payment for time off for union duties and seeking work and protective award payments under the Employment Protection Act 1975.[5]

iii) 'Accrued holiday remuneration,' i.e. sums which would have been paid in the normal course to a clerk, servant, workman or labourer had his employment continued until he became entitled to a holiday.[6]

iv) Social Security, pensions contributions and redundancy

fund contributions payable by statute during the twelve months before the date of the receiving order.

These preferential debts rank equally between themselves and must be paid in full unless the bankrupt's property is insufficient to meet them, in which case they abate in equal proportions between themselves.[7] No composition or scheme will be approved by the court which does not provide for payment in priority of all these preferential debts.[8]

The Crown is bound by the provisions of section 33, and has no claim to priority of payment except in respect of the debts mentioned therein.[9]

Apprentices An apprentice or articled clerk, who has paid a fee to the master, may, on the latter's bankruptcy, obtain a return of money, varying in amount, according to the time which has elapsed since he entered the service at the trustee's discretion (subject to appeal to the court); or the trustee may, with the apprentice's consent, transfer the indenture of apprenticeship or articles of agreement to some other person.[10]

Friendly societies A registered society has by the Friendly Societies Act 1974, s. 59, a preferential right as regards any claims for money or property by virtue of his office in the hands of any of its officers, if such officer becomes bankrupt. The right remains, although the moneys cannot be traced and are no longer in the officer's possession,[11] and although he ceased to be such officer before his bankruptcy.[12] Such a debt must be paid in priority to all the other debts of the bankrupt, including those enumerated in s. 33 of the Bankruptcy Act 1914, as amended by subsequent Acts.

Savings banks Depositors in savings banks are secured against loss by the acts or misconduct of any officer employed by a similar preferential right in the event of such officer becoming bankrupt.[13]

---

1 Bankruptcy Act 1914, s. 33.

2 Finance Act 1952, s. 30 (2).

3 The managing director of a company is not a 'clerk or servant' within the meaning of this section (*Re Newspaper Proprietary Syndicate Ltd* [1900] 2 Ch 349).

4 Insolvency Act 1976, s. 1 and Sch. 1, Part I, raised the amount to £800. Persons who have lent money to pay salaries or wages do not stand in the shoes of those who would otherwise have been preferred creditors (*Williams on Bankruptcy* (18th edn) 228). This contrasts with the priority given to such persons in the winding up of a company by s. 319 (4) of the Companies Act 1948.

5 Employment Protection Act 1975, s. 63. Ss. 64–67 provide that in respect of certain debts and contributions employees and others may claim against the

Secretary of State who is then subrogated to their claims against an insolvent employer.

6 Companies act 1947, ss. 91 and 115.
7 Bankruptcy Act 1914, s. 33 (2).
8 Ibid, s. 16 (19).
9 Ibid, s. 151 *and see Food Controller v Cork* [1923] AC 647. S. 33 also applies to deceased insolvents, the date of death being treated as the date of the receiving order. The priority given by s. 130 (6) to funeral and testamentary expenses is not affected.
10 Ibid, s. 34.
11 *Re Miller, ex parte Official Receiver* [1893] 1 QB 327.
12 *Re Eilbeck ex parte Good Intent Lodge No. 987 of Grand United Order of Odd Fellows,* [1910] 1 KB 136.
13 Trustee Savings Bank Act 1969, s. 72.

Other debts

33.41 With the exception of the above and of certain deferred debts hereinafter referred to (para. 33.45, post), all debts proved in the bankruptcy are paid *pari passu*.[1]

---

1 Bankruptcy Act 1914, s. 33 (7). If there is a surplus after paying the debts, interest from the date of the receiving order is payable on all debts proved (ibid, s. 33 (8)). Cf. para. 33.45, post.

The landlord

33.42 The landlord is in a peculiar position as regards his rent. He has no priority over other creditors, unless he has distrained. The position then is as follows:

1. If he distrains within three months before the receiving order, he must pay the preferential creditors out of the proceeds of the distress; if he suffers loss thereby, he acquires the same rights of priority as the persons so paid.[1]

2. If he distrains after the commencement of the bankruptcy, he can do so only for six months' rent accrued prior to the adjudication, and distress is not available for rent payable in respect of any period subsequent to the date when the distress was levied; where the landlord does not recover the full rent due to him by distress, he may prove for the balance as an ordinary creditor.[2]

3. If the trustee remains in possession without disclaiming, the landlord may distrain for rent accrued due after adjudication in the ordinary way.[3]

4. A landlord may take an action for possession following forfeiture of the lease for non-payment of rent without leave under s. 7 of the Bankruptcy Act 1914.[4]

1 Bankruptcy Act 1914, s. 33 (4).
2 Ibid, s. 35 (1).
3 *Re Binns, ex parte Hale* (1875) 1 ChD 285.
4 *Ezekiel v Orakpo* [1977] QB 260, [1976] 3 All ER 659, CA.

Secured creditors

33.43 A secured creditor is a person holding a mortgage, charge or lien on the property of the debtor, as security for a debt due to him from the debtor.[1] The expression therefore does not include a creditor who is secured by the guarantee, or by a mortgage charge or lien on the property, of a third person.[2] The test is would the security if given up augment the estate against which proof is made; if not, the creditor can prove for the whole debt without deducting the value of his security.[3]

The creditor may rely on his security and not prove. If he proves he has three courses open to him,[4] viz., he may:

1. Surrender his security and prove for his entire debt;
2. He may realise it, and prove for any deficit after deducting the net amount realised;
3. He may state the particulars in his proof, assess its value, and prove for a dividend on the deficit; but in this case the trustee may redeem the security at the assessed value.

Where a security has been valued and the trustee does not redeem, the creditor may require him in writing to elect whether he will do so or not, and the trustee must then, if he wishes to redeem, do so within six months. If the trustee is dissatisfied with the valuation, he may demand a sale of the security, on such terms as he and the creditor may agree or the court may fix; the creditor may, with leave of the court, amend if he can prove that he made a bona fide mistake or that the security has altered in value since he put in his proof.[4] Where the secured creditor is also the petitioning creditor, the trustee is not entitled to redeem the security at the value placed upon it in the petition; at the same time, the petitioning creditor is bound by the valuation of his security given in his petition.[5]

If it is found at any time that a creditor has omitted to state in his proof that he is secured, the security must be surrendered to the trustee for the general benefit of the creditors, unless the court is satisfied that the omission arose from inadvertence, in which case the court may allow the proof to be amended upon such terms as it considers just.[6]

Where the debtor's goods have been pledged as security, the official receiver or trustee may serve written notice of his intention to inspect the goods, and after such notice the pledgee must not realise his security until he has given the trustee a reasonable opportunity to inspect and redeem the goods.[7]

---

1 Bankruptcy Act 1914, s. 167. For security see chap. 17.
2 Where execution has not been completed by the appointment of a receiver the creditor is not secured. *Re a Debtor* (No. 39 of 1974) *ex parte Okill v Getting* [1977] 3 All ER 489, [1977] 1 WLR 1308.
3 *Re Turner, ex parte West Riding Union Banking Co* (1881) 19 ChD 105 at 112. Proof allowed against joint estate of firm without valuing security upon separate estate of partner. See also *Re Rushton, Ex parte National Westminster Bank Ltd v Official Receiver* [1972] Ch 197, [1971] 2 All ER 937.
4 Bankruptcy Act 1914, Sch. II, rr. 10–18.
5 *Re Vautin* [1899] 2 QB 549. But see *Re Button, Ex parte Voss* [1905] 1 KB 602.
6 Bankruptcy (Amendment) Act 1926, s. 11.
7 Bankruptcy Act 1914, s. 59.

Mutual dealings

33.44 It may happen that the bankrupt, X, not only owes money to a particular creditor, Y, but is also owed money by Y. In such a case when the trustee makes a claim against Y, Y is permitted to set-off against the claim the money X owes him. The rule is that if there have been mutual debts, mutual credits, or mutual dealings between the bankrupt and the creditor an account must be taken between them and a balance struck, and that balance only shall be claimed or paid; but the creditor cannot claim the benefit of any set-off where he had notice of an available act of bankruptcy at the time he gave credit to the debtor.[1] The line of set-off must be drawn at the date of the receiving order, unless the creditor's right of set-off has been stopped at an earlier date by notice of an act of bankruptcy.[1] In *re Daintrey*.[2]

The bankrupt owed a creditor £86 and, before the receiving order, the bankrupt sold his business to the creditor under an agreement whereby the price comprised a portion of the profits to be earned for three years after the sale. After three years it was found that by reason of this agreement £300 was owing to the bankrupt. *Held:* the creditor was allowed to set off the £86 owed to him against the £300.

However, the debts must be due between the same parties and in the same right, so that a joint debt owing by a partnership cannot be set off against a separate debt owing to one of the parties.[3]

The operation of the statutory provision on mutual dealings cannot be excluded by agreement.[4]

---

1 Bankruptcy Act 1914, s. 31. As to unliquidated claims, see *Jack v Kipping* (1882) 9 QBD 113. Statutory debts may be set off: *Re DH Curtis Builders Ltd* (1977) *Times* July 29.
2 [1900] 1 QB 546.
3 *Re Pennington and Owen* [1925] Ch 825.
4 *National Westminster Bank Ltd v Halesowen Presswork and Assemblies, Ltd* [1972] AC 785, [1972] 1 All ER 641, HL.

Deferred debts

33.45 To the general rule that all debts other than preferential debts are payable pari passu,[1] there are six exceptions, being cases where the claimant is postponed to the rights of other creditors until they are paid in full:

1. If there is a claim by a person other than a moneylender for agreed interest exceeding five per cent. per annum, the claim is deferred so far as it relates to interest in excess of five per cent. per annum. Accounts settled within three years before the receiving order may be re-opened if forming substantially one transaction with the debt proved and sums received by the creditor appropriated to principal and interest in the proportion that the principal bears to the sum payable as interest at the agreed rate, and if a security is realised or its value assessed after the receiving order the amount realised or value assessed must be appropriated in like manner;[2]

2. In the case of moneylenders, interest must be calculated at five per cent. per annum until all the debts proved have been paid in full. The moneylender is debarred from presenting a petition and voting at meetings, compositions and schemes in respect of that portion of his debt which represents interest in excess of five per cent. per annum.[3] The moneylender may, however, serve a bankruptcy notice on the borrower founded on a judgment which includes interest at a rate exceeding five per cent. per annum,[4] and if a petition is presented his refusal to

accept a tender of principal and five per cent. interest is not a sufficient cause for dismissing the petition.[5]

3. Where one partner of a firm is adjudged bankrupt, the claim of a creditor to whom the bankrupt is indebted jointly with the other partners, or any of them, is postponed to the claims of the separate creditors.[6]

4. Certain debts within s. 3 of the Partnership Act 1890, e.g. loans at a rate of interest varying with profits are deferred. See para. 11.05, ante.

5. Proof for money lent by a wife to a husband, or by a husband to a wife, for use in his or her trade or business is postponed.[7]

6. The trustees of a settlement which has been avoided have a deferred right to claim a dividend.[8]

Apart from these statutory provisions, it has been held that a person who authorises the use of his money as part of the capital of a business, so that it is exposed to the hazards of the business and the danger of being lost, is not in fact a creditor at all and cannot compete with the creditors of the business.[9]

---

1 Para. 33.41, ante.
2 Bankruptcy Act 1914, s. 66. In a scheme of arrangement the application of this section may be excluded (*Re Nepean* [1903] 1 KB 794).
3 Moneylenders Act 1927, s. 9 (1)..
4 *Re A Debtor* (247 of 1930) [1930] 2 Ch 239.
5 *Re A Debtor (No. 231 of 1936)* [1937] Ch 181, [1936] 3 All ER 641.
6 Bankruptcy Act 1914, s. 63. Para. 11.20, ante.
7 Ibid, s. 36. Even if a judgment has been obtained (*Re Lupkovics, Ex parte the Trustee v Freville* [1954] 2 All ER 125, [1954] 1 WLR 1234). But if any money is lent to a partnership of which the spouse is a member the right of proof is not affected (*Re Tuff* (1887) 19 QBD 88).
8 Ibid, s. 42; para 33.23, ante.
9 *Re Beale* (1876) 4 ChD 246; *Re Meade (A Bankrupt) Ex parte Humber v Palmer* [1951] Ch 774, [1951] 2 All ER 168.

Form of proof

33.46 A proof should be made as soon as may be after the making of the receiving order, and should be sent to the trustee (or official receiver). A claim need only be verified by affidavit when the official receiver or trustee so requires.[1]

When the proof is sent in, the trustee must, within twenty-eight days,[2]

1. Admit it,
2. Reject it, or
3. Require further evidence,

and if he rejects a proof, he must send written notice of his decision with the grounds thereof, to the creditor.[3] The court has power to review the decision,[4] and may expunge or reduce a proof admitted by the trustee, even on the application of the trustee himself. The trustee cannot recover payments made to a creditor whose proof is subsequently expunged or overpayments made to a creditor whose proof is subsequently reduced, but in the latter case the creditor cannot receive any further dividend on the reduced proof without giving credit for overpayments.[5]

---

1 Insolvency Act 1976, s. 5.
2 Bankruptcy Rules 1952, r. 259.
3 Bankruptcy Act 1914, Sch. II, r. 23.
4 Ibid, Sch. II, rr. 24–26.
5 *Re Searle, Hoare & Co* [1924] 2 Ch 325. But it is submitted that the creditor might be ordered to refund dividends if his proof was fraudulent.

Dividends[1]

33.47 These are payable to all who have proved, the amount depending upon what remains of the estate after payment of the expenses and the preferential debts. There may be one or more dividends, according as may be found convenient, and the time for declaration, though fixed by the rules, may be varied to suit the circumstances.[2] Due notice must be given to the creditors and to the Department of Trade, and the intention to distribute must be announced in the Gazette.

Any surplus after payment of the creditors in full with interest and the costs of the bankruptcy belongs to the debtor.[3]

---

1 See Bankruptcy Rules 1952, rr. 267–273. Bankruptcy Act 1914, ss. 62–69.
2 Ibid, rr. 269, 270.
3 Bankruptcy Act 1914, s. 69.

---

8. Compositions and arrangements

Scheme or composition

33.48 A debtor may obtain his release by the acceptance of a composition or the adoption of a scheme of arrangement; e.g. the creditors may agree to take 50p. in the £ payable by instalments and guaranteed by satisfactory persons.[1] This may take place even after adjudication in bankruptcy;[2] but as a rule it precedes this, and is consented to at a specially called meeting, which may be the first meeting. The procedure is as follows:[3]

1. The debtor must submit to the Official Receiver his proposal in writing signed by him[4] as soon as may be after the receiving order;[5]

2. The Official Receiver must then call a meeting of creditors, accompanying his notice with a copy of the debtor's proposal and report on the scheme;

3. The meeting must be held before the conclusion of the public examination;

4. If accepted at this by a majority in number and three-fourths in value of those who have proved, the sanction of the court must then be obtained to the scheme, but not till after the public examination is concluded.[6]

Approval of the court The court cannot approve the scheme if (i) it is of the opinion that the terms of the proposal are not reasonable, or (ii) it is of the opinion that they are not calculated to benefit the general body of creditors, or (iii) the scheme does not provide for the payment in priority of the preferential debts.[7]

Further, if any of the facts disentitling a bankrupt to an immediate discharge are proved,[8] the court's power to approve the arrangement is gone, unless the scheme provides reasonable security for a dividend of at least 25p. in the £ on all the unsecured debts provable against the debtor's estate; i.e. provable at the time when the scheme comes up for approval. If any creditors have released their debts, those debts can be disregarded.[9] As a general rule, the releases must be absolute and the circumstances under which they were obtained must be fully disclosed;[10] but there may be cases in which a conditional withdrawal will suffice.[11] The court will not refuse to approve a scheme on the ground of the debtor's misconduct unless it is of such a character as to make it against public policy to sanction the scheme.[12] A scheme may be approved if it seems beneficial to the creditors and there is a reasonable possibility of the statutory 25p. in the £ being paid within a short period.[13]

Effect of scheme when approved If the approval of the court is given the receiving order is discharged, and the adjudication, if made, is annulled, and the bankrupt's property reverts to himself or goes to such person as is nominated in the scheme; the debtor thereafter being released from all liabilities from which a discharge would have released him, subject, however, to the terms of the scheme. The scheme is binding on *all creditors* so far as it relates to debts due to them and provable in the bankruptcy.[14]

The trustee under a scheme is, so far as possible, in the same position as the trustee in bankruptcy; but he must adhere to the terms of the arrangement.[15]

Powers are reserved to the court to annul an arrangement if it fails to be workable, or if the debtor does not carry out his part of it.[16]

---

1 These arrangements are contractually binding despite the apparent absence of consideration: see para. 3.20, n. 7, ante.
2 Bankruptcy Act 1914, s. 21.
3 Ibid, s. 16.
4 No one can sign this proposal on behalf of the debtor (*Re (Prince) Blucher, Ex parte Debtor* [1931] 2 Ch 70, CA).
5 Usually within four days after the specified time for lodging the statement of affairs.
6 The desire of the creditors is not of itself sufficient to induce the court to approve the scheme (*Re Reed and Bowen* (1886) *Ex parte Reed and Bowen,* 17 QBD 244).
7 Bankruptcy Act 1914, s. 16. See para. 33.40, ante, CA.
8 See paras. 33.12, 33.13.
9 *Re EAB* [1902] 1 KB 457.
10 *Re Pilling Ex parte Board of Trade* [1903] 2 KB 50, CA.
11 *Re Flew Ex parte Flew* [1905] 1 KB 278, CA.
12 *Re EAB,* ante.
13 *Re Murray, a Debtor* [1969] 1 All ER 441, [1969] 1 WLR 246.
14 Bankruptcy Act 1914, s. 16 (13).
15 Ibid, s. 16 (17).
16 Ibid, s. 16 (16).

Deeds of arrangement

33.49 Creditors may make arrangements with the debtor outside the provisions of the Bankruptcy Acts and thereby avoid bankruptcy, but in such cases the rules of bankruptcy do not apply, and the debtor is released from the claims only of those who assent to the scheme. The arrangement is a contract and subject to the general law relating thereto. Any secret preference given or bargained for by any creditor entitles the others to withdraw from the arrangement.

Such arrangements will usually come within the Deeds of Arrangement Act 1914 and if they fall within the definition of a 'deed of arrangement' they must comply with that Act in order to be valid. The Act defines a deed of arrangement as any instrument, whether under seal or not, made for the benefit of creditors generally or made by an insolvent debtor for the benefit of any three or more creditors. It may be:

1. An assignment of property;
2. A deed or agreement for a composition;

and in cases where the creditors obtain control over the debtor's property,

3. A letter of licence;

4. An agreement for the carrying on or winding up of the debtor's business.[1]

A deed of any of these classes will be void unless it is registered at the Department of Trade[2] within seven days after first execution and is properly stamped.[3]

A deed for the benefit of creditors generally is also void unless assented to by a majority in number and value of the creditors before or within twenty-one days of registration. Within twenty-eight days of registration a statutory declaration must be filed confirming that the assents have been obtained.[4] Within a further seven days the trustee must give security unless a majority in number and value of the creditors dispense with it. In default the court may declare the deed void or appoint a new trustee.[5]

A conveyance or assignment for the benefit of creditors generally, is an act of bankruptcy available for three months to a creditor who has not assented to or recognised the deed,[6] but if such creditor has been served by the trustee under the deed with a notice of the execution of the deed, the time is cut back to one month.[7] The trustee should not act under the deed for three months after its execution unless all creditors have assented to it because, if the debtor becomes bankrupt the doctrine of relation back will apply and the trustee under the deed would have to account for all dealing with the debtor's property.[8]

Should the deed be void, it follows that the trustee under it must account for dealings with the debtor's property even if a bankruptcy petition is presented *after* the lapse of three months from the deed. But, where a deed of arrangement is void by reason that the requisite majority of creditors has not assented to it, or in the case of a deed for the benefit of three or more creditors, by reason that the debtor was insolvent at the time of the execution of the deed and that the deed was not registered as required by the Act, but is not void for any other reason, and a receiving order is made against the debtor upon a petition presented *after* the lapse of three months from the execution of the deed, the trustee under the deed is not liable to account for dealings with the debtor's property if he proves he did not know and had no reason to suspect the deed was void.[9]

A trustee under a deed of arrangement must account yearly to the Department of Trade and every six months to all assenting creditors. A majority in number and value of creditors can demand an audit during the administration or within twelve months of the date of final accounts.[10]

---

1 Deeds of Arrangement Act 1914, s. 1.
2 Administration of Justice Act 1925, s. 22 (1). If the deed affects land, it must also be registered at the Land Charges Registry or it is void against a purchaser of the land: Land Charges Act 1972, s. 7.
3 Deeds of Arrangement Act 1914, s. 2. A deed executed abroad must be registered within seven days after the time when it would reach England if posted within one week.
4 Deeds of Arrangement Act 1914, s. 3. The time can be extended by the court.
5 Ibid, s. 11.
6 See para. 33. 03 (1), ante.
7 Deeds of Arrangement Act 1914, s. 24.
8 However the trustee under the deed is allowed expenses incurred in complying with the Act and may be allowed by the trustee in bankruptcy remuneration for work that has benefited the estate. Ibid, s. 21; *Re Green, ex parte Parker* [1917] 1 KB 183.
9 Deeds of Arrangement Act 1914, s. 19. If the trustee acts when he knows the deed is void, he is liable to a penalty: ibid, s. 12.
10 Ibid, ss. 13–15.

---

9. Bankruptcy of partnerships and partners

33.50 As a whole the rules governing the administration of the estate of an individual apply to that of a firm, but in some respects there are variations. In ordinary cases a receiving order may be made against a firm,[1] but it operates as an order against each individual member, and the court will order discovery to be made of the names of the partners.

When a receiving order is made against a firm, the debtors must submit a joint statement of their partnership affairs and each partner must submit a statement of his separate affairs.[2] The adjudication is made as against the individuals by name and not against the firm.[3]

The first meeting is attended by the joint creditors and by the creditors of each separate partner's estate; the trustee appointed by the joint creditors is trustee of the separate estates of the partners, but each separate set of creditors is entitled to its own committee of inspection. The trustee's remuneration is fixed by each estate separately.[4]

Administration of the joint and separate estates is dealt with in para. 11.20, ante.

---

1 Bankruptcy Act 1914, s. 119; Bankruptcy Rules 1952, r. 285. If a judgment is obtained against a firm without personally serving a partner, a bankruptcy

notice cannot be served on that partner without first obtaining leave (*Re Ide, Ex parte Ide* (1886) 17 QBD 755).
2 Bankruptcy Rules 1952, r. 287.
3 Ibid, r. 288.
4 Ibid, rr. 291, 294, 296.

10. Administration of estate of deceased insolvent

33.51   The legal representative of a deceased debtor or any creditor whose debt would have been sufficient to support a bankruptcy petition if the debtor had been alive may petition to have the estate administered in the local court of bankruptcy; or if an administration on the equity side is in progress, the court may transfer it to bankruptcy.

The creditor who desires an administration order must show that there is no reasonable probability of the estate being sufficient for the payment of the debts owing by the deceased. An order cannot be made until a personal[1] representative is appointed.[2] Notice to the legal personal representative of the presentation of a petition is, in the event of an order being made, equivalent to notice of an act of bankruptcy. The executor's right of retainer is not affected.[3]

The official receiver becomes trustee, unless the creditors by ordinary resolution appoint a trustee (and committee of inspection also, if so desired), and he must pay funeral and testamentary expenses in priority to every other debt; he is entitled to have detailed information as to the assets and liabilities given him by the executor or administrator, and may ask of them any information he requires.[4]

Unliquidated damages in tort are provable.[5]

1 Bankruptcy Act 1914, s. 130.
2 *Re A Debtor (No. 1035 of 1938)* [1939] Ch 594, [1939] 2 All ER 56.
3 *Re Rhoades* [1899] 2 QB 347.
4 Bankruptcy Act 1914, s. 130; Bankruptcy Rules 1952, r. 304.
5 Law Reform (Miscellaneous Provisions) Act 1934, s. 1 (6). As to the position regarding voluntary settlements and the rights of execution creditors, see Williams on Bankruptcy (18th edn), 541–542.

11. Small bankruptcies

33.52   If the estate is not likely to exceed £4000, and a receiving order is made, the court can order a '*summary administration*,' in which case the estate is administered by the official receiver as trustee, and without a committee of inspection, but by special resolution the creditors may select a trustee and have the estate administered in the ordinary way.[1]

When a judgment has been obtained in a county court and the debtor is unable to pay, and his debts amount to not more than £2000, the county court may, without putting the estate into bankruptcy, make an order for their payment by instalments or otherwise, and either in full or to such an extent as appears practicable and subject to any conditions as to future earnings or income as the court may think just.[2] Where a person fails to make any payment required by an administration order the court may, if it thinks fit, replace the administration order by a receiving order.[3]

---

1 The procedure is regulated by s. 129 of the Act and Bankruptcy Rules 1952, r. 298. There are no local advertisements unless ordered; if no satisfactory proposals for a compromise are lodged the debtor can be adjudicated forthwith; the estate should be distributed if possible in a single dividend within six months; costs are on a reduced scale. Insolvency Act 1976, s. 1, Sch. 1, Part I, raised the maximum figure to £4000.

2 County Courts Act 1959, ss. 148–156, as amended by the Administration of Justice Act 1965, s. 20. Insolvency Act 1976, s. 13. The making of an order and furnishing of lists of creditors are no longer acts of bankruptcy. The figure of £2000 was fixed by the County Courts (Administrative Order Jurisdiction) Order 1977.

3 Insolvency Act 1976, s. 11. The minimum debt is £400.

Part XII

Arbitration

Chapter 34

Arbitrations

1. Introductory

34.01 The settlement of disputes by arbitration is governed largely by the Arbitration Act 1950 and references to sections throughout the present chapter are to the sections of that Act.

There are three ways in which arbitration may arise:

1. *By order of the court.* Under the Rules of the Supreme Court the jurisdiction or powers of the High Court can be exercised in certain circumstances by official referees or special referees or by masters, registrars, district registrars or other officers of the court. In certain circumstances, the rules authorise the whole of a case or any particular issue to be ordered to be *tried* by the referee or other officer. Moreover, any question before a court may be referred *for inquiry and report.*[1] The type of case chiefly envisaged is where prolonged examination of documents or scientific or local examination is required or where matters of account are involved. Provision was made in 1973 for an extended county court arbitral jurisdiction, largely exercised by the registrar, primarily to deal with small consumer claims.[2] The county court arbitral jurisdiction no longer requires an order of the court to bring it into effect.[3]

2. *By certain statutes* the parties are given an option to refer disputes, and in some cases the reference is made compulsory. The Arbitration Act, with the exception of certain sections, applies to statutory arbitrations except in so far as it is inconsistent with the special Act.[4] Provision is also made for arbitration in industrial disputes.[5]

3. *By consent out of court.* Parties[6] may agree to submit either present or future disputes to arbitration and the arbitrator may or may not be named in the agreement. Such an agreement is known as an *arbitration agreement* or *submission.* The agreement may be by word of mouth but the Arbitration Act only applies to written agreements, for an arbitration agreement is defined as:

'a *written* agreement to submit present or future differences to arbitration whether an arbitrator is named therein or not.[7]

---

1 Administration of Justice Act 1956, s. 15 (1). By the Courts Act 1971, s. 25, existing official referees became Circuit judges. In future no person will be appointed to the office of official referee but particular Circuit judges will be required to discharge 'official referees' business'.
2 Administration of Justice Act 1973, s. 7.
3 Administration of Justice Act 1977, s. 17.
4 S. 31.
5 Employment Protection Act 1975, ss. 1, 3 and 10. This differs in a number of ways from arbitration by agreement and the Arbitration Act 1950 does not apply. See the 1975 Act, s. 3.
6 A minor is bound by an arbitration clause if the contract as a whole is for his benefit (*Slade v Metrodent* [1953] 2 QB 112, [1953] 2 All ER 336).
7 S. 32. Many trade associations maintain arbitral tribunals and terms submitting disputes to arbitratror are common form in their standard contracts. See *Tradax v Andre* (1978) Times, 3rd March, for suggestions for reforms in commercial arbitration.

---

2. Arbitration agreements

Arbitrations and actions

34.02 Commercial arbitrations, which are usually the result of agreement out of court, are particularly useful where the issues involve expert knowledge of a particular trade and the arbitrator is chosen for his experience in that trade. But where the main issues are questions of commercial law these are frequently handled most speedily and economically by the High Court which has a special procedure for dealing with commercial causes in the Commercial Court.[1]

---

1 See *Peter Cassidy Seed Co Ltd v Osuustukkukauppa IL* [1957] 1 All ER 484, [1957] 1 WLR 273; *JH Vantol Ltd v Fairclough Dodd and Jones Ltd* [1956] 3 All ER 921, [1957] 1 WLR 136, HL; *British Imex Industries Ltd v Midland Bank Ltd* [1958] 1 QB 452, [1958] 1 All ER 264 (judgment eleven days after writ). The Commercial Court is part of the Queen's Bench Division of the High Court—it has been in existence since 1895 but only put on a statutory basis by the Administration of Justice Act 1970, s. 3.

Effect of arbitration agreement upon action

34.03 An arbitration agreement will not necessarily bar legal proceedings; but if a party commences an action the court may, on the application of the other party, stay the action if the applicant has not delivered any pleadings or taken any step in the action (except entering an appearance), there is no sufficient reason why the dispute should not be referred to arbitration, and the applicant is ready and willing to do all things necessary to the proper conduct of the arbitration.[1] The court has thus a discretion to grant or refuse a stay and in particular in cases where the court has power to give relief on the ground that the arbitrator is not impartial or that the dispute involves a question of fraud, it may refuse to stay the action.[2]

Generally speaking, the court will give effect to an arbitration agreement unless the person opposing a stay of action can prove there is good reason for allowing the action to continue.

Thus:

Where the agreement provided that a foreign court should try disputes but both parties were strangers to the foreign court and many of the witnesses were in this country the court refused a stay.[3]

If the court has refused to stay an action, or if no application to stay it has been made, the court has sole jurisdiction to decide the dispute, and it will not tolerate arbitration proceedings with respect to that dispute while the action is pending.[4]

1 S. 4 (1). And see para. 34.22, post, for Arbitration Act 1975, s. 1, for stay when the agreement contains an international element.
2 S. 24 (3).
3 *The Fehmarn* [1958] 1 All ER 333, [1958] 1 WLR 159. See also *Olver v Hillier* [1959] 2 All ER 220, [1959] 1 WLR 551 (dissolution of partnership—no stay); and *Taunton-Collins v Cromie* [1964] 2 All ER 332, [1964] 1 WLR 633, CA (no stay because one party to action not a party to arbitration agreement and multiplicity of proceedings undesirable).
4 *Doleman & Sons v Ossett Corpn* [1912] 3 KB 257, CA.

34.04 *Scott v Avery clause* Any agreement whereby the jurisdiction of the courts to determine matters of law is completely ousted, e.g. an arbitrator is given the final power to determine a question of law, is illegal. The court's statutory power under s. 21 to compel an arbitrator to submit a point of law for determination by the courts cannot be ousted.[1] On the other hand, it is lawful for parties to stipulate that no right of action shall accrue, until the amount of the debt or damages has been ascertained by arbitration—the reference to arbitration will be a condition precedent to the right to sue, and the non-observance thereof will afford a defence to the action.[2] This is known as a *Scott v Avery* clause. Despite the clause, where the court orders that the arbitration agreement shall cease to have effect (e.g. under s. 25), it may further order that a provision in the agreement making an award a condition precedent to the right to sue shall also cease to have effect.[3] It is also lawful for parties to agree that a claim shall be deemed to be waived and absolutely barred if an arbitrator is not appointed within a certain time. If such a condition is not complied with, the claim cannot be enforced either by action or arbitration.[4] But the court may extend the time if undue hardship would otherwise be caused.[5]

In *Ford v Clarksons Holidays Ltd*:[6]

> By an arbitration clause in a 'package' holiday contract, it was agreed that the decision of a mutually agreed independent arbitrator should be 'accepted by all parties as final'. When the plaintiff began an action and the defendants applied to stay the proceedings, the plaintiff contended the clause purported to oust the court's jurisdiction and that a stay should be refused because arbitration proceedings would be more expensive. *Held:* the clause did not purport to oust the court's jurisdiction and the allegation of expense, even if true, was not a proper reason for refusing a stay.

---

1 *Czarnikow v Roth, Schmidt & Co* [1922] 2 KB 478. See para. 6.09, ante.

2 *Scott v Avery* (1856) 5 HLC 811.

3 S. 25 (4). For the practice, see *Kruger Townwear Ltd v Northern Assurance Co Ltd* [1953] 2 All ER 727, [1953] 1 WLR 1049.

4 *Atlantic Shipping etc Co v Louis Dreyfus & Co* [1922] 2 AC 250. Cf *Ford & Co v Compagnie Furness (France)* [1922] 2 KB 797; *Pinnock Bros v Lewis and Peat* [1923] 1 KB 690; *Smeaton Hanscomb & Co Ltd v Sassoon I Setty Son & Co (No. 1)* [1953] 2 All ER 1471, [1953] 1 WLR 1468.

5 S. 27. See, e.g., *Liberian Shipping Corpn v A King & Sons Ltd* [1967] 2 QB 86, [1967] 1 All ER 934, 938, CA, where Lord Denning MR said that 'undue' hardship simply means excessive hardship, i.e. greater hardship than the circumstances warrant: 'Even though a claimant has been at fault himself, it is an undue hardship on him if the consequences are out of proportion to the fault.' The clause on its true construction may only bar the right to arbitration and not the substantive right.

6 [1971] 3 All ER 454, [1971] 1 WLR 1412, CA.

Construction of arbitration agreement

34.05 What is the subject matter of the arbitration agreement is a matter of construction in each case. Words referring to disputes arising 'under' or 'in respect of' a contract are widely construed and include disputes as to whether the contract has been repudiated or frustrated.[1]

If, however, a party denies the existence or the validity of the contract in toto, e.g. on the ground that it is illegal, he will be precluded from setting up the arbitration clause as a defence to an action;[2] but this does not apply where a party admits the existence of a binding contract, although he denies liability under it.[3]

It is often important to decide whether an agreement to refer a question to a third party is an arbitration agreement or not. If the intention is that the third party is to decide the question by a quasi-judical process, the agreement is an arbitration agreement. But if the third party is to use his own knowledge and skill, e.g. to make a valuation of property which is being transferred, there is no arbitration. The Arbitration Act does not apply to a valuation. The parties are contractually bound by the decision of the valuer although it can be set aside if fraudulently made or if on its face it is made on a wrong basis.[4] An arbitrator, owing to his quasi-judicial functions, cannot normally be sued by the parties.[5] A valuer is similarly protected if he is acting as a quasi-arbitrator between two parties even though not technically an arbitrator.[6]

---

1 *Heyman v Darwins Ltd* [1942] AC 356, [1942] 1 All ER 337, HL; *Government of Gibraltar v Kenney* [1956] 2 QB 410, [1956] 3 All ER 22; *The Tradesman* [1961] 3 All ER 661, [1962] 1 WLR 61.
2 *Jureidini v National British etc Insurance Co* [1915] AC 499.
3 *Woodall v Pearl Assurance Co* [1919] 1 KB 593, CA.
4 *Dean v Prince* [1953] Ch 590, [1953] 2 All ER 636, revd. on the facts [1954] Ch 409, [1954] 1 All ER 749.
5 *Chambers v Goldthorpe* [1901] 1 QB 624. But see *Arenson v Casson Beckman Rutley & Co* [1977] AC 405, [1975] 3 All ER 901; *Sutcliffe v Thackerah* [1974] AC 727, [1974] 1 All ER 859, HL.
6 *Finnegan v Allan* [1943] 1 KB 425, [1943] 1 All ER, 493, CA.

Alteration

34.06 A submission may be altered by agreement between the parties, but the arbitrator has no power to alter its terms. The court can amend so as to give effect to the real intention of the parties, but not so as to introduce new matter.

The time for making an award even when fixed by the agreement can be enlarged by order of the court, whether it has expired or not.[1]

1 S. 13 (2).

Revocation

34.07   The authority of an arbitrator or umpire appointed by virtue of an arbitration agreement (unless a contrary intention is expressed) is irrevocable except by leave of the court.[1] Such leave will be given only in exceptional circumstances such as misconduct on the part of the arbitrator and the like.[2] But in certain circumstances the court will either remove or give leave to revoke the authority of a particular arbitrator and may order that the arbitration agreement shall cease to have effect. An arbitrator can be removed by the court if he has misconducted himself or the proceedings,[3] or if he fails to use reasonable dispatch in entering on or proceeding with the reference.[4] The court will give leave to revoke the authority of an arbitrator for good cause—e.g. if he is not or may not be impartial. This is so even if the applicant knew of this when he entered into the agreement provided that the dispute had not already arisen.[5]

   Where the court has given leave to revoke the authority of an arbitrator it may appoint a person to act as sole arbitrator in place of the person or persons removed, or order that the agreement shall cease to have effect with respect to the dispute referred.[6]

   Similarly, where under an agreement to refer future disputes, a dispute arises which involves a charge of fraud against any party, the court may order that the agreement shall cease to have effect.[7]

---

1 S. 1.
2 *City Centre Properties (ITC Pensions) Ltd v Tersons Ltd* [1969] 2 All ER 1121, [1969] 1 WLR 772, CA.
3 S. 23 (1).
4 S. 13 (3).
5 S. 24 (1).
6 S. 25 (2).
7 S. 24 (2).

Assignment and transmission

34.08   An arbitration clause can be enforced by or against an assignee if the contract as a whole is assignable.[1] If the moneys receivable under a contract are assigned, an award cannot be made in favour of the assignor.[2] In such a case it may be necessary for the assignor and assignee to be joined as parties.

An arbitration agreement is not discharged by the death of any party thereto, but in such an event it will be enforceable by or against the personal representative of the deceased.[3]

If a contract to which a bankrupt is a party contains an arbitration clause, that clause will be enforceable by or against the trustee in bankruptcy if he adopts the contract.[4] In other cases, if a bankrupt was before the commencement of the bankruptcy party to an arbitration agreement which applies to some matter requiring to be determined for the purpose of the bankruptcy, the court having jurisdiction in the bankruptcy may, on the application of any other party or the trustee with the consent of the committee of inspection, order the matter to be determined in accordance with the agreement, if it is of opinion that it ought to be so determined.[5]

---

1 *Shayler v Woolf* [1946] Ch 320, [1946] 2 All ER 54, CA.
2 *Cottage Club Estates v Woodhouse Estates Co (Amersham)* [1928] 2 KB 463.
3 S. 2. The authority of an arbitrator is not revoked by the death of his appointer (ibid).
4 S. 3 (1).
5 S. 3 (2).

Illegality

34.09　A submission may be unenforceable as a contractual obligation. Thus a submission which is an integral part of a betting contract is void under the Gaming Act 1845.[1]

---

1 *Joe Lee Ltd v Dalmeny* [1927] 1 Ch 300. See para. 6.07, ante.

---

3. Arbitrators and umpires

The arbitrator

34.10　Any person may be appointed arbitrator, and an interest in the subject-matter known to both parties at the time of appointment is no objection.[1]

The agreement may name the arbitrator or arbitrators or provide how they are to be appointed, e.g. by the President of the Law Society, or even by lot. Unless a contrary intention is expressed in the agreement, it is deemed to include a provision that the reference be to a single arbitrator.[2]

If the reference is to a single arbitrator and the parties do not concur in appointing one, or if after appointment the arbitrator refuses to act or is incapable of acting, or dies, and the parties do not supply the vacancy, any party may serve the others with notice to concur in appointing an arbitrator, and if no appointment is made within seven clear days after service of such notice, the court may appoint.[3]

If the reference is to two arbitrators, and one party fails to appoint his arbitrator, either originally or by way of substitution, the other party having appointed his arbitrator may serve a notice requiring his opponent to make the appointment. If such notice is not complied with within seven clear days, the party serving it may appoint his arbitrator to act as sole arbitrator in the reference, but the court may set aside any appointment so made.[4]

Where arbitrators have been removed or their authority revoked by leave of the court, the court may appoint a person or persons to act in the place of the person or persons removed.[5]

---

1 *Johnston v Cheape* (1817) 5 Dow. 247. But see para. 34.07, ante.
2 S. 6.
3 S. 10. If the application is made by an alien resident out of the jurisdiction, the court may require him to give security for the costs of the arbitration as a condition of making the appointment (*Re Bjornstad and The Ouse Shipping Co* [1924] 2 KB 673).
4 S. 7. 'Appointment' is not complete until the nominated arbitrator is told of his appointment and he consents to it: *Tradax Export SA v Volkswagenwerk AG* [1970] 1 All ER 420, [1970] 1 QB 537, CA.
5 S. 25 (1), (2).

The umpire

34.11 If the reference is to two arbitrators, they must immediately appoint an umpire.[1] If they fail to do so, or if the umpire refuses to act, is incapable, or dies, and the arbitrators do not supply the vacancy, the court may appoint in like manner as in the case of a sole arbitrator.[2] The duties of the umpire commence when he is called upon to act, not when he is appointed. He is called on to act when the arbitrators deliver to the parties or to him a notice in writing that they cannot agree.[3] The court may order him to enter on the reference at any time.[4]

If the submission provides that each party shall appoint an arbitrator, and that the appointed arbitrators shall appoint a third, the agreement will have effect as if it provided for the appointment of an umpire; but if the agreement provides for the appointment of three arbitrators otherwise than as above, the award of any two of them will be binding.[5]

INVALID APPOINTMENT
If an arbitration agreement specifies the qualifications of an arbitrator or umpire, any award made by someone purporting to act as arbitrator or umpire who does not possess such qualifications is void and the defect in appointment is not cured by subsequent appearance of the parties before him.[6]

DUTIES OF UMPIRE
The umpire enters on the reference in lieu of the arbitrators, who, in a commercial arbitration, may give evidence before the umpire—they are not disqualified from so doing by the mere fact that they have acted in the matter in a judicial capacity.[7]

The umpire must decide the whole matter between the parties, and not particular points upon which the arbitrators cannot agree.[8] He has the same powers and is bound by the same rules as the arbitrators.

A JUDGE AS ARBITRATOR
Under the Administration of Justice Act 1970, s. 4, a judge of the Commercial Court may accept appointment as sole arbitrator or umpire if in all the circumstances he thinks fit. Fees payable are to be taken by the High Court.

---

1 S. 8 (1).
2 S. 10.
3 S. 8 (2).
4 S. 8 (3).
5 S. 9.
6 *Rahcassi Shipping Co SA v Blue Star Line Ltd* [1969] 1 QB 173, [1967] 3 All ER 301.
7 *Bourgeois v Weddell & Co* [1924] 1 KB 539; *Wessanen's Koninklijke Fabrieken NV v Isaac Modiano Bros & Sons Ltd* [1960] 3 All ER 617, [1960] 1 WLR 1243.
8 *Cerrito v North Eastern Timber Importers* [1952] 1 Lloyd's Rep 330 but see *Orion Compania Espanola de Seguros v Belfort Maatschappij Vooralgenene Verzekgringeen* [1962] 2 Lloyd's Rep 257.

4. Conduct of the proceedings

34.12 Once the arbitrator or arbitrators : ave been appointed, the first step usually is to take an appointment for directions as to preliminary steps such as pleadings, or discovery of documents. The arbitration agreement may provide that the reference is to be governed by the rules of a particular trade association. But where a custom is alleged to have grown up in a particular association which conflicts with the ordinary rules of procedure it will only be incorporated in the arbitration agreement if it is consistent with the tenor of the agreement as a whole. There can be no prescriptive right to commit an irregularity.[1]

Unless a contrary intention appears, the parties and persons claiming through them are bound subject to any legal objection to produce all documents in their possession or power which may be required and to do all other things which the arbitrator or umpire may require.[2] This entitles him to order pleadings,[3] disclosure of documents or interrogatories on oath.[4] But he cannot order security for costs.[5] In addition the court may make orders in respect of the following matters: (1) security for costs; (2) discovery of documents; (3) giving evidence on affidavit; (4) examination of witnesses before an examiner or on commission abroad; (5) the preservation, interim custody or sale of any goods; (6) the detention, preservation or inspection of any property, the taking of samples or trying of experiments; (7) interim injunctions or the appointment of a receiver.[6]

---

1 *London Export Corpn Ltd v Jubilee Coffee Roasting Co Ltd* [1958] 2 All ER 411, [1958] 1 WLR 661.
2 S. 12 (1).
3 *Re Crighton and Law Car and General Insurance Corpn* [1910] 2 KB 738.
4 *Kursell v Timber Operators and Contractors Ltd* [1923] 2 KB 202.
5 *Re Unione Stearinerie Lanza and Wiener* [1917] 2 KB 558.
6 S. 12 (6).

The hearing

34.13 The arbitrator has, with regard to the parties to the submission, some of the powers of a judge, and the proceedings resemble those of an action.[1] The arbitrator may, at his discretion, exclude persons, other than the parties, who are going to be examined before him during the time that any of the other witnesses are giving evidence. A lay arbitrator is generally allowed to have a legal adviser to sit with him or assist him during the hearing.

An arbitrator may, generally speaking, take skilled advice, but it is not advisable that he should do so without the consent of the parties. Where an arbitrator is authorised to appoint an accountant, 'if not objected to by the parties,' he may not appoint one without communicating with the parties.[2] An arbitrator skilled in a particular trade may use his own knowledge and experience, e.g. in determining the quality of goods sold and the amount of damages without hearing evidence.[3]

The arbitrator will fix the time and place of the hearing and notify the parties. If one party fails to attend the arbitrator can proceed in his absence, but he should first give distinct notice of his intention to do so.[4]

If a question arises whether the arbitrator has jurisdiction or not, it is his duty to consider the point, although if he wrongly decides that he has jurisdiction, that will not make his award good.[5]

---

1 *Re Enoch and Zaretzky* [1910] 1 KB 327.
2 *Re Tidswell* (1864) 33 Beav 213.
3 *Mediterranean and Eastern Export Co Ltd v Fortress Fabrics (Manchester), Ltd* [1948] 2 All ER 186.
4 *Gladwin v Chilcote* (1841) 9 Dowl. 550.
5 *Christopher Brown, Ltd v Genossenschaft Oesterreichischer Waldbesitzer* [1954] 1 QB 8, [1953] 2 All ER 1039.

Evidence

34.14 The arbitrator or umpire is bound to observe the rules of evidence no less than judges.[1] The arbitrator must hear both sides, and take evidence in the presence of both parties. Any practice to the contrary is absolutely wrong and is a ground for setting aside any award.[2] In the absence of agreement to the contrary, the parties are deemed to have agreed to submit to examination on oath or affirmation and that witnesses shall similarly be examined if the arbitrator thinks fit. The arbitrator has power to administer the oaths or take the affirmations.[3]

He should receive all the evidence tendered, taking notes of everything material, but if he rejects evidence under a mistake as to its value it is not sufficient ground for setting aside the award; similarly, if he receives evidence upon matters not coming within the scope of the reference, his award will not on that ground alone be set aside.[4]

He has no right to call a witness without the consent of the parties.[5]

The attendance of a witness to give evidence or to produce documents can be enforced by a writ of subpœna issued by the High Court.[6] In the case of a prisoner a writ of habeas corpus ad testificandum must be issued.[7] Any witness giving false evidence is guilty of perjury.[8]

It is not open to the parties to an arbitration to agree that the dispute should be determined on a basis of 'fairness' rather than on a legal basis. If the rule were otherwise it would not be possible for the court to decide on the statement of a special case whether there had been an error of law.[9]

---

1 *Re Enoch and Zaretzky, Bock & Co* [1910] 1 KB 327.
2 *Ramsden & Co v Jacobs* [1922] 1 KB 640, per Bray J. See para. 34.20, post.
3 S. 12 (1), (2), (3).
4 *Falkingham v Victorian Rly Comrs* [1900] AC 452.
5 *Re Enoch and Zaretzky, Bock & Co* [1910] 1 KB 327.
6 S. 12 (4).
7 S. 12 (5).
8 Perjury Act 1911, s. 1.
9 *Orion Compania Espanola de Seguros v Belfort Maatschappij Vooralgemene Verzekgringeen* [1962] 2 Lloyd's Rep 257.

Special case

34.15 An arbitrator or umpire may, and must if so directed by the court, state:

    a) any question of law arising in the course of the reference;[1] or

    b) an award or any part of an award,

in the form of a special case for the decision of the court.[2]

In stating an award in the form of a special case, the arbitrator should state the facts on which the award is based and pose the questions of law which the court is to settle. As Lord Pearson has said:

'The procedure by special case is a valuable safeguard, because without it there might grow up a system of arbitrators' law independent of, and divergent from, the law administered by the courts; and also, if different arbitrators took different views as to the meaning of a clause in a standard contract, there would be no means of obtaining an authoritative decision. On the other hand, the procedure should be kept within its proper limits, confined to questions of law, and should not be extended so as to encroach on the general finality of the arbitrator's decision as provided by s. 16 of the Arbitration Act 1950'.[3]

The court may direct a special case to be stated with respect to an interim award or on a question of law arising in the course of the reference although the proceedings under the reference are still pending.[4] If the arbitrator refuses to state a case asked for on reasonable grounds, and makes his award summarily so as to preclude an application to the court, that is misconduct, and the award may be sent back with an order to state a case,[5] or set aside.[6]

It is the duty of the parties to see that all the relevant facts are found, but the court will not construe a special case too rigidly[7] and may draw inferences of fact.[8]

These provisions do not apply to references for trial by order of the court.[9] Appeals from an official or special referee are governed by the Rules of the Supreme Court.[10]

An agreement not to require an arbitrator to state a special case is contrary to public policy and invalid because it ousts the special statutory jurisdiction of the courts to compel arbitrators to submit a point of law for determination by the courts.[11]

Where the arbitrator states his award in the form of a special case, he is functus officio, and the court pronounces judgment upon the facts found by him. It is, however, competent for an arbitrator to state his award in the form of a special case with a limited time for setting it down for hearing and with an alternative final award which is to become operative if the case is not set down within the time limited.[12]

---

1 See *Halfdan Greig & Co A/S v Sterling Coal and Navigation Corpn* [1973] QB 843, [1973] 2 All ER 1073, CA. A clear cut question of law, important and raised bona fide should normally be stated on request by a party.

2 S. 21 (1). No appeal lies from a decision of the court under para. (a) of this subsection without the leave of the court or the Court of Appeal (s. 21 (3)).

3 *Tersons Ltd v Stevenage Development Corpn Ltd* [1965] 1 QB 37 at 55, [1963] 3 All ER 863 at 872.

4 S. 21 (2).

5 *Re Palmer & Co and Hosken* [1898] 1 QB 131.

6 *Re Fischel & Co and Mann and Cook* [1919] 2 KB 431.

7 *Anglo-Saxon Petroleum Co Ltd v Adamastos Shipping Co Ltd* [1957] 2 QB 233 at 264, [1957] 2 All ER 311 at 315, CA. For decision in the House of Lords, see para. 23.18, ante.

8 *Universal Cargo Carriers Corpn v Citati (No. 2)* [1958] 2 QB 254, [1958] 2 All ER 563, CA.

9 See para. 34.01, ante.

10 See Administration of Justice Act 1956, s. 15 (2).

11 *Czarnikow v Roth, Schmidt & Co* [1922] 2 KB 478.

12 *Re Olympia Oil and Cake Co and MacAndrew Moreland & Co* [1918] 2 KB 771.

5. The award

Time for award

34.16 In the absence of a provision to the contrary in the arbitration agreement an arbitrator or umpire has power to make his award at any time[1] except where the award has been remitted for reconsideration.[2] If a time is fixed by the Act or the agreement the court has power to extend it.[3]

---

1 S. 13 (1). But a dilatory arbitrator may be removed: see para. 34.07, ante.
2 See para. 34.19, post.
3 S. 13 (2).

Form and requisites

34.17 The arbitrator should decide all matters submitted to him under the submission, but he should not go beyond them; if he transgresses in either respect the award is void.

Unless the agreement specifies otherwise, as soon as the arbitrator has executed the award, he should give notice to the parties that it is ready to be delivered.

The arbitrator may correct in an award any clerical mistake or error arising from any accidental slip or omission.[1] But if he puts down what he intended to put down, although the legal effect may be doubtful, he cannot alter his award for the purpose of expounding his meaning.[2]

All awards (unless they otherwise direct) carry interest at the same rate as a judgment debt.[3] An arbitrator is not empowered to fix whatever rate of interest he chooses so that, unless he directs that the award will carry no interest, it will carry interest at the same rate as a judgment debt.[4]

Subject to anything in the agreement the arbitrators or umpire have the same power as the court to order specific performance of any contract other than a contract relating to land or any interest in land.[5]

The chief requisites of an award are three in number, viz.:

1. *The award must be certain* in meaning, so that the parties to the reference can understand how they are affected by it; but the court will assist the parties to interpret it, if possible, and make any alterations necessary to make the meaning clear. If its meaning cannot be interpreted, the award is bad.

2. *The award must be final;* this does not prevent the arbitrator from making an interim award[6] in a proper case unless the

agreement precludes it; but any award should deal with the whole of the subject-matter to which it relates and which ought to be determined.[7]

3. *The award must be possible and reasonable, e.g.* an award that a party should deliver up a deed not in his custody or under his control would be void.

If the award is bad in part it is not necessarily void; if the good can be separated from the bad, the latter alone is void, as where an arbitrator had awarded on some matters not within the submission; but if the two parts are not separable the whole award is void.

---

1 S. 17.
2 *Sutherland & Co v Hannevig Bros* [1921] 1 KB 336.
3 S. 20.
4 *Timber Shipping Co SA v London and Overseas Freighters Ltd* [1972] AC 1, [1971] 2 All ER 599, HL.
5 S. 15.
6 S. 14.
7 *Samuel v Cooper* (1835) 2 Ad & E 752.

Costs

34.18 The costs of the reference and award are in the discretion of the arbitrators or umpire.[1] The discretion must be exercised judicially[2] but the arbitrator need not state his reasons.[3] Any costs awarded are taxable in the High Court.[4]

Any provision in an arbitration agreement that a party shall bear his own costs, or any part thereof, is void; unless the provision is part of an agreement to submit to arbitration a dispute which has arisen *before* the making of such agreement.[5]

If the arbitrator omits to deal with the costs of the reference any party may within fourteen days[6] apply to the arbitrator for an order directing by and to whom the costs shall be paid, and after hearing any party who may desire to be heard, the arbitrator must amend his award by adding thereto directions as to costs which he thinks proper.[7]

---

1 S. 18 (1).
2 *LE Cattan Ltd v A Michaelides & Co* [1958] 2 All ER 125, [1958] 1 WLR 717; *Heaven and Kesterton Ltd v Sven Widaeus A/B* [1958] 1 All ER 420, [1958] 1 WLR 248; *Ceylon Government v Chandris* [1963] 2 QB 327, [1963] 2 All ER 1.
3 *Perry v Stopher* [1959] 1 All ER 713, [1959] 1 WLR 415.
4 S. 18 (2).

5 S. 18 (3).
6 The court or a judge may extend the time.
7 S. 18 (4).

Referring back the award

34.19 The award is final and binding on the parties and persons claiming through them.[1] But the court may remit matters referred to the reconsideration of the arbitrators or umpire;[2] they must make their award within three months after the date of the order for remission.[3] The following grounds for remission have been held to be adequate:

1. Any defect sufficient to empower the court to set it aside.[4]
2. Omission through inadvertence, e.g. where a case is stated but the relevant facts have not been found.[5]
3. Formal defects.
4. Mistake admitted by the arbitrator.
5. Where new and material evidence has been discovered.

It seems, however, that the court's discretion to refer back an award is not limited exclusively to the above grounds.[6]

1 S. 16. *Middlemiss Gould v Hartlepool Corpn* [1972] 1 WLR 1643.
2 S. 22 (1).
3 S. 22 (2).
4 See para. 34.20, post.
5 *Universal Cargo Carriers Corpn v Citati* [1957] 3 All ER 234, [1957] 1 WLR 979, CA.
6 *Margulies Bros Ltd v Dafnis Thomaides & Co (UK) Ltd (No. 2)* [1958] 1 All ER 777, [1958] 1 WLR 398.

Setting aside the award

34.20 Among the grounds upon which an award may be set aside are the following:

1. Where the arbitrator or umpire has misconducted himself or the proceedings, or the award has been improperly procured.[1]

Irregularity in the conduct of the proceedings, although the arbitrator may not have acted from any corrupt or improper motive, is misconduct. Thus, an award will not stand if the arbitrator:

i) hears one party and refuses to hear the other;

ii) holds private communication with one party on the subject-matter of the reference;

iii) examines witnesses on one side in the absence of the other party, unless justifiably proceeding ex parte; or

iv) examines witnesses in the absence of both parties;

v) refuses to state a case for the opinion of the court on a substantial point of law.[2]

2. If the award is uncertain or not final.

In a reference by consent the court will not set aside the award for mistake, unless it is bad on the face of it in point of law, or such error in law appears upon some document accompanying and forming part of the award.[3]

3. If the award is based on an illegal contract.[4]

The court will not grant an application to set aside the award unless convinced of its necessity, but will rather remit the award if the error can be corrected without the expense of starting afresh.[5]

Pending an application to set aside an award the court may order any money payable under it to be brought into court or secured.[6]

---

1 S. 23 (2).

2 *Re Fischel & Co and Mann and Cook* [1919] 2 KB 431.

3 *Giacomo Costa Fu Andrea v British Italian Trading Co Ltd* [1963] 1 QB 201, [1962] 2 All ER 53. A reference in the award to the pleadings is not sufficient to incorporate them into the award and they may not be looked at when an error on the face of the award is alleged: *Belsfield Court Construction Co Ltd v Pywell* [1970] 2 QB 47, [1970] 1 All ER 453.

4 *David Taylor & Son Ltd v Barnett Trading Co* [1953] 1 All ER 843, CA. For illegal contracts see paras. 6.02, et seq., ante.

5 *Kiril Mischeff Ltd v Constant, Smith & Co* [1950] 2 KB 616, [1950] 1 All ER 890.

6 S. 23 (3).

Enforcing an award

34.21 1. An award may, by leave of the court, be enforced in the same manner as a judgment, and where such leave is given judgment may be entered in terms of the award.[1]

2. By action on the award. (This is the only remedy where the submission is not in writing.)

3. Perhaps by attachment.

The court may also grant specific performance of an award. Certain foreign awards may be enforced by action, or in the same manner as a judgment.[2] Such awards include those made between subjects of Powers who have made reciprocal arrangements with this country and are parties to a Convention on the Execution of Arbitral Awards, which was signed on behalf of His Majesty at Geneva on 26 September 1927.[3] But a foreign award is not enforceable unless it is valid and final in the country in which it was made; it must also be in respect of a matter which may lawfully be referred to arbitration under the law of England, and its enforcement must not be contrary to the public policy or the law of England.[4]

---

1 S. 26.
2 S. 36. Arbitration Act 1950, Part II.
3 S. 35.
4 S. 37.

34.22 The Arbitration Act 1975 has been passed to give effect to the New York Convention on the Recognition and Enforcement of Foreign Arbitral Awards. If a party to an arbitration agreement which is not a 'domestic agreement' commences court proceedings these may be stayed on proof of the agreement.[1] A 'domestic agreement' is one which does not provide for arbitration in a state other than the United Kingdom and to which only a United Kingdom nationals, residents or bodies corporate were party at the time when the proceedings were commenced.[2] 'Convention awards' made in the territory of a state party to the New York Convention other than the United Kingdom, are enforceable in England and Wales as court orders in accordance with the Arbitration Act 1950.[3] Enforcement may be refused if there is want of capacity; invalidity either by the law chosen by the parties or, if none, then by the law of the country where the award was made; lack of notice of the appointment of the tribunal or of the hearing; if the award deals with matters outside the scope of the submission; if the tribunal is not constituted in accordance with the agreement or, failing any such provision, in accordance with the law of the country where the arbitration took place; if the award has not become binding on the parties or if it has been suspended or set aside by competent authority either of the country in which, or the law under which, it was made.[4] Enforcement will also be refused if the award deals with matters which may not be settled by arbitration or if it is contrary to public policy.[5] If a Convention award is in part good it may be enforced to that extent.[6] Where a Convention award is also a 'foreign award' within Part II of the

Arbitration Act 1950 then the 1975 Act applies to the exclusion of Part II of the 1950 Act.[7]

---

1 Arbitration Act 1975, s. 1 (1).
2 Ibid, s. 1 (4).
3 Ibid, s. 3 (1) and Arbitration Act 1950, s. 26.
4 Arbitration Act 1975, s. 5 (2).
5 Ibid, s. 5 (3).
6 Ibid, s. 5 (4).
7 Ibid, s. 2. Part II of the 1950 Act comprises ss. 35–43 and gives effect to the Geneva Convention (ante).

Lien on award for remuneration

34.23 An arbitrator or umpire has a lien on the award and submission, and may retain them until his charges are paid. He can also recover any agreed or reasonable remuneration by action; for the appointment of a person as arbitrator in a mercantile dispute raises an implied promise by the parties to the submission to pay for his services. Thus, the unsuccessful party to an arbitration must pay the remuneration of an arbitrator appointed by the other side, if so ordered by the umpire under his award, and the arbitrator can sue for the amount in question.[1]

If an arbitrator or umpire refuses to deliver his award except on payment of the fees demanded by him, the court may order him to do so on payment into court by the party applying of the fees demanded. Those fees will then be taxed, and the sum found reasonable on taxation will be paid out of court to the arbitrator or umpire and any balance will be returned to the applicant. But no such taxation will be ordered where the fees demanded have been fixed by a written agreement between the applicant and the arbitrator or umpire.[2]

---

1 *Crampton and Holt v Ridley & Co* (1887) 20 QBD 48; *Brown v Llandovery Terra Cotta Co* (1909) 25 TLR 625.
2 S. 19.

Limitation

34.24 The Limitation Act applies to arbitration proceedings, and its operation is not affected by a term in the agreement that an award shall be a condition precedent to the right to sue. An

767

arbitration is deemed to commence when one party serves the other with notice to appoint an arbitrator or to submit the dispute to the named arbitrator. Where the court sets an award aside or, after the commencement of the arbitration, orders that the agreement shall cease to have effect, it may order that the period between the commencement of the arbitration and the date of the order shall be excluded in computing the time for the commencement of proceedings with respect to the dispute referred.[1]

---

1 Limitation Act 1939, s. 27. See generally paras. 8.08, et seq., ante.

Index